ALSO BY LYNN VINCENT

Dog Company (with Captain Roger Hill)

Heaven Is for Real (with Todd Burpo)

Same Kind of Different As Me (with Ron Hall and Denver Moore)

What Difference Do It Make? (with Ron Hall and Denver Moore)

Never Surrender (with LTG. William G. Boykin)

ALSO BY SARA VLADIC

USS Indianapolis: The Legacy (film)

INDIANAPOLIS

★

**THE TRUE STORY OF THE WORST SEA DISASTER
IN U.S. NAVAL HISTORY AND THE FIFTY-YEAR
FIGHT TO EXONERATE AN INNOCENT MAN**

LYNN VINCENT

AND

SARA VLADIC

Simon & Schuster

NEW YORK · LONDON · TORONTO · SYDNEY · NEW DELHI

Simon & Schuster
1230 Avenue of the Americas
New York, NY 10020

First Simon & Schuster hardcover edition July 2018

SIMON & SCHUSTER and colophon are registered trademarks
of Simon & Schuster, Inc.

For information about special discounts for bulk purchases,
please contact Simon & Schuster Special Sales at 1-866-506-1949
or business@simonandschuster.com.

The Simon & Schuster Speakers Bureau can bring authors to your
live event. For more information, or to book an event, contact the
Simon & Schuster Speakers Bureau at 1-866-248-3049
or visit our website at www.simonspeakers.com.

Interior design by Paul Dippolito

Manufactured in the United States of America

1   3   5   7   9   10   8   6   4   2

Library of Congress Cataloging-in-Publication Data is available.

ISBN 978-1-5011-3594-1
ISBN 978-1-5011-3596-5 (ebook)

For those who did not live to tell their stories

CONTENTS

USS *INDIANAPOLIS*

Portland-Class Heavy Cruiser

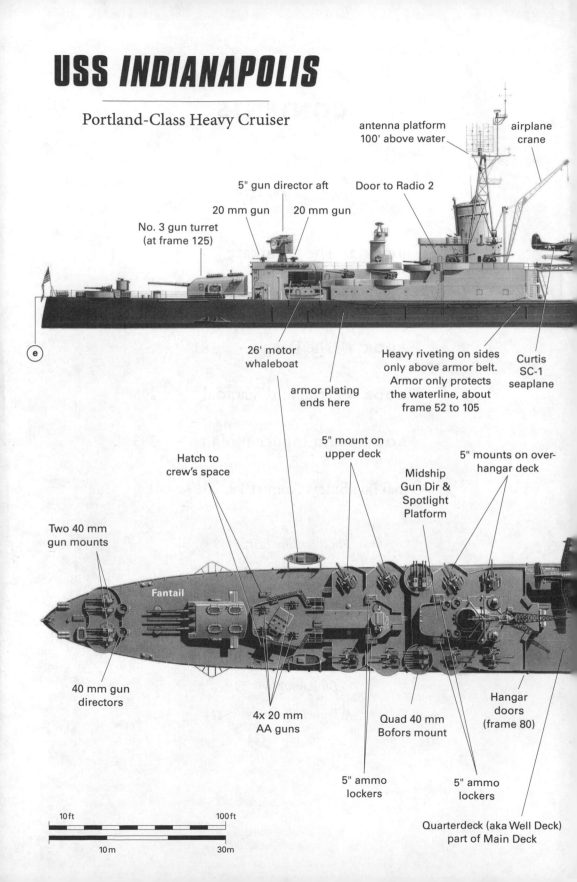

antenna platform
100' above water

airplane
crane

5" gun director aft

Door to Radio 2

20 mm gun

20 mm gun

No. 3 gun turret
(at frame 125)

e

26' motor
whaleboat

Heavy riveting on sides
only above armor belt.
Armor only protects
the waterline, about
frame 52 to 105

Curtis
SC-1
seaplane

armor plating
ends here

5" mount on
upper deck

5" mounts on over-
hangar deck

Hatch to
crew's space

Midship
Gun Dir &
Spotlight
Platform

Two 40 mm
gun mounts

Fantail

40 mm gun
directors

4x 20 mm
AA guns

Quad 40 mm
Bofors mount

Hangar
doors
(frame 80)

5" ammo
lockers

5" ammo
lockers

Quarterdeck (aka Well Deck)
part of Main Deck

10 ft   100 ft

10 m   30m

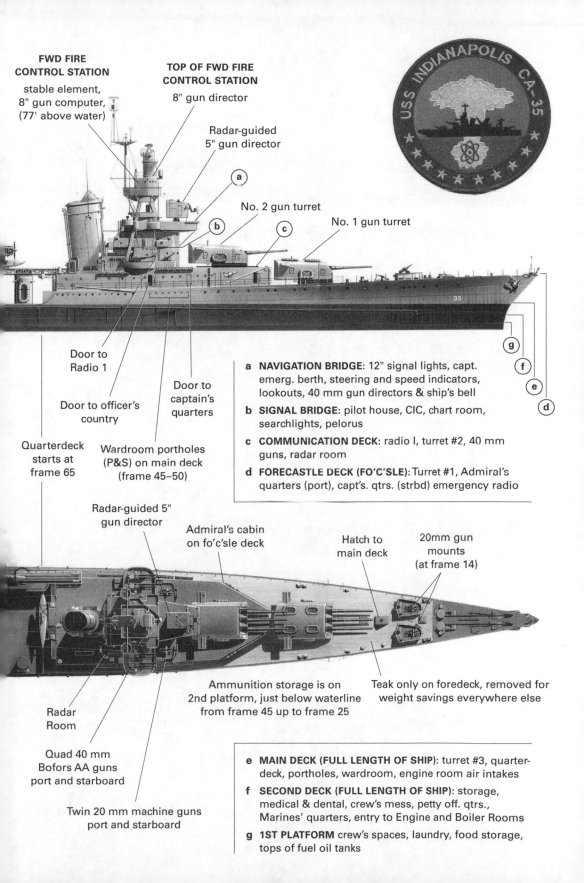

FWD FIRE CONTROL STATION
stable element, 8" gun computer, (77' above water)

TOP OF FWD FIRE CONTROL STATION
8" gun director

Radar-guided 5" gun director

ⓐ

No. 2 gun turret

ⓑ   ⓒ

No. 1 gun turret

ⓖ
ⓕ
ⓔ
ⓓ

Door to Radio 1

Door to captain's quarters

Door to officer's country

Quarterdeck starts at frame 65

Wardroom portholes (P&S) on main deck (frame 45–50)

a NAVIGATION BRIDGE: 12" signal lights, capt. emerg. berth, steering and speed indicators, lookouts, 40 mm gun directors & ship's bell

b SIGNAL BRIDGE: pilot house, CIC, chart room, searchlights, pelorus

c COMMUNICATION DECK: radio I, turret #2, 40 mm guns, radar room

d FORECASTLE DECK (FO'C'SLE): Turret #1, Admiral's quarters (port), capt's. qtrs. (strbd) emergency radio

Radar-guided 5" gun director

Admiral's cabin on fo'c'sle deck

Hatch to main deck

20mm gun mounts (at frame 14)

Radar Room

Ammunition storage is on 2nd platform, just below waterline from frame 45 up to frame 25

Teak only on foredeck, removed for weight savings everywhere else

Quad 40 mm Bofors AA guns port and starboard

Twin 20 mm machine guns port and starboard

e MAIN DECK (FULL LENGTH OF SHIP): turret #3, quarterdeck, portholes, wardroom, engine room air intakes

f SECOND DECK (FULL LENGTH OF SHIP): storage, medical & dental, crew's mess, petty off. qtrs., Marines' quarters, entry to Engine and Boiler Rooms

g 1ST PLATFORM crew's spaces, laundry, food storage, tops of fuel oil tanks

THE SHIP

SHE WAS BORN FROM soil as American as the men who sailed her. Ore mined near the Great Lakes and in the Tennessee Valley. Transported by barge and train to steel mills in Detroit and Pittsburgh. Machined and welded and hammered together in Camden, New Jersey, by tradesmen from across the forty-eight states. From her keel—forged red-hot and laid in 1930—she rose amid clang and clamor and showering sparks, unfolding bow to stern in 147 bands of high-strength steel, her superstructure climbing toward the sun until, in 1932, she parted water for the first time and was christened USS *Indianapolis*.

Indy was grand but svelte. Franklin Delano Roosevelt made her his ship of state and invited world leaders and royalty to dance under the stars on her polished teak decks. When war came, many of the sailors she carried into battle were still teenagers. They slept in bunks three high, went to chapel on Sunday mornings, and shot dice on the fantail on Sunday afternoons. They danced to Glenn Miller and sang along with the Andrews Sisters. They referred to Indy as their first love and the Queen. At least one of their wives called her "the other woman."

Indianapolis was the flagship of the World War II Pacific fleet—the largest naval fleet in the history of the modern world. Along her centerline she carried three 250-ton turrets, each hefting three eight-inch guns that could reach out eighteen miles to rake beaches, destroy pillboxes, and punch through the armor of enemy ships. Her hull bristled with two dozen 40 mm Bofors guns, some radar-aimed for lethal precision, along with thirty-two machine guns that could cloak a mile-wide circle around her in a hail of 20 mm rounds. From her decks, Fifth Fleet commander Admiral Raymond Spruance would build an island bridge that stretched west from Pearl Harbor to Japan and was mortared in the blood of nations.

By the summer of 1945, the Pacific war was churning toward its fiery climax. A new weapon had been born, a "destroyer of worlds." During the last week of July, under the command of Captain Charles B. McVay III, *Indianapolis* delivered the core of this weapon to its launch point, completing the most highly classified naval mission of the war. Four days later, just after midnight, a Japanese submarine spotted Indy and struck her with two torpedoes. Three hundred men went down with the ship. As Indy sank into the yawning underwater canyons of the Philippine Sea, nearly nine hundred men made it into the water alive. Only 316 survived.

The sinking of *Indianapolis* was the greatest sea disaster in the history of the American Navy. It was also a national scandal that would bridge two centuries. There would be a controversial court-martial. An enemy witness. Lies and machinations by men of high rank. Broken lives. Suicides.

Decade after decade, the survivors would fight for their captain, battling to correct a vulgar injustice. As Indy's story rolled forward, spanning thirteen presidents, from FDR to George W. Bush, it would inspire a filmmaker named Spielberg, an eleven-year-old boy named Hunter Scott, a maverick lawmaker named Bob Smith, and Captain William Toti, skipper of her namesake submarine. Men fought over her for decades, and no victor emerged for fifty years.

Indianapolis is a war grave now. But don't think of her that way. Roll the film backward. Watch her rise.

BOOK 1

THE KAMIKAZE

★

WORLD WAR II
PACIFIC THEATER OF OPERATIONS
SPRING 1945

1

A CRY WENT UP from the gun crew range-finders aboard the heavy cruiser *Indianapolis*: "Judy! Port side! Close aboard!"

It was a Japanese dive-bomber—a "Judy"—the third bogie of the day. The plane plunged from a slab of clouds, its long, glazed canopy glinting softly in the filtered morning light.

On the cruiser's bridge, Captain Charles McVay had the conn, with Admiral Raymond Spruance tracking the action from his high bridge chair. Both men wore khaki shirts, tieless, and soft garrison caps. Through the bridge wings, McVay, who was forty-six, could see the ships of the task group surrounding Indy in a rough ring, prows cutting cobalt seas along the same axis. Sailing closest were sixteen aircraft carriers, including *Bunker Hill, Essex, Enterprise, Yorktown, Hancock,* and *Franklin.* Farther out, the battleships and cruisers steamed, with the whole task group making way inside the sheltering embrace of a destroyer screen. A fighter CAP (combat air patrol), about thirty-two planes, fanned out over the task group.

Indy was at Condition I, general quarters, with all hands at battle stations. Bugler Glenn Morgan stood near McVay, headphones clamped over his ears, ready to relay data from critical combat stations around the ship.

The Judy kept coming, a dark-winged pill swelling against the pale dawn. Morgan watched its approach and wondered if it was another suicider. The Japanese had been crashing their planes into U.S. ships for five months, since Leyte Gulf. Most of the fellows thought they were bonkers. What kind of nut would do that, Morgan wondered, intentionally crash himself into a ship?

The Judy hurtled in, its engine thrumming past Indy's port beam toward a juicier target off her bow, the carrier *Bunker Hill*. Staccato gunfire burst like black popcorn flung across the sky as Indy's 20 mm gun crews arced their barrels with the plane's flight path. But the Judy snapped through the flak unscathed, and the pilot released a bomb. It whistled close to *Bunker Hill* but missed and pierced the sea close astern. The carrier returned fire, chewing into the plane with her antiaircraft battery. Morgan watched the bomber's shredded carcass cartwheel into the sea.

It was "L-14 Day," two weeks before the American landing at Okinawa. Task Force 58 was maneuvering at Emperor Hirohito's doorstep, just a hundred miles off Kyushu, southernmost in the slim scythe of islands that formed Japan. A land of sacred pagodas and active volcanoes, Kyushu was also home to the Japanese naval arsenal and shipyard at Sasebo, as well as major steel and arms works in the city of Nagasaki.

So far, the Empire's air reaction to Task Force 58 had been wildly aggressive. Attacks developed so swiftly that U.S. task force radar gave little if any warning. The clouds themselves seemed to spawn enemy planes, and a visual sighting by a close screen—quick, agile destroyers protecting the fleet—was often the first sign of menace. A day earlier, Japanese bombers had hit three carriers, but crews were able to patch the holes and keep their planes flying.

For the men of *Indianapolis*, fighting off single planes had become ordinary work. Since Spruance hoisted his flag aboard Indy in 1943, the crew of nearly a thousand had earned eight battle stars, not counting their last stop, Iwo Jima, where they'd helped tenderize the beach for the landing Marines.

Since his battle station was on the bridge, Morgan, a twenty-one-year-old Oklahoman, was always in the middle of the action—which is to say, the calm at the eye of the storm. Captain McVay and Admiral Spruance ran a quiet bridge, unlike the previous skipper, Captain Einar "Johnny" Johnson, a bantamweight officer who cursed loudly, cheerfully, and often.

Morgan had liked Johnson, but he wasn't so sure about McVay, who'd taken command in November. Sure, he'd just won a Silver Star for courage under fire in the Solomon Islands. But Morgan still felt that McVay didn't know much, and with his leading-man eyes and Pepsodent smile, the skipper also seemed a little snooty. The gossip was, he'd dated a movie star and married a princess.

Morning dawned in full. The air on the bridge tasted briny and cool, spring in the Northern Pacific. Morgan watched as the carriers went on offense, volleying waves of planes to strike enemy air bases at Kyushu. Launched singly, the planes formed up in swarms and arrowed toward the horizon, their props generating a low hum like venomous bees.

At intervals through the day, McVay reviewed the action report for Iwo Jima, which Yeoman Second Class Vic Buckett had typed up for his signature. The size and power of the force arrayed against Iwo Jima represented American naval power at its zenith. Buckett had recorded the bombardment of the island, which began in mid-February, as well as the weather: heavy rains had provided excellent cover for the surface fleet but played hell with the aviators. By February 19, the day of the landing, though, a high-pressure system had swept the squalls aside, and the Marines sloshed ashore under blue skies with a light northerly breeze.

McVay remembered watching hundreds of landing craft churn toward the beach. His sailors lined the rails, shouting, "Give 'em hell, boys!" Parked a few thousand yards offshore at Spruance's order, *Indianapolis* supported the landing and subsequent infantry battle with more shore bombardment, which the action report showed in detail. What the report did not show was how the fighting ashore collapsed into chaos, the Marines mired to their knees in sludgy volcanic ash and mowed down by heavy machine-gun fire. Nor could it show the moment those saltwater cowboys staked the Stars and Stripes on Mount Suribachi in full view of the attacking U.S. fleet.

McVay remembered the moment vividly: the whole fleet blasting horns, ringing bells, sailors cheering and clapping and waving their Dixie cup caps. Some men said that when they saw that flag go up they thought of home and how it surely wouldn't be long until they could sail back to their moms and sweethearts and the good old U.S.A.

The captain continued flipping through the thick sheaf of pages. The report noted that *Indianapolis* had taken no casualties at Iwo Jima and that the performance of her crew had been excellent. Satisfied, the captain scribbled his customary signature on the document: Chas. B. McVay, III.

●   ●   ●

Later in the day, Admiral Raymond Spruance emerged from the flag quarters for his daily laps around the forecastle, or "fo'c'sle,"* a superstructure just aft of the bow. Slim and tan, the admiral transmitted serenity, but his lucent blue eyes concealed an inward turbulence. At fifty-eight, Spruance vented his intensity as he had all his life, with physical exercise, usually dragging junior officers along, breathless. Sometimes he wore his khaki trousers, sometimes shorts and a T-shirt. Once, his chief of staff wrote home from the Marshall Islands that Spruance was "rigged out in a new pair of gaudy Hawaiian bathing panties."

Alone this time, Spruance charged forward along the port side, passing the No. 1 turret. Indy's crew was accustomed to his walks, and as he passed sailors polishing brass, painting, and swabbing decks, they greeted him—"Sir" or "Admiral"—with a respectful nod. He did not require that they snap to and render a hand salute. This was a ship at war, not a berthing inspection. While he insisted on efficiency, Spruance loathed commanders who burdened their men with ticky-tack formalities when there was important work to be done. On some ships, there was tension between an admiral's staff and the ship's company, with the staff seen as privileged intruders who made more work for the regular crew. There was none of that aboard *Indianapolis*. Spruance got on well with the reserved McVay just as he had with the more colorful Captain Johnson. He knew McVay to be the son of a rather difficult admiral, Charles B. McVay, Jr., a veteran of the Spanish-American War.

Today, Spruance was not content with hitting just the Kyushu airfields. He also wanted to hit Kure naval base on the island of Honshu, where an attractive chunk of the enemy's remaining surface fleet swung at anchor. Some considered such tactics overkill, and Spruance had developed a reputation for it. An aide once objected that the admiral was going to "crack a walnut with a sledgehammer." Spruance had peered over his reading glasses and said, "Roscoe, that's the way to win wars."

The admiral was famously unflappable, but found the attack on Pearl Harbor a shattering experience. Spruance revealed this only to his wife and daughter, then waited anxiously for Admiral Chester Nimitz to take

---

* Fo'c'sle is pronounced "fōksəl."

over as CincPac—Commander in Chief Pacific Fleet. After the obscenity at Pearl, America's Pacific Fleet leadership was demoralized. Spruance sensed that Nimitz would inject some sorely needed fighting spirit, and he was right. Nimitz proved bold, aggressive, confident. Energized, the Pacific fleet began to sortie out and fight back. Spruance was elated.

When he reached the foredeck, the admiral turned right and passed under the eight-inch gun barrels. A sea breeze ruffled his khakis and cooled his way. As he crossed the fo'c'sle forward, he saw a pair of sailors sitting near the gunwale. They wore Dixie cup hats, chambray shirts, and dungarees faded nearly sky-blue by a combination of sun and shipboard detergent. Spruance saw that the younger of the two men wore a cast on his right hand. Something odd protruded from the top. It looked like a wire. The admiral passed the men, hung another right, and walked aft along the starboard rail.

In June 1942, after Spruance engineered the surprise American victory at Midway, Nimitz lassoed him and made him CincPac chief of staff, then deputy commander, Pacific Fleet. Spruance quickly presided over a series of firsts: the first night carrier landing in naval history; the first to establish a rotation system for aviators in combat; the first to realize that the westward push toward Japan would require the creation of the most advanced logistics apparatus in the history of warfare. For Spruance, working for Nimitz had been an inspiration. Spruance considered the elder man one of the finest and most human characters he'd ever met. He was also the only man Spruance ever met who did not know what it meant to be afraid.

Now, with only Okinawa between his fleet and mainland Japan, Spruance saw no reason to alter his doctrine of overwhelming force. Shore bombardment of Okinawa was about to begin, with *Indianapolis* in the thick of it. The size of the landing force would be second only to D-Day at Normandy. Meanwhile, the Nazis were on the run in Europe, the Brits on the move in Burma, and General Douglas MacArthur—whose effectiveness, Spruance agreed with Navy Secretary James Forrestal, was mortgaged to his vanity—was rapidly recapturing the Philippines. The end of the Pacific war seemed just over the horizon.

Spruance completed a full lap of the forward superstructure and arrived again at the bow, where the two sailors were still sitting. Curious about the cast with the strange hardware, he detoured and walked over.

Since they were at leisure, the men jumped to their feet and rendered hand salutes. Spruance glanced at the name stenciled on the younger man's shirt. "Celaya, is it?"

"Yes, sir. Adolfo Celaya, sir."

Celaya, who was seventeen, had joined the Navy out of the tiny, dust-swept desert town of Florence, Arizona. He'd seen a lot of brass aboard and had observed Spruance doing laps for nearly a whole year. But Celaya had never spoken to him, and he was a little nervous.

Spruance nodded toward Celaya's hand. "What happened there?"

"Broke my hand, sir." Celaya glanced at his buddy, Seaman First Class Mike Quihuis, who pressed his lips into a thin line to keep from smiling. He knew Celaya was hoping the admiral wouldn't ask *how* he broke his hand.

On closer inspection, Spruance could see that the wire, about the gauge of an ordinary coat hanger, originated in the area of the boy's thumb. It rose more than eight inches from the cast and ended in a loop, resembling nothing so much as an antenna.

Spruance caught Celaya's eye and smiled. "You picking up Tokyo Rose on that thing?"

Celaya shook his head and laughed. "No, sir."

The admiral smiled again, then turned away and resumed his course to starboard.

That evening, Spruance received updates on Admiral Marc Mitscher's air strikes on the Japanese mainland. Mitscher commanded the fast carrier force known as Task Force 58. By day's end, his pilots had bested 102 enemy flyers in dogfights over Kyushu and destroyed another 275 aircraft on the ground. The fighter CAP, or combat air patrol, shot down a dozen planes over the task force, and antiaircraft batteries splashed another twenty-one. The enemy had managed to score hits on two American carriers, *Yorktown* and *Enterprise*, but damage to *Yorktown* was minor, and the bomb that hit *Enterprise* failed to detonate.

Meanwhile, the American sorties had yielded a bonus. Over the Japanese naval base at Kure, Mitscher's pilots spotted the battleship *Yamato* in the harbor. Designed as a "supership," *Yamato* was capable of fighting multiple enemy vessels at once. Lithe and muscular with minimal freeboard, the mighty vessel lurked low in the water, her vast superstructure bristling with guns. She was by far the Empire's most dangerous remaining surface threat, and Spruance wanted her off the board. By hitting both Japan's air and surface forces today and tomorrow, he hoped to disrupt interference with the Allied landing at Okinawa. Bitter experience had taught him that during the landing itself, his forces would be critically exposed.

2

MARCH 1945

Kure Naval District
Hiroshima Prefecture, Japan

HAVING COMPLIED WITH AN infuriating order to break contact with American naval targets and make for Okino-Shima, Lieutenant Commander Mochitsura Hashimoto drove his submarine back to Kure Naval Base and stormed into the office of the Combined Fleet commander in chief.

"We were within two hours of the target!" Hashimoto told a senior staff officer, referring to American ships anchored at Iwo Jima. "If another boat had been dispatched to Okino, we could have launched our *kaiten!*"

Hashimoto referred to the manned suicide torpedoes aboard his submarine, I-58.

The staff officer gazed back at him. "We didn't realize you had gotten so close."

For the thirty-seven-year-old sub commander, it was not close enough. The hour was late and the sea growing smaller. Fourteen hundred miles south of Tokyo, the Mariana Islands were hatching American bomber bases while hundreds of Allied ships heaped the islands with war matériel. U.S. squadrons at Saipan and Tinian were slinging B-29 Superfortress bombers into the sky, bound for the Japanese home islands. Only two weeks earlier, nearly three hundred B-29s had torched

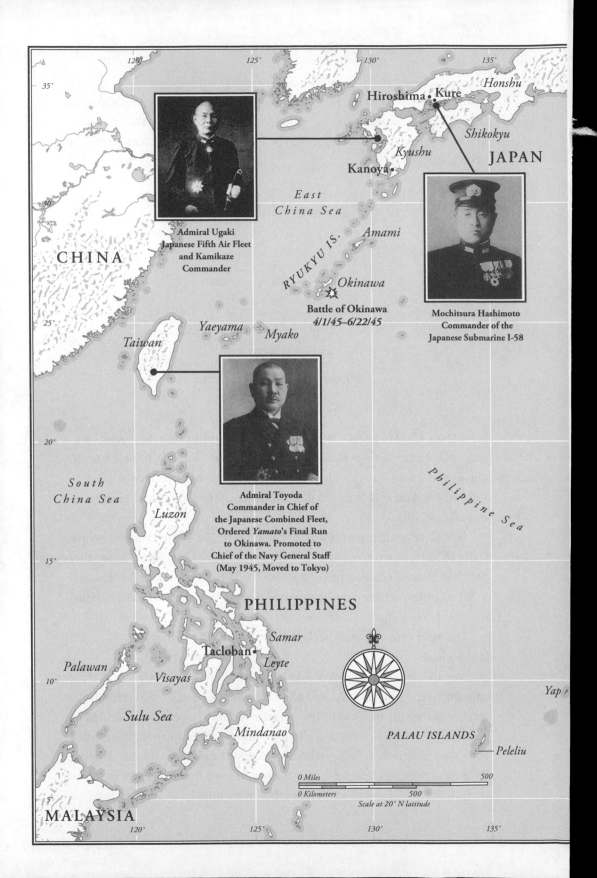

35°

120°   125°   130°   135°

Hiroshima   Kure   Honshu

Shikokyu

JAPAN

30°

Kyushu

Kanoya

East
China Sea

Amami

**Admiral Ugaki
Japanese Fifth Air Fleet
and Kamikaze
Commander**

CHINA

RYUKYU IS.

Okinawa

25°

**Battle of Okinawa
4/1/45–6/22/45**

**Mochitsura Hashimoto
Commander of the
Japanese Submarine I-58**

Yaeyama

Myako

Taiwan

20°

South
China Sea

**Admiral Toyoda
Commander in Chief of
the Japanese Combined Fleet,
Ordered *Yamato*'s Final Run
to Okinawa. Promoted to
Chief of the Navy General Staff
(May 1945, Moved to Tokyo)**

Luzon

Philippine Sea

15°

PHILIPPINES

Samar

Tacloban

Leyte

Palawan

10°

Visayas

Yap

Sulu Sea

Mindanao

PALAU ISLANDS

Peleliu

0 Miles   500

0 Kilometers   500

Scale at 20° N latitude

5°

MALAYSIA

120°   125°   130°   135°

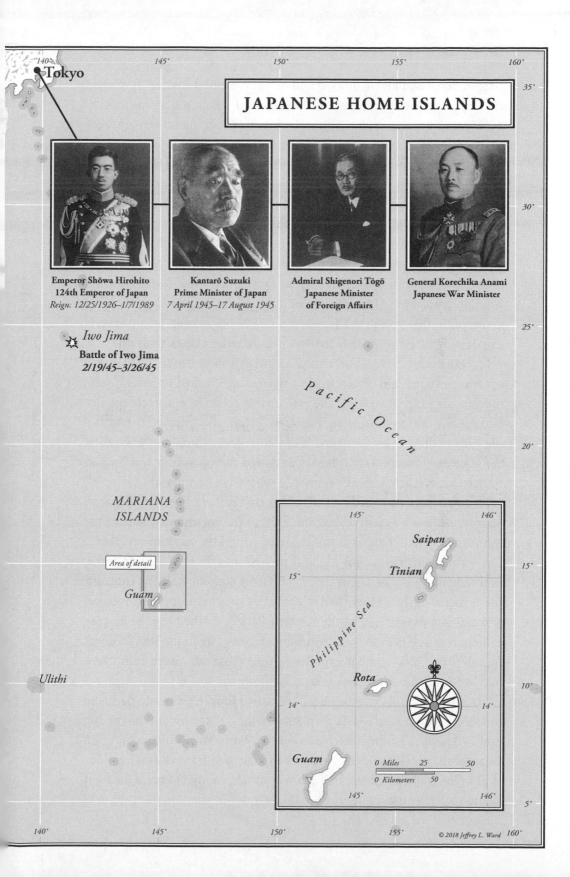

Tokyo

JAPANESE HOME ISLANDS

Emperor Shōwa Hirohito
124th Emperor of Japan
Reign: 12/25/1926–1/7/1989

Kantarō Suzuki
Prime Minister of Japan
7 April 1945–17 August 1945

Admiral Shigenori Tōgō
Japanese Minister
of Foreign Affairs

General Korechika Anami
Japanese War Minister

Iwo Jima
Battle of Iwo Jima
2/19/45–3/26/45

Pacific Ocean

MARIANA
ISLANDS

Area of detail

Guam

Ulithi

Saipan

Tinian

Philippine Sea

Rota

15°

14°

Guam

0 Miles	25	50
0 Kilometers	50	

© 2018 Jeffrey L. Ward

sixteen square miles of Tokyo, killing almost one hundred thousand civilians. Cannibal flames spread the stench of burning flesh for miles.

Meanwhile, the enemy admiral Spruance had mobilized unprecedented logistics operations, pushing fuel, ammunition, and supplies westward. His superior, Nimitz, had established a forward headquarters at Guam and based his fleet there. It was not quite at Japan's threshold, but certainly in her courtyard. Even the insufferable American general Douglas MacArthur had returned to the Philippines.

The outrageous order that sent Hashimoto speeding back to Kure and into the office of his commander in chief had pulled him from his own mission to Iwo Jima. Three weeks earlier, his two-sub attack group, Kamitake, was formed in the wake of utter failure by a three-boat group, Chibaya. In that group, the Japanese sub I-370 was sunk by an American destroyer, and another, I-368, by enemy carrier planes. Only one sub, I-44, returned to base—but barely. An American destroyer sighted her off Iwo Jima and laid on a relentless stern chase. Forced to remain submerged for nearly two days, she was unable to surface to recharge her batteries or vent to outside air. Her crew gasped like beached fish as rising carbon dioxide levels turned I-44 into a steel coffin. On the verge of suffocating his men, the captain abandoned the operation and limped back to Kure, where he was summarily relieved of command.

Immediately after the Japanese attack on Pearl Harbor, the American submarine fleet was sent to take the fight to the enemy, buying time for the surface fleet to recover from its losses. American submariners therefore gained experience quickly and proved an effective fighting force, neutralizing much of Japan's merchant and combat fleet. In contrast, the Imperial Japanese Navy had relegated its subs to resupplying men on isolated islands throughout the Western Pacific. By the time the Empire called on its sub fleet to face the American Navy late in the war, its commanders had little combat experience, and those who were competent had little patience for their less capable brethren.

Despite the Chibaya group's failure at Iwo Jima, Hashimoto had held out hope for Kamitake. His own submarine, I-58, was one of the big new B-3 series, a landmark achievement in World War II sub technology. Boats of the previous B series boasted a range of fourteen thousand nautical miles. I-58's range was half again as much, enough to press the fight against all Allied shipping, merchant or man-o'-war. Further, she was armed with the lethal Type 95 torpedo, a marvel of weaponry that used highly compressed oxygen as a fuel oxidizer. This increased the torpedo's range to nearly triple that of standard U.S. torpedoes, while nearly eliminating any telltale air-bubble wake. Hashimoto's torpedoes were the fastest in use by any navy in the world.

His boat was also fitted with the latest shortwave aerial. En route to Iwo Jima, it worked perfectly, sucking down transmissions between enemy ships. For a week, his seasoned crew played cat and mouse with America's barbarian Navy better than ever before.

Still, Hashimoto could not deny the superiority of the enemy fleet, and his countrymen had begun to wonder about their adversaries. The Americans had industrial might, yes, but surely they could not match Japanese resolve. They were farm boys and schoolteachers and factory workers, without guile or cleverness—as easy to read as a child's schoolbook. They would not fight to the death or sacrifice all as a Japanese would for *bushido*, the way of the warrior. Yet these same amateurs had nearly secured Iwo Jima. Before the war, when the Empire administered the little rock as a territory of Tokyo, only a thousand people had lived there. It was peaceful and bucolic, with one school, one Shinto shrine, and one policeman. Now the green volcanic diamond—less than eight hundred miles from Hashimoto's home, from his wife and three sons—was another stepping-stone for the Americans to invade his homeland.

The battle for Iwo was nearing its end. There would be no surrender there, Hashimoto knew. Imperial generals had known they could not prevent an enemy landing, and Japan's remaining air strength lacked the range to reach the island. So troops there had contracted into a defensive posture, hunkering in a meticulously prepared system of caves and trenches. The objective was not to win but rather to buy time to prepare for the home island invasion. What had once seemed impossible by then seemed inevitable. Still, on March 6, en route to Iwo Jima, Hashimoto put one eye to I-58's periscope. He was determined not to give up.

Hashimoto's broad, flat nose anchored closely grouped features, and his square head rode his shoulders like the turret on a tank. Grasping the periscope's training handles, he turned the barrel slowly, his gaze arcing low over the watery chop. A broken overcast hung shroudlike over the dying light.

There! To the south. The silhouette of a large enemy warship.

He announced the sighting to his crew. It was an enticing target, but it was nearly night and the ship an hour distant. Hashimoto knew he could attack it only in the absence of moonlight, or risk being sighted and sunk. Were he to attack, any errant flash of lunar light might be I-58's end. Hashimoto would not mind that, so long as he and his crew fought with honor.

Hashimoto had been the torpedo officer on a sub at Pearl Harbor, Japan's masterful first strike against America. It had been a heady time to be a Japanese sailor, and afterward, the Imperial Japanese Navy (IJN) swept down the Pacific Rim, capturing a dozen major islands and territories from the British, the Dutch, and others. In the three years since, however, Hashimoto had managed to sink only a couple of minor vessels. Now the war's end loomed and he wanted to bring home at least one major prize for the emperor. Not to do so would mean *mentsu wo ushinau.* He would lose face.

Hashimoto eyed his instruments. The warship was a tempting target, but I-58 was approaching enemy waters, and he did not want to repeat I-44's mistake. It would be best to use this unhectored interval to recharge his sub's batteries while there was still time.

He gave the order—that I-58 would recharge instead of attack—and sparked spirited objections from his crew.

"We are turning away from the enemy!" some cried. "Where is the honor in that?"

Hashimoto reminded them of I-58's mission: She was equipped with *kaiten*—manned suicide torpedoes—best for attacking *ships at anchor.*

The next day, March 7, batteries fully charged, he proceeded toward a position seventeen miles northwest of Iwo Jima. With enemy lines of communication to the south and east, Hashimoto expected defenses there to be thin. He sailed on the surface and good fortune smiled on him: As his boat plunged through a line of squalls, curtains of rain slashed visibility to nearly zero.

Perfect, he thought. If the weather held, conditions would be ideal for operating the *kaiten.*

At 11 p.m. on March 8, he stood on the bridge as the sub made way, deck awash, sea foam exploding over the bow. He expected to reach the *kaiten* launch point at 2 a.m. His suicide pilots had finished their final rituals—belongings ordered, letters written home, final prayers offered at the Shinto shrine on board. The pilots were already in their cockpits when a series of enemy radar transmissions banged in. Signals shot in from three compass points—enemy destroyers, it was almost certain. The crew went quick-quiet and Hashimoto ticked through his limited options.

He could not dive out of sight—I-58 was still three hours from the launch point, the *kaiten* manned and coupled to the deck. Armed only with the suicide torpedoes and a small, deck-mounted machine gun, she was an offensive weapon only, virtually defenseless.

Quickly, he made his decision and addressed his men in a low voice: "If we are sighted, we will dive. For now, bring drinks to the *kaiten* pilots to keep them going."

Sailors carried out the order, speaking only in whispers, guarding even their footfalls to avoid enemy sonar detection. Throughout the boat, stillness set in. From the mess deck, the smell of pickled fish crept through the quiet compartments, and Hashimoto pressed on toward the launch point, conning boldly through the rain.

An hour passed as he closed the distance to target. Two hours until launch.

Then, in the radio room, the urgent signal arrived from Japan. It was the outrageous order that would send Hashimoto storming into the commander in chief's office at Kure:

KAMITAKE UNIT OPERATION CANCELLED—I-58 IS
TO PROCEED FORTHWITH TO OKINO-SHIMA TO
ACT AS WIRELESS LINK SHIP FOR COMBINED FLEET
OPERATION TO BE CARRIED OUT MARCH 11.

Maddening! Hashimoto thought. Finally, we are at the Americans' doorstep unseen, and they are turning us away!

He could not reply by signal as the transmission would lead to immediate discovery. But who was to say he could not first launch his *kaiten*, then plot a course for Okino-Shima? Perhaps he could still take a prize for great Japan. He was weighing this possibility when a second signal broke through. It was a personal message from the Chief of Staff Combined Fleet:

OPERATION "HA" IS VERY IMPORTANT AND YOUR
ORDERS SHOULD BE FOLLOWED WITHOUT FAIL.

There had been nothing for Hashimoto to do but comply. He recalled the suicide pilots from the brink of immortality and followed orders, hating every minute of it. Now, leaving the C-in-C's office at Kure, all he could do was await new orders to the Americans' next target, Okinawa. If the enemy held true to form, the shelling there was soon to begin.

Hashimoto knew that any damage he might have inflicted on the enemy at Iwo Jima would have been small. Also, there had been those lurking American destroyers. It was difficult to say what would have happened to his boat if he had launched his *kaiten* in their presence.

But Hashimoto was certain of one thing: Above all, he had wanted to try.

3

MARCH 19, 1945

USS *Indianapolis*
Pacific Ocean
Near Kyushu, Japan

IT WAS NOT YET four in the morning when Captain McVay ordered Condition I set in his antiaircraft batteries. The skipper always set Condition I, or "battle stations," in the morning because that's when the suicide planes seemed to be most active. Indy was operating sixty miles off the coast of Shikoku, the smallest island in the Empire's homeland chain, due east of Kyushu.

Glenn Morgan had relieved the watch and was again on the bridge, wearing his headphones. He was a bugler, yes, a musician in love with newer music like Jimmy Dorsey's "Tangerine" and Glenn Miller's "String of Pearls" (he could play both perfectly on his cornet, which he had carried with him to boot camp, prompting his fellow recruits to holler at him to "go play that damn thing in the head!"). But Morgan had also fallen in love with the rhythms of a fighting ship at sea. The quartermaster barking at his strikers, boys who would be quartermasters themselves someday. The crisp calls of the OOD—Officer of the Deck—passed to the helmsman. Morgan had even learned to steer the ship himself and sometimes couldn't believe he was allowed to, him, a Bristow, Oklahoma, boy, driving the flagship of the fleet.*

Morgan loved *Indianapolis's* slim contours. Bow to fantail, she stretched 610 feet, with a beam of just 66 feet from the port rail to the starboard, and a draft of 17 to 24 feet, depending on her load. Indy was one of America's eighteen "Treaty Cruisers," the offspring of the heavy cruiser race between America, Japan, France, Italy, and Great Britain. Commissioned in 1932, she was subject to treaty displacement limitations that produced thinly armored vessels shipbuilders referred to as "tin clads." But like Morgan, the men who sailed these lithe ships often fell in love with their speed and grace.

During his 1936 "Good Neighbor" cruise to South America, President Franklin D. Roosevelt hosted guests aboard Indy one evening. Well-dressed ladies dined in the wardroom that night and danced on the quarterdeck, a polished pool of gleaming teak. But none of the ladies could rival Indy herself. Her graceful rigging fluttered with banners and pennants. Hundreds of Japanese lanterns lit her lines, shimmering against a night sky of velvet blue. Just after dark, a full moon rose, its glow accenting her white peacetime paint. Officers who were there that night remembered not the ladies, but the ship. *She* was magical.

Morgan reported to Indy in 1944 and had been aboard for a couple of months when a kid named Earl Procai reported for duty. Procai, a nineteen-year-old from Minneapolis, was a bugler second class. With another new man, Donald Mack, that made four buglers aboard.

---

* Though in overall command of the Pacific Fleet, Spruance alternated at-sea command with Admiral William "Bull" Halsey. Under Spruance the fleet designation was 5th Fleet and under Halsey, 3rd Fleet. The two admirals took it in turns, with one at sea and the other ashore planning the next operation. *Indianapolis* was Spruance's flagship. Halsey's were the battleships *New Jersey* and *Missouri*.

That meant Morgan and his best friend, Bugler Second Class Calvin Ball Emery, could quit working "port-and-starboard"—twelve hours on, twelve hours off. It cut Morgan's watchstanding in half.

Well, mostly. Morgan thought Procai was a very nice fellow, but he couldn't blow his horn worth a hoot. When Indy was in port and Procai had the watch, one of the other buglers would scoot topside to play "Evening Colors." They didn't want the other ships to hear Procai's halting, mangled rendition.

"Earl," Morgan said to Procai one day, pointing to the man's horn, "you've *got* to play this thing better." He grabbed a bugle and took Procai down to steering aft. Thereafter, a couple of times a week, Morgan and Procai hunkered down in the heat, machinery cranking, practicing the bugle calls. The horse-race trills of "Reveille," the regal notes of "Tattoo," the mournful tones of "Taps." Morgan played them all, and Procai echoed them back. The kid got to be pretty good and in the process, down there sweating it out in steering, the two got to be good friends.

As morning on the bridge unfolded, Admiral Spruance took station in his bridge chair. At 5:30 a.m., the carriers launched the CAP, followed by the first sweeps against enemy airfields at Shikoku and northwestern Honshu on the Japanese mainland. Shortly after 6 a.m., sunrise chased the night away, revealing the ships of the mighty task force as if raising a theater curtain.

At the conn, McVay ordered the OOD to maneuver on a general northeasterly line as the first enemy planes appeared in the sky. At 7:08 a.m., an enemy bomber nosed out of a cloud base at less than two thousand feet, and about a thousand feet dead ahead of the carrier *Franklin*. Indy's bridge crew watched as the pilot accelerated in a masthead bombing run. Two bombs dropped from the fuselage and sailed in twenty-five degrees off horizontal, falling through the flak of *Franklin*'s guns. The first smashed into the flight deck in the center of thirty-one planes, burst into the hangar, and exploded. The second hit the flight deck, then penetrated the hangar, where it detonated over twenty-two parked planes.

The men of Indy could see a thick pillar of black smoke erupt from the carrier, with multiple red explosions bursting at its base. Sparks and fire triggered a massive gasoline vapor explosion. Planes that had been turning up for launch were flung violently together, and their whirring props sliced each other into strips. Fire poured across the flight and hangar decks in thick sheets, fed with fuel from ruptured aircraft gas tanks.

Against the backdrop of *Franklin's* inferno, suicide planes screamed in, guns rattling. The heavy carrier *Essex* splashed one attacker. Eighteen minutes later, another plane dove on *Essex*, but missed and crashed close aboard to port. At 12:54 p.m., a Japanese Judy made another attack run on the crippled *Franklin*, but its bomb exploded short.

Soon the enemy turned its attack on *Indianapolis*. At 1:19 p.m., a Zero appeared on the starboard quarter, 4,500 yards out, altitude 4,000 feet. Adrenaline raced through the ship, an exhilarating cocktail of raw combat power and esprit de corps, spiked with a tincture of fear. Indy's gunners opened fire.

The plane dodged into cloud cover, then shot out into blue sky again, now falling with a friendly fighter on its tail. A minute later, spotters picked up another enemy fighter circling the ship. Cries went up from the rangefinder operators—"3,800 yards!" The trigger men locked onto the plane, tracing its killing path toward *Indianapolis*. Sixty seconds later, the fighter was diving toward Indy's port quarter when one of the 5-inch gun crews blew off its tail, ending the pilot's day. No time to rest, though, as another Judy zinged in for a third run on *Essex*. Again, Indy opened fire. The plane smashed into the sea on *Essex's* port beam, but McVay and his gunners couldn't tell whether they or one of the other American ships had shot it down. At 2:30 p.m., another Judy appeared directly over *Indianapolis*, at twelve thousand feet, flying port to starboard. The plane was later reported shot down, but the Indy bridge crew did not see it fall.

It was the last attack in a very busy day that dealt Spruance a significant blow. The Japanese had long targeted his heavy carriers, but with little success. Now they had hit five in a single week, with *Franklin's* fiery agony in full view of the admiral's seat on Indy's bridge.

In the end, it was never a suicider, a bomb, or a torpedo that actually sank a ship. It was water. The interior of a warship is a honeycomb of watertight compartments segmenting the space inside her skin. Corridors called "passageways" run fore and aft and also, at intervals, traverse the vessel across the beam. These are interrupted by walls called "bulkheads," into which watertight doors are built.

Each watertight door or "hatch" is equipped with a handle, or "dog."

When the door is shut and the handle turned tight, or "dogged down," it renders the door watertight. Ladders connect one deck with another, and each point of connection is equipped with a "scuttle," a small hatchway that can also be dogged down and made watertight. Compartments off passageways—such as machinery spaces, berthing, offices, chow hall, and the like—also have doors equipped with watertight seals.

Offensive weapons could only make holes in a warship. Fluid tons of seawater would then rush in to equalize pressure. When the weight of the water exceeded the ship's buoyancy, down she went.

Miraculously, *Franklin* would not go down. Casualty reports from the crippled carrier streamed in to the flag staff aboard *Indianapolis*. The total number of men killed would reach 724, with another 265 wounded. With a thirteen-degree list and three feet down by the stern, the ship was taken under tow by USS *Pittsburgh*. Soon, though, she was able to cast off her tow and proceed under her own steam, having endured one of the worst fires any warship ever survived.

4

MARCH 31, 1945

Imperial Japanese Navy Special Attack Unit
Kanoya Airfield
Kyushu, Japan

VICE ADMIRAL MATOME UGAKI stood on Kanoya airfield on Kyushu, watching as aircrews climbed into twenty-four Ginga bombers. The day was momentous. After establishing the Special Attack Unit, the "kamikaze," as the last line of defense against the American invaders, this mission would be the unit's first major test. It was a far cry from where Ugaki had been two weeks before, huddled in an air raid shelter on this same field as a great tide of enemy planes blistered his flight-line with bombs and bullets. He had not been afraid—just annoyed by all the damned noise.

Now he would strike back. Before him on the airfield stood the crews of five Kawanishi flying boats and four land-based bombers that would lead the formation, contributing advance patrols and weather reconnaissance.

Already, Ugaki's search planes were keeping tabs on an enemy battle group, including its flagship, *Indianapolis*, now fifty miles southeast of Okinawa. The group had begun bombardment of the island, preparing to seize the last stepping-stone en route to the homeland invasion, and General Mitsuru Ushijima was charged with its defense. Most Okinawans lived on the island's southern half, along green ridges thickly terraced with rice paddies and fields of sugarcane. Ushijima's garrisons had enlarged and reinforced a natural network of caves, and also dug into a chain of slit trenches and bunkers concentrated around the southern capital of Naha. Ugaki was determined to come to Ushijima's aid.

It had been a little over a month since Admiral Ugaki, who was fifty-five, took over Japan's Special Attack Unit. On February 10, he was enjoying a bottle of sake when he received a telephone call summoning him before the emperor. Two days later, His Majesty received the admiral in audience at Fukiage Imperial Garden in Tokyo—albeit in an air raid shelter due to the menacing presence of an enemy plane. The forty-three-year-old emperor was a slight, bespectacled man. In his shy way, he honored Ugaki with kind words and personally assigned him to lead the kamikaze. It was a mission Ugaki understood as key to the fate of his nation.

By the spring of 1944, Ugaki had found himself shocked at the turnabout in the war. Territory after territory lost. The ominous attrition of matériel and men. Meanwhile, Allied forces were reaching peak strength, and Ugaki felt time was running out. His beloved commander, Admiral Isoroku Yamamoto, had predicted this result. In August 1941, the admiral, who had studied briefly at Harvard and had many American friends, ascended to commander in chief of Japan's Combined Fleet. He appointed Ugaki his chief of staff. As Japan contemplated war on America, Yamamoto warned that since the Empire could not win, it should not provoke this Western leviathan. But once ordered to fight, Yamamoto, a brilliant strategist, put the full force of his intellect behind the effort. Having spent two years in Washington, D.C., as a naval attaché, he knew the American Navy well and once called it "a dagger pointed at our throat." To counter that threat, Yamamoto engineered the surprise attack at Pearl Harbor.

But the admiral would not live out the war. In April 1943, U.S. intelligence received detailed information about his flight plans. Yamamoto would be aboard one of two planes departing Rabaul, New Guinea, on the morning of April 18. Ugaki would be on the other. At 7:30 a.m., a flight of sixteen American P-38 Lightning fighters intercepted the Japanese planes and shot both down. Yamamoto was killed, a small vengeance for Pearl Harbor. Ugaki, wounded but alive, vowed vengeance for his commander and friend.

Now, as commander of the Special Attack Unit, Ugaki had ramped up both special attack recruitment and training. American pilots had already decimated Japanese airpower. Now many of the Empire's pilots were fresh from flight school, some still in their teens. Ugaki's recruits were presented with the kamikaze concept, given forms to sign, and offered a choice: They could sign their names either next to the word "eager" or next to the words "very eager." Some signed out of bravado, but others felt forced, some by peer pressure and some by ancient national traditions such as honor and love of country and family.

Some who had signed now found themselves standing before Ugaki about to make their final flight. The young men about to die had spent their last days quietly. They read and reread letters from loved ones and spent hours gazing at treasured photographs. They wrote letters home. Many tucked locks of their hair into the envelopes. Finally, they boxed up their personal belongings to be shipped to their families when they did not return.

Ugaki's executive officer, Rear Admiral Toshiyuki Yokoi, thought the whole enterprise an enormous waste. When Imperial General Headquarters issued the unprecedented order that all armed forces should resort to suicide attack, Yokoi considered it nothing less than a national death sentence. He had studied the recent string of Japanese defeats and was working to improve land-based patrol methods, eliminate enemy surprise, and build up force protection at Japanese ground installations. To him and many other commanders, the suicide strategy proved that the High Command, panicked by a string of defeats, had abandoned cool military judgment and collapsed into wild gambling.

Doctrinally, Yokoi had never believed in the soundness of suicide tactics. First, there was the physics of the matter: A striking plane could not achieve sufficient velocity to pierce the decks of America's capital ships, the largest and most important in the enemy fleet. Second, there was no way to measure success, since dead pilots could not report. Finally, the expenditure of life and matériel ran precisely opposite the goals of an operations staff, which is to maximize damage at the least possible cost.

But other senior officers agreed with Ugaki, whose thoughts had run wild seeking ways to save the Empire. Some kamikaze leaders said openly that they could afford to sacrifice two thousand men—that if just 30 percent of their pilots hit Allied targets, it would be enough. For Ugaki's part, this calculus was not as cold as it seemed. He felt deep gratitude to the pilots who sacrificed themselves, and confided this to his most trusted confidant, his journal: "It is not because I am unfeeling that I can send our young men to die with a smile . . . ," he wrote. "I had made up my mind to follow the example of those young boys some day."

5

MARCH 31, 1945

USS *Indianapolis*
Okinawa, Japan

ON MARCH 31, THE morning before Easter, Seaman Second Class L. D. Cox sauntered down Indy's second-deck passageway toward breakfast. Cox, a nineteen-year-old with a round, open face and a gap-toothed smile, was nearing the mess hall when he ran into another sailor.

Cox stuck out his hand and introduced himself. The sailor grinned and gave Cox's hand an exuberant shake. "Pole!" he said. "Pole's my name!"

Cox's eyes went wide. "Not the great Basil P. Pole from Hugo, Oklahoma?"

"Yessir, that's me!" Pole said. Then he laughed and laughed, just as he did every day when he and Cox performed this same ritual. Cox laughed, too, shoulders bouncing as he continued down the passageway. He got a kick out of Basil P. Pole, but he was pretty sure that old boy's elevator only went about halfway up.

Nearing the mess hall, Cox could already smell what was for breakfast: beans. He sighed. He wished right now he had some of his mama's biscuits and gravy instead. On the other hand, he wouldn't trade what he'd seen out here during the war. At Iwo Jima, he'd stood at the rail and watched the Marines stomp ashore. They'd been so close that if he'd looked through binoculars he felt he could have seen them fighting hand-to-hand. And when that flag went up on Mount Suribachi and the horns blew and the bells clanged, tears winked into Cox's eyes and the hair on the back of his neck stood straight up.

Now they'd been bombarding Okinawa for a week. The percussion of the big guns hammered with such intensity that many crew members developed a ringing in their ears that would last the rest of their lives. It seemed to Cox on some days that a hundred hostile planes swarmed overhead. Air and sea fused in a hash of smoke, blast upon blast, ships' gunners firing up, pilots firing down, opposing rounds slashing black Xs in the sky. Cox had seen enemy planes get nicked, their tails erupting in flame like trick birthday candles before they zoomed down to explode against the hard plate of the sea. Some had their control surfaces shot off and entered slow flat spins, pinwheeling down almost lazily to hit the water with barely a splash. Sometimes, surface gunners simply shredded planes in midair.

The persistent stench of cordite infused the crews' uniforms, their skin, even their hair. The only respite came when the ship turned to a heading with a strong wind abeam so that the smoke of the guns could be carried overboard.

Cox thought it funny that he'd signed up for all this just to meet girls.

He'd graduated from high school only three years earlier—at thirty students, his graduating class in Comanche, Texas, was famously large— and attended two semesters at John Tarleton Agricultural College. But when he turned seventeen, Cox realized he was a prime candidate for the draft, so he thought he'd better just go on and volunteer. On the road between his family's livestock farm and the college, every second telephone pole was plastered with a flyer that said, "Join the Navy, see the world!" Those flyers alternated with ones that said, "A girl in every port!"

That sounded good to Cox, and one midnight in 1943, he hopped an old train passing through Comanche and rode it to Dallas, where he raised his right hand. Another train slid him west to boot camp in San Diego, then it was on to *Indianapolis*, where he arrived at about the same time as Captain McVay.

The first time he laid eyes on Indy, Cox just stood and gawked. She was colossal. Sleek. Magnificent. He could hardly wait to get aboard. When he did, a chief petty officer assigned Cox to deck division and here he still was, six months later, doing the dirty work. Chipping paint, lugging stores, sweating in the mess hall scrubbing pans the size of the pig troughs back home. Now, he stepped one-two over the knee knocker—a watertight doorway with an oval-shaped, man-sized cutout to pass through—and entered the mess hall. He lifted his chin in greeting to three sailors, Lyle Umenhoffer, Verlin Fortin, and Troy Nunley, all hunched over their plates. Sure enough, breakfast was beans.

On the bridge, McVay ordered Indy released from formation and maneuvered to take station in column astern *Salt Lake City*, another heavy cruiser. During the weeklong bombardment leading up to D-Day, Indy and the fleet had fired more than five thousand tons of ammunition on targets at Okinawa. Now, underwater demolition teams reconnoitered the beach approaches while Mitscher's carrier planes sanitized the island's sandy skirts, laying lines of rocket fire.

McVay was the second generation of his family to fight at sea. His father, Charles B. McVay, Jr., fleeted up in an entirely different Navy, when U.S. warships proceeded mainly under sail, carried livestock as food stores, and during drills, repelled enemy "boarders" with pikes and cutlasses. The elder McVay fought first in the Spanish-American War, then commanded the armored cruiser *Saratoga* during World War I, along with a pair of battleships, *New Jersey* and *Oklahoma*. He then served as commandant of Washington Naval Yard, chief of the Bureau of Ordnance, and commander in chief, U.S. Asiatic Fleet. McVay Junior was seventy-six now and, in his retirement, had assumed the role of hanging judge. He delivered a steady stream of sharp-tongued verdicts on the younger McVay's Navy performance and demanded that he cover himself with glory befitting an admiral's son.

McVay felt the pressure, but he was charting his own course in a Navy modernized under President Theodore Roosevelt. An academy man like his father, McVay III was commissioned in 1920 and rose quickly to prestigious postings, including commanding officer of USS *Luzon*, the flagship of the Yangtze Patrol in China. An officer on the rise, he had proved himself a utility player, serving as naval aide to the high command in the Philippines, as skipper of an oiler, and as executive officer of the light cruiser *Cleveland*. There, in action in the Solomon Islands, he earned a Silver Star for gallantry. Before taking command of *Indianapolis*, McVay served as chairman of the Joint Intelligence Staff under the Combined Chiefs of Staff of U.S. and British forces, a group privy to most of the war's deepest secrets.

As a leader of men, McVay's manner was somewhat less formal than his father's. He made it a regular practice to visit his enlisted men in their work spaces and ask them how things were going. Not in an inappropriately familiar way, but one that communicated his concern. The sailors' feedback worked itself out in practical ways. When McVay learned that the morale and welfare folks were showing movies only for officers, he ordered movies to be shown for enlisted men, too. Once, he went down and had a meal in the enlisted mess. After he finished, he stopped in at the galley and told the cooks to start serving better food. He felt it was important for his sailors to know that they were as critical to the life and mission of the ship as his officers, and that he, their skipper, was looking out for them.

Now *Indianapolis* steamed ahead to a position eleven miles off an Okinawa beach called Zanpa, still astern *Salt Lake City*, about a thousand yards behind. There were no other ships in the formation.

In fire control aft, Cleatus Lebow held his cards close to his chest and fanned them out to take a peek. Liking what he saw, Lebow, a fire controlman third class, glanced up at his regular poker buddies—Murphy, Gaither, and Smitty. All four men were seated around a four-by-six steel box that held spare 20 mm gun sights. Someone had covered the box with a wool blanket.

Paul Murphy, also a fire controlman third, was the dealer this hand. Dark-haired, with an open, all-American smile, Murphy, of Chillicothe, Missouri, was one of those happy-all-the-time folks who'd never met a stranger. He reported to Indy just a few months after Lebow. Both men were twenty years old and had become good friends. Now, Lebow studied Murphy's poker face, but the eyes weren't giving anything away.

"I'm in for a nickel," Lebow said in his heavy Texas drawl.

The other fellows hooted. It was a fairly rich bet, since there was a fifteen-cent per game maximum—money enough to buy three Cokes. Murphy and Smitty matched Lebow's nickel, but Gaither folded. Lebow usually won these games and thought old Gaither probably didn't want to give him any more of his money.

Lebow checked his cards. He slipped two from his hand and slid them facedown across the wool blanket to Murphy, who flipped him two more. Smitty took a couple of cards, and Murphy dealt himself one.

Lebow had been aboard since January 1944. With eight brothers and sisters, he was from a big, churchgoing family—which meant if church was open, the Lebows were going. Still, Lebow was no pacifist. As a gunnery range-finder aboard *Indianapolis* for most of the ship's battles, he had personally helped treat Japanese defenders to the latest fad in the Pacific: the "Spruance haircut." That meant total destruction, everything in sight laid low and burning.

Wagers circled the table again. "Call," Murphy said, and pitched in another nickel.

One by one, Lebow ticked his cards down on the gun-sight box, followed by Smitty, who revealed his all at once. Murphy slapped his cards faceup on top of Lebow's, his laughter bubbling like a soda fountain. "Read 'em and weep, boys! Read 'em and weep!"

Mike Quihuis glanced at the oddball cast on Adolfo Celaya's hand. "Hey, Celaya, you still layin' off the rednecks?"

"Nah," Celaya said. "I ain't scared."

Celaya and Quihuis were walking down the port side, the skies for the moment quiet.

In 1944, with so many of his friends going off to fight the war, Celaya had decided to join the Navy. Since he was only seventeen, his father had to sign for him. After he reported to *Indianapolis*, Celeya made friends with Santos Pena and Mike Quihuis, who was also of Mexican descent. There were only a couple dozen Hispanics on the ship, a tiny minority in a crew of about twelve hundred.

In Arizona, being Mexican hadn't been a big deal. In fact, it was a Mexican kid who had given Celaya his nickname, "Harpo." The kid said Celaya's puffy hair looked like Harpo Marx's, and Celaya had decided to embrace it. But in the Navy, Harpo's brown skin was a problem. From boot camp on, it seemed to Harpo that Navy recruiters had stacked the ranks with corn-fed rednecks from the middle and southern states. They called him "Pancho" and "wetback" and wanted to know when he was going to crawl back into that hole in Mexico he'd crawled out of. The rednecks didn't care that Celaya's family had been in America for four generations.

Quihuis and Pena were older than Harpo and tried to keep him out of trouble. But the kid was full of piss and vinegar, and having friends by his side only made him bolder. It didn't hurt that Quihuis had once been the welterweight boxing champ of Arizona.

Increasingly, when the rednecks ragged Harpo, he ragged back. Then one day, after a big Texan spat out an insult, Celaya wound up a round-house and clocked him in the jaw. The Texan's nose spouted blood and he crumpled to the deck. Pena, Quihuis, and several other men grabbed Celaya and held him back.

The Texan lumbered to his feet, towering over Celaya. "I'm gonna get you, you dirty goddamned Mexican! I'm gonna get you alone someday and kill you!"

Celaya had been too happy to be afraid. He had finally given it to one of those rednecks, and good. But when he looked down at his punching hand, he saw that he'd also paid a price. A shard of naked bone poked up through his skin.

Quihuis hustled him down to sickbay, where Indy's chief physician, Dr. Lewis Haynes, examined Celaya's hand.

"How did this happen, sailor?" the doctor asked.

"Slipped and fell, sir."

Haynes got to work. He put Celaya's hand in a cast and installed the wire contraption. It was an experimental technique Haynes had never tried before, a kind of traction. Celaya hopped off the exam table to leave, but Haynes stopped him.

"Yes, sir?" Harpo said.

Haynes leveled his gaze, but a smile pushed at the corners of his mouth. "Next time you hit someone," he said, "close your fist."

Harpo's face flushed and he looked at the deck. "Yes, sir."

Now, walking down the port side, Celaya told Quihuis he'd probably get the cast off in another week. At thirty-one years old with a wife and three kids, Quihuis was as much an uncle as a buddy to Celaya, who was still only a teenager. Quihuis agreed with Pena that the kid needed to watch his mouth. After Celaya decked that Texan, Pena had pulled him aside and whispered fiercely, "If you keep up that attitude, you won't be around anymore."

"What do you mean?" Celaya said.

"I mean, some night a bunch of those rednecks are gonna grab you and throw you off the fantail. That really happens! Is that what you want?"

Apparently, Harpo did not, because Quihuis noticed that he settled down some after that, despite his big talk to the contrary.

Suddenly, the high whine of props and acceleration hit Quihuis's ears like a stinger. He froze, whipped his head skyward, and saw a suicide plane. It was headed straight for the ship.

6

MARCH 31, 1945

USS *Indianapolis*
Okinawa, Japan

THE JAPANESE PLANE, an Army Peregrine Falcon, burst through the low overcast at 7:08 a.m., whining wide open. The 20 mm gun mount on Indy's fo'c'sle unleashed a chatter of bullets. McVay charged out from the charthouse, shouting, "Who is that trigger-happy—?"

Then he heard the plane. McVay wheeled around and ordered general quarters—the signal for the crew to drop what they're doing and prepare for battle. A boatswain's whistle piped over the 1MC,* a one-way loudspeaker system that reached every compartment on the ship. "All hands, man your battle stations."

On the port side amidships, Quihuis yelled one word at Harpo: "Run!" He wanted to put some steel between them and the suicide plane and sprinted down the port side, Harpo on his heels. They plunged through a hatch and down a ladder, sliding down the handrails on their armpits, feet never touching the rungs.

Edgar Harrell, a twenty-year-old Marine corporal from Kentucky, raced to the 40 mm gun mount on the fantail. He saw the plane screaming toward the ship. It appeared to be balanced on the twin pillars of fire streaming from its guns.

On the fo'c'sle, the "trigger-happy" 20 mm gunner, Buck Gibson, kept shooting. He saw tracer rounds piercing the plane and his parents' faces flashed before him. Would he ever see them again?

On the mess deck, L. D. Cox heard the battle stations call, dropped his tray on the table, and flew out the door and up a ladder. He reached the main deck just in time to catch movement at the skyward edge of his vision. It was a suicider, and it seemed to be headed straight for him.

---

* 1MC is pronounced "One-Em-See."

•   •   •

On the 40 mm gun, Ed Harrell was ready to shoot. He was waiting for
the gun sights to connect to radar when the pilot changed course slightly,
possibly deflected by Gibson's gun. The plane now flew almost parallel to
Indy, but then seemed to lose control. It veered left, dove, and slammed
into the main deck aft with a thunderous sound, just inside the port gunwale, and a five-hundred-pound bomb dropped free of the wing. The
crash tore a hole in the main deck, four feet by five, its outboard portion
open to the air, like a bite out of the ship.

The projectile plummeted nose first through the main deck and
drilled down through the ship, just three feet inboard of her skin.

The bomb punched a sixteen-inch hole through the second deck
and kept falling. On the mess deck, Lyle Umenhoffer, Verlin Fortin, and
Troy Nunley saw it crash through the overhead and pierce the deck
eight feet from their table. The impact sprayed them in a maelstrom
of beans.

The bomb continued banging down through the ship, smashing
straight through a crew berthing compartment where Seaman First Class
Tony King saw it fall right past his bunk. The bomb kept falling, drilling
the first platform deck and cracking open the skin between frames 112
and 113 and spilling out into the sea.

Then it exploded.

The blast shook Indy with seismic force. A shock wave boomeranged
back through the bomb's exit hole, blowing its edges inward and tearing
what had been a smallish rupture into a yawning hole, four feet high and
five feet wide. Seawater and fuel oil burst up through the main deck in
a geyser a hundred feet high. The explosion caused the ship to whip so
violently that the abrupt movement snapped antennae off the foremast
and knocked the planes from the catapults.

All over the ship, men fell against bulkheads or to their knees, doused
in showers of grime and dust. Gear tore loose and clattered to the deck.
The force of the blast ruptured portions of the deck, jacked others up at
angles, buckled framing, and wrinkled Indy's skin like the corrugated
roof on a shed. On every deck, men heard the low, eerie groan of twisting steel.

The impact threw Cox into the air. The fantail plunged, and blue water washed across the stern. Seawater flooded the aft 40 mm gun-mounts. The suicide plane still hung on the rail, like a malevolent insect. From the bridge wing, Morgan saw four sailors rush to the plane, lay their hands wherever they could, and give a mighty shove. Most of the plane tumbled over the side and splashed into the sea.

Indianapolis was rapidly taking on water. A voice blared over the 1MC: "Set Material Condition Afirm." The call, which ordered the crew to secure all watertight hatches, reverberated belowdecks and echoed through every compartment.

Amid the mad scramble up the ladders was nineteen-year-old Troy Nunley, who had crawled out of the mess hall through a carpet of beans. He couldn't believe he was leaving all his stuff behind in his locker—he'd said he never would—but he had to get out, *had* to. Water was rushing down the second-deck passageway like the Mississippi River. Nunley clambered up a ladder, men on his heels, and popped out into daylight in the center of a knot of sailors. They surrounded the hatch and were shouting back down—"Come on! Come on! We have to dog it down!"—urging the climbers up with wild gestures.

Nunley heard men calling up from below, chased up the ladder by the deluge. He turned and looked down into the hatch. He could see a man submerged to his waist and another to his chest. Adrenaline flooded Nunley's body. He reached into the hatch and yanked up one man—the young bugler, Earl Procai, who was badly wounded—and then another.

The water was rising fast.

"We gotta shut it!" the men on the deck called. "We gotta dog it down!"

Nunley heard more voices from below—"Help! Help us!"

He heard another voice at his shoulder. "Water's almost to the top! We gotta dog it down! Help us!"

But Nunley couldn't. He knew it was either save the sailors below or save the ship, but he couldn't shut the hatch on those men.

Next he heard a heavy clang, the hatch slamming shut. The voices below were severed, but Troy Nunley would hear them for the rest of his life.

•　　•　　•

In sickbay, Dr. Haynes and the junior ship's physician, Lieutenant Junior Grade Melvin Modisher, were working furiously on the wounded when Harpo Celaya burst in waving his arm.

"Doc, you gotta get me out of this cast! They need me topside!"

Haynes turned from the man he was working on, sheared off Celaya's cast, and sent him on his way. Post attack musters revealed that eight men were missing, prompting officers and chiefs to organize search parties. There were twenty-one wounded, including Procai. Though Nunley had helped pull Procai clear of the flooding, the young bugler died of his wounds.

Meanwhile, Indy herself had sustained grave injuries, and the crew broke into damage control parties that sped like ambulance teams to minister to her wounds. Waterlogged compartments on the port side dragged her off-kilter, and she listed to port, eventually canting her decks seventeen degrees.

Spruance immediately expressed his suspicion that the Japanese pilot had targeted Indy, knowing she was the 5th Fleet flagship. He ordered his flag lieutenant to see whether a code book had dropped from the plane's wreckage before it was pushed overboard. A search was made, but no code book was found.

The damage to the ship was too serious for repairs at sea. On the bridge, McVay ordered the OOD,* or officer of the deck—the captain's direct representative on the bridge—to set course for Kerama Retto, an island twenty miles away. The Keramas had been the first islands Spruance ordered his forces to hit in the Ryukyu chain, part of his bold plan to secure both a seaplane base and a fleet anchorage in support of the main Okinawa invasion. The 77th Division, under Major General Andrew D. Bruce, had begun landings on March 26 and finally secured the Keramas just two days before Spruance's own ship needed safe harbor.

At 10 a.m., escorted by USS *Twiggs*, Indy cautiously spun up her starboard screws and limped to Kerama Retto under her own power. Word from underwater demolition teams was that sharp reefs fringed the islands, with treacherous coral heads lurking scant feet below the surface.

---

* The OOD (pronounced "oh-oh-dee") is the officer of the deck. A rotating crew of qualified officers take shifts or "stand watches" in this position, which is located on the bridge when the ship is under way.

The twenty-mile trip took two and a half hours. McVay guided his stricken ship gently, and once in the anchorage, nudged her into berth K-66.

Late in the afternoon on March 31, Glenn Morgan stood at attention on the quarterdeck, a silver bugle in his hand. He felt as if some evil force had peeled open his chest and plucked out his heart. His best friend, Calvin Ball Emery, and his little buddy, Earl Procai, were among nine men killed in the kamikaze strike. Captain McVay had already ordered the colors lowered to half-mast and mustered the crew to render Procai his final honors.

Indianapolis's officers and chiefs—the most senior enlisted men—stood in solemn ranks wearing long-sleeved cotton grays. Petty officers and below wore dungarees and chambray shirts. The formation bent in an L around a plain wooden box. Procai's body lay inside. An American flag lay over the box, just large enough to cover the top.

From the quarterdeck, Morgan could see the Kerama islands, some so narrow they could be measured in yards. Procai was to be buried on one of those little slivers. It was so far from his home in Minnesota, Morgan thought. From his mother and father and sisters who adored him. From the Orthodox church where Procai had performed the Ukrainian "Hopak" dance on holidays. From all the things he had told Morgan he loved.

A Marine honor guard stood at the rail, and the detail leader barked a command. Morgan fell in line with the firing party and sounded "Officers Call" on his bugle.

"Crew!" an officer called out. "Parade rest!"

The crew took the stance and Father Thomas Conway, the chaplain, stepped up wearing vestments, a lector in his left hand. He spoke scripture over the boy and administered a rite of hope and consolation.

Conway called the men to prayer and they lowered their heads. Afterward, Morgan brought the crew to attention with a bugle call. Three times, the Marine detail leader uttered a deep command: "Aim . . . fire!" The honor guard fired three volleys into the sky over the rail. Then Morgan raised the trumpet and sounded "Taps" for his dear friend. It was one of the calls they'd practiced together.

7

APRIL 1945

USS *Indianapolis*
Kerama Islands

FOLLOWING THE KAMIKAZE ATTACK, Spruance sent a message to Admiral Richmond Kelly Turner, commander of 5th Fleet's amphibious assault troops. After months of planning and with twelve hundred ships ready to strike Okinawa, Spruance himself would be sitting D-Day out.

Until the kamikaze, the lucky Indy Maru, as the men called her, had charged across the Pacific at the head of the fleet, challenged but unscarred, trailing victory in her wake. Now, though, the crew's seeming shield of invincibility was shattered. Worse, they were trapped in the Kerama Retto anchorage. Japanese doctrine called for sinking not the greatest number of ships, but the greatest aggregate tonnage. In a harbor filled with sitting ducks, *Indianapolis* was the prize bird.

Morgan found the whole thing unnerving, Indy swinging helpless on the hook and the venomous Japanese still buzzing around. "Since we've been anchored and disabled," he wrote in his contraband diary, "we've felt as though we are living on borrowed time." The crew had been warned not to keep diaries or journals lest they fall into enemy hands. But Morgan thought it would be all right since he never entered any secrets into print. "Air attacks from suicides continued last night and this morning, three more ships got hit. At first, being at war was adventurous, but after being hit, it is entirely frightening. Suicide boats are at night running in the harbor. A security watch is posted and a boat circling the ship all night continually."

With Lyle Umenhoffer and others, Morgan had escorted two sets of bodies—in canvas bags stitched by Indy's sailmaker—to one of the outlying islands for burial. On one trip, a Japanese boy ran up to him. He couldn't speak English, except to chirp, "New York! New York!" The boy gave Morgan a wooden flute. He was a friendly little kid, a bright spot in a grim errand. Then a Marine warned the funeral detail that while the island was mainly secure, rogue Japanese snipers were still taking pot-shots. Morgan hotfooted it back to the small boat that had brought them ashore and got the hell out of there.

On the night of April 1, he addressed his diary entry to his wife, Mertie Jo. A pretty brunette with wide-set eyes and a Rita Hayworth smile, she'd married Morgan just after he graduated from boot camp. Morgan recounted to his wife the loss of Emery and Procai, who lived for only a few minutes after he was found. "It doesn't seem possible that such a thing as this could happen. When you find out about it, my darling wife, I know you'll feel as I do now, for you knew little Earl and good old staunch C.B., who many a time took my watch so I could see you." Morgan ended the diary entry with his usual closing line, "I love you, Mertie Jo."

L. D. Cox was ramming a slab of steel wool back and forth in a giant cooking pan, sweat streaming south in his collar. Beside him, a mile-high pile of pots and pans climbed toward the overhead, and steam snaked up from the deep sink to cook his face. Cox let go of the wool and flipped his palm up to look at it. The steel wool had chewed his fingers bloody.

After the plane hit, he'd been sent to the scullery, where he'd been scrubbing pots and pans for two days straight. He was about to grumble aloud when he remembered the dead boys they'd buried at Kerama Retto. He decided to stop feeling sorry for himself, picked up the scouring pad, and started in again.

"Are you Loel Dene Cox?"

Cox looked up to see an unusual sight—an officer in the scullery. "Yes, sir, I am," he answered.

"I noticed in your record that you've had some college. Since that suicider, we're shorthanded up in navigation. How would you like to move from deck division to navigation? You'd work up on the bridge."

Cox tried not to sound too eager. "I'd like that, sir."

"Well, son, drop that pan and follow me."

Cox dropped the pan so fast and hard he imagined it ringing all over the ship, and in his mind, he licked that officer's boots all the way up the ladder.

Up on the bridge, he found Admiral Spruance and Captain McVay, a couple of other officers, the bugler Morgan, a yeoman named Buckett, and Lieutenant Commander Kyle "Kasey" Moore, who had been his boss up until a few moments ago.

Now this is more like it, Cox thought, though he did think he detected the skipper giving his haircut an appraising glance.

A salvage ship, USS *Clamp*, had moored alongside Indy, and her chief salvage officer worked closely with McVay's first lieutenant and damage control officer, Kasey Moore. Though "lieutenant" refers to a rank, "first lieutenant" is a Navy job title, and Moore's included supervising maintenance of the ship's hull. Now, in the wake of the kamikaze strike, Moore toured the hash of gnarled steel inside Indy's skin and, with Photographer's Mate Alfred Sedivi, snapped pictures to catalog the destruction.

Shortly after Spruance raised his flag on *Indianapolis*, he learned that Moore, of Knoxville, Tennessee, had been a respected newspaperman in civilian life. A staff writer at the *Knoxville Sunday Journal*, Moore had also traveled as a stringer for papers like the *New York Times*, taking expert photos to run with his stories. Spruance was keen to document American progress across the Pacific and quickly dubbed Moore "photographic officer." From then on Moore, Spruance, and often Sedivi, boarded a Higgins boat and bounced into the beach of every conquered island.

Moore's first trip ashore with Spruance was at Betio, Tarawa, and it marked him deeply. The island might as well have been hell. Crushed and blackened, the landscape wore the smell of death like a rotting skin. A thousand Marines and nearly five thousand Japanese had been killed. The stench was nearly unbearable and worked its way into Moore's clothes so thoroughly that he later would not be able to get it out.

With Spruance and his staff, Moore picked his way through a sprawling vista of enemy corpses that stretched away like some grotesque landscape painted by a ghoul. Some Japanese had committed *seppuku*, ritual suicide, and their intestines protruded from their bellies in putrid loops. The images cemented Moore's opinion that these men were fanatical warriors who would never surrender.

At Betio, Moore took his first pictures for Spruance, and the two would become good friends. Moore admired and respected the admiral more than any man he had ever known, loved his wry, quiet humor, and his dogged logic in the face of opposition. Of all the brass of whom Moore had taken pictures—Nimitz, Halsey, MacArthur, Fleet Admiral Ernest King—Spruance was one of the few who was reluctant to pose and never asked for copies. Along with Alfred Sedivi's, Moore's photos, processed in *Indianapolis*'s dark, cramped lab and absorbed into the Navy's immense unbylined catalog, would become some of the most iconic of the Pacific war.

But neither man had had to document major damage aboard their own ship. Now, Sedivi snapped a series of pictures while Moore took notes. Wide gashes in the decks and skin laid Indy's innards open to air and sea. Thick coatings of fuel oil clung to every surface. Multiple decks were jacked out of position, beams and framing buckled and twisted, bulkheads sheared from their stiffeners. Both the deep-sea dive locker and motor whaleboat hull had been destroyed. The explosion had also torn the No. 4 shaft completely off the ship, leaving another hole, two feet tall by six feet long.

After itemizing the destruction, Moore set an array of continuous watches. Sailors kept steady eyes on damaged areas, ready to report any signs of separation or weakening of bulkheads or watertight doors. Meanwhile, divers from *Clamp* worked to place soft patches over the holes.

On April 3, the admiral was striding across Indy's mangled fantail when the chief salvage officer from *Clamp* walked up, crestfallen. "Sorry to report, sir, my men have dropped the propeller and it's at the bottom of the harbor."

The officer braced himself for a dressing-down, but Spruance said quietly, "That's too bad." Then he kept on walking.

This development did not dismay or surprise the admiral. He had chosen *Indianapolis* precisely because she was expendable. That was not the same as being substandard—in fact, far from it. Spruance had wanted for his flagship a quick, agile vessel powerful enough to defend herself, but with enough endurance to steam between the far-flung islands in this vast theater—perhaps the largest theater in the history of warfare.

Whether his ship was taken out of the fight by the duties of command or by enemy fire, he had not wanted his withdrawal to weaken his fleet. Therefore, instead of setting up shop on a battleship or carrier, he had chosen a cruiser, and an aging one at that.

The plan now was for the ship to return to the States for repairs. The Okinawa landings had gone better than Spruance could have imagined, but he knew Japan's ceding of the beaches meant fiercer fighting ahead. On April 5, Spruance shifted his flag to the battleship *New Mexico*. Before he and his staff trooped off Indy's brow, the admiral pulled McVay aside and insisted that *Indianapolis* return quickly and resume duty as his flagship.

8

APRIL 1945

Imperial Japanese Submarine I-58
Near Okinawa, Japan

ON APRIL 2, MOCHITSURA Hashimoto put to sea with the same *kaiten* crews he'd carried in his frustrated operation against Iwo Jima. Before his departure, he made a point of asking headquarters for detailed reports of the enemy's positions off Okinawa. The Americans had already begun their bombardment there. Hashimoto was particularly keen to learn the disposition of American destroyer patrols off the island's northern shore.

Okinawa's airfields were just four hundred miles from Japan. Emperor Hirohito considered the island's successful defense critical to achieving a negotiated peace with Washington and avoiding the shame of surrender. The garrison there had used their bare hands to extend a natural cave network into a labyrinth of trenches and bunkers. As at Iwo Jima, the strategy was to lie in wait, let the invading Americans come ashore,

and then slaughter them wholesale. Japan's military leaders hoped that
if they could make America pay dearly enough for Okinawa, her leaders
would judge the blood cost of a homeland invasion too high.

How had it come to this? Hashimoto wondered. He had been born in
1909, and by the time he was of age, Japan's military was the pride of the
nation. When he graduated from the naval academy and was commissioned in 1931, the nation boasted a robust economy and a string of war
victories in Manchuria and China. This was as it should be, Hashimoto
thought then. Was not Japan the land of destiny, chosen by the gods to
lead the world? Was not even the emperor himself divine?

Now, as I-58 sailed south of Kyushu, a storm front crept in. Low
dark clouds scuttled across the skies, and a gathering sea whipped and
swelled. Hashimoto began to worry about whether he would be able to
launch his *kaiten*. In this surge, they could broach and be destroyed.

The Type 1 *kaiten*—a name that means "the turn toward heaven"—
was a modified Type 93 *sanso gyorai*, an oxygen torpedo. Each was small,
less than an arm span across and about sixty feet long, and the fate of
its pilot even more certain than that of the kamikaze. While the kamikaze might develop mechanical trouble and return to base, a *kaiten*
could not redock with its mother sub. Once the pilot boarded the torpedo and closed the hatch, there was no escape. After launch, when the
pilot reached final attack range, he surfaced to check his bearing and distance to the target via periscope and make any necessary adjustments.
He would then submerge again, arm his warhead, and proceed on his
final attack run. If he missed, he could make adjustments and try again.
If he failed altogether, he could detonate his vessel as a last resort rather
than sink to the sea bottom and slowly suffocate.

Though the *kaiten*'s creators both perished in failed underwater trials, IJN leaders had reason to see the project through. Japanese military
planners thought the heavy, long-range projectile would give smaller
vessels a mighty hammer with which to strike larger ones, such as battleships.

Hashimoto had not been able to launch *kaiten* since I-58's first war
patrol in January 1945. He remembered the send-off from Kure. As I-58's
virgin bow cleaved the harbor, the *kaiten* pilots sat on the converted hangar deck in their human torpedoes, swords held aloft, white headbands
flying dashingly in the breeze. Hashimoto watched from the bridge as a

festival of well-wishers in motorboats darted alongside, shouting good omens, prayers for success, and the names of these sailors about to sortie out and face the enemy. Beside the Japanese ensign flew another flag with the inscription "The Unpredictable Kaiten."

On that patrol, Hashimoto had driven his boat to Guam, where he lurked eleven miles off Apra Harbor, lying to, waiting, dodging American ships and planes unseen. On January 11, thirteen minutes after surfacing, I-58 intercepted enemy radio traffic warning American ships that a suspicious vessel had been sighted.

Hashimoto tensed. *Could it be us?*

If it was, there was nothing he could do about it. His boat was two hours from the *kaiten* launch point off Guam. He pressed on.

An earlier air reconnaissance report had shown twenty large and forty small transports moored in Apra Harbor. No glorious targets such as an aircraft carrier or large man-o'-war. Inwardly, Hashimoto felt sorry for the *kaiten* pilots, that they were about to sacrifice their lives for mere consolation prizes. But he rallied their spirits and counseled them each to search for the largest, most heavily loaded transport they could find. He also reminded them that the recon report was nearly thirty-six hours old. "Perhaps an aircraft carrier has come in since the report," he offered as encouragement.

Hashimoto and one of his navigators climbed up through the conning tower to the bridge and looked out over the gunnery deck where the *kaiten* were lashed to the hull. Billowing clouds sailed in a dark sky that shimmered with starlight. Two *kaiten* pilots reported to the bridge, both wearing only *fundoshi*, the traditional Japanese undergarment. Except for the ocean swell sluicing against the hull, silence spread across the moment.

One pilot gazed into the heavens. "Captain," he finally said, "which is the Southern Cross?"

Hashimoto tilted his eyes at the sky but could not find the constellation. He turned to the navigator and asked him to point it out.

"The Cross isn't showing yet," the navigator said. "It will appear soon, though, to the south."

The pilot showed no disappointment, but said simply, "We embark."

The pilots shook hands and climbed down to their *kaiten*, followed shortly by another pair of pilots, including Lieutenant Ishikawa, a young officer of twenty-two. Hashimoto wished them luck and gave them orders to board their torpedoes. Their composure at that moment struck him and would remain with him for the rest of his life.

I-58 submerged, and at 2:30 a.m., Hashimoto gave the order: "Stand by to launch."

The *kaiten* aligned their rudders with the submarine, and a half-hour later—ninety minutes before dawn—the launch began. Two suicide torpedoes shot into the sea, their pilots shouting, "Three cheers for the emperor!" just before their telephone lines were ripped from the mothership. A third pilot had communication problems and could not be heard. The fourth pilot's telephone line was working, but he jetted away from I-58 without uttering a sound.

For the next ninety minutes, Hashimoto and his crew listened on the hydrophones for clues that their brave comrades had hit their targets. A periscope search to the east showed promise—smoke, perhaps. But then again, it might have been only a dark cloud. In the end, nothing was confirmed.

That night at the evening meal, Hashimoto and his officers prayed for the souls of the departed pilots. Afterward, they attended to the young men's personal effects, which included each man's *Isho*, or "death letter," containing last thoughts. Lieutenant Ishikawa had written:

> The day of decisive action together with three other men on board has arrived. We are all well and in good spirits. . . . Great Japan is the land of the Gods. The land of the Gods is eternal and cannot be destroyed. Hereafter no matter, there will be thousands and tens of thousands of boys, and we now offer our lives as a sacrifice for our country. Let us get away from the petty affairs of this earthly and mundane life to the land where righteousness reigns supreme and eternal.

Now, so close to Okinawa, Hashimoto hoped for better success. But as at Iwo Jima, harassment by enemy fighters and bombers had again rendered him unable to charge his batteries. On April 6, he reached the area west of Amami Shima and at 1 p.m. spotted a ship, its superstructure slicing into the horizon. Though he was still close to home waters, the enemy's advance had shrunk the seas like a harshly washed garment. Hashimoto could not afford to assume the ship was Japanese. Instead, he ordered a dive.

9

***

APRIL 6, 1945

USS *Indianapolis*
Kerama Islands

ON THE MORNING OF April 6, enemy planes grazed the Kerama Retto anchorage, then banked back toward the main surface force that was still shelling the beach at Okinawa. The Japanese first targeted the outer ring of destroyers on picket duty, then swept down on the flattops at the center of the fleet. As many as twenty planes would swarm a single ship. Antiaircraft gunners shot most of them down, but pilots who managed to slip through crashed decks and superstructures, igniting infernos like the one that had torched *Franklin*. In all, ten coordinated attacks, more than three hundred enemy planes, dove on the American fleet that day, the largest coordinated suicide attack of the war. Japanese pilots dispatched by Vice Admiral Ugaki sank two destroyers, a high-speed minesweeper, and two cargo ships, while damaging dozens more.

From Kerama Retto, Indy's gunners could see oily smoke piling up over the horizon, the noise terrific even from a distance. At 4:41 p.m., they opened fire on an enemy plane sighted to the west. After nightfall, two more planes attacked Kerama's southern anchorage. One was shot down, while the other crashed an ammunition ship and exploded in a sheet of flame that seemed to reach the heavens.

The men of Indy thought Kerama Retto—"Island Chain Between Happiness and Good"—a gruesome place and wished they could get the hell out of there. The scuttlebutt was that the ship would go all the way back to the States for repairs, but some of the fellows said only to Pearl Harbor. On April 7, McVay weighed anchor, and at first it seemed he might have to shoot his way out of the little harbor. Gunners spotted enemy aircraft in the area as early as 3 a.m., and an hour later commenced firing. But at a quarter past six, the senior officer present in the anchorage gave the all clear. A half hour later, McVay stood on the bridge, sending commands down to the engine room.

Down in engineering, Commander Glen DeGrave used engines No. 1 and 2, starboard only, since the No. 3 shaft was unusable and the No. 4 screw now lay at the bottom of the sea. At half past seven, Indy passed through the northern antisubmarine net and by 1:15 p.m. had rendezvoused with the thirteen-ship task unit that would see her safely to Guam.

At the same time, a few miles to the west, Admiral Spruance was about to check off another objective on his war plan: The Japanese supership *Yamato* was crumbling under the assault of hundreds of American fighter-bombers. Twin waves of U.S. planes swarmed the mighty vessel until she resembled from the air a mastodon set upon by a pack of predators. As she made her final death roll, the ship disappeared in a great flash of light. A column of red fire shot skyward, then melted into a boiling thunderball. Aboard *New Mexico*, Spruance got word: *Yamato* was down. Her death marked the worldwide end of the battleship era—and also of Japanese surface resistance in the Pacific war.

In Tokyo, Emperor Hirohito heard the news, and for him, *Yamato*'s defeat signaled the futility of pressing on with the war. His generals, however, did not agree. They would fight to the death, even if it meant arming schoolgirls with bamboo spears. The next day, Hirohito secretly charged his new prime minister, Admiral Kantaro Suzuki, with a new mission: find acceptable means of ending the war. *Any* means short of outright surrender.

10

APRIL 1945

Alsos Mission
Stadtilm, Germany

NEARLY SIX THOUSAND MILES west of the emperor's palace, another secret mission was nearing its climax. Army Major Robert Furman arrived in Stadtilm, Germany, to find that the Nazis had beaten him to his target by two days.

Furman was chief intelligence officer for America's Manhattan Project. His mission was to learn how close the Third Reich was to developing an atomic bomb. Traveling with Samuel Goudsmit, a Dutch-American physicist, Furman landed in Stadtilm, a close-built village of steep-gabled roofs and Gothic church spires, on April 10. The pair had tracked to the town a man whose name was near the top of their target list of German scientists: Kurt Diebner, a physicist with the Heereswaffenamt, the weapons agency of the German army.

Furman and Goudsmit, key agents in a clandestine U.S. mission called Alsos, wanted to question Diebner about the state of the Nazis' quest to build a bomb. But by the time they arrived, the Gestapo had already scooped up Diebner and other scientists and whisked them away to Adolf Hitler's mountain fortress in the Bavarian Alps.

Pushing across Europe in the wake of advancing Allied troops, the Alsos mission had two main goals: to nail down the final truth about the state of German atomic science and to track down every last gram of fissionable material hidden on the continent. In Stadtilm, Diebner's group had left behind a small cache of fissionable material in the form of pressed uranium oxide, as well as an atomic "pile," or reactor. Goudsmit examined the pile and found it pathetically rudimentary. Added to the intel that had cascaded into Alsos all spring, the Stadtilm find was further evidence that the Nazis were years away from turning the doomsday theory of fission into a working weapon.

But mere evidence was not good enough for Furman's boss, Major

General Leslie Groves. The forty-eight-year-old general headed the war's most closely guarded secret, America's own bomb-building project, the Manhattan Engineering District. The specter of a German atomic weapon had haunted Groves since the summer of 1943, when Manhattan scientists working for him—including several German expatriates— raised the awful possibility.

There were signs. The Nazis' heavy-water production in Norway, for example. There were also large missing caches of uranium ore, including boxcar loads that the Germans had seized in Belgium in 1940. And what of the news that Werner Heisenberg, considered by many to be the world's foremost practicing physicist, was engaged in atomic research on Germany's behalf?

Meanwhile, American atomic experts cloistered in covert labs at the University of Chicago, the Oakridge labs in Knoxville, Tennessee, and Los Alamos in New Mexico raised an even more chilling possibility. U.S. scientists had experimented with multiple ways of making fissionable materials, all complex and time-consuming, but all successful. Could that mean there might be other methods, too? Had they missed some tiny epiphany that would unlock the secret of a simpler fission, one the enemy had discovered already?

At times, the fear swirling around these questions nearly paralyzed U.S. researchers. Very little information about the enemy effort abroad filtered stateside. The Brits, who had entered the war with a superior intelligence service, passed along an occasional nugget. But they were war-weary, focused on driving back the Axis powers, and had little manpower to devote to the collection of intelligence in so new and narrow a field. Groves, though, was a determined man. He had been charged with delivering a functional atom bomb. If that meant setting up his own intelligence apparatus, then by God that's what he would do. In August 1943, he began engineering foreign intelligence collection aimed at drilling down to the truth about the German atomic program.

That was when he summoned Major Robert Furman. A twenty-eight-year-old with cinnamon hair and a serious disposition, Furman already knew the general, having worked for him in 1941 overseeing the final stages of construction of the Pentagon. Furman had studied civil engineering at Princeton, where he became accustomed to spotting Albert Einstein's wild mane floating across the campus like dandelion fluff. For many students, Depression-era Princeton was less a laurel than a refuge. With jobs scarce and their fathers out of work, they went to college to kill time. Furman paid for his own education by working side jobs—running a theater and managing a sandwich shop. After graduation, he suffered a series of employment setbacks as three jobs in construction and civil engineering fell through.

In 1940, he was called up for Army service, where he finally realized his dream of becoming a builder. During the Pentagon project, he worked under General Groves, who remembered Furman when he needed a key man who was both tenacious and discreet.

In early autumn 1943, Furman took a seat across the desk from Groves at his office on the fifth floor of the new War Department building on C Street in Washington, D.C. The general turned to open his office safe. Inside, Furman glimpsed manuals, stacks of paper, and, oddly, a little cache of hard candy. Groves extracted a book, opened it to the final page, and directed Furman to read the last paragraph.

The major saw that the text involved the potentiality of "fission," the theory that all matter had an equivalence in, and was potentially convertible to, energy. When fission occurred layer upon layer, the theory went, in a kind of kinetic avalanche, it would produce an explosion of unprecedented magnitude. Furman was first exposed to atomic theory in the late thirties, while still at Princeton. In 1939, Dr. Otto Hahn of Germany's Kaiser Wilhelm Institute had bombarded uranium with neutrons, achieving the first laboratory example of fission. Since then, *Time* and other publications had speculated about the possibility of ripening this nascent force into an apocalyptic weapon.

Furman finished reading the passage and looked up at Groves, whose eyes were bright with the expectation of shared revelation.

"Yes," Furman said simply. He thought Groves seemed rather disappointed at his lack of surprise.

At that first meeting, Groves briefed Furman on the Manhattan Engineering District, as the project was technically known. The general explained that he needed to know what the Germans were doing in the atomic field. But he could not very well set up something so bold as a "department of atomic intelligence" without giving away the existence of the American program, even within the U.S. government itself. Instead, he wanted Furman to meet with the various intelligence agencies—

Army, Navy, OSS (Office of Strategic Services)—and find out what those agencies knew without revealing why he wanted to know it.

Furman accepted the assignment and began a crash course in atomic science. Among his tutors were Dr. Richard Tolman, a mathematical and physical chemist who had influenced Einstein's thinking on the physical dynamics of the universe, and Dr. J. Robert Oppenheimer, Groves's lead scientist at Los Alamos.

Oppenheimer told Furman that any effort to collect intelligence on the German atomic program would begin by pinpointing the whereabouts of the country's leading scientists. Find them, Oppenheimer said, and Furman would find the Nazi program. Furman made a list of every European scientist with credentials in the atomic field, a fairly simple task in so new and exclusive a discipline. Working with members of the OSS, he led missions to capture and interrogate every one of them.

For the next eighteen months, Furman proved himself intensely secretive, a quality Groves prized, and as unswerving as a bullet. Both traits cost Furman a woman he loved. When he entered the Manhattan Project, he was engaged to be married. But as he canvassed the world, he was unable to tell his fiancée where he was or what he was doing. Finally, the engagement was called off and the relationship melted away. He would later say his fiancée "suffered greatly."

By the spring of 1945, there was no one in the world apart from Groves who knew more about every facet of the Manhattan Project than Robert Furman. Now, in April, the Alsos mission was accelerating. Furman and Goudsmit had missed Kurt Diebner at Stadtilm, but other Alsos agents were closing in on Werner Heisenberg, the top scientist on Furman's list.

For Groves, the possibility of a German bomb had always been a matter of percentages. If there was even one chance in ten that the German program could produce a usable weapon, Groves was determined to obliterate it. Now that possibility had dwindled to a pinpoint, and the general was turning his attention to the mission he had long known would be the Manhattan Project's ultimate endgame: to complete the world's first atomic bombs and use them to end the war in the Pacific.

11

MAY 1945

USS *Indianapolis*
Mare Island, California

ON MAY 2, CAPTAIN McVay spotted the Farallon islands, dark dollops of igneous rock that pierced the mist just thirty miles outside the Golden Gate Bridge. *Indianapolis* was almost home.

McVay was taking her to Mare Island shipyard, where he had first taken command in November 1944. The repair period was expected to stretch into months. With the war winding down fast, it seemed Indy wasn't likely to see combat again. Still, armed forces recruiting continued apace, and McVay was slated to receive a slew of new sailors while in the yard. In all, about a third of the crew would turn over, and whatever the state of the war, these new men would need to be trained before the ship went back to sea. After yard workers repaired the damage inflicted by the kamikaze (and installed a few new bells and whistles), McVay planned to scoot down the coast to San Diego for some refresher training.

Indianapolis had gotten under way from Guam on April 15, after dropping two crew members for good: Harpo's buddy, Mike Quihuis, and Marine Corporal Donald Miller, an orderly to Spruance and McVay. Quihuis had been invited to lead a boxing program for local kids on the island. He got McVay's permission to accept, then packed his seabag and went ashore so quickly that he barely had time to say goodbye. Miller had volunteered to go help at an engineering facility. Most fellows knew that volunteering for anything in the military was a bad idea, but after the kamikaze strike Miller decided he wanted to get off the ship.

Down by two screws, Indy could only chug along en route to the States, but at least she was running under her own power. The freshwater evaporator was down. That meant drinking water was on rations and the crew had to make do with saltwater showers. At Kerama Retto, repair crews had been able to reduce the list to three degrees, but the men still felt as if they were walking in a funhouse all the way home.

Days out of Guam, grim news descended on the ship. President Franklin Roosevelt was dead. The loss of America's longest-serving president was felt around the world, but aboard Indy, where the stewards had turned down his bed and served him his meals, it felt a little more personal. Captain McVay ordered a memorial service for Monday, April 16, 1945, at 4:30 in the afternoon. Father Conway presided, and Indy's crew reflected on FDR's legacy.

Roosevelt had been president for so long that he already occupied the Oval Office when the youngest of Indy's crew were still in kindergarten. Some of her oldest hands remembered crossing the equator with Roosevelt aboard. "Crossing the line" was always a momentous event for "pollywog" sailors who had never ventured so far south. But that was the first time an American president ever served as King Neptune during the colorful initiation rite held topside, after which the "slimy wogs" were accepted into the order of "trusty shellbacks." Roosevelt even signed their shellback certificates.

This man, who insisted that all people in all nations shared Americans' entitlement to basic freedoms, was the same man who had sent this crew to war against the Nazis and the Japanese to defend those freedoms. Now he had passed on, and as the men of *Indianapolis* mourned him, the mantle of commander in chief passed to Harry S. Truman. A World War I combat veteran, the new president had a reputation as a man of moderate temperament and deep integrity.

During Indy's passage home, another pair of deaths triggered celebration on the ship. First, news flashed across the world that Benito Mussolini was dead at the hands of partisan executioners. One U.S. newspaper reported that *Il Duce*'s corpse had been hung upside down from the rafters of a gas station and its face kicked until it was "a toothless, pulpy mass." Then, about a week later, *der Führer* himself, Adolf Hitler, did the world a favor and shot himself in the head. When the news was announced on *Indianapolis*, cheers rang out all over the ship.

After Guam, with the war zone several hundred miles astern, the men began to relax. On April 22, Kasey Moore and a few other men, including the ship's dentist, Earl Henry, shot trap off the fantail, using a hand trap and a shotgun. Several men proved to be sharp shots.

After reporting aboard *Indianapolis* at Saipan in 1944, Henry, who was from Knoxville, Tennessee, had been surprised to run into Moore.

The two already knew each other: Moore, the former newspaperman, had profiled Henry for the *Knoxville Sunday Journal* way back in 1933. Already an ornithologist of note at just twenty-one, Henry was about to hang up his hobby of bird taxidermy in order to begin practicing dentistry. After mounting a collection of 137 specimens, Moore wrote, Henry was "going to quit stuffing birds to begin filling teeth." The reason: Young Henry did not think people would patronize a dentist who handled dead birds in his spare time.

Still, Henry yearned for a creative outlet. He began sketching birds and soon could produce textbook-quality drawings in chalk and pencil. Later, he graduated to painting and began committing images to canvas—belted kingfishers, ruby-throated hummingbirds, purple gallinules. His work began as anatomically accurate and graduated to the quality of fine art. One of them, "An American Eagle in the Pacific," was painted aboard Indy and reflected Henry's sentiments on the war. In it, a fierce bald eagle spread his wings across a backdrop of the Stars and Stripes, its claw clutching a bloody serpent whose tail was wrapped in a tattered Japanese flag.

One officer told Henry that while he was a fine dentist, it would be his bird paintings that would make him famous. But not at the rate he was going now, Henry feared. His wife, Jane, was pregnant with their first child and due to give birth in August. Henry had waited longer than some men to start a family and it was practically all he talked about. He had not forgotten how to paint, but with the baby due soon, he felt an urgency to finish his magnum opus, a scale model of *Indianapolis*.

Around the ship, Henry's model was famous. It was a precise duplicate of the real ship. Six feet long, this masterpiece perched on a peg that fastened it to a polished teak base. Henry had fashioned the hull and superstructure from a newer material called plastic and strung lifelines along rails formed from dental silver.

On the day of the trap shoot, McVay saw a large bird glide in on the sea breeze and land on the fo'c'sle. Birds were rare this far from land, and McVay could see that Henry was enchanted with the visitor, which had a long, snowy breast, chocolate wings, and webbed feet the color of robins' eggs. As the dentist approached carefully, drawing to within an arm's length, the bird seemed almost tame, sitting still and calmly picking its feathers.

Later, McVay phoned down to dental and asked Henry what kind of bird it was. A blue-footed booby, Henry said. McVay was surprised. Most of the men had thought it was an albatross, a sign of good luck.

At 6:19 a.m., the OOD directed the helmsman to enter the channel to San Francisco Bay and soon the ship passed under the Golden Gate Bridge. Not yet ten years old, the bridge was an engineering marvel, and passing under its signature red-orange expanse felt like a gathering in, a return to safe pasture. McVay looked forward to getting home to his wife, Louise. She was his second wife, after a marriage to Kinau Wilder, who was by marriage a Hawaiian aristocrat and the mother of his two sons, Charles B. McVay IV (known as "Quatro") and Kimo Wilder McVay.

A descendant of the original Hawaii missionaries, Kinau had been a whirling socialite. By contrast, Louise Graham Claytor, the daughter of a prominent physician, was quiet, warm, and gentle. McVay met her while serving in Washington, D.C., as chairman of the Joint Intelligence Staff and courted her assiduously for a year. When he took command of Indy, they had been married for only a few months. During the ship's brief stopover in Guam, McVay had run into Louise's cousin, Lieutenant Commander W. Graham Claytor, captain of the destroyer escort USS Cecil J. Doyle. Now McVay was ready to get home and resume his honeymoon.

The wind clipped down the channel at twenty knots, but it was not of the brutal variety that usually leeched the warmth from a sunny San Francisco day. Visibility was unusually good, the city skyline crisp against a cloudless sky. At half past eleven, McVay directed his OOD to moor the ship port side to the Mare Island ammunition depot. The slim cruiser slid gently pierside and a line-handling detail passed down ropes thick as a man's leg. Yard workers made fast the lines to bollards, mooring Indy to offload her ordnance.

Finally, on May 5, tugs nudged the ship gently through the dry dock gates. By 9 a.m., she was suspended in dry dock No. 2, her hull cradled in custom V-shaped keel blocks. Then the gates squealed shut and the water was pumped out, exposing all of Indy's wounds.

12

MAY 1945

Union Pacific Rail Line
Chicago, Illinois

KATHERINE MOORE SQUEEZED INTO the crowded dining car aboard the *San Francisco Challenger*, elated but exhausted. The Allies had just declared victory in Europe, and the headlines still blared in her head. In a nation exploding with champagne corks, confetti, and returning soldiers, it had been almost impossible to get a ticket on anything going anywhere. From Chicago, she had peppered her husband, Lieutenant Commander Kasey Moore, with a hail of telegrams. She had gotten a train . . . no, she got bumped . . . she had gotten a train . . . no, she got bumped. Finally, she managed to secure a seat on the *Challenger*, a Union Pacific/Southern Pacific line that had been upgraded to attract female passengers. But Katherine didn't care about the lounge cars and porter service, only that this *Challenger* seemed to be the slowest train ever to crawl across a continent. At times she wanted to get out and push.

Mary Moore, Kasey's eleven-year-old daughter by his first wife, would join Katherine and Kasey at Mare Island once school let out. Mary's mother had abandoned the family when the girl was two years old, and neither Kasey nor Mary had seen her since. With her mother gone, Mary's father became her whole world. Now, the war had left the girl in Katherine's care.

An attendant came by. Katherine ordered lunch and thought about San Francisco. Kasey had written to say that he'd secured for them a "house" in the Mare Island Navy Yard, really one half of a furnished Quonset hut. The other half was occupied by a new ensign, John Woolston, and his wife.

The best piece of news—Kasey was to have twenty-one days' leave.

Leave. Finally. Some time away from the other woman.

That was Katherine's nickname for *Indianapolis*—and it was not without a salting of real jealousy. Moore had joined the ship in the Aleutian Islands in 1942, seven days after Katherine married him. Since then, their marriage had been a series of brief interludes snatched from Indy's domineering schedule. Three months in the spring of 1943, and then that Christmas. A week in April of 1944, along with a week in November of the same year. That was all.

Two years into his tour, Moore was offered a transfer to another ship—Katherine had jokingly called it a newer, younger love—but Moore refused to leave his first love, the sleek, clipper-prowed mistress *Indianapolis*.

"When I'm with you," he told Katherine, "my heart is filled with joy, and I wonder how I can ever leave you. But when I'm with her, she fills my mind. She is always there. You *do* understand, don't you?"

Katherine did, but still eyed the other woman warily.

When she met Moore in college, she was an accomplished violinist with ambitions of her own. She wanted to learn to fly a plane, study at the Sorbonne and Juilliard, trek the sand around the pyramids by moonlight. Getting married was not a high priority. But when the war hit, Moore joined the naval reserve and life accelerated. With their futures now uncertain, securing their love suddenly eclipsed all else, and they made wedding plans.

At first, Moore was assigned to a public relations unit in Nashville, Tennessee. Katherine thought it was a wonderful assignment. Moore did not. One day, sitting on their front porch swing, he put his arm around her.

"I've applied for sea duty," he said.

Katherine was incredulous. She pointed out that he was thirty-three years old and didn't have to do that, being past the draft age.

"I don't want my grandchildren to ask someday, 'What did you do in the great war, Grandfather?,'" Moore said. "I don't want to say, 'I fought the war with a typewriter in Nashville, Tennessee.'"

"If you go to sea," Katherine said, "you probably won't have any grandchildren."

In the *Challenger* dining car, she gazed out the window at America's middle plains. The nation had defeated Germany, and judging by the news, was on the verge of defeating Japan. For reasons apart from war weariness, Katherine was ecstatic. There was a real possibility that the other woman would never carry away her husband again.

• • •

After drydocking his ship, McVay approved a series of rotating shore leave periods for the crew. Then he unpacked his gear at the Quonset hut he and Louise were to share on base. The honeymooners enjoyed quiet, precious hours at home and in the city, and McVay also managed to work in a fishing trip to the Russian River in Northern California.

Father Thomas Conway loaned Lew Haynes a few dollars so that the doctor could afford to go home and see his wife and kids. Then the priest used his own leave to travel the country, visiting the families of the nine men killed in the kamikaze strike. Conway had never behaved as a cloistered cleric aboard the ship, nor sequestered himself with officers, although he was an officer himself. The sailors thought of him as a man's man who was willing to pitch in and get his hands dirty if the situation required it. That worked in Conway's favor when he occasionally had to chide young sailors over their choices in life, or more often, for not writing often enough to their moms and dads back home.

Earl Henry's approved leave period was coming up and he was rushing to finish his model. He was pleased with the way the details were coming together. There was a miniature bell where Indy's real bell hung on the navigation bridge. Even the spud locker where the mess cooks stored the potatoes was fitted with a tiny copper screen. So finely crafted was this miniature *Indianapolis* that Captain McVay had once offered Henry a huge sum of money for it. But Henry wouldn't sell the model at any price. It was to be a gift for his newborn son or daughter.

Harpo Celaya headed home to Florence, Arizona, and to Delores, a dark-eyed beauty who had caught his attention before he left for the Navy. Back then, Celaya had been larger than life, and when he went off to fight the war, he kept up an air of being above it all, even at the bloodiest battle of all, Iwo Jima. Now, though, Celaya had seen how short life could be, and he wanted to share it with someone special.

Glenn Morgan was ecstatic to be reunited with his best girl, Mertie Jo. On the other hand, Morgan's bugler buddy Donald Mack beat him out for promotion to third class petty officer. Commander Johns Hopkins Janney, Indy's navigator, put Mack ahead of Morgan even though Mack had previously failed the test twice. Morgan was steamed. But he thought he might know why Janney didn't like him: Morgan was married and Janney wasn't.

One day at Mare Island, Morgan asked Janney for special liberty. He didn't have duty and wanted to go home and see Mertie Jo.

"No," Janney said. "You married men think you've got rights that other people don't."

The commander was partly right. Morgan and Mertie Jo lived on base in a Quonset hut, while unmarried men like Janney had to quarter on the ship. But none of that should have had bearing on whether Morgan could go ashore. To get around Janney, Morgan had one of his friends made him a fake ID card so that the quarterdeck watch wouldn't enter his real name in the log when he left the ship. It was a bit of skullduggery for a chance to see his wife, and McVay would discipline him for sure if he got caught. He didn't.

13

MAY 1945

Kure Naval Yard
Kure, Japan

BY MAY 1945, MOCHITSURA Hashimoto's sub was never safe, even in home waters. On May 5, five days after he tied up at his pier in Kure harbor, the skies over the seaside prefecture filled with flashing silver plate and the deep, ominous thrum of American planes. A phalanx of B-29 Superfortress bombers skimmed over the base and emptied their bellies, projectiles streaking toward earth like raptors. The Hiro Naval Arsenal was destroyed, but I-58 and the remaining IJN sub fleet escaped damage.

The Americans' new low-altitude bombing tactic was now well established. Before March, the Superfortress raiders had operated mainly at altitude, unleashing high-explosive bombs. But that changed when Major General Curtis LeMay retooled U.S. bombing tactics and tested his new doctrine with a low-altitude firebombing of Tokyo. The central target was Shitamachi, a locus of "shadow factories" that supplied materials to manufacturers of military aircraft. Shitamachi was also a downtown suburb of 750,000 people who lived in a warren of tightly packed wood-frame buildings. The attack had been like throwing torches into rice paper. The resulting blaze devoured sixteen square miles of the city and at least 80,000 souls. Since then, the enemy had sent nearly two thousand B-29s in eight separate raids, nearly all of them low-altitude firebombings. Hashimoto was watching his country literally go up in flames.

Meanwhile, the IJN's *kaiten*-equipped submarines were proving an abysmal failure. Of the four *kaiten* subs sent to Okinawa, only half returned, including Hashimoto's. Undeterred, the IJN had ordered a refit for I-58. Yard technicians were now removing her aircraft catapult and hangar so that she could carry six suicide torpedoes.

At the beginning of the war, Japan's Navy ruled the Pacific. Hashimoto remembered lying in wait off the Hawaiian coast on December 6, 1941. He was torpedo officer aboard I-24 then, and the boat lay off Oahu, concealed beneath the obscuring blanket of the sea. Through the periscope, Hashimoto had seen lights twinkling along the shore, rows of lamps on an airport, and the neon signs at Waikiki. He could hear a radio and the music sounded to him like jazz.

The next day, December 7, more than 350 fighter-bombers from six Japanese carriers stormed Pearl Harbor. With I-24 at a depth of ninety feet, Hashimoto did not see the air attack. But the ocean beneath Japan's first attack on America became dangerously turbulent, forcing I-24 to break the surface, shedding concealment and exposing her to potential attack. As he and the crew scrambled to resubmerge the boat, Hashimoto kept an eye on his watch, longing for sunset and the cover of night.

Later, the I-24 crew celebrated victory, but the truth was that Japan's submarines had failed shamefully at Pearl Harbor. Now, during I-58's Kure refit, Hashimoto was condemned to watch as America steadily carved up the remaining IJN fleet. The cascading failures angered Hashimoto, who had been fighting Japan's naval leadership for material improvements to the sub fleet since 1943. By then, the Americans had equipped all their boats with radar while Japanese crews in the forward areas longed for radar as farmers long for rain. Radar would allow Hashimoto to travel quickly on the surface and give the crew enough time to dive when they detected enemy aircraft approaching. He thought it a disgraceful state of affairs and was frustrated that more of Japan's resources had not been poured into scientific research. He felt that the struggle for sea supremacy had devolved into a fight between the blind and those who could see.

With other Japanese submariners, Hashimoto developed the view that one radar set would be more valuable than a hundred new submarines. For months in 1943, against protocol, he banged on doors and lobbied for the technology to make IJN sub warfare safer and more effective. All he got in return was approval for an allotment of one additional pair of binoculars. Disgusted, he chalked up his failure to interdepartmental rivalry and a headquarters staff that was more concerned with its image than with the safety of the men serving at the front.

Now two years had passed. Finally, IJN leaders had relented and installed radar, but not before Hashimoto watched many of his fellow sub commanders, including several he'd gone to school with, sent down to salty graves. During the Kure refit, workers fitted I-58 with Type 3 sonar and relocated her Type 22 radar to a pedestal in front of the conning tower. But when I-58 put to sea again, Hashimoto suspected that the improvements to his submarine had come too late.

14

JUNE 1945

USS *Indianapolis*
Mare Island, California

EARL HENRY COULD HARDLY believe it: He'd missed the birth of his son by five days. After spending time with Jane in Mayfield, Kentucky, he'd boarded a westbound train on June 13 and returned to Mare Island. Five days later, Earl Junior was born—nearly two months early!

Henry had been excited about the prospect of becoming a father, but he never dreamed he would be so exuberant at the news. On June 30, he received his first letter from Jane since they became parents. He read it three times and could hardly wait for another one. The best news of all was that Jane had some photographs taken of the baby and was sending him prints in the mail. The preliminary report from Henry's father-in-law was that little Earl looked like a Republican.

Henry had hoped to finish his *Indianapolis* model before going home, but that hadn't happened so it was still aboard the ship. One evening in June, Kasey Moore asked him to bring it to the wardroom. The ship's officers often hosted their wives for dinner there, and Moore wanted the new families to see the replica ship. Moore's wife, Katherine, thought Henry's model was the most beautifully crafted thing she'd ever seen.

She told Henry that Kasey's parents lived in Knoxville. "Why don't you let me take it home for you?"

Moore chimed in. "I could pack it up so it could make the trip without a scratch."

Henry smiled and shook his head. "Thank you, but it's a gift for my son. When I detach from Indy, I'm flying home and I want to take it myself."

It seemed that day might come quickly. Officers around him speculated that the war would be over in less than six months. Henry thought it might last a bit longer, but not so long that he would miss very much of little Earl's childhood. Since reporting to Indy, he had written to

Jane about everything he did and saw—the phosphorescence of plankton churning in the ship's night wake . . . showering in a warm island
rain because it was the only way to get a freshwater shower . . . the way
clear saltwater bubbled up in the island tidal pools then receded to reveal
starfish and tiny crabs and little jewel-colored fish that fed at his feet.
He wouldn't trade what he'd seen during his naval service, but now he
wanted more than anything to get back to Tennessee, to enjoy the simple
routines of home and hearth. He told Jane that if the Navy offered him a
permanent position, he'd turn it down so fast her head would spin.

As anxious as Henry was to get home, Ensign John Woolston was glad
to be aboard. Since reporting, he'd prowled the passageways on a mission: memorize *Indianapolis*. Every frame, beam, deck plate, tank, and
machinery space. Every repair locker, damage control station, door,
hatch, and dog. The twenty-year-old ensign, with a slim face, angular
jaw, and serious brown eyes, had made it his business to know the ship
better than any man aboard. So he stalked the decks, stopping to gaze
at "bulls eyes"—hyphenated alphanumerics stenciled on the bulkheads
that marked deck number, frame number, relation to ship's centerline,
and the function of a given compartment—and log them in the near-
photographic catalog that was his brain.

When Woolston reported to *Indianapolis* in May, it was actually his
second time aboard, the first occurring while he was still in grade school.
Woolston's good friend had a much older sister. She was married to a
naval officer who invited the two boys to tour the ship. Woolston took
the ferry across Puget Sound, stepped aboard, and fell in love. After the
tour, he bought his first model kit—a replica *Indianapolis* that became
his first and most treasured model. Some years later, Woolston was row-
ing the Mosquito Pass near Henry Island when he saw the real Indy
again, cleaving the Straits of Juan de Fuca on a high-speed run. Even at
a distance she was impressive, and the waves of her passage rocked his
little craft from five miles away.

Now, fresh from naval architectural and marine engineering school
at the Massachusetts Institute of Technology, Woolston had reported
aboard for duty. Taken to Captain McVay for the customary quick intro-

duction, he pegged the skipper as a gentleman of the old line, cordial but not affable, approachable but not familiar. From then on, Woolston's immediate boss was Moore. Woolston considered it paramount to continue his education in knowing the ship, in particular how the basics of watertight integrity operated on this particular vessel.

Indianapolis was designed in 1930 with a single "through-deck" along which one could pass from bow to stern without having to climb up and down ladders and make a circuitous route using multiple decks. This design made it impractical to operate completely buttoned up, with maximum watertight integrity—a state known as "Material Condition Afirm"—since the ordinary duties of sailing necessitated free movement of personnel up and down the length of the ship. Further, Condition Afirm would shut off all ventilation to interior spaces. On a ship without air-conditioning operating in the steamy South Pacific, that could kill a crew as quickly as the enemy.

Because *Indianapolis*'s hull was not heavily armored like those of most of the warships in the fleet, her designers had made judicious compromises in an effort to pack as much firepower, speed, and cruising range as possible into the ten-thousand-ton treaty cruiser limit. While her trim skin made her one of the fastest large ships in the Navy, it also meant that the bubble of steam and gas produced by an exploding torpedo could more easily crack her in two.

Woolston felt that the more he knew about the ship, the more he could do to prevent just that. And so, from bowsprit to fantail, bilge to crow's nest, he memorized it all.

Day and night in dry dock No. 2, workmen swarmed over scaffolding that climbed the ship's sides like the exoskeleton of some industrial insect. During *Indianapolis*'s 1944 overhaul, Mare Island had bustled with more than ten thousand tradesmen. Now that number had quadrupled to more than forty thousand. From that legion, scores of shipfitters, pipefitters, electricians, sheet metal artisans, coppersmiths, boilermakers, blacksmiths, and builders buzzed around Indy like bees around their queen.

Her decks and interiors echoed with the simmer of welding torches, the pounding of hammers, the laborious screech of fresh-machined parts sliding into place. The noise and dirt of this constant construction wore the crew down. Dust covered every surface on the ship, including the men's bunks and pillows. They griped to one another that they'd be glad when Indy was put back together again.

Woolston and Kasey Moore oversaw the entire process. The service schools were churning out droves of officers of varying quality, but Moore felt that in Woolston he had been dealt an ace. Though he was one of the ship's most junior officers, Woolston's educational background was proving invaluable. Moreover, in the summer between high school and MIT, Woolston had worked in the engineering department of a firm that was building mine ships for the Navy. Very quickly, Moore put him to work as a liaison between Indy's repair department and the shipyard tradesmen.

Moore himself had a fierce work ethic, and it was only at the skipper's insistence that he took a few days off to spend with Katherine and Mary. His dogged persistence may have been why, after less than three months in the yard, *Indianapolis* was ready when the Navy called her.

15

JULY 9, 1945

Manhattan Engineering District Offices
Washington, D.C.

MAJOR ROBERT FURMAN HAD eight hours to check out of his living quarters, put all his possessions in storage, jump on a plane, and embark on a mission that would usher humanity into a new age. On July 9, he sat in the Washington, D.C., offices of the Manhattan Engineering District, typing a memo that surprised even him:

```
I will leave tonight at 9:00 on the plane for Albu-
querque. Derry is wiring Oppie to expect me and to have
transportation at Albuquerque for me. I will go to
Oppie and get further instructions from him.
```

Furman was to meet Manhattan Project chief scientist Robert Oppenheimer the following morning. The mission at hand involved delivery of a "package." Considering the contents, the code word was almost comically bland. Furman continued finger-pecking the typewriter keys:

```
The package will leave Y the 14th. I will probably take
possession of the package as courier at Albuquerque
airport. Nolan and I will fly with the package. . . .
Captain Larkin will also join the party at Albuquerque
and will be Liaison Officer with the Navy. At San Fran-
cisco he will introduce me to Captain McVay. The ship
will be the Indianapolis . . .
```

General Groves had peeled Furman off a beach for this mission. Having missed the Heereswaffenamt physicist Kurt Diebner in Stadtilm, Furman and Samuel Goudsmit had flown to Göttingen. There, they examined files on German scientists and questioned another man on the target list. Then, on April 22, Groves received word that the final stockpile of missing uranium had been recovered.

The new president, Harry Truman, was in the loop now. On April 25, nearly two weeks after Roosevelt's death, Groves, with war secretary Henry Stimson, briefed Truman on the Manhattan Project. It was Truman's first full revelation of the weapon under development. One of Roosevelt's former aides told him it was powerful enough to "destroy the whole world."

With Groves and Stimson, Truman strategized. Which allies would they share the information with? How would an atomic weapon affect foreign policy decisions? In succeeding weeks, the question for Truman became one of numbers. How many lives would be lost in an invasion of the home islands of Japan, a nation that had pledged to fight to the death and that was urging its citizens to choose suicide over submission? The estimates were staggering, eclipsing by far the estimated death toll of dropping the atomic bomb. And yet scientists as distinguished as Leo Szilard were weighing in against using the new weapon. It was Szilard who in 1933 first developed the idea of the nuclear chain reaction and who, with Albert Einstein, encouraged the United States to build an atomic weapon. Now, though, on moral grounds, he opposed using it on Japanese cities and circulated a petition among Manhattan Project scientists to gather support for his position. Admiral Nimitz, who had been briefed on the bomb in February, also favored a mainland invasion. After some deliberation, Truman authorized continuation of the project and formed an interim committee to advise him on the bomb's use.

Barely more than a week after Truman learned the full extent of the Manhattan Project, its alter ego, Alsos, was drawing to a close. On May 1, Alsos agents detained Kurt Diebner near Munich, then picked up Furman's top target, Werner Heisenberg, two days later. With that, Alsos closed shop. There was no German bomb. And after nearly two years of bouncing all over Europe, Furman was overdue for a vacation.

Groves authorized him to take leave, and Furman packed himself off to a stateside beach resort. He tried to relax, to unwind in the somnolent sun, but found his respite constantly punctured as he waited on edge for word from Washington. Even as the sun warmed his skin, he knew the Manhattan offices were now focused on one thing: making final arrangements to move its first fruits, the world's inaugural atomic weapon.

Sure enough, on July 8 Furman got the word: His leave was canceled. Groves ordered him back to D.C., posthaste. His mission: to shepherd the bomb to its launch point, the island of Tinian in the northern Marianas. Once back in the capital, he didn't even have time to unpack.

Furman zipped his memo off the typewriter carriage and left the Manhattan offices to see to the storage of his belongings. He thought about Groves's brief on the bomb transport mission. There would be two planes flying the package from New Mexico to California. "If anything happens, we won't be looking for you," Groves had told him. "We'll be looking for the shipment. You're only the expediter. The purpose of having two planes is so that if one crashes, we'll know where it happened." Groves also told Furman that the cargo was "priceless." The only way it could be replaced would be by building a new bomb—which would require time that troops preparing to invade Japan could not afford.

Other than these ominous warnings, Groves remained vague about the details of the operation, which made Furman wary. Some people involved with the project wondered whether, once unleashed, this untried leviathan called fission might ignite the atmosphere itself. That was, of course, an unknown. But the effects of radioactivity were very well known, and Furman was not looking forward to spending time in close company with the package.

That evening, he drove to the airport and boarded an Army transport plane whose engines were already thrumming. He had barely taken his seat when the plane taxied into position on the runway, lurched forward in a takeoff roll, and left the earth. Furman peered out the window beside his seat and watched the city beneath him vanish.

A continent later, the rising sun slid red from behind a high sandy mountain, illuminating a runway that reclined across lonely desert flats. The plane swooped down and returned its wheels to earth. Furman picked up a car and met Oppenheimer in the city of Santa Fe, New Mexico.

Oppie suggested they chat in the privacy of his sedan. The two men sat in the parking lot of the La Fonda Hotel, a historic inn built in the pueblo style. The hotel was said to be haunted by the ghost of a judge who was shot to death in the lobby in 1867.

Furman noticed that the scientist appeared unruffled. Much of the Los Alamos scientific staff was already migrating to the Alamogordo Bombing and Gunnery Range to witness the first atomic test. Oppie was on his way there, too. The test was the culmination of years of pioneering research, untold reams of mathematical calculations, and serendipitous eureka moments. And although Furman had helped clear the way for this test, he would not be able to witness the historic moment, a test Oppie himself had dubbed "Trinity." Instead, Furman would be accompanying the core of the first operational bomb across the Pacific—a core containing some of the ore he had captured in Europe.

In the La Fonda parking lot, Oppenheimer laid out the plan. At Los Alamos, Furman was to link up with Army Captain James Nolan, the project's chief medical officer and a member of "Project Alberta," a Manhattan Project division charged with the logistics of assembling and deploying a combat-ready bomb. Although Furman was charged with the completion of the movement to Tinian, Oppenheimer explained, the Los Alamos team deemed it necessary to send along a physician fully familiar with radiation's effect on the human body. Nolan's job would be to monitor the "package's" radiation output—and to make sure that in any hysterical moment at sea, the *Indianapolis* captain, McVay, did not deem the package a threat to his men or vessel and chuck it overboard.

Furman and Nolan were to proceed by armed convoy from Los Alamos to Kirtland Air Force Base in Albuquerque, New Mexico, where they would find two planes waiting. Those aircraft would fly men and package to Hamilton Field, an airport near Mare Island. There, Furman and Nolan would secure the cargo, then meet with Admiral William Purnell, the Navy's link to the Manhattan Project; Captain Deak Parsons, the weaponeer on the aircraft that had been tapped to carry the payload; and McVay.

A finely tuned network of security officers would protect the cargo at all points along the journey. *Indianapolis* would be moored at Hunter's Point shipyard, just across the bay from Mare Island, awaiting onload of the shipment. In their interactions with the ship's crew, Furman and Nolan were to present themselves as Army artillery officers. The contents of the shipment were not to be revealed to anyone aboard *Indianapolis*, even McVay.

The briefing complete, Furman headed for Los Alamos, and Oppenheimer pointed his car toward the Trinity test site. If the two men ever crossed paths again, it would likely be in a very different world.

At Los Alamos, Furman met Captain James Nolan, his assigned contact. Nolan was a radiologist recruited to the Manhattan Engineering District by a classmate who had been recruited by Oppenheimer himself. The two men were the first doctors on-site at Los Alamos, and Nolan had gone on to become the chief medical officer at the secret base, overseeing normal medical services. In early 1945, he resigned those duties to work exclusively for Oppenheimer on radiation and related safeguards.

On July 13, a Manhattan Project security officer accompanied Furman to inspect the shipment. It was no bigger than two old-fashioned ice cream freezers—a pair of tallish buckets, each a bit narrower than a milk pail and made of shiny aluminum. The lids were bolted down, their tops fitted with eyebolts through which a pipe could be threaded when it was necessary to carry the containers any distance. Though small, the containers were deceptively dense since they held uranium, which was among the heaviest of natural elements.

One container was a dummy that Furman would use for trials and safety drills. The second container held, in essence, one-half of the first combat-ready atomic bomb—the fissionable material, but with the casement, fusing, and firing mechanism removed. This meant that the contents were inert, in theory at least. Furman noticed that no one who knew what was in the buckets seemed too sure about that.

After Furman looked over the shipment, the project security officer presented him with a piece of paper. Reading it, Furman found that it was a lengthy receipt that described the shipment in detail. At the bottom, he saw Oppenheimer's signature. The security officer told Furman to sign the receipt, acknowledging that he had taken possession of the shipment. The procedure struck Furman as ludicrous: The Army had just issued him an atomic bomb the same way it would issue him a uniform or a pistol or a mattress.

In addition to the ice cream buckets, Furman and Nolan were to take with them a large wooden crate. About the size of a Ford automobile, the box contained miscellaneous unclassified materials that were to go with the officers to Tinian. To divert attention from the package, the two officers agreed to make use of the crate. The trucks would bring it pierside, where it would be lifted aboard *Indianapolis* by crane, secured in the aircraft hangar, and immediately placed under Marine guard. It was an impressive-looking box, just the sort of thing to draw the crew's attention. When the time came to load the uranium-235, Furman and Nolan would simply have it carried aboard with their luggage.

16

JULY 15, 1945

Naval Headquarters Building
Mare Island, California

ABOARD INDY, A BOATSWAIN'S mate sounded two bells, and the 1MC crackled to life: "*Indianapolis* departing." The simple, traditional announcement meant that the captain was leaving the ship.

McVay strode off the quarterdeck, down the brow to the pier, and tucked himself into a waiting car. He was headed for a meeting with Vice Admiral William R. Purnell and Captain William "Deak" Parsons. Purnell worked directly for Fleet Admiral Ernest King. He had summoned McVay, and the captain had only an inkling of why.

On July 12, McVay learned he would not be taking Indy down to San Diego to break in his new crew after all. Instead, he was to clear her decks and make her ready for a special mission. Immediately, he canceled all leave, and for three days the crew had been trickling back to the Navy yard, reeled in from points east by a string of urgent telegrams. Some, like ensigns Donald Blum and Donald Howison, had been up in Seattle, completing ammunition-handling courses at the naval training base. McVay recalled them, too.

As these men streamed back to Mare Island, McVay took the rest out for sea trials aboard their freshly repaired ship. Two hundred fifty new men had reported to *Indianapolis* since May. For many, the sea trials conducted on July 14, a day veiled in a misty rain, was their very first time on the ocean.

In addition, half of McVay's complement of officers were new to the ship, many of them "ninety-day wonders"—commissioned through Officer Candidate School, but civilians just three months before. Vessel and crew performed the sea trial basics well, but McVay still pined for that refresher training and its no-nonsense drills. He was well aware that combat was not the time to learn how to fight your ship.

• • •

The man McVay was going to see, Vice Admiral William Purnell, had eyes the color of a Nordic lake. Like many in the tight-knit fraternity running the naval war, he was an academy grad, class of 1908. During World War I, Purnell, a native of Bowling Green, Missouri, quickly distinguished himself, commanding four different destroyers and earning the Navy Cross.

But those days of glory turned dark in World War II. Purnell was serving as chief of staff of the Asiatic Fleet when the forty-vessel force was decimated by the Japanese at the dawn of the Pacific conflict. Now, though, the war had come full circle. With the ultrasecret meeting about to take place, Purnell was poised to help decimate Japan.

The admiral had joined the effort to develop and deliver an atomic bomb in 1942. As the Navy representative on the Manhattan Project's military policy committee, he provided liaison between the Navy and General Groves, as well as such stratospheric brass as Secretary Stimson. With Groves's permission, Purnell tapped Deak Parsons to serve as director of the Manhattan Project's ordnance team. Vigorous and trim at forty-three, Parsons had a reputation as an innovator who was known to buck rules laid down for rules' sake. Within minutes of meeting him, Groves knew Parsons was just the man for the job.

Earlier in the war, Parsons served at the Naval Proving Grounds in Dahlgren, Virginia, and at the Applied Physics Laboratory in Silver Spring, Maryland. From there, he had hoped to go to sea. Instead, he found himself driving cross-country to landlocked Los Alamos in a red convertible with his wife, two blonde daughters, and the family cocker spaniel. At the secret desert lab, scientists had devised two atomic bomb designs: an implosion type using plutonium, and a gun type using uranium. Parsons's primary assignment was the assembly of the gun-type uranium bomb.

He would actually complete that job inside the belly of the *Enola Gay*, the B-29 Superfortress that would deliver the bomb to its target. Because B-29s had a proclivity for crashing on takeoff, and because the uranium bomb was so dangerous, Groves decided that the "gadget," as they called it, must be assembled in the air.

Truman, still contemplating the heavy toll exacted by the battle for Okinawa, allowed Groves's plans to speed ahead. In the final calculus, the president had decided that as terrible as it was, the bomb might have the power to prevent an invasion that would surely be more terrible than the fight for that small, rocky island.

Okinawa had cost America dearly: 36 ships sunk, 368 damaged, 763 aircraft lost, more than 12,000 soldiers, sailors, and Marines dead, drowned, or missing. More than 34,000 men were wounded, plus an additional 26,000 nonbattle casualties, primarily cases of combat fatigue, or "shell shock." The cost to Japan was even higher: more than 100,000 Japanese fighters died, as well as up to 140,000 civilians—nearly half the island's estimated prewar population.

The death toll underscored Truman's opinion that this enemy would never surrender—would risk total annihilation rather than admit defeat. Just before the official conclusion of the battle for Okinawa, Truman held a special briefing on the proposed invasion of mainland Japan, telling the Joint Chiefs that he wanted to prevent "another Okinawa." Even Nimitz, who had favored a homeland invasion as late as April, changed his position amid soaring Okinawa losses. He now supported using the bomb. Intelligence reports of thousands of kamikaze planes and suicide boats being assembled for the defense of the Japanese home island of Kyushu reinforced his new position. At the Joint Chiefs briefing in mid-June, Truman concluded that he would allow invasion plans to continue. Concurrently, he was also becoming more inclined to use atomic weapons to end the war.

As a result, Purnell and Parsons were making ready to transport the bomb even before they knew they would use it. Because General Groves felt air transport more inherently risky, the three men agreed to send the uranium-235 projectile for the bomb, dubbed Little Boy, by sea. The transport brain trust chose *Indianapolis* for the job.

Before meeting Indy's skipper, Charles McVay, Purnell and Parsons agreed to reveal only what the captain needed to know and no more. Now McVay appeared in Purnell's office, and the admiral laid out the mission.

Indianapolis would depart the next day, July 16, carrying highly classified cargo, Purnell said. The cargo would be accompanied by two Army officers, Major Robert Furman and Captain James Nolan. McVay was to make a high-speed run to Pearl Harbor, where he would drop off passengers and take on fuel. He was then to proceed to Tinian Island in the northern Marianas. During both passages, the cargo was to be kept under armed guard at all times. During neither transit was McVay to allow another ship to share the horizon with *Indianapolis*.

McVay would not be told the contents of the shipment, Purnell said. But should some emergency occur at sea, the shipment was to be saved at all costs—even before McVay's vessel or the lives of his men.

When Kasey Moore told Katherine that Indy had been tapped for a special mission, Katherine came undone. In the privacy of their Quonset hut, she mounted her protest: "But your repairs aren't even finished!"

Katherine was right. There were projects that needed buttoning up, bulkheads to paint, and the slight but persistent list the ship had developed after workmen removed an aircraft catapult. Moore had tried everything to troubleshoot the list, but the ship's clinometer mocked him. Now that they were getting under way, he'd have to correct it by shifting ballast. Also, the freshwater evaporators had turned temperamental, frustrating him to no end.

He explained to Katherine that workmen would join them as far as Pearl Harbor, and the rest of the work would be completed by the fleet auxiliaries in the forward areas. Nimitz and Spruance had emphasized front-line repairs in the Pacific theater. Spruance, in particular, did not want to hamper the fight by forcing his ships to return to mainland yards too often.

Katherine Moore didn't care what the admiral wanted. She fled into the Quonset hut's tiny bathroom, shut the door, and wept.

17

BY 2 P.M. ON July 15, the temperature at Hunter's Point had notched up into the high sixties, downright balmy by San Francisco standards. On the fo'c'sle, Dr. Lewis Haynes puffed a stogie and gazed down at the pier. It was nowhere near quitting time, but the normally bustling waterfront was dead quiet. The doctor thought that strange. As he watched, a pair of Army trucks trundled to a stop alongside the ship. During the 30-mile steam down to Hunter's Point, Captain McVay had told Haynes and other officers that Indy was going to tie up and take on some cargo. Haynes guessed that whatever that cargo was, it was in these trucks.

Far below Haynes, Coxswain Louis Erwin mustered with a working party that Louis DeBernardi had assembled on the pier. Erwin, of Chattanooga, Tennessee, had served on *Indianapolis* since her first campaign as Spruance's flagship at the Gilbert Islands in 1943. DeBernardi, a first-class boatswain's mate, had joined the Navy in 1940. He narrowly missed the horror of Pearl Harbor when his own ship sailed for Australia on December 6, 1941. As the two men watched, armed soldiers jumped down from the Army trucks. Some posted themselves like guards. Others threw open the rear flaps on one of the trucks and lowered the tailgate. Next, a pair of Army officers emerged and supervised as soldiers unloaded a wooden crate the size of an automobile.

From high above, a crane on the *Indianapolis* hangar deck lowered a line. Moving quickly, sailors in the working party wrapped the crate in cargo straps and hooked them to the line. Amid shouts and hand signals from the pier to the hangar deck, the line snapped taut. The crane hoisted its great load skyward, swung it gently over the ship, and settled it on the main deck. Another crew of sailors then pushed the crate into the port hangar.

DeBernardi then complied with an odd request: He directed two of his sailors to shoulder each end of a metal pole. Suspended from the pole were a pair of shiny metal canisters. Whatever was in them seemed heavy because the men struggled to carry it up the brow. The two Army officers followed, carrying their luggage.

McVay greeted Furman and Nolan, then ushered them directly to their quarters, a cabin occupied by Spruance's flag secretary when the admiral's staff was aboard. After pleasantries, McVay suggested a number of places aboard his vessel where the Army's cargo could be stored en route to Tinian. Furman considered the alternatives and quickly arrived at a decision. The canisters would remain in the flag secretary's cabin with him and Nolan.

Furman told McVay he would like to have the shipment bolted into place and that he would like locks with which to secure it. McVay summoned Moore, who soon had the cabin fitted with a pair of eyebolts screwed into the deck. Furman chained the containers down and locked them in place. With this arrangement, the major felt that he and Nolan could quickly remove the locks and free the containers in an emergency. Meanwhile, they would be safe, immobile, and always in view.

With this unexpected zag in Indy's schedule, Marine Corporal Ed Harrell sensed a new mood in the air, the buzz of tension. First, the canceling of all leave, then the sudden steam across the bay, followed by all kinds of strange people coming aboard. Now Harrell's commander, Captain Edward Parke, had ordered him to station guards around some mysterious cargo that had just been brought aboard.

Trailed by a small contingent of Marines, Harrell stepped into the port hangar to see what all the fuss was about. It was a crate, about five feet high and five feet wide, maybe fifteen feet long. The box had been lashed to the deck with cargo straps threaded through the pad eyes that would normally hold Indy's observation planes in place. Harrell wondered briefly what was in the box, but he didn't have time to stand around and contemplate it. He posted a private, nineteen-year-old Melvin Jacob, by the hangar with explicit instructions to make men go around to the starboard side. Harrell told the other Marines to keep everyone away, by which he especially meant curious sailors. He then left immediately to carry out the second half of Captain Parke's orders. With a single Marine in tow, he crossed the quarterdeck and climbed back up to the flag secretary's quarters, where he posted another guard.

At 8 a.m. on July 16, *Indianapolis* cast off from Hunter's Point and began the short promenade up the bay. Buck Gibson, the gunner who'd been first to fire at the kamikaze, stood topside with a group of sailors. Visibility was good in the bay, but out past Farallon Light, rough weather threatened.

As the ship made her westward turn toward the Golden Gate, Gibson looked up at the bright bridge that linked the northern and southern peninsulas like the clasp on a necklace. Gibson, who hailed from Mart, Texas, had just turned twenty-three and was war weary. He'd served on Indy since 1942, since the Aleutians, near as long as anybody aboard. He had hoped the trip back to Mare Island after the suicider would be the last time he'd pass under this bridge.

But no, he thought, here we go again.

Soon the red-orange span loomed directly overhead. As Indy slid into its shadow, a second-class gunner's mate standing beside Gibson spoke up.

"You boys take a good look at that bridge," he said, "'cause some of you ain't ever gonna see it again."

AUGUST 1997

U.S. FLEET ACTIVITIES
SASEBO, JAPAN

ONE HUNDRED FIFTY FEET below the surface of the East China Sea, Commander William Toti issued an order to his officer of the deck: "Proceed to periscope depth." Toti, the captain of the Los Angeles–class nuclear submarine USS *Indianapolis*, stood in the sub's darkened control room as the men around him began to carry out his command. Within minutes, the deck under Toti's feet canted skyward, and he listened intently to the sounds of his boat: the diving officer's quiet depth reports. The soft whir of ventilation fans. The familiar pops and creaks as Indy's hull expanded, the boat actually growing larger in response to decreasing water pressure. Toti knew her every hum and whisper.

It was August 1997 and Bill Toti, a forty-one-year-old commander from Youngstown, Ohio, was driving his boat to the American sub base at Sasebo, Japan. He and his crew of 135 had just completed Operation Keynote, a joint exercise.

En route to Keynote, Toti and his crew had paused to honor their namesake vessel, USS *Indianapolis*, the cruiser. On July 30, with the full endorsement of the Secretary of the Navy, Toti had surfaced his boat in the center of the Philippine Sea to lay a wreath in honor of the lost ship and her crew. After decades of studying the cruiser's story, he knew the official sinking coordinates by heart.

Wearing full dress whites, with a ceremonial sword hanging from his hip, Toti had climbed topside and scanned the sea. The horizon surrounded the sub in a perfect circle. Nothing now but peace and tranquility under a perfect blue sky, and yet in that terrible predawn hour in 1945, a scene of terror. Flame. Agony. In the cosmos of a tragedy, even one or two mitigating moments can turn aside unqualified disaster. But sometimes disaster is without defect, and every one of the thousand instants on which destinies turn goes terribly and perfectly wrong.

Toti first learned of the cruiser disaster at the Naval Academy in 1975. Then just eighteen years old, he was a freshman that year—a "plebe." The movie *Jaws* was a monster hit, and after Plebe Summer ended, that was the film he wanted to see. In a darkened theater in downtown Annapolis, Maryland, Toti watched, riveted, as a great white shark terrorized Amity Island. But the scene that struck him most was when Quint, the vinegar-tongued fishing boat captain, sits belowdecks with Hooper, the shark expert, and the island's police chief, Brody.

Quint and Hooper are drinking and comparing scars, their mutual disdain dissolving in a haze of booze and sea stories. Brody asks Quint about a scar on his arm. Quint's smile fades, and he places a hand on Hooper's arm. "Mr. Hooper, that's the USS *Indianapolis*."

Hooper's laughter stops like a valve wrenching shut. He stares at Quint in disbelief. "You were on the *Indianapolis*?"

Then Quint, played by actor Robert Shaw, launches into one of the most famous monologues in film history.

"Japanese submarine slammed two torpedoes into our side, Chief. We was comin' back from the island of Tinian . . . just delivered the bomb, the Hiroshima bomb. Eleven hundred men went into the water. Vessel went down in twelve minutes . . . Very first light, Chief, the sharks come cruisin'. So we formed ourselves into tight groups . . . And the idea was, the shark goes to the nearest man, and then he'd start poundin' and hollerin' and screamin' and sometimes the shark would go away . . . Sometimes he wouldn't go away. Sometimes that shark, he looks right into you. Right into your eyes. You know the thing about a shark, he's got lifeless eyes, black eyes, like a doll's eyes. When he comes at ya, he doesn't seem to be livin'. Until he bites ya and those black eyes roll over white. And then . . . ah, then you hear that terrible high-pitch screamin', and the ocean turns red, and in spite of all the poundin' and the hollerin' they all come in and . . . rip you to pieces."

Steven Spielberg's landmark thriller was the first time many Americans heard of *Indianapolis*. It was certainly Toti's first time. He had no idea then that the famous cruiser would become intricately intertwined with his life.

In preparation for the memorial ceremony, Toti's chief of the boat mustered a small detachment of sailors topside, one man bearing a wreath the crew had procured in Okinawa. The official party—the chief, Toti, and the executive officer—stood in formation at right angles to an honor guard holding rifles at parade rest.

Toti held a single sheet of paper, prepared remarks, and his face was solemn as he spoke aloud the cruiser's history—her ten World War II battle stars, her world-changing final mission—over the exact place on earth where she was thought to have disappeared.

The honor guard snapped to attention for the rifle salute.

"Aim . . . fire!"

"Aim . . . fire!"

"Aim . . . fire!"

Gunshots cracked over the sea mist, echoes rolling out across the deep.

Toti's heart had been heavy then and it was heavy now, as he pulled into Sasebo. When his crew embarked on this deployment, it would mark the last time *Indianapolis* sailed. In less than a year, the submarine he now commanded would be decommissioned. It was scandalous, really. Heartbreaking. She was in prime condition, only eighteen years old, designed to last thirty. Despite a groundbreaking and highly classified final mission, this *Indianapolis*, too, was headed for the grave.

At the Sasebo officers club, Toti's reflective mood yielded to celebration as Commander Katsushi Ogawa raised a mallet and brought it down on the lid of a wooden cask of sake. The lid splintered with a loud crack and a crowd of Japanese and American submariners sent up a cheer.

Ogawa, captain of the Japanese coastal defense sub *Narushio*, used a ladle to fill each man's square ceremonial wooden cup. He then raised his own cup to Toti. "American submarines best in the world!"

Toti bowed his head. "*Arigato*, Ogawa-san."

A large group of officers, American and Japanese, threw back their sake and cups were refilled. Toti raised his cup and offered a toast in return. "Here's to the cooperation of the Japanese and American submarine fleets, once enemies, now the best of friends!"

Ogawa broke into a broad smile and tipped back another go of sake. "*Domo arigato*, Toti-san."

The officers had gathered to commemorate the success of Keynote, which all agreed had been a smashing success. The mood around the table was ebullient, a situation the sake only improved. There were more congratulations and a review of Keynote's high points, as well as the requisite helping of sea stories. The officers roared with laughter, and there was more sake. The conversation then turned to their nations' shared past.

"Do you know much about World War II operations?" Toti asked Ogawa.

The Japanese skipper made big eyes and puffed out his cheeks as if Toti had asked whether he knew the ocean was blue. "Yes, we study this much in naval academy."

"Are you familiar with Hashimoto? Mochitsura Hashimoto, the captain of I-58?"

Ogawa nodded. "Yes, this very famous name. Everybody know Hashimoto."

"I understand he's a Shinto priest down in Kyoto now," Toti said.

In the 1970s, Hashimoto had taken over care of Umenomiya Taishya Shrine. Immediately after the war, Hashimoto worked at several Japanese businesses, including a long stint with Kawasaki Juukuo, a heavy equipment firm with a defense contract to build submarines. He also wrote a book on World War II Japanese submarine operations. It was translated into English and published in 1954 by New York publisher Henry Holt & Co. under the title *Sunk*. Commander Edward L. Beach, an American submariner who fought at the Battle of Midway, contributed an introduction. Beach, who would go on to write the bestselling submarine thriller *Run Silent, Run Deep*, noted that Hashimoto's account included withering criticism of Japan's failed submarine strategy.

What *Sunk* did not include, however, was any word on a singular event that occurred in December 1945, four months after the end of the war—an event that involved Hashimoto traveling to Washington, D.C., in connection with the sinking of *Indianapolis*.

"Do you know how I could contact Hashimoto?" Toti asked Ogawa. "I would love to talk with him about USS *Indianapolis*, the cruiser."

"I think we can learn this for you," Ogawa said.

Toti felt a tingle of excitement. Hashimoto was legendary in the submarine community. Meeting him would be like reaching back and touching history. What could he give to Ogawa to convince the old sub skipper to see him? Quickly, Toti searched his pockets for a scrap of paper, found a pen, and scribbled out a note.

> *Dear Commander Hashimoto,*
>
> *I'm Commander William Toti, the captain of USS India-napolis, an American nuclear submarine. I have your book and read it with great interest. I know the last time you encountered a captain of the USS Indianapolis, it did not go well. But I am interested in hearing your side of the story about the 1945 court martial. I would like to know if the prosecutors spoke with you before your testimony, and tried to tell you what to say. I would be very honored to meet you and get your thoughts on why you weren't believed.*

Toti slid the note across the table to Ogawa, who promised to see what he could do.

A few weeks later, the submarine *Indianapolis* entered the harbor at Yokosuka, Japan. As she made way on the surface, she looked for all the world like a half-submerged jetliner. Toti stood atop the sail and surveyed the harbor. Below him, a linehandling crew stood topside and prepared to moor the boat. He thought about the *Narushio* skipper, Ogawa, and hoped he had been able to track down Hashimoto. Toti had set aside some time to take a train down to Kyoto to meet him. He could hardly wait to get ashore.

As the time ticked down to decommission *Indianapolis*, Toti felt that a visit with Hashimoto would be a fitting bookend to history and to him personally. He had grown up with this vessel and now knew her so well that he could sense her moods. An unusual shudder. A random vibration. The slight tilt of the deck as her bow sought a new course. He first reported to Indy as a lieutenant junior grade, having volunteered because of her legacy. The boat had lost several officers to transfers, and Toti volunteered to "cross-deck," transferring from the submarine USS *Omaha* midtour. During that first assignment to *Indianapolis*, he married his wife, Karen, whom he met in Hawaii while stationed at Pearl. In 1989, he cross-decked to Indy a second time, this time because the submarine force wanted him to "split tour" as navigator in Indy after a successful tour as chief engineer in USS *Buffalo*. In 1995, Toti was serving at the Pentagon when he received new orders: he was returning to Indy again, this time to take command.

The first time Toti crossed Indy's brow as skipper, a sailor sounded two bells and announced over the 1MC: "*Indianapolis*, arriving." This was the customary way that a ship's crew acknowledged the arrival of its captain on board, and the moment produced in Toti a deep sense of reverence, one that never went away no matter how many times he heard it. He felt a profound sense of lineage and stewardship, knowing the same words had been spoken whenever Captain Charles McVay had walked up the cruiser's brow, and the skippers before him. The commanding officer of a ship carries with him not only his own crew, but all crews— not just his history aboard the vessel, but all the history that came before. Ronald Reagan used to say he never took his suit jacket off in the Oval Office out of reverence for the office of president. Toti understood that feeling completely.

The job of sub skipper came with a nearly incomprehensible level of responsibility. Infantry soldiers have significant influence on their own survival, as do sailors on a surface ship. But on a submarine, the individual sailor has no control over how effectively his vessel will fight. If the skipper screws up, there's nothing the sailor can do about it. Everyone is in the same boat, literally and figuratively. Toti contemplated that responsibility regularly, felt the weight of it every day. Commanding *Indianapolis* was the hardest and best job he'd ever had.

Now it was almost over. As the decommissioning neared, he contacted cruiser survivor Paul Murphy for the names and addresses of all the living survivors, and he wrote them each a letter:

> *Since you were never able to decommission your ship, I would*
> *be honored if you would attend the decommissioning of mine.*
> *But I have one request: that you would stand in formation*
> *during the ceremony and be a part of my crew, as one crew,*
> *the combined crew of* Indianapolis.

Responses had been trickling in, some written by family members and some in the spidery script of the survivors themselves. The ceremony would take place after the new year, in February 1998.

In the harbor at Yokosuka, Toti watched the gentle approach of a tug, dark bottomed with a white wheelhouse. The little boat closed with Indy, and linehandlers flung up a line, secured it, and nestled close to the submarine. A few minutes later, the tug nosed the sub up to the pier, where the linehandlers tied her up and Toti went ashore.

After dispensing with a few items of official business, he set off across the base and tracked down Ogawa, who immediately began flapping his arms as if waving off a landing jet.

"No, no, no!" he was saying, smiling and ducking his head deferentially. "You cannot see Hashimoto-san! He is old man, now. Too many requests."

Sensing that he was not getting the whole story, Toti waited.

"We give him your message," Ogawa said. "He know there is American submarine named for ship he sank. But he say he does not want to talk about it anymore."

Toti was taken aback, and a litany of possible explanations ticker-taped through his mind. Was Hashimoto worried that Toti might read between the lines since he was a sub captain, too? Or was his memory fading and he was afraid he would lose face if he misspoke? He was eighty-seven years old, after all. Hashimoto had visited with the survivors, Captain McVay's sons, and others involved with the cruiser's history. But maybe this was the first time since 1945 that a representative of the American Navy had asked to speak with him.

Toti peered keenly at Ogawa. "Are you sure he won't meet with me?"

Ogawa shook his head with vigor. "No! No meeting! Commander Hashimoto say, 'If the Navy don't believe me in 1945, why they believe me today?'"

BOOK 2

THE MISSION

★

PACIFIC THEATER OF OPERATIONS

AND

WASHINGTON, D.C.

JULY 1945

1

Combat Intelligence Office
Office of the Chief of Naval Operations
Washington, D.C.

FOR MONTHS, CAPTAIN WILLIAM Smedburg had been preparing detailed charts showing enemy sub positions in the Western Pacific. The day before the cruiser *Indianapolis* sailed from San Francisco, he received intelligence on Hashimoto's boat. I-58 was to be part of the "Tamon" group, a quartet of *kaiten*-equipped submarines set to sortie from Japan with one purpose: sinking Allied ships. The intel on the Tamon subs—I-58, I-47, I-53, and I-367—was classified TOP SECRET ULTRA, and Smedburg, a combat intelligence officer who worked directly for Fleet Admiral Ernest J. King, considered it hot.

ULTRA was the Allies' most highly classified program of intelligence. After VE Day in May, the combined intelligence power of the U.S. military had converged on the Pacific. At the Joint Intelligence Center Pacific Ocean Area (JICPOA)—Nimitz's intel section at Pearl Harbor—the staff swelled to eighteen hundred, with hundreds more personnel fanned out across the theater. JICPOA's largest challenge now was preparing for the invasion of mainland Japan, set for on or about November 1. Intercepts of Japanese military messages consistently disclosed that, if invaded, her armed forces planned what to Western minds seemed an Armageddon.

Japan's preparations surprised U.S. planners with their speed and intensity. The Empire had built defenses and amassed forces at Kyushu four times greater than predicted and in far less time. The manpower level for Japan's ground armies was approaching 375,000, with a confirmed total of eleven combat divisions and two depot divisions to be in place by month's end. This force was only expected to grow.

In addition, Army signals intelligence revealed that Japan had accurately guessed America's three planned mainland invasion points on the island of Kyushu. Defenses were pouring in so rapidly that Empire defenders would soon outnumber the invasion force. The demand for intel was voracious, and America's newly concentrated Pacific apparatus was churning out two million printed sheets of data each week. Much of this information coursed like lifeblood through the Allies' far-flung Pacific units via the vascular system known as the chain of command. This began with Nimitz and branched down through area commanders, such as the admirals in charge of the Mariana Islands and the Philippine Sea Frontier. From there, intel flowed down to the individual island commanders and their tenants, to task force and task group commanders, and on out to the fleet.

But information classified TOP SECRET ULTRA was different. Closely held and tightly guarded, it seeped out daily to only a tiny group of Pacific Fleet commanders. High rank alone could not earn access— even the commanding general of Army forces in Hawaii was not cleared. ULTRA's dissemination was chokepoint-narrow, and with good reason. The Japanese had proven they could change their code within twenty-four hours of suspecting it had been cracked. To accidentally tip America's hand now could tip the scales of war. But since intelligence is useless if it doesn't reach the forces that need it, sanitized versions were prepared for commanders in the field.

Since breaking the code, the Americans had collected thousands of intercepts. Each was treated as a discrete data set and "carded"—its facts typed in purple ink on a five-by-seven card with the words "TOP SECRET—ULTRA" stamped in bright red vertically in the margin.

Early on, ULTRA intelligence could be spotty, the purple lines pocked with blank underscores representing "unrecovered" details— gaps in information. By the summer of 1945, though, the American codebreakers, who were known as "magicians," had become so proficient that the language on many ULTRA cards was as plain as reading the enemy's mail.

Submarine intercepts included copious detail: the identity of the Japanese sender, the submarine's designator, its mission, dates and times of departure, its plan of movement, sometimes even grid coordinates.

On July 15, the day before *Indianapolis* sailed for Tinian, the magicians captured this intercept:

FROM CAPTAIN SUB I-58
THIS SUB WILL MOVE UP INTO THE SEA AREA WEST OF
THE MARIANAS ISLANDS AS FOLLOWS: 182000, WILL
PASS THROUGH THE EASTERN ENTRANCE TO BUNGO
SUIDOO

According to the date-time group in this intercept—"182000"—I-58 would pass through Bungo Suidoo on July 18 at "twenty-hundred" Zulu time, or 8 p.m.* Bungo Suidoo is the wide channel between the Japanese home islands of Kyushu and Shikoku, connecting the Inland Sea with the Pacific. By this point in the war, Japan had restricted her submarine activity almost exclusively to the upper reaches of the Northern Pacific, fending off the Allies' advance from Okinawa toward the home islands. However, the July 15 ULTRA intercept showed that Hashimoto would drive his boat deep into the Philippine Sea, a sprawling body of water defined within the larger Pacific by green islands sprinkled in the rough shape of an expansive horseshoe.

At the bottom of the horseshoe lies the Palau island group, seized from Japan in November 1944. The Mariana Islands, several captured during Spruance's campaigns, form the horseshoe's eastern upright. Twelve hundred miles to the west—the left side of the horseshoe when viewed from above—the Philippine Islands form the sea's opposite boundary, with the island of Mindanao in the south, then north up the chain to Leyte, Samar, and Luzon. The Ryukyu chain, including Iwo Jima and Okinawa, lay northeast of Luzon, capping the horseshoe to the north.

The magicians captured portions of I-58's projected route—first a

---

* In a naval "date-time group," the first two numbers indicated the date and the last four digits the time of day. Date-time groups were always written in "Zulu time," the military name for the global twenty-four-hour clock predicated on the time of day at the line of longitude that passes through Greenwich, England. On the twenty-four-hour clock, a time of "0000" would be midnight, 0600 ("zero six hundred") would be 6 a.m., and 1200 ("twelve hundred") would be noon. Hourly times between noon and midnight are written as 1300 (thirteen hundred, or 1 p.m.), 1400 (or 2 p.m.), and so on to 2300, or 11 p.m.

pair of unrecovered headings that Hashimoto would use on July 19 and 20, followed by a generally southerly heading thereafter:

> 192200, IN GRID POSITION "USE _____, _____".
> 200400, IN GRID POSITION "USE _____, _____".
> THEREAFTER COURSE WILL BE 160 DEGREES . . .

The blanks represented the unrecovered headings. This intel was followed by an estimate of I-58's assigned patrol area, based on a fully recovered range and a partially recovered position:

> I-58 WAS SCHEDULED TO SORTIE FROM THE WESTERN
> INLAND SEA ON 18 JULY CARRYING 6 KAITEN TO
> PATROL THE SEA AREA 500 MILES NORTH OF (PALAU?)

Smedburg, the combat intelligence officer, had been tracking the Tamon group since July 13, when intercepts first revealed the four-sub attack force, all assigned operating areas in the Philippine Sea. On his chart, he had plotted I-53 on the west-southwest line between Okinawa and Luzon, Philippines. Two more Tamon boats, I-367 and I-47, appeared on the chart farther north.

If this newly recovered information about I-58 and the islands of Palau was correct, then the sub's position by late July would be essentially astride the east-west Allied shipping lane between Guam in the Marianas on the eastern edge of the Philippine Sea, and Leyte in the Philippines to the west, a course known as Route Peddie.

Smedburg marked it that way on his enemy sub chart, and immediately put this data in the mill. At Guam, Commodore James Carter received this information. Carter was commander of CincPac Advance, a forward headquarters that Nimitz had established in order to be closer to the fighting. As he did each day, Carter initialed the intel concerning the Tamon group to acknowledge receipt.

2

JULY 16, 1945

The Pacific Ocean

INDY ROLLED FORWARD, HURDLING over the wave tops and shouldering through the troughs, her hull swelling with slow, deep breaths like the flanks of a galloping horse. Captain Charles McVay could taste the salt air on the bridge as his ship cleaved the sea at flank speed, near her maximum of thirty-one knots, or about thirty-five miles per hour. Topside watchstanders leaned toward the bow as the ship churned her own stiff breeze, while below, a small army of men tended a steaming battery of boilers and turbines.

L. D. Cox was on the bridge to stand his regular watch, but his prime mission was to get the scuttlebutt on a near disaster. Earlier, he'd been sipping coffee in the mess hall when the deck heeled wildly under his feet. Coffee splashed from his cup as he and every man around him slid, stumbled, or fell to starboard. Rumor had it that Indy had hit an unusually rough wave. Cox didn't believe that for a minute. Sure, they'd run into some rough weather just outside the Golden Gate, but the ship had been in plenty angrier seas than this. Cox slid over to the quartermaster to find out what had happened.

"It was some new kid," the quartermaster said. At the helm, the officer of the deck had a "striker," a man in training. The OOD had directed a course change, and the kid quickly turned the rudder four or five degrees, the quartermaster explained. "Nearly laid us down!"

Cox emitted a low whistle. Four or five degrees! Since transferring to navigation division, he had learned that when Indy was hauling ass, you wanted to give her only about two degrees of rudder, or risk putting her on her side. Ships of her class were notoriously top-heavy, and drastic maneuvers might cause her to roll so far that she could not recover.

Good thing it was only a close call, Cox thought, especially with General MacArthur's special-delivery scented toilet paper aboard.

That was one of the guesses on what was in the crate the Marines were guarding around the clock in the port hangar. Rumors raced around the ship, and some of the men even had a betting pool going. The crate was about the size of an automobile, so some said it wasn't toilet paper for the general, but a car. MacArthur had enough clout to demand something like that, and Cox wasn't alone in thinking that the man was such a showoff, he probably would. Others wagered the crate was full of liquor for the officers to toast the end of the war.

Glenn Morgan had heard all the rumors, too. He decided to mosey up to the port hangar to razz the Marines, whom he considered a generally high-strung bunch. He planted himself in front of the guard detail, tipped his Dixie cup back with his thumb, and let a slow, mysterious smile develop.

"I know what's in the box," he said.

The Marines smirked. "Yeah, what?" said one.

"It's a map . . . and the paperwork for the invasion of Japan."

The Marines stood fast and eyed Morgan skeptically.

"Think about it," Morgan pressed. "They've gotta have all this stuff so they'll know where they're going once they start the invasion."

The Marines told Morgan to quit beating his gums, pointing out that he didn't know any more than they did. Which was perfectly true. Of all the mysterious-crate rumors Morgan had heard, he knew for sure this one wasn't true because he'd started it himself.

Once Indy cleared the worst of the weather, McVay made his way to the flag lieutenant's quarters to check on his Army guests. They were quartered in one of the larger staterooms on the fo'c'sle deck just aft of the admiral's cabin, with a double bunk and a desk built into steel walls. Furman and Nolan were there, their curious canisters padlocked and secured to the deck with chains and eyebolts as Furman had requested.

It was then that McVay received another sliver of information. Furman revealed that Captain Nolan was not an artillery officer. He was a physician, sent on the mission to assure McVay that the material brought aboard his ship was safe.

McVay processed this revelation and thought for a moment about what the shipment might contain. Aloud, he asked whether the canisters contained bacteria.

When he did not receive an answer, he let the moment pass. "My crew and I will do everything possible to ensure safe passage of your cargo," he said.

Then McVay departed. Later, he called several key officers to the bridge. "We're on a special mission," McVay told them. "I can't tell you what the mission is. I don't know myself, but I've been told that every day we take off the trip is a day off the war."

As Dr. Lewis Haynes listened to McVay's cryptic brief, he recalled something he'd seen earlier that day. It was a dispatch circulated only among members of Admiral Spruance's staff, of which Haynes was technically a part since he was chief medical officer on the admiral's flagship. Addressed to all commanders, the dispatch stated that *Indianapolis* was operating under the authority of the commander in chief.

The new commander in chief, Haynes realized—Harry S. Truman.

Indianapolis was not to be diverted from her mission for any reason whatsoever, the message said. Haynes had signed the dispatch as required and thought, my God, what have we got that's under control of the president of the United States?

Half a world away, President Harry S. Truman held in his hand a top secret telegram from his war secretary, Henry Stimson:

> OPERATED ON THIS MORNING. DIAGNOSIS NOT YET
> COMPLETE BUT RESULTS SEEM SATISFACTORY AND
> ALREADY EXCEED EXPECTATIONS.

Translation: The Trinity test was successful. With a blinding flash and a light not of this world, mankind had entered the nuclear age.

Truman was in Potsdam, Germany, for a summit with British prime minister Winston Churchill and Communist Party general secretary Joseph Stalin. The president had already met with Churchill and taken a tour of the devastation that was Berlin. He had not yet met with Stalin, but would later size him up as a man with an aggressive agenda who was smart as hell.

The summit had multiple aims. They included establishing goals for the demilitarization, democratization, and denazification of Germany; defining the borders and governance of Poland; and hammering out a

postwar working relationship between the "Big Three" superpowers—
the Soviets, the United States, and the United Kingdom. In addition,
Churchill, Truman, and Stalin would discuss surrender terms for the
lone remaining adversary, the nation of Japan.

Truman gazed at Stimson's message and considered its implications.
Not only had the test met the most optimistic expectations of the Los
Alamos scientists, but America had truly discovered, and had possession of, the most terrible bomb in the history of the world. Truman, a
devout Christian, remembered the fiery destruction foretold in Scripture in the Euphrates Valley era after Noah and his fabulous ark. Was this
awful weapon the fulfillment of that prophecy?

3

AT MCVAY'S DIRECTION, KASEY Moore and a small group of
officers met with Furman and Nolan in their cabin. The men discussed a
range of potential emergencies that, if they materialized, could endanger
the Army cargo. The greatest danger to a ship at sea was fire, the Navy
officers explained. That could occur at any time. As a matter of standard procedure, the ship's crew was already well versed in firefighting. In
addition, the new men were under an aggressive training program that
McVay and his executive officer, Commander Joseph Flynn, had implemented to whip them into shape.

Moore and the Indy officers next explained another potential emergency: *Indianapolis* could be sunk in such a fashion that her crew would
have less than half an hour to dispose of the shipment. While newer
ships had been built to sustain underwater damage, Indy's senior officers did not believe a cruiser of her class could sustain even a single torpedo strike if hit in a vulnerable spot. In cruising condition, the second
deck—about ten feet above the waterline—was left wide open, with no
watertight compartments buttoned up to prevent through-deck flood-

ing. This was necessary for ventilation and so that the crew could quickly man their general quarters stations. But it also exposed the second deck to flooding. If that happened, the ship would either capsize or go down by the head, or bow first.

The Bureau of Ships called this an acceptable risk, and McVay and Flynn's training program for new crew concentrated heavily on damage control.

Moore and the other officers told Furman and Nolan that it would take one hell of a lucky Japanese sub commander to sink Indy so quickly as to endanger their cargo. First, the sub would have to be lying directly in Indy's path. Then its skipper would need two hits amidships, or at her center, to sink her. Even then, she would likely remain afloat for a number of hours, enabling the crew to get the shipment safely into a motor whaleboat.

The whole scenario was so unlikely as to be almost out of the realm of possibility. Still, the Navy officers didn't discount it entirely. Moore told Furman he would drill a team of sailors on getting the cargo off the ship in a hurry and would even assign alternate crews to assist. He would also set aside ropes, block and tackle, rafts, life jackets, and whaleboats for offloading the cargo in an emergency. There were plenty of extra life jackets. Moore had had a tough time getting a new supply aboard, but then received a double shipment of jackets right before Indy sailed.

Later that day, Furman heard a fire alarm ring out. A small conflagration had blazed up in a waste area. A designated firefighting team quickly doused it, but the incident underscored to Furman what Moore had said: Fire would be the most prevalent danger.

On July 16, martial music boomed through the harbor at Kure and the voices of cheering patriots rolled to Hashimoto's ears in waves. I-58 entered the swept channel and headed toward the *kaiten* base at Hirao. Hashimoto presided over a special ceremony for his six suicide pilots. As always, he marveled at their bravery.

The next morning, I-58 slipped down to the Bungo channel, where they conducted deep-sea-diving trials during which the *kaiten*'s periscopes were found to be defective. The setback sent Hashimoto back to Hirao for replacements, but his boat sailed again, in company with I-53, on the evening of July 18. That night, I-58's radarmen picked up what appeared to be a B-29 formation. Probably en route to attack the Japanese mainland, Hashimoto thought. He found himself wondering which city was in for it this time.

For weeks, the Americans had attacked with carrier task forces and shore-based bombers, softening the beach, no doubt, for the inevitable mainland invasion. The enemy's Third Fleet and Twentieth Air Wing were launching wave after wave against Honshu. Naval aircraft from the Ryukyu Islands, now controlled by the Americans, ranged over the East China Sea and along the coasts of Kyushu and southern and central Korea. Carrier task forces were also attacking the remaining Japanese surface fleet in their homeports. In the past week alone, the enemy had sunk nearly a hundred ships, and destroyed or damaged locomotives, rail yards, factories, lighthouses, oil plants, and ammunition depots. With the Americans now able to consolidate their forces in the north and west, the assault was vicious, concentrated, and relentless. Japan had not flagged in resistance, but in fight after fight, her planes fell from the sky like broken kites with soot tails. Ships not sunk were left burning.

The hour was growing desperate, Hashimoto knew, and there was nothing he could do except take the fight to the enemy. As part of the Tamon attack group, he would do exactly that, proceeding east and then south, down into the Philippine Sea. His orders were clear, the mission strictly offensive: move into the sea west of Guam and the Marianas, find the enemy, and attack.

4

ON THE SECOND DAY out of San Francisco, Cleatus Lebow almost got into a fistfight. Some fathead from another division was picking on Clarence Hershberger again. Hershberger was only eighteen, an Indiana kid who worked with Lebow and Paul Murphy in fire control. Hershberger had really wanted to be a Marine—mainly because girls really went crazy for the uniform—but the Marines wouldn't take him because he had flat feet. Hershberger was a swell fellow, Lebow thought, but a missing tooth had left a wide gap in his smile, and there were a couple of tough guys who just wouldn't stop picking on him. Finally, Lebow told them that if they didn't knock it off, he was going to let them have it.

Other than that, the ride over to Pearl was proving fast and mostly quiet—well, other than all the drills the skipper had ordered. The extra training was a good thing for the new men, Lebow thought now, sitting in fire control. As Commander Flynn had observed, the whole lot of them were "green, green, green."

Lebow had not expected to see the forward areas again, but he was not as surprised as some. While on leave from Mare Island, he'd visited his folks in Abernathy, Texas. When it was almost time to go back to the ship, a disquiet seized him. He found that he dreaded returning to *Indianapolis*, and he had never felt that way before. He confided this to his mother, Minervia, who reminded him that Jesus would be with him wherever he went. This counsel reassured Lebow at the time, but now his disquiet was back, and he still didn't know precisely what the problem was. Maybe it was those nine Indy sailors who died off Okinawa. That had really rattled him. But there had been other things—things he had not told his mother.

During the short preinvasion bombardment of Iwo Jima, Admiral Spruance had parked *Indianapolis* a few thousand yards offshore, where Lebow and Murphy joined in the shelling. Iwo had been an ugly island before, Lebow thought, barren and dominated by an ashy peak that burped steam like a stinking old drunk. Then it turned horrific.

On D-Day, February 19, Lebow watched the attack through his range-finder and could actually see the shallows turning red with the blood of American boys. The sight clawed at his heart. Then, during the bombardment of Okinawa in the last week of March, he was again looking through his range-finder at the shoreline. He swept his gaze left to right along the beach, which stacked itself into black volcanic rock that rose to form a cliff about two hundred feet high. He was inspecting the cliff when movement caught his eye.

Lebow saw a woman. She looked young to him, and Japanese. A pair of Japanese soldiers hemmed her against the cliff's edge, and in her arms she held a baby. Clinging to her leg was another child, maybe three or four years old. As Lebow watched, the soldiers pressed the woman closer and closer to the edge. Finally, with nowhere to go, she scooped the older child into her free arm and jumped to her death.

Lebow had not had time to feel much then. He thought all things Japanese were evil, especially after Iwo Jima. But enemy soldiers forcing women and children to their deaths was a new level of depravity. The memory stuck with him, made him uneasy, and probably contributed to this dread that was still parked in his gut. He hadn't known that Indy would be going back to the forward area, but now here they were. He wondered if he was also right, as he had told his mother, that something awful was going to happen.

Furman and Nolan slept and sat with the bomb. Nolan was also waging a losing battle with seasickness. He had known it would plague him and began swallowing pills to fight it even before he and Furman boarded the planes in Albuquerque. The pills made him sleepy, and he spent a great deal of time in his bunk suffering nausea so vicious that he feared he was going to die, while also fearing that he wouldn't. There was only one upside. The time Nolan spent secluded in the flag lieutenant's cabin facilitated continual radiation checks on the cargo without drawing attention to what might otherwise have appeared to be oddly frequent visits to his quarters.

Furman, meanwhile, set about absorbing the wonder of his first experience on a warship at sea. Indy rumbled along in rhythm with the sea—up, down, side to side—shuddering and thrumming with the effort. Designed to give and bend, she yielded to the tons of water that coursed around her, rolling forward with a purposeful grace, averaging thirty knots. The speed, Furman learned, was a tactic that would not only shorten the trip but also keep them safe from enemy subs. Even the fastest of the Japanese boats could only make about nineteen knots.

Each day, Furman observed gunnery practice—since he was imper-sonating an artillery officer, it seemed the thing to do. One of the ship's observation planes towed behind it a brightly colored sleeve, a kind of long windsock, and Indy's gun crews blasted away at it. Furman thought the pilots who drew the job of being shot at had a most unenviable assignment.

Despite his bent toward secrecy, Furman quickly formed friendships with several Indy officers. He especially enjoyed the Irish types—Father Conway, Moore, Flynn, and the engineering officer, Commander Glen DeGrave of Milwaukee, Wisconsin. Furman considered them all good examples of Hibernian blood, spirited men of strong convictions and good humor. Flynn, who was nicknamed "Red" for his hair, even looked the part. A 1927 Naval Academy grad, he had already been assigned to take command of another ship and hoped to catch up with her on this voyage.

The engineering officer, DeGrave, regaled Furman and Nolan with humor-leavened rants about the indignity he was about to suffer. Just as they were putting to sea, DeGrave received orders. The Navy had decided that at fifty-one he was too old for further sea duty, and he was to be put off *Indianapolis* at Pearl Harbor. DeGrave was furious about this and kept Furman in stitches with salty grousing about his impending fate.

Meanwhile, the bomb transport mission was proceeding without incident—if you didn't count the fire and the near capsize. The decoy crate seemed to be working well. The box was stenciled with Army quartermaster marks that were both indecipherable and, in every respect, misleading. Still, rumors and wagering on the contents continued. One sailor told Furman that after much deliberation, he'd hit on what was in the crate: a ransom for General Jonathan Wainwright.

The Japanese had taken Wainwright prisoner when the Americans surrendered at the Philippine island of Corregidor in the summer of 1942. To ransom the general would take something really special, the sailor allowed, since Wainwright was the highest-ranking American POW of the war. And the sailor had figured out what that special something was: The crate contained none other than the heart-stoppingly beautiful screen siren Hedy Lamarr!

Furman laughed but neither confirmed nor denied the sailor's suspicion. It was as good a rumor as any—which meant it was about as far from the truth as you could get.

5

AFTER THREE DAYS AT flank speed, Diamond Head rose into view, its jagged southern rim like teeth sawing into the sky. When the ship passed abeam the old volcano, the 1MC came to life, announcing that *Indianapolis* had just broken the speed record for the 2,091-mile passage from Farallon Light off San Francisco to Diamond Head—the whole voyage in 74.5 hours. All over the ship, the men sent up a cheer—not least because many were looking forward to beer on the beach and bronze-skinned island girls.

But after Indy moored in Pearl's green-water lagoon, McVay allowed almost no one to leave the ship. Dr. Haynes thought perhaps there were medical exceptions, and he tracked down Flynn.

"I've got a corpsman with a fractured leg," Haynes explained. "I need to offload him and transfer him to the hospital."

"Sorry, Lew, but nobody's leaving the ship," Flynn said.

Haynes insisted. "He's got a fractured ankle and he's in a cast. He really should be in a hospital."

But Flynn was equally insistent. "Like I said, nobody's leaving the ship—nobody but the yard workers and men with orders." Haynes did not press further. A rabble-rouser at the Academy, Flynn had mellowed into a man who loved a good joke but would also tell you no in a way that left little room for argument.

One man with orders to disembark was the engineering officer, DeGrave. By the time Indy tied up at the pier, he was mad as hell all over again. He had beaten "over-age" orders before, but the ones he had in his pocket now were final. He stomped down the brow having spit out only minimal goodbyes. His replacement, an ex–merchant marine named Lieutenant Richard Banks Redmayne, had served for five months as DeGrave's assistant. Now, at age twenty-seven, he would ascend to the top spot, engineering officer for the flagship of the 5th Fleet.

Indianapolis took on fuel and stores. Six hours after tying up, a line-handling crew cast off again. On the bridge, McVay rang for steam. The engine room, now under Redmayne's command, gave it to him, and the ship nosed out through the harbor gate. Haynes stood topside watching. On the way in, he'd noticed that the normally busy harbor was entirely deserted, which meant Indy could pull right up for fueling without the usual lengthy wait. Now she was sailing past a strange steel city of American ships, all just sitting outside the antisubmarine nets, doing nothing. Haynes realized then that whatever was on the hangar deck in that well-guarded crate was awfully important.

On July 23, when *Indianapolis* was halfway to Tinian, the Pacific joint intelligence center issued a ten-page submarine update, classified TOP SECRET ULTRA. Addressees on the message included eleven different Pacific commands, but with a tiny distribution: Only sixteen people would see this intelligence. The update was tabular in format and contained revisions to data that had been published on July 16, the day *Indianapolis* sailed from Mare Island.

The July 16 report had pinpointed the IJN submarine I-372 in Yokosuka, Japan. The July 23 report updated this information: Task Force 38 aircraft had sunk I-372 in Yokosuka. The new report also revised the positions of submarines in the Tamon group. Analysts charted I-47 and I-53 at Nansei Shoto, between Okinawa and the nearest of the major Philippine Islands, Luzon, and plotted I-58 in the central Philippine Sea, in the vicinity of the Caroline and Mariana Islands.

By day, flying fish leapt like dancers along Indy's southwesterly track toward the Marianas. At night, her screws spun a luminous green wake that ribboned from the stern like the trailing robe of a queen. Tinian lay about fourteen hundred miles south of Japan, and five nautical miles southwest of Saipan, appearing from the air as green as Ireland, its warm coastal waters percolating with brightly striped fish. McVay had decided to make the transit from Pearl to Tinian at twenty-four knots, and now he was well ahead of schedule.

Along with his crew, McVay puzzled over the contents of the crate, albeit along a narrower line. He knew that Purnell, the admiral who'd given him the assignment, was deeply involved in some secret project, though he didn't know just what. But considering what Furman had said about the shipment cutting time off the war, McVay knew it had to be a weapon.

In the end, it didn't matter. His job was to make sure the shipment, whatever it was, arrived quickly and safely at Tinian. Indy's weeklong steam would put her in the anchorage there on the morning of July 26. It would be a homecoming of sorts.

In June 1944, *Indianapolis* arrived off Saipan with Spruance on her bridge. The admiral's sprawling surface force, along with Admiral Mitscher's carrier planes, had just bested the Empire in the Battle of the Philippine Sea. Now the Japanese meant to defend Saipan at all costs.

America paid a high price to capture the island, losing 11,000 of 71,000 ground troops. As the Marianas invasion pressed on, Indy's flag plot, Spruance's tactical control space aboard the ship, became a smoke-filled room, the scene of grand debates on strategy and tactics. Admiral Kelly Turner and General Harry Schmidt sent 41,000 troops, mostly Marines, ashore at Tinian to face a defending Japanese garrison of 8,500. After eight days of fighting, only 313 Japanese soldiers survived.

Now Spruance's flagship was returning to the island, albeit without his flag. During the transit, McVay and Flynn continued their shipshape project with firefighting and abandon-ship drills for the new men, as well as drills specifically related to the special cargo. McVay also issued standing orders for continued gunnery practice.

Dr. James Nolan's seasickness had abated some. Since he was posing as a gunnery officer, he decided it would be prudent to at least observe some naval target practice. This though he disliked guns and was afraid of them. Moving carefully so as not to trigger another wave of nausea, he joined Furman topside, where he stood with Commander Stan Lipski, Indy's gunnery officer, and Ensign Donald Blum. As the four men watched Indy's five-inch guns eject fire and smoke, the deep concussion of each salvo thundered in Nolan's chest.

At twenty-one, Blum was the junior gunnery officer, one of the men Flynn had labeled "green, green, green." Blum reported to *Indianapolis* at Mare Island after receiving his commission through the Navy's V-12 program, a college curriculum designed to churn out a steady supply of officers to staff the war. He was among the ship's most junior officers, which was perhaps what prompted his habit of high-lighting privileges he enjoyed in contrast with the humble circumstances of the enlisted.

The gun barrels recoiled with each blast and coughed thick smoke, which the seabreeze ushered aft amid the lingering smell of explosives. Blum turned to Nolan with a question: "How big are the guns you shoot in the Army?"

The doctor froze for a moment and cursed his lack of foresight. If he was going to pose as an artillery officer, why hadn't he at least prepared himself a bit of a script? But he recovered quickly with a dash of humor. Nolan made a large circle with his hands and held it up in the air with a smile. "About this big."

Blum and Lipski burst out laughing. Nolan and Furman laughed, too, and breathed inward sighs of relief. But when they weren't looking, Blum glanced at Lipski and raised his eyebrows.

En route to Tinian, some sailors felt the skipper's extra gunnery practice was about the last thing *Indianapolis* needed. Seaman Second Class Don McCall had spent the last three years burning across the Pacific with Admiral Spruance, doing the real thing. Tall and narrow-faced, McCall had red hair that rolled back from his forehead in a thick wave that wasn't strictly regulation. He grew up in Mansfield, a speck of a town in central Illinois. His father, a strong, honest man who raised his kids to be likewise, fell suddenly ill after exposure to lime-mortar. Three days later, he was dead. McCall was only ten. After that, his mother took a job running a sewing machine for a New Deal program, the Works Progress Administration. But there was never enough money. When McCall reported to *Indianapolis*, he was eighteen years old. It was the first time he ever remembered having enough to eat. And they even paid him— eighteen dollars a month.

McCall loved the Navy and saw his first action at Tarawa. When Indy arrived there in November 1943, the island had looked to him like an emerald floating in a sapphire sea. When she left, Tarawa was nothing but stumps and smoke. In battle, Spruance always insisted on a ringside seat and often ordered his flagship positioned close to the beach rather than commanding from a distance. McCall served as an air-sea lookout on the starboard side of the bridge, where he often worked directly with the admiral on sighting enemy shore batteries for the gun crews using binoculars and Indy's "pelorus," an instrument for observing a target's bearing from the ship.

McCall saw a lot through his binoculars that he later wished he hadn't—like civilians forced to leap in droves from the cliffs at Saipan in the summer of 1944. That kind of thing had caused a lot of the fellows to despise all Japanese. McCall didn't. Peering through his glasses at savage hand-to-hand combat, he would sometimes see an enemy soldier fall and think, "That man had a family."

6

ON THE MORNING OF July 24, a few hundred miles north of Indy's track in the upper reaches of the Philippine Sea, a radarman aboard the destroyer escort USS *Underhill* picked up a bogie. It was a Japanese "Dinah," a bomber, shadowing *Underhill* and her convoy.

Commanded by Lieutenant Commander Robert Newcomb, *Underhill* (DE-682) was escorting six troopships bearing battle-weary soldiers of the Army's 96th Division after their final assault on Okinawa. Throughout the war, American shipbuilders had delivered more than 550 destroyer escorts like *Underhill* in an effort to counter Axis submarine threats in both the Atlantic and Pacific theaters. The ships were small, fast, and equipped with five-inch and three-inch guns, as well as 40 mm and 20 mm antiaircraft defenses. Destroyer escorts sailed in company with slower, less defensible ships such as transports, as well as cruisers, which were not equipped with underwater sound detection or other antisubmarine gear.

Escorts sometimes fought off IJN subs and other times sank them. Occasionally, though, a Japanese sub commander scored a direct hit on a ship under an escort's care. In those cases, the escort transformed into an ambulance on the spot and picked up surviving American crew. The Navy's policy on escort ships had evolved as combat victories compressed the hot areas of Pacific operations into the north and west. Now Nansei Shoto, the area astride the shipping lane between Okinawa and Luzon, Philippines, was one of the hottest. *Underhill* was a replacement in this convoy, which also included a number of patrol craft and sub chasers. The original escort tapped for the mission was down with mechanical problems.

Soon, the Dinah had flown close enough that *Underhill's* lookouts spotted it and sent up a cry. But the plane, it turned out, was no threat. Instead, she was a hound leading the hunters to their prey.

Within an hour, a pair of submarines snaked into the area. One laid a dummy mine—bait for *Underhill*. When the destroyer stood in to sink the mine with gunfire, the subs attacked, releasing at least two *kaiten*.

Underhill spotted one of the suicide subs on the surface. Quickly, Newcomb ordered a course change and rang for flank speed.

"All hands stand by to ram!" he said.

Underhill crashed the *kaiten* on its port side, but seconds later two explosions ripped the ship apart. *Underhill's* entire bow forward of the stack was blown off. It sailed up and splashed down to starboard, where it floated like a giant ragged buoy, sticking straight up. One hundred twelve men died in the blast, including Newcomb. Other ships in the convoy quickly scooped up survivors.

In ULTRA traffic, the sinking of *Underhill* was quickly credited to the Tamon group being tracked by Captain William Smedburg and the combat intelligence office in D.C. Viewed on Smedburg's chart, the Japanese attack occurred only a few miles from the last estimated positions of I-47 and I-53. It also occurred less than a week after I-372 was sunk at Yokosuka, where ULTRA intercepts had last placed her.

It seemed that the magicians were on a hell of a roll.

The *Underhill* intel filtered out to select theater intelligence officers and area commanders. At Guam, Captain Edwin Layton passed the information to Commodore James Carter, commander of CincPac Advance, who discussed it personally with his surface operations officer, Captain Oliver Naquin. Vice Admiral George Murray, who was the commander of the Mariana Islands, also received it, along with select senior officers in the Pacific. Properly sanitized, this information should have trickled down to commanders in the fleet.

•   •   •

As *Indianapolis* steamed for Tinian, McVay's officers and men kept themselves busy. The communications officer, Lieutenant Commander Ken Stout, and his radiomen spent time testing four newly installed medium- and high-frequency radio transmitters called TCKs. The radiomen transmitted ship to shore and back again, and the TCKs all worked perfectly.

Earl Henry had also been working hard. Since pulling out of San Francisco Bay, he'd been a one-man dental assembly line. The pale green dental chair in his examination room rolled and dipped as Indy clipped through heaving seas, but it was bolted to the deck, and Henry had become an expert at pulling his drill from a sailor's mouth in time to keep from drilling anything he shouldn't.

The Pacific humidity had turned his exam room sticky and close, but he spent full days in there trying to fill the time until he could finally get a look at his little son. Jane had mailed the photographs as promised. After Tinian, *Indianapolis* would stop in at Guam, and Henry was expecting to receive the pictures then. He chattered about them nonstop to all the officers, including the skipper.

McVay kept himself occupied inspecting personnel and berthing, accompanied by a new yeoman, Richard Paroubek, a first-class petty officer who'd joined the ship at Mare Island in June. By then, Paroubek had twenty months of shore duty under his belt, including time spent on college campuses recruiting WAVES (Women Accepted for Volunteer Emergency Service). With his Lawrence of Arabia eyes, he was good at it—plus, he joked, *somebody* had to do it. Finally, though, the Navy made him pick a sea billet. A friend in the Twelfth Naval District told Paroubek he could choose between a carrier, a destroyer, or a heavy cruiser, all under repair at Mare Island. Paroubek had lost two friends in the consuming blaze aboard USS *Franklin*, so he didn't want a carrier. And he'd heard that destroyers had suffered heavy losses around the Philippines. He chose the cruiser *Indianapolis* as the safest bet.

7

JULY 26, 1945

Tinian Island

THE SEA BREEZE BROUGHT the welcome smell of tropical land, signaling that *Indianapolis* was approaching the forty-square-mile coral lozenge referred to by Manhattan Project insiders simply as "Destination." The OOD set the sea and anchor detail, McVay rang engineering to back down the engines, and the helmsman nosed Indy's clipper bow into a basin on the island's leeward edge called Tinian Town Bay. A year earlier, Admiral Spruance had stood on Indy's bridge, overseeing the Allied capture of the island. Now, the Seabees, the Navy's construction battalion, had hewn from the rough coral ground a half-dozen military-grade runways, and trucks and Jeeps sped through a grid of city streets named for those in the New York City borough of Manhattan.

Indy's linehandlers pitched a hawser rope down to the pier, where a man looped it over a bollard. Signalmen raised the American flag on the fantail and, at the bow, hoisted the Navy jack, the white stars of the forty-eight states set in a field of blue.

As linehandlers worked to secure Indy in her mooring, McVay's new yeoman, Richard Paroubek, stood at the rail, last in a string of curious sailors. As he watched, a miniature armada of motor whaleboats and other small vessels streamed toward the ship, all of them containing a lot of brass hats. Paroubek saw, too, that the pier beyond rippled with military police. From among the small boats advancing toward the ship, a landing craft emerged. Its broad, flat topside cargo space was designed to carry tanks, but now it was empty except for a lopsided number of officers.

"You men follow me."

Paroubek looked up to identify the speaker. It was Commander Flynn. His order peeled the last three fellows off the port rail, with Paroubek at the end of the line. Just my luck, he thought. Wrong place, wrong time.

He trailed Flynn to the flag lieutenant's quarters, where he entered and saw three men. Two were the skipper's Army guests, the major and the captain. He also saw two metal canisters joined by a long pipe that was threaded through eyebolts on the canister tops. Paroubek looked at the oddball contraption and thought back to some reading he'd done. "That looks like it has to do with radiation," he murmured.

The comment met a thick wall of silence. Flynn ordered Paroubek and the other men to carry the canisters out to the fo'c'sle for offloading.

At the same moment *Indianapolis* was offloading her secret cargo, world-changing events were unfolding elsewhere on the globe. In Germany, Truman, Churchill, and Stalin had issued the "Potsdam Declaration," dictating terms for Japan's surrender. The document, which vowed "prompt and utter destruction" if the Empire did not immediately accept the terms, was a high point for Churchill amid a crushing low. At home in England, he'd just been voted out of office. Voters had lofted the Labour Party to power, and Churchill's deputy, Clement Attlee, was installed as prime minister.

Churchill's defeat would be catastrophically misread by Japan. Leaders there saw it as a weakening in the Allies' united front, a softened beachhead upon which dissent might gain ground. Foreign affairs minister Shigenori Togo banked heavily on such an outcome as he considered the Potsdam Declaration and prepared the Empire's response.

At Tinian, Ensign John Woolston was standing on the fo'c'sle when Paroubek and the others walked by with the pipe on their shoulders, like comic-book headhunters with a pair of severed heads dangling from a pole. As Indy's mysterious voyage unfolded, Woolston's attention had been focused on the large crate in the port hangar, his mind constructing then discarding possibilities. But the moment he saw the canisters, he knew what the cargo was as clearly as if the Army officers had copied him on a top secret memo. He'd read all the stories in *Time*.

An atomic weapon would explain the urgency, the secrecy, and the orders to save the cargo at all costs. It would also explain the empty harbor back at Pearl and Tinian's brass-filled harbor now. All this flashed through Woolston's mind just as Furman and Nolan walked toward him carrying their luggage. Woolston was sure that he was among a very few, if any, who had solved the mystery. Suddenly the urge seized him to tap Furman on the shoulder and say, sotto voce, "Hey, sir, how's your uranium doing?" Or something. Something that would let the Army officer know he hadn't fooled *everyone*. But Woolston knew that as junior as he was, that would be unforgivably brash. Besides, Captain McVay and Commander Flynn were standing nearby. In the end, Woolston decided he just didn't have the guts.

Meanwhile, an Indy crane operator swung out a boom trailing a hundred-yard line with a buoy tied to it. Seaman Lyle Umenhoffer, who'd escaped the mess hall when the kamikaze hit, worked with some men from deck division to hook the mysterious crate to the line. A buddy of Umenhoffer's was working the crane.

"Look at all that brass," he'd said to Umenhoffer a few minutes earlier, when both men had a bird's-eye view of the throng of gray and khaki uniforms. A startling number had the gold braid of high rank scrolling across the visors of their hats. Umenhoffer's friend said he'd never seen so many "scrambled eggs."

Umenhoffer had. On July 17, 1944, after 5th Fleet forces took Saipan, a whole galaxy of two-, three-, and four-stars clambered up a Jacob's ladder and assembled aboard *Indianapolis* to talk strategy with Spruance. The visitors included Fleet Admiral Ernest King—a *five*-star—Admiral Chester Nimitz, and a constellation of other flag and general officers sufficient to have Indy's entire crew tiptoeing around the ship for the rest of the day. Then, in January 1945 at Ulithi, Spruance resumed control of the fleet from Admiral William "Bull" Halsey in preparation for the invasion of Iwo Jima. From the decks of *Indianapolis*, Spruance would command more than a quarter-million Marines, soldiers, sailors, and airmen, including one hundred thousand ground troops. At Ulithi, so many stars graced Indy's decks to consult with their fleet commander that the introverted Spruance wrote to his wife, "I have been very busy, mostly seeing people, which I do not enjoy in large doses."

Now, as brass from every service branch watched from below, Umenhoffer's buddy carefully lowered the crate and set it on the deck of a second landing craft. While most of the crew focused on this operation, Woolston had been watching as a crane on the other landing craft lifted the canisters down to its deck. Furman and Nolan had then climbed down a rope ladder into the craft.

Woolston noticed how absurd the canisters appeared. They were, in fact, the only items on a deck thirty feet wide and a hundred feet long. This, too, matched his new theory. As he watched, the boat quickly put her stern to Indy and growled away.

8

JULY 27, 1945

Apra Harbor, Guam

ON THE MORNING OF July 27, USS *Indianapolis* dropped anchor in Apra Harbor, Guam. A boatswain's mate blew his high-pitched whistle and piped McVay ashore. A car then collected the captain for the quick ride up the coast to CincPac Advance headquarters.

Motoring northeast along the island rim, McVay could see on his left the coral-shadowed, turquoise waters of Apra, a deep-water port that was in many ways the perfect South Pacific moorage. Green strips of land wrapped like velvety arms around the blue basin, protecting it from the open sea. The channel entrance was narrow—some would say too narrow, for many ships had grounded trying to enter—but the slim access made it easy to protect the harbor from seaborne invaders.

At Tinian, McVay had received orders:

> Date: 26 July 1945
>
> From: CINCPAC Adv Hq
> To: Indianapolis
>
> Upon completion unloading Tinian, report to Port Director
> for routing to Guam where disembark Com 5th Fleet
> personnel X Completion report to PD Guam for onward
> routing to Leyte where on arrival report CTF 95 by dispatch

*for duty X CTG 95.7 directed arrange 10 days training for
Indianapolis in Leyte area.*

In plain language, the orders meant this: After Indy dropped the secret cargo at Tinian, she was to travel to Guam, then proceed west across the Philippine Sea to Leyte, Philippines. There, Rear Admiral Lynde McCormick would arrange the long-overdue refresher training for McVay's crew.

Copies of the CincPac message, date-time group 260152, streamed out to seven other addressees, including a covey of admirals—Spruance and Nimitz, as well as Vice Admiral Murray, commander of the Marianas, who was headquartered at Guam. Also copied were Task Force 95 commander Vice Admiral Jesse Oldendorf and his subordinate, McCormick, commander of Task Group 95.7.

The message should have been classified "secret," as were all warship routing messages, but was broadcast as "restricted" by mistake, lowering its importance. All addressees received the message except for McCormick, who was to arrange *Indianapolis*'s training. McCormick's radiomen made a decryption error, scrambling the numbers in "95.7" and concluding that the message was not for their boss.

McVay had not been in the forward areas since April. To get the lay of the land, he planned to call on a classmate of his, Commodore James Carter, commander of CincPac Advance, Nimitz's new Pacific Fleet headquarters. To be nearer the fighting, the admiral had chosen to stake his new claim on a bottle-green hill overlooking Agana, which Spruance and the Marines had captured a year earlier in a symbolic, full circle victory.

Three days after the attack on Pearl Harbor, with America still stunned and reeling, five thousand Japanese soldiers stormed Guam's crystalline beaches, sweeping away a garrison of four hundred U.S. soldiers. The island became the first American-held territory to fall to Japan. Then, retribution. After conquering Saipan in July 1944, *Indianapolis* took station off Guam and battered the Japanese in a thunderous symphony of shore bombardment. Sixty thousand troops—Marines, Army, and even Coast Guard—slogged ashore at Orote, Agana, and Agat. Tales of Japanese atrocities had hardened many hearts among invading U.S. ground forces. Their attitude was to take no prisoners, to give no quarter. After

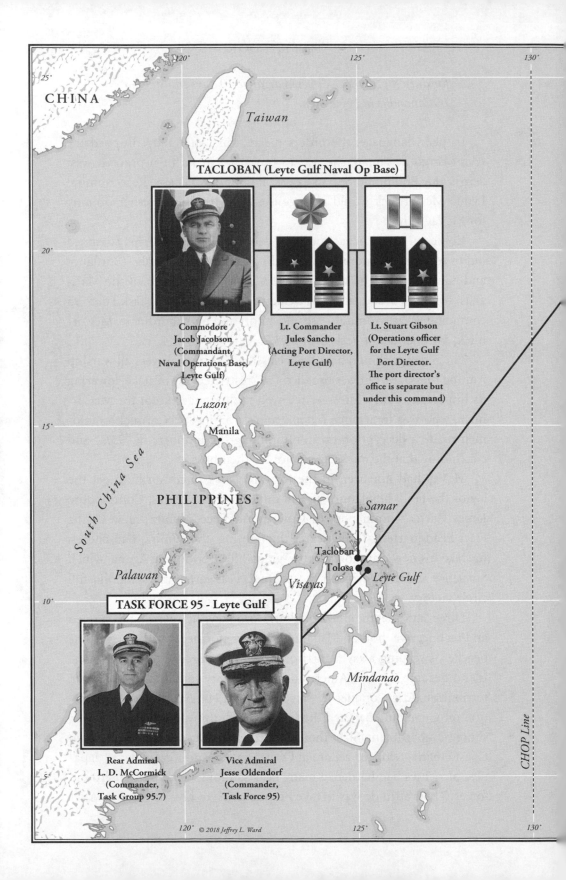

CHINA

25°

120°   125°   130°

Taiwan

TACLOBAN (Leyte Gulf Naval Op Base)

20°

Commodore
Jacob Jacobson
(Commandant,
Naval Operations Base,
Leyte Gulf)

Lt. Commander
Jules Sancho
(Acting Port Director,
Leyte Gulf)

Lt. Stuart Gibson
(Operations officer
for the Leyte Gulf
Port Director.
The port director's
office is separate but
under this command)

Luzon

15°

Manila

PHILIPPINES

Samar

South China Sea

Tacloban
Tolosa
Leyte Gulf

Palawan

Visayas

10°

TASK FORCE 95 - Leyte Gulf

Mindanao

CHOP Line

Rear Admiral
L. D. McCormick
(Commander,
Task Group 95.7)

Vice Admiral
Jesse Oldendorf
(Commander,
Task Force 95)

5°

PHILIPPINE SEA COMMANDS

TOLOSA - Philippine Sea Frontier (PhilSeaFron)

Rear Admiral
James Kauffman
(Commander,
PHILSEAFRON)

Commodore
Norman Gillette
(Acting Commander,
PHILSEAFRON)

Captain Alfred Granum
(Operations Officer for
Commodore Gillette, and
Naval Headquarters, Tacloban)

MARIANAS SEA FRONTIER HQ (Guam)

Vice Admiral
George Murray
(Commander,
Marianas)

Captain
Oliver F. Naquin
(Surface Ops
Officer Marianas)

Commodore
James Carter
(Commanding Officer,
Advance HQ, CINCPAC)

Lieutenant
Joseph Waldron
(Convoy and
Routing officer,
Naval Operating
Base Guam)

Ulithi

Guam was the hub of the Pacific Theater Operations and home of
several separate commands including Mariana Islands, Advance
HQ CINCPAC, & Naval Operations Base, Guam.

*MARIANA
ISLANDS*

Saipan
Tinian
Rota
Guam
Apra Harbor,
final port
of departure

*PALAU
ISLANDS*

0 Miles — 500
0 Kilometers — 500
Scale at 20° N latitude

135°   140°   145°
25°
20°
15°
10°
5°

twenty days of savage combat, America again controlled the island, and Indy steamed into Apra to bring Spruance ashore, becoming the first American ship to enter the harbor since the beginning of the war.

Commodore Carter served as Nimitz's assistant chief of staff and operations officer, but McVay knew him as "Jimmy." When McVay appeared in his office, the two had casual conversation. McVay explained that he had been out of the fight since Okinawa and asked Carter to catch him up on the operational situation.

"Things are very quiet," Carter said.

He did not mention, either directly or in sanitized fashion, the ULTRA intelligence on the deployment of four IJN submarines on offensive missions to the Philippine Sea. Neither did he mention that one, and possibly two, of those subs sank *Underhill*. Or that Admiral King's magicians had pinned I-58 to their maps five hundred miles north of what they suspected was Palau, near the Allied shipping lanes that crisscrossed the Philippine Sea between the Marianas, the Carolines, and the Philippines.

Instead, Carter said, "The Japs are on their last legs and there's nothing to worry about."

McVay explained his orders to take *Indianapolis* from Guam to Leyte.

"First of all, you will not be routed by this office," Carter said. "That's handled by the routing officer, Naval Operating Base Guam." He added that Nimitz was anxious for McVay and his crew to complete refresher training in Leyte so that *Indianapolis* would be ready to embark Admiral Spruance and his staff, and resume duty as the 5th Fleet flagship.

"At the rate I'm going," McVay said, "my refresher training will probably be conducted in Tokyo Bay." He was only half joking.

After visiting Carter, McVay went to have lunch with Spruance and his chief of staff, Rear Admiral Arthur C. Davis. Over the meal, Spruance told McVay he wouldn't need him for several weeks. Was there anything McVay wanted to do in the meantime? McVay said he'd like to get his refresher training in without delay.

"Go ahead," Spruance said. "When you finish that, I might send you to Manila. The rest of the staff might be there, and they can use you until I'm ready to embark. Is there anything you'd rather do?"

"No, sir," McVay said.

The admiral was in no rush, he told the captain, as he was busy working on the invasion plans for Kyushu, the Japanese island that had been nearest when Spruance sat aboard Indy and watched *Franklin* burn.

At about 4 p.m., McVay went to the routing office and huddled with Lieutenant R. C. Northover and Ensign William Renoe over a plotting board in a Quonset hut. Joseph J. Waldron, another lieutenant, listened in. Waldron was the convoy and routing officer for Naval Operating Base Guam. The plotting board depicted "Route Peddie," an eleven-hundred-mile straight shot from Guam to Leyte across the Philippine Sea. The route missed a due-west heading by just eight degrees.

McVay told the junior officers that he'd like to leave the next day, July 28.

"What speed would you like to make?" Northover asked.

The question puzzled McVay, who felt the routing officers were in a better position to make that call than he was. In addition to fuel and mission considerations, a warship's speed was also designed to reduce the threat of attack by enemy subs. With sufficient speed, a cruiser like Indy could outrun any Japanese boat.

"I haven't been out here for over two months," McVay said. "I don't know what speed you are allowed to make. Is the sixteen-knot speed limitation still in effect?"

The fleet had imposed this restriction in order to conserve fuel.

"I don't know," the lieutenant said.

McVay hoped to arrive early morning at Homonhon Island at the entrance to Leyte Gulf, he explained. He wanted to meet planes towing target sleeves and, he said, "shoot our way in."

The captain watched as Northover checked the distance, made a quick calculation, and announced his findings. If McVay wanted to reach Leyte in forty-eight hours, he would have to make twenty-four or twenty-five knots.

"If you take three days, 15.7 knots will be your SOA," the lieutenant said. SOA means "speed of advance," or the speed over the ocean bottom made good toward a ship's destination, taking into account wind, currents, and weather. Having just made high-speed runs from Mare Island to Pearl and then from Pearl to Tinian, McVay said he'd prefer to run at the lower speed to reduce wear on his engines. Northover said he would prepare the routing instructions accordingly and give them to McVay's navigator, Commander Janney.

McVay remarked he would prefer to travel in company with another ship. He had never felt that a ship without underwater sound detection equipment should travel alone, but sometimes escorts weren't available and a skipper had to accept the risk.

At Okinawa, heavy damage to destroyers and destroyer escorts had required Pacific Fleet commanders to rethink the deployment of escorts so that damaged ships could rotate into the yards for repairs. So by the time *Indianapolis* was ready to sail, escorts were being used mainly for merchants, for troopships—as with the *Underhill* escort— and for vessels traveling in the most exposed areas. Route Peddie was not considered one of these. The routing officer told McVay he would not be afforded an escort.

McVay had traveled solo many times, so he didn't give it another thought. He thanked Northover and Renoe and left the Quonset hut to return to *Indianapolis*. Still, after McVay was gone, Waldron called the offices of Captain Oliver Naquin, surface operations officer for Guam, to see whether an escort was available. Waldron was told that no escort was necessary. Given *Indianapolis*'s size and number of personnel, Waldron was a little surprised, and he said as much to Northover, adding, "At least we went through the motions."

9

ON THE SAME MORNING that McVay called at the Guam routing office, Japan's Supreme Council for the Direction of the War was also going through the motions. The council met to discuss its position on the Potsdam Declaration issued by the Big Three powers demanding Japan's surrender. In the end, the council decided not to release a position. Instead, Prime Minister Suzuki and Foreign Minister Togo of Japan agreed that the Empire would "*mokusatsu*" the declaration, which meant

to "remain in wise and masterly inactivity," or to "treat with silent con-
tempt."

Tokyo newspapers took this inaction to mean that the emperor and
his government rejected the Allies' demand for surrender, and the world
received it the same way.

Potsdam therefore had no effect on Mochitsura Hashimoto, who
had pointed his boat toward an enemy shipping crossroads where he
planned to lie in wait. There was a sector in the central Philippine Sea
where American lines of communication out of Leyte, Saipan, Okinawa,
Guam, Palau, and Ulithi converged. The area could prove a fruitful lair
from which to ambush the Allied fleet, Hashimoto thought. The inter-
secting routes covered a broad expanse, however, and he realized it was a
geographic gamble. He might miss altogether a chance to attack.

Indeed, by the time I-58 arrived on the Okinawa-Saipan route, the
ocean seemed empty of targets, so Hashimoto steamed southeast to the
Okinawa-Guam route. Night fell, and a lustrous vanilla moon created
for a time excellent conditions for attack. But the lunar glow soon melted
away and with it, opportunity. Hashimoto ordered his navigator to turn
south and proceed at speed to the east-west American sea lane that connected Guam with Leyte. Then he walked aft and slipped into the boat's
Shinto shrine to pray.

In Apra Harbor, whaleboats whisked about, ferrying food, mail, and supplies out to the anchored ships. Aboard *Indianapolis*, the duty crew that
was stuck aboard gazed longingly past the whaleboats toward a primitive beach dotted with coconut palms and banana trees that shimmered
in the wind. Some hoped to get a glimpse of one of the exotic native girls
they'd heard lived on the island. Those not ogling the beach muscled
food and supplies from the whaleboats and loaded fuel from a barge,
worried that this port visit might be truncated at any moment, as their
port call had been at Pearl. Despite the activity, the port was strangely
hushed, with ships mooring and sailing without signal, this still being a
war zone.

In the afternoon, McVay's navigator, Johns Hopkins Janney, called at
the routing office and was presented with the routing instructions pre-

pared by Waldron's team. Janney and Waldron huddled over the plotting chart and discussed the route. *Indianapolis* would depart Apra Harbor at 9 a.m. on Saturday, July 28. She was to proceed at 15.7 knots and arrive off Homonhon for antiaircraft gunnery practice on the morning of Tuesday, July 31, a distance of 1,123 nautical miles. After that, it was just under fifty miles to Leyte, where Indy was to arrive at 11 a.m.

Janney perused the printed instructions: Commanding Officers are at all times responsible for the safe navigation of their ships . . . may depart from prescribed routing when, in their judgment, weather, currents, or other navigation hazards jeopardize the safety of the ship. . . . zigzag at the discretion of the Commanding Officer.

Zigzagging was an antisubmarine warfare (ASW) tactic in which surface convoys and ships sailing alone frequently altered course to port or starboard. This standard maneuver was meant to confuse enemy sub commanders as to the true course, and also make it harder for subs to score torpedo hits. Some ASW experts argued that the maneuver had become so standard that enemy sub skippers figured it into their firing calculations.

The zigzag language and the rest of Indy's routing instructions were boilerplate, and Janney had seen it all before. He had also seen at least a portion of the attached intelligence report, which included a trio of reported submarine contacts. Janney reviewed the contacts with Waldron. All three were within 150 miles of Route Peddie, one to the north and two to the south. Janney wasn't worried about them. If additional intelligence were obtained, he knew he would receive it via the FOX schedule, a series of encrypted messages broadcast directly to ships at sea.

Back at the ship, Janney briefed McVay on the routing orders. Confirmation that there would be no escort prompted the usual banter: "Here we go again." Apart from his success with previous solo passages, McVay had sound reasons to be unperturbed about this one. Before taking command of *Indianapolis*, he headed the Joint Intelligence staff in Washington, D.C. In that post, McVay would likely have known about ULTRA and its near-real-time intel on enemy movement, and that Carter's office was privy to ULTRA's limited distribution. If Carter said things were quiet, McVay had reason to believe him. That Northover offered McVay a speed of advance as leisurely as 15.7 knots buttressed what Carter had told him—there was nothing to worry about.

At 9:10 a.m. on July 28, Kasey Moore ordered his sea and anchor detail topside, where they weighed anchor and cast off lines. On the bridge, McVay rang for steam, and *Indianapolis* sailed out of Apra Harbor. Waldron, the routing officer, transmitted a standard departure message— date-time group 280032—to his counterpart, Lieutenant Stuart Gibson, at Tacloban, Philippines. According to the message, *Indianapolis* would sail from Guam to Leyte via Route Peddie at 15.7 knots, and would arrive off Leyte on July 31 at 8 a.m. About three hours after that, *Indianapolis* would pull into port.

The Philippine Sea was so vast a territory that it fell under two naval authorities: Commander Marianas Area, Vice Admiral George Murray, headquartered at Guam; and acting Philippine Sea Frontier Commander, Commodore Norman C. Gillette, headquartered eleven hundred miles almost due west at Leyte. Gillette, an old hand who had also served in World War I, had been the Philippine Sea Frontier chief of staff since October 1944. Now, he was acting commander because his boss, Vice Admiral James Kauffman, was away on leave.

According to Guam's departure message, *Indianapolis* would, sometime on July 30, cross the "Chop" line. "Chop" was an acronym cobbled together from pronounceable letters in the term "CHange of OPerational Command." This was important. When a ship crossed that line, it was said to have "chopped" from one officer's responsibility to another's. Geographically, the Chop line was the 130-degree east line of longitude that ended Murray's jurisdiction and began Gillette's.

The day after Hashimoto intercepted the American shipping route between Guam and Leyte, an enemy aircraft popped up on radar and forced him to dive. Hashimoto wasn't worried. Radar had improved, and he no longer felt as if he were fighting blind.

It was July 28, I-58's tenth day out of Kure. The sub's innards felt hot and dank. The stale air smelled of pickled fish from the galley, diesel fuel, and sewage. Except for onions, the vegetables had run out, leaving only tinned food. The canned sweet potatoes, which most sailors agreed tasted like sand or ashes, were particularly unpopular. At an evening meal shortly after departing Kure, Hashimoto had dined with his *kaiten* crews and explained I-58's orders. The boat was to move into the Philippine Sea west of the Marianas, eventually positioning itself on a vector line of 160 to attack enemy ships off the eastern coast of the Philippine Islands. During the meal, Hashimoto and his officers toasted the *kaiten* crews, wishing them success.

Each time Hashimoto deployed the special attack boats, he found it painful. Now, though, the war was going so badly that the number of men lost in battle was increasing across the whole Japanese Navy, not just special attack units, and the sub fleet was getting the worst of it. With the possible exception of destroyers, more submarines had been lost by the Japanese Navy than any other type of craft. Losses in 1942 and 1943 had been relatively light, but in 1944, the Americans gathered themselves with the cataclysmic power of a killing storm. Since then, more than a hundred Japanese submarines had been sunk, a dozen this spring alone in U.S. attacks in the Ryukyus and, most brazenly, in the Sea of Japan itself.

Hashimoto had watched as many of his submarine school classmates were sent into the breach, never to return. With young and old alike dying in great numbers, his *kaiten* pilots' fate seemed in some ways inevitable. Perhaps their sacrifice would turn the tide of war. Or perhaps at the end of this war, everyone he knew would be dead, including his crew.

Like most Japanese, he had been trained since birth in Shinto, "the way of the gods." But he had perhaps a stronger tie to the faith than others since his family had been caring for the Umenomiya Taishya Shrine in Kyoto. Hashimoto's father was *kannushi*, the priest of the shrine, which was known for its great stone lanterns, blossoming plum trees, and towering spruce. For more than thirteen hundred years, the shrine and its stewards had honored the *kami*, or spirits, of the emperor and empress. The land and buildings had now been in Hashimoto's family for centuries. In caring for the shrine, the family maintained its links with the spirits of their ancestors, stretching back to ancient times.

Hashimoto's eldest brother had been a full colonel in the Japanese Army. He would likely have taken over the shrine after the war, but he was killed during a battle in North China. Since then, succession had been in doubt. Certainly, one of Hashimoto's older brothers—he was the fifth and last son of nine children—might take over priestly duties from their father one day. But that was a worry for another time. For now, Hashimoto sailed west along the Guam-Leyte route, hunting Americans.

When *Indianapolis* sailed from Guam, her departure message listed three "action" addressees—recipients who had some responsibility to act: Lieutenant Commander Jules Sancho, the port director at Tacloban; the Marianas shipping control office at Guam; and Rear Admiral Lynde McCormick, commander of Task Group 95.7. This time, McCormick received the message. But not having received CincPac's July 26 message about arranging training for *Indianapolis*, the admiral was confused about why Captain McVay would be reporting to Task Group 95.7.

The group had been in existence for only a few days. All the other ships that had reported to McCormick had performed strenuous duty in Okinawa and were being sent back to rest and refit for the next large amphibious operation. *Indianapolis*, on the other hand, was Spruance's flagship. McCormick thought it strange that Indy should report to him—though he supposed that the Pacific Fleet commander could send his ship anywhere he wished. McCormick would be at sea with a training group around the time Indy was to arrive at Leyte. On the other hand, he wouldn't be surprised if she were diverted to Okinawa, where the fleet was short by one cruiser.

Indy's 280032 departure message included several "information" addressees—commands with interest in, but no required action on, Indy's movement. Among them were Task Force 95 commander Vice Admiral Jesse Oldendorf, as well as Spruance, Murray, and Gillette.

On each side of the Philippine Sea, surface operations staffs were charged with tracking Indy's passage using her "PIM"—pronounced "pim"—her Plan of Intended Movement. In the Philippines, Captain Alfred Granum's operations staff entered the ship's movement data in a memo record and on the Philippine Sea Frontier's plotting board. At Guam, the Marianas surface operations staff entered *Indianapolis*'s departure on their plotting board. At that moment, responsibility for her progress passed to Captain Oliver Naquin.

A New Orleans, Louisiana, native, Naquin, forty-one, had seen more action than most. On May 23, 1939, he was skipper of the submarine USS *Squalus*, which sank during a routine training patrol. Twenty-six men drowned, but Naquin and thirty-two others were rescued after forty hours trapped on the bottom of the sea. In November 1942, he was navigator on the heavy cruiser USS *New Orleans* when a torpedo blew off 150 feet of her bow at Guadalcanal. Naquin, who received a Bronze Star for valor, seemed to have a talent for survival.

As I-58's periscope lanced through the surface chop at 2 p.m., Hashimoto leaned into the eyepiece and a surge of joy leapt through his heart. A large three-masted ship, a tanker, was creeping across the surface.

At last! he thought. *Face-to-face with the elusive enemy.*

Hashimoto gave the order to dive and nudged his boat closer to the target. Since he could not be sure of the positions of any lurking destroyers, he decided to remain out of torpedo range and instead deploy his suicide pilots.

"Numbers one and two *kaiten*—stand by," he ordered.

At 2:31 p.m., *kaiten* 2 launched. Ten minutes later, *kaiten* 1's pilot shouted, "Three cheers for the emperor," then slipped his securing band and was off.

Using his periscope, Hashimoto watched through a curtain of South Sea squalls until he could no longer see the tanker. Fifty minutes later, the sub's hydrophones picked up the sound of an explosion. Ten minutes passed and then another blast. Hashimoto gave the order to surface and swept the horizon with his periscope. But he couldn't see anything. Another squall cloaked the view.

10

ABOARD THE DESTROYER ESCORT USS *Albert T. Harris*, Lieutenant Junior Grade Jordan Sheperd peered off the starboard beam at lights blinking from a ship fourteen miles away. The staccato flashes were Morse code, and a *Harris* signalman unraveled the message: She was the merchant ship SS *Wild Hunter* and she'd spotted an enemy submarine, last known coordinates: 10-25N, 131-45E. The position was about seventy-five nautical miles south of the Guam-Leyte sea lane known as Route Peddie.

"Sound general quarters," Sheperd, *Harris*'s officer of the deck, said calmly. "Set Material Condition Afirm."

An alarm like a rhythmic clanging bell echoed out on the 1MC in urgent bursts. Every sailor on the ship hopped to and sprinted to his battle station, dogging down doors and hatches for maximum watertight integrity.

"Commence zigzagging," Sheperd said. He also ordered a second boiler brought online to generate more speed.

All this was standard procedure. *Harris* had responded to many of these calls, but this late in the war in this part of the ocean, most of them were wild goose chases. Things had been quiet for *Harris* since June, when she supported the seizure of Brunei, Borneo, under the command of Lieutenant Commander Sidney King. The ship was then reassigned to Escort Division 77 in July and had been escorting convoys between the Philippine Islands. By now, they'd learned that merchant sailors were a jumpy bunch, and their sub "sightings" almost always a bad case of nerves.

This sighting, however, was very much real. At 4:29 p.m., *Wild Hunter*, under the command of reserve lieutenant Bruce Maxwell, had sighted a periscope broad on the port beam, just three thousand yards away. The ship went to general quarters and Maxwell's gunners scrambled to their weapons, but the periscope slid quickly out of sight. Eleven minutes later, a second periscope was seen breaking the surface—dead astern and closer by a third. Maxwell's gunners fired a single shot, which landed dead on target. The periscope disappeared.

Wild Hunter transmitted two messages, six minutes apart, reporting the action. Both were received by surface operations at Tacloban,
Captain Alfred Granum's office, the same office tracking *Indianapolis*.
Granum's office then dispatched *Harris* to the *Wild Hunter* scene with
instructions to keep them advised. Now, on *Harris*'s bridge, the helmsman zigged then zagged, steering the ship at thirty-degree angles back
and forth across base course. Nearby, in the sound hut, a headphoned
sonarman sat at a console, sweeping searchlight sonar across suspect
bearings. Still, many of *Harris*'s crew couldn't help but wonder: Had
another merchant skipper summoned them to chase yet another wild
goose?

Near the bow, gunner's mates climbed up to man the antisubmarine
rocket projector mounted behind the forward five-inch gun. Each of the
weapon's twenty-four 7.2-inch-wide missiles slid onto its own rod, or
spigot socket. When empty, the rows of rods resembled spines, earning
the weapon a nickname, "the hedgehog." Adding this newer technology
had increased the Allied submarine kill rate tenfold, relegating the less-
effective depth charge to a secondary weapon.

At 6:10 p.m., topside lookouts on *Harris* spotted an object on the
horizon. But it was only a buoy, they discovered a few minutes later. After
four years of war, there was all kinds of flotsam adrift in the Pacific. Captain King ordered it sunk, and just as his 20 mm gunners obliged, Sonarman Second Class Lefebvre, sitting in the sound hut just off the bridge,
called out: "Sonar contact!" It was a strong echo that Lefebvre had been
able to pick up even amid the gunfire. "Eleven hundred yards! Target
width ten degrees!"

In the sound hut, *Harris*'s antisubmarine warfare officer James
McNulty scribbled a notation: "Bearing width 10° indicated midget submarine."

Seven hundred twenty-four miles east of *Harris*, Dr. Earl Henry decided
to split his time between catching up on dental work and finishing his
model of *Indianapolis*. During this easy passage, he was tackling both
in the dental clinic. He had moved his six-foot model there because it
was crowding his cabin mate, Ken Stout, the communications officer.
With the war winding to a close, Henry was beginning to feel an urgency

to get the project done. Theoretically, he could finish the model even if he were to detach from Indy, but that idea didn't appeal to him. It was important that the model be an *exact* replica of the actual ship, and the only way to achieve that was to finish it while he was still aboard.

Henry found himself a little distracted, though. When the mail came aboard at Tinian, he had received his usual trove. There was one letter he was looking for in particular, and when he saw Jane's distinctive script on several envelopes, he tore them all open.

Finally! In two gorgeous photographs: Earl Henry, Jr., the cutest little fellow ever born.

Henry sprinted to hunt down his closest friends on the ship, Doctors Haynes and Modisher. During off-hours, the three, plus Stout, kept up a running game of bridge during which little Earl was often a topic of conversation. They knew that Jane had delivered early and that Henry was waiting for photographs. Haynes warned the dentist not to be too concerned if the pictures weren't flattering.

"All prematures look like the wrath of God," Haynes had said.

But when Henry tracked down both docs in sickbay and handed over the snapshots, Haynes clapped Henry on the shoulder and said, "He looks grand, Earl, just grand!"

Modisher agreed. Paternal pride bloomed on Henry's face. Nothing short of effervescent, he darted out of sickbay and ran off to show Captain McVay.

Now, sailing toward Leyte, Henry figured he'd shown every officer on the ship. Stout, who had to live with him, was probably tired of hearing about it, Henry mused. He let his mind roll forward to a time when he and Jane could settle into domesticity. He was looking forward to caring for the new baby, even letting Jane catch up on all the sleep she missed while he was away.

Henry knew there could still be tough going ahead, but VE Day had certainly made the picture brighter. Now, the Allies could concentrate on pounding Japan alone. Since spring, stories had streamed into the wardroom and the dental suite of Japan's sometimes bizarre resistance. Word was, they were training schoolgirls to fight with sticks.

Who would put children on their front lines? Henry wondered. A nation like that needed to be utterly destroyed, he'd told Jane. If the fanatical resistance continued, it would be.

• • •

Aboard *Harris*, gunner's mates on the fo'c'sle fired the hedgehog, a twenty-four-missile salvo. Once airborne, the projectiles bloomed into a ring then plunged for the sea. The missiles pierced the surface in a foamy white circle 250 yards ahead of the ship and descended at a rate of twenty-three feet per second toward the sonar contact. The gun crew and bridge team stared at the water, waiting. A hit would cause the contact-fused missiles to detonate, signaled by a spectacular roar of foam exploding just off the bow.

As twilight fell, the quartermaster made a log entry:

1842—Fired hedgehog, no results.

Still, Combat Information Center personnel heard two detonations. Due to the depth of the water, McNulty thought they'd hit the sub. Suddenly, the chase was on.

The sound hut regained contact. The gunner's mates hustled to reload the hedgehog. The sonar team called out new bearings, with Shep-erd ordering the helmsman: "Come left!" or "Come right!" The quarter-master had to work fast to keep up his log:

1843—Regained contact.
1846—Commenced run.
1852—Fired hedgehog.
1857—Commenced dry run.
1925—Regained contact, commenced hedgehog attack.
1930—Fired hedgehog.
1942—Regained contact.
1947—Fired hedgehog.

Each salvo pierced the waves and disappeared without payoff. Each time the hedgehog fired, Lefebvre, the sonarman, lost contact due to sound reverberations, but as soon as these faded he quickly reacquired. After the fourth attack, *Harris*'s skipper, King, ordered an end to general quarters. This did not mean he was giving up. There were few things in the ocean that created multiple, shifting sonar returns, so King knew he had a sub—"highly probable" is the term he used in reporting to the surface operations office at Leyte. But during general quarters, all hands are manning their battle stations, and since King wanted to keep his men sharp, he backed down his posture to a war cruising watch and set material condition Baker. This allowed the crew to open some of the ship's ventilation ducts and enabled his watch teams to rotate and rest between shifts as *Harris* settled in for what looked to be a serious chase.

11

FOLLOWING *HARRIS'S* REPORT OF an enemy sub contact, Captain Alfred Granum at Philippine Sea Frontier broadcast a message marked "Urgent Secret":

> ATT HARRIS DE FOURFOURSEVEN INVESTIGATING
> PERISCOPE SIGHTING REPORTED BY SS WILDHUNTER
> REPORTS SOUND CONTACT . . . PROBABLE SUBMARINE.
> PROCEED AND ASSIST.

In light of the ULTRA information coming out of Admiral Ernest King's combat intel office, as well as the sinking of *Underhill*, the apparent spike in enemy submarine activity concerned Granum's boss, Commodore Gillette, greatly. In response, he had increased antisubmarine patrols in the area and diverted numerous ships. While Commodore Carter had told McVay at Guam that "things were quiet" and there was "nothing to worry about," Gillette would later term the fresh IJN sorties into the Philippine Sea a "recognized threat."

At Guam, both CincPac Advance (Carter's office) and Commander Marianas (Vice Admiral Murray's office) received Granum's message about *Wild Hunter* in the wee hours of July 29, just after 1:30 a.m. CincPac Advance was part of a powerful network of stations that broadcast the "FOX" schedule, an unbroken river of messages and orders that streamed out from headquarters to the fleet. In every radio shack on every ship, "guarding the FOX" was a twenty-four-hour, seven-day-a-week job. A rotating line of experienced radiomen clapped on headphones, laid hands on the typewriter, or "mill," and typed down any traffic pertinent to their vessel.

Each message came through encrypted as a series of five-character alphanumerics. When a radioman snatched a message from the stream, he typed it down and passed it to his chief, who passed it to the code-room for decryption and distribution. This was easier in theory than in practice. The FOX broadcasts were receive-only and uninterruptible. There was no way to stop the flow or ask for a repeat of anything that had been blocked by static, a fading signal, or even a watchstander's ill-timed sneeze. Still, each discreet message was numbered and all were rebroadcast again and again. If a ship afloat didn't catch an important one the first time, her radiomen might catch it again the next day. Or the day after that.

Aboard *Harris*, Lieutenant Carl Rau relieved Sheperd as officer of the deck at 8 p.m. Night pulled her blanket across the sea, and soon the only sounds interrupting the quiet were the bass hum of the ship's engines and the splash of waves breaking over the bow. Rau made his first entry in the deck log: "Steaming as before on various courses and speeds holding contact on a probable sub contact."

Six minutes later, the ship's fathometer picked up a definite sounding at eighteen fathoms—just over a hundred feet—directly below the ship. In the sound hut, the sonarman LeFebvre strained, listening. Only a man-made object could trigger so shallow a reading in a sea so deep.

Five minutes passed . . . then ten . . .

"Contact! Bearing three-one-zero, range thirteen hundred yards."

"Contact, aye," Rau called. "Fire full pattern."

Topside in full darkness, the hedgehog team launched another twenty-four-missile burst, which splashed down ahead of the ship. Again, no result.

Then, at 8:26 p.m.: "Screw beats!"

This shout from the sonarmen changed the game completely. They had identified the distinctive *chug-it chug-it chug-it* sound of submarine propeller blades. Nothing else in the sea made that sound. At 8:47 p.m., sonar heard screws again. *Harris*'s quarry was no longer a probable sub. Now it was certain.

McNulty logged the type of sonar echo: Submarine.

At 9 p.m. (2100 in military time), the ship passed directly over the submarine and lost contact due to short range. The next hour was a rapid-fire exchange of shouts—"Contact!" "Come left!" "Come right!"—between sonar and helm as the gun crew topside awaited orders to fire. Once again, the quartermaster had to scramble to keep the log current.

> 2116: Regained contact bearing 090° T range 975 yards. Making
>   dry run.
> 2118: Lost contact.
> 2130: Regained contact bearing 298° T range 325 yards.
> 2132: Lost contact.
> 2140: Regained contact bearing 042° T range 1650 yards.
> 2142: Lost contact.
> 2144: Regained contact bearing 005° T range 1500 yards.

The sub zigged and zagged beneath *Harris*, the sonar team picking up contact first off the starboard beam, then the port bow, then the starboard bow, then dead ahead. The order went up from Rau: "Prepare to fire!"

At 9:50 p.m., the hedgehog crew fired a full salvo. Sonar quickly lost then regained contact off the starboard beam. Again, the hedgehog attack failed, and King and Rau conferred. Seven salvos, 168 missiles, and as many misses. Was there something wrong with the hedgehog?

King ordered the gun crew to troubleshoot the weapon. He also made a plan: Sonar would hold contact on the sub until daylight, then make a depth-charge attack. As quickly as King made the decision, though, new sonar returns revealed the enemy sub making headway, opening distance between itself and *Harris*. Rau ordered two more salvos from the hedgehog. Again, no results. Twenty minutes before midnight, the gun crew figured out why: The weapon's gyro indicator was out of whack.

Every salvo *Harris* had fired for the past six hours had been ten degrees off target.

12

JULY 29, 1945

The Philippine Sea

FOUR HUNDRED NINETY MILES east of *Harris*, Seaman First Class Sam Lopez began the day in church and ended it shooting dice. Captain McVay had declared a "rope-yarn Sunday"—a holdover term from the days when the crew took a break from regular chores and spent time mending uniforms and hammocks. He knew his men needed a break.

In the morning, Father Conway conducted Catholic mass, with Lopez, a twenty-year-old from Monongah, West Virginia, in attendance, along with Harpo Celaya and Santos Pena. Later, Modisher and Haynes helped Conway with hymns during the Protestant service. After church, the smoking lamp was lit. The men broke out their cigarettes and looked for something to do. Some played cards, others settled themselves in the lee of a cool breeze and cracked open a book. Not Lopez, though. After three hours shooting dice, he had won so much money that he picked up his lucky dice, kissed them, and threw them overboard.

Almost due west along *Indianapolis*'s track, *Harris* and her sonarmen continued interrogating the sea. The night before, Granum's office at Philippine Sea Frontier logged *Harris*'s evaluation of the presence of an enemy sub just south of Route Peddie as "highly probable," and noted that *Harris* had attacked.

At 9:37 p.m. on July 28, Granum sent help, dispatching the destroyer transport USS *Greene* to assist in the search. *Greene* caught up with *Harris* just before 5 a.m. on July 29 and took station thirty-five hundred yards off her starboard beam. At 0755, *Greene*'s sonarmen called out, "Sonar contact!"

Eight minutes later, she commenced a depth-charge run on various headings, her gun crew rolling charges off the stern-mounted rails at intervals, bracketing the sub's last known position, trying to trap her for the kill. Floating a little over a mile away, *Harris*'s crew watched as water plumes exploded skyward. After a brief loss of contact, *Greene* regained contact and commenced a second depth-charge attack along three specific lines. But there was no hit. And then, no contact.

Greene stood down, now twenty-five hundred yards off *Harris*'s starboard beam. Just after 9 a.m., a PV-1 Ventura dispatched by Philippine Sea Frontier thrummed in and took up a circling search. By then, both ships had commenced a "retiring search plan," a series of turns that spiraled outward in an attempt to reacquire a wily enemy while tracking his presumed flight from danger.

After the adrenaline of *Harris*'s fifteen-hour close chase, the next hours were deflating. The sonarmen persevered, calling out a string of actual and possible contacts, but all of them resulted in the same anticlimactic log entry: "Non-sub."

Commander Marianas and CincPac Advance received traffic, marked Operational Priority Secret, reporting that *Harris* and *Greene* had lost contact and resumed a retiring search. *Harris*'s quarry had escaped. That meant there was an enemy sub on the loose near Route Peddie, and McVay and his men were steaming toward it.

Indianapolis was still east of the Chop line, which meant that Captain Oliver Naquin was responsible for her. But his staff at Guam took no action except to move Indy westward on their plotting board in accordance with her planned speed of advance.

For combat intelligence specialists at Guam and Pearl that day, the volume of intercepted operational and aircraft intelligence traffic was light. But ULTRA-cleared personnel did note an increase in broadcasts to Japanese submarines. The magicians were tracking Hashimoto and the Tamon group but struggling to acquire grid positions assigned to its boats. Earlier traffic seemed to indicate that I-58 was planning to patrol five hundred miles north of Palau, but the recovery of that location was only partial. An earlier Seventh Fleet assessment had concluded that all Japanese sub operations had localized in home waters. However, analysts warned that they expected an all-out submarine effort in the final defense of the Empire.

The magicians were seeing some of that now. July 29 ULTRA intercepts showed that Japan had added two subs, I-363 and I-366, to the Tamon group, and ordered them to sortie in the first week of August. The four original Tamon subs were ordered to operate within fifty miles of the Leyte-Okinawa supply route to intercept and attack enemy shipping.

Hashimoto, now eleven days out from Kure, was among the IJN skippers to receive those orders. Already deep in the Philippine Sea, nearly due east of Leyte, he decided to improvise. Surfacing his boat under an ashen overcast, he made for the intersection of the north-south line between Okinawa and Palau, and the east-west route between Guam and Leyte. That would put him at the dead center of Route Peddie.

Indianapolis was moving west-southwest, still at 15.7 knots and zigzagging, slightly south of Route Peddie and about 340 miles east of the last known position of the enemy submarine that *Harris* lost. It was a balmy day in the mid-eighties, and a three-knot wind pushed a group of bright cumulus clouds southwest, like ships sailing in company. In the afternoon, lookouts spotted the chunky silhouette of a friendly ship lumbering north.

Indy's communications officer, Ken Stout, ordered his men to hail her via the TBS, or "Talk Between Ships," a short-range line-of-sight communication system.

When contact was established,* the ship identified herself as LST-779. The acronym stood for "Landing Ship, Tank," but the irreverent joked that it stood for "large slow target." This particular ship had distinguished herself. She was the first LST to reach Iwo Jima, beaching as Japanese gunners lashed her with blistering fire. As part of her business ashore, she gave the Marines an American flag. It would be the one that the men of Indy watched being hoisted aloft on Mount Suribachi.

This day, she was conducting antiaircraft defense maneuvers, and her captain, Lieutenant Joseph A. Hopkins, warned *Indianapolis* that his ship was about to conduct firing exercises. Stout and his men acknowledged,

---

* Reports conflict as to whether the contact between *Indianapolis* and LST-779 was visual or by radio.

and the two ships, both bound for the Philippines, passed out of visual range.

In the wardroom that evening, Janney sat down to eat with Dr. Haynes, Flynn, and several other officers. Dinner was steak and strawberries, and Janney would not have been surprised if Flynn left his steak for last. The commander usually ate dessert first and encouraged others to do so as well, a policy that delighted the crew, as well as his daughters, Anne and Carleen, back home.

"A Jap sub has been spotted along our route," Janney said to the group.

Haynes's eyes twinkled. "Our escort will take care of it."

The table erupted in laughter.

Strictly speaking, Janney was not supposed to share this kind of information with the doctor, who'd been known to turn a jest into a fact, then carry it all over the ship like the town crier. That's why Captain McVay had a policy against loose talk about tactical information. But the wardroom was tight-knit while McVay usually dined alone—and besides, what other news was there to share over dinner?

As the 6 to 8 p.m. watch approached, Lieutenant Junior Grade Charles Brite McKissick made his way toward the bridge to relieve the officer of the deck. McKissick, a winsome twenty-five-year-old from McKinney, Texas, had been standing this critical watch for less than a year. Technically, he was still in training, and since the OOD was the direct representative of the skipper, he was careful not to cut any corners. Per McVay's standing orders, he had stopped into CIC (Combat Information Center) for a brief on the tactical situation and found nothing out of the ordinary.

The deck swayed under McKissick's feet. He judged the seas as somewhere between choppy and rough. Before assuming the watch, he picked up the communications board. It contained dispatches and other information for which every OOD was responsible during his watch. McKissick flipped open the metal cover and paged through the message traffic.

His eye fell on the dispatch Janney had spoken of—possible enemy submarine contact somewhere ahead. The dispatch included latitude/longitude information: 10-26N, 131-45E.

Over the past dozen hours, an equal number of messages concerning USS *Harris*'s submarine hunt had burned across the Philippine

Sea between Captain Granum's office in the Philippines and Captain Naquin's at Guam. Most were also streaming out on one or more of the FOX schedules. Salting this chatter were such troubling terms as "oil slick"—the ghost residue left on the ocean's surface by a submarine—"sound contact with engine propeller," and "evaluation positive." A message marked Operational Priority Secret noted that *Harris* attacked ten times with hedgehogs, and that USS *Greene* had joined in the hunt, contributing two depth-charge attacks. "Negative results. Lost contact," that message concluded. "Classified as probable sub."

It is unclear which hard-copy message made its way from Indy's communications office to her bridge. All that is known is that the one clipped into the silver folder was dated July 29 and that it struck McKissick as routine. If a warship routed itself around every suspected sub, he knew, the U.S. Navy would never get anywhere.

As he relieved the watch, McKissick discussed this dispatch with the off-going OOD. The two agreed that even if the sub in question was steering an intercept course, the closest it would come to *Indianapolis* would be seventy-five to a hundred miles.

Glenn Morgan was just finishing up his watch when his friend, Quartermaster Third Class Vincent Allard, showed up for the 8 p.m. to midnight watch, along with one of his strikers, the new kid, Billy Emery. Captain McVay came to the bridge and Morgan listened as he and McKissick assessed the visibility. Allard had already noticed that it was too poor even to visually determine the direction of the swells.

McVay and McKissick walked out onto the port bridge wing to evaluate the sky. Though it was still technically twilight, as the sun had set less than an hour before, the darkness was already so nearly absolute that neither man could distinguish the features of the others on the bridge, just a few feet away. In the tropics, the transition from day to night passes quickly.

McVay told McKissick that at the end of the evening twilight he could secure from zigzagging and return the ship to base course.

"Aye, sir," McKissick said.

Allard entered the captain's order in the deck log. It was standard procedure to cease zigzagging as full darkness fell when visibility was poor. The standing orders, a sheaf of typewritten pages tucked into the back of the regular night order book, required the OOD to notify the captain immediately of any changes in sea conditions or weather.

McVay departed the bridge. And when darkness fully blanketed *Indianapolis*, the helmsman began steering a straight course.

As I-58 cruised on the surface, squalls fought each other aloft but did not trouble the sea. Hashimoto had hoped to remain on the surface, but a thick marine layer clotted the area and he could see no farther than if he had been staring into the bottom of an iron teakettle. The moon would rise in two hours. Perhaps visibility would improve then. Hashimoto ordered a dive and set a westward course at a submerged speed of two knots.

He went to the wardroom, having left orders to be roused at 10:30 p.m. Two-thirds of the crew also found places to lie down, stripped off their uniforms, and sprawled naked in all corners of the sub—atop torpedoes and rice sacks, even between shelves. Silence seeped through the dimly lit boat, interrupted only by the air-conditioning plant, the whisper of hydroplanes and rudders, and the scurrying of rats. These vermin were ubiquitous on IJN submarines. A perfect plague, Hashimoto thought, impossible to keep down. He had offered twenty yen cash plus an extra night of shore leave to any man who caught and killed one. Now he stripped off his uniform, lay down in his bunk, and listened to the strange music of his subaqueous domain.

13

JULY 29, 1945

Near Midnight
The Philippine Sea

THERE WAS SCUTTLEBUTT FLYING around Radio 1 that evening. Radio 1 was the main communications shack and was located at
the base of the ship's forward superstructure one level above the fo'c'sle
deck, where Admiral Spruance did his laps when he was aboard. A sailor
leaning over the rail on the starboard bridge wing could see the door
to Radio 1. Radio 2 was much farther aft, tucked in behind the second
smokestack.

Fifteen or twenty minutes before midnight, Lieutenant Junior Grade
David Driscoll, the communications watch officer, walked from the
adjoining office into the main shack and made the gossip official: "Got a
submarine report," he said to the room. Such messages were decrypted in
the comm office then passed to the OOD, who usually shared them with
Commander Janney so that he could check the positions on his charts.

Elwyn Sturtevant, a Los Angeles native, reported to Radio 1 for the
midwatch, along with four other men. He clamped on the headphones,
sat down at the mill, and prepared to fish important messages out of the
FOX schedule flood.

Though only twenty-one, Sturtevant was an old hand by the standards of the war. A radioman second class, he'd served in the ship's
radio department since May 1943, and considered the shacks greatly
improved since the most recent Mare Island overhaul. Yard technicians
had installed several new receivers, two new transmitters, and a direction
finder to replace one that had its antenna sheared off by a friendly carrier plane at Okinawa.

The crew was in fine shape, too. A couple of new kids, Jack Miner and
Fred Hart, had reported in the yard, but a lot of the men were experienced hands, while the division officer, Chief Warrant Officer Leonard T.

Woods, was absolutely tops. All the men revered him, both as a technical expert and as a surefooted leader. Woods exuded the quiet authority of a man much older than his twenty-six years.

It was Driscoll, however, who had the duty with Sturtevant. A radioman sat near Sturtevant guarding Jump FOX, which, like the FOX schedule, was another fire hose of coded information. There were a couple of new strikers on duty, trainees in their assigned departments. Seamen Jack Cassidy and James Belcher had perhaps the most important midwatch job of all: taking care of the coffee gear.

Sturtevant registered Driscoll's announcement about the submarine but was unbothered. Driscoll seemed bland about the message. Apparently, the sub was hundreds of miles south.

Lieutenant Commander Stanley Lipski appeared on the bridge to relieve McKissick at 8 p.m. The thirty-four-year-old gunnery officer from Northampton, Massachusetts, had served as a naval attaché in Helsinki before the war, and spoke fluent Russian. He was also a former intelligence officer and naval aviator. Everyone liked Lipski because he was that rare man who was both fiercely competent and a genuinely nice fellow.

This night, he wore two hats—OOD and supervisor of the watch. With him was Lieutenant Redmayne, the engineering officer who had relieved the disgruntled DeGrave. Redmayne was under instruction as supervisor of the watch and had stood duty on Indy's bridge only about half a dozen times. Before *Indianapolis*, he had served on two seaplane-tending vessels. Indy was his first chance to serve on a capital ship. When Redmayne relieved the watch, he noticed that visibility was very poor, with no moon.

Shortly after 8 p.m., Commander Janney, the navigator, appeared briefly on the bridge to deliver the night orders, then returned between 9:00 and 9:30 p.m. The *Wild Hunter* encounter had yielded new information, he told Lipski and Redmayne. A destroyer escort and a patrol bomber (known collectively as a "hunter-killer" group) had been dispatched to chase a submarine spotted by the merchant ship. The sighting was well ahead of *Indianapolis*'s path, in an area they would pass through at about 8 a.m. the following morning.

Meanwhile, in a second-deck berthing area near the stern, Harpo Celaya curled around a woolen blanket, trying to catch some shut-eye. The sweltering Pacific heat had turned the compartment into a greenhouse. Celaya had drawn a top rack, nearest the overhead where all the heat collected with no place to escape. He was used to heat, but at home in Arizona it was the dry bake of the Sonoran Desert, not a boiling hell like out here. He tossed and turned, half-dreaming and bathed in sweat.

"Celaya . . . ?" A jostling hand accompanied the whisper. It was his new crew chief, Everett Thorpe, a watertender. Thorpe let Celaya know that he was headed topside where it was much cooler and asked his friend to join him.

Both men had the 4 a.m. watch. Thorpe suggested that one or the other of them could be responsible for making sure neither overslept. Harpo agreed. Bleary-eyed, he climbed down from his rack, dragging his blanket behind him. It was about 9 p.m. They stopped by the galley and grabbed sandwiches, then climbed up to the main deck where, it appeared, they were late to the party. The heat belowdecks had driven much of the crew to seek respite topside. Bodies lay everywhere—men tucked under the gun turrets, sprawled out on the fo'c'sle, and under nets that held dozens of life jackets. Just when it seemed they wouldn't find a space large enough to lie down, they found an empty spot on the quarterdeck.

Harpo and Thorpe sat down and started eating their sandwiches. Harpo liked Thorpe, who was from the Deep South and one of the few fellows aboard who didn't seem to notice that he was Mexican. On the run over to Tinian, the two had spent almost nine days together in the fireroom with Harpo teaching Thorpe to speak a little Spanish.

Noticing that Celaya was carrying his heavy blanket, Thorpe questioned his judgment. The temperature topside was nearly as sweltering as below. What in the world did he need a blanket for?

"I can't sleep without it," Harpo said. "It goes back to when I was a kid, and if you tease me about it, I'll have to kill you."

Thorpe laughed. The truth was that back home in the Sonoran summer, if you slept without a blanket the mosquitoes would eat you alive. But Harpo thought it was funnier to let Thorpe think the blanket was some kind of childhood quirk. When he finished his sandwich, Harpo stripped off his pants and rolled them into a pillow. He wrapped the blanket around his shoulders and lay down, staring up into the night, unconsciously toying with the St. Anthony's medal that hung around his neck. His mother had given it to him before she left his father. Harpo always wore it for good luck.

In the red light of the charthouse, McVay reviewed the plot and night orders with Janney. The ship was darkened and the door to the charthouse was open. A night breeze whispered in, humid and salt-laden. McVay stepped out onto the bridge. By now, he estimated, *Indianapolis* had hit the PIM—the Plan of Intended Movement—although with the stars imprisoned behind the overcast, they were unable to take a celestial fix to confirm. Soon thereafter, Flynn directed the ship's speed increased to about seventeen knots.

"I want to have a little bit of gravy up my sleeve in case we have to use it," Flynn said, by which he meant make up ground they'd lost while zigzagging. That was fine with McVay. It would make a difference of only a few miles, and anyway, McVay remembered what Commodore Carter said: Things were quiet.

He could feel Indy undulating through long, deep swells, along with an irregular lateral motion. Even in the darkness, he could glimpse the fitful sloshing of ghostly whitecaps. This indicated a confused sea driven by opposite-direction weather patterns potentially hundreds of miles away.

Moonrise was expected a half hour before midnight, but it was now nearly 11 p.m. and the quartermaster, Allard, hadn't seen even a hint of it yet. The bridge was so utterly dark that Allard couldn't tell his strikers apart unless he got right up in their faces. Lookout stations were fully manned: Both wings of the navigation bridge had a pair of sailors on permanent stations with mounted binoculars. There were more lookouts with binoculars one level lower on the signal bridge, as well as additional full-time lookouts with mounted binoculars at "sky amidships" near the No. 2 stack. In all, no less than twelve men with binoculars were on watch at all times.

The 20 mm and 40 mm gun crews each had a man dedicated to lookout duty, adding ten more pairs of eyes. All night long, a petty officer would make regular rounds to ensure all these men were doing their jobs instead of catching a few winks.

Having given his stateroom to Captain Edwin Crouch, a friend and fellow Academy grad who had hitched a ride at Guam, McVay retired to his emergency cabin, less than ten paces aft of the bridge. The air in the tiny space sweltered. He stripped naked and lay down in his rack. Near his head, a voice tube from the bulkhead connected him with the OOD. Murmured conversation from the bridge floated through it into the cabin and carried him down to sleep.

A few minutes before midnight, Kasey Moore relieved Lipski as supervisor of the watch and took a turn around the navigation bridge. All watchstanders were posted and alert. McVay had ordered "Yoke modified," a cruising condition normally set when there was little threat of attack. Under the standard wartime steaming condition, known simply as "Yoke," a cruiser of Indy's class was zipped up much too tightly for comfortable cruising. To seal the number of doors and hatches required for maximum watertight integrity would mean stifling both ventilation and the ability of essential watch personnel to move forward and aft.

Shortly after the war began, "Yoke modified" became the new standard for older cruisers. Aboard Indy, this configuration was more habit than prescribed. Main-deck and second-deck doors were left completely open, as were select others. While this improved the flow of air and personnel, it would also improve the flow of seawater through adjoining compartments if Indy were hit, potentially flooding the ship. The condition was a holdover from the previous skipper. Moore and McVay had discussed revising the damage control organization and procedures, even sending the ship's damage control books down to San Diego so that trainers there could prepare appropriate damage control and battle problems. But the special mission to Tinian yanked Indy out of the States so quickly that they'd had to send a messenger down to retrieve the books immediately.

On the navigation bridge, L. D. Cox had his headphones on and was ready to pass data back and forth to the engine room. It had been pitch-black when he first took the watch at midnight. Now, though, the clouds had begun to break apart, and he glimpsed quicksilver slivers of moon.

Bugler Donald Mack ducked into the charthouse to talk with the quartermaster on watch, Jimmy French. Billy Emery, a spanking new graduate of quartermaster school in Bainbridge, Maryland, was there, too. This was Emery's first ship. Since she looked to be in drydock for months and unlikely to see action again, his father, Lieutenant Commander John Emery, had pulled some strings to get Billy stationed on *Indianapolis.*

As ordered, I-58's petty officer of the watch had roused Hashimoto at 10:30 p.m. with nothing new to report. Hashimoto dressed, visited the shrine, then mounted the conning tower, where he could use the periscope.

"Night battle stations," he announced.

It was a routine order, something to keep the men on their toes. As the crew hustled to comply, he let his eyes adjust to the darkness. Hashimoto ordered the diving officer to make his depth sixty feet.

It was 11 p.m. Moonrise was nearly sixty minutes old.

"Raise night periscope," Hashimoto said.

When the instrument was just clear of the surface, he bent to the eyepiece and had a quick look around. The earth's rotation had already flung the nearly full moon high into the eastern sky. It flirted with heavy cloud cover, lunar light glinting off the heaving sea. Hashimoto could almost see the horizon. At intervals, the moon shook herself free of clouds, and he judged the light sufficient for a submerged attack.

He nudged the periscope higher, then swept the headwindow left and right, scanning carefully.

"Stand by Type-13 Radar."

Crewmen raised the antenna above the surface and detected no aircraft. With no skyborne enemy and a clean sea, Hashimoto decided to surface and look for enemy ships. He gave the order and I-58's crew leapt into motion. Alarm bells sounded. Sailors hurried to their posts.

Hashimoto snapped the periscope handles into their housing. "Surface. Blow main ballast."

High-pressure air rushed into the main tanks, expelling seawater and lifting the boat. I-58 broke the surface. When her decks were awash, the conning tower hatch was cracked open, sending a welcome stream of fresh air into the ship. Ears popped as pressure inside the boat equalized with the atmosphere.

When the pressure was fully equalized, a signalman climbed onto the bridge, followed by the navigator, who was intent on trying to take at least a partial celestial fix. The surface radar operator prepared to scan the area.

Hashimoto was still scanning through the night periscope when he heard the navigator shout, "Bearing red nine-zero degrees, a possible enemy ship!"

Hashimoto lowered the night periscope, bounded to the bridge, and raised his binoculars. Yes! There it was! A black spot on the horizon, hanging on the rays of the moon.

Hashimoto uttered a single word: "Dive."

The four men on the bridge slid down the ladder. The last man down, the signalman, pulled the hatch closed. Hashimoto manned the periscope again. The black shape was still there, clear through the head-window.

"Open the vents," he said.

As the main ballast tank vents opened, water gushed into the tanks, and I-58 slid down until the lid of the sea closed above her.

"Ship in sight," Hashimoto said.

An invisible charge shot through his crew, man to man. In the four years since he first lurked off Pearl Harbor, never had Hashimoto been in such a potentially advantaged position. The dark silhouette drew closer, but he could not yet discern the class of ship.

What if I-58 had already been detected? What if the shape was a destroyer pressing in for the kill? Thick darkness concealed Hashimoto's face from the others in the conning tower, and he worked to keep his voice composed.

"All tubes to the ready," he said. "*Kaiten*, stand by."

14

JULY 30, 1945

Midnight
The Philippine Sea

MARINE CORPORAL EDGAR HARRELL got off watch a little before midnight and decided to sleep topside again. The night before, he and a buddy named Munson had bedded down atop the No. 1 gun turret. There were a couple of big life rafts lashed to the turret's gently sloping roof, so it was nice and comfortable up there. The only problem was that it was against regulations. With Indy's interior sweltering, Harrell wanted to avoid his bunk again, but he also wanted to avoid getting busted down in paygrade. Munson had opted for the life rafts again, but there was some open deck space under the barrels of the same gun. Harrell decided to sleep there.

The night was thick and warm. Harrell spread his blanket on the steel deck and tucked his shoes under his head for a pillow. As he gazed up at the sky, moonlight sifted down through the overcast, then disappeared again. He felt tired and homesick. Harrell thanked God for His protection and asked Him to watch over his family and Ola Mae, his girl back home. The deep hum of Indy's engines and the swooshing of her wake carried him down toward dreams.

Well forward of Harrell, on the bow, Harpo's friend Santos Pena stretched out on top of a ready-box full of 20 mm ammunition and gazed up into the moonlit clouds. His lookout shift would begin shortly, but for now he welcomed the silky night breeze.

I-58's crew waited, breathless. The black shape on the horizon soon gathered itself into the shape of a triangle suspended in the moon's silver light. But looking through the night periscope, Hashimoto still could not determine her class. Neither could he see the height of her mast in order to estimate the range. This lack of data opened the door to an array of possible mistakes, and his mind ticked through them all.

Without the range, course, and speed of the target, he could not make the proper calculations to obtain a hit. If the class of ship were known, he could estimate the speed by counting the target's propeller blade frequency, but the hydrophones remained silent. And with the target pointed directly at him, its hull was masking sonar sounds. He would have to wait until the target was on a broader line of sight to ferret out its speed. Also, changes in the target's speed and course could throw off Hashimoto's aim, especially at night, so the moment of firing had to be determined in advance.

A whole kingdom of errors loomed. But if Hashimoto could keep them small and fire six torpedoes in a fanwise spread, he could ensure a hit. Even if he guessed wrong on one of the variables—or even if the target zigzagged, as it was almost sure to do.

A crisp demand interrupted his calculations: "Send us!"

It was the suicide pilots. Hashimoto had been so preoccupied with his Type 95 torpedo calculations that he had not followed up on his earlier order for the *kaiten*.

"Why can't we be launched?" the pilots clamored.

Hashimoto understood their desire. The *kaiten* could steer to the target, regardless of its speed or course. But the touch-and-go, obscured visibility would make it difficult for the pilots to home in visually on the target over a period of tens of minutes. To get a Type 95 torpedo hit, all he needed was a reasonable estimate of speed and range, along with one good bearing, and he could send his fish to their target. That was the better option here, so he decided not to use the *kaiten* unless the oxygen torpedoes failed to hit their mark.

Hashimoto put his eye to the scope again and saw the top of the triangle resolve into two distinct shapes. He could make out a large mast forward and estimated its height at ninety feet. His heartbeat quickened. She appeared to be a large cruiser, ten thousand tons or bigger. Now I-58's hydrophones gurgled to life, announcing enemy propeller revolutions that were moderately high. Using visual observations, Hashimoto adjusted and put the target's speed at twelve knots, course 260, range three thousand yards.

He alone could see all this. Without him, the crew could know nothing. As they awaited his word, straining in the deadly quiet, an exhilarating thought formed in his mind: *We've got her.*

Ensign John Woolston had the 8 p.m. to midnight watch in damage control central. Four officers rotated through the watch from dusk to dawn, and Lieutenant Hurst, the new damage control officer who'd come aboard three weeks after Woolston, usually joined the primary watchstander. He did this night, freeing Woolston to roam the ship to ensure that watch teams were doing their required inspections and setting the proper damage-control condition. Woolston emerged topside to make sure the ship was fully darkened and also took a peek at the weather. At that moment, it was a pitch-black night, and thick clouds intermittently obscured a nearly full moon.

Touring the decks, he found the ship fully darkened, with no errant lights that would paint a bull's-eye on Indy for an enemy sub. Woolston checked his watch and headed back to damage control central. At almost exactly midnight, his relief appeared, and Hurst cut Woolston loose. Gratefully, Woolston headed up to the wardroom, where he greeted the lone steward, a young black man, working behind the serving window.

"Coffee, please, and a ham sandwich," Woolston said.

He looked around the wardroom, which was roughly square with a low overhead. Several rows of long tables sat empty, surrounded by thinly padded, heavy metal chairs. Woolston mused that when he toured Indy as a kid, he had sat and eaten a sandwich in this same space.

The steward rustled up the coffee and sandwich, and slid it to the serving window. Woolston picked up the cup and plate, found a table, and sat down.

Aboard I-58, a sonarman thought he heard the clinking of dishes.* Twenty-seven minutes had passed since I-58's navigator spotted the enemy ship. It now became apparent that the target was approaching

---

* Yamada, Goro. "Sinking the *Indianapolis*: A Japanese Perspective." Interview of an I-58 crewman by historian Dan King.

off the starboard bow. He ordered the torpedo director computer set to "green sixty degrees"—the torpedoes would turn sixty degrees starboard after launch.

The target closed the distance: twenty-five hundred yards . . . two thousand . . . fifteen hundred.

"Stand by . . ." Hashimoto commanded in a loud voice. "Fire!"

At two-second intervals, six torpedoes ejected from tubes carved into the sub's forward hull, one tube after another until all six were away. A report came from the torpedo room: "All tubes fired and correct."

It was about five minutes after midnight, and six warheads streaked toward the enemy warship in a lethal fan. Hashimoto snatched a look through the periscope, brought his boat on a course parallel to the target, and waited. Every minute seemed an age.

15

THE FIRST FISH SLAMMED into Indy's starboard bow, killing dozens of men in an instant. The violent explosion ejected McVay from his bunk. The ship whipped beneath him and set up a rattling vibration that caused him to flash back to Okinawa.

Had they been hit by another suicider?

No, he thought. Impossible.

In the blink of time those thoughts took, another shattering concussion rocked Indy amidships. Acrid white smoke immediately filled McVay's emergency cabin, and he could not see. He picked himself up off the deck, felt his way to the cabin door, swung around the bulkhead, and appeared on the lightless bridge stark naked. At that moment, there were thirteen men on the bridge. Only three would survive.

· · ·

President Franklin Delano Roosevelt aboard *Indianapolis*, his ship of state.

Indianapolis sails under the Golden Gate Bridge. The ship was commissioned in November 1932, two months before construction of the bridge began.

(L to R): Admiral Raymond Spruance, Fleet Admiral Ernest J. King, and Admiral Chester Nimitz with Brigadier General Sanderford Jarman.

Cooks and bakers on liberty. In no particular order: Raymond Kinzle, Keith Owen, David Kemp, John Spinelli, Clarence Hupka, Fernando Sanchez, Sal Maldonado, and Morgan Moseley.

Kyle "Kasey" Moore (left) and Father Thomas Conway (in profile) share a moment of laughter in the *Indianapolis* wardroom. Notice that Moore is wearing his uninflated life belt, as required.

A portion of Indy's Marine detachment, 1945. Top (L to R): Miles Spooner, Earl Riggins, Paul Uffelman, Giles McCoy, and Melvin Jacob. Bottom (L to R): Max Hughes, Raymond Rich, Jacob Greenwald, and Edgar Harrell.

Liberty time: (L to R) Robert Owens Jr., Arthur Labuda, Ralph Guye, Marion Schaap, Edward Alvey Jr., Glenn Morgan, and Vincent Allard.

Adolfo Celaya (center) poses with two Marines on Guam.

During general quarters, Indy's stewards manned the guns.

CDR Stanley Lipski

LT Charles B. McKissick

LT Richard Redmayne

This photo of McVay and his officers was taken just before Indy sailed from Mare Island, California, with components of the first atomic bomb. (L to R, front) CDR Johns Hopkins Janney, CAPT Charles McVay III, CDR Joseph Flynn, CDR Glen DeGrave. (L to R, back) LCDR C. M. Christiansen; LCDR Kasey Moore; LCDR Lewis Haynes, M.D.; LCDR Earl Henry, D.D.S.; LCDR Charles Hayes.

CWO Leonard Woods

ENS John Woolston

Capt Edwin Parke
Marine Corps

Japanese Zeke exploding near USS *Essex* after being shot down by USS *Indianapolis* near Southern Honshu, Japan, March 19, 1945.

Burials at sea following the March 31, 1945, kamikaze strike on Indy.

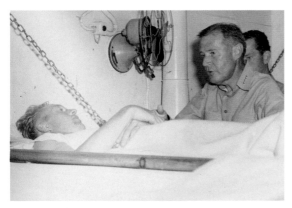

Following the kamikaze strike, Spruance visits a wounded sailor in sickbay.

Killed by Jap Suicide Pilot

Earl Procai, 19, Navy bugler, second class, was killed aboard the USS Indianapolis March 31 when a Japanese suicide plane struck his ship, his parents, Mr. and Mrs. Anthony

EARL PROCAI

Procai, 707, Tenth avenue, S. E., Minneapoli, Minn., were informed recently, the Minneapolis Times reported (clipping sent to Weekly by Rev. A. Kist).

Procai, who had been in the South Pacific area since early in 1944, was buried on Zamami island, ten miles from Okinawa.

He joined the Navy, after attending Vocational High School, in September, 1943. Besides his parents, he is survived by three sisters. Memorial services for him were held in St. Michael's Ukrainian Orthodox Church in Minneapolis.

Bugler Earl Procai's obituary.

WT3 Jimmy O'Donnell and his wife, Mary, just before Indy's final mission.

ENS Harlan Twible and his bride, Alice. The two married on June 6, 1945, the week after he graduated from the U.S. Naval Academy.

LCDR Kasey Moore and his daughter, Mary.

Seaman Dick Thelen and his father just before Thelen shipped out.

LCDR Earl Henry and his wife, Jane, at Memphis, Tennessee's famous Peabody Hotel the month before Indy's final mission. Jane was expecting.

Three members of the crew of *Enola Gay*: (L to R) Navigator Theodore "Dutch" Van Kirk, pilot Paul Tibbets, and bombardier Thomas Ferebee.

The scientists, technicians, and military leaders of the Manhattan Engineering District's Project Alberta on Tinian Island, 1945. In the second row (6th, 7th, and 8th from left) are the "Tinian Joint Chiefs," ADM William Purnell, GEN Thomas Farrell, and CAPT William "Deak" Parsons. At the end of the second row on the right (leaning forward) is Army CPT James Nolan, who, with MAJ Robert Furman, accompanied the Little Boy components aboard *Indianapolis*.

MAJ Robert Furman, Manhattan Project intelligence chief.

The Imperial Japanese Submarine I-58.

A young Mochitsura Hashimoto with his wife
and two of his three sons.

Hashimoto aboard I-58.

30 JUL 1945

From: SA TO KO 4   30 July/0048.
To : NO FU TE 27 (RI KU O Ø) (Navy Vice   JN-25-P-91
                                    Minister)
        HA SO HA O1 (KO E YA. 5) (Headquarters COMBINED NAVAL
                                    FORCE),
        SI U RI 14 (HE KI TA 1) (Comdr ADVANCE EXPEDITIONARY
                                    FORCE)
From Captain Sub I-58 (16595).
29 July at 2322 attacked and sunk one (two unrecovered groups).
Sinking confirmed. Obtained three torpedo hits. Position
(unrecovered grid).
(FRUPAC-041956-DISC-DI)   JUN 0605 Aug rec 15
        GI COMMENT: This is a revised version of item 62,
        page 41, RI Summary 311300/Q July.
                MIGAT identifies:
                        RI KU O Ø - Tokyo Bureau of Military
                                    Preparations

TOP SECRET—ULTRA

ULTRA intercept of a July 30 message from Hashimoto to his higher headquarters
reporting that I-58 had sunk an enemy ship. See diagrams pp. 204–205.

The first explosion knocked Pena off the ready-box, and he felt the ship's bow lift from the water. A brilliant yellow flash bloomed straight up from the bow and along both sides, an immense fan of fire. The spray hadn't yet settled from the first blast when the second struck farther back, near the No. 1 gun turret. Pena scrambled to his feet and looked forward. Less than ten feet from where he was standing, it looked to him as if *Indianapolis*'s entire bow was gone.

High over Pena, on watch in forward fire control near the top of the superstructure, Troy Nunley happened to have his eyes trained on the bow when the first torpedo slammed home. He saw the mammoth blast peel the bow leftward and down, opening the front of the ship from the bowsprit aft to frame 12. In the explosive flash, he glimpsed the bow's dark form hulking underwater, still attached by thin tendrils of steel like the lid of an opened tin can. Nunley, who had watched men sealed below decks after the suicide strike at Okinawa, knew instantly that any man who had been forward of frame 12 was dead.

In the pilot house, Glenn Morgan felt the deck vault up and wallop him in the back. Caustic smoke slithered in through the portholes and sucked his breath away. He flicked on his red-lensed flashlight and aimed it at his watch. It was a few minutes after midnight.

Morgan saw his good friend Ralph Guye, a quartermaster, peering at him, the red beam lighting his face in an eerie glow.

"What do you think happened?" Guye asked.

"Maybe a magazine exploded," Morgan said. But that was as wild a guess as there ever had been. In truth, he had no idea, and the uncertainty bothered him.

"Do you think we should go up to the bridge?" Guye asked. Morgan agreed and they took off.

On the quarterdeck, Harpo heard Thorpe screaming. The first torpedo blast had lifted both men off the deck. The second blast amidships sent a fireball their way. Harpo saw that Thorpe had been singed from head to toe. He himself felt as if he had just been doused in fire. His hair was gone. His eyelashes were gone. The heavy woolen blanket was gone as well. It had burned up entirely, but had saved the rest of him. Both men jumped up and ran toward their battle stations.

·   ·   ·

When the explosions rocked the ship, Clarence Hershberger woke up in midair to see a fifty-foot pillar of smoke and flame shooting straight into the night sky. In a flash, he realized this inferno was roaring up from the same hatch he'd been sleeping beside only moments before.

Hershberger hit the deck half-stunned. When he gathered himself, he noticed that his uniform was soaking wet. How could that be? He could only guess the explosions had sent a wave over the bow. If so, why hadn't it washed him overboard?

No time to think about that now. The deck was getting so hot it was beginning to burn his socks. He hotfooted it back to berthing in search of his life jacket.

Down in the officers' quarters, Dr. Haynes had been blown out of his bunk. He staggered into the smoke-clogged passageway to find the surrounding compartments engulfed in fire. He felt his way toward the wardroom, where, beyond the fire, John Woolston had been about to take the first bite of his ham sandwich when a hollow, metallic boom shook the ship. Whirling caterpillars of flame flashed in through the wardroom's two forward doors then flashed out again, as though there were a dragon in the passageway.

Woolston had just three seconds to realize that he'd been singed when the second, louder blast directly beneath him threw him to the deck. Two more sheets of flame poured in through the wardroom doors. Then the lights went out.

Hashimoto peered through his night periscope at the scene of destruction unfolding quickly before him. On the target's main and after-turrets, skyscrapers of silver water shot toward the moon. Red tongues of flame followed immediately after, tasting the night. A third column of water rose alongside the No. 2 turret and seemed to swallow the ship.

"A hit! A hit!" Hashimoto shouted, and his elated crew improvised a victory dance.

With the target now offering no threat, Hashimoto raised the day periscope and let the men in the conning tower have a look. The hydrophones then registered deep, heavy explosions—secondary blasts far greater than the torpedo strikes themselves.

"Depth-charge attack!" some of the sub crew shouted in fear.

"No," Hashimoto said, reassuring them. "It is the target exploding. There is no other enemy in sight."

Hashimoto put his eyes to the scope again and saw flashes of fire rippling across the target.

Nine thousand feet above *Indianapolis*, Army Captain Richard G. LeFrancis gazed down from the cockpit of his Douglas C-54 Skymaster at what looked like a spectacular naval battle. LeFrancis, an Army transport pilot en route from Manila to Guam, had been briefed that the Navy was planning fleet gunnery practice somewhere between the Marianas and the Philippines. His instructions were to stay clear and fly about twenty miles north of the area.

LeFrancis had a brigadier general aboard, a big cheese who worked directly for MacArthur. The captain called the general up to the cockpit to check out the action below. The senior officer took the copilot's seat and seemed to LeFrancis to really be enjoying the action.

"Looks like the target is firing back," the general remarked.

LeFrancis agreed. As the men peered down, the fireworks below were a bit surreal—spectacular, but because of the plane's altitude, entirely silent.

When Hashimoto's torpedoes struck Indy, her aviation fuel stores ignited, and a maelstrom of flame and explosions incinerated or severely burned anyone belowdecks in the forward part of the ship. The blaze torched men sleeping in sickbay, the forward enlisted berthing, the Marine berthing, and the compartment occupied by the ship's stewards. A deck above, those in officers' country were also in peril as fires ripped upward.

The Japanese Type 95 torpedo carried a huge explosive payload designed to mortally wound battleships and cruisers. The initial pressure blast was meant to buckle the ship's skin and weaken her internal framing. The warhead's second effect was to punch a cavernous, temporary hole in the ocean beneath the target. These first- and second-order effects created a kinetic ambush: With a well-aimed torpedo, the weight of both the weakened ship and the displaced water would crash back into the void and break the vessel in half.

Hashimoto's first torpedo rammed Indy's starboard bow just below the forward 20 mm antiaircraft guns. Before anyone had time to process what had happened, the explosion was over, its work done, and Indy's bow was in shambles. Ripped away between frames 12 and 13, the bow clung to the keel of the ship like a hangnail, held there by only a few threads of hull plating. Two seconds later, the second torpedo exploded below the waterline near frame 45, missing Indy's armor belt by just a few frames. The twin blasts and water cavity effects ruptured the hull, tore open the thin outer strakes, and opened the ship to the sea.

With the bow sheared off, and the propellers still pushing the ship forward, the honeycomb of exposed passageways and compartments funneled the sea into the interior of the ship. A wall of seawater surged in, drowning the men immediately behind frame 12. The main and second decks continued flooding fast, and fuel oil floated atop the seawater.

As *Indianapolis* lay broken on the surface, many men thought instantly that she was doomed. Others thought she would weather the blasts, whatever they had been.

"Hurrah!" cried one sailor who had been standing watch near the 40 mm guns. "One of the boilers blew up! It's back to the States for us!"

16

ON THE BRIDGE, MCVAY addressed the officer of the deck, Lieutenant John Orr. "Do you have any reports?"

"No, sir. I've lost all communications." Orr, agitated, added that he tried to stop the engines, but was unsure whether the order got through to the engine room.

With the steel deck of the bridge tilting slightly under his bare feet, McVay made a rapid calculation. The engine room telegraph was electrical, and it was out. So, too, were the ship's service phone, the battle phones, and even the sound-powered phones. That was it: All comms were down.

Orr told McVay he had already dispatched Lieutenant Junior Grade Paul Candalino two decks directly below the navigation bridge to tell the men in Radio 1 to send a distress signal. Orr had also sent the boatswain's mate of the watch, Coxswain Edward Keyes, to pass word that all hands were to report topside.

McVay looked at Orr. "See what other information you can get," he said, then turned to go back to his emergency cabin for clothes.

From his station a hundred feet above the waterline in the main battery director, Firecontrolman Third Class Robert Witzig saw all hell breaking loose below him: men dashing to their battle stations; others burned, broken, and screaming; the damaged bow belching smoke and swallowing water. Looking aft, he saw smoke, flames, and sparks jetting from the forward stack, and a crowd beginning to gather on the quarterdeck.

Marine Corporal Ed Harrell was headed there himself as he tried to reach his emergency station. Moving aft, he saw burned men climbing up from below, shrieking in agony. Melting flesh dripped from their faces. Bones jutted through their skin. Harrell's stomach turned at the charred stench of burned human flesh.

Harrell saw Marine Lieutenant Edward Stauffer standing near canvas bags full of life jackets secured to the bulkheads.

"Sir," Harrell called. "Permission to cut down the life jackets?"

"No," Stauffer said. "Not until we're given the orders to abandon ship." Then another burn victim staggered out onto the deck. It was the gunnery officer, Commander Lipski. Burned flesh hung from his arms and his eyes were charcoal pits in his face. "Help me," he moaned.

"Get the commander a life jacket," someone yelled, and immediately sailors rushed in and cut the canvas bags down. Yeoman Victor Buckett grabbed the kapok vests and started handing them out to the crew. Harrell grabbed one and put it on Lipski.

The quarterdeck was quickly overrun as injured men were brought up from below and from the forward parts of the ship. Amid the bedlam, the gravely injured Lipski stood calmly, ordering men to grab life jackets.

On the signal bridge, nineteen-year-old Signalman Third Class Paul McGinnis heard the keening of men being cooked alive somewhere below him. McGinnis had felt the torpedo attack as a violent shaking and donned a life jacket, just in case. Now, the excruciating screams rooted him in place and seemed as if they would never end. Then something even more horrific happened: The screaming stopped.

The signalmen around McGinnis began stowing classified papers in weighted bags to sink them. Then, oddly, another of his buddies began the ordinary chore of tidying up, sweeping up spilled sugar and grounds from around the coffee station. For a minute, McGinnis thought everything was going to be okay.

Down in the port hangar, Jim Jarvis, a third-class aviation machinist mate, had not been awakened by the explosions, but by the profound hush that followed. Usually, the blower in the hangar was so loud that it made conversation almost impossible. But when the torpedoes hit, the blower stopped and Jarvis lurched awake in the strange quiet.

Also conspicuously absent was the near-constant yapping of the 1MC, which governed ship life even in emergencies. Like the blower, it remained eerily mute, paralyzing large portions of the crew as they awaited orders.

All over the ship, men snatched up handsets for the JL Talker, a kind of telephone network and a main conduit to the bridge, and tried to get information or report what they were seeing. On the darkened bridge, Seaman First Class A. C. "Tony" King manned the JL Talker and found that he couldn't receive or send messages either. No one on the ship could talk to him, and therefore, to the officers in command.

Now dressed, McVay returned to the bridge.

"Somebody get the captain a life jacket!" Orr yelled.

L. D. Cox jumped to comply, retrieving one of the new kapok vests. He helped McVay into it then put one on himself. Cox noticed strange noises filtering up from below. The black smell of burning filled his senses, and the ship's list began to increase. None were good signs.

Another sailor asked Cox if he was getting ready to be sunk. Cox glanced at him as he secured the kapok's straps. "I'm going to be ready for anything."

Lieutenant Commander Kasey Moore, who had already been forward, returned to the bridge and addressed McVay.

"Sir, we're going down rapidly by the head," Moore said, concerned but cool. "Do you wish to abandon ship?"

Even in good conditions with the ship properly trimmed and ballasted, she would capsize rapidly if the list angle reached sixty-five degrees. Now, McVay estimated that Indy had taken a list of only about three degrees. The kamikaze had produced a bigger list, which the crew had been able to control quite easily. McVay felt confident they could do the same here.

"Not yet," McVay said to Moore. "Take another look and give me any further information."

Then McVay turned to Cox. "We're still making way," he said. "Put your headphones on and see if you can raise the engine room. Tell them to cut all power to the screws."

"Aye, sir." Cox clamped on the phones, but the circuit was dead. "I can't reach the engine room, Captain," he said.

In Engine Room 1, below the waterline in the exact center of the ship, the effects of the torpedo hits had been catastrophic. The main generators tripped out due to short circuits in the forward power lines. The lights had gone out instantly, imprisoning the men in absolute darkness. The normal whine and hum of machinery wound down to a spectral silence.

In the cavernous, three-story compartment, a few battle lanterns flickered to life. Within the first minute, Norman Roberts and William Nightingale, both first-class machinist mates, could see that the steam pressure had plunged from three hundred pounds per square inch to seventy-five. They knew that could mean only two things: One, a torpedo had struck the forward fireroom next door, triggering a colossal steam leak, and two, the men in there were dead—likely flash-boiled.

Roberts was covered with coffee. He'd been holding a full cup when the torpedo struck, and the impact blew him so high he'd hit the over-head. Now, the ventilation ducts up there were spitting red-hot sparks. Without steam pressure, the forward turbines that drove the two outer screws stopped. The propellers still turned, though, driven slowly by ocean water dragging over them, like pinwheels in the wind.

All through this, the crewmen in Engine Room 1—the forward engine room—worked to establish communication with the men in the after-engine room. After several failed attempts, Nightingale managed to get a connection and reported that he had lost the electric lead forward and had no steam. Then Nightingale's orders finally came through: start a main generator. It was the last successful transmission.

Radioman Jack Miner burst through the light-lock door between Bat-tle 2 and Radio 2 and found that the overhead lights in the back half of the ship were on. Fred Hart, a second-class radio tech, was already in the room. Miner, a nineteen-year-old from Glencoe, Illinois, had com-pleted a semester at Yale before joining the Navy to help win the war. He'd been aboard for only seventeen days. Now he stood in Radio 2, five decks above the waterline, with Hart, wondering about their next move. The ship's transmitters were located here in Radio 2, but the receivers were in Radio 1 in the forward half of the ship.

Hart saw that all the Radio 2 gear seemed to be in place except for a transmitter that was in for repair and had slid off a rack onto the deck. All the transmitter pilot lights were lit, which meant they had power.

About five minutes had passed since the torpedo strikes. Hart could feel that the ship had taken on a slight list, and that she seemed to be settling gradually. He was thinking maybe they hadn't been hit too bad when Chief Warrant Officer Leonard Woods entered the shack, burned and covered with soot.

"We're in bad shape," Woods said to the group in the room, which had grown to seven or eight men. He had been sleeping in his quarters when the explosions hit and had seen the damage forward, including a mass of flames. He suspected that the cables connecting Radio 2 with Radio 1 were severed. That meant the indicator board that would nor-mally tell Radio 2 which sending positions the main shack was going to use, and which transmitter, was dead.

Woods did not seem to notice his burns. Instead, he simply took charge. "Grab a life jacket or life belt, blow up the belts, and keep calm," he said. "Miner, power up the TBK." The TBK was a 500-kilocycle transmitter. It was always kept warmed up, so all Miner had to do was throw the power switch.

"Hart, go to Radio 1 and get our position," Woods said.

The radio chief didn't know whether Hart would be able to get to Radio 1. It was two hundred feet forward through a maze of flames, smoke, and God knew what else, up and down four ladders tilted at crazy angles, around multiple gun mounts, across the quarterdeck, and up to the comm deck. Who knew what he'd find when he got there?

Woods didn't know whether Radio 1 would be able to transmit remotely, but he did know this: The radio shacks had just become the most important compartments on the dying ship.

17

RADIO 1 WAS WRECKED. Half the operating positions had been jarred loose and a hash of receivers, furniture, and typewriters clogged the space, lit only by the dim glow of battle lamps. Two receivers in a far corner of the shack were burning, sifting smoke into the room.

Elwyn Sturtevant, Radioman First Class J. J. Moran, and the rest of the radiomen crowded into the comm office with Lieutenant Driscoll. Without ports to see outside the room, the men were concerned that the enemy was still in the vicinity and would spot any light emanating from the ship. They planned to evacuate via an interior office door that would not emit any light, but when they opened that door to exit the space, the passageway was a tunnel of fire.

"Turn around," Lieutenant Driscoll shouted. "Go out the main shack door!"

Sturtevant and the others turned to comply, but when they opened the main radio shack door, they ran into Paul Candalino, the junior officer of the deck under Orr.

"Transmit a distress message," Candalino said.

Driscoll nodded and snatched up the telephone to call Radio 2. The line was dead. He tried the squawk box. Also dead. Thinking quickly, Driscoll said to the room that someone would have to go to Radio 2 and set up two frequencies.

"Aye, sir, I'll go," Sturtevant said. Driscoll issued brief instructions and Sturtevant sped out of the shack. Driscoll, a young officer who'd been aboard for less than a year, did not send the ship's position with Sturtevant. It was an omission on which a thousand destinies hinged.

Sturtevant navigated the fiery gantlet to Radio 2, where he found Woods standing in the center of the room, issuing orders.

Sturtevant cut in. "Lieutenant Driscoll says to set up 4235 and 500 and pipe it to Radio 1."

"We're already up on 500, we'll key that from here," Woods said. "We'll pipe up 4235 to Radio 1 on Line 3. Go tell Lieutenant Driscoll."

Sturtevant dashed out, back through the bedlam toward the main shack.

Woods then moved to an emergency key that was connected to the TBK transmitter. The key was located at the starboard bulkhead. With the ship's starboard list, Woods had to adjust his footing to remain upright.

Not knowing Indy's position, he began to transmit the only message he could: SOS.

Plunged into thick darkness when the torpedoes hit, John Woolston could see nothing but sparkles of flame in the passageway that led from the wardroom to the quarterdeck. Except for mild burns, he wasn't injured, but smoke and heat were pouring into the room. He called to the steward, who answered back from within the pantry, fear in his voice. Woolston found his feet, felt his way to the serving window, and swung himself through.

"Let's find a wrench and open the ports," Woolston said. He meant to open the two steel ports that covered the pantry portholes. They needed fresh air—and fast. The steward laid his hands on a wrench, opened the forward port, and handed the wrench to Woolston. The ports opened, he and the steward thrust their heads out into the night and sucked in air that tasted cool and alive. A few moments passed as Woolston gathered his strength.

"Okay, we better climb out of here," he said.

But breathing the by-products of fire had already veiled the steward's brain to reason. "I wanna stay here and rest a little longer," he said.

Woolston knew if they stayed there, they would die. He looked down at the steward. There was no way he could lift the man to safety. He peered up at the porthole. It was small, but he was slim.

Woolston looked back at the steward again. "Don't dawdle," he said, then thrust his head and shoulders through the port's narrow circle, braced his hands on the outside, and pushed. Directly below him, he saw a dark void, a straight drop into the ocean. There was no room for a mistake.

When his hips were through, Woolston was able to spin himself faceup so that he was sitting in the porthole, facing the ship's skin. He reached up and grabbed deck lines that were strung above him. Eeling his way free, he pulled himself up to the fo'c'sle deck.

Woolston took stock. Despite billowing smoke, he could see no fires topside. Still, Indy's bow was under and she was listing badly. To Woolston, it looked like the end, but the men he could see—both officers and crew—seemed controlled. Shouting orders and rushing about, but in an orderly way. He climbed down to the quarterdeck, then up to the afterstack, which he reached by climbing a two-story ladder that canted forward as though he were climbing a hill.

On the second deck, badly injured Marines were stumbling into Mess No. 1, the compartment just aft of the Marine Corps berthing. The second torpedo had decimated the Marines' quarters, and those not killed instantly were severely burned and in shock. A corpsman ordered the men laid out on the mess tables and then circulated among them, administering morphine to relieve their pain.

The No. 4 throttleman was also in the mess, doing his best to close the auxiliary steam stop and isolate his broken boiler. He noticed that the room was beginning to fill with oily seawater and decided it was getting bad enough that he should warn the men in Engine Room 1 below. A ladder connected the mess with a hatch at the forward starboard corner of that compartment.

The throttleman yelled down the ladder well into the engine room: "Main steam line in the port side parted at the forward bulkhead and dropped down about four inches!"

Nightingale acknowledged and glanced at the clinometer, which now showed a ten-degree list. Because Indy's decks were tipping to starboard, seawater in the mess had begun pouring down the ladder well into the engine room, the way one cup in a tilted ice cube tray pours water into the next.

Nightingale assessed the situation. The electric generators wouldn't start. The auxiliary steam line aft couldn't get any steam. There was no battle power to light off the dynamo plant. Now, loose equipment was starting to tumble to the low side of the compartment.

Again, the throttleman's voice echoed down the ladder well: "Get out of there!"

Nightingale agreed and made it an order: "All hands clear the engine room," he said.

The crew surged toward the ladder but quickly found they had waited too long. As the list increased, the water streaming down the ladder swelled to a deluge, blocking their escape. They would all drown in minutes if they didn't find a way out.

Having abandoned the pilot house, Glenn Morgan and Ralph Guye had attached themselves to the tilting handrails as best they could and clambered up.

"We need kapoks," Morgan said. They stopped briefly where the life vests were supposed to be secured to a line near the bridge, but all the vests were gone.

The men looked at each other. "We've still got these," Guye said, jerking his chin toward the inflatable fastened to his belt.

The skipper and Lieutenant Commander Moore had required every crew member to carry a rubber, self-inflating life belt at all times, and always made a big deal out of it, even posting mess hall watches so that a man couldn't get chow unless he had his life preserver with him. Morgan was glad for that now. The two men quickly snapped the inflatables around their waists and headed for the bridge. Morgan was in the lead, clasping the port rail to keep upright against the list.

Aboard I-58, the suicide pilots were pleading their case. Since the enemy ship wasn't sinking, the *kaiten* pilots begged, "Send us!"

It was true. Through the periscope, Hashimoto could see no signs that he had sunk the cruiser. Despite the dark, the stricken ship would now certainly be an easy target for the *kaiten*. But what if she sank before they reached her? Hashimoto thought. That would be a waste of both men and ammunition.

A report came in that the enemy was using underwater detection gear. Hashimoto was sure he had scored three hits, but it seemed the target intended to return fire. Before the enemy could get a good contact, Hashimoto decided to dive and reload in the safety of the deep.

18

ONLY SIX TO SEVEN minutes had passed since the torpedo strikes. Roberts and Nightingale led the men of Engine Room 1 toward the gushing water that tumbled from the overhead hatch. They crowded behind the ladder that led to the No. 1 mess and looked up. There was an air locker up there, above the hatch but below the mess. It was a small crawl space that extended laterally beyond the column of the ladder well. The air locker would not fill with water unless the entire engine room was filled first. If they could reach it, they could brace themselves in the air locker one at a time and force their way up through a hatch into the mess, even as water continued to fill the space.

Each man was wearing a "Mae West" life vest, named for the curvaceous 1930s star. The vests were inflatable, but the men did not inflate them yet. Instead, as seawater crashed into the engine room, they waited. As the rising flood carried them toward the air locker, they prayed that no one up there would see the hatch open and dog it down.

Up in the mess, choking smoke danced between the battle lantern beams, and an eerie red glow seeped in from somewhere, possibly from the fires in sickbay below. The mess was already filled with injured Marines from their berthing, and even more wounded had crowded in—many scarlet-skinned with severe flash burns—who were helped there by men who were better off. One man wandered in wearing only undershorts. He was burned head to toe, and fire had singed off all his hair. The compartment was waist deep with oily water now, and a flotsam of kitchen tools and tables and benches clustered near the starboard bulkhead, drawn there by the list.

Seaman First Class Marvin Kirkland was in the mess and heard someone shout his name. When Kirkland turned to look he saw the chief damage control officer, Lieutenant Commander Kasey Moore, working to unwind a fire hose from a bulkhead rack.

"Get topside and see how much hose you can find," Moore said. Concerned about fires in the forward areas of the ship, he ordered Kirkland to get more help, and to return on the double.

Acknowledging the order, Kirkland climbed out of the tilting mess and headed for the quarterdeck. It would be the last time anyone reported seeing Moore, who would remain below, fighting to save his beloved ship.

Topside, Seaman Second Class Harold Bray had reached his battle station on the fantail when he heard the quartermaster, Jimmy French, yelling at him over the noise. "You better go, kid! She's going down!"

Bray, eighteen, had been waiting since age fourteen to get on a ship and fight the Japs. He had just finished boot camp in April, finally joined a ship, and now he was going to abandon it?

Bray hollered back, "I don't think she's going down!"

Frenchy's words just didn't make sense. How could a ship as big and beautiful as *Indianapolis* sink?

Fire Controlman Third Class Paul Murphy confronted a different question after the blasts. Murphy, Lebow's poker buddy, finally made it up to the 8-inch after-control tower, his general quarters station, and found one of his good friends, Paul Boone Mitchell, fast asleep. Murphy wondered how anyone could sleep through such a jolt.

He shoved a life jacket at Mitchell. "Take this and go to your general quarters."

Mitchell darted off. Now, near the stern and away from the damage forward, Murphy was encouraged to see hundreds of men leaning on the lifelines on Indy's port side. Their collective weight had to be in the thousands of pounds, he thought. Surely, all that weight would right the ship. Murphy ran up to the port lifelines to help.

When Seaman Sam Lopez saw this human ballasting effort, he turned to his buddy Hank McKlin and yelled, "They're crazy! This ship isn't going to tilt. It's going to sink."

But it was impossible to get the ballast men to listen, so Lopez and McKlin climbed a ladder, grabbed four rolled-up cargo nets, and hoisted them atop the port railing. Their plan was to wait for the Abandon Ship call and then slide down the side of the ship, along with the cargo nets, and swim away together.

When only a few inches of air remained, the men in Engine Room 1 inflated their Mae Wests and let the jackets propel them up into the air locker. From there, one by one, they fought their way up through the falling water, and up through the hatch into the mess, letting their jackets pop them to the surface of the mess hall flooding. Each man vacuumed in deep breaths of air and relief. Conditions in the mess were very bad, but at least they weren't lethal, as in the space they'd just escaped.

After confirming that all hands had escaped Engine Room 1, Nightingale fought the deluge of water, trying to dog down the hatch. But it was impossible and he abandoned the effort. He decided to see if he could help in the after-engine room, a carbon copy of the compartment he'd just left.

Nightingale waded out of the mess and headed toward the stern. On his way aft, he picked up a badly burned man in the passageway and carried him to the No. 2 mess, which had also become an aid station. When he climbed down into the after-engine room, the lights were on, and with the exception of wafting smoke, he could see pretty well.

"Why have you abandoned the forward engine room?" a voice said.

It was Lieutenant Redmayne, the engineering officer, who had been in the fancy crapper known as the "Head of Department Head" when the torpedoes hit.

Nightingale explained what had happened in Engine Room 1. Redmayne said no more, only turned to inspect some gauges. The list was now approaching fourteen degrees.

"Should I return to the forward engine room, sir?" Nightingale said.

"No," said Redmayne.

When Redmayne said nothing further, Nightingale exited the after-engine room and attempted to make his way forward on the port side in order to check the steam stops.

The fire control officer burst onto the bridge. "Sir, I can't get to the engine room. It's fire everywhere below."

"Go back and try again," McVay said.

Janney then appeared on the bridge, and McVay told him to take another message down to radio. "Say we've been hit by two torpedoes. Give our latitude and longitude. Say we need immediate assistance."

The instant Janney left for Radio 1, Commander Joe Flynn arrived on the bridge. "Sir, the damage is serious," he told McVay. "I recommend that we abandon ship."

McVay, who had utter regard for his executive officer's ability, assessed the situation. As the list angle increased, the clinometer needle had swung slowly toward twenty degrees. With an unknown number of compartments flooding below, the ship's stability would be seriously compromised. McVay made the mental calculations and determined that his ship was doomed. Now he had to allow enough time for his men to escape with their lives.

He turned to Orr. "Pass the word to abandon ship."

With all communications out, the abandon-ship order would have to be passed man to man.

•   •   •

The radiomen Hart and Sturtevant missed each other in their sprints between Radio 1 and 2. When Hart arrived in the main shack, he saw Lieutenant Driscoll holding a flashlight over Radioman First Class J. J. Moran. The room was dim and filled with smoke. By the wavering glow of Driscoll's light, Hart could see Moran trying to send a distress signal.

Though the transmitters were physically located in Radio 2, all were set in remote position so that they could be controlled from the main shack. But the pilot light was dark. Moran couldn't tell whether he was successfully transmitting his message, but he sent it anyway, in the blind.

Moran, who came from Johnstown, Pennsylvania, had run to Radio 1 from a forward coding room where he'd been sleeping. The passageways had been blocked with fire and smoke, so he climbed out a porthole and up the outside of the ship to reach the main shack. Now, tapping the code key, Moran sent the distress message that Driscoll had jotted down on a piece of paper.

> XRAY VICTOR MIKE LOVE—WE HAVE BEEN HIT BY TWO
> TORPEDOES . . . NEED IMMEDIATE ASSISTANCE.

He repeated each word twice and included the ship's position by latitude and longitude, still unsure if transmission was going out. Frequency 4235 had been set up for just such an emergency ever since Indy sailed from San Francisco. Moran knew the transmitter could work even with a busted pilot light, and he hoped like hell that it was working now.

Hart leaned over Moran's shoulder and copied down the message. It included Indy's designator, and also gave her position.

Returning from Radio 2, Sturtevant crowded into the room. He relayed Woods's message. "4235 is ready to go on Line 3!" Sturtevant said.

By now Hart had copied down the full distress message. He told the group he would take it back to Woods in Radio 2. Hart turned and left the shack, but he soon found he couldn't go back the way he'd come. The ship had lurched sharply to starboard, tilting the deck twenty degrees, and the quarterdeck was now awash. Hart knew the door to Radio 2 was located on the starboard side. Going back there might be suicide. Besides, that shack had probably already been abandoned anyway. Hart clambered over a gun mount and abandoned ship. With him went the slip of paper containing the last known coordinates of *Indianapolis*.

19

WHEN COX HEARD CAPTAIN McVay order abandon ship, he left the bridge. He'd heard about captains going down with their ships, and God help him, Cox didn't want to go down with him.

Clambering down to the portside comm deck, he looked over the railing. He could see the fo'c'sle deck below him and knew that if he tried to jump, he would never make it past that deck and into the water. Thinking quickly, he looked around. There! A steel hook welded to the outside of the splinter shield. He remembered vaguely that the hook was used to store gaffs—part of the equipment for retrieving seaplanes. Cox reached out, grabbed the hook, swung out as far as it would take him, then let go. He saw the fo'c'sle deck go hurtling by beneath him, then slammed into the hull and tumbled into the sea.

On the bridge, McVay took stock. Neither Candalino nor Janney had returned from the main radio shack. It was absolutely essential that someone be notified of *Indianapolis*'s location. McVay turned to Orr. "I'm going down to Radio 1."

The main shack was directly below the bridge, two decks down. On the way, McVay knew he could take a look at the part of the main deck he'd heard was split near the No. 1 turret. He could feel the list increasing, see and smell fire, and hear the din of men scurrying around the ship. But no one had given him specifics about the damage, and he could not visualize why she was going down so fast.

McVay ducked into the charthouse, where he picked up a kapok life preserver. On his way past his emergency cabin at the after end of the bridge deck, he ran into Captain Edwin Crouch, the friend who had hitched a ride to Leyte at McVay's invitation.

"Charlie, have you got a spare life preserver?" Crouch said.

McVay ducked into his cabin and grabbed an inflatable life belt. He handed it to a quartermaster named Harrison. "Blow this up for Captain Crouch," he said. McVay then continued on his mission to ensure a distress signal got off the ship. He would not see either Harrison or Crouch again.

In the after-engine room, Redmayne made a decision that would affect every man who left the ship. The chief oil king and one of his assistants reported to Redmayne and asked if they should pump fuel oil from the starboard fuel tanks overboard. Doing so would help shift ballast away from the list. Redmayne gave the order, and the oil king executed it. Great gouts of fuel oil, thick and viscous, glugged out into the sea around the ship.

Now Redmayne found himself at an impasse. While Engine Room 1 had controlled specific elements of Indy's propulsion system, the after-engine room could control all four screws. The choices Redmayne made next could determine the fate of the ship, and he was unsure of what to do. What he needed was more information from the bridge, so he decided to head up there himself. Before climbing the series of ladders that would take him out of the huge space, he turned to his men. They were to remain in the after-engine room until he returned, he said. The order was a death sentence.

In Radio 2, Chief Warrant Officer Woods was still at the emergency key. With the ship heeling rapidly to starboard, it had become almost impossible to stand. Miner and others grabbed bolted-down objects and held on. Woods braced himself against the starboard bulkhead, leaned over the key, and kept tapping out his SOS.

Peering over Woods's shoulder, Jack Miner saw the needle on the antenna circuit jumping and waving like a friend offering help. His heart soared. That meant they were transmitting! The SOS was going out!

But Hart had still not returned, and without the ship's position, it was just the SOS, again and again. Still, the TBK was a powerful transmitter. As long as the antenna meter was loading up, the signal should be heard all over the Pacific.

Indianapolis now lay in the water at a forty-five-degree starboard list. Half her main deck was awash and smoke billowed aft from the obliterated bow, carrying with it the smell of explosives. Black clouds rolled over the knots of men topside still struggling to reach the high side of the ship. Shouted orders flew through the haze against the sound of churning waters.

When Redmayne left the after-engine room, gauges showed steam pressure holding at three hundred pounds per square inch, and the No. 2 screw continued making 160 turns per minute. This propelled Indy forward and down, in a long, slow loop to port.

On various decks all along the high side, men three and four deep clung to rails, lifelines, and each other. Nightingale was there, as were Lebow and his poker buddies, Smitty and Gaither. While Lebow was climbing to the high side, the ship had taken another hard lurch and he had seen a motor whaleboat jump from its saddle, barely miss Nightingale, and crush several men against a bulkhead.

More men had begun leaving the ship, some leaping into the dark, oily sea and others walking down the hull. George Horvath, a twenty-five-year-old motor machinist mate from Ohio, was near the fantail when he saw something that would haunt him for the rest of his life. Two black stewards came racing up a nearby ladder and ran full speed toward the fantail.

"No! No! No!" Horvath screamed. "Don't do it! Don't jump!"

But it was too late. The stewards leapt over the lifeline, off the fantail, and right into the turning screws. Horvath froze, his mouth still formed in a scream, his mind unable to process what he'd just seen.

They died quickly, they died quickly, they died quickly, he thought rapid-fire.

It was the only thing he could do to reconcile himself to the horror.

•   •   •

An exterior ladder connected the after end of the bridge to the signal bridge below it. As McVay put his foot on the first ladder rung, *Indianapolis* took a sickening roll and he saw people sliding past below him. Clinging to the angled ladder, he managed to climb down. As he reached the signal bridge, the ship heeled over another fifteen to twenty degrees. The list had now passed forty-five degrees and Indy was still rolling and going down steadily by the head. By clinging to fixed objects, McVay was able to wrestle himself to the ladder leading down to the port side of the communications deck. Soon the ship seemed to steady itself at a sixty-degree list. He could see young sailors on the high side jumping overboard, some without life jackets, all with faces full of fear.

McVay pulled himself up to the lifeline where boys were leaping from the ship. "Do not jump over the side unless you have a life jacket!" he yelled. "Or go back by the stack and cut down a floater net! Throw that over the side before you jump!"

McVay heard a voice yell from above him, "That is the captain talking!" It was Orr calling down to the boys from the bridge. "Now get your floater nets and your life jackets!"

As Glenn Morgan and Ralph Guye climbed toward the high side of the ship, Morgan saw Lieutenant Orr standing outside on the bridge wing, yelling into a bullhorn, directing traffic with his free hand. "All hands, abandon ship! All hands, abandon ship!"

Morgan marveled at the young lieutenant's calm demeanor, the businesslike way he instructed the men to leave the ship in a safe manner. Orr had been through this drill before, only it hadn't been a drill. He'd been aboard the destroyer USS *Cooper* when she was torpedoed and broken in two in Ormoc Bay, Luzon, just seven months earlier. *Cooper* sank within a minute with more than half her crew lost.

Feeling Guye's hand grip his shoulder, Morgan paused and turned his head. Guye looked into his eyes. "What do you say we stick together through this?"

Morgan nodded. "Yes, let's do."

Happy to have a friend like Guye to face this with, Morgan turned and scrambled up the incline, reaching the bridge with Guye behind him. When they reached Orr, the lieutenant called over the noise. "Did you hear the word to abandon ship?"

"Yes, sir!"

Another of Morgan's buddies, the bugler Donald Mack, stood next to Orr with a plastic horn in his hand.

Morgan yelled at him, "Well, are you gonna blow that damn thing?"

"When I get orders to!" Mack hollered back.

Woolston clambered back down from the afterstack and struggled to reach the port rail, since he was climbing the deck sharply uphill. Another steward crawled up, clinging to the port rail to keep from sliding downhill. He did not have a life jacket. Woolston grabbed the steward by the arm, guided him to an open deck edge, and the two slid together into the darkened sea. Woolston and the steward splashed down into a slick of fuel oil that was clotted with unclaimed life jackets and a mass of men. Some, frozen in fear or shock, lingered in the dangerous water near Indy's keel. Others swam away to avoid the suction that a sinking ship was said to create on her way down.

Woolston helped the steward into one of the jackets and urged him to swim toward a group well away from the ship. Then Woolston struck out, swimming the strong crawl he'd learned while growing up on Puget Sound. When he felt he was out of immediate danger, Woolston stopped and turned around. The ocean was consuming *Indianapolis*.

20

WORD FINALLY MADE ITS way to Harrell's emergency station: Captain McVay had given the order to abandon ship. He knew that abandon-ship procedures called for him to leave from the high side. Turning his eyes forward, he saw that much of that part of the ship had already disappeared into the sea. Harrell found he could barely stand on the leaning deck. He could see men leaping from the ship, landing on top of each other in the water.

Harrell made his way carefully to the port side and paused there, staring down into the inky dark. Fire and screams and death raged behind him, and the oil-slathered sea heaved below him, 280 miles from the nearest land.

Terror suffused him, but he also knew that this moment had been ordained for him by his Savior. Looking down into the oil-slicked mire of the sea, he remembered Jeremiah, whom God rescued after the prophet's enemies had thrown him into a miry cistern to either drown or starve. Harrell knew only one thing to do: he cried out to God.

In the blink of an eye, his fear was replaced by a sudden enfolding peace that Harrell would remember as supernatural. The transformation was not an act of will. Instead, Harrell felt it as the warmth of divine assurance. His God was with him and would see him through.

In two long strides, he traversed the port hull to the waterline. He jumped into the water, splashing down amid the fuel oil. Immediately, his life vest leapt up around his head, and he struggled to keep his face out of the oil. Caught between the liquid darks of sea and night, Harrell plunged forward, swimming. As he cut the water, trying to escape the drag of the ship, snatches of Scripture raced through his mind, passages he'd memorized over the years: "Peace I leave with you, my peace I give unto you; not as the world giveth, give I unto you. Let not your heart be troubled, neither let it be afraid."

In that moment, Edgar Harrell knew he was going to make it.

In Radio 1, receivers the size of coffins began breaking free of the port bulkhead—which was now nearly overhead—and tumbling down the sloped deck. Seawater began pouring into the space. Moran had just finished sending the distress message again—straight through this time without repeated words—when Driscoll shouted, "Clear out!"

Sturtevant, Moran, and the rest crawled uphill, clambered over the kneeknocker and out into the passageway. One by one, the radio crew burst into the controlled chaos outside. The ship was underwater up to the comm deck and still plowing forward under steam.

Moran was standing at the forward stack when the ocean reached his waist and carried him away. Sturtevant made his way forward, where he spotted a twenty-five-man life raft still secured to the No. 2 turret. Working with three other sailors, he finally cut it down, but the deck of the ship was now nearly vertical. Throwing the cumbersome raft over the lifelines on the high side of the ship proved impossible. Instead, Sturtevant got into the raft with the others. Instantly, the force of the ocean surging back from the bow swept the raft over the aft edge of the sunken fo'c'sle, past the quarterdeck, and into the night.

Clinging to the bridge wing rail with Ralph Guye and Lieutenant Orr, Glenn Morgan could see hundreds of men clustered at the port rail below. He sensed fear spiking, coursing man to man as the port side and stern rose higher and higher above the ocean's black surface. Morgan felt time running out. He knew he had to get off the ship before she rolled.

He waved half a salute at Orr. "I'll see you later, sir!"

Morgan climbed over the rail and looked down. Below he could see the signal bridge and beside it, the pelorus—a sundial-shaped instrument on a pedestal. He should be able to slide down the overhead toward the signal bridge. But to reach the signal bridge deck, he would have to jump. If he landed on the pelorus, he might sustain an injury that would keep him from making it off the ship. He *had* to land between it and the signal bridge's steel rail—a very narrow strip.

Carefully, Morgan began his slide, then paused. Fixing his gaze on what looked like a safe spot, he jumped—and landed on target. He immediately scrambled over the rail, then slid on his shoe soles until he came to rest on the port side of the comm deck against the Bofors gun mount, its barrels now pointed straight up. Rushing water sluiced over the guns, pinning Morgan against the breech. He could feel Indy yielding to the sea. She was sinking and taking him with her.

Suddenly, a great pressure released. Morgan felt the sensation of rising and clung to the gun barrel. It felt as if he were climbing it, but the barrel was actually slipping down through his grasp as the ship dropped away. White foam and debris boiled around him. He heard men calling, screaming. Down, down, the gun slipped, until the flash guard, shaped like a funnel, passed through his fingertips. It was the last thing he touched on *Indianapolis*.

Free of the ship, Morgan found himself surrounded by rolling froth that glowed phosphorescent green, a billion plankton caught in the ship's dying churn. That was when his heart flared with a sudden and ugly clarity. He had completely forgotten about Ralph Guye. He had promised Ralph they'd stick together, then he'd leapt the rail and abandoned him. Guilt flooded Morgan's heart.

In Radio 2, Woods was still tapping out the SOS. He could hear the creaks and groans of crumpling bulkheads, feel the extremity of the list gathering speed. He knew *Indianapolis* was headed for the bottom. He waited as long as he could for orders, but none came.

"Men," he finally said to the sailors in Radio 2, "abandon ship."

Miner did not have to be told twice. Apparently, no one else did either, because by the time he turned toward the door to comply, the shack was empty. The starboard door was now located at the bottom of a sharp downhill, and Miner had to crabwalk carefully to reach it without falling. As he crawled over the kneeknocker into the passageway, he looked back a final time. The lights and power were still on. Woods had not moved. After evacuating his men, he stood fast, still keying the SOS.

At the stern railing, a stream of men abandoned ship, some jumping, some waiting for the water to get closer. Everywhere, men fought to swim away from the dying vessel, grabbing anything they could to keep them afloat. The suction pulled some men under as others barely broke free. Some felt no suction at all.

About ten minutes had passed since the torpedo strikes and the ship heeled wildly under Harpo Celaya's feet. He had not seen Thorpe since they parted ways at the quarterdeck. He knew he was going to have to abandon ship, and all he could think about was going below to his locker. He was on his way there when he ran smack into Santos Pena, who had left the bow and now was awaiting further orders by the No. 3 turret.

"Where the hell do you think you're going?" Pena said.

"I've gotta get my life jacket!"

Pena stopped him, explaining that he had just come from the forward area and the whole bow was gone. He knew they had to get off the ship and wanted to stay together.

With Pena in the lead, Harpo climbed hand over hand up the main deck aft toward the port rail, which now stood out against the sky. Both men picked their way through the lifelines and leaned out, peering into a black maw. Pena jumped first, and Harpo followed a second later. He landed hard on something—or someone. He couldn't tell.

Harpo thrashed in the midnight sea, kicking and turning in desperate circles. "Santos! Santos!" he cried. "Santos, where are you?" There was no answer.

"Santos! Santos!" he cried again.

Harpo's heart broke right there in the water when he realized that the hard thing he had landed on must have been Pena. His best friend had probably just saved his life, and now he had killed him.

The ship continued a rapid roll to starboard and lay nearly on her side. In the No. 1 mess, Norman Roberts and the rest of the men who had used their Mae Wests to escape the forward engine room now waited by a ladder to repeat the process. When the mess hall finally filled with water, they floated up past the sunken quarterdeck and out into the sea.

Redmayne, the engineering officer, never made it to the bridge. Instead he crawled out of the No. 2 mess into a passageway near the bakery. After the torpedoes hit, he had burned his right hand while shielding himself from flames. Then he tripped blindly in a passageway, fell to the scalding deck, and burned the fingertips on his left hand. Now, the radical list had turned bulkheads into decks, and a row of welder's oxygen cylinders that had once been mounted vertically lay before him like a ladder. Proceeding painfully up the cylinders hand over hand, he finally gained the main portside passageway.

The ship continued to roll, now threatening to capsize. Topside, the throng of men on the rail had to decide if they would abandon ship. Would they tempt fate in the dark with the still-turning screws, or stay put and potentially be trapped in a capsize by unseen lines, cables, and debris?

Nightingale made his choice. He clambered up the bulkhead to the 20 mm bathtub and jumped about five feet out into the water. Hundreds followed suit. Together, these men would form a group with Redmayne the senior man among them.

Seconds later, the ship rolled again, this time clear over to ninety degrees. On the main deck, gear began to tear loose and crash into sailors. Man after man lost his grip and went sliding down the deck, borne along in a cascade of debris. Gunpowder cans, life vests, rafts, furniture, crates of vegetables, and dead bodies all splashed into the water alongside the living. Again, George Horvath felt helpless as he watched injured shipmates tumble toward the starboard side to be swallowed alive by the sea.

Still fighting to reach Radio 1, McVay leapt to the fo'c'sle deck, which was almost completely submerged. He pulled himself to the lifelines, climbed through, and began walking aft. McVay had reached the No. 3 turret on the afterdeck when the surging sea swept him off the ship.

Men already in the water soon turned back to see a fearsome sight: The flagship of the fleet stood on end, her stern towering over them like a black skyscraper erected on a moon-silvered plain. They stared spellbound as Indy's massive screws kept up a lazy turning and all around her the phosphorescent water glowed like green fire.

Only twelve minutes had passed since the torpedo blasts. Now, amid a roar like waves pounding the beach in a storm, *Indianapolis* plunged straight down. McVay looked up to see men still leaping from the stern and the giant silhouettes of Indy's port screws falling directly toward his head. He thought, *Well, this is the end of me*, and then turned and began to swim. Water and hot oil slid up the back of his neck, and soon he heard a loud swishing sound behind him.

When McVay turned around to look, his ship, USS *Indianapolis*, was gone.

FEBRUARY 1998

PIER S-1A
SUBMARINE BASE PEARL HARBOR
OAHU, HAWAII

★　　★　　★　　★　　★

"SKIPPER, WE'VE GOT A problem."

The Navy chief leaned in, speaking quietly into Commander William Toti's ear. The two men were standing on the outdoor lanai at the Pearl Harbor Submarine Base officers club amid a crowd of guests that included the four admirals who led U.S. military forces in the Pacific.

It was not a good day for a problem.

Buttoned into full dress whites, Toti saw a blue Hawaiian sky arcing overhead. Around him, he heard cocktail chatter, glasses clinking, laughter—the sounds of a reception that followed the ceremony he'd been dreading for months.

Toti looked at his chief and sighed. "What is it?"

"It's the plates, sir. All the *Indianapolis* plates in the galley are gone."

Instantly, Toti's shoulders relaxed. He shook his head and laughed. As of that morning, the submarine's galley had been stacked with dinner plates bearing the boat's logo, crossed checkered flags with the designator "SSN-697" at the bottom, and "USS *Indianapolis*" at the top.

If the plates were gone, Toti knew exactly who had taken them. Technically it was theft, but no one in the entire Navy would dare call it a crime.

About thirty survivors had taken Toti up on his invitation to join him for the deactivation ceremony. That morning, the old sailors had begun to trickle in, many still hale and hearty, some pushing walkers. They wore golf shirts and dress shirts and American-flag ties. They sported CA-35 ball caps festooned with gold braid and commemorative pins. Some were round with home cooking, others thin, their trouser legs flapping around legs gaunt with age. One was dying of cancer.

The young sailors in Toti's crew greeted the survivors warmly and shook their hands with something between reverence and awe. These old salts were the stuff of legend. For more than fifty years, every sailor coming through boot camp had learned the story of their survival. The swimming pool at the Recruit Training Center in Great Lakes, Illinois, was named in their honor: the USS *Indianapolis* Combat Training Pool.

Because of the Indy disaster, every recruit now had to pass a swimming test in order to graduate from boot camp. That was not true during World War II.

For more than a decade after the sinking, the *Indianapolis* tragedy lay mostly unexamined. After more than six years of war and 60 million dead, people had seemed ready to move on. Then, in 1958, Associated Press news editor Richard Newcomb published *Abandon Ship*, a book that was part narrative, part investigative journalism. Newcomb, a Rutgers graduate, had served as a correspondent during World War II. "The story told here is not a happy one," he wrote in the book's preface, "and no official Navy imprimatur will be found upon it."

Newcomb found that while Pearl Harbor, the Bataan Death March, Okinawa, and Iwo Jima seemed burned in the public memory, the greatest at-sea disaster of the war—indeed in American naval history—had receded into obscurity. "Some people knew one part of the story and some knew another, but the myth and mystery which had grown up around the case were amazing. The lack of authentic knowledge extended even into official quarters, and was most affecting where it was most unexpected—among those who had suffered through it."

Newcomb was the first author after the sinking to interview the *Indianapolis* survivors. Many told him they had never even spoken to their families about the ordeal.

Before the deactivation ceremony, Toti's sub crew had taken some of the survivors on a tour of their namesake submarine. Later, sailors and officers assembled in ranks, and guests filed into a seating area. Toti took his place at a podium under a white awning, its scalloped edges ruffling in the trade winds. From the dais, Toti could see the glistening combination caps of his officers and chiefs, and the white Dixie-cup caps of his petty officers and seamen. The survivors, wearing their ball caps, sat in chairs in the first row, the place of honor usually reserved for admirals.

Toti squared up the pages of his speech, his heart a lead weight in his chest. Measured in commendations, his crew of 115 had proven themselves the best in the fleet. But with the Cold War long over and peace breaking out, the Pentagon had decided that America no longer needed so vast a sub fleet. Soon *Indianapolis* would be hauled up to Bremerton, Washington, to be scrapped, and Toti's crew scattered to the seven seas. In the process, he felt, the nation would lose something precious. The world that had once needed Indy had changed. That was a good thing, Toti felt, but also profoundly sad, for it seemed to him that he was not here to praise *Indianapolis*, but to bury her.

Toti glanced briefly at his notes and began. He thanked the guests in attendance and reviewed his history aboard the submarine.

"We should celebrate the ship," he said. "For she served us nobly, keeping us well and safe in a dangerous time. *Indianapolis* contributed greatly to that peace and to the end of the Cold War, and her success in that endeavor today leads to her demise. Today's peace is her legacy. But it was not always so. Our nation has known terrible war, and another USS *Indianapolis* was not fortunate enough to serve during times of peace. That *Indianapolis* was a major participant in the worst war the world has ever known. And so, I would like to honor the crew members from the cruiser *Indianapolis*, our sister ship. That ship has inspired us through the years in a way you can't understand unless you served on board."

Toti paused and let his eyes roam over the men in ball caps. As they gazed back at him, he saw a certain intensity of spirit, a warrior's fire in their eyes.

"No ship or crew in history has done more or sacrificed more than the cruiser *Indianapolis*. But we were at war, and in war, the nation calls upon its finest to perform greatly, and sometimes to suffer greatly in defense of freedom. Finally, gentlemen, I would like to correct an omission. I have observed that you never had the benefit of being able to put your ship to rest in a manner such as this. You never got to decommission your *Indianapolis*. But since our achievement was built on the shoulders of your sacrifice, I thought it appropriate that we finally correct this oversight. For our *Indianapolis* is your *Indianapolis*.

"And so it would make me very proud if you would join with my crew here today, to finally and gallantly put an end to your service, and be once again dismissed together as a crew, one crew—the crew of USS *Indianapolis*. Shipmates, as I call out your names, if you would take your station and man your watch, we will all be a crew once again."

And they did. One by one, Toti called their names—the amiably ornery ones like Glenn Morgan, seventy-four—and the not-so-ornery ones like John Spinelli, seventy-five, who served on the cruiser as a cook. Spinelli was dying of lung cancer but had made the trip anyway. There was Paul Murphy, seventy-three, and Lyle Umenhoffer, seventy, and more than two dozen others.

The old sailors took their places, standing with the young sailors in spaces that had been left between them. Toti noticed that the survivors stood at attention in exactly the right way. Though half a century had passed, they hadn't forgotten how.

At the reception afterward, Toti was chatting with guests when the chief leaned in to tell him about the missing plates.

"Don't worry about it, Chief," Toti said, smiling. "I'll take care of it."

He was still smiling when survivors Murphy and Morgan walked up and shook his hand. The men were accompanied by their wives, Mary Lou Murphy and Mertie Jo Morgan.

Toti noticed a faint protrusion in the front of Morgan's golf shirt, a slim round outline just above his belt.

"Um . . . Glenn?" Toti said.

"Yes?"

"That wouldn't happen to be an *Indianapolis* galley plate you've got in your shirt there, would it?"

Morgan's face crinkled into a sly grin. "A plate? Why, Bill, I don't know what you're talking about."

Toti laughed.

Murphy thanked Toti for inviting them, and then paused for a moment before continuing. "Me and the men have been talking," Murphy said. "Standing in formation as part of the Indy crew again is something we'll never forget."

"Paul, it's my honor," Toti said. "And I don't think those young sailors who stood with you today will ever forget it either."

After the war, Murphy had gone on to become a mechanical engineer, and Morgan a division supervisor with Texaco. Now, both were retired. Murphy fixed his gaze on Toti and turned serious. "Hey, we've all been thinking," he said, meaning the survivors. "There may never be another USS *Indianapolis* to carry on the reputation of our ship. That means you're the last captain of the *Indianapolis*. Have you thought about that?"

"Of course I've thought about it," Toti answered.

Murphy squared his shoulders and looked Toti directly in the eye. "Well, the last captain of the last *Indianapolis* needs you," he said. "And some of us think you have a duty to respond to his call."

BOOK 3

THE DEEP

★

THE PHILIPPINE SEA
JULY 30–AUGUST 4, 1945

1

Site of the Sinking

CAPTAIN MCVAY SWIVELED HIS head in the liquid darkness. He could hear other men calling out, but floated alone in a layer of fuel oil, the kind so thick it had to be heated to be transferred. The oil rocked on the surface in a gooey slab, its tarry stench climbing down McVay's throat like the caustic fumes of road construction. Beneath the oil, the water felt cool—not cold—about eighty degrees.

Storms to the north of *Indianapolis*'s track had whipped the waves into a confused state that buffeted McVay about. He looked up and saw that clouds gauzed the moon. Suddenly, a hard edge bumped him and he whirled around. It was a potato crate and he climbed aboard, straddling it. A few seconds later, two life rafts floated by, one atop the other, and McVay abandoned the crate for the rafts. Most of the wood-lattice flooring in the rafts was gone, and he could find no paddles. Then he heard voices and began yelling in their direction.

Through the dark, a voice shot back: "Is that Captain McVay?"

"Yes! Who is that?"

"It's Allard, sir!"

"Come aboard!"

Within a short time, the quartermaster had swum over, herding two young sailors, both spent and nearly unconscious. McVay and Allard worked to unstack the rafts and lash them together. Then, captain and quartermaster hauled the injured men into the second raft before crawling into a raft of their own. Both young men seemed to McVay to have ingested large quantities of salt water and oil, and they were unable to stop retching. Exhaustion finally set in, then silence. McVay kept an eye on the two stricken boys in the other raft. Soon neither was moving, and he concluded that they were dead.

•　•　•

In his haste to escape the ship's suction, Glenn Morgan hadn't had time to look around, but once he got clear, he sucked in his breath and took his bearings. The hazy moon offered little light, but he could make out a huge shadow hulking on the surface not far away. As his eyes adjusted to the darkness, the shadow resolved.

A seaplane!

Indy had carried three Curtis SC-1 Seahawk floatplanes, with one almost always sitting in a catapult, ready for launch. This one must have torn loose during the explosions and been blown clear. It was actually sitting upright on its floats.

Morgan immediately pictured himself climbing out of the drink into what was likely the only dry spot for almost three hundred miles. Wait until he told Mertie Jo when this was all over. She wouldn't believe his luck.

He dug in swimming again. He'd heard some yelling and expected to meet other men, but he did not see a single soul. When he reached the plane, he saw an empty wooden life raft floating directly under the tail. Then, in a flash, he saw his salvation slipping away. The plane's floats were damaged, and she was beginning to sink. The vertical stabilizer on the Seahawk's tail fell sideways, aimed dead center of the raft like the downstroke of an ax. As the seaplane's tail timbered toward the sea, Morgan lunged for the raft and grabbed its edge. He lifted his foot from the water, braced it against the stabilizer's edge, and pulled the raft as hard as he could. Just as the plane's tail hit the water, the raft scooted clear, and Morgan watched the seaplane sink through a flurry of black foam as quickly as a dead man with an anvil tied to his leg.

A wave of disappointment stole over him, followed quickly by a flood of gratitude. He'd lost the plane, but at least he had the raft. He climbed in and took another look around. He could still see no other survivors, but he spotted another raft. Paddling by hand, he got close enough to snag it. He lashed them together with lengths of slim line that were tied along the sides of each raft. That was when a head popped into view. Then another and another, each one black and unrecognizable, completely covered in a mucky sheath.

Several men climbed into the rafts with Morgan. The crude gray vessels resembled rectangular, canvas-wrapped doughnuts, and had wooden lattice work suspended inside them by rope mesh. While not at all dry or comfortable, they at least offered a resting place. In the case of the Indy, some of these could accommodate as many as twenty-five tightly packed sailors, all standing waist-deep on the wooden platform.

Eventually, Morgan, aided in part by Signalman Third Class Kenley Lanter from Thomasville, Georgia, and first-class radioman J. J. Moran, lashed four of these rafts together. As a bonus, they had a floater net tied alongside. The net did not offer the same type of protection as a raft, since it was really just a grid of cork floats connected at eighteen-inch intervals.

The rafts were equipped with survival kits. In them, Morgan and his new companions found meager rations, flares, fishing supplies, and some flashlights. They discussed using the flashlights to signal other survivors, but were leery. Japanese submarines had been known to lurk at a sinking site and machine-gun any survivors.

L. D. Cox hadn't been in the ocean long when he started adding to its contents. His stomach lurched again and again, and he vomited great gouts of salt water mixed with the fuel oil, which seemed to him only slightly thinner than tar. Cox had watched Indy sink from view and heard her protests, rendered in shrieking steel. It had sounded to him just like she had a soul. Bubbles the size of jellyfish jetted to the surface, and he could feel them exploding against his groin. Must be the boilers, Cox had thought.

Afterward, Cox swam right into another young sailor, who had been badly burned.

"Is that you, Cox?" the sailor asked.

Squinting in the dark, Cox realized it was one of his best buddies. "Josey?"

Cox could hardly believe what he was seeing. Clifford Josey was covered in flash burns in every place that his skin was exposed. In the dim moonlight, it looked as if his face was melting off. To avoid touching the delicate burned flesh, Cox grabbed Josey by the vest, pulled him close, and held him while they floated in the dark.

"Someone put a life jacket on me and pushed me overboard," Josey said, his voice barely a whisper.

Josey was one of the Texas boys Cox liked to hang around with. His family lived just a couple of hours from Cox's own. Now the two, both still in their teens, agitated in the wind-whipped swells like rags in the gentle cycle of a washing machine. From somewhere off in the gloom, Cox heard shouts for help. But he stayed with Josey, held him, and soothed him with talk about what it was going to be like when they got home to Texas. Josey only lived for an hour.

A little over an hour after he fired his torpedoes, Hashimoto received another report: The target's sonar* had gone silent. When his torpedomen finished reloading for a second salvo, he gave the order, "Surface the ship."

The diving officer echoed back the command, high-pressure air shot into the ballast tanks, and I-58 rose like a dirigible leaving earth. A crew member asked Hashimoto whether, once back on the surface, he would allow the crew to attack any enemy survivors.

"No," Hashimoto replied. "We have already done our job."

When his boat reached the skin of the sea, Hashimoto pierced it with his periscope and swept the headwindow in a full ring. He could see nothing. He ordered the helmsman to make for the spot where the target would have sunk. Then he looked again. Still nothing.

A ship so badly wounded could not have fled so quickly over the horizon, he thought. Though he was now certain he had sunk a major American warship, he wanted some proof, but he could not even spot any debris. With the moon tucked again behind the clouds, he could barely make out the horizon, let alone detect objects on the surface.

Frustration set in, then regret, as he knew what he had to do next. There was virtually no chance the Americans would have sent a capital ship out this far on its own, so there had to be other ships around—probably destroyers.

Wary of counterattacks, Hashimoto gave the order to turn northeast, and I-58 sailed away.

Harpo Celaya had been swimming since the ship disappeared. All around him was a strange quiet, the only sound an eerily isolated slap-

---

* Both reports to Hashimoto of *Indianapolis* using underwater sound detection were in error. Indy had no such gear.

ping of the sea against his own body. For a moment, he pictured himself from above, the only man alive for hundreds of miles, just a pinprick in a vast, watery universe. He did not know that the ocean around him was filled with other men, some whole, others mortally injured, some drifting with the swells, others thrashing for their lives. Debris floated between them—food crates, helmets, lines, buoys, gas masks, the detritus of the ship. When the first torpedo opened the bow, it ripped into the ship's stores, and the water was littered with shoes, gloves, and winter coats.

Harpo had been swimming for about fifteen minutes when he saw a floating body. Swimming closer, he could see that the dead man wore a life jacket.

Harpo swam right up to the body, which abruptly sputtered to life. "Get away from me!" the sailor yelled. "Get away!"

"What do you mean get away?" Harpo cried. "I don't have a life jacket. I need help!"

"Get away! Get away!" the sailor repeated, and struck out in a flailing crawl to put distance between himself and Harpo.

Harpo swam away, and kept swimming until he ran right into a miracle: two sailors on a raft. He made his way over. "Boy, am I glad to see you fellows," he said.

As he prepared to climb aboard, one of the men batted Harpo's arm away and roared, "Get the hell off!"

Harpo swam to the other side of the raft and tried again. The other man grabbed Harpo's shoulders and tried to shove his head underwater. Harpo fought his way loose. He kept his distance for a few moments, then cautiously made his way back to the raft. He saw a rope tied to one side, trailing down into the water. Harpo grabbed it and hung on.

Edgar Harrell found himself floating in the midnight sea with a group of about eighty men, including two other Marines. One was so badly injured that he lasted only a couple of hours. The other, Private First Class Miles Spooner, a Florida boy, was in agony. Leaving Indy, he dove into the water headfirst, and now his eyes burned beneath the viscous layer of oil that clung to his corneas like a poison skin.

To keep the waves from separating them, these survivors had latched their life vests together front to back, forming a circle. The first topic of conversation was rescue. Had an SOS gotten off before Indy sank? They tried to assure each other that one had. Besides, the Navy would miss them when they failed to show up for gunnery practice as scheduled. Harrell, who served as Captain McVay's Marine orderly, had heard the skipper discussing this appointed rendezvous. Indy was to meet the battleship USS *Idaho* on the morning of July 31—which, the men realized, was only a handful of hours away.

The conversation then turned to danger. They were reasonably sure it had been a sub that sank them, and Japanese submariners were known to be ruthless, surfacing to machine-gun survivors. Sometimes they dragged survivors onto the sub and systematically killed them by pistol, clubbing, or beheading. In 1944, half a dozen such stories had sizzled around Indy like sparks on a wire. On the other hand, Harrell and many others figured that help was on the way. There was a good chance the enemy would know that, too, and clear out of the area.

After he abandoned ship, nineteen-year-old Seaman First Class Felton Outland looked around to see four tethered life rafts almost within his reach. Only moments earlier, he had nearly suffered the same fate as *Indianapolis*. Before the order to abandon ship, Outland's friend, George Abbott, went below to look for life jackets. He returned with only one and gave it to Outland, then went to look for more. Outland started to leave the ship on the port side, but the water met him on the main deck, and as Indy plunged for the bottom, she took Outland with her.

On the way down, his feet got tangled in some kind of line and the ship dragged him under the water, deeper and deeper. Soon, the air in his lungs turned toxic and he had to expel it, bubbles jetting to the surface even as he descended into the cool, dark abyss. Just when it seemed he would never see light again, the line untangled and the kapok jacket shot him to the surface. He sucked in a great ragged breath and thanked God and George Abbott. The kapok saved Outland's life, but he would never see his friend again.

On reaching the bundled rafts, Outland did what he could to clear his eyes of diesel fuel and found one other man there, Mike Kuryla, a coxswain. He climbed aboard and together they called out to others. "This way! We have a raft!"

Soon, eighteen-year-old Glen Milbrodt, a seaman second class from Akron, Iowa, pulled himself into one of the four empty rafts, then turned to pull others aboard. One man he helped was completely naked. Feeling badly for him, Milbrodt gave him the shirt off his own back.

Soon the group swelled to seventeen men, including Robert Brundige, another Iowa farm boy, and Giles McCoy, a loud and cocky Marine. McCoy had been guarding two prisoners in the brig when the torpedoes hit. Working the jail keys quickly, he freed the prisoners and the three men bolted topside together. Now, McCoy still wore his big, heavy shoes and a .45 automatic pistol in a gunbelt on his waist.

2

JULY 30, 1945, MONDAY—SUNRISE

Five Miles from Sinking Site

SUNRISE OVER THE PHILIPPINE Sea revealed an ironically beautiful morning. Blue skies, azure seas, and what promised to be a bright tropical sun. Had someone spotted the survivors from the air, they would have seen a thick, jet-black mat of oil with clumps of men distributed throughout.

When the torpedoes hit, some men forward were blown off the ship, while others saw the bow gone and jumped over the side without orders. For the twelve minutes that *Indianapolis* was still above the surface, she continued making way. Her inboard screws—driven from the after-engine room—propelled the ship through the water in a giant leftward arc, depositing men, singly and in groups, over one to two miles on her heading of 260 degrees.

For this reason, on the morning of the first day, the survivor groups could not see each other, and many thought their group represented the only men left alive.

The currents in the area moved along at about one mile per hour and also whorled in giant, slow-moving eddies that mixed men and debris as if all were caught in a slow-motion butter churn. Some men drifted together, others apart. Two men within shouting distance in the morning might be a quarter-mile apart by afternoon—or vice versa.

Still, the men would never again be in such close proximity as they were this first day.

Already, the survivor groups had drifted about five miles generally west-southwest. About 300 to 400 of the 880 or so initial survivors had coalesced into one large group. Mostly bobbing in life jackets or treading water, this group included John Woolston, Dr. Haynes, Dr. Modisher, Father Conway, and Captain Parke, commander of Indy's Marine detachment. It was Parke who had detailed Harrell to post guards around Major Furman's crate. Now, in the water, he immediately took charge, and the men, who had been safe on their ship one minute and the next cast adrift in the open sea, were glad of it.

They could hear the Marine captain yelling orders to be on the lookout for buoys, which might hold telephones to be used by downed pilots who crashed at sea. With his booming voice and the help of Conway and Haynes, Parke organized these hundreds of floaters into one great mass. Each man put his arms through the life jacket of the man in front of him so that back to front, the group formed a large ring. The injured, and those without life jackets, were put in the center where Haynes and Modisher could look after them.

At first light, Parke took stock of the group's resources, which, apart from life jackets, consisted of a single line of rope, about a hundred feet long.* Though the seas were calm, rolling swells and shifting currents threatened to drag the group apart. Parke ordered the men to shape the

---

* There have been varying accounts from different survivors as to the actual length of the line used to corral the group, but most standard heavy cruiser life rings had

line into a ring. Those with life jackets were to tie themselves to the line, and those without jackets were to hang on. The procedure was simple, but it kept the men together and gave them something to focus on, a strategy that would prove to save lives.

Modisher had been sleeping near the bow when the first torpedo struck, and he awoke to the whistle of a lethal blade. The explosion had launched a porthole cover from the hull plating and it went sailing past his head like a guillotine. He jumped down from the middle rack and peered out the open porthole but could see only steam and smoke and hear the sounds of chaos. The doctor donned a life jacket and dashed to the quarterdeck, where he found a melee of badly burned men. He found an emergency kit, but there wasn't much he could do except to dispense salve and pain medicine. He wished he had some now. Several men in his floater group were catastrophically burned.

There was not much the doctors could do medically, but Haynes and Modisher encouraged the men to fight their salt water– and oil-induced nausea and to refrain from vomiting. They needed to conserve both energy and fluids, since no one knew how long they'd be adrift before rescue arrived.

The pearl light of dawn revealed to Harpo Celaya that his group had swelled in the night to more than a hundred men. At least two more rafts and two floater nets had joined the flotilla, and now he hung on to his little line and watched a bizarre carousel of desperation: castaways crabbed over the rafts and nets in swarms, swamping them until they dumped everyone and sank, only to pop to the surface again. The process then repeated.

Finally, Chief Clarence Benton swam forward to short-circuit the chaos. "All right, everyone off the rafts unless you're injured or without a life jacket. Everyone else can hang on to the sides."

Benton, all of twenty-eight, was not the senior man. A number of officers had joined the group, including Ensign Donald Blum, who'd

---

throw lines measuring approximately one hundred feet. A ring formed from such a line would measure about thirty feet across.

watched gunnery practice with the Army officers on the way to Tinian, and Ensign Harlan Twible, one of the new officers who had joined the ship at Mare Island. Twible had graduated from the Academy, gotten married, and reported to *Indianapolis* all in the space of a single month.

There were also two other ensigns, a seasoned warrant officer, and a few chiefs. Lieutenant Richard Redmayne was the SOPA—the Senior Officer Present Afloat, literally—but with everyone disguised in fuel oil, he did not declare himself. Chief Benton, who hailed from a small town in New Mexico, stepped into this break in the chain of command. The men, for the most part, obeyed him.

Rejected from the rafts, Celaya floated in exile. He hadn't gotten along with too many men while on the ship, and he wasn't sure things would change for the better out here. Grief gnawed at his mind as he replayed his leap from the ship and mourned his friend, Santos Pena. After the two original raft passengers fought him off the previous night, another pair of survivors tried to force their way aboard but were also repelled. Then so many survivors swarmed the raft that the two men couldn't hold them off any longer.

Among this larger group was Redmayne. He had muscled his way aboard the raft and remained there, nursing his burned hands. Redmayne spent the dark early morning hours watching as a couple of chiefs directed the men to collect any useful supplies from the water and put them in the rafts—water casks, ration tins, malt tablets. They would be divided equally and distributed later. From time to time, he asked men nearby their name and rank. Surely, someone would outrank him and take charge of the group. In a group this large, under these circumstances, officers might be targets, and self-preservation called for cagey tactics. He would bide his time.

In the same group were Lebow's poker buddy Paul Murphy and Lindsey Wilcox, a second-class watertender who had worked in the fireroom, deep in Indy's belly. If he had not been relieved ten minutes before the torpedoes struck, he would have been killed. At twenty-one, Wilcox was a newlywed. He gave thanks to God and repented of every last sin he could think of, including the time he stole a pie from his grandmother's kitchen window.

·   ·   ·

Glenn Morgan, who had rescued a single raft from under the seaplane, now had a small armada of four rafts, a floater net, and twenty men. The rafts slid up and down the long, glassy swells while smaller waves smashed over the sides. This group was near the McVay rafts but could not see them, as the swells towered overhead like walls, blocking their sight. At intervals, Morgan thrust his head over the edge of his raft and retched. It wasn't seasickness. It was the fuel oil. Only in the morning did he realize that he, like his mates, was lacquered in it.

Morgan didn't recognize everyone in his group. Three he knew well—Moran and Lanter, who shared his raft, and Lieutenant (junior grade) Howard Freeze, the senior man in the group. Morgan had stood watch with Freeze and thought him a fine officer. Freeze, who abandoned ship in his underwear, sat in the raft adjacent. Morgan saw that the lieutenant's skin glowed a frightening pink, as if he'd been flash-fried.

Morgan rested in water to his waist, but the top layer of the Western Pacific was warm enough. To get more of their bodies clear of the water, the men took turns sitting on the raft's edges, but only one or two at a time. Any more would push the raft deeper, causing the water to rise chest-high on the men still seated inside.

A bag lashed to the lattice held several small kegs of water and a pouch of survival gear. There was a first-aid kit, cans of Spam, fishing kits, malt tablets for controlling thirst, some hardtack, a hatchet, and small enamel cups. The bag also contained signaling mirrors, four-by-eight-foot pieces of canvas, and—most promising—flares. They were ten-gauge flare shells with a primitive little firing tube operated by a plunger.

"Morgan, fire off a few of those," Freeze called from his raft, calm and reserved despite the severity of his burns.

"Yes, sir," Morgan said. He loaded one of the green shells into the tube, held it straight up, pulled the plunger, and let it go.

The tube coughed smoke and a little green ball of fire sailed into the sky, reminding Morgan of a one-shot Roman candle. Quickly, he reloaded and fired a red flare and then a white one and watched them climb, too. But their fire looked anemic in the blazing sunlight, and Morgan doubted they could be seen at any distance at all. He checked the remaining supply of flares. There were only four or five.

"Sir, why don't we save the rest of these," he said to Freeze. "Let's wait until dark."

Freeze agreed, and remarked to one of the men that his pain level was such that he wished he had a large supply of morphine. "I'd rather die from too much morphine than die of these burns," he said.

Then Freeze fell silent. Morgan could see that he had lapsed into shock.

MONDAY—DAY
Harman Field, Guam

Something about the naval battle he'd seen the night before was bothering Army pilot Richard LeFrancis. The action he and MacArthur's general saw splashing like fireworks against the midnight sea had not looked to them like gunnery practice. In fact, it looked more like a large ship being sunk.

After landing his plane at Harman Field on Guam, LeFrancis caught a ride over to the Navy end of the island and tracked down a commander. He described the events of the night before, adding that the general thought he'd seen the ship firing back. The Navy commander told LeFrancis that he was unaware of any gunnery practice scheduled for that area, and that LeFrancis and the general had probably not seen the kind of action LeFrancis described.

Having done his due diligence, LeFrancis hitched a ride back to the Army side of Guam and for the time being let it go.

Ten Miles from the Sinking Site

As the morning sun warmed the Pacific waters, Gunner's Mate Buck Gibson held a dying boy in his arms. The two sailors sprawled half out of the water on a floater net not far from the Redmayne group, the second-largest gathering of men. Dozens of desperate survivors had swarmed the flimsy island, and Gibson had to fight for a place to hang on as the net surged up and down in ten- to twelve-foot swells. He was surrounded by blackened faces, so coated with filth that he couldn't tell who they were, not even the kid in his arms.

When Indy tipped sideways and boxes started sliding, Gibson had donned an old horse-collar life jacket and tossed a floater net over the port side. Before he abandoned ship, he ran into his buddy Tommy Meyer, of Marlin, Texas.

"I'll make you a deal," Gibson shouted. "If you don't make it, I'll go see your folks in Marlin. If I don't make it, you go see my folks in Mart." The two men shook on it, but Gibson hadn't seen Meyer since. Now he cradled this younger sailor, whose right arm had been boiled crimson and black and smelled like cooked meat.

"Help's on the way," Gibson murmured softly, his Texas accent thick as sausage gravy. "How old're you, anyhow?"

"Seventeen," the boy murmured.

"Well . . . help's on the way."

"You don't have to keep saying that. I'm not afraid to die."

Gibson marveled. For three years he'd been afraid. Strafed and shelled and dive-bombed until he'd gazed down from Indy's decks at the dark, swirling sea, and feared it might swallow him whole. Now he saw fear everywhere he looked, but this kid lay peacefully and did not complain.

On the far side of the floater nets, about a hundred yards away, Buck's good buddy, coxswain Cozell Smith, clung to a single life vest along with Joseph Dronet, who could not swim. Dronet wasn't the only one. Clarence Hupka, a baker, and Verlin Fortin, a watertender, had both served aboard Indy for nearly two years, but the Navy hadn't taught either of them to swim. Both vowed to learn quickly.

Without a life jacket of his own, Smith had stayed afloat all night by attaching himself to Dronet. During the morning, he spotted Gibson and his group in the distance, hanging on to something. He swam for it and found the group clustered around a floater net, barely holding on to the edges, clinging to one another. Those without life jackets clambered on top of those who did, piling themselves three and four men high. Smith found this situation no better than the one he'd left, but he was too exhausted to swim back. He thought about something his father had said when he joined the Navy after completing the tenth grade.

"Do you know what I'm signing?" his father had asked as he scribbled his signature on Smith's Navy application.

Smith, then seventeen, replied in know-it-all fashion that yes, he knew: His father was signing his permission for Smith to join the Navy.

"No!" his father said. "I'm signing your death warrant."

Now, Smith supposed his father had been right.

Viewed from above on these rolling blue dunes, the survivor groups were now spread over several miles of open sea, still connected by thick, winding mats of fuel oil. Three separate groups—Richard Redmayne's, Glenn Morgan's, and Felton Outland's—would form around three different quartets of rafts with varying numbers of attendant floater nets. Several groups of raftless swimmers formed as well, some with floater nets, some with only the life jackets on their backs. The largest group with only life jackets was the one that included Haynes, Woolston, Conway, and Parke. But over the coming days, more than a hundred men would drift away from the Haynes group to join others, or form their own.

Ed Harrell's swimmer group floated among those toward the north. With the sun full up, Harrell could see that about a third of the men in his group had died during the night. He and others removed their dog tags and vests and relinquished their bodies to the deep. But many of the dead refused to leave, and soon the fifty or sixty men still living found themselves swimming with a school of corpses.

By contrast, the McVay group, among those toward the southwestern edge of the survivor map, enjoyed a relative oasis. They had connected with another raft and floater net bearing five more men, bringing McVay's castaway crew to a total of nine souls. Also, the men found on their rafts two good paddles, a Very flare pistol with a dozen flares, and a large sheet of canvas. There was a box of matches, too, but it had soaked through, rendering the contents mostly useless. They also salvaged some tubes of ointment and a few morphine syrettes from an emergency kit that was otherwise ruined.

Later in the morning, McVay spotted a pair of rafts in the distance. They popped into view when McVay's raft topped the wave crests, then disappeared when it slid down into the troughs. The nearest of the new rafts was about fifteen hundred yards away, and someone aboard was yelling for help. But the seas had grown rough and his men were so exhausted from swimming for their lives that McVay knew they could not attempt to paddle over.

As Monday wore on, the McVay group floated near an emergency rations can and scooped it aboard. Food! Beautifully packed, with a double tin top to prevent water from seeping in, it contained several cans of Hormel Spam, along with malted milk tablets and tins of biscuits. McVay looked over the rations and did some quick math.

"I will open one Hormel tin per day," he announced, adding that he would divide the twelve ounces evenly. He also calculated that each man could have two malted milk tablets and two biscuits per day. Rationed this way, he thought the provisions could last up to ten days.

Late that day came the most important find of all: a three-gallon water breaker. The men heaved it aboard. McVay examined it, then tested the water and found it salty. The breaker had apparently developed a hairline crack and admitted the sea, making the water nearly undrinkable. McVay decided not to tell the men. Instead, he announced that he would take charge of the water and save it until someone absolutely needed a drink.

The men floated and waited, and McVay, ever in control of the situation, asked questions of them one at a time, bidding them to answer to the group. John Muldoon, a first-class machinist's mate, said he'd found his way to this small assembly with John Spinelli in a busted-out life raft. Spinelli, a cook, sat shirtless while George Kurlich, a fire controlman, was stark naked. Kurlich told his raft mates that he'd abandoned ship directly from the showers. From then on, the men kidded him: "Hey, George, did you at least turn off the shower before you jumped over the side?"

3

JULY 30, 1945, MONDAY—DAY

Tinian Island

ALL THINGS CONSIDERED, LIFE on the island of Tinian agreed with Major Robert Furman. The Army had quartered him in a pyramid tent in sight of the ships at sea. The chow hall food was crude, but there was plenty of it. And he was pleasantly surprised at the available drinks and confections. Every week, each man received five glasses of cool beer.

When *Indianapolis* pulled into Tinian Town Bay on July 26, the first thing Furman did was search the faces of the assembled brass for news on the Trinity test. He saw in their eyes the determined glint of success. After the crane lowered the canisters into the waiting landing craft, Furman and Nolan climbed down a rope ladder—a maneuver Furman found tricky—and dropped into the boat. Once ashore, the shipment was carefully packed into a truck and shuttled to an assembly area under the charge of Captain William "Deak" Parsons and Project Alberta.

Francis Birch, a naval officer who would supervise Little Boy's assembly, signed for the canisters. Then, perhaps for the first time since being recalled from his beach vacation, Furman took a long, deep breath and relaxed. He had passed the baton. Now, Parsons and the fifty-one Los Alamos scientists, engineers, technicians, and administrative officers of Project Alberta would complete the final leg of the race that Furman had been running since 1943.

First, the assembly. The weapon for which he had transported the fissionable material consisted of a gun that would fire one mass of uranium 235 at another. An initiator would then inject a burst of neutrons, triggering a chain reaction and a titanic accumulation of energy that would ultimately cause the bomb to blow itself apart and shower Armageddon on the target city. In its final form, the weapon would be only ten feet long and twenty-eight inches across. The scientists had dubbed it "Little Boy."

Second, the delivery, aboard a B-29 bomber of the 509th Composite Bomber Squadron. Her pilot, Colonel Paul Tibbets, Jr., had named the plane after his mother, *Enola Gay*.

Furman believed the bomb mission just. Too many lives had been lost already. While he was shepherding nuclear scientists for Groves during the development of the bomb, one young scientist received a letter from his father, an infantry officer fighting at the front in Italy.

"This is some pretty horrible stuff I'm going through over here," the father wrote.

The scientist wrote back, "Well, just hang in there. . . . I can't tell you what I'm doing, but it's going to end the war."

"Glad to hear it," the father replied. "But is there any chance it could be tomorrow or the next day? I don't know whether I can last much longer."

He did not last, but died instead.

Though this bomb was unprecedented in lethality, Furman believed using it would save hundreds of thousands of lives—perhaps millions—both American and Japanese.

For now, though, he found himself on this tiny coral rock, bunked down between an ex-policeman and future tree surgeon on one side and a member of the Massachusetts bar on the other. When no business pressed, Furman wrote letters to his folks or joined Captain Nolan to explore the beaches and shallows. Once, the pair ventured out past a sandy coastal shelf, over a ring of sharp coral rocks, and into crystalline water that flashed with a rainbow of tropical fish.

The Philippine Sea

Floating near Buck Gibson's group, Seaman Second Class Curtis Pace was used to seeing silver barracuda flashing beneath his feet. But when a shadow larger and more menacing passed close below him, Pace panicked, kicking and flailing until a shout snapped his frenzy.

"What the hell is wrong with you?"

Turning, Pace saw a young sailor with horror in his eyes.

"Nothing," Pace said. He didn't want to scare the kid. "Thought I saw something, that's all. Musta been all the oil in my eyes."

The kid relaxed. Pace glanced down in time to see a shark whip its tail once and its dark silhouette melt in with the predator squadron flying through the water below.

The sharks had been visible down there for a while. Scores of them cycloned in water columns that were clear as crystal for at least fifty feet before receding into sapphire. Many were likely oceanic whitetips, the most common ship-following shark and considered the most dangerous shark of all. The Japanese called them *yogore*, the word an assembly of *kanji* characters that convey the ideas of "pollute," "defile," and "rape."

Usually loners, whitetips will gather in large packs around plentiful food, like jackals around the weak in the Serengeti. Bronze in color with paddlelike pectoral fins, they swim so slowly as to appear nonchalant, almost lazy. But once aroused, they are utterly relentless.

For now, the sharks around Pace seemed content to circle and wait, advancing in aggressive curiosity then retreating to await opportunity.

Evening came, the sky still bright but fading. A few hundred yards from Pace, Haynes and Parke kept the floaters organized. The group had formed into concentric rings expanding outward from the center, where the most gravely injured men remained sheltered—those dragging broken limbs, bleeding from wide gashes, or blinded with burns.

Haynes and Modisher swam from man to man offering any help they could, which was almost none since they had no supplies. Soon Haynes came upon two sailors taking turns holding up a severely injured man. It was his good friend, the gunnery officer Stanley Lipski. His eyes seemed boiled in their sockets. What remained of his hands appeared as charred meat clinging to bones.

"Lew, I'm dying," Lipski murmured. "Tell my wife I love her, and that she should marry again."

"I will, Stan," Haynes whispered.

Haynes stayed near, offering words of reassurance. Supported only by partially saturated life vests, Yeoman Dick Paroubek and Signalman Third Class Frank Centazzo held Lipski's hands up out of the water and kept his legs flat so that they would not dangle and cause him any more pain.

Stanley Lipski took a long time to die. When he finally let go, Haynes cut away his life jacket and let his friend, one of the most respected officers aboard *Indianapolis*, slip silently into the deep. Haynes, Paroubek, and Centazzo watched Lipski recede, down and down, until he disappeared.

"The Lord is my shepherd," someone began, "I shall not want. He maketh me to lie down in green pastures. He leadeth me beside still waters . . ."

Like a flame passed from one candle to the next, the Twenty-third Psalm spread from man to man, those who knew it joining in, voices rising until the benediction glowed warm over the spot on earth where Lipski left this life.

Combat Intelligence, CincPac, Pearl Harbor

Under the somnolent sway of palm trees outside a two-story plantation-style building not far from the Pearl Harbor shipyard, a set of stairs led down to an unremarkable and windowless basement office. There, on the afternoon of July 30, CINCPAC's ULTRA magicians intercepted a message: The captain of the Tamon group submarine I-58 was reporting to his high command that he'd sunk . . . something.

I-58 had attacked on 29 July at 2332, the message said. "Sinking confirmed. Obtained three torpedo hits."*

The code men decrypted everything they could, but there were two parts of the transmission they could not recover—the type of ship sunk and the location.

Sometimes, Japanese sub commanders exaggerated their successes, hoping to curry favor or save face. The most likely scenario was that it was another enemy hoax—the Japanese had been known to fabricate sinking reports, hoping to bait American rescuers into a trap.

In any case, the intercept was one of about five hundred processed that day. Without a vessel type or location of the alleged sinking, there wasn't much to go on. Still, the magicians put the intercept into the mill for processing. Linguists checked the Japanese-to-English translation, then the message was delivered to Captain Smedburg in Combat Intelligence and to other stations around the world.

Also on July 30, Commander Amphibious Forces Pacific (COM-PHIBSPAC) tried to raise *Indianapolis* for a planned test of the ship's

---

* Hashimoto obtained only two torpedo hits.

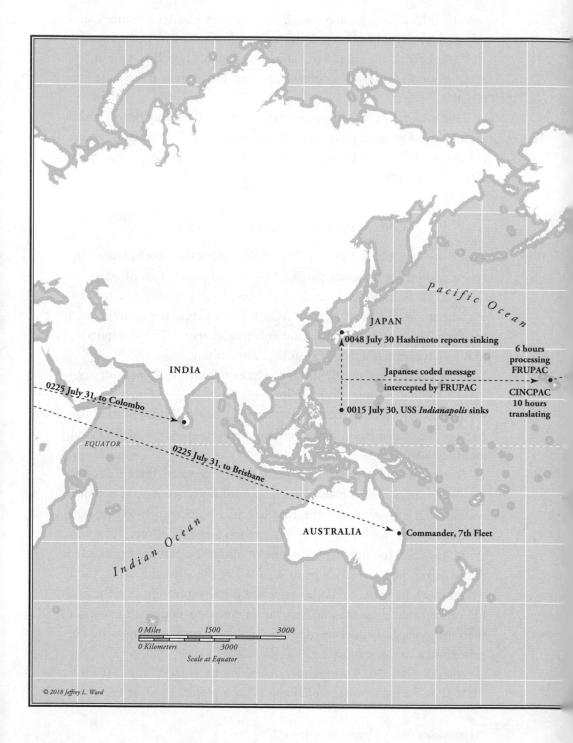

Pacific Ocean

JAPAN

0048 July 30 Hashimoto reports sinking

6 hours
processing
FRUPAC

Japanese coded message
intercepted by FRUPAC

CINCPAC
10 hours
translating

INDIA

0225 July 31, to Colombo

0015 July 30, USS *Indianapolis* sinks

EQUATOR

0225 July 31, to Brisbane

Indian Ocean

AUSTRALIA

Commander, 7th Fleet

0 Miles   1500   3000
0 Kilometers   3000
Scale at Equator

© 2018 Jeffrey L. Ward

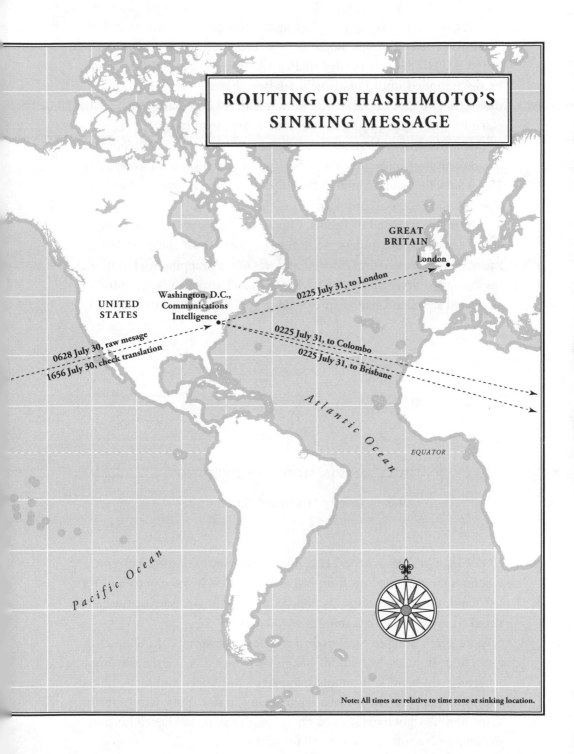

ROUTING OF HASHIMOTO'S SINKING MESSAGE

GREAT BRITAIN

London

0225 July 31, to London

UNITED STATES

Washington, D.C., Communications Intelligence

0628 July 30, raw mesage

1656 July 30, check translation

0225 July 31, to Colombo

0225 July 31, to Brisbane

Atlantic Ocean

EQUATOR

Pacific Ocean

Note: All times are relative to time zone at sinking location.

new radio teletype equipment. When the test failed, COMPHIBSPAC asked for a relay through Radio Guam. That test also failed, prompting COMPHIBSPAC to notify CincPac Advance that radio checks would be discontinued until *Indianapolis* advised that she was ready for further tests. The CincPac Advance communications officer was not unduly alarmed. Maybe the ship's new receivers weren't working.

Meanwhile, operations staffers at Leyte had been tracking *Indianapolis* on their plotting boards. Using McVay's planned speed of advance of 15.7 knots, they approximated the ship's position and moved her west along Route Peddie accordingly.

On the eastern end of Peddie, Captain Naquin's staff at Guam consulted Indy's routing orders. According to her Plan of Intended Movement, she had crossed the Chop line and was now Philippine Sea Frontier's responsibility. Several hours later, when the clock struck the time of Indy's estimated arrival at Leyte, Guam would simply wipe her off their map.

4

———

JULY 30, 1945, MONDAY—EVENING

Ten to Twenty Miles from Sinking Site

COZELL SMITH WAS STILL floating in Buck Gibson's net group when a shark barreled up from below and locked its jaws onto Smith's left hand. Instantly, Smith was pulled under. A single, horrific thought shrieked in his head: *I am going to be eaten alive!*

The shark dragged Smith ten feet below the surface. Enveloped in a storm of bubbles, he held his breath and shoved at the shark's snout with his right hand. The animal snapped its head back and forth, holding Smith's arm in viselike jaws while trying to saw it off with its teeth. Then Smith's right hand slipped on the shark's skin, and he felt his middle finger jab a soft spot and go all the way in.

Suddenly, the shark let go. Smith popped through the surface gasping, his hand shredded and bleeding. He struck out swimming in a wild race back to the nets.

The men on the nets had seen the attack. "No! Get away! Get away!" they cried, terrified of the chum line that streamed from Smith's hand.

As he neared the group, they kicked him and clubbed him with arms and fists. But the shark attack had charged Smith with adrenaline and he bulldozed through the group, climbing over men's bodies like a rat fleeing fire. He landed in the middle of a net, where a sailor whipped out a knife and began slashing at him. Smith threw up his arms to protect his face and body. Suddenly, he realized the man would kill him, just like the shark. He fought his way back into the water and swam clear of the treacherous group, where he floated about a hundred feet away, his only company a dead body that bobbed facedown beside him. Not having a life jacket or anything to support him, Smith clamped his right hand around his left wrist and held it that way for a long time, kicking his feet to keep his head above water.

Just out of sight of the Gibson net group, L. D. Cox saw a giant shark shoot up from below and snatch the man next to him, life jacket and all, the attack so close that the splash curled over Cox like a breaking wave. Instinctively, he ducked and squeezed his eyes shut against the spray. When he opened them again, his buddy was gone.

Several swells over from the Haynes group, gurgling screams tore the air. Seaman First Class James "Denny" Price and his friend Seaman James King pulled up their legs as sharks ripped into the outer circle of their group. King, severely injured in the sinking, decided he couldn't take it any longer. Pulling free from Price, he shucked his life jacket and dove beneath the surface to end his own life, but Price dove down and caught him before he could get away. It was the third time King had tried it. A nearby friend questioned Price's sanity. Why did Price keep risking his own life to go after King?

Price could only reply, "It's the right thing to do." Now, to keep King from giving up again, Price grabbed his life jacket and wrapped it around them both. They huddled together as the sharks chewed into the group. Price could feel them hitting his feet, and he shivered with revulsion. There were so many now, he was practically walking on their backs.

In the Redmayne group, Harpo Celaya knew all about the sharks.

Hours before, they had set up a patrol beneath him, their rough hides grazing his legs as they reconnoitered. He knew that if he actually saw a shark, he might come undone, so he clung to his rope and refused to look down. Then he heard an unearthly sound, a scream unlike any he'd ever heard a man make. The sharks had eaten another sailor.

Sometime later, relief arrived when a friendly face swam up. It was Fred Markmann, a watertender from New Jersey. Harpo had always thought Markmann looked a little like Popeye. He even had the famous forearms. Now he was in bad shape, in both body and spirit. Celaya offered to share his rope.

"I hurt my leg bad, Celaya," Markmann said. "I don't think I'm gonna make it."

"Don't talk like that. We'll be back ashore having a beer before you know it."

"That ain't gonna happen."

The sun was falling fast. For the next few hours, Markmann seemed intent on making his own prediction come true. He pushed away from Harpo several times and tried to swim off to die. But Harpo kept after him, pulling him back to the relative safety of their little length of line.

Harpo's throat stung with thirst. Unconsciously, he sucked on his St. Anthony's medal, which seemed to help. Just yards away, a tiny group of men on one of the rafts had begun to guzzle from the meager water supply and stuff their faces with hardtack. The trouble was that no one man could do anything to stop them. The raft men were packed in so tightly that moving was next to impossible without exerting a week's store of energy. Nor did any officers step forward, including Redmayne, although by now he had identified himself as an officer to Harlan Twible, a junior ensign. Twible wanted to take charge but feared overstepping Redmayne's seniority.

Finally, surrounding sailors began to yell for justice. Once again, it was Chief Benton who swam up and took charge. He asked the men to stop consuming the crackers and water. They'd likely be in the water for some time, he said, and it was necessary to save the provisions and ration them equally. This worked for the time being.

Glenn Morgan's stomach executed a final hard squeeze, ejecting green bile from his mouth. After that, the nausea subsided. The other men were beginning to feel better, too, and conversation set in. The first topic was what the men had seen and heard before Indy went down, and how they got off the ship. It was Moran's story that interested Morgan most.

"I was ordered to send an SOS," he said, "and I did it. From Radio 1." The men sat in their raft, undulating waves lapping at the edges.

"How do you know it went out?" Morgan said.

Moran shot him the glance one shoots at a complete lunkhead. "You can always tell. There's a meter that shows whether the signal's going out. It didn't show where I was, but it was showing in Radio 2. Sturtevant was in there. He saw it."

Another voice chimed in. It was Fred Hart, the radio technician who got the ship's position from Radio 1, but abandoned ship before taking it to Woods. Hart sat in the adjacent raft, next to Lieutenant Freeze. He knew there was power to the transmitters in Radio 2 because he turned on a small AC generator as soon as he entered the compartment. And if Sturtevant saw the antenna meter loading up in Radio 2, Hart felt there was absolutely no reason why the SOS message wouldn't have gotten out.

"Just because a signal went out doesn't mean anybody received it," Moran countered.

Moran's realism didn't dampen Morgan's spirits. The whole fleet would be looking for them!

Meanwhile, a shark had already found them. Earlier, Moran had spotted a large dorsal fin slicing the wave crests. The shark—someone dubbed him Charlie—was a dark olive green, seven or eight feet long, with a head about a foot wide. Charlie commenced a steady orbit around the flotilla and was still there as swells carried the rafts into their second night adrift.

Don McCall, the sailor who first had enough to eat after joining the Navy, floated alone just past the outskirts of the Haynes group. His body temperature was dropping. He thought of his hometown library, where there had been a fine old potbelly stove. After his father died from lime-mortar exposure, McCall and his sister sometimes had to swipe coal from passing trains in order to heat their house. Other times, McCall spent winter days in the library, devouring books. Now, shivering under the cold moon, he concentrated on the library stove, and the people he'd met in stories. He remembered the crew from *The Rime of the Ancient Mariner*. Tortured with thirst, and with their ship snagged in the sweltering equator doldrums, the crew lamented:

> *Water, water, everywhere,*
> *And all the boards did shrink;*
> *Water, water, everywhere,*
> *Nor any drop to drink.*

McCall found that he was growing thirsty, too. Up the swells carried him, and down again, the cool sea glittering like treasure in the moon's fairy light. McCall was not tempted. He knew from his books not to drink it.

5

JULY 31, 1945, TUESDAY—MORNING

Sixteen to Thirty-two Miles from Sinking Site

THE CASTAWAYS HAD BEEN in the water for about thirty hours and in the Haynes group, Captain Parke's main objective was to keep everyone together. Many men had dozed on and off through the night, fitful spells of sleep snatched from a waking nightmare. Parke swam around the huge ring of floating sailors, encouraging and assisting, comforting the men who were injured or burned. More than once, he gave away his own life jacket to support exhausted survivors and treaded water until he found an empty one. The wounded quickly grew to rely on the Marine's comforting presence, and the sound of their moans and pleas became as constant as the slap of water against the men.

"Captain Parke!" they called. "Captain Parke!"

Haynes, meanwhile, had begun ranging out from these swimmers to see how he could help other groups. Making rounds beyond the outskirts, he swam up to Denny Price, who was on one of the three Gibson group nets. The young seaman was still holding tight to his friend King, whom he had saved again and again because it was the right thing to do.

Haynes examined King. "He's gone, son," he said to Price. "It's time to let him go." Heartbroken, Price unwrapped the life jacket that had bound him with his friend and watched King's body sink slowly down, feetfirst. King's head was tilted back, eyes open, and he seemed to Price to be staring upward as he sank. Price thought he could see right down into the dead boy's soul.

Some men on a raft in the Redmayne group began hogging down rations again. Then, just after sunrise, Twible, Benton, and an ensign named Eames tried to ration a small amount of food to each man—half a cracker and one malted milk tablet. Even then, some men managed to filch more than their share, while others got none. This drove Radioman Jack Miner crazy. But with the rafts and nets overfilled with men, the scoundrels were out of his reach and there was nothing he could do but stew in anger. Miner had a plan, though. He also had a knife. If the time came when he could get off his net with ease, he was going to kill the filchers—or worse.

Buck Gibson kept thinking about fried chicken and being picked up by a destroyer. As dawn seeped up to light the second morning, Gibson knew the burned boy still lay beside him on the floater net because he'd reached out all through the night to be sure. But as the sun rose in full, Gibson saw light fall on bare bone. Something had eaten the boy's broken leg during the night and the gnawed end now jutted from the net into the water. Gently, Gibson jostled him. He was dead. Gibson did not share this with the sailors near him. He had already planned to keep the boy on the net even if he died. At least that way he could return his body to his family.

The sky grew brighter, and someone initiated a count-off. Gibson discovered there were 167 men in his group, which had now added two more floater nets that were within shouting distance. Because he was a gunner's mate, Gibson knew that *Indianapolis* was scheduled for gunnery practice off Leyte. He passed the word along the nets: If they could hold on for just a day or two, help would be coming. Gibson's experience and certainty gave the men around him hope.

The Gibson nets were beginning to drift apart. Having fled one net in the group, Cozell Smith was happy to find another, more hospitable net about a hundred yards away. After the shark tried to tear off his left hand, Smith had used only his right to remove the life jacket from the dead sailor who'd been keeping him company. Using the jacket as support, he kicked over to a new net and found his friend Seaman Curtis Pace, along with Denny Price, who was deep in thought over losing King. With them was Joseph Mikolayek, a twenty-four-year-old tough guy from Detroit. The good-humored Mikolayek had always taken his job seriously, and that meant caring for his men, who included Pace, Price, and Smith. Having attained the ripe old age of twenty-four after serving two years aboard Indy, the "old man" was revered by the younger sailors. Smith was relieved to find his character hadn't changed in the water. Seeing Smith's damaged hand, Mikolayek quickly tore off part of his shirttail and created a makeshift bandage.

In Glenn Morgan's group, Kenley Lanter sat in a raft with a seaman second class named Harold Shearer, a twenty-four-year-old from Canton, Ohio. Shearer sat motionless on the latticework. After the torpedoes hit Indy, he was climbing a ladder toward the quarterdeck when he grabbed a superheated railing to keep from falling. Now burned strips of flesh hung from his arms, which he held straight out before him like a monster in a Boris Karloff picture.

In the afternoon, J. J. Moran spoke to Morgan quietly. "Have you had any water?"

Morgan said that he hadn't. Moran said he hadn't either. The two men looked to another raft, where they knew some sailors had opened one of the water kegs and begun drinking from it. Until Moran mentioned it, Morgan hadn't paid attention to how much of the group's remaining water was already gone.

"All right, attention all hands," Moran said. "From this point on, our remaining water will be rationed. We will issue ourselves equal amounts,

three ounces in the morning and three ounces at night. Those cups from
the survival gear have graduated measurements. Use them. The Spam
and hardtack will also be rationed."

It was the first time since the sinking that anyone in the group had
asserted some kind of authority. Lieutenant Freeze was too badly burned
to take charge. That left the group with six petty officers and Moran, a
first-class radioman, the senior man. Being a first-class on a warship was
a big deal—nearly all the way up the enlisted food chain, with only a
chief being higher. A first-class had earned his chops. He started at the
bottom chipping paint just like everyone else and worked his way up to
both leadership and technical expertise. When a first-class told a junior
man to do something, that sailor didn't ask questions.

No one asked Moran questions now or challenged him. Why should
they? Morgan thought. The rationing plan was simple logic. But it was
more than what Moran said—it was the way he said it. There was a firm-
ness in his manner, a conviction that inspired confidence. Morgan felt
comfortable with the parameters Moran laid down. It was then that
Morgan noticed for the first time that the volcanic burn in his eyes had
begun to subside. For the first time, he was beginning to feel that, all
things considered, he was actually in pretty good shape.

To pass the time, he began experimenting with one of the signaling mirrors they'd found tucked into the survival kits. In the movies, heroes were
forever using mirrors to flash bursts of sunlight, sending messages over vast
distances. These survival-kit mirrors were rectangular, about three inches
by four, and had a tiny cross of clear glass cut in the center. Morgan found
that when the sun was in front of him, he could catch its reflection in the
mirror. Then, by peering through the little cross, he could aim the reflected
light at a target—the edge of his raft, for example. For longer distances, he
held up his other hand and aimed the cross there. He thought maybe if he
sighted the cross on his hand then aligned his hand with a more distant
target—say, an aircraft or a ship—he might be able to signal for help.

The McVay group had slept in turns through Monday night, then began
Tuesday by counting a collection of visitors. The trio of sharks that had
mustered around the rafts the previous day had now grown to five. As
the climbing sun chased the chill from their bones, McVay led the men in

prayer. Though the warmth was welcome, it also melted the fuel oil so that what had clung in the men's hair now ran down their faces and into their eyes. It was impossible to wipe away the insoluble mess, and the burn was nearly insufferable. With venomous fury, it stung for the first ten minutes the eyes were open. Then, perversely, it stung again the next time they were closed. McVay had gotten fuel oil in just one eye and could see with the other. He checked in with his men frequently to ask how they were doing.

With a day to rest and fortified by their rations, the men had recovered some pep, and none had significant injuries. McVay decided they would paddle over and link up with the man in the nearest raft who had been calling for help. Digging in with paddles, the straggling flotilla inched up each liquid hill and sledded down its back, only to be buffeted in the other direction by a new swell. It took four and a half hours to paddle fifteen hundred yards. It turned out that the man yelling for help was physically fine, just understandably lonely.

After that, McVay decided to reconfigure the spacing of the rafts and directed the men to lengthen the lines that tied them together. He hoped to expand their footprint on the ocean to improve their chances of being spotted from the air. During the first two days, the group had seen several planes, some of them likely patrol bombers on regular sector searches for enemy craft. At night, their red and green navigation lights flickered in the sky like close planets amid a blanket of stars. Only in darkness did McVay direct the men to fire flares. Their green fire speared the night, carrying the men's hopes up into the sky. But time after time, the flares flamed out unseen.

Once, McVay's heart tripped faster when he saw an aircraft emit a revolving white light. *They've seen us!* he thought. But the plane flew on, its lights stitching themselves into the sparkling firmament. Knowing that pilots and aircrews are preoccupied with flying their planes, McVay was unperturbed, and he tried to encourage the men.

"They probably won't see us until they realize we're missing," he said. Apart from that, McVay was basing his hopes on ships, not planes, and he did not believe that any would reach the area until sometime on Thursday.

Otha Alton Havins, a second-class yeoman, and another sailor did their part to keep up the castaways' spirits. Both had been part of Indy's aviation unit barbershop quartet. On Tuesday afternoon, they harmonized a couple of popular choruses: "I Want A Girl (Just Like the Girl Who Married Dear Old Dad)," and a GI's song made popular by the Andrews Sisters just after the start of the Pacific war:

> *Don't sit under the apple tree with anyone else but me,*
> *Anyone else but me, anyone else but me, no, no, no!*
> *Don't sit under the apple tree with anyone else but me*
> *Till I come marching home.*

Later that day, the flotilla bumped into a block of butter and the men plucked it from the water. Then they spotted another large, floating can. Thinking it was another ration can, McVay expended considerable time and effort trying to reach it. But when the men pulled it aboard, they found that it was an empty 40 mm ammo can. Maybe they could use it as a catch basin for rain, someone suggested. They decided to keep it aboard.

Giles McCoy and Felton Outland watched their shipmates float away, unsure they had made the right decision. The day before, they had been part of a tight cluster of four rafts secured with short lengths of rope. But every wave bashed them together in a violent version of bumper boats. Prevented from sleeping by the unpredictable jolts, their uniforms chafed, and the rafts threatened to break and fail. Making matters worse, the men on one of the rafts had begun to lose their minds and the men on the other three rafts were afraid of what they might do. Finally, on Tuesday, unable to rest, they decided to cut all the rafts free.

Now as the eddies sent the little craft off to four separate fates, dead bodies and sharks coursed through the spaces between them. Outland had weakened to a pitiful state, so McCoy, with his loud mouth, took charge of the men on his raft: Payne, Brundige, Gray, Kemp, and Outland. Mike Kuryla, on one of the other rafts, had been against splitting up. Some thought that maybe he'd been right.

In the raft group where Miner dreamed of knifing the filchers, Lieutenant Redmayne's mind was also steadily slipping away. As the survivors neared the forty-eight-hour mark, all were exhausted. But Redmayne had lapsed into a half-slumber in which reality fused with phantasm. At intervals, he cried out, "I need to get to the engine room!"

Roughly sixty men now occupied the rafts in this group, with another sixty to eighty clinging to nets. Many sailors had already succumbed to their injuries and sunk silently below the waves. Over the past twenty-four hours, the rafts and nets had slowly drifted apart, like dandelion seeds caught in a breeze. Ensign Eames and those around him represented the fringe of this group, which was separated from the Haynes group by a few hundred yards.

Haynes, Parke, Modisher, Conway, and others worked tirelessly to keep their group peaceful and unified, but Redmayne's group lacked strong leadership. And while other raft groups were faring better because they had some supplies, the rations in Redmayne's group triggered fights and hoarding.

On Tuesday, the pilferers struck again, snatching rations from rafts and gorging themselves on water and malt tablets. Ensign Twible reported this to Redmayne, who pulled himself together and made his rank known.

"I'm Lieutenant Redmayne, the chief engineer, and it turns out that I am the senior officer in the group," he announced to the men nearby. But it was too late. With chiefs outranking officers and thieves on the loose, the chain of command had long since broken down. Besides, what did rank mean out here in the middle of the Pacific? Redmayne was mainly ignored, and most men who found rations among the flotsam kept them.

Floating in a sagging life jacket, Ensign Donald Blum observed this chaos and decided it was time for a new strategy. Clearly, Redmayne had no authority, and Blum had never had much regard for enlisted men. He decided that if someone in this group was going to survive, it was going to be him. He gazed up at the rafts and saw that they were still completely full. Uninjured, he had not qualified for a seat on a raft under Chief Benton's plan. But Benton was enlisted, and Blum was an officer. Blum bided his time until he saw a sailor's lifeless body pushed gently off a raft. This was his opportunity. Blum quietly took the dead man's vacated seat and began to refine a plan.

6

JULY 31, 1945, TUESDAY—AFTERNOON/EVENING

DICK THELEN, AN EIGHTEEN-YEAR-OLD from Lansing, Michigan, was battling nausea. The accumulation of oil and salt water in his gut had triggered it. Riding ten- to twelve-foot swells, up and down, up and down, hour after hour made it worse. He wondered how much more of this they could take.

Earlier in the day, Thelen had been relieved to swim into Robert Terry, a fellow seaman. The two had joined Indy at Mare Island on the same day less than two months earlier and had become fast friends. Now, floating at the far fringe of the Haynes swimmer group, they vowed to watch each other's backs. But their vigilance couldn't stop the horrifying screams that erupted when sharks took their shipmates, or the unrelenting pain of hunger and severe dehydration. It was hard not to lose hope.

Thelen had already seen many around him give up and slip beneath the waves. But each time he was tempted to follow them, he remembered his father's face. Before Thelen left for his assignment to *Indianapolis*, his father grasped his hand firmly, looked him in the eye, and said, "Dick, I want you to come home."

Thelen promised he would, though at the time he thought the promise unnecessary, the war being almost over. Now, though, he could hear his dad's voice and feel his firm grip. Thelen wouldn't give up. He couldn't. He had promised his father.

A short distance away, Father Conway began calling for any Catholics in the group to swim toward him. Thelen, a strong Catholic, swam over and joined a group that had grown to more than twenty-five men. Conway took time to talk to each of them in turn, hear their confessions, and give them last rites. A tremendous peace settled over Thelen. If rescue didn't come, and the Lord took him now, it would be okay.

Many in the Haynes group felt that Conway's spiritual offerings helped them more than anything the doctors could do at the moment.

The priest's efforts comforted Dick Paroubek's soul so greatly that the yeoman felt he could relax for the first time since the ship went down.

Marine Corporal Edgar Harrell's swimmer group was in desperate shape. Their numbers had dwindled from eighty to forty, with many of those who died joining the crowd of corpses that refused to float away. The living men's tongues had begun to swell in their mouths, and the magnitude of their thirst became a torture conceived by demons. Overcome, some drank from the ocean, furtively at first, then blissfully as if bending their heads to take great quenching mouthfuls from a clear mountain lake. Others, more circumspect, succumbed to the deception that salt could be strained from seawater. These men teamed up, one holding a patch of torn clothing over his mouth and the other pouring water through.

It didn't matter; all the seawater drinkers died painful deaths. A lack of fluid intake increased salt levels in their bodies, triggering the natural response of greater thirst. When they took in no fluid to decrease salt levels, water rushed out from their cells to do the job. Brain cells tore loose from their rightful locations, impairing judgment just enough to cause the men to seek poisonous relief. Thirst begged their hands to administer water to dilute the salt that was poisoning their bodies. They obliged with seawater, introducing more salt and increasing their thirst to the point of mindless lust. Blood vessels tore and fluid built up in the brain, causing seizures and insanity. They vomited and foamed at the mouth. Some died of kidney failure. Others' brains short-circuited violently, as when a tree branch hits a high voltage power line.

Harrell watched, horrified, as young men, full of life and laughter and pranks just a day and a half before, went out of their heads. Surrounded by water, his thirst unbearable, he clenched his teeth against the cool seduction and prayed. In his head, he recited Psalm 23. "The Lord is my shepherd. I shall not want . . ."

Harrell felt strength leaving his limbs, but his buddy Spooner was worse. The other Marine's eyes were now so inflamed that they literally bulged from their sockets, making it impossible for him to close them. The constant slap of waves splashed salt on the raw surfaces of his eyeballs. The light of the sun sparked excruciating pain.

The day spun out cruelly, the men suspended in the troughs between waves with no soothing grace, only thirst, pain, heat, blood, sharks, and the coppery rotting stench of dead men. Finally, Spooner told Harrell that he planned to end his own life.

Harrell looked into the burned and swollen death mask that was his friend's face. "How will you do it?"

"I'll dive down so far that I'll drown before I come back up."

Harrell put his hands on his buddy's shoulders. "Spooner, listen to me. There are only two Marines left in this group, and when everyone else is gone, you're going to be with me. I know in my heart that God is going to deliver us and we're going to survive this together."

Harrell didn't know if he'd gotten through. Quickly, he turned Spooner's back to him and firmly fastened the other Marine's life vest to his own. As night set in, Harrell's vigor ebbed steadily, leeched away in the grip of creeping hypothermia. His mind drifted from the gruesome reality of liquid death and half-eaten corpses to the edge of unreason.

Tinian Island
Northern Marianas

By the time the castaways had been in the water for three days, two storms were gathering off mainland Japan. On July 26, the day *Indianapolis* dropped her secret cargo at Tinian, military weather forecasters began tracking Typhoon Eva, a storm with projected winds that could top seventy miles per hour. The second storm was incubating at Tinian itself, and if not for Eva would have been unleashed on August 1.

Little Boy had been ready for deployment the day before, on July 31, and was missing only a quartet of cordite charges that were kept separately for safety on takeoff. But Eva's northerly track would take her over Okinawa in the Ryukyus and just south of Kyushu, Japan. So the Little Boy launch was put on hold in search of better weather.

Captain Deak Parsons and Admiral William Purnell, the officers who had briefed McVay on the bomb transport mission in San Francisco, had returned to the tiny island. Purnell, an assistant chief of naval operations, was Fleet Admiral King's personal representative at Tinian. With Parsons and Brigadier General Thomas Farrell, Groves's deputy for operations, Purnell formed a triumvirate that the three jokingly called the "Tinian Joint Chiefs." Except, in terms of power, it was no joke. Together, the three men held in their hands the lives of tens of thousands of Japanese civilians, as well as those of an estimated one million Japanese and American troops.

For Parsons, it was personal. The number of casualties at Okinawa had scaled a height he could scarcely fathom. Also, his kid brother, Bob, an eighteen-year-old Marine Corps private, had barely survived the Battle of Iwo Jima. On his way to Tinian, Parsons had stopped to visit his brother at the naval hospital in San Diego. One whole side of Bob's face was crushed, and a rock had been driven up through his right eye, which doctors had replaced with a piece of pink plastic.

During his two years with the Manhattan Project, Parsons's driving aim had been to bring a swift end to the war. That goal was now within reach. On July 31, three of Colonel Paul Tibbets's fifteen B-29 Superfortresses—the planes that formed the secret squadron known as the 509th Composite Bomber Squadron—took off from Tinian. The planes sped to Iwo Jima, a distance of 730 miles, dropped a dummy unit, and practiced the daredevil turn designed to get the *Enola Gay* clear of the blast radius when she dropped the real thing. After the test, Parsons declared training complete, and General Farrell sent a message to Groves: The first atomic bomb was ready for combat deployment.

7

AUGUST 1, 1945, WEDNESDAY

Philippine Sea

THOUGH THEIR SHIP HAD plunged to the sea bottom nearly three days before, for many in the Haynes group, Wednesday dawned a day of celebration. Their beloved Indy had not sunk after all! She was anchored just below the surface—and there were treats to be had: Ice cream sundaes! Candy bars! Ice-cold Coca-Cola! The men dove happily down to take their pick. Not far off, a hotel was discovered suspended on the water, and anyone could enjoy an hour of rest there in the one available bunk if he just waited his turn in line. So far, the line was only fifteen men deep, because some had found an even better option: an A&W root beer stand with free floats served by beautiful pinup girls.

Captain Parke chased down one hallucinating man after another as they dove down to the imaginary ship or struck out for the root beer stand that lay just beyond the rolling wave crests. It was never-ending work, more than any one man could handle in such circumstances, but the Marine would not give up. Parke had worked without ceasing for days, rounding up stragglers, trying to keep the group together until, late on the third day, he too succumbed to hallucinations. The Marine broke from the group and struck out swimming. Some heard him yelling, as if at a group of attackers, perhaps some imagined Japanese. Finally, Parke collapsed, dead of exhaustion.

The loss of their brave watchman stunned those men still in their right minds. If Parke couldn't hang on, what hope did the rest of them have? And now that he was gone, whom could they trust?

From eighty souls to seventeen. By Wednesday morning, August 1, that's how far the count in Harrell's group had fallen. Sunrise elevated their body temperatures slightly and they were grateful for the warmth. But as the bright orb climbed, it turned unfriendly, scorching their heads. No one talked much. Dehydration had puffed up their tongues so that their words came out as if their mouths were stuffed with cotton batting. Wearing only waterlogged life jackets, the group rode the swells low, chins now resting in the sea. Up, down. Up, down. The only sounds, the slosh and slap of water that seemed larger than the sky.

At midmorning, one man broke the silence with a prayer. Another man followed. Soon, every still-sane man in the group had taken a turn, pleading with God for deliverance. Harrell looked at his watch. It was about 10 a.m.

The prayers continued for three hours. Not rote prayers, not learned ones. Humble and genuine supplication, punctuated by impassioned stories about loved ones who waited for them at home. Lapsed men who had perhaps never prayed beyond their childhood bedsides now cried out, specks in a monstrous wasteland, unseen except by the only One who *could* see. This they hoped with a fervency that burned hotter than the sun.

Minutes later, a miracle: A large swell buoyed the group above the wave tops. In the distance, they saw another group of survivors, and with them, what appeared to be a makeshift raft.

Aboard the McVay rafts, the men sat quietly, up to their waists in the water. All that could be said had been said. Now, the hours ticked by, suspended in an obscure stillness. Long, rolling swells lifted the flotilla, but a receding pattern of identical swells, like giant furrows in a plowed field, kept them from seeing very far. There was almost no wind and the sun bore down as if through a magnifying glass. Vince Allard, the quartermaster, had cut apart a piece of the loose canvas and made cornucopia hats, which kept the sun off their heads. During the heat of the day, the men pulled the hats down over their ears, pulled up their life jacket collars to cover their necks, and kept their hands under cover. The layer of fuel oil coating their bodies kept the rest of their skin from frying, as did a layer of butter.

McVay served lunch: a piece of onion, two malt tablets, and a half-inch square of Spam. Perhaps not wanting to be the first to show weakness, no one asked the skipper for water. McVay estimated that he had five or six days of sparse rations left. He had done a lot of saltwater fishing and could see silver schools of bonita and small mackerel wheeling and glinting beneath the surface. Allard, who had grown up near Washington's Okanogan River, turned out to be the best fisherman of the bunch. The best thing about the fishing was that it stirred excitement among the castaways. The group watched Allard with interest, cheering him on when fish ventured near his hook and bit. But McVay was dubious about the edibility of the catch, and would not let the men eat it.

In the Redmayne group, the days stretched out and a leaden lethargy blanketed the barely conscious men. Denied rest by his stinging and injured eyes, Petty Officer Eugene Morgan sat on one of the floater nets and squinted and blinked at the scene around him. Water. Sharks. Exhaustion. Death. More water. Fellows giving up, swimming away. Others trying and failing to stop their shipmates.

Several times, men desperate for a reprieve had come to Eugene Morgan, intent on swimming off to a phantom island. Looking into their eyes was like looking into a vacant house. It was as if their souls had already exited their bodies.

The day before, Eugene had been keeping his eye on a floater net some distance away bearing more than a dozen men when the sharks attacked in a tornado of fins and froth. Eugene sat bolt upright and watched in horror. Around him, men clamped their hands over their ears to block out the nightmare screams that crescendoed just before their crewmates disappeared.

Now, Eugene considered his own waterlogged floater net and shifted to find a more comfortable position. Through his burning eyes, he caught a glimpse of an object in the distance. It looked like a canvas bag. To cut down on the pilfering, Chief Benton had directed that all supplies be gathered on a raft bearing only officers. Had one of the bags of provisions escaped from the raft again? Eugene's floater net, which was attached to the officers' raft, was drenched, uncomfortable, and always getting tangled, yet he felt reluctant to leave it. But in this case, he decided that the risk might be worth the reward. He extricated himself from the net and paddled toward the object.

He'd been right: After a few moments of effort, he wrangled what turned out to be a canvas bag of rations. He headed back toward the officers' raft, but as he got close, something hit him hard. Eugene spun wildly around, expecting to find another man after his prize, but he saw instead a streaking fin and felt cool water accelerate around his groin. Looking down, he saw that his skivvies were gone, torn from his body by a shark. Terror filled Eugene's chest. Clutching the rations, he scrambled back to the group before the predator could return for a second bite.

Eugene squinted, blinked, and made his way over to the nearby officers' raft, where he turned over the bag of provisions that had cost him his underwear. A sailor named Anthony, a pharmacist's mate, noticed how bad Eugene's eyes had become and called him to the sickbay raft. Eugene gladly complied, reckoning that a few inches of cork might offer a bit more protection than a holey old net. On the sickbay raft, he noticed a can or two of provisions tucked down under the water by everyone's legs, their lids punched in to prevent them from floating away. Eugene found it merely curious that this small treasure had escaped the inventory system the officers had put in place for the entire group. But other men seethed over the fact that all the supplies were now under the officers' control, and they vowed to kill the hogging sons of bitches when they all got ashore.

Glenn Morgan's group began the day with a solemn task: burying Howard Freeze. The pain of his severe burns had sent the young lieutenant into a mild hysteria. Tuesday evening, he had fallen asleep exhausted, and when Fred Hart tried to wake him, he couldn't. Freeze was dead. But there were a lot of sharks circling the rafts, and the men decided to wait until Wednesday to bury him. Hart and others gently slipped off the lieutenant's ring and watch—keepsakes for his family—and slid his body over the side. Morgan could not watch.

Long, silent hours drifting on the vast blue plain had given Morgan plenty of time to think. When Moran said the SOS went out but it was possible no one had heard it, Morgan had rejected the idea. Now, he was beginning to think the radioman had nailed it. It was clear that rescue was not coming. This realization seemed to be spreading through Morgan's group, which now contained nineteen men in four rafts. Bravado and optimism had given way to an irritable pall.

Earlier that morning a rain squall had soaked the group but also provided fresh water. They managed to catch about a gallon of it in one of the canvas sheets. Eagerly, those nearest dipped in enamel cups for a drink, but immediately spat it out. The water was brackish. Not as salty as the sea, but too salty to drink, made so by the dried sea salt that lay invisible on the canvas. The men used the remaining rainwater to rinse the canvas clean. Another squall hovered in the distance, hanging from the sky like a veil.

Morgan noticed fevered activity on another raft whose occupants had used their four-by-eight canvas and the two raft paddles to rig a sail.

"What are you fellas doing?" Moran said.

"We're gonna sail over toward where those lights came from last night and find out what's going on," one man said.

Morgan hadn't seen any lights, but now his eye caught a sudden movement. It was Harold Shearer. He had been sitting in his own raft near the side of Morgan's. Now Morgan watched Shearer clamber quickly to the opposite side, where he tumbled into the sea. Lanter and another sailor lunged to the side of the raft, grabbed handfuls of Shearer's shirt and dungarees, and hauled him back aboard.

"What are you *doing*?" Lanter yelled.

"You're not going to put *me* in a bag and throw me over!" Shearer babbled, delirious.

Morgan could only deduce that when Shearer saw the men in the other raft fashioning their canvas into a sail, he thought they were making him a bag for burial at sea. Shearer had seen it before. They'd all seen it when those nine men died after the suicide strike off Okinawa. Indy's sailmaker had used canvas to make body bags and sewn all the dead men inside them.

Shearer began an uncontrolled shivering and lapsed back into silence.

"We have to get him out of the water or he'll get pneumonia," Moran said. "Let's bring him over to this raft." Except for the last of the evaporating rainwater, Morgan and Moran's raft was dry.

"Yeah, well, where are we gonna put him?" another sailor said.

Moran eyed him. "You're gonna trade places with him."

"Like hell I will! Why don't you or Morgan go over there instead?"

Moran squared his body toward the sailor. Low and even, he said, "Get over there, and do it now." Then he softened his tone. "We'll take turns."

With Lanter's help, Morgan and Moran pulled Shearer onto the dry raft. Morgan dug a morphine syrette from their first-aid kit and replaced Shearer's shivering with a deep sleep. The sulking sailor spider-walked over to Shearer's raft and sat down in water waist deep.

AUGUST 1, 1945, WEDNESDAY—AFTERNOON

In the Redmayne group, Ensign Donald Blum was wrestling a monster called sleep—not normal sleep, but the sleep of the damned. After nearly seventy-two hours with few rations and little rest, he found himself nodding off constantly. Balanced on the edge of consciousness, he struggled to determine whether he was trapped in a nightmare. Sometimes, when Blum was certain he was awake, he had to work hard to separate reality from hallucinations. He obsessed over drinking water and conjured images of fresh-grown tomatoes from his mother's victory garden back home.

When the waves crested, the men on the southern edge of this group could glimpse men in the water to the south, but did not know who they were.

Near Blum, Ensign Twible wanted to do something to help the men, so he ordered them to pray. Many did, while others learned the Lord's Prayer for the first time. Electrician's Mate Second Class William Drayton had heard the words many times, but it was in the extremity of this plight that he finally understood their meaning.

Blum, though, wasn't so sure about any kind of higher power. He'd heard men praying since the beginning of this calamity—the Lord's Prayer, asking God for rescue, and so forth. Now men were talking of heaven. The idea just didn't register with Blum. If God was going to rescue them, why had he put them in this mess in the first place? In the end, Blum believed the only one he could count on was himself. He had finalized his plan: He would convince the others to send him, along with a raft of supplies, to search for land.

In the same group, Harpo Celaya's three-day attempt to avoid eye contact with the sharks ended abruptly. One of the huge predators burst through the surface into the air, thrashed at the apex of its flight, and eyeballed Celaya on its way down like some kind of carnivorous acrobat. The sudden, aggressive appearance of the shark marked a turn in the behavior of the group. Moments earlier, a sailor had lunged for Harpo and demanded sexual congress in the lewdest terms. Then, men began attacking each other with fists and knives, fighting savagely, spilling fresh blood into the water. This attracted more sharks. Now forced to acknowledge their presence, Harpo looked down and saw them, a deadly horde twisting like a cyclone scant feet below.

Fred Markmann still clutched the little line he shared with Celaya, but he was fading fast. Harpo paddled over to Redmayne's raft and begged the lieutenant to let Markmann aboard.

"No!" Redmayne said, and pushed Harpo away. When Harpo made it back to Markmann, he heard someone speaking Spanish. He shook his head to clear his ears. But yes, it was definitely Spanish.

Harpo wrapped the rope tightly around Markmann's hand, grabbed his friend's shoulders, and looked him square in the eyes. "Stay here," he said. "I'll be right back."

Harpo swam toward the Spanish-speaking voice and when he reached the raft where it was coming from, joy and relief flooded his heart.

"Celaya!" Santos Pena cried. "¿*Cómo estás, mi amigo? ¡Pensé que estabas muerto!*"

Celaya reached up to hug his friend. "I thought you were dead, too!"

With Pena was their buddy Sal Maldonado, a baker. The three men laughed and poured out their stories, each flushed with elation. As it turned out, Pena had been in the Redmayne group the whole time. After fifteen or twenty minutes, Harpo told Pena about Markmann. "I have to get back," he said. "Stay safe."

Brimming with good news, Harpo paddled back to his regular spot by the raft, but Markmann was gone. Harpo spun in a desperate arc, scouring the sea with his eyes, scissoring his legs to get higher in the water. Finally, in the distance, he caught sight of Markmann looking back at him from atop a high swell. He was waving goodbye.

8

HAROLD SHEARER SAT STONE-STILL next to Kenley Lanter, his scorched arms still thrust ahead like the Mummy. Morgan saw that his eyes remained fixed in a distant stare and wished there was something he could do for him.

Lanter seemed to read his mind. "Hey, the bandages in the first-aid kit are sopping wet, but it might help Shearer's arms if we wrap them. What do you say?"

Morgan signaled his agreement by climbing carefully over to Lanter's raft to help. Lanter dug out the bandages, which turned out to be not only soaked, but also black, covered with fuel oil. When he unfurled them, however, they seemed clean inside. Morgan found some mineral oil in the first-aid kit and poured it over Shearer's burns. To apply the bandages Lanter and Morgan had to lift the sagging strips of burned flesh, cradle them in the bandages, then wrap the whole mess around Shearer's raw arms. Throughout this operation, Shearer seemed almost oblivious.

Several men in the group had waterproof watches. That meant they knew what time it was and could institute a formal chow call. They implemented Moran's rationing policy by carefully dividing a single can of Spam into nine or ten equal slices and then tossing the empty can over the side. Each man was issued a single slice, along with two hardtack wafers. This feast they washed down with three ounces of water.

During Wednesday's lunch, Morgan watched as Charlie the shark cruised closer, the way he always did at mealtime. The oily residue left in the empty Spam cans seemed to excite him. Charlie's approach appeared casual, almost friendly. When the shark came within a foot or so of the raft, Morgan slid from his seat on the edge back down into the relative safety of the latticework. Charlie closed the distance and, with one sweep of his tail, lifted his head completely out of the water and onto the edge of the raft— right where Morgan had been sitting. The shark paused for a moment, then eased himself backwards into the water and swam quietly away.

Morgan sat, stunned . . . until his mind drifted to other worries. They had now been in the water for three nights and three days. Doubt replaced his earlier confidence: What if rescue didn't come? How long could they hold out? He had tried the raft fishing kits, which were stocked with dried bacon and colored yarn for lures. Not even Charlie was interested. But a man on another raft was getting better results.

It was Jim Belcher, a radioman striker who'd grown up fishing in Alabama. Morgan looked over to see him spitting partially chewed malt tablets into the water. Belcher had been sleeping in his skivvies on the deck starboard of turret 2 when the first torpedo hit. It was the first time he'd ever slept outside his own quarters, and the second torpedo hit the bunk area where he had slept every night before. At eighteen, he was only a seaman, just a gopher really, but now he was in his element. He used a dip net from the emergency kit to catch a small and wriggling purple fish, which he then used to lure larger silverfish, scooping them from the sea with his net. Lanter used his knife to clean and filet the catch then diced it into small pieces, which he served on the edge of his raft.

Not every man accepted this offering. Morgan tried a few pieces, mostly out of prudence. Best to test the available groceries before the other food ran out. He was surprised to find the fish easy to chew and the taste not half bad. The day's catch boosted his confidence about their prospects for survival.

•   •   •

Buck Gibson wasn't nearly as hopeful. Having witnessed several gruesome shark attacks, the men on his floater net continued fighting each other for space. Some had begun to ignore the injured and badly burned, letting those near death float away toward the sharks.

Just out of sight, the men in Denny Price's group were terrified. Their waterlogged life jackets no longer held them up. Their faces were getting dangerously close to the surface, and they realized that the jackets that had saved their lives to this point might drown them in the end. They had knotted themselves into the vests to avoid accidentally slipping out of them, and now they were difficult to remove. With tender, peeling fingers, the men clawed at the knots. Some were unable to unravel the ties, their hands nearly useless after days of submersion. Moreover, small fish constantly nipped at their fingers and toes, and several men had exposed bone.

Mikolayek, who earlier had helped Cozell Smith bandage his shark-bitten hand, now helped Smith and others untie their vests and take them off. The men then held on to the vests, or sat on them, to keep their heads above water.

Also in this group, Verlin Fortin, who had quickly learned to swim, was struggling to stay afloat in his own vest when his best friend swam up and made an announcement. He was done with this nonsense and had decided to take a drink of ocean water. The next seconds seemed to last an age. Fortin watched his best friend dive below the surface to take his drink—but before he could, a shark plowed up and snatched him away. Fortin cried out, not in fear but with a voice that rose up clear and strong all the way from his belly: "Five days!" he vowed. "I'm going to make it five days, and if rescue doesn't come, I'll drink the water, too."

Lyle Umenhoffer floated in his life jacket near the Haynes group, but on a far fringe. His little group had dwindled to fifteen men. To discourage sharks—which seemed less inclined to tear into a mass of men—they tried to float in a tight knot with the weakest and most badly injured at the center. That put Umenhoffer on the outer ring, where he had an eye-level view of the man-eating horde. The small ones, three to four feet long, seemed the most aggressive and were tensed to hunt. These were opportunists, snatching and shredding any man who detached himself from the group.

The largest sharks stretched sixteen to twenty feet long. One moment, these behaved like gentle and curious giants, nosing up close to inspect the men with black, unblinking eyes. The next moment they attacked, their steel-trap jaws snuffing out a man's life before he could draw a breath to scream.

Umenhoffer had developed a technique for dealing with the sharks. He would wait until one of them cruised just alongside, then he would kick it, hard, in the flank, and the startled shark would dart away. He had administered at least ten such blows, and it worked every time.

Late Wednesday, Umenhoffer heard a voice from the main body of the Haynes group. "Hey! Does anybody over there know how to pray?" He looked over and saw a sailor waving his arms and hollering. He repeated the question: "Is there anybody over there who knows how to pray?"

Umenhoffer traded looks with the man next to him. Those who knew it had been praying the Lord's Prayer for three days. It had gotten so that Umenhoffer was pretty sure that any man who was an atheist when the ocean closed over *Indianapolis* wasn't one now.

"Well," he said, "I've prayed before in my life, but not really. I don't know what kind of prayer they want."

"Me, neither," the other man said.

"Well, let's swim over there and see what they want."

When they arrived, it became clear. Doc Haynes was struggling to hold Father Conway in his arms. The priest was delirious, blessing the doctor while hitting him on the chest and forehead. Unhinged by salt-water poisoning and exhaustion, Conway had been seen raving the sacrament of the last rites over men who weren't yet dying—a last, loving, irrational attempt to seal them against damnation. Haynes, to whom Conway had loaned money at Mare Island so that he could go home to his family, was the last in this chain.

Umenhoffer could see that the priest was close to death. It would not be long before his life was stolen away like those of so many other good men. The sailor who had called them over wanted to know if either of them knew how to pray Catholic last rites. Umenhoffer said he'd try. With his buddy now holding Conway, Umenhoffer was whispering a beginner's benediction when the priest jettisoned the sailor with a final thrust of his arms. Before anyone could stop him, Indy's beloved shepherd slipped beneath the surface and disappeared.

9

AUGUST 1, 1945, WEDNESDAY—AFTERNOON

Philippine Sea

BY WEDNESDAY AFTERNOON, the men had been floating in the ocean for sixty-four hours, but they remained just as oily and dirty as when their awful journey began. The castaway groups were spread out on the water, still connected by the long, winding streak of fuel oil. Those unlucky enough to be without rafts, like the Haynes group of swimmers, drifted steadily along, powered only by currents. These men formed the northeastern end of the line. Groups like Redmayne's, with a loosely assembled paddy of rafts and floater nets, made up the center. Groups composed mainly of rafts, like McVay's five-raft flotilla, were now about sixty miles from the sinking site and migrating southwest, pushed by the wind about thirty miles ahead of their slowest-moving shipmates.

In the Redmayne group, Donald Blum listened to men around him waxing ecstatic over gleaming rescue ships they saw on the horizon and the cool, fresh drinks available just below the surface. In his own impaired state, Blum had to think long and hard to separate these delusions from reality. There were only about forty left in his group—down from two hundred—and four rafts. Many had died while others simply drifted away as the shape and composition of all the survivor groups continued to shift with winds and currents.

Blum decided that most of the men in his group were out of their minds. Fights erupted, some of them fatal to one or more combatants.

Earlier that morning, word had filtered back that men on a raft some distance away were holding down another man and trying to have their way with him. It was not the only such incident. A man in charge of one of the rafts called over to Lieutenant Redmayne that things were getting pretty bad in his group. In a rare lucid moment, Redmayne sent Ensign Eames to deal with the problem. Returning shortly, Eames reported that some men were making advances on an injured radarman. Redmayne asked everyone around him to pray.

His plan now firm, Blum prepared to put it into action. He began questioning men around him, measuring their mental fitness, and soon had gathered a small group of reasonably sane sailors. Then Blum convinced Redmayne that he and his little crew needed to break off from the larger group and head toward Ulithi or Palau to get help. Of course, he would need a significant portion of the rations and supplies to succeed on such an important mission.

Twible overheard this conversation and thought the plan ill-advised. It didn't seem smart to spread the men out further. It was an especially bad idea, he thought, to give so small a group such a large share of the supplies. But Twible didn't want to overstep Redmayne's authority, even if the lieutenant was barely rational. That night, with his crew and provisions rounded up, Blum separated a raft from the group. With a paddle as a makeshift mast and a tarpaulin as a crude sail, the vessel got under way and sailed out of Twible's and Redmayne's sight.

Several wave crests and less than a mile away, Blum brought the voyage to a halt. His objective had never been to make land, but to separate himself from a group whose hallucinations had grown dangerous. Blum himself had been shoved underwater once and also received a sock on the jaw. Both incidents scared the hell out of him.

Blum and the men in his new group came to an agreement: If any of them began to hallucinate, they would be shoved off the raft. Seeing or talking of imagined things would not be tolerated. To Blum, this seemed only prudent. It was a raw case of survival of the fittest.

Buck Gibson noticed that the sharks preferred the dead. A battle of size raged around him. Small fish of all kinds would swarm a corpse until a shark swooped in, scattering the school-fish in colorful explosions as it tore the body in half. The schools then darted in again, coalescing around leftover pieces, nibbling the flesh from dismembered bones.

Before the Navy, Gibson had lived in the country his whole life. Those fish chewing on bodies reminded him of hogs eating ears of corn. But he had no reference point for what he saw next.

Insane with thirst, a man in his division used a knife to cut the throat of another sailor and drink his blood. Then Gibson saw another man cut someone's wrist.

"Look!" someone yelled. "He's eating his arm!"

As this cannibalism unfolded, heaving swells rose and fell, blocking Gibson's vision at intervals. Between them, in the troughs, he saw one man eating another, the glimpses between swells like a stop-frame film from hell.

Not far from Gibson, a well-respected coxswain took on a task that few others could stomach. Earlier that day, after watching delusional men commit unspeakable acts of violence, he made a pact with those around him. These men, who had served in his division and were his closest friends on the ship, agreed to end the life of any man who became dangerous to others. This agreement would include themselves, the ones who made the pact. Should they fall victim to hallucinations and become a threat, they, too, would be taken out. There were innocent men dying, victims of others who had lost their minds. They agreed something had to be done, or none of them would make it.

A few of the men carried five-inch utility knives. They agreed that head-locking a man and inserting the knife into the flesh under his armpit would be the most humane way to kill a friend.

After making the pact, this small group of men agonized as they played judge, jury, and executioner for shipmates who descended into delirium. When a man cried out "Dirty Jap!" or "Shark!" and launched himself at another, the respected coxswain or another man took his knife and performed the coup de grâce.

Prayers broke out in the group after these bloody judgments, among both the protected and the protectors. Silently, men were thankful their shipmates had been stopped from killing others. But each death tortured the man doing the killing, stealing a piece of his soul.

Leyte Gulf Naval Operations Base
Tacloban, Philippines

As dusk fell on the Philippines on August 1, Lieutenant Stuart Gibson noticed that *Indianapolis* had not arrived as scheduled. He had first noticed Indy's absence at sundown the day before. But he did not report this to his superior, Lieutenant Commander Jules Sancho, the port director, because he did not feel that the nonarrival of a combatant ship sailing independently was his concern. Of course, he had begun to have doubts about what was and wasn't his concern. Recently, his rating officer, Commander Forrest Tucker, had written him a scathing performance evaluation.

"This officer performs his duties willingly, but is indecisive, frequently becomes bewildered and 'rattle brained,'" Tucker wrote. "He has been a Port Director Watch Officer, a duty requiring qualifications which he does not possess to a degree necessary. It is believed he would do better in a position requiring less originality and responsibility."

That had been eight weeks ago. Gibson was so shocked by the evaluation that he wrote a rebuttal and sent it to the Bureau of Naval Personnel. He didn't know what had gotten into Tucker.

Working for the port director, Gibson's job was to track merchant shipping, not combatants, who were thought to be able to take care of themselves. So much so that CincPac Advance had in January issued Confidential Letter 10CL-45, which stated explicitly: "Arrival reports shall not be made for combatant ships."

The purpose of that directive was to reduce the flow of routine message traffic during a time period when preparations for the invasion of Japan were anything but routine. Officers were expected to be able to distinguish between what was and was not routine as a matter of common sense. Gibson thought about that with respect to *Indianapolis* and concluded this: If he wasn't supposed to report the arrival of combatant ships, he supposed that meant *non*arrivals, too.

10

AUGUST 1, 1945, WEDNESDAY AFTERNOON

AFTER THE HARRELL GROUP'S desperate prayers produced the seeming miracle of a makeshift raft, they found that the raft men were on a mission: They were going to swim to the Philippines. These men, none of whom Harrell recognized, were adamant that the Navy wasn't looking for *Indianapolis*. If anyone *was* looking for them, these sailors argued, they would already have been found.

Harrell didn't want to admit it, but he suspected they were right. The raft crew's logic was this: The closer they got to the Philippines, the better the chance they'd be rescued.

"Do any of you want to go with us?" one of the raft men said.

Harrell looked at their little vessel. It was really a pair of 40 mm ammo cans and four produce crates lashed together with strips of torn cloth—not at all seaworthy. But what was on top of the raft had already caught his attention: a pile of kapok life vests, some with wear still left in them. The raft crew had removed the vests from dead men and pulled them aboard to dry out. Harrell's kapok was so waterlogged that it was barely keeping his head out of the water. Designed to last forty-eight hours, it had lasted more than sixty and was almost spent. The fresher ones aboard the raft seemed another answer to prayer.

"I'm going to join them," Harrell told Spooner.

"If you go, Harrell, I'm going with you," Spooner said.

Harrell and Spooner did their part to get closer to the Philippines. Towing or pushing the makeshift raft, all the travelers kicked and paddled west, buoyed less by actual progress on their impossible quest than by the vigor men feel when they take hold of their own destinies.

During the journey, Harrell bumped into a crate of potatoes. The brown orbs oozed rot almost to their cores, but the men were able to peel away the putrid flesh to reveal edible centers. They ate their fill, and Harrell stuffed the leftovers in his pockets.

Night fell, blade-swift. The sun's residual warmth bled quickly away.

Later, near midnight, Harrell heard voices in the distance. The whole group commenced kicking, steering their raft toward these new sounds shooting out of the night. Soon, they met another knot of survivors, and Harrell's heart swelled when he saw someone he knew. It was Lieutenant McKissick. Harrell had gotten to know the jovial Texan while serving on the bridge as Captain McVay's orderly. Unlike some officers who lorded it over the enlisted, McKissick was helpful, making sure Harrell had all the tools he needed to do a standout job for the captain.

It didn't take long for Harrell to see that McKissick had taken charge of his own small group, and that the men had willingly let him. Harrell handed over some of the leftover potatoes. After a bit of reasoning with McKissick, the two groups joined forces in the westward press.

For Harrell, it seemed God was blessing his group's three-hour prayer vigil. That is, until he passed out in exhaustion and awoke to find himself floating in a debris field of human parts—and Spooner gone.

Harrell removed his life jacket, which was too waterlogged to hold his head out of the water, and now sat on it, riding low in the water amid carnage so putrid he could taste the rotting stench on the air. Somehow, he and Spooner had become separated in the dark. In fact, the entirety of the two recently linked survivor groups had vanished except for McKissick and a dead sailor who floated facedown in the chum.

Harrell berated himself. Why hadn't he held on to his friend tighter? They were Marines! he'd told Spooner. He remembered his promise: If Spooner agreed not to give up, they'd both make it through. Now he was gone. Harrell thought about trying to find him, but knew he was too weak to make a serious effort. And Spooner's eyes had puffed up into such blazing scarlet sores that he'd never be able to find Harrell.

Spooner's dead anyway, Harrell reasoned. And soon I will be, too.

Harrell rode his precarious perch up and down the swells with McKissick nearby. Blood swirled in the water and human debris stretched as far as they could see. The dead sailor tagged along, facedown and cruciform, brushing against them occasionally as if to remind Harrell and McKissick that he was part of their group, too.

• • •

Lieutenant Redmayne had begun hallucinating the previous night and had only worsened. He commenced taking small, furtive sips of ocean water, and shortly after, screaming maniacally. He tried several times to leap from his raft, often shouting his favorite refrain: "I have to get to the engine room!"

Finally, Ensign Twible grabbed him and stabbed him with a morphine syrette. Then, to ensure Redmayne's safety, Twible tied him to his own vest so he couldn't jump again. Now, on Thursday, the lieutenant remained unresponsive, and Twible believed himself to be the last officer still in control of his faculties. Still, he didn't have the energy to do much of anything. The best he could do was wait for help to come and try to keep Redmayne alive.

Richard Stephens and Florian Stamm had both served on Indy for more than a year. Now they watched as their once large and close-knit floater net group came undone. Around them men drowned or were eaten— or sometimes one and then the other. Stamm, whose mind was unraveling as quickly as the group, had his friend Louis DeBernardi to thank for his survival. DeBernardi, who had helped crane Major Furman's crate aboard at Mare Island, was also Stamm's supervisor. Now, any time Stamm started acting crazy, DeBernardi would slap the hell out of him, bringing him back to his senses. Stephens, on the other hand, turned inward in order to hang on. He thought of his family and their farm back in Alabama, and dreamed of toiling at the livestock chores he once loathed. It was a simple life, but he'd do anything to get back there.

On the periphery of the Haynes group, John Woolston saw glimpses of a swimmer approaching from the far distance, just the top of a head and some splashing every few seconds. As with all the other swimmers around him, his life jacket floated lower and lower, and he had trouble seeing more than a few feet in any direction. The troughs and crests of the passing swells opened and closed the sight line. In rare intervals, he could tell the swimmer was definitely approaching. Finally, he could make the man out. It was his roommate, Ensign Eames.

After breaking up the lewd behavior in the Redmayne group, Eames had had enough. He caught a break when a high swell lifted him and he saw another survivor group several hundred yards away. It turned out to be the Haynes group, and when Eames made it over, he related the debaucheries taking place in the group he'd left behind. Then Eames swam away. It would be the last time anyone reported seeing him.

That night, a gurgling scream ripped Woolston from a light doze. He jerked his head up to see two sailors tangled and fighting. "There's a Jap here, and he's trying to kill me!" one was shouting.

A bright moon frosted the sea, and Woolston could pick out the men as clearly as if someone had switched on a light. He yanked his legs horizontal and swam toward the men to break it up. But the violence spread like a virus to the next man and the next, and suddenly it was a melee, water churning, men shrieking and thrashing and growling curses. Woolston saw men clubbing each other, pushing other men's heads under the waves and holding them down.

Dr. Haynes also found himself in the middle of this all-out combat. Parke had been a restraining force, a governor on the idling engine of man's basest instincts. But his death had thrown the throttle wide open. Around Haynes, the free-for-all gained intensity, fueled by hallucinations and insanity. He untied himself from the hundred-foot line and pushed away from the man next to him. He urged others to do the same.

When Woolston reached the edge of the brawl, he broke two men apart. Wrapping his arms tight around the aggressor, Woolston yelled fiercely in his ear, "Hey, calm down! Calm down! He's your buddy. Look at him! He's not a Jap, he's your buddy!"

Gradually, the sailor went slack in his arms. Then Woolston heard another scream, swam toward it, and repeated the process. He could not say how long the chaos lasted or how many fights he broke up, but he knew he had not been able to reach them all in time. The storm died gradually, cycling down until an eerie quiet spread across the group. Men who had formerly hung together now backed away from each other, tense and wary.

Atrocities ravaged most of the groups that Wednesday night, a brief season of madness from which many would not emerge alive. In Cozell Smith's group, the water was littered with bodies, including those whose friends had executed them under the pact. Already nearing his own breaking point, the respected coxswain in the group, who perhaps shouldered the greatest burden and stepped up when others couldn't, found himself in an unbearable position. One of his closest friends, Curtis Pace, was losing his grip on reality. Pace was the man who had seen sharks early on but fibbed about it to a kid nearby because he didn't want to scare him. Now, the coxswain swam over and found Pace exhausted and rambling.

The coxswain treaded water and wrestled with himself. To this point, he had been the enforcer of the group, but Pace was a good friend. Was he really a danger to anyone?

"You have to do it, man," came a voice from his side. "It's just a matter of time before he goes out of his head completely and comes after one of us. We all agreed. Even him."

The coxswain locked eyes with another man who shared the burden of the pact, and saw a message there. He then whirled on the sailor who had urged him to take Pace out.

"I'll do you before I do him," the coxswain snapped. Then he drew back his arm and slapped Pace so hard that he came to his senses. To keep their friend out of danger, the three men linked arms for the rest of the night, praying that all this would end soon, and that at least they would die together.

11

AUGUST 2, 1945, THURSDAY—MORNING

Philippine Sea

WILBUR GWINN COULD HARDLY believe it: The new antenna was already broken. Flying over the Philippine Sea in his Lockheed PV-1 Ventura bomber, Wilbur "Chuck" Gwinn, a lieutenant junior grade, was already an hour behind schedule. It was the new aerial weight they were testing. Designed to extend the Ventura's trailing antenna wire, the weight was supposed to improve long-range radio communications. So far, though, it had been nothing but a pain in the neck.

Gwinn had taken off early that morning from his base in Peleliu, Palau, at the very bottom of the horseshoe archipelago that formed the Philippine Sea. Before commencing their regular sector search for enemy craft, Gwinn's crew had reeled out the antenna wire. The new weight lasted all of two minutes before snapping off, leaving the wire to whip and twirl in the wind. Gwinn had to make a one-eighty and return to base to get a new one installed. At 9:10 a.m., he rolled down the runway again, determined this time to wait until he was well under way in his sector to test the blasted thing again.

Now it was just after 11 a.m. Gwinn, call sign Gambler 17,* was 350 miles almost due north of Palau, cruising at three thousand feet, straight into the sun. Under the hard glare, the Philippine Sea appeared as smooth and reflective as a foil sheet. At this altitude, he could see twenty square miles at a glance. His crew reeled out the antenna wire again. So far, so good.

Spoking out from the southern rim of the Philippine Sea, the unofficial backwater of the war, these ho-hum sector searches clashed with Chuck Gwinn's passion for excitement. Born on a California ranch nestled between the Santa Cruz and Diablo Mountains, he had always been an up-and-comer. While still in his teens, he went to work for Douglas Aircraft, simultaneously studying at the University of Southern California. In 1943, at age twenty-one, he earned his Navy wings and became a test pilot. Now, at twenty-four, Gwinn was an aircraft commander in the patrol-bomber squadron VPB-152, his PV-1 Ventura the race car of the Pacific patrol fleet.

Gwinn's chief radioman, Bill Hartman, popped up on the intercom with bad news: The antenna weight had broken off again.

"Our long-range radio is now inoperative, sir," Hartman said, exasperated. Gwinn sighed. This time, the weight had lasted five minutes.

Gwinn turned the controls over to his copilot, Lieutenant Warren

---

* Aircraft call signs are pronounced one number at a time. Gambler 17 would be spoken "Gambler One Seven."

Colwell, and ducked out of the cockpit into the Ventura's belly. The burbling hum of her two-thousand-horsepower engines filled his ears. Behind the plane, the antenna wire whirled and snapped like a ringmaster's whip. If the boys didn't get it under control, it might lash the Ventura's tail and damage it.

Gwinn scowled. "Johnson, Hickman, reel that thing in."

Joe Johnson was Gwinn's plane captain, the enlisted man in charge of the aircraft's material condition. Herb Hickman was the aviation ordnanceman aboard. Gwinn watched as they retracted the wire, but he was not one to give up. There was a window in the Ventura's deck. Maybe Johnson and Hickman could pull the antenna wire through it, then attach it to something inside the fuselage to make it trail properly.

"Here, sir, try this," Johnson said.

It was a piece of rubber hose. Gwinn attached it to the end of the wire, and the crew paid it out again, into the Ventura's slipstream. Gwinn bent down and peered through the window to take a look—and almost as quickly leapt to his feet again and dashed for the cockpit.

"What's the matter?" Hickman shouted over the propeller noise.

Gwinn shouted back, "Look down and you'll see!"

Nearly four days in the water had sanded away the sharp edges of John Woolston's reason. The morning of the fourth day, he knew two things. One, he was extremely hungry, and two, there was food in the water. He could look down and see it: a swarm of sharks circling not far below, right there for the taking.

Woolston had seen other men hit by sharks, had heard their bubbling screams. He'd been wondering vaguely why he hadn't been attacked. Probably his gray uniform made him blend in with the water.

Woolston bobbed gently in his sodden life jacket. The sun baked his head, but the water was cool and incredibly clear. He gazed down through wavering shafts of sunlight and measured the predators with the practiced eye of an engineer. They were big—twelve feet, give or take—and also delicious-looking. A few bites out of one of those and he could last out here a lot longer. But, invisible as he was, how could he get the sharks to come?

As a kid, he'd fished a lot in the San Juan Islands. He recalled that he always caught more with live bait because the wriggling attracted the fish. What could he use?

His toes! Quickly, Woolston stripped off his socks. He saw that his feet, contrasted against his uniform, were parchment white and spotlit by the sun. Perfect! He thrust his toes toward the sea bottom and began wiggling them at the sharks.

Take the bait, was all he could think. *Take the bait!*

He felt ebullient, poised for a breakthrough, giddy with hope. Woolston kept this up for a few minutes, but the sharks persisted in ignoring his toes. Then, slowly, his feet got tired. Finally, he gave up and put his socks back on.

In Gwinn's Ventura, Herb Hickman pasted his face to the window and peered down at the ocean. It took about twenty seconds before waves, almost imperceptible at this altitude, lifted sunlight back to his eyes. Then he saw what had Gwinn excited. It was an oil slick. Probably a Japanese sub had crash-dived in an attempt to hide when her skipper picked up the Ventura. But the enemy skipper could not hide his telltale trail.

Hickman's heart rate picked up to a fast staccato. Their routine patrol had just turned into a search-and-destroy mission.

In the cockpit, Gwinn climbed into his seat and swung the plane around, tail to the sun. Now he could see more clearly. He put the Ventura into a diving turn and asked Colwell if the radar was showing anything.

"Nothing," Colwell shouted. "It's like glass down there—you can't see a thing."

Gwinn issued orders to his crew: "Arm depth charges. Open the bomb bay doors."

Hickman prepared the charges—there were six aboard, 325 pounds each—and Gwinn nosed the plane down until her belly skimmed the ocean at nine hundred feet, no higher than a brooding thundercloud in a close storm. Galvanized, he flew the oil slick as if it were a road map—a shining, black path that would lead him to the enemy.

•   •   •

Resignation had set in among McVay's group of castaways: They would likely die out here. The previous day, McVay told the men that they had now drifted out of the shipping lane, reducing even further their chances of being seen. He did not tell them he had ceased to hope. Whenever conversation lapsed in his ragged fleet, images of the disaster spun through his mind. He thought of the men he knew—Moore, Flynn, Janney, the dentist Earl Henry. Henry's perfect model of Indy, a gift for the new baby boy he would never meet, now lay on the sea bottom in the belly of the real ship.

McVay mourned his sailors. In his mind, he could see every single man. Silently, he called the roll, knowing they could never answer again.

Soon the men spotted a large cardboard box floating near the rafts. They paddled over and discovered that it was a case of Lucky Strike cigarettes. A couple of men pulled it from the sea, ripped it open, and passed a carton to each man. Yeoman Alton Havins searched through his and found a treasure—a single dry cigarette, about half of which could be smoked. Other men also found smokable butts. But how to light them with the matches ruined?

They came up with a plan: They'd rip the collar from a kapok jacket, toss it in the 40 mm ammo can they'd found, and fire a flare into the can to start a little fire. They pleaded with the captain to let them do it.

McVay thought it over. The flares had proven too low and dim to signal an aircraft. Why not let the boys enjoy what might be their last real pleasure in this life? He gave his consent and the sailors let out a little whoop.

As Thursday ticked by, Morgan gazed over at the next raft and watched Harold Shearer. He sat motionless, with a vacant stare, arms thrust out, bandages grimy with fuel oil. Morgan felt sorry for him. Shearer was already in tremendous pain, but then to keep holding his arms aloft that way? It must be sheer misery. Morgan didn't think he could hang on much longer. He also did not know that the next day, August 3, was Shearer's birthday. He would turn twenty-five—if he lived that long.

For his part, Morgan felt almost good. Given their predicament, a ride on a soggy raft was pretty cushy compared with the alternatives. He let his mind drift, daydreaming.

Would they survive? Yes, he thought. Though it seemed against reason, he had little doubt. Surely a rain squall would blow in at some point. They could catch water in the canvas and replenish the kegs. And with the fish they were catching, Morgan felt they could hold out for a long time. Add in a little luck, and they'd be all right.

"Hey, Morgan."

Lanter's voice roused him from his trance.

"Look," Lanter said, jerking his chin toward the horizon. "Do you see it?"

Morgan turned his eyes toward the line that divided sky and sea. He squinted, focused. Squinted and refocused. Then he saw it, a black speck moving back and forth, just above the horizon.

"I see it," he said. "Is it a bird?"

"I don't think so."

Morgan locked his gaze on the speck. It didn't act like a bird, but oscillated left then right again in straight lines. Still, it was awfully small.

"I guess it's a bird—" Morgan started to say when the speck flashed a glint of light.

"Hell, it's a *plane*!" Lanter cried.

In the rafts, all hands swiveled to look—all except for Shearer, who did not seem to care. The rest of the men set up a murmuring. Where most had sat mute and sphinxlike, now anticipation bubbled up. Nineteen pairs of eyes locked onto the mystery plane and did not let go.

12

LIEUTENANT GWINN FOLLOWED THE oil slick for about fifteen nautical miles before reaching its tip. He was about to order Hickman to release the first depth charges when he noticed a strange lump in the smooth, black surface. Then more anomalies, dozens more, resembling nothing so much as bumps on a cucumber. What in the world were they?

"Secure from bomb run," he ordered over the intercom. The Ventura zoomed low over water, and the bumps resolved into the last thing Gwinn expected to see—people!

He checked the time—11:18 a.m.—and pulled his yoke to bring the plane around for another pass. He and Colwell counted heads—ten, twenty, thirty.

Gwinn descended to three hundred feet to take a closer look. Now he could easily see oil-covered men waving, splashing, slapping the water. The crew in the belly of the plane stared down through the bomb bay doors. Hickman was so astonished he would later have no words to describe the feeling.

A thought arrowed through Gwinn's mind: ducks on the pond. Who were these people? During his preflight brief, he'd been told of ships passing along the route between Guam and Leyte. The oil slick was huge and seemed to indicate that a large vessel had been sunk. But there had been no mention of a sinking during his brief, and none since he'd been airborne. Were these Americans?

"Men in the water!" Gwinn shouted over the intercom. "Drop the life raft. Drop sonobuoys." He hoped someone in the water would know how to use the buoys to communicate.

Quickly, Gwinn and Colwell calculated a dead-reckoning position and passed it to Chief Hartman, who at 11:25 a.m. transmitted a coded dispatch to VPB-152, their patrol squadron at Palau, and to all ships in the area:

THIRTY SURVIVORS SIGHTED. SEND ASSISTANCE.

Gwinn continued his visual probe of the oil slick, flying low enough to see, but not so low as to rattle the men in the water with his propeller wash. Soon, he spotted another group of men, this one large, as many as 150. Incredible. The Ventura crew dropped another sonobuoy and took a LORAN fix—or Long Range Navigation position. At 12:45 p.m., Gwinn had Chief Hartman send another coded message: Gambler 17's position—11-54N, 133-47E—along with the new count of survivors and a request for rescue ships.

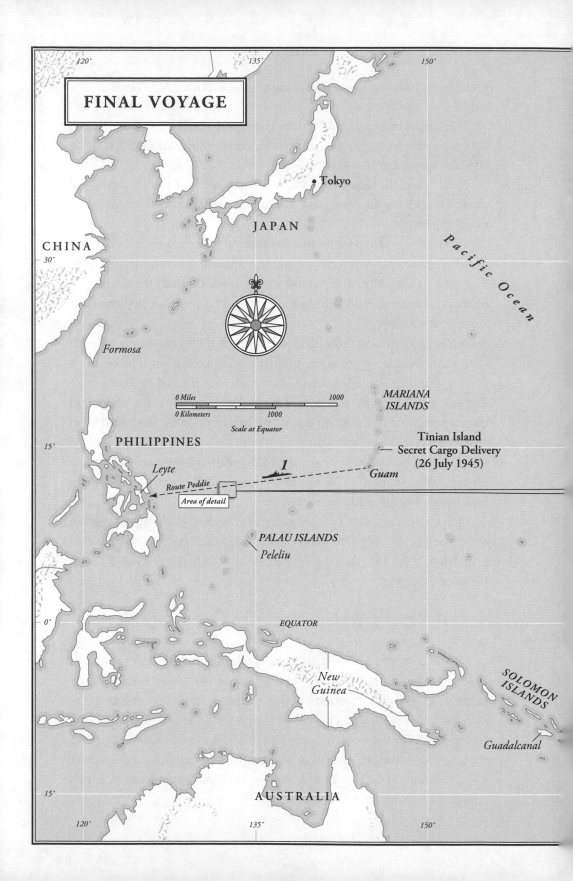

FINAL VOYAGE

Tokyo

JAPAN

CHINA

Pacific Ocean

Formosa

MARIANA
ISLANDS

PHILIPPINES

Tinian Island
Secret Cargo Delivery
(26 July 1945)

Leyte

1

Route Peddie
Area of detail

Guam

0 Miles 1000
0 Kilometers 1000
Scale at Equator

PALAU ISLANDS
Peleliu

EQUATOR

SOLOMON
ISLANDS

New
Guinea

Guadalcanal

AUSTRALIA

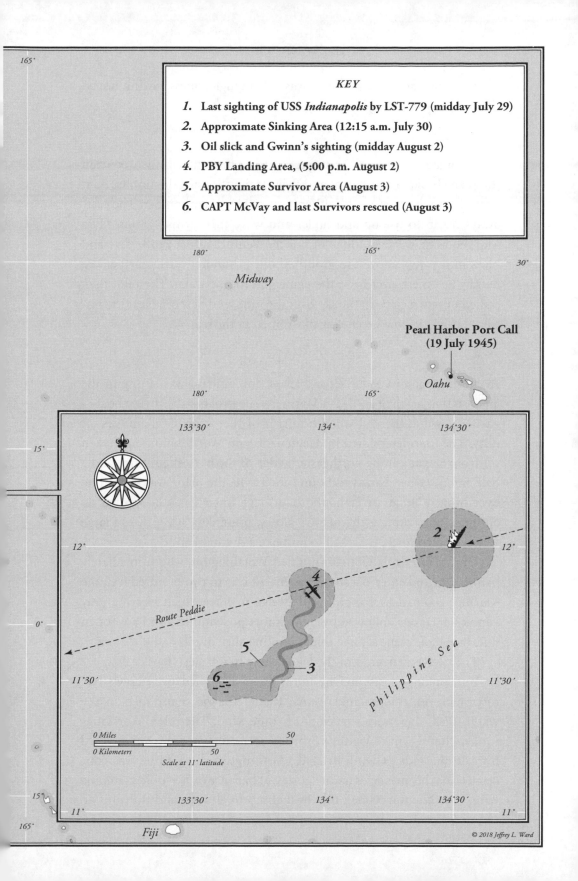

KEY

1. Last sighting of USS *Indianapolis* by LST-779 (midday July 29)
2. Approximate Sinking Area (12:15 a.m. July 30)
3. Oil slick and Gwinn's sighting (midday August 2)
4. PBY Landing Area, (5:00 p.m. August 2)
5. Approximate Survivor Area (August 3)
6. CAPT McVay and last Survivors rescued (August 3)

165°

180°   165°   30°

Midway

**Pearl Harbor Port Call
(19 July 1945)**

Oahu

133°30′   134°   134°30′

15°

12°   2   12°

4

Route Peddie

0°

5   3

Philippine Sea

11°30′   11°30′   6

0 Miles   50
0 Kilometers   50
Scale at 11° latitude

15°

165°   133°30′   134°   134°30′

11°   11°

Fiji

© 2018 Jeffrey L. Ward

The long-range antenna wire was still a tangled mess. Gwinn hoped the transmission was going out.

The Morgan group had barely begun using their signal mirrors when the plane broke off its patrol and flew straight toward the flotilla. As it neared, it took shape as a PV-1 Ventura—a U.S. Navy bomber! The castaways began to whoop and holler and wave their arms. Elation filled Morgan as he watched the pilot put the Ventura into a gentle dive and buzz in low just above the group. About a hundred yards farther on, he saw an object eject from the plane and hit the water. The pilot then pulled up, cut a circle in the sky over the rafts, and flew off. Near the flotilla, a bright yellow-green ring blossomed in the sea.

Aviation Machinist Mate Second Class Jim Graham was sitting in the after-station hatch of a PBM-5 Mariner—a patrol bomber flying boat—gazing down at the vast smooth mirror of the ocean. Graham was off duty. The Mariner, piloted by Lieutenant Sam Worthington, had taken off from Saipan (at the northeastern edge of the horseshoe) three and a half hours earlier. Now westbound for Leyte, the plane was skimming over broken clouds at eight thousand feet when Graham spotted an anomaly. Interrupting the ocean's glossy, boundless sweep was a large yellow-green blotch. It looked to him like a dye marker.

On the intercom, Graham notified Worthington, who immediately banked left and entered a steep descent. At one to two hundred feet, the Mariner zoomed over a group of twelve to fifteen men wearing gray kapok life jackets, followed by more knots of swimmers and a wooden raft, the whole scene set in a thick, winding slick of oil.

The twelve-man crew of the plane came to full alert: Japs!

But looking closer, maybe not. Was it a ditched B-29 crew? No: too much oil. Had a tanker sunk, then? No: too many men in the water. Well, they were survivors of some kind. The pilot, Worthington, spotted Gwinn's Ventura orbiting some distance away and raised him on the radio. Gwinn briefed Worthington and said he was concerned that his messages hadn't gone out because of his fouled antenna wire. Worthington replied that he'd climb to altitude and transmit an all-points message. His crew kicked out yellow life rafts and jackets, water breakers, and a "Gibson Girl," a portable emergency radio. Then as Worthington climbed, his radioman hopped to and began a continuous transmission to Leyte.

Seaman Harold Bray, the sailor who hadn't believed the quartermaster, Frenchy, when he said Indy would sink, was floating on the fringes of the Gibson floater net group when he saw objects falling from Gwinn's Ventura. One of them splashed down nearby and Bray swam to it, charged with hope. It was a sonobuoy, but having been at sea for all of two weeks, he had never seen one before.

Bray shook it, listening for the slosh of drinking water. Hearing none, he inspected it more closely. Was it some new kind of lifesaving gear? Did it contain food? Finally, he decided he didn't know what to do with the damned thing and cast it away. If it wasn't water, food, or a raft, it was useless.

Bray stared up again at the plane in the sky. It seemed to be flying away. *Don't leave us!* he screamed in his mind, or maybe even out loud.

Adrenaline burst forth in Ed Harrell's body as if from a geyser.

"I hear a plane!" he cried, heart pounding.

"So do I!" McKissick yelled.

Chuck Gwinn's Ventura had finally reached the part of the twenty-five-mile oil slick where McKissick and Harrell floated in the muck. Harrell began to wave his arms, to cry, to splash, to pray. McKissick joined in as thoughts sped through Harrell's mind, a chorus of hope. Just as it seemed the aircraft would pass over their heads and fly on, the pilot made a dive.

The plane was a PV-1 Ventura, and it flew low over the two screaming men, who were now triumphant. They'd been seen!

The Ventura circled back in a low oval and shoved out a life raft. It tumbled from the sky and splashed down about a hundred yards from McKissick. Before flying off, the pilot ratified their joy by rocking his wings, a universal aviation sign used to acknowledge a friendly.

McKissick made his way to the raft, followed by Harrell, who paused on the way to say a farewell benediction over the dead sailor who'd been traveling with them.

Though planes had flown over so high and so often than the men in his group had begun to ignore them, when Harpo Celaya saw the Ventura, he knew they'd been saved. Joy overtook him, and a surge of relief flushed tears from his eyes. He laughed and screamed. He thought of his Arizona home, his mother and father, Dolores. But as the Ventura flew off, he realized he had to be careful. He hadn't been rescued yet, and he was damned if he was going to get this close, then drown like Markmann—or become lunch for a shark.

13

AUGUST 2, 1945, THURSDAY—DAY

Peleliu Airfield, Palau

AT PELELIU, LIEUTENANT COMMANDER George Atteberry, commanding officer of the patrol bomber squadron VPB-152, intercepted a transmission from one of his pilots flying up around Route Peddie. Knowing how long the coderoom jockeys took to decrypt things, Atteberry decoded it himself, saving hours. The message was garbled, something about men in the water. Probably some flyers. He drove over to another outfit, VPB-23, a squadron of Catalina flying boats. Atteberry hunted down the duty pilot, Lieutenant Adrian Marks.

Atteberry knew Gwinn could only circle the rescue area to the limit of his fuel capacity. It wouldn't be a good idea for him to return to Peleliu before another plane arrived on-scene to relieve him. Without eyes on the survivors at all times, they might never be found again. Marks would have to leave immediately, Atteberry said.

Marks and his crew climbed into his PBY-5A Catalina flying boat, a thick-bodied seaplane with a distinctive "parasol" wing. Unlike planes designed with two wings, one attached to each side of the fuselage, a parasol wing is a single, wide airfoil held above the fuselage by struts—like a biplane, but without the lower wing. The Catalina's large twin propellers were mounted side by side near the center of the wing just aft of, and above, the cockpit. This high placement kept the engines clear of ocean spray. The Catalina was a patrol plane, but when deployed for rescue—one of its primary missions—it was known as a "Dumbo."

On the runway, Marks assumed the call sign Playmate 2, turned up his engines, and purred off to the north. The time was 12:42 p.m. About a minute later, Atteberry took off from Peleliu in a Ventura, call sign Gambler Leader.

From the word Marks received from Atteberry, another Ventura was circling a life raft up near Route Peddie. Marks assumed a plane had ditched. Probably one of the carrier boys, needing both assistance and consolation. Marks and his copilot, Irving Lefkowitz, were to fly to the scene and relieve the Ventura on station. Marks half-expected to drop some equipment, spend half a day circling a lone survivor, then vector in a ship to scoop him out of the drink. Even that would be a hell of a lot more interesting than cooling his heels on the island. For three days, he'd been listening to Glenn Miller records and flipping through novels while his last mission gnawed at his brain. On July 30, he and his crew had flown out over the ocean in search of a downed aircrew, but came up empty. Failure was an unusual experience for Marks, and it left a sense of disquiet in his chest.

By age twenty-four, he had graduated from Northwestern University and Indiana University Law School, passed the bar, married the daughter of the chief justice of the Indiana Supreme Court, and accepted a commission as an ensign in the naval reserve. Stationed at Pearl Harbor when the Japanese attacked on December 7, 1941, Marks served on a ship that fought back. The following year, he earned his pilot wings, and now, at twenty-eight, had logged untold hours in the Dumbo, most of them rescuing less fortunate pilots who had lost their airplanes to the sea.

Though Atteberry launched after Marks, his plane was faster and he was already ahead. Marks was only eighty miles north of Palau, north-bound in trail of Atteberry, when he spotted a destroyer escort steaming south below him. At altitude, the ship and its wake appeared as a thin, straight mark in the sea, as if an invisible child were tracing a white line with a stick. When Marks was overhead, the ship hailed him on the radio, just an acknowledgment of friendly forces, utterly routine. The ship turned out to be USS *Cecil J. Doyle*, and the skipper an acquaintance of his, Lieutenant Commander W. Graham Claytor, a fellow lawyer from Indianapolis. *Doyle* was en route to Kossol Passage, at the northern end of the Palau chain, after an unsuccessful joint sea/air submarine hunt. Marks told him about the men in the water up near Route Peddie.

"You're probably going to get rerouted up there," Marks said, his voice scratching over the frequency.

Claytor thought Marks was probably right. Whoever was in the water, somebody had to fish them out. It wouldn't be Marks's Dumbo, since open-sea landings were both dangerous and forbidden. And it could take hours for new routing orders to crawl through clogged official channels. Claytor thought it over. He didn't have orders, but . . . ?

On *Doyle*'s bridge, Claytor told his officer of the deck to reverse course and increase speed to twenty-two knots. He'd worry about the paperwork later.

Sam Worthington's Mariner orbited over the rescue scene for two hours and forty minutes, then pushed for Leyte. Thirty minutes later, the crew sighted a lone swimmer in his skivvies swimming west. But there was nothing they could do because they had already pushed out all their life-saving equipment.

Graham, the crewman who first spotted the dye marker, was heartsick. Here was this brave guy trying to swim for it, and they had nothing to offer him. Worthington's radioman transmitted the position and remained over the swimmer until Worthington knew Leyte had a navigational fix. Then, with fuel running low, he had no choice but to press for Leyte. With a prayer and a salute, the Mariner crew flew on. The swimmer never even looked up.

• • •

At eight in the morning on Thursday, August 2, the surface control officer at Philippine Sea Frontier—a Lieutenant Green—looked over his
Expected Arrivals. *Indianapolis* appeared on the list, but had not arrived.
If she hadn't pulled in by now, she wasn't going to, Green thought. He
dashed off a memo to the plotting section: Could he remove *Indianapolis*
from the board? The reply came five hours later: no. There were reports
coming in. Men in the water.

A rising dread had begun percolating at commands around the
Philippine Sea. At Leyte, the surface operations officer, Captain Alfred
Granum, learned that Indy should have arrived three days ago and had
not. From Peleliu and the aircraft on-scene, Frontier commander Norman Gillette learned of men in the water. He, too, discovered that *Indianapolis* was missing. Gillette sent a message to Guam:

INDIANAPOLIS HAS NOT ARRIVED LEYTE X ADVISE

Though brief, his dispatch vibrated with dawning panic. It sped to
all stars around the Pacific: Admirals Nimitz, Murray, McCormick, and
Oldendorf; to Commodore Carter at Guam; and to *Indianapolis* herself.
Gillette may have been hoping that Lieutenant Waldron's Guam departure message had been a mistake, that the great ship had actually never
left port.

But no. Guam replied to Gillette that Indy had indeed departed
Guam for Leyte—nearly a week ago. Perhaps, then, *Indianapolis* had
reported to McCormick for training? Gillette sent the admiral a plainly
worded query:

HAS INDIANAPOLIS REPORTED TO YOU

McCormick's reply was equally plain:

NEGATIVE.

14

AUGUST 2, 1945, THURSDAY—DAY

Philippine Sea

MARKS AND LEFKOWITZ WERE still flying north over the open sea in the Dumbo that Atteberry had dispatched from Peleliu. At 2:10 p.m., they received a second message from the Ventura that was already flying up around Route Peddie: There were 150 survivors in the water.

How many? Marks thought.

That couldn't be. There had been no word of a sinking, and if there really were that many ducks on the pond, the Navy would certainly know about it. This message was probably just as garbled as the first one. Still, he passed the information to Claytor on *Doyle* and increased his airspeed.

Aboard *Doyle*, Claytor heard the pilots' chatter. One hundred fifty men in the water? He called the engine room. "What can you do to give me more speed?"

The ship was already steaming at flank speed and running hot. Down in the fireroom, Coxswain Charles Doyle was wetting down shafts with a fire hose to keep from burning up a bearing. He heard the chief engineer tell Claytor that he could coax a couple of more knots if he overrode—or "gagged"—the safety relief valves. The safeties were designed to relieve pressure so that the boilers didn't explode. Gagging them was dangerous, and only the captain could order it done.

In the fireroom, the chief engineer hung up with Claytor and turned to Doyle. "Gag the safeties," he said.

On the bridge, Claytor made radio contact with Atteberry at 2:35 p.m., and *Doyle* assumed the call sign Birddog One. A half hour later, Marks began picking up signals from Atteberry's plane, and just before four in the afternoon, had Atteberry's Ventura in sight. But he was not prepared for what he saw next—men. Not dozens of them—scores. Maybe hundreds.

Marks raised Atteberry on the radio: "Gambler Leader, Playmate 2."

"Playmate 2, Gambler Leader, go ahead."

"I am on station and have the survivors in sight."

"Roger, Playmate 2. There are a lot of them scattered over a wide area. Do not drop any equipment yet. I want to show you the area first, then you can decide how to deploy your rescue gear."

Atteberry was concerned that Marks might drop all his gear to the first group in the water, not realizing there were more. Many, many more. Flying in trail of Atteberry, Marks took in the footprint formed by the survivor groups, which now spread over twenty-five square miles.

Skimming over the whitecaps at a recon altitude of just a couple of hundred feet, Marks, Lefkowitz, and their navigator, Ensign Morgan Hensley, saw a dot pattern of oil-covered men. Most were clustered together in groups of ten or more. Some clung to life rafts, others, in sodden vests, only to each other. Many floated alone. Groups composed primarily of rafts now formed the leading edge of a motley survivor convoy that continued its west-southwest drift. Though Marks didn't know it, these groups had now blown eighteen to twenty miles south of Route Peddie, and nearly eighty miles from the sinking site. At the opposite end of the oily residue, thirty to forty miles northeast, the swimmers and those less exposed to the wind formed the tail end of the troupe. These men remained nearly on Route Peddie, but about forty to fifty miles from where they began their slow journey.

Marks was shocked at the sheer scope of the disaster unfurling before him. He started to encode a message, then stopped. There were rules about information security, but he decided that in this case rules should be broken. He sent a message in plain English:

BETWEEN ONE HUNDRED AND TWO HUNDRED
SURVIVORS AT POSITION REPORTED. NEED ALL
SURVIVAL EQUIPMENT WHILE DAYLIGHT HOLDS.
MANY SURVIVORS WITHOUT RAFTS.

Marks gave the message the highest-possible priority—the same category as an enemy contact report. His radioman sent the message in the clear and reported an immediate "Roger" from Peleliu. What the radioman couldn't know was that the officer who received the message at Peleliu did nothing. He did not pass the message to Marks's skipper, or to anyone else. He simply sat on it.

Marks tipped the Dumbo's big wing port and starboard, cutting a trail behind Atteberry. Surveying the scene, he marveled. Out here in the open sea, the odds that these men would be spotted were so minute as to be unbelievable. What were the chances that the Ventura would fly directly over the survivors? From a normal sector-search altitude, the head of a man floating in the water would be less than a speck, as undetectable as the diameter of the cross-section of a human hair seen endwise from across a room. In a word, invisible.

While conducting a sector search, a pilot could take in twenty square miles at a glance—a box covering four hundred miles. Under these conditions, even spotting the oil slick had been miraculous. The sea that day was preternaturally smooth—the term "like glass" was not hyperbole. It would take sunlight hitting the oil exactly right at the exact moment the crew had been looking at that exact spot for them to distinguish the black slick from the hundreds of miles of dark blue ocean that surrounded it.

Marks considered the odds that these men had been spotted one in a billion.

Three hundred miles west, the men of the high-speed transport ship USS *Bassett* had settled in for a quiet watch, the topside crew monitoring the race between the ship's bow wave and a spirited school of dolphins. Then Radioman Third Class James Bargsley received a message from the Philippine Sea Frontier, marked URGENT. There were 150 men in the water, and *Bassett* was to proceed at best speed to assist.

The skipper, Lieutenant Commander Harold J. Theriault,* ordered, "All ahead, flank speed," and his crew snapped into action. The medical department came to full alert. In the galley, mess cooks began prepping light foods and fruit juices. The ship carried a complement of smaller boats called LCVPs, which stood for Landing Craft, Vehicle, Personnel,

---

* Pronounced "terry-oh."

and were used mainly in amphibious operations to beach troops and equipment. Now, though, their shallow drafts and flat, bargelike decks would prove perfect for hauling near-dead men from the sea.

Intrigue stirred *Bassett*'s crew: survivors in the water from a mystery ship? Which ship could it be?

Commands ashore were beginning to ask the same question. In short order, *Bassett*'s radiomen received a second message: The first vessel on-scene was to advise Peleliu and all addressees what ship the survivors were from and the cause of the sinking.

After leading Adrian Marks on an aerial tour over the survivors, Atteberry signaled the Dumbo's reconnaissance complete. Marks knew that no ship would arrive in the area until midnight. He decided to drop his gear, focusing on the survivors who had only life jackets. At 4:05 p.m., the crew opened a hatch and began shoving out life rafts, water casks, and other supplies. Rescue was their primary mission, and they were accustomed to the procedure.

Then came a moment when Marks knew normal procedures would not be enough. His crew saw a man floating alone. Moments later, the man was gone, taken by a shark.

Sunblind and exhausted, Seaman First Class Dick Thelen heard Marks's plane and saw a large rectangular shadow tumble from its belly.

A raft! And only about fifty yards away!

Thelen, his friend Robert Terry, and two more buddies from the Haynes group agreed to swim for it. After floating without food or water for more than a hundred hours, each stroke of Thelen's arms felt like flopping a cast-iron post into the water, each kick as if his legs were made of stone. Out front, he made it to the raft, where some other men had already clambered aboard.

Thelen looked back for his friends and was surprised to see one of them still some distance away, clutching his chest, his face a mask of agony. Then, in a blink, he disappeared. Thelen clutched the edge of the raft, shocked. Was it a heart attack? He glanced around wildly, looking for the other men. He saw no one but Terry, still swimming, slowly closing the distance.

Terry's arms smacked weakly against the swells like toy paddles. He was struggling to stay afloat. Thelen wanted to go back and help, but he was so spent he feared he would drown. But that was okay because Terry was only ten feet away now.

"Come on! Come on!" Thelen yelled, stretching out his arm toward his friend. "You're gonna make it!"

The encouragement was no sooner out of Thelen's mouth than his insides seized. A shark reared out of the water and snatched Terry from sight.

Thelen clung to the raft, shaking all the way down to his feet. Certain he would be next, he waited to be eaten. But minutes piled up one upon the other, and death did not come for him.

Why them and not me? he asked himself in anguish.

The sun was falling. The men already on the raft were too weak to pull Thelen up, and he was too weak to pull himself aboard. He hung on to the raft's edge and berated himself for agreeing to swim for it. Maybe if they'd all stayed with their group, his friends would still be alive.

As the afternoon wore on, more planes arrived from Peleliu, dropping rafts and survival gear, which fell from the sky like a life-giving rain. With the help of his friend Clarence Hupka, Cozell Smith made it to a raft despite his shark-shredded hand. On the edges of Smith's group, Cleatus Lebow and Clarence Hershberger also watched objects tumble from the sky, including big tins of water. Many of these burst on impact, spilling their pure contents into the poison sea. Lebow's throat burned with thirst and watching the tins break drove him over the edge.

He let go of the floater net and swam away. He had made it some distance when Hershberger caught up to him and hauled him back to the net. Lebow waited awhile then struck out again. Hershberger splashed after him and pulled him back a second time. If Lebow broke away again, Hershberger said, he'd have to let him go because he wouldn't have the strength to go after him. "What are you doing, anyway?"

Lebow's eyes lit up. Among all that gear dropping from the plane, he'd seen a box of B-29 bomber parts, Lebow said. "We can put an airplane together and fly home!"

Hershberger peered into his friend's overbright eyes and considered this for a moment. "Cleatus, it's getting dark," he finally said. "Let's wait until morning and do it then."

"Okay," Lebow said simply. In the tilted logic of his delirium, the idea was just rational enough to save his life.

15

ABOARD HIS DUMBO, MARKS made a rebel decision. He keyed his mic and raised Atteberry.

"Gambler Leader, Playmate 2."

"Playmate 2, go ahead."

"I'm going to attempt an open-sea landing."

"Roger that."

Atteberry knew the rules against such an operation. An open-sea landing was little more than a controlled crash into the backside of a wave. A Dumbo was designed with sufficient buoyancy to remain on the surface, but it had no pontoons or floats on which to land. Instead, the plane landed in the water on its belly. This model weighed fifteen tons, and initial contact with the water was always violent, usually popping rivets, or worse, opening seams in the hull. At stall speed and with near-zero lift, the pilot had little control of the aircraft after first impact. Sometimes it took the strength of both pilots to hold the cockpit control column fully back in order to keep the plane from pitching over nose first and diving toward the bottom.

But like Marks's crew, Atteberry had seen the plight of the men in the water. He also knew that no ships would arrive until at least midnight. He could see that there were many survivors who wouldn't last that long.

Atteberry agreed to orbit above Marks and help him find a spot to land where his crew could help the most survivors.

Circling in the Dumbo, Marks and Lefkowitz assessed the conditions: The wind was due north, with swells a dozen feet high. Marks transmitted the news to Peleliu:

> WILL ATTEMPT OPEN-SEA LANDING. P.V. CIRCLING THE
> AREA.

This time, the message arrowed straight to his squadron skipper, who, without benefit of Marks's previous message, blustered and raved, wanting to know what sort of fool stunt Marks thought he was up to. Everyone in the Dumbo squadrons viewed an attempt to land on the open sea as an event that merited equal measures of cursing and prayer. The word "attempt," though, was to Adrian Marks an almost foreign concept. There was little he had tried in life that he had not achieved. It did not matter to him that open-sea landings were against regulations, nor that he had never even practiced one. Men in the water were dying, and he was in a position to save them. He dared the ocean to defy him.

In the belly of the Dumbo, Marks's crew strapped themselves in tight. This was going to be dicey.

Just after 5 p.m., against a lowering sun, Marks drew on everything he knew and every ounce of courage he had. He executed a power stall into the wind and slammed his airplane belly first into the back of a huge swell. The Dumbo's hull screeched in fury, emitting all the sounds of an accident. The crew pitched forward, safety harnesses crushing their chests. The ocean rejected the plane, batting it fifteen feet back into the air. Marks and Lefkowitz rocked aft, heads whiplashed against their seatbacks. The propellers roared in protest, and for a moment the plane hung suspended over the whitecaps.

Fighting physics, Marks gripped the control column with both hands. The Dumbo's belly smashed into the wave and it bounced again—but not as high this time. Marks wrestled the controls, willing the plane to obey. Finally, the Dumbo breached the swell's shining skin. Blue water sprayed up over the cockpit windshield and slid away again as the sea gave way grudgingly, as though surrendering to an invasion.

Playmate 2 settled into the ocean, rivets popping from her hull. In the rear of the plane, the crew looked at each other and exhaled. They were still alive.

The sun dipped lower, painting the water with fire. No one wasted time. Marks's navigator, Ensign Hensley, assessed the damage. Seawater squirted into the cabin through open seams and showered down through cracks in the overhead hatches. Inverted showers spouted up through the rivet holes and seams below. Hensley worked with the plane captain to stuff pencils and cotton into the voids. Water streamed into the radio compartment at a slow but steady rate. They couldn't stop the leak, so Hensley set up a bailing rotation that would ultimately produce about a dozen buckets per hour.

Lefkowitz went aft to organize the rescue party while Marks remained in the cockpit, the Dumbo undulating underneath him like a pelican riding swells. Over the radio, he and Atteberry talked out a plan. They agreed that the men in groups, even those with only life jackets, stood a better chance of surviving the night than those who were floating alone. They decided that Marks should water-taxi near the lone swimmers and pull them aboard. They did not know that every man in the water had been there for more than four days.

Since Marks could not see over the twelve-foot swells, Atteberry circled overhead to guide him. The operation was halting at first. Hensley stood in the open hatch on the starboard side of the plane, with the boarding ladder lowered. When Marks taxied near a survivor, Hensley threw out a life ring with a line attached to it. But the men in the water were so weak that few could hold on to the ring as the taxiing plane dragged it by. When they did manage to hold on, they could not climb the ladder by themselves.

Hensley was not a big man, but he had wrestled in college and rippled with muscle. He hoisted each man aboard using brute strength. The first man he pulled aboard was James Smith, a seaman second who had been serving his time in the brig—with five days' bread and water—up until a few short hours before the ship sank. Hungry, tired, and sick of what he'd witnessed over the past four and a half days, he pushed his way toward the plane and made sure Marks didn't pass him by. But once aboard, the crew didn't have time to find out who he was or what ship had sunk before Smith passed out.

•   •   •

John Woolston saw the plane in the water, shed his leaden life jacket, stretched out his arms, and swam toward his future. When the plane was just a few yards away, he saw a life ring sail from an open door and hit the water nearby. Woolston reached out to grab it, but missed and the ring floated away. He had overestimated his strength. Now, without the jacket, he was barely staying afloat. If he couldn't make the plane, he was finished. Weakly, Woolston treaded water, and the next thing he knew, he was airborne. Hensley had reached down from the open hatch, scooped Woolston from the drink, and pitched him over his head into the cargo bay like a sack of flour.

As the rescue proceeded, the airmen were shocked at the condition of the survivors: They were emaciated and blistered, broken-limbed and burned to the bone, some missing whole sections of skin. Many screamed in agony when Hensley grabbed their arms to haul them aboard. Marks wagered that many of them would not have survived another night.

He was astonished when some of the survivors said they were from USS *Indianapolis*, and that they'd been sunk just after midnight on July 30. This was August 2. How was it possible that no one had known *Indianapolis* was missing?

Marks was still in contact with *Doyle*, but he didn't dare blurt out over the radio that *Indianapolis* had been sunk. He also did not have time to code a message about the survivors' identity. There were still too many men in the water, and too many sharks. Instead, he urged Claytor on the radio to make his best possible speed.

"There may be enemy submarines in the area," Marks warned. "Use caution."

Marks kept up his taxi. In an effort to save the singles, he passed knots of astonishingly skeletal men who called out, "Water!" and "Save us!" Then, when Marks taxied past, their cries changed to "Wait!" and "Don't go!"

Their angry, desperate pleas tore at his mind. Who was he to pick and choose lives to save? Who was he to play God?

One of the men yelling was Lyle Umenhoffer. Wearing a pneumatic life belt himself, he had a man on each side of him and was holding their heads out of the water so that their sodden vests didn't pull them under.

When he saw the big Dumbo heading toward his little group, Umenhoffer's heart soared—and then the plane taxied right by.

"Hey!" he shouted. "How about us?"

Hensley stood in the open hatch on the starboard side of the plane and yelled in reply, "We'll be back to get you!"

At that, Umenhoffer felt the fight return to his limbs. They'd been identified! They were going to be saved. There was no way he would let go of his buddies now.

Late in the afternoon, the McVay group spotted yet another plane. But this one, well to the south, was behaving differently, circling. Then other planes joined in. For the next few hours, the McVay group watched the aircraft orbit.

"There must be other survivors," someone said.

Apparently it was just their small group that had drifted this far north, McVay said. What he did not say was that this meant they were in a terrible fix. The circling plane had moved steadily farther south. If it kept moving south and his group kept moving north, it looked as though they would not be found.

Charles McKissick swam to the Dumbo and climbed in, then directed Marks back to Harrell. The Dumbo's massive wing towered over the Marine like a great, sheltering roof, and its throaty engines blocked all other sound. Hensley pulled Harrell aboard and the aircrew stacked him against a bulkhead where other survivors were wedged in like cordwood.

Harrell stared at the other men, oil-drenched and skeletal, until a series of metallic bangs caught his attention. It was a survivor whacking a can of green beans on a deck bolt to try to open it. The man's pounding appeared all the more desperate because his eyes were a pair of bulging red sores.

Harrell's heart flipped in his chest. It was Spooner!

Spooner managed to punch a hole in the can, and began sipping from it.

"Hey, Marine," Harrell said. "How about sharing some of that with me?"

"Leave me alone!"

"Spooner, it's me! Harrell!"

Beneath his tortured eyes, Spooner's face split in a grin, and he nearly leapt into Harrell's lap. Overjoyed, Harrell thanked God for letting him keep his promise to his brother Marine. Then the two men shared the best drink either one of them would ever have: warm green bean juice from a can.

As darkness descended on *Doyle*, Graham Claytor laid on speed. Marks had been right. Claytor did receive a secret dispatch ordering all available fleet units to the scene of some awful disaster. *Doyle*'s radiomen received the message an hour after Claytor headed that way on his own.

Claytor, a summa cum laude graduate of Harvard Law 1936, had never cottoned to the status quo. After Harvard, he'd had his pick of lucrative Wall Street law firms but chose instead to clerk for U.S. Appeals Court Justice Learned Hand and then for Supreme Court Justice Louis Brandeis in D.C. With war looming in 1941, he tried to join the Navy, but was rejected as too old. Then an enterprising recruiter found a special program for overage volunteers with seagoing experience.

Did Claytor have seagoing experience, the recruiter wanted to know?

Yes, Claytor said. He had sailed the Chesapeake Bay in his own boat.

That was all the recruiter needed. Now, at thirty-three, Claytor had two seagoing command tours under his belt. His long, serious face reminded people a little of the actor Humphrey Bogart, and like Bogart, Claytor's eyes were susceptible to a twinkle.

Claytor still did not know which ship had sunk. At 4:33 p.m., a dispatch from Peleliu had indicated that two more rescue vessels were steaming to the scene, USS *Madison* and USS *Ralph Talbot*. At 6:30 p.m., he received a new dispatch with updated information from both Peleliu and the planes, including corrected positions. Claytor adjusted course accordingly.

Over scratchy airwaves, he had maintained constant contact with Marks and Atteberry since early afternoon. He monitored Marks's open-sea landing, and Atteberry's overhead vectors. He knew about the sharks, and about the men being pulled onto Marks's plane.

Doyle's chief engineer called the bridge from the engine room, wanting to know how long Claytor intended to keep up flank speed. Some of the ship's line bearings were getting hot and he'd changed the oil on them several times, the engineer said. "We can't keep this speed up or we're going to blow the engines."

"If they blow, they blow," Claytor replied, surprising his crew. "We've got men in the water."

16

IN THE WATER, THE dead outnumbered the living. Men continued to expire so quickly that it became almost impossible to move around without having to shoulder through shoals of corpses.

Floating among the dead, Aviation Machinist's Mate Jim Jarvis yearned to be on that rescue plane. Even though only a few hundred yards separated him from safety, he just didn't have it in him to swim. Ensign Thomas Brophy, however, felt differently. The twenty-one-year-old officer was among those in Redmayne's group who had chosen not to reveal their rank. In fact, Harlan Twible hadn't even realized Brophy was in his group until the ensign broke away swimming for the Dumbo.

"Come back!" Twible yelled. "Come back!"

Watching Brophy's weak strokes, Twible didn't think he would make it. But Brophy kept swimming.

Twible tried again. "Come back, Ensign, that's an order!"

Brophy made it only halfway to the plane. His strength faltered and he slipped below the waves, one of many who spent their last strength swimming for the refuge of Marks's plane and drowning instead.

Dusk fell, siphoning precious light from the rescue scene. There were now thirty survivors aboard Marks's Dumbo. In addition to James Smith, Harrell, Spooner, McKissick, and Woolston, Marks had scooped

up quartermaster Bob Gause and coxswain Louis Erwin. Marks also circled back for Umenhoffer and his buddies. A number of men were also
hauled from a raft, but it was too late for twenty-one-year-old radarman
Art Leenerman. The Dumbo was getting crowded, and Hensley wanted
to reserve the space aboard for living survivors. The aircrew left Leenerman's lifeless body in the raft and attached it by a line to the plane. At
least they could return his body to his family.

Now, Marks peered aft. His aircraft had become a trauma ward so
packed with wounded, starving, dehydrated sailors that it was nearly
impossible for his crew to navigate in the cabin without stepping on survivors. Still, the Dumbo was the only island of refuge for almost three
hundred miles. After some discussion, Marks and Lefkowitz agreed that
the plane's sprawling wing could hold more survivors. There were fifteen hundred square feet of room up there, more than the floor space
in many a house. But to save any more men, they would have to hurry.
Night came suddenly this close to the equator. Even Marks's strength of
will couldn't change that.

He turned and addressed the survivors. "You men up front, crawl out
on the wing."

Umenhoffer realized what the lieutenant was trying to do. While
open saltwater ulcers covered Umenhoffer's legs, he was better off than
some. With help from below, he hoisted himself through an overhead
hatch and squeezed through the engineer's crawl space out onto the
broad surface of the wing. Soon, others began to follow.

A bold violet glow clung to the western sky. Stars winked awake in the
east. The Dumbo pitched and rolled, rising and falling with the swells. It
quickly became apparent that those on the wing were in danger of sliding
right back into the water again, perhaps never to be found. Marks's crew
pulled out lengths of parachute cord and lashed the men down. Working
by Thursday's last light, Hensley and the crew were able to bring aboard
two dozen more men, bringing the number of rescued to fifty-three.

Just before night fell, another Dumbo arrived on-scene and landed in
the water. But the pilot, R. C. Alcorn, had time to rescue only one man.
Over the objections of his crew, Alcorn refused to water-taxi for fear he
would run down survivors in the dark.

•   •   •

The Dumbo operations were far outside the McVay group's field of view, but the captain and his men saw another plane. It was a big one, and excitement rippled across the rafts. Yeoman Havins thought the plane was definitely moving closer, but the sun was sinking fast. The men took turns standing on the edge of one of the rafts and waving a piece of canvas like a surrender flag, their legs held fast by the others. Careless of the circling sharks, each man eagerly took a turn. The plane drew closer. Hope and joy sparked across the flotilla like electric current. They were going home!

Then, suddenly, the sun dropped away. The purple twilight meshed with the surface of the sea, and the plane faded away to the south. The men slumped down in their rafts, heartbroken. Pulling the rafts close, they reviewed their situation. They had not lost hope, they agreed, and were certain the pilot would return the next day.

Marks's Dumbo rode the swells enveloped in darkness that was remarkably complete. There was no moon. Thick clouds scudded in to blot out the stars. In the plane's belly, men lolled against the bulkheads. Some moaned in pain. Others, out of their heads, babbled wild stories. The day after the sinking, one said, a landing craft had picked up thirty men and sailed away, leaving everyone else to die. Another man said a seaplane had landed on the water, picked up several survivors, and abandoned the rest.

Streaming a sea anchor from the bow to slow the plane's drift, Marks let the Dumbo bob up and down in the hulking sea. He had hoped to use his landing lights and an Aldis lamp, a handheld light used to send Morse code, to continue looking for survivors. But the height of the swells made that impractical, and like the other Dumbo pilot who had picked up just one man, he feared running over men in the water.

In the rear of the plane, the crew thought they had run out of fresh water until a thorough search turned up a partially full water breaker in the radio compartment. Someone poured the water into a kettle and passed it up top, where a crew member picked his way carefully down the wing, rationing the precious liquid to four or five men at a time. The kettle was then passed below, refilled, and the process begun again. As the crewman on the wing took the last of the water down the line of men in the dark, he worried that he wouldn't be able to figure out where in the line he had left off. He was surprised when, despite their misery, voice after voice in the darkness said the same thing: "I've had mine."

Their honesty moved Marks deeply. Conduct like that is not indoctrinated through military training, he thought. It is learned at an early age, in Sunday school and in a home where honesty is a way of life.

Marks could hardly believe all that he had witnessed so far. Life rafts and flotsam attached to his plane, every container of supplies broken open, water and oil on the bulkheads inside and out, men strapped to the wing with parachute cord like so much vacation luggage on an automobile. It was a hell of a mess.

Time ticked toward midnight. The wind picked up, chilling the air. The crew had long since dispensed the last drop of water. Marks knew there were men in his plane near death. As the hours passed, he could hear them crying softly with thirst and pain.

17

BOILERS CHURNING HOT, USS *Doyle* sliced through the sea with the urgency of a bullet. Over the radio, Claytor had heard that Marks collected more than fifty men, and also about the second Dumbo. This meant there were at least a hundred men still in the water on this blackest of nights. Claytor imagined their terror. How many would be lost to cold or sharks? How many would simply give up hope?

At 10:42 p.m., Claytor issued an order that no man aboard had ever heard before: "Turn on the searchlight and point it at the sky."

Claytor's officers and sailors were stunned. At night, the crew of a warship made a religion of keeping it dark, skulking around under dim red lights, even hiding the orange glimmer of their cigarettes.

Some on the bridge were aware of Marks's warning about possible submarines in the area. Allowing any light to escape the ship was like painting her with a bull's-eye for the enemy. Still, they understood. *Doyle* was more than an hour away from the survivors, and Claytor wanted the men in the water to see the light, dig deep, and hang on just a little longer.

A sailor complied with the skipper's order and the ship's twenty-four-inch searchlight streamed skyward, piercing the night with a perfect tower of brilliant white. Standing topside, Charles Doyle gazed up at this unprecedented beacon and hairs stood up on the back of his neck. Like the rest of the crew, he trusted his captain. He also knew that for the first time in his Navy service, his ship had just become the brightest target in the Pacific.

When Marks saw *Doyle*'s light on the southern horizon, he decided he had never seen a finer example of American courage. Claytor knew there might be enemy subs—Marks had told him so himself. And yet the *Doyle* captain had resolutely trained his searchlight at the sky.

The reaction on the Dumbo was electrifying.

"Look!" Marks said to the men crying for water and clinging to life. That light they saw was a destroyer on its way. There was water on aboard, and doctors. Rescue was coming soon.

And as he watched, joy and relief washed across their faces. They settled back against the bulkheads and gazed upon that lovely light, now certain of their salvation.

Doyle's light had a similar effect on men still in the water. Lebow and Hershberger's group had dwindled from 130 to 35, and they had almost given up hope. But when Hershberger saw the luminous tower, he realized for the first time that he was going to make it.

L. D. Cox's group began with about thirty men, and Cox had watched two-thirds of them die. Then, when he saw Marks's plane taxi past at a distance, he assumed he and the rest of his group were doomed. But when he saw *Doyle*'s beacon, it was as though a light switched on in heaven. Around him, fresh fire surged in the men, a sudden, burning will to live.

In Morgan's group, depression had also set in. After Lanter spotted the plane earlier in the day, they had all watched and watched as it skated back and forth on the horizon. Then darkness came, erasing it from the sky, and with it their hope. Then *Doyle*'s searchlight appeared, and Morgan felt chills race up his spine. It was the most beautiful thing he'd ever seen.

Far to the north, McVay, too, saw *Doyle*'s light arrowing straight up. He did not know that the man who'd ordered this beacon was his wife's cousin, Graham Claytor.

Doyle plunged toward the survivors, her searchlight making intermittent sweeps ahead to avoid running anyone down. Claytor told his OOD to proceed directly to the two Dumbos. Just before midnight, a lookout spotted a pistol flare in the distance, but they could not investigate it because they had reached Marks's wallowing plane. Ten minutes later, *Doyle* lowered a whaleboat over the side, and it motored over.

The winds were friendly—a gentle breeze from the north-northwest—but the seas were rough. Whitecaps splashed salt water into the whaleboat as her bow bit into the midnight sea. There was a boatswain and a bowhookman aboard, and when the whaleboat reached the plane, each man threw up a line. The Dumbo crew began lowering survivors down from the wing.

The transfer operation was wild and precarious. The whaleboat's steel hull bashed against the plane's thin skin, forcing the boatswain to shove a bumper between them to cushion the blows. The boat crew reached up as high as they could to haul the survivors down into the boat, then tucked them under a canopy to shield them from the wilding sea.

At half past midnight, the first survivors arrived alongside *Doyle*. At the fantail, the whaleboat crew shoved from below and the topside crew pulled from above as load after load of survivors was hauled aboard. There was a cargo net draped over the fantail. Those who could not climb it were hoisted in a sling fashioned from canvas and lines. Sailors in dungarees shepherded the ragged castaways belowdecks.

The last Indy sailor to be pulled up was Art Leenerman, whose corpse Marks had been towing behind the Dumbo in a raft. Just as the canvas sling crossed *Doyle*'s rails, Leenerman sputtered awake, shocking his rescuers. No one was more shocked than Leenerman, who had passed out lost at sea and woke up wrapped in canvas and flying across the fantail of an unknown ship.

Meanwhile, Claytor huddled with his communications officer. One of the men transferred from the Dumbo had delivered possibly the last news Claytor expected to hear: "I am from the *Indianapolis*, and we sank five days ago."

Claytor was astounded. *Indianapolis*? That was Charlie McVay's boat! And these men had been in the water for four days and five nights? How could that be? Claytor's mind sped to his cousin, Louise. Had her husband survived? Claytor had his communications officer draft a secret message.

HAVE ARRIVED AREA. AM PICKING UP SURVIVORS
FROM USS INDIANAPOLIS (CA 35) TORPEDOED AND
SUNK LAST SUNDAY NIGHT.

The message, addressed to the commander of the Western Carolines Submarine Area, landed like a bomb in the upper echelon of the Pacific Fleet. Within hours, the hard copy of his transmission was covered in bold, red pencil marks:

HOLD, DO NOT SHOW.

ADMIRAL EDWARDS AND REAR ADMIRAL BIERI WANT
ANY INFORMATION AVAILABLE ON POSSIBLE SPECIAL
ASSIGNMENT OF CA 35.

LOCATION SHEET SHOWS HER IN PORT PHILIPPINE
AREA.

Someone scribbled over the message classification:

PROBABLY TO BE UPGRADED TO TOP SECRET.

18

AUGUST 3, 1945, FRIDAY—JUST AFTER MIDNIGHT

Philippine Sea

IT WAS FULL DARK when *Bassett* neared the position described in the message traffic. Cloud cover blocked all starlight. At the helm, Albert Lutz, the quartermaster, steered the ship through pelting rain and a pitching black sea. The OOD ordered speed reduced first to fifteen knots, then slower, until finally the boilers were allowing only enough steam to make way. The ship crept toward the unknown in extreme darkness, guns at the ready in case of attack. The air on the bridge was so charged with tension that Lutz felt as if he were in the middle of a Hitchcock film.

Captain Theriault had already brought the crew to general quarters. It was possible that the mystery ship had been sunk by an enemy sub. Given that this vessel still had not been identified, it was also possible that the whole thing was a Japanese trick, and *Bassett* was sailing into an ambush. It would not have surprised Theriault for a Japanese sub to put a few expendable men in the water to attract a fake rescue, then lie in wait to sink the rescue ship. He ordered his lookouts to keep sharp eyes abeam while the sonar hut below the flying bridge kept pinging ahead, searching for steel targets lurking off the bow. Both radar and sonar returns were empty. Still, Theriault proceeded with extreme caution.

For weeks, *Bassett* had been on antisubmarine patrol, but a lot of the men were pretty sure they would have to head north soon, with the invasion force, to face the Japanese up close. The whole of America's military might was now aimed at the enemy's home islands. Allied bombers had continued torching ports, factories, earthworks, rail yards, and airfields, reducing vast sections of the Empire to rubble and fire. And yet the Japanese would not surrender.

As a result, *Bassett*'s crew felt poised at the brink of Armageddon, and most were not terribly thrilled to be under Theriault's command. Ensign Malcolm Smook knew Theriault to be the only officer aboard without a college education, and felt the skipper walked around with a chip on his shoulder.

Lutz considered the man both an elitist and a coward. Earlier that year, when *Bassett* was ordered to the Battle of Okinawa, Theriault pleaded illness. The ship's doctor signed off on his removal from the ship. Lutz, who was thrilled to see him go, ushered Theriault aboard an LCVP and watched as the boat ferried him a short distance to a merchant ship, which was to take him to the rear. When Theriault arrived at the merchant vessel, he indicated to its crew that since he was now a naval officer, some of the civilian seamen should carry his bags. One of them gave Theriault the finger. If he wanted to come aboard, he could carry his own damn bags. Lutz and some buddies watched the scene from *Bassett* and applauded.

Now the *Bassett* crew fanned out along the rails to look for these reported survivors. Officers ordered Bill Van Wilpe and a couple of his mates to the bow, armed with binoculars. Van Wilpe, a nineteen-year-old from Ringwood, New Jersey, was a quiet, brainy farm boy the approximate size of a redwood tree. Though he served as a gunner's mate, Van Wilpe didn't enjoy the adrenaline rush of naval gunnery as some of the other men did. The 5-inch gun was so loud he swore it loosened the wax in his ears.

But Van Wilpe did love being at sea. If the Navy hadn't drafted him, he would have joined the merchant marine. Now, reaching the bow, Van Wilpe manned the port side, put the glasses to his eyes, and commenced scanning the night.

William Claytor's ship was a hive of motion. The condition of the survivors stunned the *Doyle* crew. The Indy men were emaciated and shark-bitten. Some had lost as much as forty pounds. Their skin looked like burned bacon and was pocked with oozing sores. Many were delirious. Belowdecks, ministrations began: small sips of water and fruit juice. Light food if they could tolerate it. The sponging away of thick coatings of fuel oil, which could not be removed except with diesel. Then, showers and clean skivvies.

The men of *Doyle* gave up their bunks for the men of *Indianapolis*, most of whom dropped into the sleep of the dead. Two-thirds of the men Marks's crew rescued were stretcher cases, but every one of them was still alive.

Meanwhile, on the bridge, Claytor had ordered the engine room to make bare steerageway, and the helmsman guided the ship as it crept forward through the thicket night. Signalmen scanned the water with searchlights. Sailors lined the rails and kept their eyes peeled for more survivors.

Just after 1 a.m., *Doyle* lookouts spotted another searchlight to the north. Her signalmen challenged the vessel and received a response: She was USS *Bassett*.

Aboard *Bassett*, the wrenching shouts of a half-dozen lookouts tore the silence. "Life raft, port beam!"

Soon a pair of LCVPs was waterborne and en route. Ensign Jack Broser, of Brooklyn, New York, captained LCVP 1 with Coxswain Jack Paul as his boat crew engineer. Broser held a battle lantern aloft. Its battery-powered glow illuminated the rolling swells, revealing strange creatures just below the surface—jacks, trevally, and other huge blue-water fish. There was no telling what else lurked down there in the dark.

Peter Wren, a twenty-five-year-old ensign from Richmond, Virginia, commanded LCVP 2, and he was first to reach survivors. It was a large group—seventy-five to a hundred men—floating in the water, and they were nearly impossible to see. Wren's hookman, a young man still in his teens, held up a battle lantern. Its narrow beam danced over the survivors like an old-time stage light, picking out oddly dark faces punched with white eyes.

Were these men American or Japanese?

Wren drew a .45 pistol from his belt and shouted down from his boat, "Who are you, and what ship are you from?"

"Just like a dumbass officer!" came the shouted reply. "Asking dumb-ass questions!"

Wren knew then that these were definitely American sailors.

"Okay, then, what ship are you from?" he called back.

"Shove off, ya dumb bastard! Who needs ya?"

Impressed that the men still had spirit, Wren directed his coxswain to come about to the lee side of the blackened mass and made ready to start pulling them aboard. But there were too many for his boat to handle alone. As the coxswain came about in the dark and the hookman trained the battle lamp on the bobbing heads, Wren struggled to get out a radio call for help. In the six- to eight-foot seas, the radio gear worked at the swell tops but fuzzed into uselessness in the troughs. Finally, he got his transmission off. Then, in a series of partial messages snatched on the wave crests, he put it together that Broser was on his way.

Wren's coxswain motored close to the floater group, swells rocking the boat like a carnival ride. Wren leaned over the gunwale and grabbed a man under the arms. He pulled—hard—and felt the man's flesh and muscle begin to pull away from his bones. The survivor let out a scream, and Wren quickly shifted his grip to the man's life vest. With another swell and a giant heave, Wren was able to get him into the boat.

Soon, Wren saw the light of Broser's battle lamp dancing against the water in the near distance. LCVP 1 plunged down a swell, approaching the survivor group from the side opposite Wren. Broser cut his engines and drifted up to the oily pack of bobbing heads. But due to the lousy radio, he still didn't know what he was looking at.

"Identify yourselves!" Broser called out. "What ship are you from?"

"Indianapolis!" came the cry.

But the faces before him were completely covered in oil, and Broser was still leery. "What city do the Dodgers play in?"

"Brooklyn! *Help us!"*

Satisfied, Broser ordered his coxswain to pull parallel with Wren on the opposite side of the survivors. But one of them mistook the boat for the enemy.

"Japs!" a survivor cried out, and swam for his life.

Instantly, Broser doffed his hat and gunbelt and dove over the side. He chased down the survivor, headlocked him, and dragged him back to the boat.

On the other side of the survivor group, Wren's boat was full. It was time to motor back to *Bassett*. But when he looked back to find her homing lights, all he saw was an unbroken obsidian veil, no star or glimmer of light anywhere. In seas this rough, there was no way he could get back to the ship.

•   •   •

At the same moment Wren was wondering how to get back to *Bassett*, her bridge was the scene of a showdown. Lieutenant R. S. Horowitz, the OOD, heard Wren's voice scratching over the radio, asking him to turn on a searchlight. But nearby, an argument had broken out between Captain Theriault and several officers.

A few minutes earlier, a seaman had called out, "Look at that fish!"

The sailor had spotted a shark. But "fish" is also Navy slang for "torpedo." Theriault, who had parked his ship where another had possibly just been torpedoed and sunk, lunged for the engine-order telegraph and dialed it to all-ahead full.

"Get the LCVPs aboard!" he yelled. "Let's get the hell out of here!"

The engine room was about to comply when another officer reset the telegraph, canceling Theriault's order.

"No way," the officer said. "We're going to stay here until we get every survivor aboard."

Theriault repeated his order. *Bassett* was to leave the area immediately. But the other officers physically blocked the skipper's path to the fantail, where the rescue effort was being coordinated, and gave him only one open avenue: to his quarters.

Around this time, Bill Van Wilpe, the big farm boy, headed for the fantail and happened upon a group of officers. He saw Theriault with an officer walking behind him, and another on each flank. Officers do not give way to enlisted, so Van Wilpe got out of the way to let the group pass. He didn't know what had happened, but it looked to him as though the captain was a prisoner.

Aboard *Doyle*, Claytor continued his patrol for survivors. The destroyer escort inched ahead through heaving seas, her searchlights trawling over the surface. Sailors lined the rails, eyes straining to spot something, anything, where there was mostly nothing. Meanwhile, other ships established voice contact with *Doyle*. In the hours after midnight, USS *Madison* and USS *Ralph Talbot* checked in.

At 3 a.m., shouts went up as two rubber rafts and seventeen pairs of eyes blinked against *Doyle*'s roving lights. Claytor's crew brought these survivors aboard. At a quarter to five, the searchlight picked out two more rafts, and *Doyle*'s crew saved twenty-two more men.

•   •   •

Peter Wren bounced his LCVP over troughs and crests, the belly of his boat filled with men near death. Once *Bassett*'s officers quelled Theriault's plan to flee the area, Horowitz, the OOD, ordered the searchlight switched on. Broser's boat was full, too, but he had agreed to remain with the survivors still in the water so that they would not feel abandoned.

Ensign Malcolm Smook watched from the bridge as Wren pulled alongside *Bassett*'s port rear quarter in seas so wild that they sometimes lifted his boat higher than the ship. A Jacob's ladder hung over the ship's side and waves smashed over the fantail as *Bassett* sailors tried to pull survivors aboard without crushing them between the LCVP and the ship.

The rescue continued as Wren and Broser skippered the LCVPs round robin between the survivors and the ship. The number of Indy men aboard *Bassett* climbed—twenty, forty, sixty—with the seas growing more turbulent as night pressed toward dawn. After one of Broser's return trips, Van Wilpe lumbered down the port side and, with his immense wingspan, helped haul men up and over the side. It didn't take him long to realize that the LCVP crews must be having a hell of a time fishing these men out of the water. He asked to be relieved from his current duties so that he could help rescue survivors. Permission was granted, and Van Wilpe clambered down the Jacob's ladder and into Broser's boat.

The rescuers shoved off again and soon the coxswain had motored to an area adrift in blackened faces. Van Wilpe quickly saw why it was taking so long to pick up survivors. Half the boat crew had to sprawl spreadeagle over the stern while the other half of the crew held on to their legs. The stern men dangled their torsos and arms from the boat, and tried to snatch oil-slicked survivors from the treacherous, tossing sea. Van Wilpe assessed the futility of the situation. He didn't ask Broser, but simply leapt into the foaming sea.

Broser, who had been in the water and knew full well the danger, went wild. "Van Wilpe! What the hell are you doing? Get back aboard this boat right now!"

Broser didn't know it, but Van Wilpe could swim like a water rat. Within moments, he had wrapped his fire-hose arms around half a dozen men and hauled them to the boat as easily as Gulliver dragging Lilliputians.

Broser was still yelling. "Dammit, Van Wilpe, get back aboard, *now*! That's an order!"

Van Wilpe and his charges roller-coastered in the massive swells. "Sir!" he shouted up, "It would be a lot easier if you'd come down here and help me!"

Broser stopped yelling. In the light of the battle lamp, he glared down at this big, insubordinate lug hugging six soot-faced, emaciated men. Then, for the second time, Broser took off his gunbelt, stepped up to the port side, and dove in.

Tossed in the oily sea, Van Wilpe and Broser swam through a mix of torn and blackened men, many of whom were corpses. Sometimes it was difficult to tell the difference. Van Wilpe prodded and poked, looking for signs of life. When it seemed a man was dead, he pushed the body away and moved on, heartsick. What if he was wrong? Some of the living men, crazed and fearful, fought him savagely. Others were convinced they needed no help at all. All Van Wilpe could do was drag them, sputtering and fighting, back to the boat. Broser had already climbed back aboard when Van Wilpe brought another group to the stern.

The ensign yelled down, "Okay, Van Wilpe, climb aboard."

Treading water, Van Wilpe craned his neck and looked the situation over. There was no more room for survivors aboard the LCVP, but he didn't want to abandon the ones in the water.

"No, sir! You take those men back to the ship!" he called up to Broser. "I'll stay here until you get back!"

Angry when Van Wilpe first leapt into the water, Broser was now apoplectic. Feet planted wide in the stern, he unleashed a torrent of orders and threats. Van Wilpe argued his case: These men were so close to rescue that he didn't want them to lose hope. Since there was no way to force the big man back into the boat, Broser again conceded. He ordered the coxswain to pull away slowly so as not to fling too much wake on Van Wilpe and his flock.

The survivors did not wait quietly. One man yelled that he was going below for food and plunged under the surface. Another said he was going down to berthing to write a letter home. Each time, Van Wilpe surface-dived and had to swim down five feet in the dark to haul the man back up. Soon he began to throw up the oil-laced salt water, and this retching was sapping his strength. It seemed forever before Broser motored up again, and Van Wilpe was glad to see him.

When all the survivors were loaded into the LCVP, Van Wilpe climbed aboard, too, and the coxswain steered for *Bassett*. Curtains of rain swept in, lashing the boat in torrents. As it neared *Bassett*, a giant swell tipped the boat nearly on her side. Three survivors fell back into the sea and vanished. Aboard *Bassett*, the crew gasped at the cruel twist of fate visited upon these men, so close to survival and now lost again. And they were astonished when they saw a huge form fight his way to the edge of the LCVP and leap overboard.

It was Van Wilpe again. He dove beneath the mountainous swells and disappeared. The *Bassett* crew scoured the surface with binoculars. Then Van Wilpe broke the surface, gasping for air, all three survivors wrapped in his enormous arms, all three alive.

19

DURING THE EARLY MORNING hours of August 3, *Bassett* rescued 151 men, the most of any rescue ship. Harold Bray was hanging on a floater net outside the Redmayne group with another new sailor, Fireman Apprentice Second Class Dale Krueger, when he heard an LCVP motor up. He squinted up into the glare of a bright light as a voice behind it called to him like an apparition: "Hey, sailor! Can you climb aboard?"

"Hell, yes!" Bray called back.

He didn't care whose voice it was—he was getting on that boat. But when he tried to clamber up, his strength failed him, and a *Bassett* sailor had to pull him over the gunwale. The boat seemed like heaven to Bray, as dry and clean as anything he had ever laid eyes on.

Bassett also pulled twenty-five-year-old Jimmy O'Donnell aboard. A third-class watertender who'd been aboard Indy for five major battles, O'Donnell had stayed alive in the water by sticking close to his group of fifteen men and refusing to give up—no matter what. Aboard *Bassett*, some sailors offered to help O'Donnell walk to the head. "No, I'm okay," he said. Then he took two steps and hit the deck.

The men of *Bassett* also rescued Santos Pena, as well as Harpo Celaya, plucking the latter out of the water with a giant hook. When Celaya got aboard the ship, he'd hoped for a gallon of ice water, followed by a feast. Instead, he got a lukewarm ounce every few minutes, followed by small helpings of chicken broth, all administered as carefully as medicine. Finally, sleep drew Harpo down like a magnet.

Bassett also collected Lebow, Hershberger, and Lebow's buddy Paul Murphy, as well as Don McCall, L. D. Cox, and the radioman Jack Miner, the last man to see the heroic Chief Warrant Officer Woods standing fast at the key, tapping out the SOS. Men from the main body of the Redmayne group also wound up on *Bassett*, including Chief Benton, who would be awarded the Navy and Marine Corps Medal for his leadership in the water. Ensign Donald Blum, who secured a provisioned raft and sailed it a mile from the Redmayne group, was taken to the bridge. He told officers there that the survivors were from *Indianapolis*.

As the early morning hours wore on, many men remained in the water. More rescue ships arrived, including the high-speed transports *Ringness* and *Register*, bringing the total number of surface vessels on-scene to seven. Since *Madison*'s skipper, Commander Donald Todd, was the senior officer present afloat, he took charge of the scene. As the morning unfolded, a phalanx of search planes appeared. Todd assigned each a sprawling slab of ocean, and the pilots buzzed off to commence box-pattern searches.

With both passenger capacity and medical resources stretched beyond limits, *Bassett* requested permission to depart the scene then headed west to the new hospital facility at Samar. The remaining rescue ships would transport the rest of the survivors south to Peleliu.

Just after sunrise, the McVay group spotted a plane to the north,* and the men were so excited they refused the skipper's daily offering of rations.

---

* Because McVay first sighted rescue planes to his south, he believed his survivor group was the farthest north. But, though planes were searching to his south, rescue ships' logs and the testimony of *Ringness* skipper William Meyer show that at rescue

Instead, they locked their eyes on the aircraft as the pilot carved a giant airborne square. The easterly leg brought the plane closest to the group, filling each man's chest with hope. McVay had just decided that the aircrew would surely spot them on the next sweep when George Kurlich, the sailor who had abandoned ship naked, piped up.

"Fellas, do I see a ship bearing down on us, or am I hallucinating?"

As one, the flotilla crew whirled to see what was behind them. It was, in fact, two ships, both steaming up from the south at high speed and nearly on top of the rafts.

"Well, to hell with planes!" someone said. "These people will pick us up!"

One vessel, USS *Ringness*, already had a cargo net hanging from its starboard side. Yeoman Havins, the barbershop quartet singer, had promised God that if he were rescued, he would become a minister. Now he was so overcome with joy that he was ready to try walking on water to reach the ship.

When *Ringness* pulled alongside the rafts, the other vessel, USS *Register*, continued north in search of more survivors. Each man in the McVay group climbed the *Ringness* cargo net under his own power. Once aboard, a sailor met them and offered cigarettes. Another man named John Jarman helped McVay shuck his oil-slicked life jacket, which Jarman tossed onto the pile of others heaped on the deck. Seamean Al Lederer and Bill Fouts attended to the survivors as they were brought aboard, one by one. McVay remained on the fantail until all his men were aboard, while a hospital corpsman named Goodfriend collected vital statistics on the survivors. Jarman then escorted McVay into the interior of the ship to meet the skipper, Lieutenant Commander William Meyer, who offered McVay his sea cabin as a place to rest.

Three hours later, his assigned search area thoroughly scoured, Meyer felt he could leave the bridge long enough to look in on his guest. McVay was dismayed to learn that *Ringness* had found only thirty-nine survivors.

Meyer said that a report of *Ringness*'s rescue efforts was due to *Madison*'s skipper, Commander Todd. Would McVay like to include any details of the sinking in Meyer's report?

McVay's group was at the leading westerly edge of all the survivor groups and also the farthest south.

Meyer reminded McVay that a court of inquiry would certainly be held, and that details of the moments before the sinking were bound to come out.

McVay hesitated. When Indy was hit, had she been zigzagging? Under the standing orders, it was possible that Lieutenant Orr, *Indianapolis*'s OOD, had recommenced zigzagging. But McVay couldn't be sure—he had been asleep. If conditions necessitated zigzagging, McVay was sure Orr would have ordered it done without hesitation. But there were some officers who would initiate zigzagging then go inform the captain, and others who would inform the captain first. McVay could not be sure which kind Orr was—or had been, if he was among the dead. In any case, he felt the responsibility lay with himself.

The two men discussed it at length. Finally, McVay agreed to Meyer's draft message. It included the lat/long where McVay's group was rescued, the number of total survivors aboard *Ringness*, the suspected cause of the sinking, and the fact that *Indianapolis* had not been steering a zigzag course.

Through the long watches of the night, *Doyle* rescued a total of ninety-three men, including those from the two Dumbos, as well as the doctors, Modisher and Haynes; McVay's yeomen, Paroubek and Buckett; and Keyes, the brave coxswain who had gone belowdecks after the torpedoes hit to order all hands topside. *Doyle* also rescued Jim Jarvis, Dick Thelen, and Bill Akines, a seaman second class. Akines would later say that if Commander Claytor had not aimed his searchlight at the sky, he would not have lived.

USS *Register* picked up twelve survivors, including Troy Nunley, who had been floating alone with watertender Joseph Van Meter, riding a rolled-up floater net, cowboy style, for four days. USS *Dufilho* spotted and rescued a lone survivor, Seaman Second Class Francis H. Rineay, and transferred him to *Register* before continuing search efforts. Also transferred to *Register* were the twenty-four men picked up by USS *Ralph Talbot*, including Clarence Hupka and Cozell Smith, as well as Curtis Pace, who had linked arms with his buddies the previous night, hoping only to die together. All three men lived.

On Friday, August 3, sunrise lit the pair of floating Dumbos, their pilots having spent the night aboard their planes. Alcorn was able to take off from the water. But between the open-sea landing and bashing hulls with *Doyle*'s whaleboat, the damage to Marks's aircraft was substantial. Marks considered it too hazardous to attempt a takeoff. He radioed Claytor, who sent the whaleboat to retrieve the Dumbo crew and any salvageable gear.

At 8 a.m., Marks stood aboard *Doyle* and watched as his plane—just hours ago a precious sanctuary for fifty-three men—was first burned, then sunk with 40 mm gunfire.

Ringness scooped Glenn Morgan's group from the water. Almost as soon as Morgan climbed aboard, he heard a familiar voice shouting his name. It was Vince Allard, the quartermaster he had worked with so closely on the bridge of *Indianapolis*. Morgan's heart warmed to see that his friend had made it, too. Their spirits soared further when *Ringness* storekeeper Roy McLendon handed each of them new clothes and a shaving kit.

After a shower and a breakfast in bed of two sunny-side eggs, Morgan was ordered to rest, but he couldn't. Once he realized that there were dozens more survivors, he bounded up and down the rows of bunks looking for Ralph Guye. Still tortured that he'd abandoned Ralph after promising to stick with him, Morgan's chest swelled with hope that each face he saw would belong to his friend. But none did.

Soon, Morgan got word that Captain McVay wanted to see him, and he reported to Meyer's quarters. Happy to see each other, Morgan and McVay chatted briefly about the sinking, then the captain asked Morgan to get a list of all survivors aboard *Ringness*.

"Aye aye, sir," Morgan said, and left.

Morgan grabbed a pen and paper and jotted down the names of all the men in his own survivor group. He knew he'd just survived an epic disaster and would want to remember his mates. Then he tracked down the running list of all survivors that *Ringness* personnel had prepared and returned it to McVay. It was the last time he would see his captain for fifteen years.

As August 3 unfolded, more search planes streamed into the area and commenced a series of expanding- and moving-square searches. As aircraft scoured the seas to the north, west, and south, rescue ships sped to additional survivor groups pinpointed by pilots.

RESCUE OPERATIONS

USS *RALPH TALBOT* (DD-390)
24 Rescued

Outland/McCoy/Milbrodt
RAFT GROUP
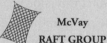

- Started with 4 rafts, and 19 men (including some Marines).
- Split up the rafts, leaving Kuryla's group Tuesday evening, in hopes of being spotted.
- Outland's raft was the final group of survivors rescued.
- Picked up by *Ringness* on the evening of August 3.

Pace/C. Smith/Hupka
FLOATER NET GROUP

- Rescued by *Talbot* & transferred to Register.
- Only had one floater net among them.
- Started with approximately 120 men (includes Gibson group).

McVay
RAFT GROUP

- Started with 3 rafts & 9 men, but took on another raft with 1 sailor. Ended up with 4 rafts, 1 floater net and 10 men.
- The rafts were spread apart approx. 75 feet.
- Had various supplies and rations.
- Picked up 10:20am Friday, August 3.
- Rescued by *Ringness*.

Kuryla
RAFT GROUP

- Split apart from the Outland raft group on Tuesday evening.
- Kuryla and the 4 men on his raft were rescued by *Register*.

G. Morgan
4 RAFTS AND 1 FLOATER NET

- 20 men in the group the first night.
- Only officer was Lt. Freeze, who died.
- Rescued by *Ringness*.

Singles

- Men floating on rolled up floater nets or objects that kept them out of the water.
- Rescued by *Register*.
- A lone survivor, S2c Rineay of New Orleans was rescued by the USS *Dufilho*, and transferred to the *Register*.

USS *DUFILHO* (DE-423)
1 Rescued

USS *REGISTER* (APD-92)
12 Rescued

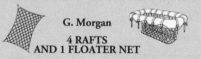

USS *RINGNESS* (APD-100)
39 Rescued

← to *Leyte*, 650 miles

to *PALAU ISLANDS*, 280 miles

USS *BASSETT* (APD-73)
151 Rescued

2 CATALINAS
Adrian Marks - 53 Rescued
R. C. Alcorn - 1 Rescued

USS *CECIL J. DOYLE* (DE-368)
39 Rescued

Gibson
FLOATER NET GROUP

- Not far from Redmayne's Group.
- Started with approximately 120 men (includes Pace group).
- Men were piled on to the 2 floater nets or hung on to the sides.
- Rescued by the *Bassett*.

Haynes/Conway/Parke
SWIMMERS

- Largest group (started with about 400 men)
- Comprised mostly of men who left from the port side, and who abandoned ship earlier than those in the Redmayne group.
- Divided up into smaller groups but were never that far apart as a whole.
- Furthest northeast.
- Rescued by *Doyle* or Marks's PBY, with one rescued by Alcorn's Catalina.

Redmayne/Celaya
RAFTS, NETS, AND VESTS GROUP

- Comprised mostly of men who left from the starboard side, or jumped toward the starboard side from the high side rails when the ship was at 90 degrees on her side. Jumped before McVay & Outland, but after Haynes.
- Second largest group, started with more than 200 men.
- 4 rafts, several nets.
- Had the most supplies of any group, but the men did not work together or get along.
- Rescued by the *Bassett*.

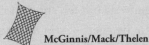

McGinnis/Mack/Thelen
FLOATER NETS & SWIMMERS

- A few hundred yards from Haynes.
- Estimated to start with about 140-150 men.
- The majority were attached to floater nets.
- Most of these men had some encounter with Dr. Haynes. Either started with the Haynes group and ended with McGinnis, Mack, and Thelen, or started here and left to join with Haynes.
- Rescued by *Doyle* or PBY.

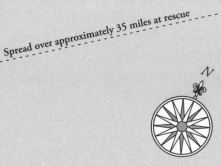

Spread over approximately 35 miles at rescue

N

ADDITIONAL RESCUE & RECOVERY
SHIPS PRESENT

•

USS *HELM* (DD-356)
USS *RALPH TALBOT* (DD-390)
USS *MADISON* (DD-425) - SOPA
USS *FRENCH* (DE-367)
USS *AYLWIN* (DD-355)
USS *COCKRELL* (DE-366)

Late on Friday afternoon, Felton Outland, Giles McCoy, and four raft-mates were sitting quietly, sifting their thoughts. Theirs was the group that had begun with four rafts and nineteen men, but cast off the lines and went their separate ways. Since then, Outland's and McCoy's raft had drifted well south of the massive rescue operations that were now taking place, and they could see none of it. As far as they knew, they were alone.

It had become hard to hold on. The day before, one of the men succumbed to delirium and leapt overboard. He tried to swim away but was rescued by a member of the group. Another man urinated into an empty Spam can, then drank the contents. Meanwhile, their raft had been sinking an inch each day.

Evening came. Outland was dreading another cold night adrift when an intruder suddenly pushed into their midst. A plane, flying low and fast, thrummed over the group and dropped dye markers. Not long after, *Ringness*'s huge bow appeared above them.

Almost before Outland's bleary mind could comprehend what this meant, the after-part of the ship was slipping past. A heaving line flew out over the gunwale but fell short of Outland's raft. Terrified that he would miss rescue by mere feet, Outland lunged for the tail end of the line, latched on, and held tight. He would not let this ship escape his grasp. The men of *Ringness* dragged Outland's half-dead company aboard on the evening of August 3, the fifth full day after *Indianapolis* sank.

On August 4, Lieutenant Chuck Gwinn, the Ventura pilot who first spotted the survivors, took off from Peleliu to rejoin the search. That afternoon, Lieutenant Commander George Atteberry, the Ventura squadron skipper who had first received Gwinn's message and dispatched Marks to the scene, received by hand a dispatch from the commander of the Western Carolines Sub Area. At dawn on August 5, the dispatch said, the rescue ships were to form a scouting line on a bearing of 108 degrees and steam north-northeast from a specific point of origin at a speed of fourteen knots. The planes were to fly overhead to assist and search out to a radius of one hundred miles.

The mission had changed from search and rescue to the recovery and identification of bodies. The five men on Felton Outland's raft were not only the last *Indianapolis* survivors pulled from the water, but also the last Americans of World War II to be rescued at sea after enemy action.

JANUARY 1999

SPRINGFIELD, VIRGINIA

COMMANDER WILLIAM TOTI TURNED a page and cursed his choice of late-night reading. He sat in his study, a fat Navy report open on his desk—a report that inferred that Captain Charles McVay was a coward and a liar.

It was well past midnight. Toti's Springfield, Virginia, home was dark and quiet. Karen and the kids were asleep upstairs. He would've liked to get some sleep, too, but the thick sheaf before him, spotlighted in the glow of a brass banker's lamp, made that impossible for the moment.

Since his conversation with survivors Paul Murphy and Glenn Morgan at the deactivation ceremony at Pearl Harbor, Toti had been keeping the promise he made that day.

"We want you to help exonerate our captain," Murphy had said at the reception.

In 1945, Fleet Admiral Ernest J. King ordered that Charles B. McVay III stand trial for the loss of *Indianapolis*. In the half-century since, an army of supporters—journalists, survivors, and, lately, even a sixth-grade kid—had been trying to prove the Navy wrong.

No one had yet succeeded.

Toti understood why the survivors wanted him on the team. As a sub skipper, he was uniquely positioned to analyze Hashimoto's attack and evaluate whether McVay's actions had been appropriate. It all made sense, but Toti dreaded it just the same. Not because he feared controversy or the work entailed, but because over the years he had read virtually every book, article, and document ever written on the cruiser's sinking. He worried that everything that could be said had already been said. And he was fairly certain that in the end, the survivors weren't going to like what he had to say.

Toti had discussed his struggle several times with his wife, who was more cautious than he by nature.

"These men are our friends," Karen said. "If there's any chance you're going to make them mad, then maybe you shouldn't do it."

"But how can I *not* do it?" Toti said. "I was an Indy captain. I sailed the same seas as McVay. I have imagined those events through his eyes too many times. And as a submariner, I've imagined the opposite side of those same events over and over again through Hashimoto's eyes."

Then, that day at the reception, Toti had looked at the fire in Murphy's and Morgan's eyes and known there was no way he could turn them down.

"Of course," Toti had told them. "I'll look into it."

After the deactivation ceremony, Toti and his crew spent ten months preparing the submarine *Indianapolis* for the boneyard, a meticulous (and laborious) process that broke Toti's heart. Then it was time for new orders. He and Karen wanted to stay in Hawaii near her family, while Toti transferred "up the hill" to Pacific Fleet headquarters. But a four-star admiral preempted those plans.

Toti had served in Admiral Don Pilling's orbit during an earlier Pentagon tour, when Pilling had only one star. Fast-forward five years and three more stars, and the admiral was now Vice Chief of Naval Operations. Pilling was a man with an easy sense of humor and a brain the size of a warship. After graduating fourth in his 1965 academy class, he went on to earn a PhD in mathematics from the University of Cambridge. He spent most of his sea duty on smaller surface ships, rising to command USS *Dahlgren*, a destroyer, then Cruiser Group 12, and then Sixth Fleet naval strike forces in southern Europe. Throughout his career, Pilling remained a scholar, even serving a fellowship at the Brookings Institution. The joke around the Pentagon was that if he dropped his briefcase, math books, and not Navy paperwork, would fall out.

The admiral had noticed Toti during his first Pentagon tour, when *Indianapolis* completed a mission so highly classified that Toti would not be able to talk about it for the rest of his life. After *Indianapolis* was deactivated, Pilling put out the word that he wanted Toti as his special assistant. And what the vice chief wants, the vice chief gets. So Toti, Karen, and their kids, Sara and Billy, flew east and moved into a brick colonial in Springfield, Virginia. The place was small, but after bouncing around Navy duty stations for more than a decade, it was their first real house, and they loved it.

Now his family was upstairs asleep, and Toti was doing what he'd been doing on nights and weekends for an entire year. He'd reread every book written about Indy and her tragic end, as well as the court-martial transcript and reams of testimony that survivors had given at the Navy's supplemental investigation in late 1945. He had been searching for a hidden answer, something a sub skipper might spot that had eluded the survivors for decades. He hadn't found anything new—until this report that was now robbing him of sleep.

It was the Navy's latest legal analysis of the sinking and the court-martial of Captain McVay, prepared in response to a request by Senator Richard Lugar of Indiana. To get a copy, Toti had stopped by the Offices of the Judge Advocate General at Washington Navy Yard—the scene of McVay's 1945 court-martial—and asked for it.

Along with the report, he had received a salvo of condescending glances from attorneys in the room: *Oh, this sub driver thinks he's a lawyer now.*

At more than seventy-two thousand words, Commander R. D. Scott's report was a book in itself. It dealt with lofty constitutional principles as applied to civilian control of the military, the separation of powers, and the attenuation of individual rights in the military. When the report first appeared in 1996, it infuriated the *Indianapolis* survivors, who felt it not only perpetuated myths and misinformation, but added to them. Toti tended to agree. For one thing, Scott, a Navy JAG, had included his own assessment of Hashimoto's submarine attack on *Indianapolis*. If McVay had been zigzagging, Scott reasoned, Hashimoto's torpedoes would have missed, end of story.

Toti, a sub commander, thought that analysis somewhere between naive and preposterous. Submarine warfare was not some kid's game where, when your torpedoes miss, words pop up on your radar screen flashing GAME OVER, and you pack up and sail home. Toti reasoned that if Hashimoto's first salvo had missed, he would simply have repositioned and fired again. At McVay's 1945 court-martial, Captain Glynn Donaho, the only submarine expert brought to the stand, had said the same thing.

In some cases, Toti thought Scott had become transfixed by his own prose. For example, after his rescue, McVay testified that as his ship rolled catastrophically to starboard, he was swept overboard. Scott wrote, "The Navy has never challenged Captain McVay's uncorroborated account that he did not go down with his ship because he was swept over the side by a wave, notwithstanding apparent conflicts in his testimony."

Here, Toti knew, Scott was suggesting that it was McVay's duty to go down with his vessel, a notion that had no foundation in naval regulation or even naval tradition. Not only that, Scott was implying that McVay, a man who had won a Silver Star for gallantry, was lying about how he wound up in the water, while inexplicably telling the truth about other details that would surely damn him.

As a seagoing captain himself, Toti found this personally offensive, and it washed away any lingering reluctance to help the survivors clear their skipper's name. It was Richard Newcomb, the Associated Press news editor and author of *Abandon Ship*, who first triggered the survivors' efforts. Newcomb was the first to explore the legitimacy of McVay's court-martial and to reveal publicly for the first time the mechanics of his conviction. In writing his book, Newcomb scoured naval records, questioned Navy officials, and also interviewed the two captains, McVay and Hashimoto.

In 1958, *Abandon Ship* stirred the hearts of the survivors, and in 1960 they held their first reunion. They held another one every five years until 1995, when the reunions became more frequent. To a man, the survivors believed McVay was innocent. Many family members of men lost at sea felt the same way. Galvanized by Newcomb's research, the men, their families, and supporters began rattling cages. Writers and lawyers and lawmakers parsed the arguments over the captain's actions, his trial, and its outcome. Many accused the Navy of a cover-up. The word "scapegoat" was frequently invoked.

U.S. senator Spark Matsunaga of Hawaii read the *Indianapolis* story into the Congressional Record, and McVay's adult sons, Kimo and Quatro, campaigned on their father's behalf. Kimo even wrote to President Ronald Reagan and Vice President George H. W. Bush. But American presidents, the sons were told, had no authority to set aside a military court-martial. Meanwhile, McVay's court-martial was legally correct, JAG officers had ruled, the verdict legally sound. Therefore, nothing could be done.

In 1990, hope for exoneration flared briefly with the publication of *Fatal Voyage* by *Washington Post* foreign correspondent Dan Kurzman. But again hope quickly faded.

Between 1990 and 1995, the Murphys—Paul and Mary Lou—along with Glenn and Mertie Jo Morgan, Jimmy and Mary O'Donell, L. D. Cox, Dick Thelen, and others, pressed even harder toward two goals:

building a permanent monument to honor the *Indianapolis* dead and clearing their captain's name. In 1995, they saw the first dream achieved when a stately granite monument to the ship's final crew was erected beside the Canal Walk in the city of Indianapolis, Indiana.

Still, the survivors did not rest. Instead, they plied the halls of Congress. Wearing buttons and other Indy memorabilia, they met by appointment with their state representatives and senators and presented their case for exonerating McVay. Lawmakers were always gracious, according the survivors the respect they were due. After each trip to Washington, the Murphys in particular were sure that this would be the time they put the ball in the end zone. But each time, as had been the case through five decades, their efforts came up short.

Toti closed R. D. Scott's noxious report, switched off the banker's lamp with a little brass chain, and climbed the stairs toward bed. He knew how heavy the weight that hung around McVay's neck must have been. A captain develops a relationship with both his vessel and his crew. Toti himself had become intimately familiar with his Indy and her shifting moods. He wondered how losing her—how losing his men, his officers, his friends—would have felt. He wondered whether he could learn to live with it even as it tore him apart.

Toti imagined McVay's life a nightmare from the moment Hashimoto's torpedoes blew off Indy's bow. Something beyond a nightmare, really—a realm for which there was perhaps no word. He imagined McVay in the courtroom at Washington Yard, a base his father, the flinty admiral, had once commanded. Toti had been to that courtroom, had seen its imposing austerity.

He imagined himself in McVay's position, a cruiser commander in a victorious Navy, having played a key role in that victory by delivering the Little Boy components to Tinian. Knowing that as the world settled into a costly peace, he had become the public symbol of one of the American Navy's most devastating defeats, a disgraceful counterpoint to his nation's epic victory.

Toti imagined McVay still fighting, still reliving those torpedo blasts, still replaying his own decisions, wondering if there was anything else he could have done.

BOOK 4

TRIAL AND SCANDAL

★

PACIFIC THEATER OF OPERATIONS

AND

WASHINGTON, D.C.

AUGUST 5, 1945–JUNE 30, 1949

1

AT BASE HOSPITAL NO. 20 on Peleliu, sixteen reporters crowded around Captain McVay and scribbled furiously as the skipper, his skin still scorched and windblown, described the horrors of those days at sea. Malcolm Johnson, a Navy-accredited war correspondent, noticed that McVay had the presence of mind to ask that a stenographer be provided to transcribe the interview. The captain's story was vivid and detailed, and Johnson thought the transcript would make one heck of a read.

The reporters asked pointed questions, the most consequential of which was, "Why was no search begun?"

"That is my sixty-four-dollar question," McVay said with more than a trace of indignation. "And I intend to ask it."

The news that *Indianapolis*'s crew had languished for days in the open sea hit Johnson with a seismic jolt. He listened as McVay's frustration bubbled up.

"We were due at our anchorage at 1100 hours [on Tuesday]. I should think by noon or 1300, they would have started to worry," the captain said. "A ship that size practically runs on a train schedule. I should think by noon they would have started to call by radio to find out where we were, or if something was wrong. So far as I know, nothing was started until Thursday."

Johnson was an experienced reporter who had covered the Pacific war from inside the theater. McVay left no doubt in his mind that he believed a search should have been instituted within twenty-four hours of his ship's becoming overdue. Johnson jotted down this fact in his notes.

AUGUST 6, 1945

Major Robert Furman and a knot of officers and scientists leaned toward a radio like young trees in a gale. The *Enola Gay* was returning to Tinian from Hiroshima, her bomb bay triumphantly empty. In the preceding days, tension had stretched like a tightwire over Tinian as poor weather, military strategy, and diplomatic chess moves delayed the order to strike. But fifteen seconds after 9:15 a.m. on August 6, *Enola Gay*'s bomb bay doors opened and the weapon known as Little Boy dropped free, hurtling toward Hiroshima.

Colonel Paul Tibbets and his crew counted off the seconds until impact. When they hit "forty-three," the sky flashed white and a jolt rocked the plane. On the ground below, as many as 140,000 souls perished.

Now, news tumbled from the radio about the B-29's success. As the plane neared her final approach to Tinian, Furman broke away and joined the stream of celebrants flowing down to the airfield. About two hundred men—officers, enlisted, scientists, and technicians—began lining the taxiway. A throng of dignitaries had gathered as well. The most senior was General Carl "Tooey" Spaatz, commander of U.S. Strategic Air Forces. After VE Day, Spaatz transferred over from Europe, where he had worked directly for General Eisenhower. During the final climactic drive to defeat Hitler, Spaatz, who was then Strategic Air Forces commander in the European theater, convinced Eisenhower to make serial strikes on the Reich's oil supply his top air priority.

"The chimera of one air operation that will end the war . . . does not exist," Spaatz argued then. His comment would prove prescient: In the Pacific theater, it would take two.

Furman watched as *Enola Gay* touched down in a thrum of propeller noise and taxied to her coral hardstand through a gantlet of cheers. Tibbets, Captain Deak Parsons, and the rest of the crew descended the ladder. B-29s had a tendency to crash on takeoff. Parsons's job had been to arm Little Boy midflight so as not to accidentally blow Tinian off the map.

"Attention to orders!" a voice cried out. The crew and all in uniform snapped to attention.

Spaatz marched up and awarded the Distinguished Service Cross to Tibbets, pinning the medal to his flight suit.

Tibbets then said a few words to his men. "We have accomplished today what the 509th was organized to do," he said. "We saw a Jap city and wrecked same."

As Furman looked around, he could see that the men of the 509th were nearly overcome with emotion. Speaking of the medal Spaatz had just pinned on his chest, Tibbets let his eyes roam over the whole squadron. "I owe it to you," he said, then praised every division individually, from the cooks and mechanics to the utility workers and office staff. "No one could do anything without you."

After the airfield ceremony, a day of celebration unfolded. It was, Furman thought, a display of food, drink, and entertainment equal to what any remote, ultrasecret, womanless island could have mustered. But soon, black news cast a shadow over his sense of mission accomplishment. Word was bouncing around the Allied archipelago that *Indianapolis* had sunk. The news grieved Furman. He had grown fond of the naval officers—the first lieutenant, Kasey Moore. The executive officer, Joe Flynn. Stan Lipski, the gunnery officer. Had any of them survived?

Days later, the press descended on Tinian for limited interviews with the *Enola Gay* crew and Project Alberta scientists. It was then that Furman released the information crediting *Indianapolis* and her crew with the dangerous transport of the atomic bomb materials from San Francisco to Tinian. He thought they deserved that much. But someone higher in the food chain put that revelation on ice.

AUGUST 7, 1945

An entire day had passed since seventy thousand structures in Hiroshima were leveled by the first atomic bomb, but most Japanese leaders seemed largely unfazed. The Japanese Army released an underwhelming communiqué stating that Hiroshima was attacked by "a small number of B-29s" causing "considerable damage" and that "a new type of bomb" had been used. Details, the communiqué said, were now under investigation.

The Japanese government took no other action except to send a fact-finding team to Hiroshima, and to delay any further response to the previously ignored Allied surrender terms issued at Potsdam until the team returned. It was clear that the Americans were following through on their vow to rain "prompt and utter destruction" on Japan if she failed to surrender. But the Empire had weathered devastating B-29 raids before, including the apocalyptic firebombing of Tokyo in March that destroyed sixteen square miles and killed between 80,000 and 130,000 people. How was this attack on Hiroshima different? The Supreme War Council could obtain very little reporting except for news that a single bomb had essentially wiped the city from the earth.

Sixteen hours after the Little Boy blast, Truman released a statement from the White House that removed all doubt about what had happened. "It is an atomic bomb," Truman said. "It is a harnessing of the basic power of the universe. The force from which the sun draws its power has been loosed against those who brought war to the Far East." He reminded the world that the terms offered from Potsdam were meant "to spare the Japanese people from utter destruction." If Japan did not now accept those terms, "they may expect a rain of ruin from the air, the like of which has never been seen on this earth."

In view of the Americans' new weapon, Foreign Minister Togo urged Emperor Hirohito to accept the terms of the Potsdam Declaration. The emperor agreed. The tragedy of Hiroshima must not be repeated, he said. Togo was to tell the prime minister, Suzuki, that he must find a way to terminate the war without delay. Suzuki called an emergency meeting of the Supreme War Council, which included the top leaders of Japan's military, but was told that the council had "more pressing business" to attend to.

The Army, long opposed to surrender, then busied itself with suppressing the news seeping in from Western sources that the Allies had, with Potsdam, offered the opportunity to surrender. Through a combination of news censorship and government propaganda, many Japanese citizens believed that although they were starving and living in constant fear of the ominous shadow of B-29s, their nation was still on the verge of victory. But the war council had found that it could not suppress America's attempts to communicate with the Japanese people through a campaign of direct mail.

Newspapers and leaflets written in the Japanese language and printed on Saipan were loaded into bomb casings designed to open at four thousand feet and release a blizzard of information. Since at least July 27, the day after Potsdam, Superfortress crews had been papering the countryside, informing the people of the true state of the war and urging them to evacuate cities targeted for air raids. On August 1, B-29s dropped one million leaflets over thirty-five cities, warning civilians to evacuate areas scheduled for bombing within the next few days. The names of targeted cities appeared in Japanese writing under a picture of five airborne B-29s releasing bombs. Before the war's climax, U.S. planes would drop 63 million leaflets over the country. But even after Hiroshima, the Japanese military portrayed them all as propaganda and warned its citizens that anyone caught in possession of these enemy lies was subject to arrest.

On August 7, some Indy survivors landed at Base Hospital No. 18 on Guam. There, news of the atomic strike and its connection to Tinian Island zipped through the wards like a firecracker string. Finally, the mystery was solved. One by one, the survivors understood the sudden departure from Hunter's Point, the secrecy, the strange drills, and the presence of the two Army officers who had sailed with them.

At Guam, McVay submitted to another press interview, this one with three reporters. Leo Litz of the *Indianapolis News*, George McWilliams of the International News Service, and Paul Hughes of the *Louisville Courier-Journal* sat with the captain on a portico overlooking the Pacific. McVay sat in a wheelchair, a notebook in his hand. Already, he had been ordered to file a report on the sinking and had been writing down events as he remembered them.

"My guess is that the *Indianapolis* was hit in an underwater torpedo attack," McVay told the reporters. He went on to explain how, as soon as he got to the bridge, he tried to get word down to other parts of the ship. "But all the lights were out and I found that the explosion had paralyzed the communications system. I sent word to the radio room to see that the calls went out for help and later myself went to see about messages."

At first, McVay said, he was not sure the ship would sink. But as the ship began to list sharply, it became clear that she suffered from "serious, gaping damage."

Litz, McWilliams, and Hughes also interviewed Dr. Haynes at Guam. He sat with them, his hands bound in bandages. "I'm still in a daze," Haynes said, relating the horrors of four days drifting at sea. The reporters asked the doctor whether he had any criticism of McVay's actions.

No, he said. "It was the most terrible thing that could be imagined, and everywhere there was confusion. Nothing worked—fire and blast had severed all wires—and it was impossible to make any kind of progress from one place on the ship to another."

Paul Hughes went on to talk with several more survivors, all of whom expressed their unqualified support for the captain.

Admiral Spruance arrived at the hospital bearing Purple Hearts, and McVay accompanied the admiral as he bestowed medals on the wounded. Those who were able stood to receive their awards. Others received theirs lying in bed. Conflicting emotions tore through the men. Seaman Don McCall didn't think he deserved the honor. Joseph Kiselica, a big, tall fellow from Connecticut, seethed with resentment. "I'm proud of you," Spruance told Kiselica as he affixed the Purple Heart to his chest.

Kiselica wasn't proud at all. Not of what the Navy had done to him. And not of what the Navy had done to his shipmates, some living but most dead. First they ignore us for four days, he thought. Now they want to pin medals on us. Kiselica, a second-class machinist's mate, didn't dare say anything to the admiral, but after that day, he never wore his Purple Heart again.

When Spruance and McVay got to the quartermaster, Bob Gause, the captain said, "If you decide to stay in the Navy, I'll see to it that you make chief."

"Thank you, sir, but no thanks," Gause said. After what he'd just been through, he was going to get out of the Navy double-quick and go home to Florida.

Letters from home caught up with the men. Cleatus Lebow, who had felt that strange dread about returning to Indy at Mare Island, received one from his mother.

"I had a dream," Minervia wrote. "I heard you call me, and I got up from bed and went out on the porch to get you. Papa came out and got me and put me back to bed. It was midnight. At 12:15, I heard you call me again, and I got up and went out again to find you."

After Lebow read the letter, he looked at the date. His mother had written it on July 29, the day before the ship sank.

As the survivors' health improved, they asked to be allowed to let their families know they were still alive. The Navy let them—after a fashion. They were given a sheet of Red Cross stationery and a strict set of rules: They were not allowed to mention their whereabouts, the fact that *Indianapolis* had sunk, their nurses or doctors, or refer in any way to the ordeal they'd just survived.

And so Machinist's Mate George Horvath wrote lies to his wife:

> *I'm still doing all right and getting along, or maybe I should*
> *say I'm getting settled to the routine life at sea. Three meals a*
> *day and a couple of watches to stand. Sounds thrilling, don't*
> *it? I love you—George.*

At least, Horvath thought, Alice Mae and their two boys would know he was okay.

Also back at Guam, Malcolm Johnson and the other reporters drafted their articles. At Peleliu, Johnson's first look at the survivors had scored his memory like a diamond cutting glass. Some were still bleeding, skin boiled and aflame, faces blistered over, some missing chunks of flesh, others unable even to speak. In the perverse gallows ethos of journalism, the sinking of *Indianapolis* was a "great" story, full of drama, tragedy, and heroism, with particulars almost too awful to believe. But it was also an important story that revealed flaws in the Navy's system of tracking its ships.

Was it possible, Johnson wondered, that as the last, climactic fight loomed to the north, complacency had set in among senior officers in the rear? Was the Navy guilty of negligence on a catastrophic scale?

Through official channels, Guam public affairs personnel asked the Navy Department whether the journalists' stories about the sinking could be released from Guam. The reply came back: no. They would have to first be sent to Washington. Johnson prepared his story accordingly. Soon, his piece, along with those of the rest of the Guam press corps, was en route to D.C. by air.

2

AUGUST 9, 1945

ON THE MORNING OF August 9, Japan's Supreme War Council awoke to find that the number of their enemies had increased by one: They were now at war with the Soviets, too. The Soviets had informed Japan in April that they would not be renewing the neutrality pact the two nations had signed in 1941. The pact was not set to expire until 1946, but after Japan's *mokusatsu* of the Big Three Powers' Potsdam Declaration, the Soviets decided to accelerate their diplomatic break and announced that as of August 9, "The Soviet Union will consider herself in a state of war against Japan."

Within hours of this declaration, awful wheels were set in motion. *Bockscar*, a B-29 carrying a twenty-one-kiloton plutonium weapon dubbed Fat Man, rolled down the runway at Tinian. The decision to use the second bomb, made two days before at Guam, was not aimed at annihilating the enemy. It was psychological warfare, calculated to suggest that America had an endless supply of these apocalyptic weapons and would use them to systematically incinerate Japan unless she surrendered. It was follow-through on President Truman's warning in his August 6 declaration after Hiroshima: "We are now prepared to obliterate more rapidly and completely every productive enterprise the Japanese have above ground in any city."

At 10:58 a.m., *Bockscar* released Fat Man over Nagasaki and seconds later, the light of a thousand suns flared in the cockpit. Between 40,000 and 75,000 Japanese people on the ground perished.

For the survivors of *Indianapolis*, the deployment of history's second atomic bomb delayed an event that would reverberate for decades into the future. Admiral Chester Nimitz had ordered a court of inquiry into the circumstances surrounding Indy's sinking. The admiral ordered the court convened on August 9. But the Nagasaki strike—and the climactic combination of strategy and diplomacy that heralded the end of the war—pushed that date back to August 13.

Loosely speaking, a naval court of inquiry is a fact-finding body, much like a grand jury. In this case, the aim was to find out what happened to *Indianapolis*, why, and who was to blame.

Via naval message, Nimitz informed Vice Admiral Charles A. Lockwood, commander of the Pacific submarine force, of his position as president of the court. Nimitz also appointed to the court Vice Admiral George Murray, commander of the Marianas Islands. The proceedings were to take place in Murray's offices at Guam.

It could be argued that Murray, as the divert authority east of the Chop line, had an inherent conflict of interest. But rescue efforts had wrapped up only four days earlier and the circumstances of the sinking were still murky. No one was yet talking about the implications of the hunter-killer operation conducted by USS *Harris*. No one was talking about the positively identified submarine she had chased for a dozen hours dead ahead of *Indianapolis*. No one was talking about any responsibility that might lie with Murray for not having diverted *Indianapolis*, or even alerted McVay to the storm of message traffic that warned of a protracted antisubmarine chase in his path.

Or if anyone was talking, it was below official radar. After the sinking, Hashimoto had disappeared to the north, his role in events as yet unknown. But once the epic disaster of *Indianapolis* came to light, officers on both sides of the Philippine Sea must have wondered whether the enemy submarine chased and lost by *Harris* and *Greene* was responsible.

Meanwhile, at Murray's headquarters, a series of grim lists took shape. One was a roll of missing *Indianapolis* personnel. Page 1 alone bore the names of Paul Candalino, the officer Lieutenant Orr sent to Radio 1 with a distress message, Father Conway, Commander Flynn, Lieutenant Freeze, Commanders Lipski and Janney, Kasey Moore, and the Marine commander, Captain Parke. Also on page 1 was Orr himself, who had calmly manned a bullhorn and policed "abandon ship," though he had more reason than most men to leap quickly from the second vessel that had sunk from underneath him in less than a year.

This list, typed in thick black Pica, stretched on for eighteen single-spaced pages. Husbands, fathers, brothers, sons, uncles all swallowed by the deep. Other, overlapping lists arrived from rescue ships, all of which had ended their search for bodies on the day of the Nagasaki strike. USS *French* reported bodies found and assigned each a number.

"Body No. 20 . . . no identification tags, rings, watch or other means of identification. Body unclothed except for a pair of socks unstenciled. Body 5' 11" black hair, no distinguishing scars or marks. Body very badly mutilated by sharks and decomposed.

"Body No. 22 . . . no identification tags, rings or watch. Had identification bracelet but it was lost overboard while removing it from the arm of the body."

There were many such men and boys, unidentified and unidentifiable. Recovery vessels consistently reported the disfiguring impact of ravaging sharks. Other names on *French*'s list of the dead were, in their way, poignant, their personal effects revealing bits and pieces of young lives cut short. Carl Emerson Mires, for example, had in his pocket a wallet containing nine photos, his Navy ID, a news clipping, an address book, and another treasure—his Certificate of Domain of Neptunus Rex, the mark of a "Trusty Shellback," a sailor who has made passage across the equator. Mires, though, had made his final passage, and *French* recorded him as Body No. 27.

All such lists would make their way to the office of Admiral Louis Denfeld, Chief of Naval Personnel, whose staff would cross-reference them and match the names of the missing with those confirmed dead.

At the Guam hospital, the survivors had two nurses, one they loved and one they hated. The latter was a steel-jawed Valkyrie who stalked the wards with the mien of a warden. The men called her "Old Blood and Guts." The other nurse was Eva Jane Bolents. Each day, Eva Jane glided down the rows of beds, administering mercy. She tended the men's wounds with alcohol and soothed their chafed skin with powder. Eva Jane gave them back rubs and foot rubs, making sure they were cared for throughout the night. Before they left the hospital, several of the men proposed marriage.

Lyle Umenhoffer was busy with other things, in particular, counting his money and his blessings. The day the ship sank, he had withdrawn $250 from his ship account. Through all the days in the water, the money survived in his wallet intact. At Peleliu, Umenhoffer had laid it out bill by bill on his hospital bed to dry. Now it occurred to him that all payroll and any cash aboard, along with all the accounting records, had gone down with the ship. A lot of the fellows in the hospital had literally nothing but the clothes on their backs.

One survivor, Seaman First Class "Big Ed" Brown, of Sioux Falls, South Dakota, received a surprise visit from his brother, Jim. Each brother learned for the first time that the other was involved in delivering the killing blow to Japan. While Ed had helped transport components of Little Boy to Tinian aboard Indy, his brother, a twenty-four-year-old Army sergeant, was attached to the 509th, the secret B-29 squadron that dropped the bombs on Hiroshima and Nagasaki. Ed had known Jim was at Tinian, but with only three hours in port, Ed had no time to look him up. Now the brothers were astonished to learn they'd both played a role in ending the war.

Ed Brown wasn't the only survivor with a visitor from Tinian. Lying in his hospital bed, Ensign John Woolston was surprised when Major Robert Furman appeared at his side. As soon as he could break free, Furman had hopped a plane from Tinian to Guam. His mission had been a success, but the crew of *Indianapolis* paid a catastrophic price. Had they not been tapped to transport his canisters, he knew, the whole crew might be in San Diego for refresher training right now, sitting out the balance of the war on some sun-swept beach. Furman wanted to at least visit the survivors, shake their hands, and thank them for what they'd done for their country.

He'd already visited with Lewis Haynes, who confided the terrible news that only one of the Irish officers Furman had grown fond of had survived. Furman thought it a queer trick of fate that DeGrave's most egregious humiliation, being put off the ship, probably saved his life.

Now, Furman stood beside Woolston and thanked him for his role in the mission. Though wildly junior to the major, Woolston knew he'd never have this chance again. He told Furman about his epiphany at Tinian, about smothering his impulse to ask him about the mystery canisters.

The young ensign's lips curved into a smile. "What would you have done, sir, if I had asked you about the uranium?"

Furman froze and looked down at Woolston, his face a cipher. Then he turned his back and left. Robert Furman had been a locked vault since 1943. He would not let his concern for the survivors cross the line into speculating about a security breach that never happened.

On the night of August 9, with Nagasaki still burning, the Big Six of the Japanese Supreme War Council convened for their third meeting of the day. A bright line still divided those who would accept peace and those who favored fighting on. Worse, the council was deadlocked, with three members dug in firmly on each side. Ending the war would require, if not unanimity, at least consensus on the council—more hawks would have to agree with the doves.

Prime Minister Suzuki and Foreign Minister Togo knew what had to be done. They would have to break historical precedent and involve the emperor. Members of this council had recently reigned unopposed over much of the Pacific. This night, they met deep under the imperial palace in a bomb shelter that was sweltering and claustrophobic. At ten minutes to midnight, the emperor appeared, ready to determine the fate of Japan. Crammed tightly into the hot little space, Hirohito's counselors mopped sweat from their brows with white handkerchiefs and kept their eyes averted respectfully away from His Majesty.

After reading the Potsdam Declaration aloud, Suzuki summarized the two prior meetings that had also resulted in deadlock. He then apologized to the emperor for requesting his presence. But with the council in stalemate and even Suzuki's cabinet divided three ways on surrender, it was necessary, the prime minister said. Breaking with centuries of protocol, Suzuki asked the emperor to weigh in.

Hirohito absorbed all this quietly. Then, after a long, painful stillness, the council listened in devastated silence as their sovereign spoke the unthinkable.

"Continuing the war can only result in the annihilation of the Japanese people and a prolongation of the suffering of all humanity," the monarch said, his voice soft and controlled. "It seems obvious that the nation is no longer able to wage war, and its ability to defend its own shores is doubtful. That is unbearable for me."

The emperor had long pressed Suzuki to find a way to end the war, but the war council members had remained intractably opposed to anything resembling surrender. Now, nearly 2 million people, military and civilian, were dead, and another 8 million wounded or homeless. And in addition to Hiroshima and Nagasaki, more than 40 of his nation's 206 municipalities had been completely destroyed. Tokyo and thirty-seven other cities had lost more than 30 percent of their developed areas. Meanwhile, every major city in the country had suffered damage, save the Kyoto historic temple area, which American leaders had avoided out of respect. The emperor now declared it enough.

"The time has come to bear the unbearable," he said. "I give my sanction to the proposal to accept the Allied proclamation on the basis outlined by the foreign minister." The emperor then exited the room without another word.

The war council sat mute and shell-shocked. How could Great Japan admit defeat? they wondered. Would not people all over the land commit *seppuku*, die with honor rather than surrender in shame? Though Hirohito had voiced his opinion, his counselors were still charged with making a final decision. Many military leaders suspected that the emperor was under the spell of traitors, and some even whispered of a coup. When they heard the emperor's shameful words this night, how long would it be until those leaders rose up and overthrew him?

3

AUGUST 13, 1945

AT 10 A.M. ON August 13, Admiral Charles Lockwood convened the Nimitz-ordered court of inquiry. Though eleven days had passed since the survivors were spotted, the public had not been told that *Indianapolis* was lost. Even the next of kin of those lost at sea remained in the dark, although telegrams would go out later that day.

In addition to admirals Lockwood and Murray, the court was composed of Rear Admiral Francis Whiting and Captain William E. Hilbert, a Navy judge advocate, or lawyer. There would be forty-three witnesses called before the court. In addition, throughout the proceedings, Lockwood and the court would name a number of "interested parties"—men not quite accused of anything, but rather put on notice.

Right away, Captain Charles McVay asked the court for permission to make himself an interested party. Even while skippering his little fleet of rafts with its castaway crew, he had known what was coming. At Peleliu after rescue, he sat on the porch of an old friend's Quonset hut, staring out at the sea, grieving for his lost men and knowing that the Navy would try to hang the sinking around his neck. As an interested party, McVay would have the right to counsel, the right to be present for all testimony, and the right to introduce material into the record in the same manner as a defendant. He could even cross-examine witnesses. By naming himself an interested party, McVay secured himself a front-row seat at what otherwise would have been a closed-door proceeding.

In addition to his new status, McVay was also the first witness. The court asked him sixty-seven questions, eliciting a recitation of events as he remembered them. The court also asked if the ship had been on a zigzag course, to which McVay replied, "No, sir."

McVay noted that the night had been dark and visibility poor, and that no intelligence was given to him about any submarine threat. McVay's routing orders permitted him to cease zigzagging and steer a straight course under such conditions. But under questioning, he had to admit that his standing orders for the OOD did not include a directive to start zigzagging if conditions improved.

"Other than concerning the actual rescue of yourself and the party you were with," said Hilbert, the judge advocate, "have you any observations to make with regard to the rescue operations?"

"Nothing except that I wish to call attention to the interval of time which elapsed from the time the ship was due in Leyte to the apparent commencement of rescue operations," McVay said.

The next witness was Commander John Corry, an aerologist who was assistant officer in charge of Fleet Weather Central. Corry proceeded to paint a picture of weather on the night of the sinking that was postcard perfect. The weather was "excellent," Corry said, citing "all reports available." He then delivered a wordy technical soliloquy on ceiling and predicted visibility.

McVay stepped in instantly to cross-examine him, asking what he meant by "predicted" visibility, then forcing Corry to admit he was referring to conditions forecast and not actually observed.

"Your information related to the night of July 29 . . . was not a factual description of what the weather was in the twenty-five-mile area, was it?" McVay said.

"No," Corry admitted. "It was not a factual statement."

The next witness called was Lieutenant Joseph Waldron, the routing officer at Guam. The court asked him about Route Peddie and *Indianapolis*'s routing instructions, a total of thirty questions. After Waldron was dismissed, and the next witness entered, so did the whiff of corruption.

Captain Oliver Naquin was the surface operations officer at Guam when Indy sailed. His superior was Vice Admiral Murray, who now sat on the court. Naquin took his seat in the witness chair.

"In your capacity as surface operations officer," said Hilbert, "if there has come to your attention data on the presence of mines and submarines in the general area between Guam and Leyte, please produce such data for the period 1 July to 9 August."

"I have it here in a chart with tabulated data appended," Naquin said.

On the chart, Naquin indicated blue triangles denoting reported mines and red crosses that represented submarine contacts. He had drawn in Route Peddie and the approximate location where *Indianapolis* sank.

Naquin's chart was presented to McVay and to the court and entered into evidence.

"Can you tell us how many sightings were made along the Peddie line during the period covered?" a member of the court asked.

"My records indicate we had reports on one submarine contact, possibly sonar, by the *Madison*, on July 12," Naquin said.

This was an outright lie.

Like his counterpart Captain Alfred Granum at Leyte, Naquin had been addressed on all message traffic regarding USS *Harris* and her protracted chase of an enemy submarine along Indy's route on July 28 and

29. Naquin was also in possession of Smedburg's ULTRA intelligence, including the information on the Tamon group, and specifically that I-58 was known to be operating west of the Marianas.

The court then asked Naquin, "Would you judge that the estimate of submarine dangers along the route from Guam to Leyte at the time of the sailing of *Indianapolis* was considered to be heavy or light? . . . particularly precarious or nominal?"

"I would consider the calculated risk as practically negligible," Naquin said.

On Monday, August 13, in Mayfield, Kentucky, Jane Henry, the *Indianapolis* dentist's wife, was ready to turn in for the night when the telephone rang. Little Earl was already tucked in for the night, and Jane hurried to the upstairs extension to stop the ringing. Jane and the baby were staying with her parents, George and Bessie Covington, at their home on Eighth Street until Earl Senior came home. In a recent letter, he'd wondered at length about what they'd do after the war was over—where they would live, where he would work. In the last letter Jane received, he'd gushed about the photos she'd sent of little Earl and then said he felt America seemed to be closing in on victory. Wouldn't it be wonderful, he wrote, if the war was over by the time *Indianapolis* returned to the States?

Jane snatched up the phone before it woke the baby and heard her father's voice, already on the line. He had answered downstairs just before she had. The caller was Uncle Buck—Dr. Claude Buckner—a relative by marriage who had practiced dentistry with Earl before he left Knoxville to go on active duty.

"George, we are so sorry to hear the news," Uncle Buck was saying.

"What news?" Jane heard her father say.

Buck paused, and to Jane he seemed unsure whether to continue. "Horace and Arletta just got a telegram today from the Navy," Buck said, referring to Earl's parents. "It says Earl's missing in action."

Jane's insides went cold, and her legs seemed to turn to water. She raised a hand to brace herself against the wall.

"We haven't received any telegram like that," said George, who happened to be the Mayfield postmaster. He expected they would have received something of such high importance, but supposed that it might have reached Knoxville first before their small town.

Jane couldn't believe what she was hearing. Hot tears of bewilderment and grief spilled down her face. Quietly, she hung up the phone and fled to find her mother.

The next morning, George Covington walked the short distance to the Mayfield post office, assisted by a cane. He had called two of Jane's friends, and they were at the house already, to be with her in case the news was as bad as Buck had said. At the post office, George found what he hoped he would not: a telegram from Western Union. He read it and hobbled back to Eighth Street, the thin slip of paper riding in his breast pocket like a stone.

Back at home, Jane read the telegram through a curtain of tears.

> I DEEPLY REGRET TO INFORM YOU THAT YOUR HUSBAND, EARL O'DELL HENRY, LIEUTENANT COMMANDER USNR, IS MISSING IN ACTION 30 JULY 1945 IN THE SERVICE OF HIS COUNTRY. YOUR GREAT ANXIETY IS APPRECIATED AND YOU WILL BE FURNISHED WITH DETAILS WHEN RECEIVED. TO PREVENT POSSIBLE AID TO OUR ENEMIES PLEASE DO NOT DIVULGE THE NAME OF HIS SHIP OR STATION UNLESS THE GENERAL CIRCUMSTANCES ARE MADE PUBLIC IN NEWS STORIES.

At first, Jane couldn't catch her breath. Pain spread across her chest and down into her gut. The shock felt like electricity coursing through her bones. Her friends leaned in to console her, but in truth there was no consolation, only a splinter of hope. She didn't know what had happened to *Indianapolis*, but she did know Earl was a good swimmer. If the ship had sunk, maybe he had been able to make it to an island somewhere.

She clung to this thought as the morning passed. Then, outside, a church bell in town began to ring. It did not stop, but kept on, its insistent peal floating down Eighth Street in joyous song. Another bell joined, and another, until it seemed every church tower in Mayfield had joined in some kind of rapturous chorus. Soon, car horns joined in, followed by full-throated shouts—men, women, and the high, sweet voices of children.

George opened the door to see people spilling out of their homes, laughing and crying and embracing.

Even inside the house, Jane could hear their words: "Japan surrendered! The war is over!"

She looked down at the wrinkled telegram in her hand and wept.

Eight hundred seventy-eight other families, enough people to populate a couple of small towns, received a version of the message sent to Jane Henry. Many, including Cleatus Lebow's mother, Minervia, received a telegram stating that *Indianapolis* had gone down with "100 percent casualties." Unaware that "casualties" can refer to injury as well as fatality, Minervia and many other mothers thought their living sons were dead.

Mary O'Donnell had anxiously waited for her husband, Watertender Third Class Jimmy O'Donnell, to return to Indianapolis, the cruiser's namesake city. When Indy abruptly departed for the forward areas back in July, Mary had stood on the Golden Gate Bridge and watched her carry Jimmy away. From that moment on, a premonition haunted her: A telegram with Jimmy's name on it would be coming for her. Not one to panic, she'd pushed the feeling aside. And then the wire came. She called several friends and wives she'd met at Mare Island and quickly discovered that the entire crew was missing in action.

Lieutenant Commander John Emery, father of Bill Emery, the young quartermaster striker who joined *Indianapolis* at Mare Island, received the same telegram as the Henrys—his son was missing in action and he was to await further details. Five years earlier, John Emery and his wife had lost their five-year-old son, Billy's brother, to spinal meningitis. Now, Emery did not intend to sit still for uncertain news about the death of a second child.

Unlike most *Indianapolis* families, he had contacts. Resources. Connections. Immediately, he sat down and wrote a letter to his friend Herb Armitage, who was serving in the Pacific theater. Could Armitage find Emery some answers about Bill? At Guam, a friend of Armitage's tracked down Quartermaster Vincent Allard, who had been Bill's supervisor. The news wasn't good. Allard had last seen Bill on the bridge wearing a life jacket. No one had seen him since.

When this word reached John Emery, guilt compounded his grief. Believing that *Indianapolis* would likely sit out the rest of the war, he had pulled strings to get his son assigned to her. Now he asked himself, what had he done?

As *Indianapolis* families received news that their loved ones were missing, twenty-four men gathered again in the small, hot bunker with Emperor Hirohito to receive his final pronouncement on the war. The day after the war council's August 9 meeting, Japan had agreed to accept the Potsdam Declaration—but with a caveat: The emperor was to remain sovereign.

In response, Truman ordered continued bombing runs over military targets. For days, Hirohito's advisors were again deadlocked, this time on new terms for surrender. Though Japan's government rested on the cooperation of monarchy, military, and civil institutions, the emperor's word carried the force of deity, and on August 14 he declared fifteen years of war enough.

"If we continue the war, Japan will be altogether destroyed," Hirohito told his war council, assembled again in the cramped palace bunker. "Although some of you are of the opinion that we cannot completely trust the Allies, I believe that an immediate and peaceful end to the war is preferable to seeing Japan annihilated."

Hirohito was not worried for himself, he said, but rather for the many thousands of his countrymen who had died fighting, or who were wounded, homeless, and impoverished, with few resources to rebuild. He promised to do everything he could to help them, and with that, asked his men to write a radio script announcing Japan's surrender. He would deliver it in his own voice in a national broadcast.

Concluding his remarks, Hirohito stood and exited the bunker. When he was gone, his counselors burst into uncontrollable sobs. Some collapsed to the ground, kneeling in grief, fearing for the fate of their emperor, whom they regarded as a god. But on that day, Hirohito appeared as an ordinary man, broken down by the long years of war.

The emperor himself understood the power his radio broadcast would hold. Apart from his cloistered government, few had ever heard his voice, "the voice of the Crane."

At Guam, the court of inquiry ground on. Of the 316 *Indianapolis* survivors, only twenty testified. Besides McVay, there were four other officers: the engineering officer, Lieutenant Redmayne, as well as Gunner Horner, Twible, and Blum. The senior surviving watch officer, Lieutenant McKissick, did not testify. Nor did Ensign John Woolston, the surviving damage control officer, or Dr. Lewis Haynes, the most senior surviving officer besides McVay. Fifteen enlisted survivors also testified. As the judge advocate examined members of his crew, McVay periodically asked questions of his own.

The court then zeroed in on why the operations and shipping control staff at Leyte did not report *Indianapolis* overdue. Witnesses included acting Philippine Sea Frontier commander Commodore Norman Gillette. Under questioning, Gillette did not mention the Philippine Sea Frontier War Diary for July 1945, or its entry for July 28 concerning the merchant ship "Walk Hunter" (*Wild Hunter*, misspelled). The diary entry noted that the vessel reported a periscope sighting at 10-25N 131-45E, and fired on it. Then:

> The HARRIS (DE-447) was ordered to the scene and obtained a sound contact evaluated as highly probable. She attacked and was joined in the operation by APD-36 and a plane of T.U. 75.1.2. Contact was lost at 290600 and the search was later discontinued.

In fact, *Harris* had evaluated the contact as a certain submarine. Given the ensuing storm of message traffic, and the fact that *Harris* launched fifteen separate attacks on her target, the war diary entry seemed strangely minimalist. Gillette signed it on August 13, the day before the court of inquiry began.

The court lasted until August 20, and its officers delved deeply into the failure of Lieutenant Stuart Gibson and his superior, Lieutenant Commander Jules Sancho, to report *Indianapolis* overdue at Leyte. A string of officers from both Guam and Leyte filed into the hearing room, one by one, to be grilled on the subject.

Gibson told the court that he knew by dusk on Tuesday, August 1, that *Indianapolis* was overdue, and that he did not report it. At this news, the court made him an "interested party" and read him his rights. Immediately, Gibson requested an attorney.

Gibson's superior, Sancho, told the court he did not know *Indianapolis* had not arrived. Sancho's superior, Commodore Jacob Jacobson, said his officers had no duty to report *Indianapolis* at all, because she was scheduled to report to Admiral McCormick for training.

Philippine Sea Frontier operations officer Captain Alfred Granum said his officers assumed that Indy had arrived but did not check to be sure. Granum blamed this on 10CL-45, the governing policy on reporting the arrival of combatant ships. The policy, issued in January 1945, stated that "arrival reports shall not be made for combatant ships." 10CL-45's implication, Granum argued, was that *non*arrival reports should not be made either.

10CL-45 was drafted by Commodore James Carter, the old friend with whom McVay had met before sailing, in the same building where the court of inquiry was taking place now. It had been Carter who told McVay that "the Japs are on their last legs and there's nothing to worry about."

Now Carter told the court that both McCormick and Leyte should have realized something was amiss, and had a moral obligation to report it.

What was not discussed was the string of intelligence and communication failures that led to something being amiss in the first place—failures of which Carter, Gillette, and Naquin, as well as Vice Admiral Murray, a member of the court, were well aware.

4

AUGUST 15, 1945

ON WEDNESDAY, AUGUST 15, headlines—bold, all caps, and glorious—unfurled in newspapers across the nation:

New York Times: JAPAN SURRENDERS, END OF WAR!

Orlando Morning Sentinel: PEACE: JAPS QUIT

Cincinnati Enquirer: WAR ENDS AS JAPAN QUITS. TODAY, THURSDAY ARE LEGAL HOLIDAYS

Western radio broadcasters also heralded the surrender news, and that is where, on August 15, kamikaze commander Vice Admiral Matome Ugaki learned for the first time that Great Japan now suffered before the world in humiliating defeat. The emperor himself addressed the nation via radio at noon. Ugaki was the commander who had sent the kamikaze planes—including the one that crashed Indy—against the U.S. fleet at Okinawa. Now, due to a poor signal, he could not understand Hirohito's broadcast very well, but he could guess most of its sickening detail. As one of the officers His Majesty had entrusted with a nation-saving mission, Ugaki's heart filled with shame.

Six months earlier, Ugaki had written in his journal that he would one day follow the example of the young kamikaze. Now that time had come. He had not personally received a cease-fire order, so he told his men to prepare Suisei planes at Oita airfield immediately.

At four in the afternoon, his men were to meet him there to drink the farewell cup. Ugaki sat down and made a final entry in his journal. He hoped that "all the Japanese people will overcome all hardships expected to come in the future, display the traditional spirit of this nation more than ever, do their best to rehabilitate this country, and finally revenge this defeat in the future. I myself have made up my mind to serve this country even after death takes my body from this earth."

With that, Ugaki ended his war diary and commended it to a friend for safekeeping with instructions that it never fall into enemy hands. Then he headed for Oita airfield by car and found there eleven Suisei dive-bombers, engines already turning. On the tarmac, twenty-two aircrew stood ramrod straight, heads wrapped in white bands, each of their foreheads ablaze with a flat red disc, the emblem of the rising sun.

Looking them over, Ugaki softened. He gave an order to reduce to five the number of planes that would accompany him. But Lieutenant Tatsuo Nakatsuru would have none of it.

"We can't stand by and see only five planes dispatched," Nakatsuru told the assembly. "My unit is going to accompany him with full strength!"

Ugaki climbed up on a stand in front of the aircrew. Already, he had stripped his uniform of all insignia, including his rank. "Will all of you go with me?" he said.

The flying men raised their right hands skyward and cried as one: "Yes, sir!"

Minutes later, the crews boarded their bombers. As his plane taxied, Ugaki waved farewell to his staff, who stood on the tarmac, eyes brimming with tears. Ugaki was headed for Okinawa, where so many of his countrymen had lost their lives. He would ram the arrogant American ships and display the real spirit of the Japanese warrior.

Once airborne, the attack group arrowed south and disappeared. At 7:24 p.m., Ugaki transmitted his final message from the sky: "The emperor, *Banzai!*"

Ugaki was not the only Japanese military officer to learn of the surrender via the press. That evening, Hashimoto was standing on the bridge of his submarine, scanning the horizon for targets on passage from Okinawa, when he was asked by his senior wireless rating officer to come down a minute. Noticing that the man looked ready to burst into tears, Hashimoto reluctantly followed him to the wardroom, where they had more privacy.

"Look what's come," the officer said. It was a communiqué announcing the end of hostilities. Hashimoto took a minute to reflect on the situation and concluded that it must be some kind of newspaper stunt or military demarche. He informed those present that until an official order arrived, they would remain vigilant and continue to fight.

Returning to the special craft base two days later, Hashimoto spotted a motorboat from shore coming out to his sub and knew the moment had arrived. With his crew assembled on the upper deck, Hashimoto glanced at the now empty *kaiten* chocks and, with tears in his eyes, began reading aloud the imperial press communiqué announcing the end of the war.

On the same day, reporter Malcolm Johnson was at Guam, about to board a ship for Japan, when he heard some outrageous news. While banner headlines about the end of the war were plastered on the front page of every newspaper in the States, papers ran another, smaller headline, some below the fold:

CRUISER *INDIANAPOLIS* SUNK.

Johnson was livid. The Navy had not waited for his story about *Indianapolis*, nor that of any other reporter. Instead, it had released its own version—conveniently, Johnson thought, on the same day that President Truman announced the end of the war.

Johnson and the other reporters complained bitterly to the brass at Guam, who even raised a little protest themselves. The correspondents' stories, reported from the scene, were en route to Washington per the Navy's previous instructions, Guam officials pointed out to Washington. Couldn't the release have been held up until they arrived?

Johnson regarded the reply as cryptic. It amounted to: "Sorry, but we can't possibly hold up the story."

Why not? he wondered. They'd been holding it up for nearly two weeks. It was August 2 when Lieutenant Gwinn first spotted the men in the water. Now it was August 15. Why would the Navy sit on the sinking story for all that time, but now release its own version of events rather than wait for those written by reporters on the scene?

·   ·   ·

On CincPac Hill in Guam, amidst the questioning about routing orders, overdue ships, and submarine risk, the court of inquiry also elicited narratives of the sinking itself, as well as the days and nights in the water. The twenty survivors who testified told of the horrors they had witnessed, as well as acts of heroism and cowardice, such as the hoarding of food and water. After seven days of testimony, Vice Admiral Lockwood brought the proceedings to a close. Days later, the court issued a document titled "Finding of Facts."

The first section, "Narrative," related the departure of *Indianapolis* from Guam and the events of the sinking. Most of this was accurate: the failure of McCormick's radiomen to properly decode the departure message, the explosions, McVay's appearance on the bridge, Flynn's assessment of the damage, and McVay's attempts to send a distress message via Radio 1.

"It is believed, however, that no distress message ever left the ship due to damage to radio equipment and loss of power."

The conditions endured by the men of *Indianapolis* were summarized in three bullet points:

- The Commanding Officer was washed overboard while standing on the ship's side about frame 110, and swam to an empty life raft.
- The survivors kept themselves afloat in life rafts, floater nets, and life jackets and were assembled in four groups of varying sizes, which, when finally discovered, were dispersed along a line about twenty miles long.
- Food and water and medical supplies were found in the rafts and in the water, but in many cases water was brackish and medical supplies wet with salt water.

Following the narrative portion of the court's conclusion was a section called "Facts." The listing was an adequate recitation of events. But in some respects the court seemed to contradict both the "Facts" and itself in the next section of its findings, titled "Opinions."

For example, the "Facts" stated that "testimony regarding visibility and whether or not the moon was shining is conflicting. Likewise, testimony is conflicting as to whether or not the sky was overcast." But the court's "Opinions" stated that "visibility on the night in question was good with intermittent moonlight."

The court found that both Radio 1 and Radio 2 attempted to transmit distress signals, but could not due to equipment damage—but then concluded that McVay "incurred serious blame for failure to send out a distress message."

As though casting seeds across a fertile field, the court's opinion spread blame for the delay in reporting *Indianapolis*:

- To Rear Admiral McCormick's communications staff, who garbled the ship's departure message.
- To communications staff that attempted to test the radio teletype on July 30, could not raise the ship, and simply gave up rather than trying to achieve communications by other means.
- To the failure of any naval activity at Leyte Gulf to inquire as to Indy's nonarrival.
- To the ambiguity caused by Commodore Carter's weakly worded instruction on tracking combatant ships.
- To Jules Sancho, the port director at Tacloban, and his lieutenant, Stuart Gibson, who noticed *Indianapolis* missing and took no action.

But then, the court concluded that the *primary* reason for the delay in reporting the ship missing was "the failure or inability of the ship to transmit a distress message." This, in effect, blamed *Indianapolis* herself for the agony the delay would visit on the men in the water, despite the damage to the radio gear that the court itself acknowledged.

But none of this was as strange as the court's logic surrounding McVay's decision to allow his OOD, McKissick, discretion about whether to steer a zigzag course. Number 35 in the "Opinions" section stated that while the court had yet to establish it conclusively, its opinion was that *Indianapolis* had been torpedoed. This was coupled with the court's opinion that despite conflicting testimony, visibility was good with intermittent moonlight, and McVay's failure to zigzag was a contributory cause of the loss of the ship. "This opinion, however, cannot be given full weight," the court wrote, because the enemy had radar, "making an accurate attack relatively simple, whether a ship is zigzagging or not."

In the end, however, enemy radar, discretion to zigzag, and damaged radio equipment did not matter to Murray and the court. They recommended to Nimitz that McVay be brought to trial by general court-martial for "culpable inefficiency in the performance of his duty" and "negligently endangering the lives of others."

5

AUTUMN 1945

Washington, D.C.

AFTER GUAM, CHARLES MCVAY returned to his home on Connecticut Avenue in Washington, D.C., and reunited with Louise. It was not the homecoming he'd hoped for. After serving on the Joint Intelligence Committee, commanding a flagship, and earning a Silver Star, he had been well positioned for the climb to commodore. Instead, he was fairly sure his career was over.

McVay had known it the moment *Indianapolis* disappeared beneath the waves. During the long, sweltering days in the water, he spun out consequences in his mind, not knowing the specifics, but imagining the broad outlines. Aboard *Ringness*, when he finally agreed with Captain Meyer to include "not zigzagging" in that initial naval message, he suspected he had sealed his own doom.

Far worse than any career consequences, though, were the images of the men who'd died on his watch. He remembered them constantly, torpedo-blasted and flailing in the oily muck, the whites of their eyes glowing with a visceral strain of fear. He thought about the sacrifices of men like Captain Parke. He'd heard the story of Parke's heroism, swimming between the men in Haynes's group, encouraging them, keeping order, until he died fighting what he believed to be another threat. On September 8, McVay submitted to Navy Secretary James Forrestal a recommendation that Parke be awarded the Navy Cross for extraordinary heroism. But it was a travesty that this young man had died at all.

When speaking with reporters at Peleliu on August 5, McVay had been angry—why hadn't search and rescue been launched within a day of his ship's failure to report to Leyte? "That's my sixty-four-dollar question, and I intend to ask it," he'd told Malcolm Johnson and the other journalists. Then, at the Guam court of inquiry, McVay had himself declared an interested party and promptly made pointed examinations of several witnesses. But by September 16, when he spoke with reporters again, this time in Washington, his defiant tone had vanished.

He said he still wasn't sure what had happened to *Indianapolis*, but that the "three disinterested men" of the court of inquiry and the "men in Washington, including Admiral Purnell, who have been sifting the facts, are in a better position to tell what happened than any of us who were on the ship."

McVay's new contrition bordered on maudlin: "I was in command of the ship, and I am responsible for its fate. I hope they make their decisions soon and do what they want to with me."

In an interview Purnell gave the same day, the admiral seemed ready to oblige. He was the officer who, with Captain Deak Parsons, briefed McVay on the bomb mission the day before *Indianapolis* sailed from Mare Island. Now Purnell told reporters that it was a submarine that sank Indy in a "typical night radar attack." The sub had been "lying dead" beneath the surface and "sent home its torpedoes" using radar.

Purnell's assessment appeared in the *New York Times* on September 18. The tone of his comments, a reporter wrote, "suggested that though the magnitude of the *Indianapolis* loss was greater than in most instances, its characteristics were similar to numerous other losses." According to Purnell:

> The crew knew there was a submarine in the surrounding waters, and there was a hunter killer group after it. . . . The submarine moved to another area from which it was originally noticed, and that was that. The ship ran right over the top of the submarine.

Where Naquin had lied at the Guam court of inquiry about the true nature of the submarine threat on Route Peddie, and Gillette dodged discussing it, Purnell was telling the *New York Times* plainly that the sub chased by *Harris* and *Greene* had escaped to sink *Indianapolis*. In

another month, the naval inspector general would state that the precise
cause of the sinking had still not been determined. But here was Purnell,
an assistant Chief of Naval Operations under Fleet Admiral Ernest King,
already shaping public perception, casting unsubtle blame. To wit: The
crew knew of the danger, did nothing, and blundered right over the top
of an enemy submarine.

Timed in concert with the official death notifications that were about
to stream out across the country, Purnell's words had the ring of an
omen.

Fleet Admiral Ernest King, meanwhile, was not happy. The Guam court
of inquiry had failed, he believed. Too few witnesses called, too little evidence uncovered, too many questions unanswered.

Why was *Indianapolis* proceeding unescorted? he wanted to know.
Why was Route Peddie chosen? Were there alternative routes? Why were
no escorts available, and if available, why were they not provided? And
what responsible officer made the decision either way?

In fact, King found the entire court of inquiry inadequate in both
scope and discovery. That notwithstanding, he felt there was plenty of
blame to go around. The ship was not up to snuff with regard to interior
discipline, organization, and administration, King believed. At Leyte,
Lieutenant Stuart Gibson should have taken intelligent action when
he noticed *Indianapolis* overdue. Instead, he did nothing. Commodore
Carter's confidential letter prohibiting arrival messages for combatant
ships was clearly faulty and a primary reason for the delay in reporting *Indianapolis* overdue. There were more contributors to the disaster,
including Gibson's superior, Lieutenant Commander Jules Sancho, who
was ultimately responsible for Gibson's actions on his watch, as well as
Rear Admiral McCormick's communications staff with their garbled
decoding of Indy's departure message.

And yet, in his view, none of this excused Captain Charles McVay.
This put King at direct odds with his Pacific Fleet commander, Chester
Nimitz. After reviewing the results of the Guam court of inquiry, Nimitz
said he viewed McVay's failure to zigzag as an error in judgment, but not
one that scaled the heights of culpable negligence.

King did not agree. At this point, the fleet admiral was looking at the loss of two warships—*Underhill* and *Indianapolis*—both torpedoed in the closing days of the war due to the same failure to put ULTRA intel to tactical use, with a total loss of more than a thousand men. Even now, notices of the *Indianapolis* dead were appearing in newspaper after newspaper, the grim news echoing through hundreds of townships like the tolling of a bell.

The *Glendale Press Newspaper* in Los Angeles, California, reported the death of Radioman Second Class Paul Dollins. In Ohio, the shocking death of twins Albert and William Koegler was shared in the *Cincinnati Enquirer.* The *Seymour Tribune* announced the death of Fire Control-man Third Class Thomas Leon Barksdale in Indiana. In Council Bluffs, Iowa, Fireman Second Class Roy Edward Rhoten . . . in Milford, Iowa, Marine Lieutenant Edward Stauffer . . . in Jasper, Tennessee, Fireman Aulton Newell Phillips . . .

Dothan, Alabama. Pampa, Texas. Salisbury, Maryland. Fitchburg, Massachusetts. Rochester, New York. Troy, Ohio. It seemed there was no corner of the nation untouched by the loss.

Someone had to answer for it. On September 25, King fired off an acerbic five-page memo to Forrestal. It contained two recommendations. First, that Forrestal launch an investigation into the routing of *Indianapolis* and the garbled receipt of her departure message by Rear Admiral McCormick's task group. And second, that Captain Charles McVay be tried by general court-martial.

On September 29, from his temporary office in Washington, McVay wrote to Lieutenant Commander John Emery and his wife, who lived in Mill Valley, California.

"The exact manner in which your son met his death is not known," McVay wrote, "but it is believed that he went down with the ship. . . . The surviving officers join me in the expression of wholehearted sympathy to you in the great loss which you have sustained."

McVay was in the middle of writing 879 such letters, and each one weighed on his soul. He was grateful not to bear the burden alone. His yeoman, Vic Buckett, had been assigned to the bureau and tasked with updating the records of Indy's crew.

A total of 67 officers and 812 enlisted men had been reported as missing in action. Even now, though, there were families still holding out hope. Word had trickled back to McVay of wives clinging to the idea that their husbands were strong swimmers—perhaps they'd been able to paddle to an island and were simply marooned? The time came for him to lay these hopes, and his men, to rest.

On September 17, he had walked into the Washington, D.C., offices of Admiral Louis Denfeld, Chief of Naval Personnel, and submitted a signed statement. All personnel not previously reported as survivors, the statement said, should be considered deceased. On the basis of this missive, more than eight hundred registered letters would make their way from Washington into the pouches of mail carriers to be delivered, unwanted, to homes in forty-seven states.

Now Buckett was helping McVay manage the onslaught of mail pouring in from families of the dead. Some letters were vicious, blaming McVay for their loss. One family was particularly bitter. Anna Flynn, the widow of McVay's executive officer, Commander Joseph Flynn, sent letters to McVay that seemed penned in acid. Flynn had been on the verge of taking command when *Indianapolis* went down—would *already* be in command if he could've connected with his follow-on ship somewhere amid Indy's final port calls. The commander had two daughters, Carleen, six, and Anne, fourteen. Anne adored her father, idolized him, his Irish humor, his playful "dessert first" policy. She was proud of his stature in the cloistered world of the Navy bases where she grew up. As he climbed the ranks, his privileges expanded. Anna and her girls had a driver and a nanny and household help, wholly provided for in officers housing. All that was receding quickly into the past. The Navy told Anna she had six months to vacate officers housing. She would receive a small, onetime death benefit. She had no training, no vocation. Within a year, Commander Flynn's wife and daughters would slide from privileged to penniless. Anna blamed McVay.

Other families of the dead wrote McVay simply to ask if someone could come and talk to them about their loved ones' last moments. The captain asked Buckett if he would do that, and the yeoman agreed, traveling to multiple states to visit with wives, children, siblings, and parents. When Buckett had not known a crew member, he went anyway and told the family all he could in an effort to relieve the black pit of grief made paradoxically deeper when left empty of details. Dr. Haynes also invited grieving family members to his home, providing what comfort he could.

For a certain family, only one thing would provide comfort: to see McVay hang. Thomas Brophy was the father of Tom Brophy, Jr., the ensign who drowned at the cusp of rescue as he tried to swim to Adrian Marks's plane. When Brophy Senior heard McVay was back in Washington, he sped down from his New York home, presented himself in McVay's temporary office, and demanded an interview. McVay said that he had an important engagement on his calendar and couldn't see Brophy.

That was the extent of the conversation—from Brophy's point of view, at least. From McVay's, he had been dealing with angry and distraught family members for weeks. It was late in the day, he was exhausted, and Louise was waiting for him.

In any case, Brophy was incensed. He got into his car and followed the captain to his engagement, only to learn it was a cocktail party. The father of the dead ensign sat in his car and seethed. How dare McVay be so cavalier when Brophy's son, the light of his life, was dead? Brophy, a wealthy advertising executive, was an important, well-connected man with seats on several charitable boards and government councils. He knew that legally, McVay was on the verge of destruction. Over the next several weeks, Brophy would use all his influence, contacting Forrestal and even President Truman, to ensure that destruction was complete.

Although it may have appeared so to Brophy, McVay was not avoiding the difficult task of meeting with family members. In October 1945, Katherine Moore took a train to Washington, D.C. Captain McVay had asked to see her. For most Americans, VJ Day had been a day of celebration. For her, it marked the dawn of widowhood. Like treasures drawn from a hope chest, she found herself pulling out her memories, turning them this way and that. Those precious spring months in 1943, and Christmas the same year. That week in April of 1944, along with the following November. Now she had a new memory to add, the two months at Mare Island before Indy's last voyage. Katherine's heart ached. Five sweet parcels of time. Would they be enough to sustain her?

After the train deposited her in Washington, Katherine sought out

McVay, who regarded her sadly. "Mary is an orphan now," he said of Kasey Moore's daughter.

It was true. Mary's mother had abandoned her years earlier, and now her adoring father was gone forever. Mary was devastated, and literally clung to the last photograph of her father. In it, Kasey looked down at her, knightlike in dress whites, and Mary gazed back up with a loving smile. As for Katherine, she had married Kasey for Kasey—a newspaperman, dashing and independent, with his own convertible sports car. Katherine had hoped to travel with him, see the world. Instead, she was a widow left to raise a daughter not her own.

McVay then told Katherine of his own grief. "Every day of my life, I will see the faces of the men I lost and realize anew that I lost a $40 million ship that others had commanded successfully and safely. . . . I will probably live a long, long time as punishment," McVay said.

He was wrong about that.

6

AFTER A WEEK'S DELAY, Secretary Forrestal concurred with King's recommendation for what would be called a "supplemental investigation." This investigation was assigned to the naval inspector general, Admiral Charles P. Snyder, one of the few flag officers who had been around even longer than King.

Snyder was no lawyer. Born in West Virginia, he graduated from the Naval Academy in 1900, a year ahead of King, and received his commission as an ensign in 1902. During World War I, he commanded the Pacific Fleet flagship, USS *Oregon*, as well as a cruiser and a transport. He then climbed through a series of prestigious postings, including president of the Naval War College and then commander of Battleships, Battle Force—second in command of the U.S. fleet.

The supplemental investigation of the sinking of *Indianapolis* convened on Wednesday, October 31, at 11:05 a.m. in Snyder's D.C. offices. Assistant Inspector General Captain Charles E. Coney and Commodore Thomas Van Metre would interview a total of forty-eight witnesses. Their mandate was narrow: to probe the routing chosen for *Indianapolis*, considerations regarding escorts, and the receipt of Indy's departure message by Rear Admiral McCormick's communications staff.

Coney was a veteran of much tougher duty than this. As former commander of MacArthur's flagship, the light cruiser *Nashville*, he'd carried the general into many battles and was in command in October 1944 when MacArthur landed in Leyte, fulfilling his most famous promise, "I shall return."

Now in Snyder's offices, Coney interrogated his first witness: Captain William Smedburg, combat intelligence officer working for Admiral King. Coney asked Smedburg just six questions before learning of the chart Smedburg's office had prepared in early July, the one showing the position of the Tamon group submarines.

"We knew there were at least four Japanese submarines operating in the general area between the Japanese Islands, the Marianas, and the Palau group and the Philippines," Smedburg said. "We had the positions of those submarines rather closely estimated, we think. One of our estimated positions was so close that the point which was the center of her estimated patrol station was within a very few miles of the position where the DE *Underhill* was sunk on the 24th of July, 1945."

Coney replied, "I note from your chart that the Japanese submarine I-58 is apparently the one which was closest in proximity to the point where the *Indianapolis* was eventually sunk. Is that correct?"

"That is a position that we have assigned to I-58 based on information that we had at the time. . . . We have learned that the submarine I-58 reported to her commander that she sank a ship . . . on the 29th of July. We don't know from her report what ship she sank."

Over the next three weeks Coney and Van Metre interviewed a range of witnesses, including Commander E. S. Goodwin, operations officer for the Chief of Naval Communications, and *Indianapolis* officers Blum, McKissick, Woolston, and Haynes. A number of enlisted men also testified during this period, including Chief Gunner Harrison.

Coney and Van Metre drilled hard and deep, their questions at turns probing and challenging. During the investigation, information emerged that the U.S. Coast Guard vessel *Bibb* and a Navy cargo ship, *Hyperion*, received fragmentary distress signals on the night Indy sank, and these reports were made part of the investigation.

As the inquiry proceeded, Van Metre sent Snyder, the inspector general, periodic updates, which Snyder then assimilated into progress reports for Admiral King. Both Van Metre's and Snyder's prose and conclusions were unflinching. Neither man hesitated to report facts that might not bode well for the Navy.

On November 8, personnel chief Admiral Denfeld wrote to Forrestal. In light of emerging testimony, he recommended that McVay's court-martial be delayed until the supplemental investigation was complete.

On November 9, in his own memo to Forrestal, Admiral King concurred. The calendar then rolled forward one day, and in that twenty-four hours everything changed.

On November 10, Snyder received a memo from Van Metre. By then, thirty-five *Indianapolis* survivors had been questioned, including eight officers. Their testimony, Van Metre wrote to Snyder, made it "necessary to call as witnesses officers attached to the Headquarters of the Commander Chief Pacific Fleet, officers on the staff of the Commander Naval Base Guam, on the Staff of the Commander Naval Base, Leyte, on the Staff of the Commander Philippine Sea Frontier; and possibly from the Staff of the Commander Marianas. . . . It now also seems possible that Rear Admiral Oldendorf may be required to report before this investigation, and certainly Rear Admiral McCormick will be interrogated."

Van Metre expected these interrogations would not be completed until sometime during the first half of December. McVay himself had not been interviewed, Van Metre wrote. That interview was to take place on the coming Wednesday, November 14.

Upon receiving Van Metre's memo, Snyder wrote immediately to King. Testimony from Captain Smedburg and officers of the Navy intelligence section "indicates a failure in the naval organization in Guam and Leyte to use resources and information at their disposal." Snyder ticked off examples:

- Guam failed to provide escort, although they had information of active submarine operations in the area to be traversed.
- Guam failed to take action on a Fleet Radio Unit Pacific intelligence coup, which indicated a Japanese submarine had sunk a vessel in the vicinity in which the *Indianapolis* was known to be.
- At Leyte, the Philippine Sea Frontier organization failed to keep track of the *Indianapolis* and take action when that vessel failed to appear after a scheduled time, even though it was known to them through Fleet Radio Unit Pacific activities and other intelligence reports that submarines were operating in the area where the *Indianapolis* was and that a report of a sinking had been made by a Japanese submarine.

It is unknown whether King already had the information that Leyte knew of a sinking. Snyder learned of this from Van Metre on November 2. Within a half hour of the recorded time of Indy's sinking, the skipper of the Japanese submarine, I-58, Snyder wrote, "which was known to be operating in the general area through which *Indianapolis* was then passing," sent a message to his headquarters that he had sunk an American warship.

Under questioning, Smedburg had told Van Metre that he introduced into the intelligence machinery a paraphrased copy of the dispatch:

From Captain Sub I-58 . . . attacked and sunk one (two unrecovered groups). Sinking confirmed. Obtained three torpedo hits. Position (unrecovered grid).

Translated, this meant that the magicians had not "recovered," or intercepted, information on the type of ship sunk or its location. Nevertheless, Van Metre wrote to Snyder, "Since information of this importance is immediately transmitted by Combat Intelligence to the Commander of the area in which the occurrence took place, it became apparent that if the customary procedure was followed in this case, this important intelligence should have been passed to CincPac for further investigation."

Following up on this testimony, Van Metre visited Commander

Goodwin at the Combat Intelligence Center on Massachusetts Avenue. Goodwin consulted the record and provided Van Metre with a timeline of how I-58's intercepted message was tracked. After it was first received, it was "immediately put into the mill for processing." After a "check translation" to ensure it had been decrypted and properly translated from Japanese, it was delivered to Smedburg in Combat Intelligence, to Commander 7th Fleet, and to at least two other international stations.

Goodwin's info made clear to Van Metre that Nimitz's intelligence staff had the information of a reported sinking by July 30 at 4:46 p.m. local time, in the area where the ship went down. At this time, the men of the *Indianapolis* had been in the water for less than one day.

About ten hours later, news that a sinking had occurred reached the offices of Admiral King. That occurred the day Indy was supposed to arrive in Leyte, July 31—two days before rescue began. It is unclear whether King himself received this intelligence.

In Van Metre's opinion, these revelations threw "new light on the matter of the delay in making the search for the survivors of the *Indianapolis*, which seems to involve deeply the headquarters of the Commander in Chief, Pacific Fleet."

In plain English, Nimitz's combat intelligence staff, as well as King's own, had clues that *Indianapolis* was down within hours of the event. Though critical information was missing—the type of vessel and its location—it was no great stretch to check on the welfare of ships passing through the area where I-58 was known to be.

In his November 10 memo to King, Inspector General Snyder passed along Van Metre's assessment of the additional witnesses he felt it necessary to call: "[I]t now appears to be necessary to interrogate a number of officers, including some of considerable seniority . . . as to why action was not taken on certain information which apparently was in their possession relative to the non-arrival of the *Indianapolis* in Leyte, and the failure of the organizations under their command to take appropriate action in the case."

Someone, Snyder or Van Metre perhaps, created a chart in pencil showing just how high up the food chain these interrogations would go:

At Pearl Harbor: Rear Admiral McCormick and Commodore E. E. Stone, Nimitz's assistant chief of staff for communications.

At Guam: Vice Admiral Murray, commander of the Marianas, who had sat in judgment at the court of inquiry in Guam.

At Leyte: then-acting Philippine Sea Frontier commander, Commodore Norman Gillette.

At San Diego: Rear Admiral Oldendorf and Commodore Carter, who had told McVay that all was "quiet" in the Philippine Sea.

At Washington: Nimitz's chief of staff, the well-respected Vice Admiral Soc McMorris, and Nimitz's combat intelligence officer, Captain Edwin Layton.

It is unclear whether Admiral King saw this penciled chart, but with Snyder's enumeration of failures, he could have created his own. What *is* clear is that on the same day that King received Snyder's memo, he revised his earlier opinion and dashed off a handwritten note to Snyder:

> Comment on the feasibility of bringing C.O. *Indianapolis* to trial
> *now.*

7

FOR DECADES, HISTORIANS WOULD wonder why King reversed himself. Perhaps families of the lost, such as the influential Brophys, brought pressure, wanting McVay to be held accountable. But King was not known as a man to bow to pressure. In fact, when pushed, King pushed back—harder. Also, he had already made the decision to court-martial McVay.

Historians would entertain a second possibility: As a young officer, King was reprimanded by McVay's father while serving under him in the Asiatic fleet. Some, including old Admiral McVay himself, wondered whether King was seizing the chance to settle an old score. He was known to be vindictive. But if motivated by vendetta, why order additional investigation into the sinking of *Indianapolis*? The Guam court of inquiry had delivered to King any warrant he might have needed to provide cover for revenge. In ordering the supplemental investigation, which would rove far and deep, King seemed genuinely to be trying to get to the truth.

Snyder replied to King's one-line note the same day. He believed, he wrote, that McVay wished to have the court-martial delayed because he felt that the Navy's investigation would reveal information "in his interest" and "additional facts favorable to his case." Nevertheless, Snyder added, "Should you desire to bring Captain McVay to trial before my investigation is completed it is, in my opinion, entirely feasible to do so."

Snyder suggested that a summary of the case completed to date could be prepared, together with a list of witnesses still to be interrogated, along with a brief explanation of the reason for calling them. These could be submitted to Admiral Denfeld. Any outstanding witnesses could then be called by either the prosecution or the defense during the court-martial.

It is impossible to know what additional information King received, whether by phone or personal meeting, the day he reversed himself. But Snyder's word that day on timing seems relevant. Van Metre would probably not finish interrogating the senior officers on the penciled list until sometime during the first half of December. Those officers had belonged to the "same small club" for decades, and King belonged to it, too.

Before World War II, the United States Navy was a small, insular organization, chummy and even a bit decrepit. Although families moved often, they tended to sail in and out of one another's orbits through common postings at the major ports, or on staff duty in Washington. Annapolis was the primary source of commissioning, and most Academy grads made the Navy a career. Most officers knew most other officers to one degree or another, and they eventually served with one another, too. Their families also knew each other—their children attended school together and grew up romping in the backyards of "Officers Country" at naval installations around the world. As one historian wrote, "They formed a close, intimate community with common interests and enduring friendships."

The men at whose feet Snyder had laid potential culpability read like a Who's Who of that intimate community:

Charles "Soc" McMorris had been a distinguished cruiser commander at Guadalcanal. In 1943, King bumped aside an underperforming admiral in charge of cruiser-destroyers and subbed in McMorris, who had just received his flag. Later, McMorris relieved Spruance as Nimitz's chief of staff. He was there at the reorganization of Pacific Fleet forces into the 3rd, 5th, and 7th Fleets under Spruance in August 1943.

At Guadalcanal, McMorris served under George Murray, commander of Task Force 17. Murray, a consummate gentleman with a near spotless record, was "Naval Aviator No. 22" and instrumental in the emergence of carrier air. Both he and King were in the same 1927 "class," as it were, of carrier air leadership that burst onto the scene after Congress authorized its formation in 1926. Murray commanded the carrier USS *Enterprise* during key Pacific battles. A year before Indy sank, King hand-selected him as Commander Air Forces Pacific. Murray had relinquished that post only weeks before he assumed command of the Marianas, where he was serving when Indy sank.

Jesse B. Oldendorf, commander of Task Force 95, was a battleship commander of the old school who had also been a key commander at Guadalcanal and Saipan. Oldendorf assisted in the merging of the battleship squadrons and the new carrier air wings, taking the fleet into a new age. He fought his ships at the Marshalls, Palau, the Marianas, and Leyte, and he was wounded at the Battle of Okinawa.

Lynde McCormick and George Murray were in the same Academy class, 1911. In 1941, McCormick was serving as assistant war plans officer under Admiral Husband Kimmel when Pearl Harbor was attacked. Nimitz retained McCormick on staff, where he served as war plans officer for key battles, including Guadalcanal. From October 1943 to March 1945, he served on King's staff, as assistant chief of naval operations for logistics and plans, and accompanied King to the second Yalta conference, preparatory to ending the war.

These men, charted on the penciled witness list, had remade the Navy in their own image. They were the metalsmiths of a new global sea power, hammering out fresh strategies and tactics, deploying the largest fleet in history to win the worst war in history against arguably the most brutal and cunning enemy in history. Indeed, they would be celebrated as naval heroes for generations to come.

Murray and Oldendorf were so highly regarded that they had personally accepted the Japanese surrender. Just four weeks earlier, New York City had honored Nimitz with a ticker-tape parade that led up Broadway from Battery Park to City Hall, where he was greeted by Mayor Fiorello La Guardia and addressed the crowd from a stage built to resemble the bow of a ship. Four million people turned out.

Now, in the afterglow of victory, Nimitz's chief of staff and other leading lights of the Pacific war would be dragged out in open court to testify about the failures Snyder had enumerated—failures that had led to the death of nearly nine hundred men on the eve of victory, and more than a thousand if you tallied *Underhill* under similar intel failures. Unless . . .

. . . the court-martial were to take place before the admirals could testify in the supplemental investigation. By bringing McVay to trial immediately, King could ensure that the admirals' testimony, not slated for completion until mid-December, would never reach the public ear. In addition, he could prevent the introduction of potentially mitigating and even exonerating testimony, improving the odds of a guilty verdict. Whether either of these was King's aim remains unclear, but by pushing the court-martial ahead, he would achieve both.

Already, drumbeats signaling high-level failures were beginning to emerge in the press. Though the war was over, syndicated columnist Bill Cunningham had been in receipt of some troubling letters from service members around the world. Some asked for help, others cited dangers and injustices. "Something ought to be done," Cunningham wrote, "and I've decided to do, at least, something."

What he had decided to do was turn his nationally syndicated column, "Cunningham's Comment," into a homeland version of the celebrated "B Bag" feature in the military newspaper *Stars and Stripes*. The B Bag published anonymous letters to the editor in which enlisted troops could get gripes off their chests without fear of retribution. Though operated from inside the War Department, *Stars and Stripes* was editorially independent and had no bigger supporter throughout the war than General Eisenhower himself. The B Bag earned troops' trust by publishing items like a fall 1944 letter from a soldier who asked how it was that though the European theater was in the middle of a supply crisis, a shipment of five thousand cases of whiskey had somehow made it to officers' messes throughout the continent.

The very first time Cunningham decided to emulate the "B Bag" was the same day King reversed himself. In his November 10 column, Cunningham mentioned two cases. The first concerned a Marine unit in postbomb Nagasaki that was quartered in a ramshackle building with a surplus of rats and lice, but no fresh food. The second he called "Case of Cruiser."

"Case No. 2 concerns the loss of the USS *Indianapolis*, and the charge that a major Navy disaster, and a piece of major Navy criminal negligence was deliberately covered by withholding the announcement until it could be blanketed by the headlines of V-J Day," Cunningham wrote.

Recounting Indy's no-escort sail into submarine waters, he continued, "When she failed to rendezvous with a DE off the Philippines or make contact with an anti-aircraft plane on the appointed morning, nothing was done and evidently shoulders were shrugged. . . . Who and where is the officer or bureau responsible for that, and what action was taken? None."

At this date, the public knew little of any failures on high with respect to *Indianapolis*. Cunningham received this complaint from a crew member of one of the rescue vessels. He had also heard from the mother of a young officer who survived for days in the water—one of those who died the afternoon of August 2, after rescue was finally under way. How could she draw any comfort from her son's sacrifice, the mother wrote, when his life and those of hundreds of men around him could have been saved if the Navy had been alert? "Those agonizing hours my child suffered will not let me rest."

The day Cunningham's first B Bag column ran, Forrestal called his special assistant, Edward Hidalgo, into his office. Wagging his finger at Hidalgo, Forrestal said, "Eddie, I've been reading about the McVay case in the papers. We don't need that kind of publicity. Do whatever you can to put an end to it. Find out the truth . . . get rid of this sensationalism."

First thing on Monday, November 12, Forrestal walked into his office to find King's original note, agreeing to the delay of McVay's trial. By day's end, though, King and Forrestal had conferred. There would be no record of their conversation, only of the result, another handwritten memo by King:

12 Nov 45
THE SECRETARY DIRECTS THAT GENERAL COURT
MARTIAL OF C.O. INDIANAPOLIS BE PROCEEDED
WITH AT ONCE . . .

8

NOVEMBER 1945

Washington Navy Yard
Washington, D.C.

ON NOVEMBER 21, CAPTAIN Thomas J. Ryan signed a copy of the order convening McVay's court-martial and naming him as judge advocate, or prosecutor. The trouble was, the Navy had not yet been able to decide on charges. Still, Ryan reported to the office of the judge advocate general, Rear Admiral O. S. Colclough, and began to review materials in the case.

Ryan knew McVay, who had been two years ahead of him at the Academy. Afterward, Ryan was posted in Japan when, on September 1, 1923, the worst earthquake ever to hit the nation shook Yokohama and Tokyo into splinters. The temblor triggered a forty-foot tsunami that swept ashore and drowned thousands. As aftershocks and wind-whipped fires tore through Yokohama's streets, Ryan and another man plunged into the wreckage of the city's Grand Hotel and rescued a woman pinned beneath a heavy beam and a tumble of masonry.

Later that year, a photographer snapped a photo of Ryan in full-braid dress uniform receiving from President Calvin Coolidge the Medal of

Honor for that rescue. With his clear brow, full lips, and strong chin, Ryan had the look of a superhero.

He and McVay later fought in the same World War II campaign, at Kolombangara in the Solomon Islands, in 1943. Now the two would meet again, with Ryan on his way up and McVay, it seemed, on his way down.

The judge advocate general, Colclough, was busy weighing a litany of potential charges. He presented them to Forrestal:

Failure to ensure that the communication department was maintained in a proper condition of readiness for emergency transmission.

But radioman J. J. Moran's testimony before Van Metre and Coney revealed that the radio rooms were modernized at Mare Island, properly tested, and that McVay's radiomen were both experienced and proficient.

Failure to keep a sufficient lookout for enemy submarines.

But testimony by Chief Gunner Harrison and others showed that all watch stations were properly manned.

Failure to issue and cause to be effected orders needed to maintain watertight integrity.

But *Indianapolis* had been sailing in Yoke Modified, a cruising condition common to ships of her class.

There were other potential charges, but these too conflicted with testimony and documents already in evidence. As Colclough cast about for something that would stick, it was decided that "failure to zigzag" could easily be proven since no one disputed that *Indianapolis* was steering a straight course when she was hit. Zigzagging, of course, had been at McVay's discretion. But discretion is not a defense for poor judgment, which King felt McVay's had clearly been since the 5th Fleet flagship now lay at the bottom of the sea.

Colclough also zeroed in on a second charge: failure to order "abandon ship" in time. The problem with this charge was that a great deal of evidence to the contrary was provided at the court of inquiry. Hence, to secure a guilty verdict on this charge, he wrote to Forrestal, "It must appear that the accused did not use due care in deciding that more time was needed to ascertain the extent of the damage." Ironically, Colclough acknowledged to Forrestal that if McVay had *immediately* ordered abandon ship instead of waiting as he did to get more information, that could have prompted disciplinary action for giving up the ship too soon. Still, Colclough urged Forrestal to add the second charge, even if it might be disproven.

"This specification is recommended, however, on the grounds that its use will permit Captain McVay to clear himself of criticisms made in the press. . . . Full justification for ordering a trial on Charge II springs from the fact that this case is of vital interest not only to the families of those who lost their lives but also to the public at large."

Translation: To try McVay only on Charge I, failure to zigzag, would afford neither the families nor the public a chance to hear the story of the sinking of *Indianapolis*, since McVay could simply plead guilty and end the trial before it began. Charging the captain with the second specification would impel him to defend himself. In this way, Americans still demanding answers for this last, catastrophic blow of the war would receive them.

That much was true—but those answers would be filtered through a forum in which the thrust of inquiry was focused on one man and one man alone. On November 29, Forrestal adopted Colclough's recommendation, issued the charges against McVay, then had the captain placed under arrest. Military authorities did not place the captain in jail, but the arrest restricted his movements to Washington, D.C.

The trial was to take place at Washington Navy Yard, a base once commanded by McVay's father, and was set to begin on Monday, December 3. That gave McVay four days to prepare his defense.

The announcement of an unprecedented trial sparked preparations to match. A construction crew worked through the weekend transforming a large room on the top floor of Building 57 into a space fit for a spectacle. Carpenters, electricians, and shipfitters expanded the gallery to accommodate up to two hundred spectators. Three weeks before, Forrestal had bemoaned media attention. Now, though, workmen hammered together a special section for the press.

McVay had been assigned a defense attorney—John Parmelee Cady, a Navy captain. Like Ryan, Cady had been at the Academy with McVay. His classmates at first considered him a pious, serious young man, hailing as he did from the Puritan confines of Rhode Island. In his plebe year, Cady's go-to rule book was his Bible. By his second year, though, he had relaxed a bit, and by his third, he had become, according to his peers, "well encrusted with salt." So salty was he that in the summer of 1921, his exploits during a midshipmen's practice cruise became the stuff of legend. In the Norwegian city of Christiania, Cady drank too much pilsner with a fetching blonde "Norske," then nursed the resulting hangover by hanging his head out a porthole all the way to Lisbon. After the Naval Academy, Cady took a law degree at George Washington University, graduated in 1932, and promptly failed the bar. He later passed, but by the time of McVay's trial, he really no longer even wanted to be a lawyer. Worse, he found himself involuntarily assigned at the last minute to a nationally watched trial.

Cady visited Admiral Snyder's office to examine the accumulated record of the supplemental investigation. There, he found testimony and evidence numbering more than a thousand pages. He chain-smoked his way through as much of the material as he could, and technically had access to all of the facts. But while the machinery of the prosecution had had months to sift mountains of evidence and build its case, Cady had just ninety-six hours to wrap his brain around it all and make an argument.

On November 30, the day after Forrestal convened the court-martial, Inspector General Snyder boiled it all down in writing for King, including the chain of intelligence failures that set conditions for the Indy disaster and that had nothing to do with McVay:

- The supplemental investigation had corroborated McVay's conclusion that the Philippine Sea was safe, as told to him by Commodore Carter and the Guam routing office. The Guam operations officer, a commander named Lawrence, stated that he had not received any information from higher echelons and considered Route Peddie safe.

- Intelligence had been received in King's offices, and presumably in Nimitz's and Murray's, that there was a considerable increase in Japanese submarine activity to the west of Guam in the Philippine Sea. "It would appear," Snyder wrote, "that the increased tempo of submarine activity in this area would have dictated a revision" of policies concerning escorts.
- The hunter-killer antisubmarine operations that commenced shortly after Indy's departure "would have appeared to have been sufficient reason" for Vice Admiral George Murray to divert *Indianapolis*, "but no action was taken."
- Snyder reiterated the failure of several commands to follow up on the intercept of Hashimoto's sinking message, and to check on *Indianapolis*'s safety.
- Both CincPac Advance (Carter's office) and Commander Marianas (Murray's office) failed to pass down the ULTRA intelligence showing the location of I-58 west of Guam—or if the information was too highly classified—take action themselves.

Snyder's summary then ticked off a list of culprits for the delay in reporting the loss of *Indianapolis*. He mentioned McCormick, Sancho, and Oldendorf, but focused particularly on Commodore Norman Gillette at Leyte: "Although his headquarters presumably had been given the intelligence of increased enemy submarine activity in the Philippine Sea, and despite the additional fact that the failure of the *Indianapolis* to arrive was known to his watchstanders, he took no action until after the survivors were sighted."

Among Snyder's conclusions was this: Despite having had to forgo refresher training to transport "extremely high priority freight" on short notice, "testimony of all survivors indicates that the ship was working hard every day to attain top efficiency condition, and while there was a considerable percentage of new personnel, the morale and discipline were excellent, which was further evidenced by the splendid behavior of the crew after the explosions until the ship sank."

In addition, Snyder wrote, it might be difficult to prove that zigzagging would have improved the security of the ship, given that Carter and Murray also failed to inform McVay of the increased tempo of Japanese submarine operations.

Snyder's memo, the fruit of his long familiarity with the facts of the case, might have been all Captain Cady needed to successfully defend Captain McVay. But the memo was addressed only to Admiral King, and its admissions of the culpability of still other admirals would remain a matter of private correspondence.

When Cady accompanied McVay into the courtroom for the first time on December 3, McVay appeared pale but composed. Louise McVay accompanied her husband. Dark-haired, with a broad forehead and quiet, wide-set eyes, she walked beside him up the courtroom aisle, then broke off to take a seat in the newly expanded gallery. McVay proceeded through the bar to the defense table, passing Ryan, who acknowledged him with a nod. Seated with Ryan was Lieutenant Carl Bauersfeld, an attorney assigned to assist the prosecution.

Instead of the throng of the spectators the Navy had expected, only about forty people had shown up. Wire service reporters and photographers were setting up in the space reserved for press.

There were seven members of the court, and they formed the civilian equivalent of a jury. The president, Rear Admiral Wilder Baker, took his place at the front of the room, flanked by two commodores, Paul S. Theiss and William S. Popham, and a convocation of captains: Homer Grosskopf, John Sullivan, and Charles Hunt. The seventh man on the court, Captain Heman Redfield, was absent the first day due to a travel delay.

McVay gazed up at the court, his face taut and set, but he betrayed no emotion. He had many unanswered questions. During questioning at the inspector general's office, McVay had been shocked to learn of the hunter-killer operation led by USS *Harris*. According to Coney and Van Metre, at least two of his officers had seen a message about a submarine contact somewhere in Indy's vicinity. By instruction, every message of that nature was routed to him immediately, day or night, with a copy also going to the OOD. And McVay was appalled to hear that Commander Janney had, against policy, apparently spoken of this message in the wardroom. Why hadn't Janney, an experienced senior officer, informed him, too?

McVay couldn't ask him, of course. Janney, his head of navigation, was dead, lost at sea just like Moore, Lipski, and every one of his department heads save Redmayne and Haynes.

It embarrassed McVay to still be walking the earth alive, to have been the oldest officer on the ship and find that no line officer between himself and a reserve lieutenant had survived. While on the raft, he thought it would have been easier to have gone down with his ship. What he dreaded then now lay dead ahead.

Beside him in the courtroom, Cady was smoking a cigarette. A current of tension flicked through the air. At the head of the room, each member of the court was duly sworn. Ryan then addressed Cady: "Does the accused have any objection to the charges against him?"

Cady stubbed out his cigarette and stood. "Yes."

The first charge against his client, "through negligence suffering a vessel of the Navy to be hazarded," stated only a conclusion while failing to state an offense, Cady said. "Negligence" implied knowledge that should have been acted on and was not, and there was no proof that McVay had such knowledge.

Ryan jabbed back. First, it was not necessary that the charge meet the technical precision of a common law indictment. It need only show the court's jurisdiction over the accused and the alleged offense. Second, the charge aligned with similar charges made in courts-martial past. Third, McVay had been "fairly apprised" of the offense with which he was being charged.

Cady fine-tuned his objection: The negligence charge set out as a fact what was a mere conclusion of the government—that Captain McVay was making passage to an area in which enemy submarines might be encountered. "There is no proof that the accused had knowledge of this alleged fact," Cady said. "To charge Captain McVay with negligence of duty, it is necessary to set up the essential elements upon which his duty can be judged."

"It will be necessary to bring into evidence," Ryan replied, "whether or not the accused had, or should have had, knowledge that he was proceeding through such an area. In my opinion, it is not necessary to allege that fact in the specification now before the court."

The lawyers battled to a draw, and Rear Admiral Baker ordered the courtroom cleared. Louise McVay willed her features to remain composed and pleasant, but her eyes betrayed her anxiety as she exited the courtroom with the rest of the banished.

After a brief discussion, of which no record was made, the court reconvened. Louise filed in and resumed her seat in the gallery. Baker delivered the court's ruling: "Captain Cady's objection is not sustained. The charges and specifications are in due form and technically correct."

Ryan had scored his first victory. He addressed Cady again, "Is the accused ready for trial?"

"No, the accused does not feel he was provided sufficient time in which to properly prepare a defense, having only received the charges and specifications on November 29."

Cady requested an adjournment of—inexplicably—only one day, and it was granted. The court adjourned, and reporters flocked around McVay like pigeons. He neither preened nor objected, but accommodated them patiently, turning his head as photographers shouted his name.

9

THE FIRST THING MCVAY did on Tuesday, December 4, was answer the two charges against him: "Not guilty."

The court had reconvened on the top floor of Building 57, this time with all seven members present. Louise sat again in the gallery. Journalists crowded the press area, notepads and pens at the ready. The court reporter, a yeoman first class, placed his fingers on the stenotype and keyed three words: "The prosecution began."

Ryan called as his first witness Lieutenant Joseph J. Waldron, who had been the routing officer at Guam. Waldron told the court that the routing instructions furnished McVay by his office included a list of recent enemy contacts. He also testified that the number of contacts was "about normal" and did not indicate excessive submarine activity. Waldron seemed to be telling the truth as he understood it. But at a secret proceeding taking place on the other side of Washington Navy Yard, another witness seemed determined to tell the whole truth only when pinned to a wall.

Captain Oliver F. Naquin was under interrogation in Admiral Snyder's office, where the supplemental investigation was still under way. By the time Ryan called Waldron to the stand in Building 57, Naquin had been dodging and weaving for an hour. The survivor of two sunken vessels, he was being questioned by Captain Coney, the former skipper of MacArthur's flagship. It was a clash of iron-willed men.

Coney first established that Naquin had responsibility at Guam for safe passage of combat vessels, as well as for diverting ships in peril. He then asked Naquin what intelligence information he received as surface operations officer. Naquin first hedged, saying he had access to the "normal" contact reports and "general intelligence information."

Coney: Were you given all information available in this regard . . . regardless of its classification . . . Secret, Confidential, Top Secret, ULTRA Secret, as well as just ordinary information?

Naquin: Yes.

Coney: What use did you make of this information?

Naquin: As I have just stated, it was placed on my board to keep me apprised of the situation, except ULTRA information, which I kept in the highest of confidence.

Coney: To whom did you disseminate this information?

Naquin: I didn't disseminate it to anyone.

He didn't see any need to pass this information along since others were also receiving it, he said.

Coney: Did you know that the USS *Underhill* was sunk by an enemy submarine?

Naquin: I believe she was presumed to have been—I don't know how she was sunk.

Coney: Did you see a dispatch which indicated the *Underhill* had been sunk by a submarine and possibly special equipment had been used in the sinking?

Naquin: I don't recall that dispatch.

Coney: I show you CincPac Advanced Headquarters Blue Summary 260451, of July 1945, which is a detailed account of the sinking of the *Underhill*, and her operations at that time. . . . Have you seen that dispatch?

Naquin: Yes, I have seen this one.

Coney: From these dispatches, then, were you cognizant that there was an enemy submarine operating in the Western Pacific, also, though it may not have been on Route Peddie?

Naquin: Yes, this sinking, however, was not in the Marianas.

Coney: When you received this information of the sinking of *Underhill*, did you pass it on to anyone?

Naquin: I do not recall.

Coney: Were you informed that four enemy submarines were, during the month of July, operating on offensive missions in the general area of the Western Pacific, bounded by Guam, Palau, the Philippines, and the Southern islands of the Japanese group?

Naquin: Yes, I had such information. . . .

Coney: One of these submarines was operating in the near vicinity of Route Peddie. Did you know anything about that?

Naquin: As a result of these reports, we had assigned to us a hunter-killer carrier and four destroyers, but whether or not it was assigned prior to this sinking, I do not recall.

Was one of these vessels USS *Harris*? Coney wanted to know.

"I do not recall," Naquin said.

Coney then asked whether he had passed the ULTRA information about the four enemy subs to any ship leaving Guam.

"I don't recall that I had any occasion to pass that particular information."

What about USS *Harris* "hunting down a submarine" near Route Peddie? Did Naquin know anything about that?

> **Naquin:** I don't recall that incident.
>
> **Coney:** I have here CincPac Advance Headquarters Blue Summary of the 28th of July, which is addressed to all commands . . . [which] reported that antisubmarine operations are in progress at 10-26 North, 131-10 East, after sighting and sonar contact. Would you have seen this?
>
> **Naquin:** Yes, I would have seen this.
>
> **Coney:** Would you have plotted this position on your chart?
>
> **Naquin:** Yes, I would have done so.

Here, Coney began a merciless sifting of Naquin's inaction. If he knew *Harris* was hunting a submarine—a sub that had been both *seen* and *heard* along Route Peddie just ninety miles ahead of *Indianapolis*'s route extended—would this not have prompted him to consider diverting her?

> **Naquin:** No, I think not, as long as there was an ASW vessel working on it at the time—in contact with it.
>
> **Coney:** Did you pass this information on to the *Indianapolis* on one of her intercept schedules?
>
> **Naquin:** No, I did not.

Naquin argued that *Indianapolis* would normally receive such information, and because of that, he had no responsibility to pass it along.

> **Coney:** Was this enemy activity during the month of July increasing or on the decline from normal enemy activity in that area?
>
> **Naquin:** I don't know that you can classify one sinking as increasing or decreasing. It was an isolated incident.

It is unclear whether Coney viewed this answer as genuine, cagey, or obtuse. In any case, Coney spelled it out for him as though rehearsing the alphabet for a child:

> **Coney:** While there was only one sinking, you knew there were four submarines operating in the area. Is that more submarines than are normally operating there, or less, or approximately the same number?
>
> **Naquin:** I would say that that would be more than average.
>
> **Coney:** Did you give that fact any special consideration in connection with the sailing of the *Indianapolis*?
>
> **Naquin:** I did not, as I did not sail the *Indianapolis*.
>
> **Coney:** But immediately upon her sailing, she was then your responsibility. Did you give that fact any consideration, in so far as your responsibility for her was concerned?

Naquin's answer seemed cavalier. "I did not feel that the reported activity jeopardized the safety of her sailing. . . . A great deal of stuff reported never materialized."

10

BACK AT BUILDING 57, the first survivor to testify was Lieutenant Charles Brite McKissick, who had been in the water with Ed Harrell. McKissick had first reunited with his wife back home in McKinney, Texas, and now was stationed at Washington Navy Yard. To testify, he'd only had to walk across the base.

McKissick told the court how, as officer of the deck on watch from 6 to 8 p.m., he had ceased zigzagging at the end of evening twilight per instructions from Captain McVay. He then gave a dramatic account of being thrown from his bunk by a violent explosion, escaping from belowdecks, and as the ship keeled over, ordering all men in his vicinity to abandon ship.

Ryan asked, "During the time you were on watch that day . . . did you know that the ship was pursuing a course that would pass through an area in which enemy submarines might be encountered?"

"Objection!" Cady said from the defense table. "Calls for a conclusion on the part of the witness."

Ryan rephrased his question, and Cady withdrew his objection.

"Yes, sir," McKissick said, "I knew that the ship eventually would pass through an area in which the ship might encounter submarines. I would like to clarify that statement by saying that it was—I had seen a dispatch which indicated that there was a possible enemy submarine contact somewhere in the radius of five hundred miles of our position."

"Where did you see that dispatch?" Ryan asked.

"The dispatch was on a communications board that was kept on the bridge for the officer of the deck to review before going on watch. It was kept in a metal folder there. It was kept on the bridge at all times."

The lieutenant continued, saying the position of the possible submarine was seventy-five to one hundred miles south and two hundred miles ahead. It was the approximate position of the *Harris* chase. On further questioning, McKissick revealed that when he stopped by CIC, the combat information center, before taking the OOD watch, the plotting chart contained no indication of enemy subs. This meant that though someone had posted the hunter-killer message in the metal folder on the bridge, either it had not been routed through the Indy's combat information center, which tracked enemy contacts, or personnel there had failed to plot the location of the submarine chase.

McKissick also testified about the visibility on his watch: "At times I could see fairly well on deck and other times it was almost totally black."

Ryan then asked again about the sub contact on the dispatch board. What was its distance from the ship's approximate location during the time McKissick was on watch?

McKissick: The closest the ship would come to that contact would be . . . seventy to one hundred miles.

Ryan: And having made that estimate, did you take into consideration a submarine on the surface at night proceeding on an opposite course from that steered by *Indianapolis*?

McKissick said he and the off-going officer of the deck did one better: They assumed that the sub mentioned in the dispatch might actually target their ship and calculated how close it could get.

At that, Cady rose to cross-examine McKissick. He zeroed right in on the charge that his client, McVay, had hazarded his vessel by failing to zigzag.

Cady: Did you question the orders from the captain to stop zigzagging at the time they were given to you?

McKissick: No, sir ... I did not question the orders of the captain ... I didn't feel like it was anything unusual.

Cady: What was the visibility at that time?

McKissick: Well, the visibility at that time—of course, there were heavy clouds ahead, and it was partly cloudy overhead. At the time I ... came off watch, there was no moon. The visibility was very poor. It was a very dark night.

Cady: Was it customary on the ship to cease zigzagging after evening twilight?

McKissick: Yes, sir, it was customary as I recall. We did it all during the war at the end of evening twilight and if the visibility was poor. It was customary, as I recall, to cease zigzagging and resume base course.

Cady then sought to establish that McVay had clear rules by which his OODs should operate.

Cady: Can you testify to whether or not the standing orders contained any instructions to the officer of the deck to notify the captain in case of any change in weather conditions, visibility, or so on?

McKissick: I can testify definitely that those instructions were in the standing night orders, that if there was any change in the condition of the sea or the weather or any tactical change, it must be reported to the captain immediately.

Cady: Was it your habit to do so?

McKissick: I hadn't been standing watches for too long—about six to nine months—consequently, I did my best to abide by every rule, and I had no hesitation, of course, in notifying the captain of such events, even in daylight, during rain squalls or anything. It was my practice to notify the captain of such occurrences.

Cady returned to the subject of the message-board submarine.

Cady: At the time when you saw this dispatch that you spoke of, did it cause you any concern as to the safety of the ship?

McKissick: No, sir, I considered the position of the submarine and the position of the ship to be a great enough distance at which—as to cause no alarm. . . . [W]e received dispatches all through the war much to the same effect. When any of them were that far away, we didn't feel unduly alarmed at such a report.

Other survivors, including Lieutenant Richard Redmayne, the engineering officer, gave the court similar assessments: The night was dark, visibility poor, information about submarine contacts routine, and zigzagging did not seem necessary.

Then Dr. Lewis Haynes was called to the stand. When the torpedoes hit, Haynes said, he was blown out of his bunk and onto his desk. The second explosion filled his room with flame. "I turned to leave my room and got started toward the passageway when there was a large blast down the passageway. I ducked back into my room and felt the flames swish around me. I held my life jacket in front of my face."

The room was on fire, Haynes said, and his forehead was burned. He knew he had to get out. But when he looked for escape—via a ladder, a passageway, and other rooms—there was fire everywhere he turned.

"I got in the wardroom. It was filled with a red haze and the heat was intense. I could feel myself being overcome, probably from the gases, and about halfway across the wardroom, I did fall to the deck. I fell on my outstretched hands, and the deck at that point was very hot, and my hand sizzled, and it was very severely burned. The pain shocked me to my feet."

In the press area, reporters scribbled furiously. This was the most dramatic testimony of the trial so far.

Haynes told the court that he crossed the wardroom, feeling his way along the bulkhead, then collapsed into an easy chair and relaxed. "I thought that that was the end, and it was going to be easy, and then someone who was standing over me said, 'My God, I am fainting!' and fell on me."

That scared Haynes to his feet again. He found an open porthole, poked his head through, and vacuumed fresh air into his lungs. When his head cleared, Haynes was able to climb to the battle-dressing station in the port hangar, where rows of wounded men had already collected. That was when he joined the chief pharmacist's mate and began administering morphine.

When the time came to abandon ship, Haynes said the water below him was "black with men."

Ryan: About how many men were . . . originally in the group of survivors of which you were a part?

Haynes: I would say that the group of swimmers was made up of between three and four hundred men.

Ryan: About how many of that group were rescued?

Haynes: I believe the *Cecil Doyle* picked up ninety-three out of that group.

Ryan: What happened to the remainder?

Haynes: Well, more than twenty died the first night from burns and injuries—

"Objection!" It was Cady. "This line of questioning and this testimony is not connected with the issues in the case."

An argument ensued and Rear Admiral Baker again cleared the court. When the court reconvened, Baker announced that any testimony regarding deaths in the water following "abandon ship" should be avoided unless it was directly connected with any possible inefficiency of the accused.

The ruling would prove ironic. Cady feared testimony about the gruesome days in the water would work against McVay. He had won the point, but at a cost he had perhaps not fully calculated. Haynes, having survived in one of the largest swimmer groups, could've testified to the horrors suffered by the crew after McVay's alleged hazarding of the ship—tragedy and drama that would have been of keen interest to newspaper editors, whose columnists had already assigned the blame for the epic death toll to the Navy and not to McVay. Instead, newspapers the following day ran headlines about Haynes's conversation with Commander Janney in the wardroom, as well as Redmayne's testimony that Janney had briefed the watch officers about an enemy submarine ahead.

"Officers Standing Night Watch Told Sub in Vicinity," wrote the *Evening Press* of Muncie, Indiana. "Indianapolis Night Watch Had Been Warned of Prowling Sub," wrote the Green Bay, Wisconsin, *Press-Gazette.* "Officers of Lost Cruiser Were Told About Nip Sub," wrote the *Leader* of Wilkes-Barre, Pennsylvania.

A couple of witnesses after Haynes, Ensign John Woolston took the stand. Woolston had spent much of his time in Guam after the sinking, writing the official war damage report for *Indianapolis.* When called to the court-martial, Woolston thought he would be testifying as a survivor, and was surprised to find himself transformed, mid-testimony, from eyewitness to expert witness.

Ryan elicited from Woolston a raft of technical details, such as Indy's cruising condition, repair party status, and damage to the ship. Like McKissick, and the bugler, Donald Mack, who testified before him, Woolston told the court that he heard the order to abandon ship.

"There was plenty of time to abandon ship in an orderly fashion after the word was passed, with little danger to the men," Woolston said. "However, because of the lack of power communications within the ship, it was difficult for the men far aft to hear the word."

11

ON DECEMBER 5, CAPTAIN Ryan continued his prosecution, calling a procession of witnesses to the stand.

Indianapolis supply officer John Reid, a lieutenant commander, gave a dramatic account of his last moments on the fantail. "There seemed to be . . . at least eight hundred men clinging to the life line. The ship was listing rapidly and the men were attempting to go over the side." Reid tried to stop them. "Finally, it seemed impossible to do anything but go over the side, so the men did, and I . . . fell back against a turret, and finally, the ship just went down from under me."

Reid, the senior officer on the fantail, said he did not tell the men there to abandon ship, because for the first several minutes, he did not think Indy would sink. Other officers and chiefs also testified that they thought at first that the ship might remain afloat. This buttressed McVay's not-guilty plea to Charge II, failure to order abandon ship in time—which, of course, the prosecution had expected. Reid also testified to the visibility as seen from the fantail: broken clouds, which created a "hazy effect" when clouds were over the moon.

> **Ryan:** When the clouds were not over the moon, what was the condition?
>
> **Reid:** That was very rare, but at such times it was bright.

The question of visibility was key, since naval instructions required skippers to zigzag in times of good visibility or moonlight. Ryan attempted to elicit testimony in support of Charge I—that McVay had hazarded his vessel by failing to zigzag—while Cady tried to counter it.

> **Cady:** Did you actually see the bright exposed surface of the moon?
>
> **Reid:** At intervals, yes.

Cady: At intervals?

Reid: Rarely.

Ensign Ross Rogers, Jr., a junior division officer, said he didn't notice either the moon or visibility when he came on watch just before mid-night at "sky amidships," a high platform near the center of the ship. He noticed only that it was dark.

Ryan: Did you [notice it] at any subsequent time?

Rogers: Later on, sir, I was ordered to watch the sea for enemy submarines, and I could see the reflection of the moon in the water.

Ryan: Was this before you finally left the ship?

Rogers: Yes, sir, it was.

Chief Gunner Cecil Harrison said it was "a dark night" with a moderate ground swell and a light wind.

Ryan: How far would you estimate that you could see, in thousands of yards, from your height?

Harrison: About three thousand yards.

Ryan: What could you see at that distance?

Harrison: It would be limited—it would have to be a large vessel, the size of a destroyer. Nothing that was low in the water, I do not believe, could have been seen.

Durward Horner, a warrant gunner, told Cady under cross-examination that even after the ship was hit, it was so dark topside that he couldn't recognize his own gunnery officer, Commander Lipski. "I think I knew him more by shape than anything else." Horner said he never saw the moon. Then Ensign Donald Blum took the stand.

Ryan: Did anything unusual occur during the night of 29–30 July, 1945? If so, what was it?

Blum: The ship sank.

At Blum's blunt summary, a wave of soft laughter rolled through the gallery and the press. Blum then testified that he had been on watch at the sky amidships platform and "could see the fantail and the forward stack with no trouble. I could distinguish people walking around on the fantail."

And so it went, with testimony on Charge I swinging like a pendulum between McVay and his accusers. Some men recalled periods of luminous moonlight and lucid visibility—one sailor even recalled seeing the horizon—while others remembered a coal-black night with no moon at all. On Charge II, testimony regarding the abandon-ship order came down heavily in McVay's favor, as Admiral Colclough had predicted. By day's end on Thursday, December 6, Ryan had called twenty-two witnesses, some of whom told tales of heroism and narrow escape.

But no individual testimony was as chilling as the collective calculus of death that had begun with John Woolston:

Q: Are you the senior surviving officer in damage control?

A: Yes, sir. I am the only surviving officer.

Radioman J. J. Moran:

Q: Are there any surviving officer personnel of the communications department?

A: No, sir. There are none.

Seaman First Class Raymond Jurkiewicz:

Q: How many enlisted personnel were in CIC at that time?

A: Three, with me.

Q: How many of that number, three enlisted and two officer personnel, survived?

A: I did.

Q: Will you repeat that, please?

A: Just me. Just myself.

Witness after witness underscored this grim fact: Of the 1,195 souls aboard *Indianapolis*, three of every four men died.

12

COMMANDER MOCHITSURA HASHIMOTO STOOD atop a run of aircraft loading stairs and looked out at a foreign land: Washington, D.C. It was 8:45 a.m. on December 10. In the custody of an American naval officer, Allan Smith, a lieutenant junior grade, Hashimoto had boarded a naval transport plane in Oakland and flown all night—twelve hours with a single stop in Olathe, Kansas.

The victor had summoned the vanquished. The Navy had called Hashimoto to testify in the court-martial of Captain Charles McVay. Hashimoto had been promoted to the rank of commander four months earlier, but now he wore civilian clothes, a slouch hat and an ill-fitting dark suit. A photographer snapped Hashimoto, so dressed, at the top of the loading stairs, and that was the picture that would appear on the front pages of American newspapers.

While he was waiting for departure in Oakland, personnel from the Office of Naval Intelligence interrogated Hashimoto. He kept expecting to be clapped in irons to await trial as a war criminal. Perhaps the Americans would even execute him. His greatest fear, though, was never seeing his wife and sons again. But American officers repeatedly assured him that his trip to America was no trick. He would return to his family soon and safe, he was told. Still, he worried.

Hashimoto descended the loading stairs with Smith in trail, and a

flock of reporters pressed in, armed with cameras and pens and questions. On the tarmac, Hashimoto heard Smith tell reporters that Hashimoto did not speak much English. Kyodo, a Japanese news service, had
reported on December 8 that Hashimoto was going to Washington.
The Associated Press picked up the brief item, and newspapers all over
America began following the story. The next day, the United Press elaborated: The judge advocate had called the Japanese officer to verify that
Indianapolis had been torpedoed. By December 10, readers from coast to
coast had learned that Hashimoto was "short, stocky, and swarthy." By
December 11, reporters were calling him a "star witness."

Some Navy brass used the press to push back against Hashimoto's
court-martial appearance—albeit while keeping their names out of the
papers, perhaps so as not to run afoul of King and Forrestal. "Several
high-ranking naval officers" pointed out to reporters that Japan had
been "the enemy" until only very recently, and that Japanese accounts of
the war had frequently proven untrue. The subscript: Anything this Japanese witness might say in court could not be trusted. Meanwhile, stories
of Japanese atrocities were still fresh. The Bataan Death March, images
of Japanese soldiers using U.S. prisoners of war for bayonet practice, the
wholesale murder of civilians. Of 27,000 American POWs, 40 percent
died in captivity.

Meanwhile, there was no precedent in U.S. military justice for calling a member of a defeated enemy to testify against an American officer. Op-ed writers cried foul. Of particular interest was the opinion of
nationally syndicated columnist Robert Ruark, who wanted to know
why Hashimoto wasn't simply deposed in Japan. Perhaps, he suggested,
McVay's court-martial "was beginning to sag in reader appeal."

Now, Marine guards hustled Hashimoto from the airport to the Navy
Yard. He felt like a prisoner, but Lieutenant Smith had told him that
was not the case. Though most of his guards treated him with kindness,
others ran him through with daggered stares. In these eyes, Hashimoto
read hatred and disgust. He understood enough English to know they
regarded him as something between vermin and a monster.

Three days later, Hashimoto donned a blue suit provided by the Navy,
and a Marine guard detail escorted him to Building 57. He had been

unable to bring with him any official documents from I-58. All were destroyed when the IJN surrendered the submarine to the Americans in September. Now, Hashimoto waited outside the courtroom. Inside, a war was under way.

For the defense, Captain Cady rose and addressed Admiral Baker. "If the court please, I wish to make formal objection to the idea of calling one of the officers of the defeated enemy who, as a nation, have been proven guilty of every despicable treachery, of the most infamous cruelties, and of the most barbarous practices in violation of all of the laws of civilized warfare, to testify against one of our own commanding officers on a matter affecting his professional ability and judgment.

"I am sure I express the feeling of every American citizen, especially those who so recently fought against the Japanese, in protesting this spectacle. This objection is not, and cannot, be based on any legalistic grounds, since our lawmakers have never imagined through the centuries of Anglo-Saxon law any such grotesque proceedings."

"If the court please," Ryan replied, "the judge advocate regrets exceedingly that emotional aspects to the introduction of this witness are being stressed in this court. It is not the intention of the judge advocate, and he would resent asking this witness—anybody's asking this witness—to give any opinions as to the honor or the actions of the accused in this case."

Ryan said he believed Hashimoto's testimony was necessary to a decision in the case—he wanted the court to hear, in essence, the details of the Japanese commander's attack. "In order to guarantee accurate answers . . . we intend to request the court to swear him with the oath according to our law, and the oath which will bind him in his own country, which will make him subject to prosecution if it develops that he does not give true evidence before this court."

The prosecutor then headed off any objection to the propriety of Hashimoto's testimony. "It is a matter of record, in both our Navy Department and our War Department, that there are many cases of members of our armed forces having been tried by courts-martial and in the proceedings of those courts-martial, enemy aliens testified before the court."

The attorneys lashed back and forth. Ryan cited precedent indicating that he was only performing his due diligence as judge advocate. In a previous case, he noted, a judge advocate was found to have erred in not allowing the testimony of a pair of "notorious prostitutes."

Cady countered by saying that since Hashimoto was not a Christian, he might be incapable of abiding by the standard oath to tell the truth. The defense introduced a Naval Courts and Boards text that said persons outside the Christian religion should take "additional ceremony or acts as will make the oath binding on the conscience of the person taking it."

This was a concession by Cady, which he then immediately shot down as inadequate: "However, I submit to the court how, under the circumstances, can there be any pains of penalties of perjury upon such a witness, an enemy alien of a defeated nation who has no standing in this country at all. There are numerous questions as to the veracity of the Japanese as a race, and it is a question for the court to determine how he may be placed under oath or affirmation to tell the truth."

Ryan spoke up quickly: He was sure naval authorities could ensure that Hashimoto suffered pain were he to perjure himself. Then Ryan noted that the alternative oath he was suggesting Hashimoto take applied also to "heretics or atheists, those who have no religion."

"It appears the proper procedure would be to bring in the proposed witness," Cady said, "and to examine him as to his understanding of the truth and falsehood, the meaning of perjury."

All parties agreed. First a translator was brought in, Francis Royal Eastlake, an American who had been born in Japan and lived there for eighteen years. Eastlake gave his qualifications, which included familiarity with the oath administered in Japanese courts-martial and civil courts. The sides agreed that Hashimoto would be brought in and examined: Did he understand what it meant to tell the truth?

The door to the courtroom opened and the room hushed. The audience was now nearly quadruple what it had been in previous days of testimony. At least 150 spectators had crowded in to see Hashimoto up close.

When the controversial witness shambled in, Associated Press reporter Arthur Edson was shocked. This Japanese warrior, who claimed to have struck the worst blow against the Navy since Pearl

Harbor, looked to Edson about as ferocious as a chocolate milkshake. Escorted by a glowering Marine guard, Hashimoto stood stiffly at attention and bowed to the court before taking a seat in the witness chair.

Eastlake: Hashimoto, what is your religious belief?

Hashimoto (via Eastlake): I am a Shintoist.

Eastlake: What do you know of the meaning of truth and falsehood?

Hashimoto: I am fully aware of the difference between truth and falsehood.

Eastlake: What happens in your religion if you tell a falsehood?

Hashimoto: Should I happen to utter any falsehood, I will have to pay for it. I mean I will be punished for it.

Hashimoto delivered his answers with customary Asian reserve, so softly that neither the spectators nor reporters crowding the courtroom could hear him speaking Japanese, but only Eastlake's English translation.

Eastlake: Does your religion include a belief in a life hereafter?

Hashimoto: I believe that the soul exists after death.

Eastlake: Do you know what perjury means?

Hashimoto: [I have] full knowledge of it.

Eastlake: Is there punishment in Japanese law for perjury?

Hashimoto: I don't know all the details, but I believe that there is punishment.

Eastlake: Are you listed on any of the lists of war criminals for any of the Allied powers?

Hashimoto: To my knowledge, my name is not on any list of war criminals.

After this testimony, the court ruled Hashimoto competent to take the oaths. The president of the court administered both, and Hashimoto signed his name in ink, both in English and in Japanese. Looking on, Edson, the AP reporter, thought Hashimoto's pants too short and his chair too big. He had to sit on its edge and lean forward to put his feet flat on the floor. He looked to Edson not like a fierce warrior but like a man applying for a job as a night watchman.

> Ryan: Have you received any threats or promises of any kind, which might tend to influence you to give any particular kind of testimony?
>
> Hashimoto: I have received neither threats nor promises to put any—to try to influence me to bear witness one way or the other.

After establishing Hashimoto's duties and position on the night of July 29–30, Ryan began to probe the details of his attack. Hashimoto delivered his answers in Japanese, which were translated for the court by Commander John Bromley. While Eastlake was a civilian familiar with Japanese law and ethics, Bromley could translate the technical details of naval warfare.

Hashimoto told the court that he surfaced, supposing that the visibility had improved and the moon would be out. "I discerned a dark object and crash-dived immediately," he said. "I then swung my ship around to head in its direction." The object was ten thousand meters away, bearing ninety degrees true, he continued. He headed toward the object and prepared to fire torpedoes and launch *kaiten*.

Ryan asked whether Hashimoto could draw from memory a rough sketch showing the relative positions of the target and I-58 from the time Hashimoto first sighted *Indianapolis* until he fired his torpedoes.

"Yes," Hashimoto said. "Roughly."

He stood and sketched out the general movements of his attack, and this was entered into the court record.

Cady rose and addressed the witness. "When did you depart for this patrol?"

Hashimoto replied that he made passage from Kure to Hirao to load his *kaiten*, then departed Hirao on July 20.

Cady gestured to a nautical chart. "Can you trace on this chart your approximate course from then until the place you last testified to?"

Hashimoto obliged. On the chart, he traced a line heading about 160 degrees from the Japanese home islands. It was the same heading captured by the ULTRA magicians in intercepts describing I-58's assigned course. Cady could not have known this. Instead, he seemed to be zeroing in on another possibility not yet fully explored.

With the faintest scratching noise, Hashimoto's pencil kept traveling south-southeast until he neared the 140th line of longitude about six hundred miles west of the Mariana Islands. Here, he drew a line due south and then southwest on a heading of about 200, to intersect a small slice of ocean due east of Leyte and just over three hundred miles north of Palau.

Again, I-58's track comported precisely with intelligence in the possession of Naquin, Carter, and Gillette, and available to Admiral Murray, in the two weeks leading up to Hashimoto's attack on *Indianapolis*. Cady may have read in general terms about this intelligence in the testimony taken by Coney and Van Metre, but the ULTRA intercepts themselves were still highly classified. And so, the significance of Hashimoto's sketch, developing like a Polaroid in full view of the court, was hiding in plain sight.

The Japanese commander completed his drawing, tracing a final line that headed about 260, except for an odd jag to the south. This appeared as a sudden "V" in an otherwise westerly course. Hashimoto had also jotted dates along the entire track.

Cady pointed to the jag in I-58's route. "I would like to ask you how you know, and how you can remember, this abrupt break, this break in your course at the point marked '7/28.'"

This was where, on July 28, he attacked a tanker, Hashimoto said. After sending his *kaiten* pilots into eternity, and uncertain of the results, he had headed slightly north. The position was more than a hundred miles east of the hunter-killer op kicked off on the 28th by *Wild Hunter*. If Cady had been on the verge of arguing that the Philippine Sea Frontier had had I-58 in its grasp during the *Harris* chase, Hashimoto's chart proved they had not.

But if Cady had been able to connect the dots, a darker indictment loomed.

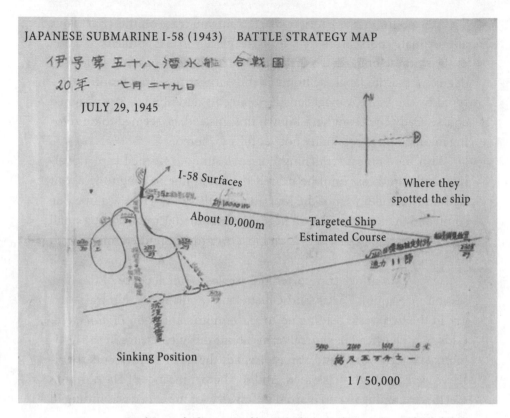

JAPANESE SUBMARINE I-58 (1943)   BATTLE STRATEGY MAP

伊号第五十八潜水艦 合戦図

20年   七月二十九日

JULY 29, 1945

I-58 Surfaces

Where they
spotted the ship

About 10,000m

Targeted Ship
Estimated Course

Sinking Position

1 / 50,000

Hashimoto's diagram of his attack on *Indianapolis*.

Along Route Peddie, where Carter had said all was quiet, where Waldron's routing officers confirmed it by suggesting a speed of 15.7 knots, where Naquin testified that the risk of hostile subs was "practically negligible," Hashimoto's chart revealed that there had lurked not one enemy submarine, but two.

The chart also put the lie to Admiral Purnell's *New York Times* musing that Indy had blundered over the top of a sub her officers knew about. Meanwhile, officers on each end of Indy's route had information on one or both subs and failed to pass it to Cady's client, McVay.

At Leyte, Captain Alfred Granum dispatched *Harris* in response to the *Wild Hunter* periscope sighting. *Harris*'s hunter-killer operation spun off a series of messages that bounced between Leyte and Guam and used the terms "highly probable" sub and "propeller beats." At Guam, Naquin had information on *both* the enemy subs in Indy's path:

He knew about the *Harris* chase, as he revealed to Coney when pressed, and he had the ULTRA intel on the Tamon group. Also at Guam, Carter's and Murray's offices had the ULTRA intel stating that I-58 was operating west of the Marianas. Murray, who sat in judgment of McVay at the Guam court of inquiry, was the divert authority east of the Chop line. Yet he did not divert *Indianapolis*, although, as Snyder told King, the Tamon group intel appeared to be sufficient reason to do so.

Testimony and message traffic proving some of these things were available to Cady, but buried in a five-month tower of evidence. But Murray's testimony in the supplemental investigation was taking place almost concurrently with Hashimoto's court-martial appearance, and Carter would not testify until December 18. Thus, Cady did not have all the facts—a direct result of King's decision to court-martial McVay before all the evidence was in. And so, even as Hashimoto's sketch laid the truth bare, Cady was unable to connect the dots, and the moment passed.

Hashimoto's testimony continued. "I then started to proceed to another point, the intersection of the lines connecting Palau and Okinawa and the line connecting Leyte Gulf and Guam." It was while patrolling this area, he said, that he encountered *Indianapolis*.

Looking on from the press area, Edson could detect in the Japanese officer's words neither pride nor humility. As he watched this small, soft-spoken man, he kept saying to himself, "Here is a fellow who commanded a three-hundred-foot submarine. Here is the guy who was a constant threat to U.S. shipping and lives." Edson had to keep reminding himself in order to believe it.

Next, Cady elicited a series of technical details about Hashimoto's attack. He had radar, but didn't use it. He had sound gear, but it wasn't working very well. His torpedoes traveled at a speed of forty-eight knots. They were set at a depth of four meters.

Cady: Was the target zigzagging at the time you sighted it?

Hashimoto: At the time of the sighting of the target, there was an indistinct blur, and I was unable to determine whether it was zigzagging.

Cady: Was it zigzagging later?

Hashimoto: There is no question of the fact that it made no radical changes in course. It is faintly possible that there was a minor change in course between the time of sighting and the time of the attack.

Cady: Would it have made any difference to you if the target had been zigzagging?

There was a pause. Cady repeated his question, the fulcrum of his defense: "Would it have made any difference to you if the target had been zigzagging?"

Hashimoto answered in Japanese, and Bromley translated this way: "It would have involved no change in the method of firing the torpedoes, but some changes in the maneuvering."

At this moment, disquiet pierced Hashimoto's heart. He understood English well enough to think, *That's not what I said, exactly.* Bromley's rendering did not convey to the court what Hashimoto meant: *I was in a perfect position. I would have hit the target no matter what.*

After landing in D.C., he had met with Ryan and Cady, separately and in private. Each had posed the same question Cady just asked, and Hashimoto told both men flatly that it wouldn't have mattered if *Indianapolis* had been zigzagging. Now, though, instead of asking Hashimoto to clarify, or reframing the question to elicit the answer he'd received pretrial, Cady inexplicably moved on.

Capitalizing on the moment, Ryan stood. "Did you use radar which was in your ship at any time in relation to the sinking of this ship about which you have testified?"

No, Hashimoto answered. Radar was not used from the time of the crash-dive until after the attack was completed.

"Did the radar assist you in any way to pick up this target?"

Again, the answer was no.

It was, for Ryan, a bull's-eye. Admiral Snyder's earlier analysis had suggested enemy radar may have negated the need to zigzag. But Hashimoto hadn't used radar either to sight or track *Indianapolis*. He used only his periscope, the specific tactic for which zigzagging had been designed.

Suddenly, Hashimoto's testimony was over. He stood and bowed again to the court. One of the Marine guards, Captain George Cordea, stepped forward to escort him. At six-three and more than two hundred pounds, Cordea was a veteran of the savage battle at Guadalcanal in which Japanese troops killed more than seven thousand Marines.

Edson heard him say to another Marine, "I gotta take this monkey back."

13

WHEN THE DEFENSE BEGAN on December 15, Cady immediately attacked the charge that McVay failed to issue a timely order of "abandon ship." He called to the stand several sailors who testified to hearing the order between eight and ten minutes after the torpedoes struck, and in time to properly execute it. Cady then proceeded to the zigzagging charge, zeroing in on moonlight and visibility. He called to the stand Seaman First Class A. C. King.

King said he was on the bridge with L. D. Cox at the time of the explosions. Visibility was poor and he never saw the moon.

Ensign Harlan Twible also took the stand. "It got so dark I had to request that the gun captain inform me if there was a man on the shield looking out over the sea," he said. When it came time for Twible's relief, he added, he looked down toward the quarterdeck and could make out only dark shapes, with not even enough detail to discern whether a given shadow was one man or two.

Others testified to their actions that night—John Bullard, a shipfitter striker, Ensign Don Howison, Dr. Melvin Modisher, and more. Compared to prosecution witnesses, the time that defense witnesses spent on the stand was notably brief. Cady moved them in and moved them out. Ryan, meanwhile, asked only scant questions, perhaps remembering a war maxim attributed to Napoleon: Never interrupt your enemy when he is making a mistake.

The court recessed on Sunday, December 16. On Monday, Cady

called Captain Oliver Naquin to the stand. Coney's grilling of Naquin in the supplemental investigation had produced ample material for McVay's defense, and Cady had access to that testimony. It would have been standard procedure for defense counsel to review a witness's prior statements before calling him to the stand in open court. But if Cady had this information, he did not use it.

> **Cady:** What is your estimate of the risk of enemy submarine activity at this time, at the end of July, along the route the *Indianapolis* was to proceed?
>
> **Naquin:** I would say it was low order.
>
> **Cady:** I'm sorry, I didn't understand.
>
> **Naquin:** I would say that it was very low order . . . very slight.
>
> **Cady:** Was there at any time any question in your mind of diverting the *Indianapolis* after she sailed?
>
> **Naquin:** There was not.

Admiral Baker and the court intervened with questions of their own.

> **Court:** You have just stated that your estimate of the danger of submarine attack on the *Indianapolis* was very slight. Had there not been reports of submarines in that area?
>
> **Naquin:** Yes, we had had reports of submarines. At the investigation in Guam in this case, I furnished a chart showing the recent submarine reports.

Naquin did not mention that this chart was wildly incomplete. Instead, he continued, telling the court that the reports on his chart were not borne out by sinkings and "as a result such reports were downgraded." Naquin gave his reasons for that, repeating the refrain about jumpy merchant skippers seeing phantom submarines.

But *after* the merchant ship *Wild Hunter* reported back-to-back periscope sightings, the *Harris* hunter-killer team reported a sound contact in message traffic on which Naquin, at Commander Marianas, was copied. Then *Harris* also reported a temporary target oil slick slightly north of Route Peddie. An hour after that, the search unit sent another message: "sound contact with engine propeller . . . evaluation positive." All this message traffic was part of the supplemental investigation. And on December 4, Naquin told Coney under questioning that he gave submarine contacts reported by naval vessels, rather than merchant ships, a "high grade."

Why did he not give a high grade to *Harris*'s "positive" report *with* propeller beats, ninety miles ahead of *Indianapolis*'s track? Cady might have asked. Especially in light of ULTRA intel that placed an enemy sub on offensive maneuvers in that vicinity? And when the *Harris* search unit reported that it had made multiple hedgehog attacks on this submarine before losing contact, how did Naquin grade the sub report then? Given the information at hand, why didn't he, the divert authority for Route Peddie east of the 130th line of longitude, divert *Indianapolis*?

But Cady did not ask these questions. And where he had lodged vigorous objections during the testimony of Ryan's witnesses, he let Naquin's testimony stand unchallenged.

Neither did Cady call to the stand Commodore Norman Gillette, acting commander of the Philippine Sea Frontier. Five days earlier, Gillette had told Coney and Van Metre, "We assumed there were submarines in that area, and we had our patrol vessels that were on submarine patrol in the vicinity of 130 degrees East, 11 North, to proceed to that area."

Gillette told investigators he recalled that one of his antisubmarine patrols did "make a report of a submarine contact," and that the Frontier received ULTRA intel on enemy contacts "continuously."

Van Metre: Did all of this activity represent an increase or a decrease from normal?

Gillette: An increase.

Van Metre: Did this increase in activity cause you any particular concern?

Gillette: Yes, sir. We were greatly concerned . . . constantly diverting shipping, increasing patrols in those areas, established a hunter-killer group, sent tankers into the area to fuel the patrol vessels so they would not have to leave their station. . . . [W]e were concerned and we used all the forces we could make available to meet this recognized threat.

"Recognized threat." There it was, a phrase that contrasted wildly with Naquin's assertions of a "practically negligible" and "very slight" risk. It also contrasted with information delivered to McVay in Carter's office, the routing office at Guam and during Indy's passage along Route Peddie. A "recognized threat" would likely have figured heavily in McVay's "discretion" on whether to zigzag.

Discretion, another word for judgment, can always be questioned, even prosecuted, and the Navy was prosecuting McVay for being negligent in his. But Cady had it right on the first day of the court-martial. "Negligence" implied knowledge that should have been acted on and was not, and there was no proof that McVay had such knowledge. In Gillette's testimony before Coney and Van Metre, though, was ample proof that others had such knowledge and did not share it with McVay. But again, with just four days to prepare a defense and Gillette's testimony occurring late in the court-martial, Cady may not have been able to review it.

On that score, the admirals still taking their turns before Coney and Van Metre across the base were busy blaming each other. Gillette said it would have been Guam's responsibility to divert *Indianapolis*. Murray said Indy had passed into Leyte's jurisdiction—this, though he later said that "technically," the ship was still in his area. Murray also averred that he did not know about the four submarines of the Tamon group, though Commodore Carter's combat intel officer, Captain Layton, said Murray had that information. Neither was Murray informed of the *Wild Hunter* sighting and *Harris*'s antisubmarine operation, he said.

But if McVay was to be held negligent for not acting on information he did not have, should Murray not have been held negligent for not acting on information that he did have? Murray didn't seem to think so. He suggested that McVay's lack of information was his own fault. He should've come to Murray's offices and asked his staff for additional intelligence to supplement his routing orders. Lots of skippers did, he said.

Rescue pilot Wilbur "Chuck" Gwinn, who spotted the Indy survivors.

Pilot Adrian Marks, who landed his PBY-5 Catalina in the open sea to rescue Indy survivors.

USS *Cecil J. Doyle* skipper W. Graham Claytor (center) and his crew.

When found, survivors Troy Nunley (left) and Joseph Van Meter (right) were "riding a rolled-up floater net cowboy style, with sharks circling," their USS *Register* rescuers reported.

USS *Bassett* rescuer Seaman Bill Van Wilpe.

An *Indianapolis* survivor is transported to an ambulance from Base Hospital #20 at Peleliu.

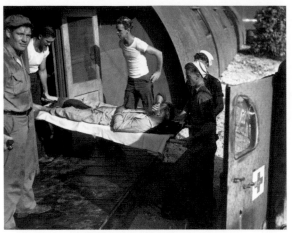

(L to R) Bernard Bateman, A. C. King, and Erick Anderson, recuperating at Base Hospital #20, Peleliu, August 5, 1945.

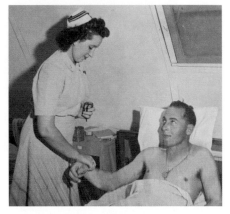

Known for her kindness, Eva Jane Bolents treats Vincent Allard at Base Hospital #18, Guam. Several survivors proposed marriage to Eva Jane.

ADM Spruance awards Purple Hearts to survivors (L to R) Glenn Morgan, J. J. Moran, and Louis Bitonti.

Emperor Hirohito meets with his War Council.

VADM Matome Ugaki prepares to make his final flight, August 15, 1945.

Japanese forces surrender in the Philippines. On the near side of the table, at center, is the Japanese commander GEN Tomoyuki Yamashita. Across from Yamashita, second from the left, is LTG Jonathan Wainwright, who, as Allied Commander, surrendered at Corregidor Island in 1942 and became the highest-ranking American POW of the war. At the opposite end of the American side of the table is Commodore Norman C. Gillette, who can be seen just to the left of Yamashita's head. Gillette was acting Philippine Sea Frontier commander when *Indianapolis* sank.

During the court-martial, Hashimoto draws a chart showing his track from Japan to the Philippine Sea.

McVay during his court-martial.

Surviving officers and sailors called to testify at the court-martial of Captain McVay.

Thomas Ryan, the Navy judge advocate, or prosecutor, who tried McVay.

These key figures were at odds over McVay's court-martial. ADM Ernest King and Navy Secretary James Forrestal (left and center) supported the trial. ADM Chester Nimitz (right) did not.

McVay receives warm greetings from the survivors and their wives at the first survivors' reunion in July 1960.

McVay and his wife, Louise, at the 1960 reunion.

Indy's "5th Division" at the 1960 reunion (L to R): R. B. McLain, Felton Outland, Louis Bitonti, Robert Schaffer, William Simpson, Norman Krueger, Richard Stephens, Bryan Blanthorn, Donald Beatty, Talbert Green, and Archie Farmer (lower front).

Senator John Warner of Virginia.

Senator Bob Smith of New Hampshire led the Senate effort to exonerate McVay.

Rep. Julia Carson (D-Indiana) at left, and Rep. Joe Scarborough (R-Florida) in gray suit, look on as a young Hunter Scott advocates exoneration for CAPT McVay. Survivor Buck Gibson (in American flag shirt) is in the background, along with McVay's son, Kimo (in red blazer).

ADM Donald Pilling, Vice Chief of Naval Operations.

CAPT William J. Toti, the last skipper of the submarine *Indianapolis*.

(L to R): Unidentified, Eugene Morgan, Glenn Morgan, Richard Paroubek, Mike Kuryla, John Spinelli, Buck Gibson, Bob McGuiggan, Cleatus Lebow, Paul Murphy, and Lyle Umenhoffer stand before SSN-697, the cruiser *Indianapolis*'s namesake sub.

Mochitsura Hashimoto (center) served as a Shinto priest in his later years.

From the deck of the submarine USS *Ohio*, Jason Witty, grandson of Indy survivor Eugene Morgan, spreads his grandfather's ashes near the site of the sinking, fulfilling Morgan's final wish that he be returned to the waters of the Pacific with his lost shipmates.

Survivor Donald McCall with LtCol (Ret.) Oliver North.

Hashimoto's granddaughter Atsuko Iida and her sons at the 2005 survivors' reunion.

(L to R): At the 2005 survivors' reunion, Mel Jacob, Vic Buckett, Harold Bray, Navy secretary Gordon England, Jim Jarvis, and Woodie James.

L. D. Cox rides in the 2005 survivors' parade in downtown Indianapolis.

Art Leenerman (left) and Earl Riggins share the survivors' book.

Admiral Soc McMorris, however, would later say that he considered it "sufficient" for McVay to have visited only the routing office. He did not "feel it should have been necessary" for McVay to pay a second visit to Murray's staff.

Meanwhile, Murray said, communications personnel on Carter's staff had tried to raise *Indianapolis* to test radio-teletype gear and were not successful. "Therefore, the knowledge of the movement of the *Indianapolis* and its failure to establish communications with CincPac's headquarters was known by personnel other than the intelligence personnel, but so far as I know, no one on my staff."

Translation: Murray's staff didn't know Indy might be missing, but Carter's staff should have. At the same time that the admirals were blaming each other in secret, the court-martial of Captain McVay was proceeding in public. Whether or not it was King's intention to protect other admirals by trying McVay before Coney and Van Metre finished grilling them, the decision was bearing fruit.

14

FOR ALL THE ANEMIA of the defense so far, Cady had an ace in the hole: Captain Glynn Robert Donaho. A fifteen-year submarine veteran and wolf pack commander, Donaho had sunk twenty-eight enemy vessels and in 1942 was awarded the Navy Cross for offensive action as skipper of USS *Flying Fish*. Cady established these bona fides before the court, and Donaho was accepted as an expert on submarine operations.

Cady: Did you ever fire at a vessel which was not zigzagging in these patrols you have made?

Donaho: Not to my knowledge.

Cady: Did you ever fire at an unescorted target?

Donaho: Yes, one.

Cady: Based on your experience as outlined above, what is your opinion on the value of zigzagging as affecting the accuracy of torpedo fire?

Donaho: With our modern submarines, fire control equipment, high speed torpedoes, a well-trained fire control party, and with torpedo spreads, I didn't find that zigzagging affected the results.

Ryan stood to cross-examine the witness.

Ryan: Can you state whether or not the Japanese submarines had as good fire control and tracking equipment as you had in our submarines?

Donaho: I know they had high speed torpedoes, radars, and I know they had . . . six torpedo tubes. . . . [W]e always gave the Japanese credit for having as good equipment as we have had.

Ryan: You mentioned radar as one of the bases for your statement. Would you have used radar in tracking the target and obtaining data for your attack?

Donaho: It all depends on the range. It depends on the visibility.

Ryan: Assuming you did not have the use of radar, would you still answer as you did, for the question of ten thousand yards and being ahead of the target at night?

Donaho: I would.

Ryan fine-tuned his question: Without radar, at ten thousand yards and a target speed of twelve knots, would it have been more or less difficult for Donaho to obtain the proper firing position if the target had been zigzagging?

Donaho's answer seemed clipped and a bit impatient, as though he were educating a dilettante. "We started off this war without radars. We were sinking ships without them. There were many times when we did not have radars due to matériel damages, breakage, failures on patrol, and we sank ships just the same. Being on the track of a target with . . . periscopes and sound gear, and spreading out torpedoes, I think the results would have been the same."

"That was not my question, if you please, Captain Donaho," Ryan said coolly. "Under the conditions stated by the accused, would it have been more difficult for you to obtain the proper firing position if the target had been zigzagging?"

"No. Not as long as I could see the target."

"Then are you telling this court that if the target had been zigzagging at the time you sighted it, and up until the moment you fired, you would not have been required to make any more calculations than if the target had been on a steady course? Is that what you wish to tell this court?"

"No, sir. If the target had been zigzagging, I would have had to change my setup in my torpedo data computer to meet the new course, or the new speed, from my sound gear."

"Well, then, are you now saying that you would have had to make considerably more calculations if the target had been zigzagging than if she were not? Is that correct?"

Ryan seemed to have scored a point . . . until Donaho fired back. Despite increased calculations, he said, he could have fired on Ryan's hypothetical zigzagging ship within ten seconds. In fact, Donaho said, "You always expect a target to zig, and you anticipate what is going to happen on the next leg. I have personally found that a target *not* zigzagging would have confused me."

As Ryan and Donaho sparred, momentum careened between the prosecution and defense, back and forth, like the swings of a wrecking ball. Ryan suggested that Donaho was discounting entirely the merit of zigzagging as an antisubmarine tactic. Donaho said Ryan's questions were too black-and-white. When pressed, Donaho said, "I maintain a qualified submarine captain does not have to have a target steer a straight course to get his torpedoes to hit."

Ryan bore down: "Could you give the court some good reason for the zigzag plans set out in the current Tactical Orders and Doctrines? Could you give any reason why all those things have been done if zigzagging makes no difference to a submarine captain at all when he is attacking a surface ship?"

Here, Donaho was forced to admit that the captain of a surface ship, when executing a zigzag—that is, steering toward or away from a torpedo—had a fifty-fifty chance of making matters better or worse. Even then, though, in some cases, he might have been better off steering a straight course.

Ryan did not concede. He showed the court a rough sketch and began to describe a detailed hypothetical firing situation. Cady objected and lost.

Suppose, Ryan said, that a ship on a zigzag course were heading away from Donaho at a forty-five-degree angle and a rate of seventeen knots. The next zigzag took the ship even farther from Donaho, at twenty or more additional degrees, and he hasn't been able to recalculate a firing solution. And the target "makes seventeen knots all this time, and you are submerged," Ryan said. "What effect would those changes have on the accuracy of your torpedo fire?"

"I would probably miss," Donaho said.

"Pardon?"

"I would probably miss."

Ryan continued hammering, forcing Donaho to admit that zigzagging did have some value.

That was only true, though, *after* torpedoes were fired, Donaho countered.

Cady stood and brushed Ryan's hypotheticals aside. He described instead the actual firing position in which Hashimoto found himself with respect to *Indianapolis.*

"Assuming, Captain, that original setup that we first put to you, where you found yourself about ten thousand yards ahead and on the base course, and that you had contact by periscope in that position ahead for about twenty-seven minutes. Would a zigzag of the target have made any difference to your ability to make a successful attack?"

"Not as long as I could see the target for twenty-seven minutes," Donaho answered, referring to the length of time Hashimoto had Indy in sight.

Ryan jumped up and displayed to the court a classified zigzag plan. "Assuming that the target had been following this zigzag plan, is your answer still the same?"

Donaho: Yes.

Ryan: Supposing, Captain Donaho, that your submarine and the target were not keeping the same time. Would that have made any difference to you?

Donaho: No, sir.

Ryan: Your answer is "no"?

Donaho: Yes.

With this last exchange, the momentum had swung decidedly in McVay's favor. Cady stood, hoping to keep it there.

Cady: Is it disconcerting to you as a submarine commander to have a ship, a target, zigzag?

Donaho: Yes, because you may be—just before firing, a zigzag throws your calculations off, and you have to get a new setup.

And with that, the wrecking ball smashed into the defense. Donaho had endured more than fifty questions, triple that of any other defense witness. Amid the storm of Ryan's sometimes condescending cross, he had held his course, maintaining at all times that zigzagging was only minimally useful. But this, his last answer, undercut all he had said before. Cady, and McVay with him, fell victim to a classic tactic of opposing counsel: keep a damaging witness on the stand long enough for him to make a fatal mistake.

Recognizing the moment, Ryan stood and addressed the court. He had no further questions. And after one more witness, the trial of Captain Charles McVay was over.

15

ON DECEMBER 19, 1945, in Marlton, New Jersey, Oliver F. Bower listened to the McVay verdict on the radio: guilty. Of hazarding his ship by failure to "zigzag."

Bower, an ordinary citizen, was astounded—not at the verdict itself, but rather at the news that a key witness for the prosecution had been Commander Mochitsura Hashimoto, the Japanese submarine captain who sank McVay's ship. Bower couldn't believe that the United States Navy had dragged a representative of America's defeated enemy to testify against a well-known and decorated naval officer.

Galvanized, Bower immediately sat down at his typewriter and tapped out a letter to Navy secretary James Forrestal. "I am not attempting to judge the right or wrong of the case," Bower wrote. "In my opinion it was, to say the least, pure discourtesy if not an insult to call the Japanese officer from his home all the way to Washington to testify in this trial. Knowing the Japanese to be what they are it is very doubtful that even under our oath and the Japanese oath such a person could be trusted to tell the truth. I sincerely believe that he would welcome an opportunity to see one of his former enemies squirm under a conviction in which this foreigner had played a part."

Bower's letter sailed down to Washington, D.C., arriving amid a blizzard of less civil-sounding protests addressed to Forrestal and to President Harry S. Truman. Mail arrived in droves from ordinary citizens, veterans, even mothers of the war dead.

Mrs. Jack Hunt of Wichita, Kansas, lost her son, Fireman First Class Jack Culver, in the Pacific when a kamikaze crashed his destroyer. "I am writing this because I am so outraged (as plenty of other Navy mothers must be) at the idea of having a 'dirty Jap' brought over to testify against one of our Navy men." Mrs. Hunt was sure McVay had done the right thing by his crew, but even if he hadn't, even if her son had been killed on the *Indianapolis*, "I still feel that I would never want his commander hauled into court with any lousy Jap to say anything against him."

World War I veteran Russell Chase of Marblehead, Massachusetts, didn't stop at one protest letter, but informed President Truman that he had also written to two senators, a congressman, Secretary Forrestal, and the judge advocate general of the trial board.

The government directed all these letters to the Navy, which replied via form letter.

In Washington, D.C., Representative Edith Rogers of Massachusetts and Representative Henry D. Larcade, Jr., of Louisiana each protested Hashimoto's testimony in fiery speeches on the floor of the U.S. House. Larcade called McVay's court-martial "a blot on the Navy that will never be erased" and deplored the "despicable Japanese commander" of the submarine that sent McVay's ship to the bottom.

Blistering headlines also followed the Navy proceeding, including op-eds from respected newspapers such as the *Chicago Sun* and the *New York Herald Tribune*. A column in the *New York World-Telegram* repeated the opinion of unnamed naval officers that McVay was a "fall guy for higher-ups."

In an op-ed that ran in the *Pittsburgh Press*, war correspondent Malcolm Johnson, who had been among the first reporters to interview McVay after the sinking, weighed in. Johnson reminded readers of the survivors' "nightmarish days in the open sea" and laid out for readers how Washington had scotched his story along with all the others. How the news of Indy's sinking, delayed for nearly two weeks, was suddenly revealed on VJ Day. At Guam, he had asked himself why. In light of the court-martial, the answer now seemed clear. In Johnson's opinion, the Navy had deliberately sabotaged the efforts of correspondents to get complete, detailed stories into their own newspapers, calculating that on VJ Day, of all days, the joyous news of Japanese surrender would render the *Indianapolis* disaster a comparative footnote. Johnson would go on to win a Pulitzer Prize for other investigative work. For now he had to content himself with outrage.

For many families of the lost, the court-martial verdict produced outrage of a different sort. It ratified their belief that McVay was to blame for their suffering. Dorothy Josey Owen, of Granbury, Texas, lost her older brother, Clifford Josey, in the sinking. Josey had been friends with L. D. Cox, who held his fellow Texan in the water for an hour before he died of severe burns. Dorothy remembered her brother as blond, handsome, and likable. She loved the affable way he wore his Dixie cup on the back of his head. Now he was gone, and her entire family laid his death at McVay's feet. After all, the Navy had said he was to blame.

Admiral Wilder Baker and the military court sentenced McVay to lose two hundred numbers toward his advancement to admiral. Put plainly, this meant the Navy would move two hundred men of McVay's rank ahead of him for promotion. The court forwarded that sentence to King and Forrestal with a recommendation for clemency based on McVay's previous outstanding record.

Following the court-martial, four other officers received letters of reprimand: Gillette and his operations officer, as well as Stuart Gibson, who failed to report Indy's nonarrival. His superior, acting port director Jules Sancho, received a letter of admonition. However, all four of these letters were subsequently withdrawn. It was as if they had never happened. Meanwhile, no one at Guam—Carter, Murray, or Naquin—was disciplined for their failure to provide McVay with the intel in their possession.

King retired from the Navy in December 1945 shortly after McVay's court-martial concluded. The new chief of naval operations was Chester Nimitz, who had not agreed that McVay should be tried in the first place. In 1946, Nimitz recommended to Forrestal that McVay's sentence be set aside. The secretary concurred and remitted the sentence in March 1946.

In April, in a quiet ceremony at the Potomac River Naval Command, McVay was awarded the Bronze Star Medal for courage displayed at Okinawa during the kamikaze strike on *Indianapolis*, three months before she sank. News of the award was not released through regular Navy public relations channels, but only as an item of "local interest" by the Potomac River command.

The slight could be construed as a bellwether: McVay's career was ruined. He would never again serve in command. Instead, he was assigned as chief of staff to the commandant of the Eighth Naval District in New Orleans, where he served his remaining time in uniform. In June 1949, in conjunction with his retirement at the age of fifty, McVay was promoted to rear admiral. This "tombstone promotion," the military equivalent of a gold watch and a swift kick out the door, occurred four months before McVay's father died. The old man's son had finally been awarded a star.

After leaving the life that was his family legacy, McVay carried his fate with stoic resignation. While many retired naval officers kept in contact, became members of auxiliaries and service organizations, and attended reunions of their units and Academy class, McVay let his military service fade from view. But grief did not fade for the families of the lost, and many undertook a campaign never to let McVay forget it. While their son or brother or father or husband had disappeared into the deep, McVay, in their view, had received a slap on the wrist and a lifetime pension.

Letters arrived in his mailbox in envelopes that seemed sealed with venom:

> If it weren't for you, my son would be 25 years old today!
> If it weren't for you, I'd be celebrating Christmas with my husband!
> If it weren't for you, my girls would have a father!

At first these rants came weekly from families like the Brophys, the Joseys, and the Flynns. Then they tapered down and came mainly around Christmas and other milestone dates, such as the anniversary of the sinking or birthdays of those lost at sea. But they never stopped. Not all families of the lost blamed McVay. But in the ensuing decades, many dunned the captain with hateful letters that arrived like due-bills that could never be paid.

JULY 1960

INDIANAPOLIS, INDIANA

AS HIS PLANE DESCENDED into Weir Cook Airport in Indianapolis, Indiana, Charles McVay sat in a seat beside Louise and found that dread filled his heart. It was a familiar emotion, having settled into his chest more than six months earlier, when he received a letter from his former Marine orderly, Edgar Harrell. There was a survivors reunion coming up—their first—to be held July 30 and 31, 1960, on the fifteenth anniversary of the sinking.

"As program chairman, we would like to extend to you a very special invitation to be guest speaker at our banquet," Harrell wrote. The reunion was to take place at the Severin Hotel in Indianapolis.

McVay was at his home in New Orleans when he received the invitation. He sat on the letter for more than a week. He couldn't help but wonder how these men would receive him. The Navy had ruled the tragedy his fault, and that was the official truth as far as the public was concerned. Many families seemed to agree, judging from the mail he still received on a regular basis after all these years. Countering these opinions was Richard Newcomb's new book, *Abandon Ship*, for which McVay had given interviews. Newcomb argued that McVay was railroaded, but the retired skipper had no way of knowing how many people had read it.

Finally, McVay summoned his courage and jotted a note back to Harrell in early December 1959, managing to inject a little humor despite his misgivings:

> Please do not reserve more than fifteen minutes for my talk. I feel certain that is sufficient time for anyone at such a function.

After the tumult of war, the court-martial, and his stint working in the Eighth Naval District before retirement, McVay settled into the comparatively tame world of insurance. From where he had once stood, working shoulder to shoulder with admirals like Spruance and at the threshold of promotion to commodore, it was a long fall. Still, the Navy and its ethics were in his blood, and he had passed them on to his sons, Kimo and Quatro. After half a lifetime in the service, McVay was shocked to learn that the business world was different—that corporate integrity had gradations, "degrees" of honesty. Despite permission from colleagues to cut corners, he never did. There was right and there was wrong, and that was that.

The airliner turned off the runway and began its taxi to the terminal. Through the windows, McVay could see men running out to the tarmac to park the plane and chock her wheels. The dread settled all the way into his belly, but it was too late now. The McVays gathered their things and melted into the line of passengers to deplane. A stewardess opened the forward hatch, admitting a blast of warm, humid air.

Outside, the ground crew had rolled up some loading stairs. When McVay stepped out of the plane, he saw something odd: twin lines of people, scores of them, men and women. They formed a path across the tarmac to the terminal, and when McVay neared the bottom of the stairs, someone shouted, "Attention on deck!"

Amid the crowd, the surviving crew of *Indianapolis* snapped to attention. Tears welled in McVay's eyes. He had not known what to expect, but he had not expected this. As he made his way forward, Louise at his side, he saw faces transformed by time, boys who had become men and men who had entered middle age. Someone began clapping, then another and another, and soon McVay found himself walking toward the terminal through a channel of smiles and fountains of applause.

Out in the parking lot, the welcoming party divided itself into twenty-five cars and caravanned back to the hotel. Giles McCoy, of Indy's former Marine detachment, chauffeured the McVays. Back at the Severin Hotel, an opulent chandelier of Austrian crystal presided over the lobby, and a marble staircase led the way to upper floors. McCoy, one of the main reunion organizers, presented McVay with the nametag he would wear for the weekend. It read: "Rear Admiral Charles B. McVay III."

McVay gazed at it for a moment, as if peering at a photograph of a stranger. He handed the nametag back to McCoy with a gentle smile. "Let's have it say 'Captain,'" he said. "I was an honest-to-goodness captain, and I never was really a rear admiral."

Quickly, McCoy had the new nametag written up and pinned it to McVay's jacket, both men smiling as a newspaper photographer snapped a picture. There were reporters everywhere, in fact. A press room was set

up in the Severin, and a public relations firm had stocked it with reporting essentials: press releases, photographs, and hot coffee.

The weekend spun out in a flurry of activity, all of it affectionate, welcoming, and laudatory. On July 30, McVay sat for a press conference with
Indiana congressman Joseph Barr, followed by a live radio interview on
WXLW with McCoy. Mayor Charles Boswell proclaimed July 30 and 31
"USS *Indianapolis* Survivors Memorial Reunion Days," and asked that
all city flags be flown at half-mast. Louise and the other survivors' wives
turned themselves out in pretty summer dresses, hats, and gloves, and
were whisked off to a formal tea at Butler University. The former Dumbo
pilot Adrian Marks, now an attorney in Frankfort, Indiana, gave a speech
to survivors and guests, as did the author Newcomb and assistant chief
of naval operations Admiral Redfield Mason. But the brightest star, the
person everyone wanted to talk to, was Wilbur Gwinn, the PV-1 Ventura
pilot who first spotted the survivors, the man they called their "angel."

Amid the whirlwind of organized events was a long, unplanned
interlude that proved the most important of the entire weekend. McVay
and the men, more than two hundred of them, gathered on the rooftop
of the Severin. There, they embraced with tears and caught up with one
another's lives.

It had been fifteen years since they'd last been together, arriving in
San Diego Bay's deep-water channel aboard USS *Hollandia*, a small
escort carrier, on September 26, 1945. The ragged remains of Indy's crew
that day manned the rails of the baby flattop, their floating home since
leaving the base hospital at Guam. Most of their faces showed joy and
relief, but guilt and depression lurked here and there, nascent cancers
that would one day metastasize.

As *Hollandia* passed the familiar landmarks—the jetty, Ballast Point,
downtown San Diego—the 1MC crackled to life. Docking was immi-
nent, and the *Hollandia* crew were to muster topside in dress blues. Not
the *Indianapolis* crew, though. Most wore ill-fitting, borrowed under-
shirts and dungarees instead of pressed Navy crackerjacks and Dixie
cup caps. They'd lost everything to the deep—wardrobe, payroll, and
all. Senior ensign Don Howison looked forward to buying some new
clothes, but first he'd have to get some money. Most of his crewmates

had the same problem. The men had assurances that they'd enjoy thirty days of "survivor leave" with paychecks in hand once they arrived on base. But which base? They had no idea.

Edgar Harrell, his buddy Spooner, and the other seven surviving Marines thought their welcome was a bit lackluster. A lone military policeman pointed the Marines away from vehicles decorated with Welcome Home banners and toward an ordinary bus. Stretcher cases like Machinist Mate First Class Roberts, who barely escaped Engine Room 1, went directly to Balboa Naval Hospital.

The rest of the crew hailed a waving crowd and admired the decorations on the vehicles that clarioned, "Survivors of the USS *Indianapolis!*" Some men welcomed the festivities, overjoyed to be home in a world at peace. Others remained conflicted, including John Woolston, who wanted to know why the Navy was parading them around "when all we've done is lose a ship."

As the buses rumbled toward downtown San Diego, Seaman First Class Sam Lopez, who'd thought the men crazy for trying to use their weight to right the ship, mourned his childhood friend Harry Linville. Lopez and Linville joined the Navy together and had spent the last two years aboard Indy. Both had survived the kamikaze attack, but Linville was killed in his sleep when Hashimoto's torpedo slammed into his berthing compartment. Other survivors also thought of the friends they'd lost. With only 316 men left, it was easy to be reminded that 879 were missing.

The buses paraded on through the cheering crowds, and onlookers walked along right beside them. There were smiles and blown kisses, and survivors stuck their heads and arms out through the windows, waving at well-wishers, some reaching for the hands of good-looking girls. A perfect stranger walked up to the bus and handed Louis Erwin and Lyle Umenhoffer a pair of cold beers.

Aviation Machinist Mate Jim Jarvis, who was awakened after the torpedo strikes by the sudden silence in the port hangar, couldn't help but chuckle. His good friend from the aviation division, Joe Kiselica, the Connecticut sailor who resented his Purple Heart, had found his way onto one of the convertibles out in front. Kiselica looked just like Douglas MacArthur. Somehow he had rustled up a corncob pipe and was yelling out to the crowd, "I have returned!" The crowd whooped and hollered.

By the end of the next day, most of the men had found a train out of town. Seaman First Class Dick Thelen couldn't wait to see his father, whose face he had remembered in the water every time he was tempted to give up. When he finally arrived home in Michigan, Thelen wrapped his father in a crushing hug and told him, "Dad, you brought me home."

While aboard *Indianapolis*, Salvador Maldonado made friends by sharing cookies and baked goods from the ship's bakery. But when he was finally home, he just couldn't adjust. When his sister, Aurora, finally suggested he do some baking "just like you did on the ship," she didn't know what she had unleashed. Accustomed to baking for nearly twelve hundred men, Maldonado whipped up twenty pies at a time. He didn't know how to make just one.

For many of the men, returning home meant reaching for some kind of "normal" that remained stubbornly out of reach. There wasn't any notion of "post-traumatic stress" or counseling. Doctors admonished the survivors to just forget about the experience and move on. A good fraction did just that, starting careers as firemen, policemen, salesmen, and engineers. Despite the ministrations of parents and wives, others faltered and stumbled. Some, like Clarence Hershberger, turned to drinking. After surviving the sinking and saving Lebow's life, Hershberger went home to find that while he was in the water, his father had cheated on his mother and abandoned the family. The weight on his nineteen-year-old shoulders proved too much.

No matter their circumstances, all the survivors had one thing in common. No one talked about the tragedy. But now, in Indianapolis, together for the first time since arriving in San Diego in September of '45, they shared their stories.

For years, Bob Gause, the former quartermaster, would jolt awake at night, screaming and bathed in sweat, nightmare images of circling sharks melting away in the wakeful darkness. Gause's first job out of the Navy was as a sponge diver and commercial fisherman, and he made it his personal mission to kill every shark he could find. If he found baby sharks trapped in his nets, Gause dragged them into his boat and took grim satisfaction in watching them die. Every time he remembered the faces of the shipmates he'd lost, it renewed his thirst for vengeance.

James Belcher, the crack fisherman who helped supply food to Morgan's raft group, had remained in the Navy and married Toyoko Inoue, a Japanese woman from Sasebo. For Toyoko, life in America was difficult at first. Her Asian features and thickly accented English sometimes drew disdain from Americans. Some were garden-variety racists. Others still nursed anger over the war. Belcher, who had more reason than most to cling to his animus against all things Japanese, wondered: If I can forgive, why can't they?

Some men struggled with alcoholism and rage, and some seemed unable to hold a job. Louis Campbell, an aviation ordnanceman, never escaped the shame of things he'd done in the water to survive. Others simply moved on. Ensign John Woolston, for example, was still a naval officer and would go on to design the Thresher-class submarine.

Among the youngest survivors present was Granville Crane, who was thirty-three. Crane reported to *Indianapolis* in April 1943 at the age of sixteen and was aboard for eight of the ship's "thriller battles," as he later called them. Floating in the Haynes group, Crane clung to his Christian faith, praying aloud constantly but making no bargains with God. After the ordeal, thankful to be alive and back home with his family, he became a pastor. Now, he was slated to give the benediction that would close the reunion's main event, a formal banquet to be held the following evening.

For Felton Outland, the hardest part of being at the reunion was that the men he wanted to see most were those who hadn't made it out of the water. Outland had told no one about his ordeal until he met a beautiful young woman named Viola on a blind date. One day, they were sitting on the beach at Nag's Head, on North Carolina's Outer Banks. They had been seeing each other for three or four months by then, and Viola thought Felton was unusually quiet. Finally, he broke his silence. With his molasses Carolina drawl hushed against the sound of the rumbling breakers, he told Viola the story of those awful days in the water. Not all of it. Just enough for her to know that it was part of who he was.

Felton and Viola married and settled in among the green plains of Sunbury, North Carolina, where Outland took up farming. When Newcomb's book *Abandon Ship* was published, many survivors devoured it, hungry for the whole story. But Outland wouldn't touch it. He didn't think he could stand to relive the horror. But Viola read it, and Outland didn't mind when she asked a question now and then.

One day in early 1959, he surprised her. "I want to go on a trip," he said.

"Where are we going?"

"I want to look up some of the buddies I was on the raft with."

There was one fellow in particular he wanted to look up, Outland said, a Marine named McCoy, the last man to join his raft group. Outland had been the one to pull McCoy from the water. "I don't remember his first name, but he told me his people live in Missouri," Outland told Viola.

It was a spur-of-the-moment trip. The Outlands climbed into their '55 Ford, drove to Viola's sister's tobacco farm through a biblical rain, and dropped off their kids. Then they drove west over winding two-lane roads that cut through the country where President Eisenhower's spanking new interstate system had not yet spread its net.

When the Outlands reached Kentucky, they stopped to visit the Abbotts, George's parents. Outland shared the story of how George had sacrificed his life jacket, saving Outland's life. The Abbotts wept, but were grateful to know their son had died a hero. Outland then asked to use their phone to call ahead to St. Louis in search of McCoy. The Abbotts insisted on covering the long-distance charges.

An operator picked up, her voice scratching over the line. "Long-distance information, St. Louis."

"Uh, yes, ma'am. I'm looking for a man named McCoy."

There was a pause, then: "Sir, we have two hundred McCoys in St. Louis. I'm going to need a little more information. Do you have a first name?"

"Well, to tell you the truth, I don't remember his first name. But he was a Marine in the war, and we both survived the sinking of the USS *Indianapolis.* We spent five nights in the water together. I haven't seen him since then, and I'm trying to get in touch."

Outland heard a noise of amazement through the phone. Then the operator said, "Well, sir, I will certainly help you find him!"

And she did.

The informal reunion of Outland and McCoy sparked a nationwide effort. "If you thought enough of me to come look me up," McCoy told Outland when they met in St. Louis, "we're *all* going to have a reunion."

McCoy, who had become a successful chiropractor, wrote letters to as many survivors as he could track down. The effort spread to Michigan and to Dick Thelen, who had lost three friends while swimming for a plane-dropped raft at the cusp of rescue. Thelen's wife, JoAnne, had a gift for rallying troops. She, too, wrote scores of letters, and with her husband crisscrossed their corner of America tracking down survivors.

Now, fifteen years after being pulled from the water, they were finally together again. The rooftop reunion spilled down into the Severin's lounge, where questions and answers floated through the cigarette haze over highballs and beer. Did you see this? Do you remember that? Even when the bar closed, the men stayed, their laughter like a balm, their tears beginning—just beginning—to disinfect psychic wounds that had plagued them for years.

George Horvath had always wondered who helped him onto a raft when a shark was chasing him. That night, he found out. For Horvath, it was the beginning of healing. The next night, for the first time since August 1945, he slept without the recurring nightmares in which Indy's black stewards leapt from the fantail and smashed into the still-spinning screws.

When Adrian Marks spoke on the first night of the reunion, Outland stood up and walked out of the room, leaving Viola at their table. He knew Marks's speech would be vivid and detailed, and he could not bear to hear it. But the next night, when the time came for McVay to give his remarks, Outland remained. He wanted to hear his captain.

After a warm introduction, McVay rose to walk to the dais and his men, the men of *Indianapolis*, rose with him, sending him forward on waves of applause. At the platform, McVay paused to collect himself, then reached inside his dinner jacket and pulled out his notes. He looked out at the room where five hundred people waited, ladies in their evening wear, men in suits and dinner jackets, the men's expressions a mixture of affection and respect, as if he were still their commanding officer.

"You have been very kind to invite me to be with you tonight," McVay began, "and it is with a feeling of humility and respect that I thank you for the privilege of being your speaker on this occasion. . . . As you know, I was the last commanding officer of the USS *Indianapolis*. In talking with you, please think of me as a . . . spokesman for the ship of which we were all so proud. Please think of me, too, as a shipmate, who shared with you good fortunes and ill fortune."

Indianapolis was "a great ship with a distinguished record in both war and peace," McVay said. "She gained her reputation not because of her design or her machinery, but because of you who fought [on] her."

He recalled for the men, who knew it well, and for the assembled guests and press who perhaps didn't, Indy's lengthy pedigree: Bougainville, the Solomons, Lee, Attu, the Gilbert Islands, the Marshalls, Kwajalein, Eniwetok, Palau, Yap, Ulithi, Woleai, the Philippine Sea, Guam, Tinian, the Western Carolines, Lingayen Gulf, Mindoro, Okinawa, Gunta, and the home islands of Japan. *Indianapolis*'s war record read like a résumé of much of the struggle for the Western Pacific.

McVay asked the men to imagine what *Indianapolis*, the ship herself, might say to them if she could. He told them he thought she might say:

> Thank you for turning out in so great a number tonight. I want to tell your wives and your families how proud I am of you. By your presence here tonight, you're telling me and your shipmates who are not with us that what you stood for in war still means much to you in peace. You still believe that freedom is worth fighting for.

Don McCall, now thirty-five, sat in the audience with his wife, Rita, and listened. He had been a seaman second class when the ship sank, the Navy the best life he'd had to that point, after growing up fatherless during the Depression. But after Indy went down, he left the service and became a brick mason. He just didn't think he could ever go back to sea again.

McCall hadn't wanted to come to the reunion. Every man he'd known aboard *Indianapolis* had been killed. But Rita had insisted, and she'd been right. Even though he had to introduce himself to the other survivors, he found that all were instantly like his closest kin, bound together by an experience that no one who had not been there could ever fully understand.

BOOK 5

AN INNOCENT MAN

★

WASHINGTON, D.C.

SUMMER 1999

1

Officers Athletic Club
The Pentagon, Washington, D.C.

COMMANDER WILLIAM TOTI'S RUNNING shoes pounded against the hard asphalt of the Pentagon's north parking lot, and when he looked up ahead, he found he was already looking at Admiral Don Pilling's back. Toti started most mornings here, as he had since coming to work for Pilling, and the two men often commenced their workouts at the same time. Pilling was more than a decade Toti's senior, but he was taller, faster, and a natural athlete, so it usually wasn't long before the white-haired admiral left Toti in the dust.

In the fifteen months since Toti reported to the Pentagon, the two men had developed a collegial working relationship, not familiar but warm. Pilling had a blue-blooded way about him. He didn't tolerate preening juniors. He had never set foot in a Walmart. He was famous for never dialing his own phone. Toti found this aristocratic air a bit intimidating until he got to know the man. Toti grew to understand that Pilling was neither effete nor arrogant. It was only that his intellect was in such a constant state of multitasking that he seemed to orbit at altitude, separated from those who operated on a more ordinary plane. Don Pilling was simply smarter than almost everyone around him, but unselfconsciously so, and keenly appreciative of others' gifts.

The admiral was aware of Toti's research on behalf of the *Indianapolis* survivors. But Toti had not shared with Pilling the fruit of his efforts: an article he'd submitted to *Proceedings*, a prestigious publication of the United States Naval Institute (USNI). The institute, a private military association with offices on the campus of the Naval Academy in Annapolis, is a nonpartisan forum for debate on issues of national security and defense. *Proceedings*, USNI's flagship publication, had been continuously published since 1874. While wholly supportive of the Navy, the peer-reviewed magazine was known for its independence. Over the decades, its editorial board had reviewed, accepted, and published many articles that clashed with both official policy and unofficial orthodoxy, sometimes to the consternation of military brass.

These facts made *Proceedings* a perfect destination for Toti's piece, which he had titled "The Sinking of USS *Indianapolis* and the Responsibilities of Command." He could have just announced his findings to the survivors, but he wanted to publish them first, to allow critics to poke holes and throw stones. After more than a year of research, Toti's position did not precisely mirror the survivors' opinion that the Navy's court-martial of McVay was flawed. Still, it challenged the Navy JAG office's oft-repeated opinion that the court-martial was "sound and remedial action is not warranted," as Commander R. D. Scott had written in the JAG analysis that had angered Toti.

From the books he had read about *Indianapolis*, Toti at first thought there had been a great deal of serendipity in I-58's attack. There was some of that—but there was more. Toti's research enabled him to actually reconstruct the attack: what Hashimoto could see through his periscope. What position he took up. The details of his torpedo spread. Toti even connected with an astronomer who was able to pinpoint the phase and position of the moon.

This research convinced Toti that not only did Hashimoto have fate on his side, he also surfaced in what amounted to a perfect firing position, then executed a textbook approach and attack. From Toti's perspective as a sub commander, the Japanese skipper's probability of success was almost as certain as sunrise. Hashimoto was going to get a hit.

For Toti, this changed the calculus. With the outcome virtually guaranteed, the question was no longer whether McVay had hazarded his ship, but rather, what he could have done to prevent Hashimoto's strike. At I-58's range and firing position, the Indy skipper's options declined dramatically. And without knowing that Hashimoto was there and poised to fire, McVay's options were essentially zero. Even a random zig-zag at just the right moment would not have saved *Indianapolis*.

Hashimoto would not and did not shoot when *Indianapolis* was broadside to him. A submarine commander in 1945 had no active homing systems. Once his torpedoes were away, he had no means to control them. What Hashimoto had to do was try to determine the target type, estimate her course and speed, and fire not where *Indianapolis* was, but where he expected her to be—with or without a zig.

To account for the potential of a zig, Hashimoto fired a spread of six torpedoes with two degrees of separation. What Toti figured out was that if there was no zig, torpedoes 2 and 3 would strike home. If Indy sped up, it would have been torpedoes 1 and 2 that scored. If Indy did zig, or if she slowed down, torpedoes 4 and 5 (or less likely, torpedo 6) would hit. In any case, Hashimoto was hoping for a couple of hits, and that's exactly what he got. As Captain Glynn Donaho had testified at McVay's court-martial, in that scenario, zigzagging would have been of no value whatsoever.

In 1945, and for the next fifty years, the Navy claimed that McVay was not charged and convicted for any deficiency that led to the sinking of *Indianapolis*. In fact, prosecutors built a case that *Indianapolis* was hazarded before she was ever detected by I-58, and would have been hazarded if Hashimoto had never seen her.

In other words, McVay's failure to sail a zigzag course, in and of itself, represented a hazard to his ship, and it was that charge—not the sinking—on which he was convicted. Toti recognized this as a legal fiction. In fifty years, no one had asked the Navy this: If *Indianapolis* had sailed a straight course and reached Leyte safely, would McVay have been court-martialed?

The answer was obvious: of course not. So, legal gymnastics aside, McVay was convicted not of hazarding his vessel, but of having it sunk from under him. Another question then followed: If a ship without anti-submarine capability was sunk by a submarine in a war zone, can the captain of that ship be held responsible?

The answer to that question is yes.

This was where Toti's thesis diverged from the opinion of the men who had asked for his help, and, ironically, converged with Commander Scott's. In his *Proceedings* article, Toti quoted a captain who explained how the Navy's principle of accountability for the safety of one's crew derived directly from the American tradition of the citizen-soldier.

The Founding Fathers explicitly rejected the European tradition of a professional officer caste that puts its own stature and survival above that of troops forcibly drawn from the peasantry. Instead in our democracy, the military leader's authority over his troops was linked to a parallel responsibility to them as fellow citizens.

Accountability is a severe standard: the commander is responsible for everything that occurs under his command. Traditionally, the only escape clause was an act of God, an incident that no prudent commander could reasonably have foreseen. The penalties of accountable failure can be drastic: command and career cut short, sometimes by court martial.

Severe, indeed. So severe that a naval commander is charged with detecting and correcting problems *before* they manifest in failure.

"Captain McVay's ship was lost," Toti wrote. "He failed to take 'all necessary measures' to protect his ship. And in our system of responsibility of command, it does not matter whether that action would have been effective—he should have tried. That is why he was found guilty."

So on one count, Scott was right: McVay's conviction was legally sound. But did that make it just? Toti argued that it did not.

To prosecute McVay was like prosecuting the parents of a child who dies in an accident. Like the captain of a ship, parents are ultimately responsible for every aspect of their children's lives. Yet the parents of a dead child have suffered enough and, absent the grossest kind of negligence or malfeasance, prosecuting them would achieve no justice.

And so it was with McVay—because of the unique, all-encompassing nature of the responsibilities of command, he may indeed have been culpable for *Indianapolis*'s misfortune, even though there was nothing he could have done to avoid it. It had been argued for decades that he was *not* responsible and that therefore his court-martial was improper. Toti saw it another way: McVay was responsible, and yet to court-martial him, though technically legal, was manifestly unjust.

Such subtle distinctions meant little to the survivors. As they aged—some now in their nineties—many wondered whether they would live to see their exoneration quest fulfilled. Already, it was too late for McVay. On November 6, 1968, in the early afternoon, he dressed in his usual uniform of a pressed khaki shirt and matching pants. At 12:30 p.m., he walked out the front door of his home on Winvian Farm in Litchfield, Connecticut, sat down on a stone step, put a .38 revolver to his temple, and pulled the trigger.

Some said it was a crumbling marriage, his third, that drove McVay into irredeemable despair. That may have been true in part, but Kimo and Quatro told Toti they thought it was *Indianapolis*. For twenty-three years, McVay had borne silently the torture of those 879 deaths, his guilt and grief swelling in that eternal river of hateful letters. Before ending his life, he had confided in his housekeeper, Florence, about nightmares that had lately plagued him, dark dreams that teemed with circling sharks.

Charles McVay took a long time to die. With his third wife, Vivian, inside the house, he lay on the steps, breathing heavily for half an hour before McVay's gardener discovered him. At a nearby hospital, an emergency surgeon pronounced McVay "legally dead but still alive," a condition that may well have described the old skipper before he put the gun to his head. McVay finally succumbed to his head wound at 4:05 p.m.

For Toti, McVay's death gave rise to a special kind of regret. The man had given so much for his crew, for his country. His last mission helped change the course of the war, maybe even world history. Toti wished that somehow he could have made a difference for McVay before it was too late.

McVay was not the only *Indianapolis* survivor to end his own life. At least a dozen more committed suicide within a few years after the sinking. In a sense, the telegram the families received announcing that Indy had sunk with "100 percent casualties" was true. Even among the survivors, no man who went into the water was the same man who came out.

By the time Toti completed his run, Admiral Pilling had long since disappeared into the locker room. Toti wondered how Pilling would react to his conclusions concerning McVay and *Indianapolis*. The *Proceedings* editorial board had accepted his article for publication. Toti, though technically a representative of the office of the chief of naval operations, had submitted his article without asking permission from his boss, the vice chief. Careerwise, maybe not the safest move. Though he had tried to present a nuanced argument, there were some admirals in the naval hierarchy who were famously linear thinkers. A man was either a team player or he wasn't. For those officers, Toti's writing clearly placed him in the latter camp. And perhaps also in the camp of a precocious Florida eighth-grader named Hunter Scott.

Hunter (no relation to Commander R. D. Scott) had gotten involved with the survivors while researching the *Indianapolis* story for a school history fair project. Over the past two years, he had single-handedly brought more attention to Indy's story and the survivors' exoneration battle than anyone before him. Hunter's was a pitch-perfect human interest story: Young boy helps old men in their lifelong quest to correct historic injustice. The whole situation was absolutely made for TV— and that's where Hunter had been: on *NBC Nightly News* with Tom Brokaw, *Good Morning America, Today*, and more. The list was long, and the Navy brass wasn't happy about it.

Hunter had done remarkable things, Toti felt, and all the more remarkable because he was now only thirteen years old. Ironically, though, it was that very fact that had backfired to extend decades of inertia. In arguing that today's admirals were still somehow in league with the admirals of 1945, Hunter was sincere. But he was also irritating the very people whose help he needed to exonerate McVay. He was calling on the Navy to overturn McVay's court-martial, which was for the Navy a Catch-22. On the one hand, it was not in the Pentagon's power to overturn a legally sound court-martial. On the other, nobody in the Navy wanted to appear to be beating up on a kid.

2

JUNE 1999

Offices of Senator Bob Smith
Dirksen Senate Office Building
Washington, D.C.

"LOOK, BOB, I RESPECT you, I'm on the committee with you, but come on," Senator John Warner was saying. "This is some kid's school project. Is this really worth a hearing before the Senate Armed Services Committee?"

Warner's response was typical of the uphill battle Senator Bob Smith had been fighting for a year. That's how long it had been since Smith, a New Hampshire Republican, first spied a line item on his daily agenda that stopped him cold.

"What's this?" Smith said, and shot a quizzical look at his legislative assistant, John Luddy. "'USS *Indianapolis* and Hunter Scott?'"

That had been in April 1998. Luddy had been sitting on the opposite side of Smith's dark, polished desk. Through a window in the Dirksen Senate Office Building suite, both men could see budding spring trees along Constitution Avenue, and beyond them, the imposing dome of the Capitol.

"It's a meeting with the survivors of the USS *Indianapolis*, sir," Luddy said.

A former Marine Corps infantry officer, Luddy was Smith's senior advisor on military affairs. He summed up in a few lines the ship's story, the court-martial of McVay, and the survivors' long fight to exonerate their captain.

"Hunter Scott is an eighth-grader. He's a constituent of Joe Scarborough's." Scarborough was a congressman representing Florida's 1st Congressional District.

Smith, a fifty-eight-year-old former history teacher, knew of *Indianapolis* only from the scant information he'd read in textbooks. "Okay, I get it that the survivors are still trying to clear their captain," he said. "But what's an eighth-grade kid got to do with it?"

It started with a grade-school history project, Luddy explained.

Hunter's interest in *Indianapolis* was triggered in 1996 when he sat down with his dad to watch his dad's favorite movie, *Jaws*. It wasn't the first time he'd seen the film. But this time, when the fishing boat captain, Quint, told the horrible tale of surviving the sinking of *Indianapolis*, Hunter really listened. As soon as the scene was over, he stood and faced his dad. "Is that a true story?"

"Yes," his dad said, smiling. "And please move from in front of the TV."

But Hunter was fascinated and pressed for more information. He needed a topic for his school history fair and felt he had found one. His father, a high school principal, promised to take Hunter with him to the University of West Florida library, where he was working on his PhD dissertation. But even university-level history books yielded only a few lines of information about the Navy's greatest sea disaster. Surprised, Hunter's dad next showed him how to search microfiche for newspaper articles from 1945. There the boy found more, but only the high points, and those repetitive and without context. The internet, in 1997, was also not very useful.

That was when Hunter decided to try to contact the survivors. He put an ad in Pensacola's Navy newspaper. Maurice Bell, a survivor living in nearby Mobile, Alabama, replied. Hunter traveled to interview Bell, who was seventy-one at the time, and with Bell's help, the project took off. By the time Hunter learned of *Indianapolis*, the survivors had been holding reunions for more than thirty-five years. Bell gave Hunter a list of all living survivors. Over the course of a year, the boy called or wrote to every single man. Though some turned him down, many wrote back, eager to share their stories. Some had never even told their families about those terrible days at sea. Hunter, then just eleven years old, was the first to hear their pain.

He began sending the survivors a questionnaire he had prepared. Many answered it and sent it back, some with mementos and photographs. Their stories galvanized the boy: the horror of friends dying in their arms, the terror of the sharks. Survivor Paul Murphy called it "fear beyond words."

For his history fair project, Hunter printed out news articles from 1945. He obtained a map of the South Pacific and marked the location of the sinking. He even wrote to Hashimoto, who responded with a few kind words and a photograph of himself as a young commander, standing at the periscope aboard I-58. The project grew to include enough documentation to fill two three-ring binders.

From all the material Hunter collected, one theme emerged that he had not expected. To a man, the survivors were still outraged over the treatment of their captain. Hunter won his school history competition. Then Joe Scarborough, his congressman, decided to put Hunter's project on display in his office, and that attracted the attention of local reporters.

Senator Smith listened with interest as Luddy summed up, saying that Hunter Scott had been all over the news. It started with a couple of appearances in 1997. The following year, Hunter appeared on all the major network evening news broadcasts, plus Fox and CNN, as well as all the major morning shows. *George* magazine had even named the kid one of its "20 Most Fascinating Men in Politics." Luddy then explained that Hunter's evidence of McVay's innocence had convinced Scarborough to craft a 1998 resolution declaring the sense of Congress that McVay's court martial was unjust. The measure had failed, but Hunter and the survivors weren't giving up.

Smith sat back, fascinated—with both the kid and the subject matter. He had great respect for veterans of McVay's era. Smith's father, an Annapolis graduate, had been a Navy pilot during World War II. He died in a plane crash just a few months before *Indianapolis* sank. Smith was a Navy veteran himself, having served two years on active duty, one in Vietnam.

A couple of hours later, Smith, Luddy, and a small knot of legislative staffers greeted Hunter Scott and a handful of survivors in the senator's large conference room. Introductions were made: Glenn Morgan, a seventy-six-year-old Texan, had brought Mertie Jo, his wife of fifty-five years. Paul Murphy, who was now seventy-five, and his wife Mary Lou hailed from Colorado. Smith also met survivor Mike Kuryla and his wife, Lorraine, and survivors Bob McGuiggan, Dick Paroubek, Dick Thelen, and Woodic James.

Hunter and the survivors took seats at the long conference table, and Hunter laid out for Smith the case for exonerating Captain McVay. Smith's first impression was that the kid seemed about twenty-five years older than his actual age of thirteen. He spoke with authority and without referring to the notes he carried in a ring binder as thick as a phone book. At intervals, Hunter asked the survivors to speak to specific issues, and Smith was struck by the way these grizzled World War II heroes took his lead. The boy was knowledgeable, organized, and passionate, and the survivors were knowledgeable, determined, and sincere. Together, Smith thought, they made a hell of a team.

Hunter had already helped push legislation to the U.S. House. Though the bill hadn't passed, Smith admired the boy's devotion to a cause larger than himself and identified with his refusal to give up. The senator's scheduler had allotted thirty minutes for the *Indianapolis* meeting, but two and a half hours flew by as Smith listened and asked questions, fascinated. Then Hunter came to the bottom line. Joe Scarborough was sponsoring a new bill in the House concerning McVay. Would Smith sponsor a Senate version?

This draft legislation, Senate Joint Resolution 26, would declare the sense of Congress that the court-martial charges against Captain McVay were "morally unsustainable," and his conviction a "miscarriage of justice that led to his unjust humiliation and damage to his naval career." SJR 26 also declared that "the American people should recognize Captain McVay's lack of culpability for the tragic loss of the USS *Indianapolis* and the lives of the men who died as a result of her sinking."

Smith considered all that he'd heard. Privately, he felt that if Hunter and the survivors were right, then a grave injustice had been done—one the survivors had been trying to undo for fifty years. Aloud, Smith said he appreciated all that had been shared about *Indianapolis* and Captain McVay. He promised only that he and his staff would dig deeper.

That had been a year ago. Since then, Smith's staff had been drilling down into the truth about the loss of *Indianapolis*. The senator had assigned one member of his staff to work exclusively on the project, reading case files and taking statements from survivors. Smith himself also spent a lot of time with his nose in the books.

He admired young Hunter Scott for the work he'd done to get the survivors this far. Beyond that, though, Smith's question became about the survivors: Were they right? Maybe. Or maybe McVay screwed up. Maybe he *should've* been court-martialed. These were the questions that Smith and his staff were running down for themselves. Over five decades, documentation had swelled to include newly declassified material, such as the ULTRA intelligence program, as well as legal analyses, scores of articles, and a number of full-length books. The latest of these, *Fatal Voyage* by Dan Kurzman, was published in 1990.

While conducting research for a book about the atomic bomb, Kurzman, a former NBC News and *Washington Post* correspondent, came across Navy documents related to the *Indianapolis* story. His wife encouraged him to dig deeper.

His discoveries and the resulting book energized Quatro and Kimo McVay, especially the latter. Gregarious and larger than life, Kimo still lived in Hawaii and made his living as a promoter, exporting Hawaiian talent to the rest of America. His most famous client was Don Ho of "Tiny Bubbles" fame. The Olympic champion surfing legend Duke Kahanamoku was Kimo's partner.

In addition to his letter-writing campaigns, Kimo made a typically audacious move: He invited Mochitsura Hashimoto to Honolulu to meet with the survivors of the ship he sank. Hashimoto accepted. The meeting took place on December 7, 1990, Pearl Harbor Day. Honolulu papers ran with the story. Tears flowed at the Arizona Memorial that day, but also warmth and forgiveness and an understanding that all the men present, including Hashimoto, had only been acting in the service of their countries.

Finally, Kimo enlisted the help of a wealthy retiree named Mike Monroney. A former Washington, D.C., lobbyist, Monroney still had close ties to Congress, not including the fact that Smith's military liaison, John Luddy, was Monroney's son-in-law.

Monroney also had a personal reason for helping with the exoneration of McVay. He had just missed going on *Indianapolis*'s final, fatal cruise. As a young sailor assigned to the ship, he fell ill just before she sailed and his orders were changed. With this history, as well as Monroney's twin ties to Congress, Kimo was counting on him to help drum up interest in the new exoneration effort on the Hill.

After more than a year of research, Smith landed firmly on the side of the survivors. He decided to move forward and ask his fellow members for a hearing before the Senate Armed Services Committee. These senators included John McCain of Arizona, Rick Santorum of Pennsylvania, Jeff Sessions of Alabama, Joe Lieberman of Connecticut, and Ted Kennedy of Massachusetts.

Their response was universal, nonpartisan, and almost identical to Senator Warner's: *Seriously? I get what you're trying to do here, Bob, but this is a kid we're talking about. Is this really worth activating the machinery of the U.S. Senate?*

For Smith, it was a good question, a challenging question, and he didn't take it lightly. He'd had to come to terms with that himself. He wondered what his father would have thought of his quest. Smith himself held the Navy close to his heart. During his Vietnam tour, he served aboard ship. He had seen many brave pilots launch from aircraft carriers into the fiery maw of battle. Some of them didn't make it back. All of that was part of Smith's identity. He was known in the Senate as a conservative maverick, pushing "unpopular" causes, such as citizen gun rights and unborn children's right to life. And yet he was also a great respecter of tradition. The quest to exonerate McVay created a conflict between the two: respect for the authority and traditions of the Navy, which had reviewed the case for decades and always reached the same conclusion, and a cause unpopular in Washington but precious to a bunch of old men and a kid.

To secure an Armed Services Committee hearing for Hunter and the survivors, there was only one man he really needed to convince: Warner, the committee chair. But Warner, who had once served as Navy secretary, was opposed just like everyone else—just as another Navy secretary with an even more intimate connection to *Indianapolis* had been. USS *Cecil J. Doyle* skipper W. Graham Claytor, who had charged without orders to the sinking site to spearhead the rescue, served as Secretary of the Navy under President Jimmy Carter. He, too, had demurred on taking any action on the McVay affair.

The sinking of *Indianapolis* was second only to Pearl Harbor as the Navy's greatest loss in World War II, Warner reminded Smith. It had been litigated and relitigated, and the conclusion was always the same. And now some kid was going to swoop in a half-century later with new information that was supposed to change history? That simply didn't make sense. Warner didn't want to embarrass the Navy, and he didn't want to embarrass the committee or himself.

"John, look, if you can't chair the hearing, I'll chair it on your behalf," Smith said. "But would you just agree to the hearing and listen to these men and this boy? I mean, if an eighth-grade kid can come in here and feel this strongly about it, and these veterans are all here standing up for their captain, we at least owe them the right to be heard."

"But the Navy's already decided this," Warner objected. "We're going to stir up a hornet's nest that doesn't need to be stirred up. And I don't want to give them the impression that we're trying to overturn the court-martial."

"We're not trying to overturn anything," Smith said. "We're going to listen. That's all we're going to do. Exoneration comes later, if you agree with it. If you don't agree with it, we won't do it."

3

THURSDAY, SEPTEMBER 9, 1999

Offices of the Navy Staff
The Pentagon
Washington, D.C.

THEY HAD BEEN GOING at it for more than an hour, a dozen or
so khakied Navy officers sitting around a conference table in a room on
the fourth deck of the Pentagon's E Ring. Notebooks were open, sheets
of paper scattered around the table. Windows in the room opened to an
inner void space between the building's D and E Rings, but Bill Toti was
wishing they overlooked something else—the Pentagon helipad, Arling-
ton Cemetery—anything that might distract him from the agitating,
round-in-circles arguments he was suffering through this morning.

The lineup was eleven to one. So it was no surprise that the one—
Toti—was losing.

"No, no, *no*," a Navy lawyer said to Toti. "You *cannot* say that!"

The lawyer's reference was to a single line in testimony Toti had written, to be delivered before the Senate Armed Services Committee in the
matter of USS *Indianapolis* and Captain Charles McVay. After months of
wrangling, Senator Bob Smith had finally secured his hearing. The committee had summoned witnesses to testify in support of—and against—
exoneration, including the chief of naval operations. It had fallen to
Admiral Don Pilling, Toti's boss, to testify on the CNO's behalf.

In mid-July, when Pilling learned he was going to testify, he had
called Toti into his office. "You know this story better than anybody on
the Navy staff, so I want you to write my testimony," Pilling said.

Toti was astonished. Whether by serendipity or providence, it seemed
his life intersected again and again with the cruiser *Indianapolis*. From
the time he first saw *Jaws* at age eighteen and learned of the cruiser's fate
to his three tours aboard her namesake sub, to the survivors' plea for
help—all these factors were engineered by outside forces, none through
any maneuvering of his own. Now, somehow, Toti found himself, a for-

mer *Indianapolis* captain, perfectly positioned to help restore the reputation of *Indianapolis*'s most famous captain. After all his history with that storied ship, her crew, and her captain, he now found himself aligned with the senior Navy officer designated to testify before Congress on matters Toti had studied his entire adult life. He thought, yet again: you can't make this stuff up.

Pilling knew Toti was a friend of the survivors. He knew Toti's view of the court-martial. Toti had finally given the admiral a copy of the *Proceedings* article in which he concluded that although the court-martial might have been technically correct, it was nevertheless unjust. Pilling liked the piece and told Toti he thought the tone was "finely nuanced" and "about right." Pilling told Toti it would be okay to write his testimony using the article as a foundation—testimony he would deliver to Senator John Warner and the Senate Armed Services Committee as the official position of the Navy.

"This is yours," Pilling said the day he gave Toti the assignment. "Make it right."

Incredible. Toti had had to work to keep his mouth from falling open. Pilling was one of the smartest men Toti knew, someone with a strong sense of justice. The planets were aligned so perfectly, how could it not go right this time?

He jumped into the job, putting in twelve to fifteen hours a day. There were others at work, too, some seeking McVay's complete exoneration in the legal sense, something for which there was no provision of law. McVay's son, Kimo, young Hunter Scott, and many survivors fell into this camp. Meanwhile, another camp—mostly representing the Navy—wanted nothing changed at all. They believed that any modification to McVay's record would constitute a rewriting of history. Both sides would fight hard to win—or at least not to lose.

In the end, Toti produced what he thought was a third option—not declaring the court-martial of McVay wrong per se, but suggesting that in retrospect the court-martial was unjust for many reasons having to do with the presentation of evidence, and that the trial generated no lessons learned or remediation that could prevent similar future disasters. Therefore the court-martial served no purpose, and with the benefit of twenty-twenty hindsight, should not have been pursued.

Toti's proposal carefully avoided indicting the Navy with words like "scapegoat" or "cover-up" as had so much literature in the past. It was a compromise Toti thought the Navy could live with, a way the Navy could restore McVay and honor the survivors while still saving face. He submitted the testimony to Pilling, who read it and declared the tone, again, "about right."

But the lawyer now in the room with Toti didn't think it was about right at all. In fact, he didn't think it was even in the same neighborhood as right.

The meeting in progress was a prep session for the hearing, which was scheduled for Tuesday, September 14, just five days away. Present were this JAG lawyer, who was a captain, and two more Navy lawyers of lower rank, all sitting across from Toti at the large conference table. There was also a commander from the office of legislative affairs, or "OLA," and two PAOs, public affairs officers.

The session, which involved the linear dissection of the testimony Toti had written for Pilling, was supposed to last an hour. Now, well into hour two, the PAOs were fairly placid, the OLA somewhat less so. The JAG captain, however, was nearly apoplectic.

The line of testimony riling the lawyer was this:

We cannot change history, but with the benefit of twenty-twenty hindsight, we can say that the court-martial of Captain McVay likely did not have the intended effect for the Navy, and were we to do it today, we would probably do it differently.

"If Admiral Pilling says this, it will open the Navy to litigation risk," the captain was saying.

"From *who*?" Toti shot back, incredulous.

"The descendants of the lost at sea!"

Inwardly, Toti rolled his eyes. Did the JAG really believe in this paper tiger? Or was he intentionally exaggerating the litigation threat to preserve the status quo on McVay? Toti thought maybe it was time to dial back the temperature in the room a bit.

"Look," he said, "my dad was a lawyer my entire young life, and now he serves as a judge. My whole upbringing, I was surrounded by the law. I don't hate lawyers. Quite the contrary—I understand why you do what you do. But I have to tell you your argument just doesn't make sense."

One of the PAOs cut in and changed the subject. "Commander Toti, what do you think will be the reaction of the people in the hearing room to Admiral Pilling's testimony?"

It was public affairs' job to anticipate backlash and either head it off or be prepared to manage it. Many survivors and their families would attend the hearing, represented by young Hunter Scott, who would also testify. Several survivors would testify in their own right, along with the author Dan Kurzman. Admiral Pilling would appear for the Navy, along with Dr. William S. Dudley, director of naval history, and Rear Admiral John D. Hutson, Judge Advocate General of the Navy.

"I can't give you a guarantee, but I'm pretty sure that if he gives this testimony, there will be shouts of glee," Toti said. "The survivors' reaction will be something like, 'Finally!' This is a chance for them to see that the Navy is willing to say, 'We're human, and we're willing to admit that maybe, just maybe, in this case we made a mistake.'"

The JAG made a noise of condescension, and Toti fixed him with a glare. "Do you even understand why the survivors are so agitated about this? For fifty years, they feel the Navy has just made things up."

He reminded the lawyer about the latest legal analysis by another JAG lawyer, Commander R. D. Scott, which included intimations that McVay lied about how he got off the ship. "You guys are supposed to stick to the law," Toti said to the JAG. "Tell me, on what tenet of the law was that opinion based?"

Another lawyer spoke up. "It's not the law, per se. He was making an argument. If it can be shown that a witness has shaded the truth in small ways, a jury can sometimes be persuaded that the witness isn't telling the truth in larger ways."

"Well, it was a stupid thing to include," Toti said. "I think it just adds weight to the survivors' opinions that the Navy is still grasping for evidence that McVay was somehow at fault, fifty-plus years after the fact."

No one in the room disagreed, but the JAG captain eyed Toti across the table. "Commander Scott doesn't think you're a very good lawyer."

Toti sighed. "And between the two of us, I'm the only one who actually commanded a ship." Turning to the PAOs, he said, "Look, I'm not trying to convince the lawyers. This is the court of public opinion. Lawyers don't have a monopoly on the truth."

After two hours, the meeting broke with the lawyers no closer to approving Pilling's testimony. The next day, Friday, the group was to reconvene, this time with the admiral in attendance. Overnight, Toti made some modifications to Pilling's statement, adding a few things, softening others.

By the start of Friday's session, Toti and the lawyers had come to agreement on almost everything. They entered the office of the vice chief of naval operations, with its long mahogany conference table near the entrance door. Pilling took his place at the head of the table, with Admiral Hutson and the JAGs to his right and Toti immediately to his left.

The group conferred on the expected flow of the hearings, concluding with a review for the admiral of the one remaining point of disagreement:

> We cannot change history, but with the benefit of twenty-twenty hindsight, we can say that the court-martial of Captain McVay likely did not have the intended effect for the Navy, and were we to do it today, we would probably do it differently.

The JAG captain reprised his argument from the day before. Toti reprised his. Pilling listened. Then, Admiral Hutson, who would also be testifying at the hearing, weighed in. He supported his JAG officers' position, he told Pilling.

Well, that's it, Toti thought. I'm dead in the water. But he kept his face impassive, put his elbows on the table, and folded his hands under his chin. There was a long silence as Pilling gazed down at the written testimony and considered all that had been said. Then he raised his head and fixed his blue eyes on Admiral Hutson.

"I'm perfectly comfortable with making this statement," he said.

Toti had to raise his fingers to cover his mouth in order to shield a wide grin. The Navy was finally going to say what everyone has been thinking for fifty years! Even beyond winning the point, he was happy to see things work the way they were supposed to work: The lawyers were supposed to give advice and assess risk, but then the line officers were supposed to factor in a holistic, operational perspective. And it happened just that way—the process at its finest.

After giving the JAGs a moment to recover, Pilling wanted to know what questions he should anticipate from the senators. Toti had prepared for the worst-case scenario. He knew all the arguments cold and did not want his boss to be caught flat-footed. So he had drafted a series of "murder board" questions—the kind of questions used to practice for a moot court or cross-examination. Questions that usually turn out be more difficult to answer than those that actually materialize.

Toti had titled the list *List of questions that could be asked that we don't have answers to.* There were about ten of them, and the group around the conference table tossed them back and forth with Pilling.

For example: As former chairman of the intelligence committee of the Combined Chiefs of Staff, wouldn't McVay have been aware of the ULTRA program? And if so, wouldn't he have known that people like Commodore Carter had ULTRA access? And that if Carter said there was nothing to worry about, wouldn't it have been reasonable for McVay to conclude that there was, in fact, nothing to worry about? Would that not explain why McVay told Commodore Van Metre during the supplemental investigation, "The knowledge which I possessed indicated to me that there was little possibility of surface, air, or sub-surface attack; in fact, no possibility."

Another murder-board question: The Navy's latest legal analysis suggested that McVay should have gone down with this ship. Is that the Navy's policy—that captains should go down with their ships? If not, how did that statement make it into an official Navy report?

There was also this: Combat intelligence intercepted Hashimoto's report that he had sunk an enemy ship, but the Navy did absolutely nothing to follow up on that report. That failure resulted in nearly twice the loss of life as the charge McVay was convicted of, hazarding his vessel. What operational commander was held accountable for those deaths? Or doesn't accountability apply to admirals?

Finally, there was the question Toti had asked in his *Proceedings* article: If McVay was not court-martialed for losing his ship, but for hazarding it by failing to zigzag, would he have been court-martialed if he had sailed a straight course and reached Leyte safely?

The lawyers suggested possible responses, which were actually platitudes and not answers. Soon the hour grew late and the workweek was done. The admiral gathered his things, including his "night reading book," a massive binder he took home each evening. It was filled with briefing items that covered the vice chief's vast range of responsibilities. This night, Toti tucked in a fat packet of materials related to *Indianapolis*, including the murder-board questions. Pilling would review it all over the weekend.

The hearing was now four days away. With Pilling in the survivors' corner, Toti felt that for the first time in more than half a century, their quest to win justice for their captain had a good shot at success.

On Saturday morning, September 11, Toti was at home with Karen and the kids. The college football season was in week three and Navy was playing Kent State. Toti had his living room television tuned to ESPN for the pregame. Outside, the morning had shrugged off a cool start and was climbing toward the low eighties under crisp blue skies. It was shaping up to be a gorgeous day.

With the hearing on McVay's court-martial three days away, Toti felt he had done all he could do. He'd spoken with the survivors, who knew about Admiral Pilling's testimony and were hopeful. Paul Murphy would be the survivors' de facto spokesman. Toti had helped him prepare his testimony. Senator Bob Smith, meanwhile, had been working closely with Hunter Scott, and with Kimo McVay's friend, Mike Monroney, the former D.C. lobbyist. In the run-up to the hearing, Monroney hosted a cocktail party and invited key members of both houses of Congress to meet the survivors. Handshakes, photographs, martinis—the Beltway recipe for goodwill.

Toti's phone rang, a corded landline on an end table next to the sofa. Keeping his eyes on ESPN, he picked up the receiver. "Hello?"

"Bill?"

"Yes?"

"This is Admiral Pilling."

If life were a sitcom, Toti would have pulled the phone away from his ear and stared at it in disbelief. The odds against the admiral calling him at home were astronomical, and on a Saturday even higher. Whatever it was, it couldn't be good. Instinctively, Toti stood.

"I'm going to have to change my testimony," the admiral said.

Toti's voice was cautious. "What aspect?"

"Pretty much all of it."

Toti's heart sank. He sat back down.

"I'm going to have to stick to the party line," Pilling said.

"Why?"

At this point, some senior officers would have groused about the way of things—politics, turf wars, dusty sacred cows. Pilling was not that type of man.

"I just wanted you to know," he said.

But Toti knew his boss was being pressured. Even a four-star has people to answer to. Toti gazed out his family room window at the sky, the leaves just tipping toward autumn. Pilling had always said he wanted him to shoot straight.

"Respectfully, sir, this isn't going to go down well with the survivors," Toti said. "They're going to be at that hearing, listening to you say the same thing the Navy has always said. It's going to get ugly."

Toti pictured Paul Murphy and Dick Thelen especially. Those two would fire back, both barrels. For them, five nights in the water outranked four stars.

"I think you're right about that," Pilling said.

There was a second problem. As the CNO's office always did when preparing to speak before Congress, Toti had already sent the testimony to senate staffers. Both Warner's and Smith's people had already read it, and thought the approach gentle, nuanced, and the right one for the Navy to take.

"Now we're going to go back to two senators and tell them, never mind, the Navy is going back to Plan A," Toti warned. "I don't think that will go down well either."

Especially, he thought, since Warner never wanted this hearing in the first place. The senator had feared exactly this scenario, embarrassing the committee by dragging the Navy through the same old mud, but this time at the behest of a teenager.

Again, Pilling agreed. "But my hands are tied. That's what we're going to have to do."

"Yes, sir. Thank you, sir." Toti hung up the phone.

He knew Pilling was right: That's what they were going to have to do. The question was, should Toti do more than that? Pilling's phone call was so uncharacteristic, so far out of left field, as to be bizarre. Was there an unspoken message there, something for Toti to read between the lines?

The hearing was three days away. The survivors might not ever get this close again. Toti thought over his options for the better part of the afternoon, watching Navy beat Kent State. Then he picked up the phone and called Mike Monroney.

4

TUESDAY, SEPTEMBER 14, 1999

Senate Committee on Armed Services
Dirksen Senate Office Building
Washington, D.C.

WHEN SHE WALKED INTO the Senate Armed Services Committee hearing room on Tuesday, September 14, the first thing Mary Lou Murphy noticed was the prevalence of gleaming wood paneling that covered the walls. Its rich, dark tones lent the chamber a decorous aura, suggesting that business of consequence was conducted here. The second thing Mary Lou noticed was all the security. Uniformed Capitol Police guarded all the entrances and exits. She could only imagine what security precautions might be like for a really high-visibility hearing.

But she quickly got over being impressed. Over the weekend, Commander Toti had called her husband, Paul, with the bad news about Admiral Pilling. The Navy would be sticking to its guns after all.

Aides and staffers streamed into the room, along with survivors, family, and supporters. Eleven survivors had paid their own way to be here, and assembled reporters scribbled notes about their appearance. They wore blue jackets bearing an image of Indy on the back. Beneath the ship was a row of ten stars, one for each of her World War II battles. Some wore their blue USS *Indianapolis* ball caps, brims covered with gold braid.

Mary Lou saw a film crew at the back of the room, their cameras stamped "C-SPAN." She was standing near one of the witness tables up front with Paul and Hunter Scott, the boy who'd set this whole thing in motion. The three turned to see Toti enter the room, trailing a tall, patrician man with white hair, blue eyes, and the gilded stripes of a four-star admiral on his sleeve.

Paul Murphy caught sight of Pilling, too, and eyeballed the admiral all the way from the door to a witness table where a nameplate marked his spot.

Toti dropped off the admiral's briefcase and came over. Murphy wrapped him in a cheerful bear hug. "Good morning, Bill! Good to see you. What the hell's wrong with your boss?"

Toti smiled and shook his head. "I haven't had time to figure that out yet. He's a really smart guy, and I don't know why things are happening the way they are."

"Well, it's going to get ugly in here today. I hope none of it splashes on you."

Toti hoped so, too, but not in the way Murphy meant.

After the surprise Saturday morning phone call from Pilling and a day of deliberation, Toti sat with Karen in their kitchen and talked through the situation over dinner.

"Why did he call me at home?" Toti wondered aloud. "Was he trying to tell me something without telling me something? Without spelling it out?"

"Maybe he just wanted you to know," Karen offered.

"If that was the case, he could have waited until Monday. He's not accountable to me."

"He knows how hard you've worked on this. He knows how much the survivors mean to you."

Karen was right about that. That's why Toti had had to telephone Paul Murphy and tell him about the admiral's reversal. Toti talked it over with Monroney before making that call.

"I can't let Paul walk into the hearing room and get walloped with such a nasty surprise," Toti told Monroney over the phone.

"That's true. What are you going to tell him?"

"I'm going to tell him that I failed. That I tried to make it right, but that in the end, I failed."

Toti had next called Murphy, who was hopping mad and vowed to tell all the other survivors of this perfidy. Then, as Toti hung up with Murphy, the seed of an idea began to take root.

There were those questions he had prepared for Admiral Pilling, the "worst-case scenario" questions. Monroney had seen them.

Toti let the idea marinate for twenty-four hours, then called Monroney again. "Remember those murder board questions?"

"Yeah?"

"Well, there are really no good answers for those questions. Even the JAGs couldn't come up with any, and I think they tend to prove the survivors' case. Could you get them directly to Smith, not to one of his staffers?"

"Absolutely."

It was important that Toti keep his fingerprints off the questions. If Smith used them in the hearing and anyone asked Toti where the senator got them, Toti would certainly own up. But it would be better for everyone if no one noticed remarkable similarities between the questions Toti had batted around with Pilling and the JAGs, and any that Smith asked Pilling during the hearing.

"Should we send them to Senator Warner, too?" Toti asked.

"You know, Warner's got a temper," Monroney said. "If he thinks Pilling is going to say one thing and he says another, he might get pretty angry."

"Would that be good or bad?"

"That depends on whether you're in Senator Warner's firing line."

Now, in the hearing room, Toti looked up as Senators Smith and Warner, along with Max Cleland, of Georgia, and Olympia Snowe, of Maine, entered the room. There was a general shush and shuffle as witnesses and spectators settled into their places.

Unlike many present, Warner was the survivors' contemporary. He had enlisted in the Navy in January 1945, right out of high school, and left the following year as a third class petty officer. He then joined the Marine Corps, serving during the Korean War. Since then, the senator had made an art of marrying well—or at least conspicuously—first wedding Catherine Conover Mellon, the banking heiress, and then Elizabeth Taylor.

Warner walked first to the witness tables and then through the gallery and greeted each survivor. He then returned to the front of the room and took a seat at the center of a raised semicircular bench studded with microphones. As he looked out over the room, Warner's face appeared chiseled from stone, his eyes hawklike under dark, low-set brows. The senator gave off the air of a man not to be trifled with.

He brought the hearing to order, praising the courage of the men who were aboard Indy "that fateful night," and particularly those present in the hearing room. "It was a very moving experience for me to go back and shake their hands," Warner said.

When *Indianapolis* sank, he had just completed recruit training at Great Lakes Naval Station and was in radio technician school in Chicago, the senator told the room. "In my generation, seventeen-, eighteen-, nineteen-year-old sailors were training to come and join you at what appeared to be, at that time, an inevitable invasion of Japan. In the wake of the tremendous losses of ships and men in the Okinawa campaign, that was a sobering future for my generation, but we looked forward, in many respects, to coming out and joining those that had gone before us and fought in the heroic battles of the Pacific."

Warner continued. "Today, we will share a chapter of that history. I think it is very important that we do so, as a reminder to this generation of Americans, living today in peace and tranquility and prosperity, that that prosperity and peace was earned through the sacrifices of so many men and women in World War II."

The senator then smiled and turned his attention to Hunter Scott. "This is my twenty-first year in this senate," he said. "I have been in many, many hearings but I think you are the youngest witness that I ever encountered. I hope, irrespective of how this concludes, that you will consider a career in the Congress of the United States someday in the future. I think you have got the makings of a darned good senator."

Hunter beamed. "Thank you," he said.

Warner then introduced Murphy, Harlan Twible, and author Dan Kurzman.

"Before we begin, I want to acknowledge that the committee has received a number of written statements from survivors who will not be testifying here today."

There were twenty-two of those statements, including entreaties from Buck Gibson, who held a dying teenager on a floater net; John Spinelli, who floated for five nights and four days on a raft with Captain McVay; Donald Mack, the bugler who was on the bridge with McVay when Hashimoto's torpedoes hit; Kenley Lanter, who was in the raft group with Glenn Morgan; and Frank Centazzo, who heard McVay shouting to all in earshot to abandon ship and later held the dying Commander Lipski in his arms.

According to the statement of Harold Eck, a former seaman second class, he had prayed daily for over fifty years that the injustice done to McVay would be corrected, removing "the blood of the lost lives" that was placed upon his hands. Dorothy Josey Owen also submitted a statement. Owen's whole family blamed McVay for the loss of her brother, Clifford, but changed their minds after books presenting other facts came to light. L. D. Cox's statement averred that he did not know of a single survivor who wouldn't have been proud to serve under McVay again, and Cleatus Lebow's statement said, "It is not right for one man to bear all the blame for the mistakes of so many others."

All these statements would be entered in the day's record.

Warner smiled down from the bench. "Now, Mr. Murphy, if you would be kind enough to do the old-fashioned drill . . . stand and be accounted for, gentlemen."

Dr. Giles McCoy rose. "I was a PFC in the Marine Corps aboard the *Indianapolis*. We had thirty-nine Marines aboard, and we did security."

"As you sound off, gentlemen, remember the old days," Warner said amiably into the mic. "A little louder with your voice."

James Belcher stood and claimed his hometown: Waynesboro, Virginia. "On board ship, I was a radioman striker."

Next, Woodie James stood up. "I was a coxswain, First Division, gun captain on the center barrel. I boarded in October of 1943, and stayed there . . . until the excitement."

At James's wry understatement, chuckles rippled through the room. One by one, the men stood, elderly now but lacking no fire. Bob McGuiggan, a gunner's mate striker on the five-inch gun, then a cannonball gunner. Mike Kuryla, fire control. Paul McGinnis, signalman. Jack Miner, radio technician. Richard Paroubek, yeoman.

Warner then asked Murphy to invite the survivors to sit down front, and Murphy did.

Smith spoke up. "I believe that Mr. McVay's son is also here. Could we introduce him?"

Murphy looked to the back of the room. "Charles McVay IV, where are you?"

"Mr. McVay," Smith said, "if you would come down in the front, that would be great."

Quatro made his way forward, and when he passed through the bar, Toti read his face. Quatro's eyes did not transmit awe at being summoned to the head of a great chamber before an august body. Instead, they contained a veiled skepticism. Not ungracious, just realistic. It was the face of a man who had endured a half-century of disappointment.

5

WARNER CALLED THE FIRST witness, Hunter Scott. Though an athlete and already five-foot-nine, Hunter had the likably lanky look of a teenage boy who has not yet grown into his hands and feet.

Hunter introduced himself to the committee members and told them how he became involved in the effort to exonerate McVay. He then held up a memento he'd brought. "With me, I carry one of my most precious possessions. This is Captain McVay's dog tag from when he was a cadet at the Naval Academy. As you can see, it has his thumbprint on the back. I carry this . . . in memory of a man who ended his own life in 1968. I carry this dog tag to remind me that only in the United States can one person make a difference, no matter what their age."

Hunter was in the middle of quoting Thomas Jefferson when, at the bench, Warner covered his microphone, leaned to his right, and whispered to Smith, "Good God, Bob, how old is this kid?"

"Fourteen," Smith said. "Can you believe it?"

Hunter concluded his testimony by noting that since he began his quest in 1996, twenty survivors had passed away, leaving only 134 still living. "Please restore the honor of their ship while some of those men are still alive to see the dream become a reality."

Warner gazed down at the boy. "That completes your testimony, Mr. Scott. Well delivered."

The next witness was Paul Murphy. Still sitting behind Admiral Pilling, Toti could see Murphy in profile on the other side of the aisle separating the Navy witnesses from the ones for McVay. White-haired and usually ready with a smile, Murphy's face was deadly serious. He looked down through his glasses and began to read his statement.

Murphy pointed out that the survivors in attendance represented about 10 percent of those still living. "But I can tell you that their presence here today speaks for all of the 316 who lived through those dreadful days. Two Ohio survivors who had planned to drive here today were Bernard Bateman and Albert Morris. I am sad to tell you that Bernard Bateman died last Friday. Morris is going to stay there and attend his funeral today. Now we have 134 who are left. We have lost seven or eight survivors since January. Our time is almost up."

Murphy then laid out a bullet-point list of reasons the survivors believed the sinking of *Indianapolis* was beyond McVay's control.

"Mr. Chairman, the loss of the *Indianapolis* remains the greatest sea disaster in the history of the United States Navy. This was an embarrassment to the Navy because they never even noticed we were missing until survivors were spotted, quite by accident, four days later. So they made our skipper take the blame to avoid admitting mistakes which were not his."

Murphy was sidling up to the "scapegoat" argument, Toti noticed.

"My twenty-page written statement is devoted, in part, to commenting on and challenging recent Navy reports; specifically, one published in June of 1996, which attempts to defend Captain McVay's court-martial and conviction. These reports greatly angered those of us who read them. They contained falsehoods, statements taken out of context, and plain mean-spirited innuendos about our skipper and others who have attempted to defend him. . . . The Navy report contained personal attacks on Captain McVay's character. They were unwarranted, and in most instances, unrelated to the charges against him. On behalf of the men who served on the *Indianapolis* under Captain McVay, I would like to state our deep resentment and ask: Why is the Navy still out to falsely persecute and defame him?"

There it was, Toti thought, the ugliness beginning to splash.

Among the next witnesses was author Dan Kurzman. An iron-chinned journalist of the old school, Kurzman was used to political subterfuge. In 1952, he broke the story that a failed assassination attempt on King Farouk of Egypt was being kept secret. In 1966, President Lyndon Johnson's State Department accused Kurzman of unethical behavior, a charge that was later crushed beneath the hammer of facts, forcing State to issue a formal letter of apology.

In researching the story of *Indianapolis*, Kurzman told the committee, he met many survivors whose character and courage represented "the true naval tradition and would make anybody proud of the Navy. But sadly, I discovered there was another Navy: a small, but powerful one, composed of highly ranked naval figures who were great fighters, but somehow lost their moral perspective. That's what this hearing is all about. The conviction of Captain McVay was a dark episode in the illustrious history of the U.S. Navy, and today, still casts a shadow over its image."

Kurzman had spent hours hunkered down in the National Archives and found there what he referred to as "the smoking gun." It was a memorandum from Edward Hidalgo, the special assistant Navy Secretary James Forrestal had once told to make the sensationalism go away. The memo said, "The causal nexus between the failure to zigzag and the loss of the ship appears not to have a solid foundation."

Hidalgo, Kurzman said, had spoken with a legal expert about a response to an appeal by McVay. The expert favored additional language to the effect that McVay was convicted of a "super technical charge." But it was felt that such language would tend to imply an apology for having convicted him at all.

Kurzman also interviewed Hashimoto, who said that McVay had been a victim of bad luck. I-58 and *Indianapolis* happened to meet at a rare moment when the degree of visibility permitted a torpedo strike.

This bad fortune might never have befallen McVay if he had been given an escort and proper intelligence.

Kurzman ended his testimony with a pair of powerful questions. "Is the American democratic system so inflexible that an injustice cannot be rectified? Is the U.S. Navy, which so gloriously helped conquer the enemy, incapable of conquering itself?"

6

SENATOR BOB SMITH THOUGHT the hearing was going well. Warner, sitting to Smith's left, had been impressed with young Hunter Scott. He was also clearly moved by the passionate testimony of the survivors, Smith noted—Murphy, as well as McCoy, and Twible, who had tried to help keep order in the Redmayne raft group.

On the bench before Smith was a sheaf of materials, including a sheet of paper given to him by Mike Monroncy. Smith called the first witness for the Navy.

Dr. William Dudley, the director of naval history, went first. Dudley delivered a lengthy history of the *Indianapolis* sinking, court of inquiry, and court-martial based on commercially published books and Navy press releases. Dudley cited one primary source, McVay's September 1945 oral narrative on the sinking.

Next, Admiral John D. Hutson testified. Hutson, the judge advocate general counsel of the Navy, told the committee that he had personally read the entire record of the trial. "I conclude that the proceedings were fair and provided the due full process of law."

Hutson argued that while modern courts-martial are, in effect, criminal trials, courts-martial before 1950 were much different affairs. Such proceedings often incorporated "the fixing of accountability and resolving vexing issues of command and discretionary action." The head JAG's testimony was brief, and he referred the committee to a detailed written statement in which he refuted the claims of Hunter Scott and the survivors.

"Thank you, Admiral Hutson," Smith said. "Admiral Pilling?"

Commander Bill Toti squared his shoulders to the bench. For an awful moment, he wondered what in the world he'd been thinking. He was an upwardly mobile officer on the verge of making captain. But this subterfuge could get him fired as Pilling's assistant, or at least reprimanded.

Karen had pleaded with him not to do it—"It's too dangerous," she'd said—but he'd done it anyway. Now, part of him thought he should have listened to his wife.

On the other hand, his long study of *Indianapolis* and McVay had convinced him that a grave injustice had been done, and that the survivors would never again get this close to righting that wrong. In the end, he'd made his decision—to work against his own boss, but, he hoped, in favor of history.

"Senator, thank you for the opportunity to appear here today and address the committee," Pilling said, smooth and polished as always. "I also have a brief statement. Then we will be ready to respond to your questions."

Pilling noted that the investigation after the sinking of *Indianapolis* revealed the Navy's weaknesses: in how ships were routed and tracked; in the quality of survival equipment; and in the material condition of Indy herself, an older ship.

The admiral then echoed Toti's *Proceedings* article on the absolute responsibility of a commanding officer for his ship. "Admiral McVay understood these concepts perfectly. After his rescue, he told reporters . . . 'I was in command of the ship and I am responsible for its fate.'"

Pilling addressed the charge on which McVay was convicted: hazarding his vessel by failure to steer a zigzag course. He emphasized that McVay was not court-martialed for the sinking, but rather for poor judgment. His decision to steer a straight course increased Indy's vulnerability to a submarine attack. Whether a zigzag course would have prevented the sinking was an open question, the admiral said. But it was clear to him that it would have "shifted the odds" in Indy's favor.

Finally, Pilling noted that McVay was a courageous officer decorated for action in combat. He also lauded the crew's heroic struggle to survive. "I understand and applaud that those men, the survivors of *Indianapolis*, should defend their captain against what some see as an unfair attack on a valiant naval officer. I hope that my comments may help to make clear that the court-martial . . . was not undertaken to attack him, but to defend the crucial principle of command accountability."

At the head of the chamber, Smith spoke into his microphone. "Thank you very much, Admiral. I understand the position that all of you are in. I respect it. I want you to know that. It is not my style to try to attack here and to demean in any way. I am trying to be objective. I have done a lot of research, not as much as some others, such as Mr. Scott, but in reading your statement, Admiral Pilling, it is weak."

Toti winced: *Here it comes . . .*

"Not the statement, but the court-martial," Smith continued. "Let me just say why. . . . There were hundreds of American ships sunk out there in the war. Nobody was court-martialed for the sinking of his ship other than Captain McVay. . . . Based on your own testimony, you are saying it was a judgment that they court-martialed him for, not the zigzag, not the sinking of the ship. You had the commander of the submarine who sank the ship, the Japanese officer, testify at the court-martial that 'I popped up with my periscope and there he was, and I sank him. Zigazgging would not have made a difference.' So let me ask you a point-blank direct question: Was Captain McVay to blame for the sinking of the USS *Indianapolis*? Yes or no?"

"As I said in my statement, sir, he was not tried for the sinking."

"So if he was not tried and court-martialed for the sinking," Smith countered, "then he was court-martialed for a judgment he made not to zigzag. . . . If it is seven hundred ships that sank, did we look at every single one of those sinkings and look at the judgment of those captains prior to that? Did we analyze each one of those?"

Since coming to work for him, Toti had learned that certain things happened to the admiral's face when he got angry. First, his face would go completely stoic. Then the corners of his mouth would start to curl up. Some people would mistake this for a smile. In the next stage, Pilling's face would begin to turn red. That was happening now.

Smith continued hammering. "Did we say, 'Well, he did not zigzag, he did zigzag, he did know this, he did not know that?' I do not think we did. . . . It is, to me, bizarre that one individual would be court-martialed on a judgment. Would any of you gentlemen wearing the uniform like to be court-martialed on an error in judgment that had no direct impact on the loss of lives? How would you feel if that were you or your son?"

"If I could just respond, Senator," Pilling said. "In the first place, as the judge advocate general pointed out, the role of a court-martial before 1950 was very different."

"I understand that."

"The second thing I would point out is that Fleet Admiral King— I mean, Nimitz—said he should not go to court-martial, but he should receive a letter of reprimand for a judgment error."

"Well, that's a big difference, let's face it. A big difference between a letter of reprimand and a court-martial. But you said that the Navy had a number of weaknesses. That is the term you used in your statement."

"Right."

"The way they noted and tracked ships, and weaknesses in survival equipment on board," Smith said. "But it is interesting that when the Navy talks about their mistakes, they are not mistakes, they are weaknesses. When we talk about a possible mistake in judgment by Captain McVay, it is a court-martial offense."

Smith now turned his guns on Hutson, the JAG: Were any of the men who allegedly received an SOS from *Indianapolis* court-martialed?

Smith was referring in part to the SOS messages reportedly received by the Coast Guard vessel *Bibb* and USS *Hyperion*. A search of radio logs and dispatch files revealed that *Bibb* received no such message. A January 1946 memorandum from *Hyperion* indicated that the ship received messages "indicating the loss of *Indianapolis*" sometime before August 4, 1945. The rescue began on August 2, and the memo does not say that the messages related to Indy were distress messages.

Over the years, additional information about distress signals arose, including an account by a sailor named Clair B. Young. In 1955, the *Los Angeles Times* and *Saturday Evening Post* ran ten-year retrospective articles on the loss of *Indianapolis*. Young came forward. He said that at half past midnight on July 30, 1945, he was a seaman on watch at the Quonset hut quarters of Commodore Jacob Jacobson, commander of Naval Operating Base (NOB), Leyte Gulf, Philippines, when a messenger approached him with an urgent radio dispatch. Upon reading the message, Young saw that it appeared to be a garbled SOS from "CA 35" that included the ship's location and condition. According to Young, he woke Jacobson, who read the message and said, "No reply at this time. If any further messages are received, notify me at once."

In 1955, Young wrote to the chief of naval operations about the "lost distress signal" and shared his recollection of those events. Later, in a 1991 personal letter to Kimo McVay, Young added new information: He had noticed "a strong odor of alcohol" in Jacobson's room and, a few days after the incident, Young noticed "CA 35" on the Ships Present board in the port director's office. But he felt there was nothing he could do about it because others already knew about the SOS.

Another man, Donald Allen, wrote to Hunter Scott in 1998. In 1945, Allen was a teenage sailor serving on limited duty at Tacloban after having suffered a heat stroke near New Guinea. On the night of July 29, Allen wrote, he was standing watch in the officer of the deck's Quonset hut at Philippine Sea Frontier when a radioman came in bearing an *Indianapolis* SOS that included the ship's position. According to Allen, a duty officer sent two seagoing tugs to the rescue, but these were recalled hours into their journey by Commodore Norman Gillette. An examination of PhilSeaFron's logs for the period shows that two seagoing tugs were indeed dispatched on July 29—but in response to a large convoy caught in a storm between Okinawa and Luzon, not in response to *Indianapolis*.

A third sailor, Russell Hetz, wrote a letter to Hunter in 1998. According to Hetz, *LCI-1004*, the landing craft to which he was assigned, received two distress messages from *Indianapolis*, eight and a half minutes apart. Six weeks later, an officer with "a lot of clout" came aboard and ripped the pages relevant to the distress calls out of the landing craft's log. Later investigation, however, showed that LCI-1004's logs appear complete.

It is true that the Philippine Sea Frontier operations plot showed that Indy had arrived in Leyte Gulf. Could the messenger Clair Young reported have been sent by the OOD where Allen was standing duty? Possibly. Since Jack Miner saw the Radio 2 antenna needle jump, it is not out of the question that multiple stations could have received Indy's distress message. However, the power was out in Radio 1 and in Radio 2, Chief Woods was able to send an SOS but not the ship's position. The distress call Hetz reported did not involve coordinates. Could that have been Woods's signal? That is also possible. And yet a conspiracy involving all three reported distress calls would have had to drop a now seventy-plus-year cone of silence over the Sea Frontier radioman and the duty officer who dispatched the tugs that Allen reported were in response to *Indianapolis.* The tug crews and their captains, as well as the landing craft radioman and its captain, would also have had to keep quiet. In addition, someone would have had to falsify LCT-1004's log in order for historians to later find it complete, and both commodores Jacobson and Gillette would have had to knowingly sign falsified war diaries for NOB Leyte Gulf and Philippine Sea Frontier, neither of which mentions a distress signal from *Indianapolis.* During the sinking investigation, the communications logs of all stations involved in the sailing and loss of *Indianapolis* were searched, and no SOS message was found.

Now Hutson answered Smith's question. "No, sir," he said. "There were no other courts-martial related to the tragic loss."

"The perception is that [McVay] was court-martialed because the ship went down and 1,200 sailors went into the water," Smith said. ". . . Frankly, I think you have to ask yourself, honestly . . . if the ship had not sunk, and Captain McVay had entered port, would he have been court-martialed?"

It was a direct hit. Toti, who had always been short, now wished he were shorter. He knew—*knew*—Pilling must surely recognize Smith's question as the same one Toti had presented during the hearing prep the previous week. Toti expected that any second, Pilling would turn around and scorch him with a knowing glare: *busted.* But Pilling did not.

Smith's question to Hutson explicitly addressed an assertion in Hutson's written statement. The admiral disputed what he called "the popular misconception" that McVay was brought to trial for having his ship sunk in combat, when he was actually court-martialed for hazarding his ship. "In fact," Hutson had written, "the actual loss of the ship was not an element of either of the two charges referred against Captain McVay."

The Navy had long held this position, and while it was technically true, the handwritten notes of Lieutenant Carl Bauersfeld cast the issue in a different light. Bauersfeld was assistant counsel to Captain Thomas Ryan, the lead prosecutor in the case. In the winter of 1945 while preparing for trial, the lieutenant created a "proof matrix," written in two columns on the lined sheets of a yellow legal pad. In the left-hand column Bauersfeld listed for Charge I against McVay—that of negligently hazarding his vessel—seven separate elements of proof. For example, one element was that McVay was captain of *Indianapolis*. Another was that the ship had been sailing unescorted. In the right-hand column, he listed the evidence that Ryan could use to prove each one.

As written by Bauersfeld, the seventh element of Charge I was this: "He [McVay] . . . through said negligence did suffer the said U.S.S. *Indianapolis* to be hazard[ed]." Next to this specification, the lieutenant wrote, "This may be proved by showing ship was torpedoed by expert witness."

The expert witness, of course, was Hashimoto. When the Japanese commander was en route to Washington, D.C., in December 1945, United Press International reported on his arrival. The wire service repeated the Navy's claim that Ryan had called Hashimoto not to testify against McVay, but to verify that *Indianapolis* had indeed been sunk by a submarine. But according to Bauersfeld's notes, that was only semantically true. Ryan actually called Hashimoto in order to convict McVay.

In the conclusion of his written statement, Hutson asserted that according to "the record of trial, 54 years of naval correspondence, and history, Captain McVay was never charged with losing his ship." The prosecution's notes, however, indicate that McVay likely had to lose his ship in order to be charged. Without Hashimoto's testimony, the cause of the sinking was inconclusive. Without the sinking, "hazarding" could not definitively be proved. And without hazarding, the rest of the charges against McVay might have collapsed for lack of foundation.

In the hearing room, the sparring continued. Senator Warner and Dr. Dudley, the historian, weighed in. Punches and counterpunches. Warner seemed troubled by some of the Navy's assertions and he said so.

Senator Smith pointed out that Captain Oliver Naquin made a judgment not to share the ULTRA intelligence on the Tamon group. The Pacific Fleet chose not to investigate I-58's report of sinking an enemy ship—another judgment. Why, Smith wanted to know, was McVay prosecuted for an error in judgment while those responsible for equally—or more—fatal judgments were not? Again, the query echoed Toti's murder board questions.

Finally, Smith said, "There is an injustice here. We should change injustices, not rewrite history, but change injustices." He gazed down at the admirals. "That man wore the uniform, just like you wore it. He was one hell of an officer. He would not have been given that bomb to take to the *Enola Gay* if he was not, as has already been stated. I think to punish him—and he endured punishment that none of us could ever understand and paid the ultimate price for it. We have a chance . . . to make it right. Not to overturn a court-martial. Not to demean the reputations of any of the other officers who may have made errors in judgment. Just to simply say we made a mistake. The court-martial was a mistake. . . . It was an injustice done to a good man."

When the hearing was over, Toti helped Pilling gather his paperwork, then crossed the aisle to say goodbye to the Murphys. Quiet congratulations bubbled among the survivors. The hearing had gone as well as it possibly could have, they felt. The weight of testimony had clearly come down on the side of passing the Senate resolution.

Toti didn't say so, but he knew there was still a towering obstacle to passage: Senator John Warner. During Warner's term as Navy secretary, he'd had the opportunity to take action on McVay's court-martial, but chose not to. Would he now support a bill that, in essence, did what he had refused to do while he was in charge of the Navy? Or would he recoil from appearing to change his position?

It would still be up to Warner whether to take the exoneration resolution to the senate floor for a vote. Would he?

JULY 2005

THE WESTIN HOTEL
INDIANAPOLIS, INDIANA

AT THE WESTIN HOTEL in Indianapolis, the vast lobby buzzed with the festive air of a state fair midway. Sixty-two of the ninety-two living survivors arrived to warm greetings and supporters from all over the globe. World War II exhibit tables lined a wide, carpeted hall. Survivors posted themselves at book-signing tables. A thirteen-foot-long scale model of *Indianapolis* dominated the lobby, drawing crowds. More than eight hundred people bounced between exhibits and little clusters of admirers gathered around the old Indy sailors to hear their stories.

At the ship model, survivors recounted the night of the tragedy, pointing to the port rail or the fantail or the quarterdeck. "This is the last place I touched her," they would say. "This is where I abandoned ship."

Exactly sixty years had passed since the sinking, and two years since the last formal reunion. But this, 2005, was a banner year. The acting secretary of defense, Gordon England, would be the speaker at the reunion's main event, the formal banquet on Saturday night. England was the highest-ranking member of the defense department ever to keynote a reunion. His presence validated the survivors' long fight for McVay.

That fight did not end with the Senate Armed Services Committee. After the hearing, two months passed as Senator Bob Smith and his new military legislative aide, Margaret "Ducky" Hemenway, battled the Pentagon. Every time Ducky sent draft exoneration language to Senator Warner's office, a more powerful aide there disemboweled it. That's because Warner was under heavy Navy pressure to leave McVay's culpability alone. Repeatedly, Smith appealed to Warner to take SJR 26 to the floor for a vote, and Warner's answer was always the same: no.

In the end, the man who finally persuaded Warner was the same one who sank *Indianapolis*. In November 1999, Mochitsura Hashimoto wrote a letter to Warner. The letter expressed Hashimoto's dismay over the fact that McVay was ever tried in court.

I have met many of your brave men who survived the sinking of the *Indianapolis*. I would like to join them in urging that your national legislature clear their captain's name. Our peoples have forgiven each other for that terrible war and its consequences. Perhaps it is time your peoples forgave Captain McVay for the humiliation of his unjust conviction.

When he received Hashimoto's plea, Warner was so astonished that he called Smith to his office to show him the letter in person. For Warner, it was the final weight on the scale. He decided to take the exoneration resolution to the Senate floor. On October 12, 2000, the measure passed. It was the same day of another naval sea disaster, when terrorists attacked the USS *Cole* in Yemen, killing seventeen sailors and wounding thirty-nine more.

House Joint Resolution 48 also passed, and with stronger exoneration language. But even after President Bill Clinton signed the legislation, his Navy secretary, Richard Danzig, refused to enter the language in Captain McVay's record. There was no movement until George W. Bush took office and appointed a new Navy secretary, Gordon England.

Months later, England met with Toti to discuss the history of the exoneration battle. Then he met with Senator Smith, who asked him to allow the amendment of Captain McVay's service record.

"It will be done," England told the senator. "You have my word." Secretary England then directed the chief of naval operations to enter the following language into McVay's record:

1. in light of the remission by the Secretary of the Navy of the sentence of the court-martial and the restoration of Captain McVay to active duty by the Chief of Naval Operations, Fleet Admiral Chester Nimitz, that the American people should now recognize Captain McVay's lack of culpability for the tragic loss of the USS *Indianapolis* and the lives of the men who died as a result of the sinking of that vessel; and

2. in light of the fact that certain exculpatory information was not available to the court-martial board and that Captain McVay's conviction resulted therefrom, that Captain McVay's military record should now reflect that he is exonerated for the loss of the USS *Indianapolis* and so many of her crew.

The survivors did not trust the Pentagon to make the entry in McVay's record, so they asked that Toti be allowed to do it. While reviewing McVay's record, Toti was surprised to find an entry about McVay's Bronze Star, the one awarded him at the Potomac River command in 1946, for action on *Indianapolis* three months before she sank. The record entry said, in error, that in 1946, McVay's whereabouts were unknown and that his medal had been "returned to stock."

Toti knew about the valor award McVay had received for action in the Solomon Islands, but not about this second honor. He showed the service record entry to Secretary England, who asked Toti whether McVay had any living relatives.

Only Charles B. McVay IV—"Quatro"—Toti said. "Kimo died two months ago." Kimo had lived to see Congress exonerate his father, but not long enough to see it become a matter of official Navy record. He died of cancer in June 2001, at the age of seventy-three.

"Present the medal to Captain McVay's living son," England said.

Toti called on Quatro and presented him with the Bronze Star. Quatro was shocked to learn that his father had won a second award for courage under fire. Apparently, McVay had not told his boys about this new honor, perhaps out of shame for having lost the ship on which he earned it.

Quatro was in attendance at the 2005 reunion, smiling and greeting survivors and families. Toti was also there, one of a slate of guest speakers that also included Lieutenant Colonel Oliver North. Toti was a captain now, having put on his eagles in August 2000, two months before Admiral Don Pilling retired from active duty. Toti never learned whether Pilling was caught off guard in the September 1999 Senate hearing—or whether he intentionally "threw the game" with his surprise Saturday phone call.

Survivors who had made the trip to Indianapolis ranged from Harold Bray, at seventy-eight the baby of the bunch, to the oldest, Thomas Goff, who was ninety-eight. One survivor didn't have to travel at all. Jimmy O'Donnell, whose wife watched Indy pass beneath the Golden Gate as the ship left the States for the last time, was the only survivor from the cruiser's namesake city.

L. D. Cox and Glenn Morgan were at the reunion, too. After the war, the two remained close friends, their kids growing up together, their families spending holidays with each other in Texas. Cox and Morgan sometimes spoke together, telling their survival story at VFW halls and civic organizations.

All of these old friends gathered, and the mood in the Westin lobby was ebullient. Paul Murphy, who had retired as an engineer, now used a wheelchair. But this day he jumped out of it, laughing. "I don't need this thing today!" he said to a young woman standing with him. "You get in and I'll give you a ride!"

The woman, a filmmaker and friend of the survivors who was taping the day's events, sat down in the chair and Murphy took her for a spin, a half-chewed cigar hanging out of his mouth and laughing like a kid.

A young Japanese woman had also come to the reunion. Her name was Atsuko Iida, and she was the granddaughter of Commander Mochitsura Hashimoto. Like Kimo, the old Japanese submarine commander had lived to see McVay exonerated. But he died two weeks later, at the age of ninety-one. Initially nervous about attending the ship's reunions, Atsuko worried about upsetting the families of Indy's lost at sea. This year, though, encouraged by her husband, Jahn, she had brought along her two young sons and her mother, Commander Hashimoto's daughter. This would be the first time the Hashimoto family met so many people connected to *Indianapolis*.

In the lobby, Atsuko and hundreds of others queued up at a long row of rectangular tables stacked with hardcover blue books. *Only 317 Survived*, a collection of first-person accounts written by the survivors and edited for publication by Mary Lou Murphy. Visitors snapped them up two and three at a time and cheerfully waited in line to get their heroes to sign them.

Survivor Ed Harrell had also just published a book, *Out of the Depths: A Survivor's Story of the Sinking of the USS* Indianapolis. Harrell had written it with his son, David, a pastor, and so was signing two books that day.

The day passed in celebration. The next night, before the banquet, the young filmmaker was walking past the model of *Indianapolis* when another man in a wheelchair began to speak. It was Bob Bunai, a former signalman first class. At ninety-six, Bunai was the second-oldest living survivor. For sixty years, he had refused to speak about the disaster. Even in the survivors' new book, Bunai's entry was short and sweet:

> I joined the Navy to see the world. Since we were too busy fighting
> a war, I didn't see the world.

Now, suddenly, in a reedy voice that crackled with years, Bunai stood and began to tell his story. Quickly, the filmmaker swung up her camera. After more than a half-century of silence, it was as if someone had flipped a switch. With his family standing nearby, Bunai spoke for twenty minutes straight, finally unburdening his soul about those terrorizing days in the water. His voice climbing high with passion, Bunai reached such a fever pitch that he tottered and nearly fell. Family members caught him and lowered him gently back into his wheelchair.

But Bunai wasn't finished. He shook his finger at the filmmaker's lens, and his voice crescendoed. "For sixty years, I cried! I cried a lot! But now . . . I ain't gonna cry anymore!"

The old gentleman's sentiment reflected that of all the survivors. For sixty years, they had gathered to fight for three things: to remember their brothers lost at sea, to build a monument honoring that sacrifice, and to exonerate their captain. Over the decades, they were faithful to their first purpose. The second goal took exactly half a century. Now, finally, McVay's record reflected his innocence. Their quest was complete.

At the banquet that night, a procession of speakers paid homage to the *Indianapolis* survivors, the families of the lost at sea, and also the rescuers, many of whom had come. To close out the evening, per long tradition, Glenn Morgan climbed onto the stage as he did each year to lead the crowd in singing a final song, "God Bless America."

Morgan stepped up to the microphone. "Now, we haven't done this before," he said, "but what I'd like to do is to have all the children come up here."

The banquet hall broke into applause as the children and grandchildren of survivors and lost-at-sea families began streaming toward the stage. School-age children weaved their way through the banquet tables, while parents led their preschoolers by the hand.

"That's right, come on, y'all," Morgan said from the stage, beckoning.

From a table near the front where she sat with her husband and sons, Atsuko Iida watched the children wending their way forward. She glanced at her own two boys, unsure.

Suddenly, the Indy families seated around her began motioning her toward the stage, encouraging her with smiles: "Yes, Atsuko! You, too! Go up there . . . go!"

Nervously, Atsuko stood. Taking her sons by their hands, she began making her way toward Morgan and the large group of gathering children.

In this hall, there was no more room for hatred. In those war years, families on both sides had been torn. Hashimoto may have claimed a victory in the war's final moments, but he returned home to find his country in ashes. And the survivors' joy over America's victory was swallowed up in the trial they endured.

Now, though, they were healing. There would always be scars, a part of each man locked forever inside his beloved ship. But over the decades, their wounds slowly knit closed, each reunion a touch of balm on the pain.

Atsuko reached the front of the room with her boys. At the microphone, Morgan sang the first notes. Five hundred people watched with smiles and tears as Hashimoto's family and the *Indianapolis* families joined together and sang, as one.

The End

FINAL LOG ENTRY
AUGUST 19, 2017

USS *INDIANAPOLIS*
THE PHILIPPINE SEA

EIGHTEEN THOUSAND FEET BELOW the surface, a "remotely operated vehicle," or ROV, whirs across the seafloor, heading for what is known technically as the next "seafloor anomaly." Festooned with lights, painted garishly yellow, and wrapped in metal nerf bars, the high-tech vehicle looks more like a portable generator than a seagoing vessel. Driven by a joystick in a control room at the other end of a six-kilometer-long cable, the vehicle hovers several meters over the seafloor, slowly motoring up to a triangle-shaped object embedded in the silt below. Orbiting its unusual quarry, the ROV's camera resolves an object that has been shrouded in darkness for seventy-two years. The number 35 pops out of the inky black, as crisp as the day it was painted.

"That's it Paul, we've got it. The Indy!"

"Paul" is philanthropist and Microsoft cofounder Paul G. Allen, whose team on August 19, 2017, found what many argue is the most important American military shipwreck to be discovered in a generation: USS *Indianapolis*. Allen owns the ultra-high-tech research vessel *Petrel*. Five days before the discovery, ROV pilot and researcher Paul Mayer sat alone in a Mark V inflatable boat. On a sea like a glass sheet, without so much as a puff of wind to ruffle the surface, Mayer waited under the glaring tropical sun. He was fishing, for both actual fish and clues about the local currents.

Mayer and Robert Kraft, *Petrel*'s director of subsea operations, and their team had for weeks scoured the area where Indy was said to have sunk. But time and again, the ship's remote sonar scans had come up empty. That got Mayer and Kraft puzzling over the currents in the area. Now, a windless day presented an opportunity to check how both *Petrel*—a gleaming-white, three-thousand-ton ship—and the diminutive Mark V would respond to local currents.

The *Petrel* team had been working to locate *Indianapolis* for weeks, but the effort had started many months before. To guide their underwater exploration, they made meticulous charts of Indy's speed of advance (SOA), looked at the relative positions of the 1945 rescue locations to back-project their potential origins, and reviewed old records in search of clues. In the end, the SOA calculations proved to be most fruitful—so much so that they ultimately allowed *Petrel* to succeed where others had failed.

With an autonomous underwater vehicle, or AUV, the team searched thousands of square miles of uncharted Pacific Ocean terrain—soaring mountains and plunging canyons as high and deep as their counterparts in the Hindu Kush. *Petrel* researchers divided this terrain into a set of grids. Equipped with a sophisticated mapping sonar, the AUV returned massive, high-resolution panoramic images of the sea bottom, which the crew then sifted for anomalies that looked man-made, or that didn't seem to fit the surrounding seafloor.

After weeks of searching, Grid 19 ultimately held the prize. The discovery came late at night. Initial, telltale images began filtering back to the on-duty crew and sparked a mounting excitement. First, a potential debris field, with signs of larger objects that appeared inorganic. Definite signs of wreckage.

Kraft was informed, and upon seeing the images, couldn't lower the ROV fast enough. The AUV returned sonar data to *Petrel*. The ROV would return live video. Kraft had a good feeling, but once the ROV was launched, it would take three to four hours to reach the bottom.

Slowly, the ROV made its descent. When it reached fifty-five hundred meters—three and a half miles below the surface—the explorers got their first glimpse of the once-proud flagship of the 5th Fleet.

The *Petrel* crew, some of whom are retired Navy men themselves, watched in reverence. This vessel was much more than a shipwreck, and every one of them took a moment to pay his respects.

The discovery of the bow came first, and then, after another AUV pass, the whole debris field was laid out before them. The panoramic sonar image revealed a number of astonishing facts. The bow, ultimately separated as a result of Commander Hashimoto's torpedo attack, had crashed into the seafloor more than a mile northeast of the rest of the hull. The main portion of the hull sat on the sea bottom, pointed to the southeast. Remarkably, the main part of the ship rested upright on the seafloor in a crater of its own making, hundreds of feet wide, surrounded by a spiderweb of giant cracks that look exactly as though Indy had slammed into a windshield.

Lack of oxygen, near-freezing temperatures, and the absence of light had preserved *Indianapolis* so perfectly that it seemed she could have gone down the same day she was discovered. Remarkably detailed photos and videos collected by the *Petrel* crew show everything from helmets and shoes to cases of Colgate and individual pieces of dinnerware scattered across the seafloor. The expedition returned iconic images of Bofors guns, rifled five-inch gun barrels, and victory tallies still fresh as the day they were painted. Even turret No. 3 somehow stayed in its barbette.

The heavy cruiser did suffer some major damage during its descent to the seafloor. While the bow definitely separated at frame 12, as several eyewitnesses attested, the next 13 frames of the forward structure are also missing, as if the ship were chewed into small pieces all the way back to frame 25 in front of turret No. 1. Whether this was an effect of onboard fires, explosions, or the sheer force of the ship falling through the water column is a mystery.

The two forward turrets, held in only by gravity and their 250-ton bulk, tumbled from the hull and embedded in the mud. The forward structures above the communications deck, including the radio room, the signal bridge, the navigation bridge, the air target designation platform, the main 8-inch director, and the radar antennae were all wrested from the hull. Torn clear of the ship, they lay mostly facedown and crumpled in a detached pile on the seafloor amidst a tangle of lines and cables.

Examinations of the wreck show two torpedo strikes (frames 12 and 45), not three as Hashimoto thought he saw. Hull plating blown outward in the forward sections of the ship indicate that internal explosions may account for what Hashimoto thought was a third hit.

The wreck, considered a war grave, still belongs to the Navy. Recognizing its importance, the Naval History and Heritage Command had invested some forethought in how to announce its discovery. They engaged former *Indianapolis* submarine captain and honorary survivor William Toti to deliver the news to the nineteen survivors still living at the time. With only a four-hour head start before the official public announcement, Toti worked together with this book's coauthor, Sara Vladic, to spread the word. And then, on August 19 at 9 a.m. PST, Paul

G. Allen broke the news of his team's discovery, unleashing a torrent of reactions across the world.

"Holy God!" said survivor Dick Thelen, then ninety years old. "I never thought this day would come in my lifetime." Echoes of his life's motto came to his mind. "I'm glad they didn't give up until they found it."

Edgar Harrell expressed what a great gift this was, as he prepared to celebrate his seventieth wedding anniversary later that day with his wife, Ola Mae, who was his sweetheart before he sailed on Indy's final voyage.

After Indy was found, calls went out across the country to survivors and family members of those men who were lost at sea, and their reactions, although varied, had the same tone. Amazement followed by reverence. Finding the ship provided a measure of peace, but it didn't change the outcome. There was happiness, but not jubilation.

For the families of the lost at sea, the news stirred high emotions, bringing back memories many had sealed away for decades. After nearly three-quarters of a century, children, nieces, nephews, and grandchildren were finding the peace that their parents and grandparents had sought for so many years.

Earl Henry, Jr., the son of lost-at-sea dentist Lieutenant Commander Earl Henry, Sr., was puzzled at his own emotions regarding the discovery. He had never met his father, and had heard only his voice via an old recording kept by his mother, Jane. Even so, he felt more connected to his father than many children who had lost a parent in the sinking. Once he had time to absorb the news, his emotions unexpectedly broke through. After a lifetime of uncertain longing, he finally knew where his father was. The discovery provided fresh fire for Earl Junior's longtime efforts to preserve his father's memory. He travels the country, sharing his father's stories and artwork. It is a fitting tribute to the way Henry proudly showed little Earl's picture to everyone on the ship.

A couple of weeks after the discovery, the Petrel team fanned out to visit some survivors in their homes. Paul Mayer paid a special visit to ninety-three-year-old survivor Louis "Kayo" Erwin, a fellow resident of Chattanooga. Seventy-two years earlier, Kayo had been part of the deck gang that loaded the atomic bomb onto the ship at Mare Island. As he sat in his comfortable chair surrounded by family, Kayo watched as Paul showed new images of the little cubbyhole on the port side where he had hung his hammock just minutes before the torpedo strike. Having spent two years aboard *Indianapolis*, Kayo sat in stunned awe. The images were so clear, it was easy to remember the last gun he had fired and the last place he touched on the ship.

John Woolston, now a retired Navy captain after an illustrious career as a chief engineer, also hosted a quartet of guests in his Honolulu home. There, Rob Kraft and Paul Mayer traded looks with Janet Greenlee, keeper of the AUV's detailed sonar image of the wreck site. They were deciding whether to reveal the image to Woolston and his close friend, honorary survivor Kim Roller. The team is so dedicated to preserving the sanctity of the site as a war grave that they have used cloak-and-dagger techniques such as spoofed GPS readings on video feeds and turning off the *Petrel*'s locator to disguise Indy's true location.

But this man, they felt, deserved to know. Greenlee pulled out a broad sheet of paper and spread it across the coffee table. Woolston, who doesn't take naps, show weakness, miss work, or catch colds, was on high alert. It would be the first time he would lay eyes on Indy since 1945.

As he surveyed the image of the ship, so startlingly vivid and well preserved, he breathed the same comment again and again: "Fantastic."

The next day, seated in the wardroom of the USS *Missouri* in Pearl Harbor, John got a private showing of the ROV video from the wreck. His engineer's perspective brought to life small details about the wreckage and its state of preservation. He found the portholes in the officers' wardroom of particular interest. After dropping his sandwich and locating a wrench with the steward, the portholes had saved his life all those years ago. He wanted to see them again, curious about their size and how he might have fit. As all gathered around the monitor, Woolston opined in a rare deadpan tone, "Maybe I made them bigger in my mind so my hips would fit through."

The room erupted in laughter. Minutes later, many in the room held back tears as Woolston recounted holding dying shipmates in his arms in the very same waters where these images had been taken.

Eighteen thousand feet below the surface, the ROV's thrusters rotate it away from the wreck for the last time. Recalled to its mothership on the surface, the boxy vehicle takes its host of lights, cameras, and sensors with it. Once again, darkness envelops the ship's proud lines, and

Lieutenant Commander Kasey Moore's first love readies herself for night operations.

Lights out on deck, her hatches are open to keep her compartments cool on a steamy tropical night. Her teak foredeck is clear, ready for the footfalls of sailors on watch. Leaning just slightly to starboard, it's as if she's cresting a wave, shrugging off another swell on her way to an important mission. Guns trained toward the sky, *Indianapolis* is ready for all that might challenge her, forever on patrol.

FINAL SAILING LIST
USS *INDIANAPOLIS*

ABBOTT, George Stanley, S1

ACOSTA, Charles Mack, MM3

ADAMS, Leo Harry, S1*

ADAMS, Pat Leon, S2

ADORANTE, Dante William, S2

AKINES, William Roy, S2*

ALBRIGHT, Charles Erskine, Jr., Cox

ALLARD, Vincent Jerome, QM3*

ALLEN, Paul Franklin, S1

ALLMARAS, Harold Dean, F2

ALTSCHULER, Allan Harvey, S2*

ALVEY, Edward Wuites, Jr., AerM2

AMICK, Homer Irwin, S2

ANDERSEN, Lawrence Joseph, SKD2

ANDERSON, Erick Thorwald, S2*

ANDERSON, Leonard Ole, MM3

ANDERSON, Sam General, S2

ANDERSON, Vincent Udell, BMl

ANDERSON, Richard Lew, F2

ANDREWS, William Robert, S2*

ANNIS, James Bernard, Jr., CEM

ANTHONY, Harold Robert, PHM3

ANTONIE, Charles Jacob, F2

ANUNTI, John Melvin, M2*

ARMENTA, Lorenzo, SC2

ARMISTEAD, John Harold, S2*

ARNOLD, Carl Lloyd, AMM3

ASHFORD, Chester Windell, WT2

ASHFORD, John Thomas, Jr., RT3*

ATKINSON, J. P., COX

AULL, Joseph Harry, S2

AULT, William Frazier, S2*

AYOTTE, Lester James, S2

BACKUS, Thomas Hawkins, LT (jg)

BAKER, Daniel Albert, S2

BAKER, Frederick Harold, S2

BAKER, William Marvin, Jr., EM2

BALDRIDGE, Clovis Roger, EM1*

BALL, Emmet Edwin, S2

BALLARD, Courtney Jackson, SSMB3

BARENTHIN, Leonard William, S2

BARKER, Robert Craig, Jr., RT1

BARKSDALE, Thomas Leon, FC3

BARNES, Paul Clayton, F2

BARNES, Willard Merlin, MM1

BARRA, Raymond James, CGM

BARRETT, James Benedict, S2

BARRY, Charles, LT (jg)

BARTO, Lloyd Peter, S1*

BARTON, George Sydney, Y3

BATEMAN, Bernard Byron, F2*

BATENHORST, Wilfred John, MM3

BATSON, Eugene Clifford, S2

BATTEN, Robert Edmon, S1

BATTS, Edward Daniel, STM1

BEANE, James Albert, F2*

BEATY, Donald Lee, S1*

BECKER, Myron Melvin, WT2

* Survivor   ** Survived, but died shortly after rescue   *** Passenger

BEDDINGTON, Charles Earnest, S1

BEDSTED, Leo Alfred Kergaard, F1

BEISTER, Richard James, WT3

BELCHER, James Robert, S1*

BELL, Maurice Glenn, S1*

BENNETT, Dean Randall, HA1

BENNETT, Ernest Franklin, B3

BENNETT, Toney Wade, ST3

BENNING, Harry, S1

BENTON, Clarence Upton, CFC*

BERNACIL, Concepcion Peralta, FC3*

BERRY, Joseph, Jr., STM1

BERRY, William Henry, ST3

BEUKEMA, Kenneth Jay, S2

BEUSCHLEIN, Joseph Carl, S2

BIDDISON, Charles Lawrence, S1

BILLINGS, Robert Burton, ENS

BILLINGSLEY, Robert Frederick, GM3

BILZ, Robert Eugene, S2

BISHOP, Arthur, Jr., S2

BITONTI, Louis Peter, S1*

BLACKWELL, Fermon Malachi, SSML3

BLANTHORN, Bryan, S1*

BLUM, Donald Joseph, ENS*

BOEGE, Raynard Richard, S2

BOGAN, Jack Roberts, RM1

BOLLINGER, Richard Howard, S1

BOOTH, Sherman Chester, S1*

BORTON, Herbert Elton, SC2

BOSS, Norbert George, S2

BOTT, Wilbur Melvin, S2

BOWLES, Eldridge Wayne, S1

BOWMAN, Charles Edward, CTC

BOYD, Troy Howard, GM3

BRADLEY, William Hearn, S2

BRAKE, John, Jr., S2

BRANDT, Russell Lee, F2*

BRAUN, Neal Fredrick, S2

BRAY, Harold John, Jr., S2*

BRICE, R. V., S2

BRIDGE, Wayne Aron, S2

BRIGHT, Chester Lee, S2

BRILEY, Harold Vinton, MAM3

BRINKER, David Allen, PFC USMC

BROOKS, Ulysess Ray, CWT

BROPHY, Thomas D'Arcy, Jr., ENS

BROWN, Edward Augustus, WT3

BROWN, Edward Joseph, S1*

BROWN, Orlo Norman, PFC USMC

BRUCE, Russell William, S2

BRULE, Maurice Joseph, S2

BRUNDIGE, Robert Henry, S1*

BRUNEAU, Charles Albino, GM3

BUCKETT, Victor Robert, Y2*

BUDISH, David, S2

BULLARD, John Kenneth, S1*

BUNAI, Robert Peter, SM1*

BUNN, Horace G., S2

BURDORF, Wilbert John, COX*

BURKHARTSMEIER, Anton Tony, S1

BURKHOLTZ, Frank, Jr., EM3

BURLESON, Martin Lafayette, S1

BURRS, John William, S1

BURT, William George Allan, QM3

BURTON, Curtis Henry, S1*

BUSH, John Richard, PVT USMC

BUSHONG, John Richard, GM3

CADWALLADER, John Julian, RT3

CAIN, Alfred Brown, RT3

CAIRO, William George, BUG1

CALL, James Edward, RM3

CAMERON, John Watson, GM2

CAMP, Garrison, STM2

CAMPANA, Paul, RDM3

CAMPBELL, Hamer Edward, Jr., GM3*

CAMPBELL, Louis Dean, AOM3*

CAMPBELL, Wayland Dee, SF3

CANDALINO, Paul Louis, LT (jg)

CANTRELL, Billy George, F2

CARNELL, Lois Wayne, S2

CARPENTER, Willard Adolphus, SM3

CARR, Harry Leroy, S2

CARROLL, Gregory Krichbaum, S1

CARROLL, Rachel Walker, COX

CARSON, Clifford, F1

CARSTENSEN, Richard, S2

CARTER, Grover Clifford, S2*

CARTER, Lindsey Linvill, S2*

CARTER, Lloyd George, COX*

CARVER, Grover Cleveland, S1*

CASSIDY, John Curran "Jack," S1*

CASTALDO, Patrick Peter, GM2

CASTIAUX, Ray Vernon, S2

CASTO, William Harrison, S1

CAVIL, Robert Ralph, MM2

CAVITT, Clinton Columbus, WT3

CELAYA, Adolfo Uvaldo, F2*

CENTAZZO, Frank Joseph, SM3*

CHAMNESS, John Desel, S2*

CHANDLER, Lloyd Nyle, S2

CHART, Joseph, EM3

CHRISTIAN, Lewis Enoch, Jr., WO

CLARK, Eugene, CK3

CLARK, Orsen, S2*

CLEMENTS, Harold Preston, S2

CLINTON, George William, S1*

CLINTON, Leland Jack, LT (jg)

COBB, William Lester, MOMM3

COLE, Walter Henry, CRM

COLEMAN, Cedric Foster, LCDR

COLEMAN, Robert Edward, F2*

COLLIER, Charles Rives, RM2*

COLLINS, James, STM1

COLVIN, Frankie Lee, SSMT2

CONDON, Barna Theodore, RDM1

CONNELLY, David Fallon, ENS

CONRAD, James Patrick, EM3

CONSER, Donald Lynn, SC2

CONSIGLIO, Joseph William, FC2

CONWAY, Thomas Michael, LT (Rev)

COOK, Floyd Edward, SF3

COOPER, Dale, Jr., F2

COPELAND, Willard James, S2

COSTNER, Homer Jackson, COX*

COUNTRYMAN, Robert Earl, S2

COWEN, Donald Rodney, FC3*

COX, Alford Edward, GM3

COX, Loel Dene, S2*

CRABB, Donald Calvin, RM2

CRANE, Granville Shaw, Jr., MM2*

CREWS, Hugh Coachman, LT (jg)

CRITES, Orval D., WT1

CROMLING, Charles John, Jr., PLTSGT
   USMC

CROUCH, Edwin Mason, CAPT***

CRUM, Charles Junior, S2

CRUZ, Jose Santos, CCK

CURTIS, Erwin Eugene, CTC

DAGENHART, Charles Romeo, Jr., PHM2

DALE, Elwood Richard, F1

DANIEL, Harold William, CBM*

DANIELLO, Anthony Gene, S1

DAVIS, James Clark, RM3

DAVIS, Kenneth Graham, F1

DAVIS, Stanley Gilbert, LT (jg)

DAVIS, Thomas Edward, SM2

DAVIS, William Holmes, PFC USMC

DAY, Richard Raymond, Jr., S2

DEAN, John Thomas, Jr., S2

DeBERNARDI, Louie, BM1*

DeFOOR, Walton, RDM3

DeMARS, Edgar Joseph, CBM

DeMENT, Dayle Pershing, S1

DENNEY, Lloyd, Jr., S2

DEWING, Ralph Otto, FC3*

DEZELSKE, William Bruce, MM2*

DIMOND, John Nelson, S2

DOLLINS, Paul, RM2

DONALD, Lyle Herbert, EM1

DONEY, William Junior, F2

DORMAN, William Burns, S1

DORNETTO, Frank Paul, WT1

DOSS, James Monroe, S2

DOUCETTE, Roland Ordean, S2

DOUGLAS, Gene Dale, F2*

DOVE, Bassil Raymond, SKD2

DOWDY, Lowell Steven, CCM

DRANE, James Anthony, GM3

DRAYTON, William Harry, EM2*

DRISCOLL, David Lowell, LT (jg)

DRONET, Joseph E. J., S2*

DRUMMOND, James Joseph, F2

DRURY, Richard Eugene, S2

DRYDEN, William Howard, MM1*

DUFRAINE, Delbert Elmer, S1

DUNBAR, Jess Lee, F2

DUPECK, Albert, Jr., PFC USMC

DURAND, Ralph Joseph, Jr., S2

DYCUS, Donald, S2

EAKINS, Morris Bradford, F2

EAMES, Paul Herford, Jr., ENS

EASTMAN, Chester Steve, S2

ECK, Harold Adam, S2*

EDDINGER, John William, S1

EDDY, Richard Leroy, RM3

EDWARDS, Alwyn Curtis, F2

EDWARDS, Roland James, BM1

E'GOLF, Harold Wesley, S2

ELLIOTT, Kenneth Albert, S1

ELLIOTT, Harry William, S2

EMERY, William Friend, S1

EMSLEY, William Joseph, S1

ENGELSMAN, Ralph, S2

EPPERSON, Ewell, S1

EPPERSON, George Lensey, S1

ERICKSON, Theodore Mentzer, S2*

ERNST, Robert Carl, F2

ERWIN, Louis Harold "Kayo," COX*

ETHIER, Eugene Edwin, EM3*

EUBANKS, James Harold, S1

EVANS, Arthur Jerome, PHM2

EVANS, Claudus, GM3*

EVERETT, Charles Norman, EM2

EVERS, Lawrence Lee, CMM

EYET, Donald Archie, S1

FANTASIA, Frank Alfred, F2

FARBER, Sheldon Lee, S2

FARLEY, James William, S1

FARMER, Archie Calvin, COX*

FARRIS, Eugene Francis, S1*

FAST HORSE, Vincent, S2

FEAKES, Fred Atkinson, AOM1*

FEDORSKI, Nicholas Walter, S1*

FEENEY, Paul Ross, S2

FELTS, Donald J., BM1*

FERGUSON, Albert Edward, CMMA*

FERGUSON, Russel Myers, RT3

FIGGINS, Harley Dean, WT2

FIRESTONE, Kenneth Francis, FC2

FIRMIN, John Alden Homer, S2

FITTING, Johnny Wayne, GM1*

FLATEN, Harold James "Hap," WT2*

FLEISCHAUER, Donald William, S1

FLESHMAN, Vern Leslie, S2

FLYNN, James Madison, Jr., S1

FLYNN, Joseph Ambrose, CDR

FOELL, Cecil Duane, ENS

FORTIN, Verlin Laverre, WT3*

FOSTER, Verne Elmer, F2*

FOX, William Henry, Jr., F2*

FRANCOIS, Norbert Edward, F1*

FRANK, Rudolph Anthony, S2

FRANKLIN, Jack Ray, RDM3

FREEZE, Howard Bruce, LT (jg)

FRENCH, Douglas Orrin, FC3

FRENCH, Jimmy Junior, QM3

FRITZ, Leonard Albert, MM3

FRONTINO, Vincent Fred, MOMM3

FRORATH, Donald Henry, S2

FUCHS, Herman Ferdinand, CWO

FULLER, Arnold Ambrose, F2

FULTON, William Clarence, CRMA

FUNKHOUSER, Robert Morris, ART2*

GABRILLO, Juan, S2*

GAITHER, Forest Maylon, FC2

GALANTE, Angelo, S2*

GALBRAITH, Norman Scott, MM2*

GARDNER, Roscoe Wallace, F2*

GARDNER, Russel Thomas, F2

GARNER, Glenn Richard, MM2

GAUSE, Robert Pritchard, QM1*

GAUSE, Rubin Conley, Jr., ENS

GEMZA, Rudolph Arnold, FCO3*

GEORGE, Gabriel Vincent, MM3*

GERNGROSS, Frederick Joseph, Jr., ENS

GETTLEMAN, Robert Alfred, S2*

GIBSON, Buck Warren, GM3*

GIBSON, Curtis Woodrow, S2

GIBSON, Ganola Francis, MM3

GILBERT, Warner, Jr., S1

GILCREASE, James, S2*

GILL, Paul Edward, WT2

GILMORE, Wilbur Albert, S2

GISMONDI, Michael Vincent, S1

GLADD, Millard, Jr., MM2*

GLAUB, Francis Anthony, GM2

GLENN, Jay Rollin, AMM3*

GLOVKA, Erwin Samuel, S2

GODFREY, Marlo Roy, RM3

GOECKEL, Ernest Stanley, LT (jg)

GOFF, Thomas Guy, SF3*

GOLDEN, Curry, STM1

GOLDEN, James LaVonne, S1

GONZALES, Ray Adam, S2

GOOCH, William Leroy, F2*

GOOD, Robert Kenneth, MM3

GOODWIN, Oliver Albert, CRT

GORE, Leonard Franklin, S2

GORECKI, Joseph Walter, SK3

GOTTMANN, Paul James, S2

GOVE, Carroll Lansing, S2

GRAY, Willis Leroy, S1*

GREATHOUSE, Bud R., S1

GREEN, Robert Urban, S2

GREEN, Tolbert, Jr., S1*

GREENE, Samuel Gile, S1

GREENLEE, Charles Iams, S2*

GREENWALD, Jacob, 1st SGT* USMC

GREER, Bob Eugene, S2

GREGORY, Garland Glen, F1

GREIF, Matthias Daniel, WT3

GRIES, Richard Charles, F2

GRIEST, Frank David, GM3

GRIFFIN, Jackie Dale, S1

GRIFFITH, Robert Lee, S1*

GRIFFITHS, Leonard Sylvester, S2

GRIGGS, Donald Ray, F1

GRIMES, David Elimer, S2

GRIMES, James Francis, S2

GRIMM, Loren Everett, PFC USMC

GROCE, Floyd Vernon, RDM2

GROCH, John Thomas, MM3

GUENTHER, Morgan Edward, EM3

GUERRERO, John Gomez, S1

GUILLOT, Murphy Umbroise, F1

GUYE, Ralph Lee, Jr., QM3

GUYON, Harold Louis, F1

HABERMAN, Bernard, S2

HADUCH, John Martin, S1

HALE, Robert Baldwin, LT

HALE, William Franklin, S2

HALL, Pressie, F1

HALLORAN, Edward George, MM3

HAM, Saul Anthony, COX

HAMBO, William Perrin, PHM3

HAMMEN, Robert, PHOM3

HAMRICK, James Junior, S2

HANCOCK, Thomas Andrew, PFC USMC

HANCOCK, William Allen, GM3

HANKINSON, Clarence Winfield, F2

HANSEN, Henry, S2

HANSON, Harley Clarence, WO*

HARLAND, George Alfred, S2

HARP, Charlie Hardin, S1

HARPER, Vasco, STM1

HARRELL, Edgar Alvin, CPL* USMC

HARRIS, James Davis, F2

HARRIS, Willard Eugene, F2

HARRISON, Cecil Manly, CWO*

HARRISON, Frederick Elliott, S2**

HARRISON, James McLaurin "Mac," S1

HART, Fred Junior, RT2*

HARTRICK, Willis Boomer, MM1

HATFIELD, Willie, S2*

HAUBRICH, Cloud David, S2

HAUSER, Jack Isaac, SK2

HAVENER, Harlan Carl, F2*

HAVINS, Otha "Alton," Y2*

HAYES, Charles David, LCDR

HAYLES, Felix, CK3

HAYNES, Lewis Leavitt, LCDR*

HAYNES, Robert Albert, LT

HAYNES, William Alexander, S1

HEERDT, Raymond Edward, F2

HEGGIE, William Arnold, RDM3

HEINZ, Richard Anthony, HA1

HELLER, John, S2*

HELLER, Robert Jacob, Jr., S2

HELSCHER, Ralph John, S1

HELT, Jack Edward, F2

HENDERSON, Ralph Lewis, S1

HENDRON, James Raymond, Jr., F2

HENRY, Earl O'Dell, LCDR

HENSCH, Erwin Fredrick, LT*

HENSLEY, Clifford, SSMB2

HERBERT, Jack Erwin, BM1

HERNDON, Duane, S2

HERSHBERGER, Clarence Lamar, S1*

HERSTINE, James Franklin, ENS

HICKEY, Harry Todd, RM3

HICKS, Clarence, S1

HIEBERT, Lloyd Henry, GM1

HILL, Clarence Max, CWT

HILL, Joe Walker, STM1

HILL, Nelson Page, Jr., LT

HILL, Richard Norman, ENS

HIND, Lyle Lewis, S2*

HINES, Lionel Gordon, WT1

HINKEN, John Richard, Jr., F2*

HOBBS, Melvin Dow, S1

HODGE, Howard Henry, RM2*

HODGINS, Lester Byron, S2

HODSHIRE, John William, S2

HOERRES, George Joseph, S2

HOLDEN, Punciano Aledia, ST1

HOLLAND, John Francis, Jr., PFC USMC

HOLLINGSWORTH, Jimmie Lee, STM2

HOLLOWAY, Andrew Jackson, S2

HOLLOWAY, Ralph Harris, COX

HOOGERWERF, John, Jr., F1

HOOPES, Gordon Herbert, S2*

HOPPER, Prentice William, S1

HOPPER, Roy Lee, AMM1

HORNER, Durward Richard, WO*

HORR, Wesley Alan, F2

HORRIGAN, John Gerard, F1

HORVATH, George John, F1*

HOSKINS, William Orson, Y3*

HOUCK, Richard Eugene, EM3*

HOUSTON, Robert Garvis, F1

HOUSTON, William Howard, PHM2

HOV, Donald Anthony, S1

HOWISON, John Donald, ENS*

HUBBARD, Gordon Roy, PFC USMC

HUBBARD, Leland Russell, PFC USMC

HUBELI, Joseph Francis, S2*

HUEBNER, Harry Helmut, S1

HUGHES, Lawrence Edwin, F2

HUGHES, Max Meredith, PFC* USMC

HUGHES, Robert Alexander, FC3

HUGHES, William Edward, SSML2

HUMPHREY, Maynard Lee, S2

HUNTER, Arthur Riles, Jr., QM1

HUNTLEY, Virgil Clair, CHSCLK

HUPKA, Clarence Elmer, BKR1*

HURLEY, Woodrow, GM2*

HURST, Robert Huntley, LT

HURT, James Edward, S2

HUTCHISON, Merle Byron, S2

IGOU, Floyd, Jr., RM2

IZOR, Walter Eugene, F1

JACKSON, Henry, STM

JACOB, Melvin Carl, PFC* USMC

JACQUEMOT, Joseph Alexander, S2*

JADLOSKI, George Kenneth, S2

JAKUBISIN, Joseph Sylvester, S2

JAMES, Woodie Eugene, COX*

JANNEY, Johns Hopkins, CDR

JARVIS, James Kenneth, AMM3*

JEFFERS, Wallace Mansfield, COX

JENNEY, Charles Irvin, LT

JENSEN, Chris Alstrum, S2

JENSEN, Eugene Wenzel, S2*

JEWELL, Floyd Raymond, SK1

JOHNSON, Bernard John, S2

JOHNSON, Elwood Wilbur, S2

JOHNSON, George Glen, S2

JOHNSON, Harold Bernard, S1

JOHNSON, Sidney Bryant, S1

JOHNSON, Walter Marion, Jr., S1

JOHNSON, William Albert, S1*

JOHNSTON, Earl Rankin, BM2

JOHNSTON, Lewis Eugene, S1

JOHNSTON, Ray Francis, MM1

JOHNSTON, Scott Albert, F2

JONES, Clinton Leroy, COX*

JONES, George Edward, S2

JONES, Jim, S2

JONES, Kenneth Malcolm, F1

JONES, Sidney, S1*

JONES, Stanley Fairwick, S2

JORDAN, Henry, STM2

JORDON, Thomas Hardin, S2

JOSEY, Clifford Odell, S2

JUMP, David Allen, ENS

JURGENSMEYER, Alfred Joseph, S2

JURKIEWICZ, Raymond Stanley, S1*

JUSTICE, Robert Eugene, S2*

KARPEL, Daniel Larence, BM1

KARTER, Leo Clement, Jr., S2

KASTEN, Stanley Otto, HA1

KATSIKAS, Gust Constantine "Gus Kay," S1*

KAWA, Raymond Phillip, SK3

KAZMIERSKI, Walter, S1*

KEENEY, Robert Allen, ENS

KEES, Shalous Eugene, EM2*

KEITH, Everett Edward, EM2

KELLY, Albert Raymond, S2

KEMP, David Poole, Jr., SC3*

KENLY, Oliver Wesley, RDM3*

KENNEDY, Andrew Jackson, Jr., S2

KENNEDY, Robert Arthur, S1

KENNY, Francis Joseph Patrick "Pat," S2

KENWORTHY, Glenn Willis, CPL

KEPHART, Paul, S1

KERBY, Deo Earl, S1*

KERN, Harry Gilbert, S1

KEY, S.T., EM2

KEYES, Edward Hiram, COX*

KIGHT, Audy Carl, S1

KILGORE, Archie Clinton, F2

KILLMAN, Robert Eugene, GM3

KINARD, Nolan Dave, S1

KINCAID, Joseph Ercel, FC2

KING, Anthony Christopher "AC," S1*

KING, Clarence, Jr., STM2

KING, James Thomas, S1

KING, Richard Eugene, S2

KING, Robert Harold, S2

KINNAMAN, Robert Leroy, S2

KINZLE, Raymond Arthur, BKR2*

KIRBY, Harry, S1

KIRCHNER, John Howard, PVT USMC

KIRK, James Roy, SC3

KIRKLAND, Marvin Foulk, S1*

KIRKMAN, Walter William, SF1

KISELICA, Joseph Frederick, AM2*

KITTOE, James William, F2*

KLAPPA, Ralph Donald, S2*

KLAUS, Joseph Frank, S1*

KLEIN, Raymond James, S1

KLEIN, Theil Joseph, SK3

KNERNSCHIELD, Andrew Nick, S1

KNOLL, Paul Edward, COX

KNOTT, Elbern Louis, S1

KNUDTSON, Raymond Arthur, S1

KNUPKE, Richard Roland, MM3

KOCH, Edward Chris, EM3*

KOEGLER, Albert, S1

KOEGLER, William, SC3

KOLAKOWSKI, Ceslaus, SM3

KOLLINGER, Robert Eugene, S1

KONESNY, John Matthew, S1

KOOPMAN, Walter Frederick, F2

KOPPANG, Raymond Irwin, LT (jg)

KOUSKI, Fred, GM3

KOVALICK, George Richard, S2

KOZIARA, George, S2*

KOZIK, Raymond, S1

KRAWITZ, Harry Joseph, MM3

KREIS, Clifford Eddie, S1*

KRON, Herman Edward, Jr., GM3

KRONENBERGER, William Maurice, GM3

KRUEGER, Dale Frank, F2*

KRUEGER, Norman Frederick, S2*

KRUSE, Darwin Glen, S2

KRZYZEWSKI, John Michael, S2

KUHN, Clair Joseph, S1

KULOVITZ, Raymond Joseph, S2

KURLICH, George Robert, FC3*

KURYLA, Michael Nicholas, Jr., COX*

KUSIAK, Alfred Meciuston, S2

KWIATKOWSKI, Marion Joseph, S2

LABUDA, Arthur Al, QM3

LaFONTAINE, Paul Sylvester, S1

LAKATOS, Emil Joseph, MM3

LAKE, Murl Christy, S1

LAMB, Robert Clyde, EM3

LAMBERT, Leonard Francis, S1

LANDON, William Wallace, Jr., FCO2

LANE, Ralph, CMM*

LANTER, Kenley MacKendree, SM3C*

LaPAGLIA, Carlos, GM2*

LaPARL, Lawrence Edward, Jr., S2

LAPCZYNSKI, Edward William, S1

LARSEN, Harlan Doyle, PFC USMC

LARSEN, Melvin Robert, S2

LATIGUE, Jackson, STM1

LATIMER, Billy Franklin, S1

LATZER, Solomon, S2

LAUGHLIN, Fain Heskett, SK3

LAWS, George Edward, S1*

LEATHERS, William Ben, MM3

LeBARON, Robert Walter, S2

LEBOW, Cleatus Archie, FCO3*

LEENERMAN, Arthur Louis, RDM3*

LEES, Henry W., PFC USMC

LELUIKA, Paul Peter, S2

LESTINA, Francis Joseph, S1

LETIZIA, Vincencio, S2

LETZ, Wilbert Joseph, SK1

LeVALLEY, William Delbert, EM2

LEVENTON, Mervin Charles, MM2

LeVIEUX, John Joseph, F2

LEWELLEN, Thomas Edgar, S2

LEWIS, James Robert, F2

LEWIS, John Robert, GM3

LINDEN, Charles Gerald, WT2

LINDSAY, Norman Lee, SF3

LINK, George Charles, S1

LINN, Roy, S1

LINVILLE, Cecil Harrison, SF2

LINVILLE, Harry Junior, S1

LIPPERT, Robert George, S1

LIPSKI, Stanley Walter, CDR

LITTLE, Frank Edward, MM2

LIVERMORE, Raymond Irving, S2

LOCH, Edwin Peter, S1

LOCKWOOD, Thomas Homer, S2*

LOEFFLER, Paul Eugene, Jr., S2

LOFTIS, James Bryant, Jr., S1*

LOFTUS, Ralph Dennis, F2

LOHR, Leo William, S1

LOMBARDI, Ralph, S1

LONG, Joseph William, S1

LONGWELL, Donald Jackson, S1

LOPEZ, Daniel Balterzar, F2*

LOPEZ, Sam, S1*

LORENC, Edward Richard, S2

LOYD, John Francis, WT2

LUCAS, Robert Andrew, S2*

LUCCA, Frank John, F2*

LUHMAN, Emerson David, MM3

LUNDGREN, Albert David, S1

LUTTRULL, Claud Ancil, COX

LUTZ, Charles Herbert, S1

MAAS, Melvin Adolph, S1*

MABEE, Kenneth Charles, F2

MACE, Harold A., S2*

MacFARLAND, Keith Irving, LT (jg)

MACHADO, Clarence James, WT2

MACK, Donald Flemming, BUG1*

MADAY, Anthony Francis, AMM1*

MADIGAN, Harry Francis, BM2

MAGDICS, Steve, Jr., F2

MAGRAY, Duwain Frederick, S2

MAKAROFF, Chester John, GM3*

MAKOWSKI, Robert Thomas, CWT

MALDONADO, Salvador, BKR3*

MALENA, Joseph John, Jr., GM2*

MALONE, Cecil Edward, S2

MALONE, Elvin Cary, S1

MALONE, Michael Leo, Jr., LT (jg)

MALSKI, Joseph John, S1*

MANESS, Charles Franklin, F2

MANKIN, Howard James, GM3

MANN, Clifford Eugene, S1

MANSKER, LaVoice, S2

MANTZ, Keith Hubert, S1

MARCIULAITIS, Charles, S1

MARKMANN, Frederick Henry, WT1

MARPLE, Paul Thomas, ENS

MARSHALL, John Lucas, WT2

MARSHALL, Robert Wallace, S2

MARTIN, Albert, S2

MARTIN, Everett Gilliland, S1

MARTTILA, Howard William, PVT USMC

MASSIER, George Arcade, S1

MASTRECOLA, Michael Martin, S2

MATHESON, Richard Robert, PHM3

MATRULLA, John, S1*

MAUNTEL, Paul John, S2

MAXWELL, Farrell Jacob, S1*

McBRIDE, Ronald Gene, S1

McBRYDE, Frank Eugene, S2

McCALL, Donald Clifton, S2*

McCLAIN, Raymond Bryant, BM2*

McCLARY, Lester Earl, S2

McCLURE, David Leroy, EM2

McCOMB, Everett Albert, F1

McCORD, Edward Franklin, Jr., EM3

McCORKLE, Ray Ralph, S1

McCORMICK, Earl William, MOMM2

McCOSKEY, Paul Franklin, S1

McCOY, Giles Gilbert, PFC* USMC

McCOY, John Seybold, Jr., M2

McCRORY, Millard Virgil, Jr., WT2*

McDANIEL, Johnny Alfred, S1

McDONALD, Franklin Gilreath, Jr., F2

McDONNER, David Pious, Jr., F1

McDOWELL, Robert Earl, S1

McELROY, Clarence Ernest, Jr., S1*

McFALL, Walter Eugene, S2*

McFEE, Carl Snyder, SC1

McGINNIS, Paul Wendle, SM3*

McGINTY, John Matthew, S1

McGUIGGAN, Robert Melvin, S1*

McGUIRE, Denis, S2

McGUIRK, Philip Arthur, LT (jg)

McHENRY, Loren Charles, Jr., S1*

McHONE, Ollie, F1

McKEE, George Edward, Jr., S1

McKENNA, Michael Joseph, S1

McKENZIE, Ernest Eugene, S1*

McKINNON, Francis Moore, Y3

McKISSICK, Charles Brite, LT (jg)*

McKLIN, Henry Theodore, S1*

McLAIN, Patrick Joseph, S2*

McLEAN, Dougald Bruce, EM3

McNABB, Thomas, Jr., F2

McNICKLE, Arthur Samuel, F1

McQUITTY, Roy Edward, COX

McVAY, Charles Butler, III, CAPT*

McVAY, Richard Calvin, Y3*

MEADE, Sidney Howard, S1

MEHLBAUM, Raymond Aloysius, S1

MEIER, Harold Edward, S2

MELICHAR, Charles Harry, EM3

MELVIN, Carl Lavern, F1

MENCHEFF, Manual Angel, S2

MEREDITH, Charles Everett, S1*

MERGLER, Charles Marlene, RDM2

MESSENGER, Leonard John, PFC USMC

MESTAS, Nestor Anastasio, WT2*

METCALF, David William, GM3

MEYER, Charles Thomas, S2*

MICHAEL, Bertrand Franklin, BKR3

MICHAEL, Elmer Orion, S1

MICHNO, Arthur Richard, S2

MIKESKA, Willie Wodrew, S2

MIKOLAYEK, Joseph, COX*

MILBRODT, Glen Lavern, S2*

MILES, Theodore Kerr, LT

MILLER, Artie Ronald, GM2

MILLER, George Edwin, F1

MILLER, Glenn Evert, S2

MILLER, Samuel George, Jr., FC3

MILLER, Walter Raymond, S2

MILLER, Walter William, B1

MILLER, Wilbur Harold, CMM

MILLS, William Harry, EM3

MINER, Herbert Jay, II, RT2*

MINOR, Richard Leon, S1

MINOR, Robert Warren, S2

MIRES, Carl Emerson, S2

MIRICH, Wally Mayo, S1

MISKOWIEC, Theodore Francis, S1

MITCHELL, James Edward, S2*

MITCHELL, James Hamilton, Jr., SK1

MITCHELL, Kenneth Earl, S1*

MITCHELL, Norval Jerry, Jr., S1*

MITCHELL, Paul Boone, FC3

MITCHELL, Winston Cooper, S1

MITTLER, Peter John, Jr., GM3

MIXON, Malcom Lois, GM2

MLADY, Clarence Charles, S1*

MODESITT, Garl Elsworth, S2*

MODISHER, Melvin Wayne, LT (jg)*

MONCRIEF, Mack Daniel, S2

MONKS, Robert Bruce, GM3

MONTOYA, Frank Edward, S1

MOORE, Donald George, S2

MOORE, Elbert, S2

MOORE, Harley Edward, S1

MOORE, Kyle "Kasey" Campbell, LCDR

MOORE, Wyatt Patton, BKR1

MORAN, Joseph John, RM1*

MORGAN, Eugene Stanley, BM2*

MORGAN, Glenn Grover, BGM3*

MORGAN, Lewis E., S2

MORGAN, Telford Frank, ENS

MORRIS, Albert Oliver, S1*

MORSE, Kendall Harold, LT (jg)

MORTON, Charles Wesley, S2

MORTON, Marion Ellis, SK2

MOSELEY, Morgan Millard, SC1*

MOULTON, Charles Calvin, S2

MOWREY, Ted Eugene, SK3*

MOYNELO, Harold Clifton, Jr., ENS

MROSZAK, Francis Alfred, S2

MULDOON, John James, MM1*

MULVEY, William Robert, BM1*

MUNSON, Bryan Cahill, PFC USMC

MURILLO, Sammy, S2

MURPHY, Allen, S2

MURPHY, Charles Thomas, PFC USMC

MURPHY, Paul James, FC3*

MUSARRA, Joe, S1

MYERS, Charles Lee, Jr., S2

MYERS, Glen Alan, MM2

MYERS, H. B., F2*

NABERS, Neal Adrian, S2

NASPINI, Joseph Anthony, F2*

NEAL, Charles Keith, S2

NEAL, George M., S2

NEAL, William Frank, PFC USMC

NEALE, Harlan Benjamin, S2

NELSEN, Edward John, GM1*

NELSON, Frank Howard, S2*

NEU, Hugh Herbert, S2

NEUBAUER, Richard, S2

NEUMAN, Jerome Clifford, F1

NEVILLE, Bobby Gene, S2

NEWCOMER, Lewis Willard, MM3

NEWELL, James Thomas, EM1

NEWHALL, James Franklin, S1*

NICHOLS, James Clarence, S2*

NICHOLS, Joseph Lawrence, BM2

NICHOLS, Paul Virgil, MM3

NIELSEN, Carl Aage Chor, Jr., F1

NIETO, Baltazar Portales, GM3

NIGHTINGALE, William Oliver, MM1*

NISKANEN, John Hubert, F2

NIXON, Daniel Merrill, S2*

NORBERG, James Arthur, CBM*

NORMAN, Theodore Raymond, GM2

NOWAK, George Joseph, F2

NUGENT, William Gerald, S2

NUNLEY, James Preston, F1

NUNLEY, Troy Audie, S2*

NUTT, Raymond Albert, S2

NUTTALL, Alexander Carlyle, S1*

OBLEDO, Mike Guerra, S1*

O'BRIEN, Arthur Joseph, S2

O'CALLAGHAN, Del Roger, WT2

OCHOA, Ernest, FC3

O'DONNELL, James Edward, WT3*

OLDEREN, Bernhard Gunnar, S1

OLIJAR, John, S1*

O'NEIL, Eugene Elbert, S1

ORR, Homer Lee, HA1

ORR, John Irwin, Jr., LT

ORSBURN, Frank Harold, SSML2*

ORTIZ, Orlando Robert, Y3

OSBURN, Charles William, S2

OTT, Theodore Gene, Y1

OUTLAND, Felton James, S1*

OVERMAN, Thurman David, S2*

OWEN, Keith Nichols, SC3*

OWENS, Robert Seldon, Jr., QM3

OWENSBY, Clifford Cecil, F2

PACE, Curtis Edward, S2*

PACHECO, Jose Cruz, S2*

PAGITT, Eldon Ernest, F2

PAIT, Robert, BM2

PALMITER, Adelore Arthur, S2*

PANE, Francis William, S2

PARHAM, Fred, ST2

PARK, David Ernest, ENS

PARKE, Edward LeRoy, Capt. USMC

PAROUBEK, Richard Anthony, Y1*

PASKET, Lyle Matthew, S2*

PATTERSON, Alfred Thompson, S2

PATTERSON, Kenneth George, S1

PATZER, Herman Lantz, EM1

PAULK, Luther Doyle, S2*

PAYNE, Edward Glenjoy, S2*

PAYNE, George David, S2

PENA, Santos Alday, S1*

PENDER, Welburn Morton, F2

PEREZ, Basilio, S2*

PERKINS, Edward Carlos, F2*

PERRY, Robert J., S2

PESSOLANO, Michael Richard, LT

PETERS, Earl Jack, S2

PETERSON, Avery Clarence, S2*

PETERSON, Darrel Erskine, S1

PETERSON, Frederick Alexander, MAM3

PETERSON, Glenn Harley, S1

PETERSON, Ralph Renny, S2**

PETRINCIC, John Nicholas, Jr., FC3

PEYTON, Robert Carter, STM1

PHILLIPS, Aulton Newell, F2

PHILLIPS, Huie Harold, S2*

PIERCE, Clyde Alton, CWT

PIERCE, Robert William, S2

PIPERATA, Alfred Joseph, MM1

PITMAN, Robert Fred, S2

PITTMAN, Almire, Jr., ST3

PLEISS, Roger David, F2

PODISH, Paul, S2*

PODSCHUN, Clifford Albert, S2*

POGUE, Herman Crawford, S2*

POHL, Theodore, F2

POKRYFKA, Donald Martin, S2

POOR, Gerald Melbourne, S2*

POORE, Albert Franklin, S2

POTRYKUS, Frank Paul, F2

POTTS, Dale Floyd, S2*

POWELL, Howard Wayne, F1

POWERS, R. C. Ottis, S2

POYNTER, Raymond Lee, S2

PRAAY, William Theo, S2

PRATHER, Clarence Jefferson, CMM

PRATT, George Roy, F1

PRICE, James Denny, S1*

PRIESTLE, Ralph Arthur, S2

PRIOR, Walter Mathew, S2

PUCKETT, William Charles, S2

PUPUIS, John Andrew, S1

PURCEL, Franklin Walter, S2

PURSEL, Forest Virgil, WT2

PYRON, Freddie Harold, S1

QUEALY, William Charles, Jr., PR2*

RABB, John Robert, SC1

RAGSDALE, Jean Obert, S1

RAHN, Alvin Wilder, SK3

RAINES, Clifford Junior, S2

RAINS, Rufus Brady, S1

RAMIREZ, Ricardo, S1*

RAMSEYER, Raymond Clifford, RT3

RANDOLPH, Cleo, STM1

RATHBONE, Wilson, S2*

RATHMAN, Frank Junior, S1

RAWDON, John Herbert, EM3*

REALING, Lyle Olan, FC2

REDD, Robert Frank, PVT USMC

REDMAYNE, Richard Banks, LT*

REED, Thomas William, EM3

REEMTS, Alvin Thomas, S1

REESE, Jesse Edmund, S2

REEVES, Chester O. B., S1*

REEVES, Robert Arnold, F2

REGALADO, Robert Henry, S1

REHNER, Herbert Adrian, S1*

REID, Curtis Franklin, S2*

REID, James Edgar, BM2*

REID, John, LCDR*

REID, Tommy Lee, RDM3*

REILLY, James Francis, Y1

REINERT, Leroy, F1

REINOLD, George Harold, PFC USMC

REMONDET, Edward Joseph, Jr., S2

REYNOLDS, Alford Pago, GM2*

REYNOLDS, Andrew Eli, S1

REYNOLDS, Carleton Clarke, F1

RHEA, Clifford, F2

RHODES, Vernon Lee, F1

RHOTEN, Roy Edward, F2

RICE, Albert, STM1

RICH, Garland Lloyd, S1

RICH, Raymond Anthony, PFC* USMC

RICHARDSON, John Richard, S2

RICHARDSON, Joseph Gustave, S2

RIDER, Francis Allan, RDM3

RIGGINS, Earl, PVT* USMC

RILEY, Junior Thomas, BM2

RINEAY, Francis Henry, Jr., S2*

ROBERTS, Benjamin Ellsworth, WT1

ROBERTS, Charles, S1

ROBERTS, Norman Harold, MM1*

ROBISON, Gerald Edward, RT3

ROBISON, John Davis, COX*

ROBISON, Marzie Joe, S2

ROCHE, Joseph Martin, LT

ROCKENBACH, Earl Arthur, SC2

ROESBERRY, Jack Roger, S1

ROGELL, Henry Tony, F1

ROGERS, Ralph Guy, RDM3*

ROGERS, Ross, Jr, ENS*

ROLAND, Jack Anderson, PHM1

ROLLINS, Willard Eugene, RM3

ROMANI, Frank Joseph, HA1

ROOF, Charles Walter, S2

ROSE, Berson Horace, GM2

ROSE, Francis Edmund, PFC USMC

ROSS, Glen Eugene, F2

ROTHMAN, Aaron, RDM3

ROWDEN, Joseph Geren, F1

ROZZANO, John, Jr., S2

RUDOMANSKI, Eugene William, RT2

RUE, William Goff, MM1

RUSSELL, Robert Avery, S2**

RUSSELL, Virgil Miller, COX*

RUST, Edwin Leroy, S1

RUTHERFORD, Robert Arnold, RM2

RYDZESKI, Frank Walter, F1

SAATHOFF, Don William, S2*

SAENZ, Jose Antonio, SC3

SAIN, Albert Franklin, S1

SALINAS, Alfredo Antonio, S1

SAMANO, Nuraldo, S2

SAMPSON, Joseph Raymond, S2

SAMS, Robert Carrol, STM2

SANCHEZ, Alejandro Vallez, S2

SANCHEZ, Fernando Sanchez, SC3*

SAND, Cyrus Harvey, BM1

SANDERS, Everett Raymond, MOMM1

SASSMAN, Gordon Wallace, COX

SCANLAN, Osceola Carlisle, S2*

SCARBROUGH, Fred Richard, COX

SCHAAP, Marion John, QM1

SCHAEFER, Harry Winfield, S2

SCHAFFER, Edward James, S1

SCHARTON, Elmer Daniel, S1

SCHECHTERLE, Harold Joseph, RDM3*

SCHEIB, Albert Eddie, F2

SCHEWE, Alfred Paul, S1

SCHLATTER, Robert Leroy, AOM3

SCHLOTTER, James Robert, RDM3

SCHMUECK, John Alton, CPHM*

SCHNAPPAUF, Harold John, SK3

SCHOOLEY, Dillard Alfred, COX

SCHUMACHER, Arthur Joseph, Jr., CEM

SCOGGINS, Millard, SM2

SCOTT, Burl Down, STM2

SCOTT, Curtis Marvin, S1

SCOTT, Hilliard, STM1

SEABERT, Clarke Wilson, S2*

SEBASTIAN, Clifford Harry, RM2

SEDIVI, Alfred Joseph, PHOM2

SELBACH, Walter Herman, WT3

SELL, Ernest Frederick, EM2

SELLERS, Leonard Edson, SF3

SELMAN, Amos, S2

SETCHFIELD, Arthur Lawrence, COX*

SEWELL, Loris Eldon, S2

SHAFFER, Robert Patrick, GM3*

SHAND, Kenneth Wallace, WT2

SHARP, William Hafford, S2*

SHAW, Calvin Patrick, GM2

SHEARER, Harold James, S2*

SHELTON, William Enloe, Jr., SM2

SHIELDS, Cecil Norris, SM2

SHIPMAN, Robert Lee, GM3**

SHOWN, Donald Herbert, CFC*

SHOWS, Audie Boyd, COX*

SIKES, Theodore Allan, ENS

SILCOX, Burnice Rufus, S1

SILVA, Phillip Gomes, S1

SIMCOX, Gordon William, EM3

SIMCOX, John Allen, F1

SIMPSON, William Edward, BM2*

SIMS, Clarence, CK2

SINCLAIR, James Ray, S2*

SINGERMAN, David, SM3

SIPES, John Leland, S1

SITEK, Henry Joseph, S2*

SITZLAR, William Clifton, F1

SLADEK, Wayne Lyn, BM1*

SLANKARD, Jack Crocker, S1*

SMALLEY, Howard Earl, S1

SMELTZER, Charles H., S2*

SMERAGLIA, Michael, RM3

SMITH, Carl Murphy, SM2

SMITH, Charles Andy, S1

SMITH, Cozell Lee, Jr., COX*

SMITH, Edwin Lee, S2

SMITH, Eugene Gordon, BM2

SMITH, Frederick Calvin, F2*

SMITH, George Robert, S1

SMITH, Guy Nephi, FCO2

SMITH, Henry August, F1

SMITH, Homer Leroy, F2

SMITH, James Wesley, S2*

SMITH, Kenneth Dean, S2

SMITH, Olen Ellis, CM3

SNYDER, John Nicholas, SF2

SNYDER, Richard Redheffer, S1

SOLOMON, William, Jr., S2

SORDIA, Ralph, S2

SOSPIZIO, Andre, EM3*

SPARKS, Charles Byrd, COX

SPEER, Lowell Elvis, RT3

SPENCER, Daniel Frederick, S1*

SPENCER, James Douglas, LT

SPENCER, Roger Herbert, S1*

SPENCER, Sidney Ancil, WO

SPINDLE, Orval Audry, S1

SPINELLI, John Anthony, SC2*

SPINO, Frank Joseph, PFC USMC

SPOMER, Elmer John, SF2

SPOONER, Miles Lewis, PVT* USMC

ST. PIERRE, Leslie Robert, MM2

STADLER, Robert Herman, WT3

STAMM, Florian Marian, S2*

STANFORTH, David Earl, F2

STANKOWSKI, Archie Joseph, S2

STANTURF, Frederick Robert, MM2

STAUFFER, Edward Henry, 1ST LT USMC

STEIGERWALD, Fred, GM2

STEPHENS, Richard Park, S2*

STEVENS, George Golden, WT2*

STEVENS, Wayne Allen, MM2

STEWART, Glenn Willard, CFC*

STEWART, Thomas Andrew, SK2

STICKLEY, Charles Benjamin, GM3

STIER, William George, S1

STIMSON, David, ENS

STONE, Dale Eugene, S2

STONE, Homer Benton, Y1

STOUT, Kenneth Irwin, LCDR

STRAIN, Joseph Mason, S2

STRAUGHN, Howard Vernon, Jr., CPL
USMC

STREICH, Allen Charles, RM2

STRICKLAND, George Thomas, S2

STRIETER, Robert Carl, S2

STRIPE, William Stanley, S2

STROM, Donald Arthur, S2

STROMKO, Joseph Anthony, F2

STRYFFELER, Virgil Lee, F2

STUECKLE, Robert Louis, S2

STURTEVANT, Elwyn Lee, RM3*

SUDANO, Angelo Anthony, SSML3

SUHR, Jerome Richard, S2

SULLIVAN, James Patrick, S2

SULLIVAN, William Daniel, PTR2

SUTER, Frank Edward, S1*

SWANSON, Robert Herman, MM2

SWART, Robert Leslie, LT (jg)

SWINDELL, Jerome Henderson, F2

TAGGART, Thomas Harris, S1

TALLEY, Dewell Emanuel, RM3*

TAWATER, Charles Hoyt, F1*

TEERLINK, David Sander, CWO

TELFORD, Arno John, RT3

TERRY, Robert Wayne, S2

THELEN, Richard Peter, S2*

THIELSCHER, Robert Turner, CRT

THOMAS, Ivan Mervin, S1*

THOMPSON, David Alvin, EM3*

THOMSEN, Arthur August, PFC USMC

THORPE, Everett Nathan, WT3

THURKETTLE, William Clarence, S2*

TIDWELL, James Freddie, S2

TISTHAMMER, Bernard Edward, CGM

TOCE, Nicolo, S2

TODD, Harold Orton, CM3

TORRETTA, John Mickey, F1*

TOSH, Bill Hugh, RDM3

TRACY, Richard Irwin, Jr., SGT USMC

TRIEMER, Ernst August, ENS

TROTTER, Arthur Cecil, RM2

TRUDEAU, Edmond Arthur, LT

TRUE, Roger Glenn, S2

TRUITT, Robert Edward, RM2

TRYON, Frederick Braum, BUG2

TULL, James Albert, S1

TURNER, Charles Morris, S2*

TURNER, William Clifford, MM2

TURNER, William Henry, Jr., ACMMA

TWIBLE, Harlan Malcolm, ENS*

UFFELMAN, Paul Roland, PFC* USMC

ULIBARRI, Antonio Dejesus, S2

ULLMANN, Paul Elliott, LT (jg)

UMENHOFFER, Lyle Edgar, S1*

UNDERWOOD, Carey Lee, S1

UNDERWOOD, Ralph Ellis, S1*

VAN METER, Joseph William, WT3*

WAKEFIELD, James Newell, S1

WALKER, A. W., STM1

WALKER, Jack Edwin, RM2

WALKER, Verner B., F2*

WALLACE, Earl John, RDM3

WALLACE, John, RDM3

WALTERS, Donald Henry, F1

WARREN, William Robertson, RT3

WATERS, Jack Lee, CY

WATSON, Winston Harl, F2

WELLS, Charles Orville, S1*

WELLS, Gerald Lloyd, EM3

WENNERHOLM, Wayne Leslie, COX

WENZEL, Ray Gunther, RT3

WHALEN, Stuart Denton, GM2

WHALLON, Louis Fletcher, Jr., LT (jg)

WHITE, Earl Clarence, TC1

WHITE, Howard McKean, CWT

WHITING, George Albert, F2*

WHITMAN, Robert Taft, LT

WILCOX, Lindsey Zeb, WT2*

WILEMAN, Roy Weldon, PHM3

WILLARD, Merriman Daniel, PHM2

WILLIAMS, Billie Joe, MM2

WILLIAMS, Magellan, STM1

WILLIAMS, Robert Louis, WO

WILSON, Frank, F2

WILSON, Thomas Beverly, S1

WISNIEWSKI, Stanley, F2*

WITTMER, Milton Robert, EM2

WITZIG, Robert Marian, FC3*

WOJIECHOWSKI, Maryian Joseph, SM1

WOLFE, Floyd Ralph, GM3

WOODS, Leonard Thomas, CWO

WOOLSTON, John, ENS

WYCH, Robert Arthur, PFC USMC

YEAPLE, Jack Thomas, Y3

ZINK, Charles William, EM2*

ZOBAL, Francis John, S2

SOURCES:

U.S. World War II Navy Muster Rolls, USS *Indianapolis*, March–October 1945

U.S. Marine Corps Muster Rolls, 1798–1958

U.S. World War II Draft Registration Cards, 1938–1945

U.S. Navy Casualties Books, Combat Naval Casualties, 1776–1945

U.S. WWII Draft Cards Young Men, 1940–1947

USS *Indianapolis* Final Sailing List, Compiled August 17, 1945

Manila American Cemetery Database

Headstones & Cenotaph information from Findagrave.com

APPENDIX A

Rescue Ships

USS *BASSETT* (APD-73) Redesignated as a Charles Lawrence–class high-speed transport. Commissioned 23 February 1945. Lieutenant Commander Harold J. Theriault USNR in command at time of rescue. Rescued 151 men.

USS *CECIL J. DOYLE* (DE-368) John C. Butler–class. Commissioned 16 October 1944. Commanding officer at time of rescue: Lieutenant Commander William Graham Claytor, Jr., USNR, who became Secretary of the Navy in 1977. Rescued 93 men (including the 53 men brought on board from Marks's PBY and one survivor from Lt. Alcorn's Catalina).*

USS *DUFILHO* (DE-423) John C. Butler–class. Commissioned 21 July 1944. Commander A. H. Nienau, USNR, in command during rescue.

Nienau, who was circulation man for the *Seattle Star* before the war, pieced together radio messages regarding "debris in the water" and sped to the debris coordinates. Arriving after dark, *Dufilho* lookouts spotted a lone survivor, Seaman Second Class Francis H. Rineay of New Orleans. While the whaleboat was picking up Seaman Rineay, *Dufilho*'s sonar picked up a strong sonar contact only nine hundred yards away. Concerned that the Japanese submarine might still be lurking in the area, *Dufilho* attacked with depth charges and hedgehogs. After twenty minutes with no evidence of a destroyed submarine, *Dufilho* picked up the whaleboat and survivor and commenced screening for the rescue operation until 4:15 p.m. the following day, when she was released to return to Leyte.

---

* *Doyle*/PBY count taken from USS *Cecil J. Doyle* action report, August 2–4, 1945.

USS *RALPH TALBOT* (DD-390) Bagley-class destroyer. Launched 31 October 1936 and commissioned 14 October 1937. Lieutenant Commander Burns Walling Spore in command at rescue. Rescued 24 men.

USS *REGISTER* (APD-92) Converted to a Crosley-class high-speed transport, 17 June 1944. Commissioned 11 January 1945. Commanding officer at time of rescue: Lieutenant Commander Furman, John Rockwell, USNR. Rescued 12 men.

USS *RINGNESS* (APD-100) Redesignated a Crosley-class high-speed transport, 17 July 1944. Commissioned 25 October 1944. Lieutenant Commander William C. Meyer, USNR, in command at time of *Indianapolis* rescue. Rescued 39 men.

SEARCH & RECOVERY SHIPS

USS *MADISON* (DD-425) Benson-class destroyer. Launched 20 October 1939 and commissioned 6 August 1940. Commander Donald Wooster Todd, Jr., was commanding officer at the time of rescue, and also Senior Officer Present Afloat.

USS *ALVIN C. COCKRELL* (DE-366) John C. Butler–class destroyer escort. Commissioned 7 August 1944. Lieutenant Commander Merrill M. Sanford, USNR, in command at rescue.

USS *AYLWIN* (DD-355) Farragut-class destroyer. Launched 10 July 1934 and commissioned 1 March 1935. Lieutenant Commander Karl Frederick Neupert in command at the time of rescue.

USS *FRENCH* (DE-367) John C. Butler–class destroyer escort. Commissioned 9 October 1944. Lieutenant Commander T. K. Dunstan, USNR, in command at rescue.

USS *HELM* (DD-356) Gridley-class destroyer. Commissioned 16 October 1937. Earned eleven Battle Stars in World War II. Commanding officer at time of rescue was Lieutenant Commander Albert Francis Hollingsworth.

APPENDIX B

Journey with Indianapolis
by Sara Vladic

I became captivated by the USS *Indianapolis* story when I was about thirteen years old. I was watching a documentary with my dad, and they mentioned one line about the ship that stuck with me. "The ship carried the bomb and was lost at sea, leaving the crew of nearly twelve hundred men abandoned at sea for five days." I couldn't believe it was a real event when I heard about it, and if it was, how could something so important be reduced to one line? I had to know more. I went to my local library and started searching. There was very little information to be found, but it was indeed a true story. I thought it would make a great movie, and I couldn't wait to see it come to the screen. At the time, I knew I wanted to make movies, but I figured someone else would make it long before I was old enough to do so.

Jump forward eight years. After graduating college and realizing nobody had told the story yet, or at least no one had done it justice on the screen, I began reaching out to the USS *Indianapolis* survivors—and the real journey began. I never imagined that the research materials gathered in order to write a screenplay would someday turn into a full-length documentary, and lead to a book. That was nearly seventeen years ago, and at the time, around 117 survivors were still alive.

It was surprising to learn that many people had written books and attempted to make movies without ever interviewing those men who lived through it. Time and time again, I found that I was blessed to be put in a situation where these men became my friends and trusted me with their stories when they hadn't shared them with anyone else for more than fifty years.

A few years passed, and even though my desperate desire to tell this story increased, the possibility still seemed extremely remote. Until that day when I met with Paul and Mary Lou Murphy at Denny's in Las Vegas. I arrived prepared to spend whatever time and money it took (from the senior deal menu because, at the time, that was about all I could afford) to convince them that I would be the one to tell their story. What I didn't realize was that they were going to beat me to the punch. Paul sat in that crowded diner and said, "Sara, I've been talking to the guys, and we've decided. . . . You're the one we want to tell our story." There were many prayers answered that day. And it would take another book to tell you about all of them, but there's no question that I now had a specific purpose, and there was no way I was going to let these men down.

Now's the part of my story that everyone should know. I wanted to give up, probably a hundred times (maybe a thousand), but if nothing else, these men taught me there was no such thing as giving up. This was only punctuated by the fact that on those days when I would cry out, asking God why He tasked me with something so huge and then made it "impossible," I would hear from one of the survivors almost immediately, asking me how I was coming along with their story, and how I was doing. It might be a call, or a letter, or just some small thing that dangled the carrot enough to keep me going. This happened EVERY. SINGLE. TIME. And then, when it got even harder, and I'd be working eighteen-hour days, and chunks of time would pass with no breakthroughs, and someone from Hollywood would attempt to shut me down or "ruin me" . . . I'd pray. And ask my close friends and family to just pray for a clear path, or wisdom. Something! What else could I do? I was young, not really experienced in that industry yet, and not even close to rich, but then time after time, something out of this world would happen that made no sense. And there would be a breakthrough that would lead me one step closer to dream becoming a reality. So I trucked on.

In the following years, I had written an event series screenplay, but it kept coming up that we needed a book, so that it could be marketed as a "based on" story. Now what, God?

After several starts and stops down various avenues, I asked those close friends and family for more prayers, and then asked if anyone knew any authors I could speak with who might be able to help me with some advice. Through my mother-in-law, I was connected with Lynn. What

I didn't know at the time was that Lynn had been praying for an epic World War II story to work on as one of her next projects.

Eventually, we decided to meet, and from the moment she rode up on her Harley and walked up to me, I knew—and I can't explain it, other than to say God told me right then and there that she would somehow be part of this journey.

And boy, was he right. Together Lynn and I got to work. We collected additional research material via trips to the National Archives, the Naval War College, the Naval Institute, the Indiana Historical Society and War Memorial, and lots and lots of web searches and additional interviews and reading journals and diaries of those involved. We were both elbow-deep in learning about Indy, and we played our role as writers and researchers, each becoming subject matter experts in our own right. The book resulted from a joint effort that was above and beyond anything we imagined.

During my seventeen-year journey with *Indianapolis*—from dream to series screenplay to documentary and now to this book—I have made some of the best friends I've ever known, and have been adopted by the survivors and their families as a granddaughter and keeper of their legacy, and was made an honorary survivor, a title I don't take lightly. It was for them that I made it through this rocky roller-coaster of a process, and for them that I'll keep fighting to make sure the story is told as it should be. It's so much more than just a cheap thriller about a massive shark attack. My hope is that when readers finish this book, they will have a complete understanding of the importance and legacy of this great ship, and those final months of the war. I want them to know the crew, and to understand how ordinary seventeen- and eighteen-year-old kids fought and paid the price for our freedom. And that those same teenagers grew up, started families, and continued their fight to exonerate their captain, never once asking for recognition themselves.

METHODOLOGY

Our hats are off to the authors who tackled this epic story before us. We'd like to mention four in particular: Richard Newcomb, author of *Abandon Ship*, was the first writer to recognize the importance of the *Indianapolis* story, to realize that an injustice had occurred with respect to McVay, and to write the story in long form. Raymond Lech, author of *All the Drowned Sailors*, was the first writer to pull together reams of primary sources in a single volume and to write the story based strictly on those sources. Dan Kurzman pounded the pavement to produce fresh reporting some fifty years after the sinking, and shared our love for digging deep into primary sources. Finally, Doug Stanton, author of *In Harm's Way*, was first to interview literally scores of survivors and then write, in his words, "a survival story" that focused on the ordeal the men faced while adrift at sea.

Following in the wake of these greats, we faced a humbling task. Our aims were several: to write an accessible and human naval history that placed Indy in her proper historical context, reminding today's readers that hers is more than a sinking story. *Indianapolis* was the ship from whose decks Spruance built his island bridge from Pearl Harbor to Japan and won the Pacific war, a victory that has relevance today for every American. We also wanted to range out and show the Japanese point of view. We hoped to treat men like Ugaki, Hashimoto, and Hirohito, though they were enemies at the time, as men who acted with sincere conscience and conviction. We wanted to share with readers for the first time the inside story of how superspy Major Robert Furman shepherded a world-changing weapon to its launch point. Furman's story shows the final braiding together of the European and Pacific conflicts that led to the end of the war.

Stories like that of *Indianapolis* are necessarily told by survivors. We wanted to tell the survivors' stories while also focusing deeply on men who were lost at sea, developing them as full human beings so that read-ers could experience what it must have been like to lose them. We wanted to fully explore the drama of the rescue, and honor the brave men who sped to the scene to save their brothers-in-arms. We wanted to touch on the home front, to delve deeply into the grief experienced by the families of Indy's lost sailors and officers, and also to explore the lifelong impact of the sinking on the men who survived it and their families. We also wanted to tell for the first time the full story of the exoneration of Cap-tain McVay.

Ironically, we did not set out to tell the story of the investigation and court-martial. But our deep dive into primary sources, particularly cor-respondence among the admirals, revealed a tale of injustice that begged to be told. It was a story that went beyond scapegoating to an institu-tional wall of silence that, while not a conspiracy, proved a shield for the powerful. After all these decades, we have that in writing, from Admi-ral Snyder to Admiral King, listing the culpability of men who far out-ranked McVay but who were never held to account.

Primary sources are the lifeblood of this book. Fact by fact, we were determined to build the story from scratch and have attempted to pro-vide copious documentation. We haunted the National Archives, the Naval War College, the Library of Congress, Ancestry.com, Newspapers .com (for contemporaneous history), and Fold3.com, an online data-base of military records that operates in conjunction with the National Archives. We visited libraries housing collections of the private papers of historical figures. To experience Indy herself, we visited Quincy, Massa-chusetts, and clambered up and down the ladders of USS *Salem*, the only World War II heavy cruiser still afloat. We tapped memoirs, letters, dia-ries, and journals to bring alive the men's thoughts as they lived and died and develop the stories of men lost at sea. There were scores of formal interviews of survivors, rescuers, families, and friends, as well as families and friends of those lost at sea.

It evolved that Lynn's continuing research and focus centered more on the storylines involving the bomb transport, Admiral Spruance, Cap-tain McVay himself, the court-martial, and the exoneration, along with naval history and protocol. Her service in the Navy helped a great deal in understanding this part of the story. Lynn also concentrated on develop-ing the stories of historical figures. Sara focused on the personal stories of the crew and their families, the sinking itself, and the men's time in the water. Sara and her husband, Ben, a mechanical engineer, also concentrated (or should we say geeked out?) on the history, construction, and technical specifications of the ship itself, as well as mining new information that only became available in late 2017 because of the discovery of the wreck of *Indianapolis*. The providential timing of that event allowed us to lay to rest forever exactly what happened during Hashimoto's fateful attack.

In our telling, there is a key element that cannot be underestimated: Sara's seventeen-year relationship with the survivors and their families. This relationship began in 2001, and then continued in 2005 with formal interviews, which evolved into hundreds of more intimate conversations during which survivors revealed information that they'd never shared with anyone before. Over a decade and a half, Sara crisscrossed the country visiting the men and their families, attending birthdays, hometown ceremonies honoring the survivors, and sadly, dozens of funerals. Her relationship with the survivors grew past "interviewer" and "filmmaker" to supporter, then friend, then honorary survivor, and in many cases, even honorary granddaughter. This critical relationship became a window into the deeper truths of the men's 1945 ordeal as many survivors decided to share details, often horrific, that they'd once sworn to keep bottled up forever.

These Greatest Generation heroes were of a different time, when men did not complain about their circumstances, but simply bore up. Several, though, wanted to finally unburden themselves and found in Sara a sympathetic listener whom they knew they could trust to keep new details private. Those stories do not appear in this book. Other men, though, nearing the ends of their lives, told Sara that they wanted the whole truth known before it was too late.

NOTES

PROLOGUE

2 *Only 316 survived*: Hulver, Richard, and Sara Vladic. "Setting the Record Straight: Loss of the USS *Indianapolis* and the Question of Clarence Donnor," *Proceedings*. U.S. Naval Institute. March 21, 2018. In 2018 author Sara Vladic teamed up with Dr. Richard Hulver at the Naval History and Heritage Command to investigate the final crew numbers of the *Indianapolis*. It was concluded through extensive research that Radio Technician 2nd Class Clarence Donnor, previously thought to have been a passenger on the final sailing crew and lost at sea, departed from the ship just hours prior to her final sailing. Instead, he received orders to report for officer training at Fort Schuyler, NY. After confirming details of the transfer in Donnor's personnel records and matching that to the crew list records compiled in August of 1945, Vladic and Hulver finally determined that 1,195 men sailed on *Indianapolis*, and 316 survived.

BOOK 1: THE KAMIKAZE

Chapter 1

5 *plane plunged from a slab of clouds*: Action Report, Nansei Shoto Operations (Phase 1) 18 March–7 April 1945, USS Indianapolis. Naval War College. Record Group 23, (NANSEI), 8–9. Also: *War Diary*, USS Indianapolis, March 1945. Naval War College Record Group 23. (MARCH WAR.)

5 *Spruance tracking the action*: Buell, Thomas B. *The Quiet Warrior: A Biography of Admiral Raymond A. Spruance.* Boston, MA: Little, Brown, 1987. Print. 373.8. (QUIET.)

5 *Sailing closest were sixteen aircraft carriers*: NANSEI, 3–4. QUIET, 373.

5 *Morgan stood near McVay*: Interview with Glenn Morgan. "Legacy On-Camera Interviews with Survivors, Survivors Families, and Families of Men Lost at Sea," 2005–2016, conducted by Sara Vladic. (LEGACY.)

6 *whistled close to Bunker Hill*: NANSEI, 9.

6 *Task Force 58 was maneuvering at Emperor Hirohito's*: NANSEI.

6 *the Empire's air reaction*: QUIET, 373.

6 *crew of nearly a thousand*: Muster Roll of the Crew of the USS *Indianapolis*, March 31, 1945, certified by Commander Flynn and approved by Captain Charles McVay III on

April 3, 1945. Recapitulation sheet. According to the Muster Roll, the ship's complement at the end of March 1945 and carrying forward was 996 men.

6　*helped tenderize the beach*: Action Report, Iwo Jima Operations, 8 February–5 March 1945, USS Indianapolis. Naval War College. Record Group 23. (IWO OPS.)

6　*wasn't so sure about McVay*: LEGACY. Morgan interview.

6　*won a Silver Star for courage*: *Military Service Record of Rear Admiral Charles B. McVay III*, obtained from the National Archives via Persons of Exceptional Prominence program. October 2016.

7　*American naval power at its zenith*: QUIET, 351–52.

7　*Buckett had recorded the bombardment*: IWO OPS, 1–42.

7　*"Give 'em hell, boys"*: LEGACY. Clarence Hershberger, LEGACY interview.

7　*the performance of her crew had been excellent*: IWO OPS, 32.

8　*At fifty-eight, Spruance vented his intensity*: QUIET, 212.

8　*"gaudy Hawaiian bathing panties"*: Ibid., 266.

8　*not content with hitting just the Kyushu*: Ibid., 373.

8　*"walnut with a sledgehammer"*: Good, Roscoe F. letter to Commander Thomas Buell re: Admiral Raymond S. Spruance. N.D. Naval War College. MSC 37, Thomas Buell Collection, Box 4.

9　*sorely needed fighting spirit*: QUIET, 109.

9　*saw a pair of sailors*: LEGACY, Celaya interview.

9　*Spruance quickly presided over a series of firsts*: See generally QUIET.

9　*finest and most human characters*: Ibid., 185.

10　*"Broke my hand, sir"*: Account of Admiral Spruance's interaction with Celaya is based on LEGACY interviews with Celaya. Also: Interview with Harpo Celaya by Lynn Vincent in Florence, Arizona. August 2015. (LV-CELAYA.)

10　*his pilots had bested 102*: Appleman, Roy Edgar. *Okinawa: The Last Battle*. Washington, D.C.: Historical Division, Dept. of the Army, 1948. Print. Reprint 1971, 15. (OKINAWA.)

10　*"supership," Yamato was capable of fighting*: Mitsuru, Yoshida. *Requiem for Battleship Yamato*. Annapolis, MD: Naval Institute Press, 1999.

Chapter 2

11　*stormed into the office of the Combined Fleet commander in chief*: Hashimoto, Mochitsura. *Sunk: The Story of the Japanese Submarine Fleet, 1941–1945*. New York: Holt, 1954. (SUNK.)

11　*B-29s had torched sixteen square miles*: "Bombing of Tokyo and Other Cities." World War II Database. Accessed June 16, 2016. Article covers 19 February–10 August 1945. Also: History Chanel. "Firebombing of Tokyo (This Day in History)." History.com. Accessed June 26, 2016. http://www.history.com/this-day-in-history/firebombing -of-tokyo.

14　*Spruance had mobilized unprecedented logistics*: QUIET, 190.

14　*his own mission to Iwo Jima*: SUNK, 194.

14　*American submarines therefore gained experience quickly*: Interview with Captain Bill Toti, former skipper of the Los Angeles–class submarine USS *Indianapolis* (SSN-697).

14　*His own submarine, I-58*: Potts, J. R. "IJN I-58—History, Specs and Pictures—Navy Ships." (IJN I-58.)

15 *his countrymen had begun to wonder*: Hastings, Max. *Retribution: The Battle for Japan, 1944–45*. New York: Alfred A. Knopf, 2009, 370. (HASTINGS.)

16 *torpedo officer on a sub at Pearl Harbor*: SUNK, 21.

16 *"We are turning away from the enemy!"*: SUNK, 197.

16 *plunged through a line of squalls*: Ibid.

17 *He could not dive out of sight*: SUNK, 198.

17 *Maddening! Hashimoto thought*: Ibid.

17 *who was to say he could not first launch his* kaiten: SUNK, 198.

18 *Above all, he had wanted to try*: Ibid.

Chapter 3

19 *"go play that damn thing in the head!"*: Morgan, Glenn Grover. "A WWII Bugler Tells His Story." Memoir. 28 Sept. 2011. 36 Pages. (GM-BUGLER)

19 *one of America's eighteen "Treaty Cruisers"*: Pike, John. "Treaty Cruiser." GlobalSecurity.org. Accessed March 8, 2016.

19 *a kid named Earl Procai reported for duty*: Procai story related in: Morgan, Glenn Grover. "Story of Suicide Plane Attack" Memoir. 28 Sept. 2011. 3 Pages. (GM-KAMIKAZE.)

20 *Spruance took station in his bridge*: QUIET, 373.

20 *At 5:30 a.m., the carriers launched the CAP*: NANSEI, 9.

20 *dead ahead of the carrier* Franklin: USS *Franklin* narrative based on USS *Franklin* (CV-13) Bomb Damage report Honshu, 19 March 1945. Bureau of Ships, Navy Department. United States Naval War College Archives. Figures for men killed and wounded from ussfranklin.org, accessed online October 17, 2017.

21 *carrier* Essex *splashed one attacker*: NANSEI, 9.

21 *falling with a friendly fighter on its tail*: Ibid.

21 *third run on* Essex: NANSEI, 10.

21 Franklin*'s fiery agony in full view of the admiral's seat*: QUIET, 373.

Chapter 4

23 *all the damned noise*: The Ugaki narrative is based on the admiral's war diary: Ugaki, Matome, Donald M. Goldstein, and Katherine V. Dillon. *Fading Victory: The Diary of Admiral Matome Ugaki, 1941–1945*. Annapolis, MD: Naval Institute Press, 2008. (UGAKI.)

23 *Ugaki felt time was running out*: UGAKI, 361.

24 *"a dagger pointed at our throat"*: Hull, Michael D., "Admiral Isoroku Yamamoto: Japan's Naval War Leader." Warfare History Network. Accessed online 19 January 2017. Yamamoto's quotation has been rendered variously, including "a dagger pointed at our hearts."

24 *vowed vengeance for his commander*: UGAKI, 360.

24 *sign their names either next to the word "eager"*: Day of the Kamikaze, Smithsonian Channel. February 8, 2008, United Kingdom. Director: Peter Nicholson.

24 *spent their last days quietly*: Ibid.

24 *nothing less than a national death sentence*: Yokoi narrative based on: Yokoi, Toshiyuki. "Kamikazes and the Okinawa Campaign." *Proceedings*. U.S. Naval Institute. May 1954. Vol 80/5/615.

25 *run wild seeking ways to save the Empire*: UGAKI, 531.

25 *"send our young men to die with a smile"*: UGAKI, 550.

Chapter 5

26 *"Not the great Basil P. Pole"*: L. D. Cox narrative based on interviews with L. D. Cox. LEGACY.

27 *hunched over their plates*: Interviews with Umenhoffer, Fortin, and Nunley. LEGACY.

27 *McVay ordered Indy released from formation*: NANSEI, 24.

27 *carried livestock as food stores*: McVay, Charles B., Jr. *Autobiography*. Papers of Admiral Charles B. McVay, Jr. Library of Congress.

28 *had assumed the role of hanging judge*: USS *Indianapolis: Ship of Doom*. Produced by Bill Van Daalen. Chip Taylor Communications.

28 *rose quickly to prestigious postings*: Biography of Rear Admiral Charles B. McVay III, U.S. Navy (Retired). This biography was printed on the letterhead of Headquarters Eighth Naval District, Federal Building, New Orleans, Louisiana.

28 *no other ships in the formation*: NANSEI, 24.

28 *Lebow held his cards*: Lebow and Murphy narrative based on interviews with Cleatus Lebow and Paul Murphy. LEGACY.

29 *Celaya and Quihuis were walking*: Narrative of Celaya and Quihuis during the kamikaze attack is based on: Quihuis, Mike. "Mike Quihuis Diary." Diary. July 22, 1944–November 26, 1945. Handwritten. (KIWI.) Also: LEGACY. Celaya interviews.

30 *stacked the ranks with corn-fed rednecks*: Clemans, Charles. *Harpo: War Survivor, Basketball Wizard*. Tucson, AZ: Wheatmark, 2009. Print. 29. (HARPO.)

30 *Quihuis and Pena were older*: LV-CELAYA.

30 *"get you alone someday and kill you"*: HARPO, 31.

30 *naked bone poked up through his skin*: LEGACY. Celaya interviews.

31 *"Next time you hit someone"*: HARPO, 31. Also: LV-CELAYA.

Chapter 6

32 *burst through the low overcast*: NANSEI, 24.

32 *"Who is that trigger-happy—"*: GM-KAMIKAZE, 2.

32 *his parents' faces flashed before him*: Murphy, Marylou, and USS *Indianapolis* Survivors. *Only 317 Survived!: USS* Indianapolis *(CA-35): Navy's Worst Tragedy at Sea—880 Men Died*. Indianapolis, IN: USS *Indianapolis* Survivors Organization, 2002. 174. (317.)

32 *L. D. Cox heard the battle stations call*: LEGACY. L. D. Cox interviews.

33 *Ed Harrell was ready to shoot*: LEGACY. Edgar Harrell interviews.

33 *The bomb punched a sixteen-inch hole*: Bomb damage report taken from NANSEI. 29–32.

33 *the ship to whip*: USS *Indianapolis* (CA-35) Report of War Damage, 31 March 1945, prepared by Mare Island Naval Yard, 6-8.

34 *four sailors rush to the plane*: GM-KAMIKAZE, 2.

34 *"We have to dog it down!"*: LEGACY. Troy Nunley interviews.

35 *musters revealed that eight men were missing*: Deck Logs, USS *Indianapolis*, March 1–March 31, 1945. National Archives, College Park, Maryland. Record Group 24. Box 4839. (MARCH LOG.)

35 *Spruance immediately expressed his suspicion*: QUIET, 378.

35 *finally secured the Keramas*: Isely, Jeter A., and Philip Axtell. Crowl. *The US Marines and Amphibious War: Its Theory, and Its Practice in the Pacific*. Princeton, NJ: Princeton University Press, 1951. Print. (WAR.)

36 *a silver bugle in his hand*: GM-KAMIKAZE.

36 *among nine men killed*: Muster Roll of the Crew of the USS *Indianapolis*, March 31, 1945, certified by Commander Flynn and approved by Captain Charles McVay III on April 3, 1945. Report of Changes, 29. MM3c Winston Hayden Arnold, QM3c Marvin Eugene Douglass, Bug2c Calvin Ball Emery, MM1c John Morris Garhart, QM3c Matt Anthony Klucaric, QM3c Richard Clarence Kuchenbach, Y3c Epifanio Lobato Jr, Bug2c Earl Peter Procai, and QM3c Byron Emery Smiley were killed in the kamikaze attack on March 31, 1945.

36 *render Procai his final honors*: MARCH LOG.

36 *Procai was to be buried*: Department of the Navy, letter to the parents of Earl Procai. March 5, 1948. In 1948, Congress undertook an effort to return America's war dead to their families. As a result, bugler Earl Procai was returned to his family, and to the home he loved so much, in Minnesota.

Chapter 7

37 *Spruance himself would be sitting D-Day out*: QUIET, 378.

37 *wrote in his contraband diary*: Morgan, Glenn Grover. "Glenn Morgan Diaries." January 1–April 25, 1945. Handwritten by Glenn Morgan, and retyped by Sharon Morgan and Ben Huntley. (GM-DIARIES.)

38 *gave Morgan a wooden flute*: GM-KAMIKAZE.

39 *dubbed Moore "photographic officer"*: Moore, Katherine D. *Goodbye, Indy Maru*. Knoxville, TN: Lori Publications, 1991, 27. (MARU.)

39 *it marked him deeply*: MARU, 64–67.

40 *respected the admiral more than any man*: Ibid., 55.

40 *document major damage aboard*: MARCH WAR, 29–32.

40 *my men have dropped the propeller*: QUIET, 379.

41 *On April 5, Spruance shifted his flag*: Ibid.

Chapter 8

41 *On April 2, Mochitsura Hashimoto put to sea*: SUNK, 201.

41 *Hirohito considered the island's successful defense*: HASTINGS, 369.

42 *if they could make America pay dearly enough*: Ibid.

42 *"the turn toward heaven"*: SUNK, 177.

42 *Type 93 sanso gyorai*: Information on the *kaiten* human torpedoes is based on "Kaiten Special Attack Submarine," Combined Fleet. Accessed October 1, 2016. http://combinedfleet.com/ships/kaiten. The authors of this site, Japanese submarine experts Bob Hackett and Sander Kingsepp, were extremely generous and helpful as we researched the Japanese fleet for this book. See also: SUNK, 177–79.

42 *swords held aloft, white headbands flying*: SUNK, 180.

43 *suspicious vessel had been sighted*: Ibid., 185.

43 *"which is the Southern Cross"*: Ibid., 186.

44 *jetted away from I-58 without uttering a sound*: Ibid., 188.

44 *Lieutenant Ishikawa had written*: Ibid., 189.

Chapter 9

45 *more than three hundred enemy planes*: "Kamikaze." U-S-History.com. Accessed online October 15, 2016. http://www.u-s-history.com/pages/h1740.html.

45 *At 4:41 p.m., they opened fire*: *Deck Logs*, USS *Indianapolis*, 1 April –30 April 1945. Record Group 24. Box No. 4839. National Archives, College Park, Maryland. (DECK APRIL.)

46 *by 1:15 p.m. had rendezvoused*: DECK APRIL.

46 Yamato *was crumbling*: Mitsuru, Yoshida. *Requiem for Battleship* Yamato. Annapolis: Naval Institute Press, 1999.

46 *Hirohito secretly charged*: Hando, Kazutoshi. *Japan's Longest Day.* 1990 ed. Vol. Eighth Printing. Tokyo: Kodansha International, 1967. (LONGEST.)

Chapter 10

47 *Nazis had beaten him*: Powers, Thomas. *Heisenberg's War: The Secret History of the German Bomb.* New York: Knopf, 1993, 413. (HEISENBERG.)

47 *clandestine U.S. mission called Alsos*: See generally HEISENBERG.

47 *a small cache of fissionable material*: HEISENBERG, 412.

48 *specter of a German atomic weapon*: Ibid., 218–28.

48 *what of the news that Werner Heisenberg*: Ibid., 113–15.

48 *fear swirling around these questions*: Ibid., 218.

48 *Furman already knew the general*: the account of Furman's relationship with General Leslie Groves is based on: Papers of Robert Furman. Library of Congress. Robert Furman's writing on Manhattan Engineering District, c. 1982, Papers of Robert Furman, Library of Congress [MED]. Also: "How to Carry an Atomic Bomb." Furman's remarks and reflections on the Alsos mission, the Manhattan Project, and his role in events, July 1985. (CARRY.)

49 *a little cache of hard candy*: "Draft: August 5, 1985." Remarks prepared about the fortieth anniversary of the dropping of the first atomic bomb. Papers of Robert Furman, Library of Congress. (DRAFT.)

50 *began a crash course in atomic science*: HEISENBERG, 219.

50 *the engagement was called off*: Interview with Robert Furman, Chief of Foreign Intelligence and assistant to General Lloyd Groves, Manhattan Project, February 20, 2008. Voices of the Manhattan Project, a joint project of Atomic Heritage Foundation and the Los Alamos Historical Society Online at: http://manhattanprojectvoices .org/oral-histories/robert-furmans-interview. Accessed March 25, 2016. (FURMAN ATOMIC.)

Chapter 11

51 *gotten under way from Guam on April 15*: DECK APRIL.

52 *Captain McVay ordered a memorial service*: Ibid.

52 *American president ever served as King Neptune*: Roosevelt served as King Neptune sometime between November 18 and December 15, 1936. Inbiblio. USS *Indianapolis* Memorial Dedication Program, 4.

52 Il Duce's *corpse had been hung upside down*: "Mussolini's Body Strung Up, Kicked, Spat Upon." *Pittsburgh Press*, April 30, 1945. Newspapers.com image of original.

52 *"toothless, pulpy mass"*: Ibid.

52 *shot trap off the fantail*: Henry, Earl O., Sr., letters to his wife, Jane Henry, May 22, 1944–July 27, 1945. Letter of April 24, 1945. Dr. Henry wrote more than 160 pages of letters to Jane. He would pass away three days after his final letter, in which he wrote to Jane that he had finally received photographs of his newborn son, Earl O. Henry, Jr.: "Baby-angel, those two wonderful pictures came today, and I am delighted as I can be over them! Considering that he is a premature baby, he looks mighty good." Letters courtesy of Earl O. Henry, Jr. (HENRY LETTERS.)

53 *Moore, the former newspaperman, had profiled Henry*: Moore, Kyle C. "Mounting Birds Is Not Stuff Business Says Youngster Who Must Stop," *Knoxville Sunday Journal*, August 6, 1933.

53 *McVay saw a large bird glide in*: HENRY LETTERS. Letter of April 24, 1945.

54 *At 6:19 a.m., the OOD directed the helmsman*: DECK APRIL.

54 *Kinau had been a whirling socialite*: Kurzman, Dan. *Fatal Voyage*. New York: Atheneum, 1990. Print. 5. (FATAL.)

Chapter 12

55 *Katherine Moore squeezed into the crowded dining car*: The account of Katherine Moore's travel to Mare Island is based on: Moore, Katherine D. *Goodbye, Indy Maru*. Knoxville, TN: Lori Publications, 1991. (MARU.)

57 *Father Thomas Conway loaned Lew Haynes a few dollars*: "Oral History with Capt. (ret.) Lewis Haynes, MD, USN," U.S. Navy Medical Department Oral History Program, June 5, 12, 22, 1995, 16. (BUMED.)

57 *Harpo Celaya headed home to Florence, Arizona*: HARPO, 32.

57 *Donald Mack beat him out for promotion*: Morgan, Glenn Grover. "A WWII Bugler Tells His Story." Memoir. 28 Sept. 2011. 36 Pages. (GM-BUGLER.)

Chapter 13

58 *filled with flashing silver plate*: "Bombing of Tokyo and Other Cities." World War II Database. Accessed June 16, 2016. Article covers 19 February–10 August 1945.

59 *The central target was Shitamachi*: History Chanel. "Firebombing of Tokyo (This Day in History)." History.com. Accessed June 26, 2016. http://www.history.com/this-day-in-history/firebombing-of-tokyo.

59 *Hashimoto had seen lights twinkling*: The account of Hashimoto at Pearl Harbor is based on his recollections in SUNK, 27–32.

60 *Hashimoto developed the view that one radar set*: Hashimoto's fight for sub modernization is related in SUNK, 164–75.

Chapter 14

61 *On June 30, he received his first letter*: HENRY LETTERS. June 30, 1945.

61 *Katherine, thought Henry's model*: MARU, 99.

61 *he had written to Jane about everything*: See generally, HENRY LETTERS.

62 *turn it down so fast her head would spin*: HENRY LETTERS. Letter of July 26, 1945.

62 *Ensign John Woolston was glad to be aboard*: LEGACY and other interviews with John Woolston by the authors 2012–17.

62 *actually his second time aboard*: Ibid.

63 *Woolston's immediate boss was Moore*: Ibid.

63 *quadrupled to more than forty thousand*: "Mare Island History." City of Vallejo, California, website. Accessed online December 12, 2017. http://www.visitvallejo.com/about-vallejo/mare-island-history.

Chapter 15

64 *he sat in the Washington, D.C., offices*: Departure Memorandum written 9 July 1945. Papers of Robert Furman, Library of Congress.

65 *"Derry is wiring Oppie to expect me"*: Robert Furman handwritten account of bomb transport, undated. Papers of Robert Furman, Library of Congress (FURMAN HW); Departure Memorandum written July 10, 1945, Papers of Robert Furman, Library of Congress (FDN).

65 *final stockpile of missing uranium*: HEISENBERG, 417.

65 *Harry Truman, was in the loop now*: Norris, Robert S. *Racing for the Bomb: The True Story of General Leslie R. Groves, the Man behind the Birth of the Atomic Age.* New York: Skyhorse Publishing, 2002. (RACING.)

66 *circulated a petition among Manhattan Project scientists*: Gest, Howard. "The July 1945 Szilard Petition on the Atomic Bomb." Departments of Biology, and History & Philosophy of Science. Indiana University, Bloomington, Indiana. A memoir by a signer at the Oak Ridge Laboratory.

66 *Alsos agents detained Kurt Diebner*: HEISENBERG, 425.

66 *He tried to relax*: Robert Furman's writing on transporting the atomic bomb aboard USS *Indianapolis*, undated. Papers of Robert F. Furman, Library of Congress. (FOI.)

66 *"We'll be looking for the shipment"*: Ibid.

66 *the cargo was "priceless"*: Ibid.

67 *spending time in close company with the package*: Ibid.

67 *Oppie suggested they chat*: The account of Furman's meeting with Oppenheimer and Nolan is based on Furman's written account of his journey from Washington, D.C., to Tinian Island via Santa Fe and Los Alamos, New Mexico, and Mare Island and Hunter's Point, California. Private Papers of Robert Furman. Library of Congress. (FOI.)

68 *two old-fashioned ice cream freezers*: Ibid. Historians have noted that a manifest for the truck that would carry the bomb components away from Los Alamos described the shipment as three crates containing, in total, several tons of material. Furman's account of two canisters and a single crate matches the eyewitness accounts of the *Indianapolis* crew, including Harrell, DeBernardi, Erwin, Paroubek, Woolston, and scores of others.

69 *one-half of the first combat-ready atomic bomb*: FOI, 5.

69 *have it carried aboard with their luggage*: FOI.

Chapter 16

70 *On July 12, McVay learned*: "Personal Narrative" by Captain Charles B. McVay, III, USN, Sinking of USS *Indianapolis*, recorded 27 September 1945. Command File World War II. Indiana Historical Society. (MCVAY NARRATIVE.)

71 *the Navy representative on the Manhattan Project's*: "William R. Purnell." Atomic Heritage Foundation. Accessed June 14, 2016. www.atomicheritage.com.

71 *Purnell tapped Deak Parsons*: Rhodes, Richard. *The Making of the Atomic Bomb.* New York: Simon & Schuster, 1987, 477. (RHODES.)

72 *the bomb might have the power to prevent an invasion*: Frank, Richard B. "Downfall: The End of the Imperial Japanese Empire." New York: Random House, 1999, 242. (DOWNFALL.)

72 *Okinawa had cost America dearly*: "Battle of Okinawa." Battle of Okinawa. http://www.globalsecurity.org/military/facility/okinawa-battle.htm. (PHASES.)

72 *wanted to prevent "another Okinawa"*: United States Department & State Foreign Relations of the United States: Diplomatic Papers: The Conference of Berlin (the Potsdam Conference), 1945. Vol. 1. Washington D.C.: U.S. Govt Printing Office, 1945.

72 *allow invasion plans to continue*: Vasey, Lloyd R. "President Truman and the Atomic Bomb: Setting the Record Straight." Center for Strategic and International Studies. Accessed December 13, 2017. https://www.csis.org/analysis/pacnet-45-president-truman-and-atomic-bomb-%E2%80%93-setting-record-straight.

72 *Groves felt air transport more inherently risky*: FOI.

72 Indianapolis *would depart the next day*: MCVAY NARRATIVE, 1.

73 *Katherine came undone*: The account of Katherine's upset over Indy's departure is based on: MARU, 138.

Chapter 17

74 *Dr. Lewis Haynes puffed a stogie*: Stanton, Doug. *In Harm's Way: The Sinking of the USS* Indianapolis *and the Extraordinary Story of Its Survivors.* New York: H. Holt, 2001, 29. (IHW.)

74 *Coxswain Louis Erwin mustered with a working party*: The account of Erwin and DeBernardi is based on LEGACY interviews (Erwin) and the men's own accounts in 317.

75 *shoulder each end of a metal pole*: 317.

75 *McVay greeted Furman and Nolan*: FOI.

75 *have the shipment bolted into place*: Ibid.

75 *Harrell stepped into the port hangar*: Harrell, Edgar, and David Harrell. *Out of the Depths: An Unforgettable WWII Story of Survival, Courage, and the Sinking of the USS* Indianapolis. 2nd ed.: Bethany House, 2014, 52–53. (DEPTHS.)

76 *"some of you ain't ever gonna see it again"*: 317, 175.

AUGUST 1997, U.S. FLEET ACTIVITIES, SASEBO, JAPAN

79 *Commander William Toti issued an order*: Account of Toti's port calls at Sasebo and Yokosuka based on interviews with Toti, 2012–2017.

84 *Since you were never able to decommission*: William Toti, Letter to Survivors, 1997.

BOOK 2: THE MISSION

Chapter 1

89 *For months, Captain William Smedburg had been preparing detailed charts*: Investigation of Sinking of USS *Indianapolis.* By order of the Chief of Naval Operations, 6 December 1945. Smedburg testimony, 2. (CONEY.)

89 *the combined intelligence power*: Holmes, W. J. *Double-Edged Secrets: U.S. Naval Intelligence Operations in the Pacific During World War II.* Annapolis, MD: Naval Institute Press 1979 (e-Book), 212. (HOLMES.)

90 *churning out two million printed sheets*: HOLMES, 229.

90 *High rank alone could not earn access*: Ibid., 62.

90 *Japanese had proven they could change their code*: Ibid., 63.

90 *purple lines pocked with blank underscores*: Description of ULTRA cards is based on the authors' examination of hundreds of ULTRA cards on file at the National Archives, College Park, Maryland. Office of Naval Intelligence, Intercepted Enemy Radio Traffic & Related Documentation, [Japan] Naval Vessels. Record Group 38, Boxes 1386–87. (ULTRA 1 and ULTRA 2. See Bibliography for a full description of this record.)

90 *codebreakers, who were known as "magicians"*: Frank, Richard B. "Why Truman Dropped the Bomb." From the August 8, 2005, Issue: Sixty Years after Hiroshima, We Now Have the Secret Intercepts That Shaped His Decision. Aug 8, 2005, Vol. 10, No. 44.

91 *"From Captain Sub I-58"*: Excerpts from the I-58 ULTRA intercept are taken from a card filed in ULTRA 1, dated 15 July 1945.

92 *Smedburg . . . had been tracking the Tamon group since July 13*: The authors found that the earliest appearance of the Tamon group in ULTRA traffic was 13 July 1945.

92 *Carter initialed the intel concerning the Tamon group*: CONEY. Layton testimony, 529. Carter testimony, 594.

Chapter 2

93 *"Nearly laid us down"*: LEGACY: L. D. Cox interviews. Survivors Robert Witzig and A. C. King also said Indy was nearly put on her side while carrying the atomic bomb components.

94 *men even had a betting pool going*: LEGACY: testimony of multiple survivors.

94 *to check on his Army guests*: Robert Furman's writing on transporting the atomic bomb aboard USS *Indianapolis*, undated. Papers of Robert F. Furman, Library of Congress. (FOI.)

95 *what have we got that's under control of the president*: "Oral History with Capt. (ret.) Lewis Haynes, MD, USN," U.S. Navy Medical Department Oral History Program, June 5, 12, 22, 1995. 17. (BUMED.)

95 *Operated on this morning. Diagnosis not yet complete*: RHODES, 685–86.

95 *a man with an aggressive agenda who was smart as hell*: McCullough, David G. *Truman.* New York: Simon & Schuster, 1992, 419. (TRUMAN.) Also: The History Channel. Accessed online December 9, 2017. http://www.history.com/this-day-in -history/truman-records-impressions-of-stalin.

96 *Was this awful weapon the fulfillment of that prophecy?*: Ferrell, Robert, ed. *Off the Record: The Private Papers of Harry S. Truman.* Harry S. Truman Library in Independence, MO. Truman's July 25, 1945 diary entry reads: "We met at 11 A.M. today. That is Stalin, Churchill and the U.S. President. But I had a most important session with Lord Mountbattan & General Marshall before then. We have discovered the most terrible bomb in the history of the world. It may be the fiery destruction prophesied in the Euphrates Valley Era, after Noah and his fabulous Ark."

Chapter 3

96   *The men discussed a range of potential emergencies*: The account of the discussion between Indy's officers and Furman and Nolan is based on Furman's writing about the transport of the bomb parts. FOI.

97   *down by the head*: That is, to sink bow first.

97   *a special ceremony for his six suicide pilots*: SUNK, 214.

97   *I-58 slipped down to the Bungo channel*: Ibid., 215.

98   *the enemy had sunk nearly a hundred ships*: Pacific Dispatches, Commander in Chief Chart Room Files, July 1–August 15, 1945. Record Group 38, Box 83, National Archives, College Park, Maryland. (CHART ROOM JULY.)

98   *His orders were clear*: SUNK, 216.

Chapter 4

98   *Lebow almost got into a fistfight*: LEGACY: Lebow interviews.

99   *the whole lot of them were "green, green, green"*: MARU, 134.

99   *Lebow watched the attack*: LEGACY: Lebow interviews.

100   *Furman and Nolan slept and sat with the bomb*: Furman FOI.

101   *a most unenviable assignment*: Ibid.

101   *formed friendships with several Indy officers*: Ibid.

101   *The decoy crate seemed to be working well*: Ibid.

101   *beautiful screen siren Hedy Lamarr!*: FOI. Hedy Lamarr was also a mathematical genius who lent her considerable talent to the war effort by working alongside Albert Einstein to help design torpedo proximity fuses.

Chapter 5

102   *the whole voyage in 74.5 hours*: Lech, Raymond B. *All the Drowned Sailors*. New York: Stein and Day, 1982, 8. (ADS.)

102   *"I've got a corpsman with a fractured leg"*: BUMED, 18.

103   *well-guarded crate was awfully important*: Ibid.

103   *joint intelligence center issued a ten-page*: "Ultra and the Sinking of the USS *Indianapolis*: A Paper Given to the Eleventh Naval History Symposium." 1993: Richard Von Doenhoff. (U&S.)

103   *make the transit from Pearl to Tinian at twenty-four knots*: Lech, Raymond B. *All the Drowned Sailors*. New York: Stein and Day, 1982, 6.

104   *arrived off Saipan with Spruance on her bridge*: QUIET, 304. In a controversial decision, Spruance chose to remain off Saipan in order to guard against a Japanese flanking attack, rather than pursue the Japanese carrier fleet, which had been spotted within range of Admiral Marc Mitscher's air forces. Spruance's contemporaries, including Mitscher, lamented an opportunity lost to deal a potentially game-changing blow to the Japanese carrier fleet. Though Japanese aviation losses in the battle rendered enemy carriers all but impotent, Spruance later regretted his decision, which, ironically altered U.S. doctrine with respect to Japanese threats against American amphibious operations. According to Spruance biographer Thomas Buell (*The Quiet Warrior*), Japanese commanders later correctly surmised that American commanders would aggressively pursue the enemy fleet. Thus, during the Battle of Leyte Gulf, Admiral William "Bull"

Halsey charged off after a decoy carrier, allowing the Japanese to flank him—the exact scenario Spruance had been trying to avoid at Saipan.

104 *Since he was posing as a gunnery officer*: Interview with Robert Furman by author Richard Newcomb, Hotel-Stacy Trent, May 17, 1957.

105 *his habit of highlighting privileges*: 317, 38–59.

105 *"About this big"*: LEGACY: Donald Blum interviews.

105 *McCall had spent the last three years*: LEGACY: Don McCall interviews. Also: telephone interview, February 18, 2017, and 317, 294–97.

Chapter 6

106 Underhill *picked up a bogie*: The account of the sinking of USS *Underhill* is based on: Crum, Jay. "Brief History of the USS *Underhill*." About USS *Underhill*. Accessed October 5, 2016. http://www.ussunderhill.org/html/about_uss_underhill.html. Also: Dace, Stanley W., Chief Boatswain's Mate. "Brief History of the USS *Underhill* DE-682." About USS *Underhill*. http://www.ussunderhill.org/html/about_the_uss _underhill.html. (UNDERHILL.)

106 *delivered more than 550 destroyer escorts*: "Destroyer Escorts." Destroyer History Foundation. Accessed October 19, 2016. http://destroyerhistory.org/de/.

107 *In ULTRA traffic, the sinking of* Underhill: ULTRA 2. CONEY, 2. Smedburg testimony.

108 *TCKs all worked perfectly.* CONEY, 366–67. Hart testimony.

108 *one-man dental assembly line*: Henry, Earl O., Sr., letters to his wife, Jane Henry, May 22, 1944–July 27, 1945.

108 *McVay kept himself occupied*: 317, 394.

108 *lost two friends in the consuming blaze*: 317. Paroubek, 395.

Chapter 7

109 *leeward edge called Tinian Town Bay*: Podoll, Ensign Erling. "LCTs 354 & 991 at Tinian." (PODOLL.)

109 *Paroubek, stood at the rail*: 317. Paroubek, 395.

109 *pier beyond rippled with military police*: PODOLL.

109 *"You men follow me"*: 317. Paroubek, 395.

110 *"That looks like it has to do with radiation"*: Ibid.

110 *"Potsdam Declaration," dictating terms*: "Potsdam Declaration: Proclamation Defining Terms for Japanese Surrender Issued, at Potsdam, July 26, 1945." National Science Digital Library. Accessed at http://nsdl.oercommons.org/courses/hiroshima -remembered-com-documents-about-the-bombing-of-hiroshima-and-nagasaki /view, July 27, 2017.

110 *catastrophically misread by Japan*: LONGEST, 9.

110 *the moment he saw the canisters*: The account of Woolston's epiphany at Tinian regarding the nature of Furman's cargo is based on LEGACY: John Woolston interviews, and subsequent telephone, email, and personal interviews conducted by the authors.

111 *"Look at all that brass"*: The account of Umenhoffer at Tinian is based on LEGACY interviews, and additional telephone and personal interviews conducted by Sara Vladic.

111 *assembled aboard* Indianapolis *to talk strategy*: QUIET, 320.

111 *climbed down a rope ladder*: Furman FOI.

Chapter 8

112 *the perfect South Pacific moorage*: Description of Apra Harbor courtesy of Captain William Toti, USN (ret.).

112 *At Tinian, McVay had received orders*: From Port Director, Guam, to Commanding Officer, USS *Indianapolis* (CA 35). Routing Instructions. 28 July 1945. Lech, Raymond B. *All the Drowned Sailors.* New York: Stein and Day, 1982, 8. (ADS.)

113 *Copies of the CincPac message*: Ibid.

113 *McCormick's radiomen made a decryption error*: McCormick, Rear Admiral L. D. to Commander in Chief, U.S. Pacific Fleet. Subject: Court of Inquiry regarding loss of USS *Indianapolis* (CA 35). 1. Indiana Historical Society.

113 *planned to call on a classmate of his*: Charles B. McVay III, handwritten draft of speech for the Indianapolis survivors' first reunion. July 30, 1960. 2. Courtesy of Captain Bill Toti, USN (Ret.) via Kimo McVay. (REUNION.)

113 *to be nearer the fighting*: QUIET, 394.

113 *Japanese soldiers stormed Guam's crystalline beaches*: "Battle for Guam. The Pacific: Lost Evidence," http://jifeed.net/trends/watch/vid88VNJA9pT_e3M.

116 *"Things are very quiet"*: REUNION, 2.

116 *went to have lunch with Spruance*: Ibid.

116 *working on the invasion plans for Kyushu*: REUNION, 3.

117 *McVay went to the routing office*: Exchange between McVay and routing office personnel is taken from: REUNION, 3. CONEY. McVay testimony, 298–303.

118 *prefer to travel in company with another ship*: CONEY, 331. McVay testimony.

118 *was told that no escort was necessary*: CONEY, 510. Waldron testimony.

118 *"At least we went through the motions"*: CONEY. Waldron testimony, 521.

Chapter 9

118 *the Empire would "mokusatsu" the declaration*: LONGEST, 14–17.

119 *arrived on the Okinawa-Saipan route*: SUNK, 216.

119 *slipped into the boat's Shinto shrine to pray*: Ibid.

119 *Janney, called at the routing office*: CONEY. Waldron testimony, 513.

120 *Commanding officers are at all times responsible*: Routing Instructions. 28 July 1945. Enclosure B-6.

120 *Janney reviewed the contacts with Waldron*: Ibid. Enclosure A. Also: CONEY. Waldron testimony, 513.

120 *"Here we go again"*: CONEY. McVay testimony, 300.

120 *McVay had reason to believe him*: Ibid., 305.

121 *buttressed what Carter had told him*: CONEY. McVay testimony, 299.

121 *the Chop line was the 130-degree east*: CONEY, 564. Murray testimony.

121 *aircraft popped up on radar and forced him to dive*: SUNK, 216.

122 *the vegetables had run out*: SUNK, 217.

122 *positioning itself on a vector line of 160*: ULTRA 2. Submarine intercept dated 15 July 1945.

122 *he found it painful*: SUNK, 182.

122 *more submarines had been lost*: Records of the 7th Fleet, Anti-submarine Warfare Reports. Record Group 38, Box 198, National Archives, College Park, Maryland. (7th FLEET.)

122 *many of his submarine school classmates*: SUNK, 145.

122 *perhaps a stronger tie to the faith*: Atsuko Iida, granddaughter of Mochitsura Hashimoto. Email and on-camera interviews conducted by Sara Vladic, 2014–16.

122 *in Hashimoto's family for centuries*: Ibid.

123 *confused about why Captain McVay would be reporting*: CONEY, 535. McCormick testimony.

123 *had performed strenuous duty in Okinawa*: Ibid.

123 *included several "information" addressees*: USS *Indianapolis* Departure Message Date-Time Group 280032 Port Director Guam to SCOMA, PD Tacloban, CTG 95.7; COM 5th Fleet, COMMARIANAS, CTF 95, CINCPAC BOTH HQ, COMWESCAROLINES.

123 *entered the ship's movement data in a memo record*: CONEY, 551. Gillette testimony.

123 *entered* Indianapolis's *departure on their plotting board*: CONEY, 491. Naquin testimony.

123 *responsibility for her progress passed to Captain Oliver Naquin*: CONEY, 506. Naquin testimony.

124 *had seen more action than most*: "Remembering the USS *Squalus* 75 Years Later." Naval History Blog. May 22, 2014.

124 *navigator on the heavy cruiser USS* New Orleans: Ibid.

124 *Face-to-face with the elusive enemy*: Account of I-58 firing *kaiten* on a three-masted ship is based on SUNK, 217.

Chapter 10

125 *Jordan Sheperd peered off the starboard beam*: Deck Logs, USS *Albert T. Harris*, 24 July–29 July 1945. National Archives, College Park, Maryland. (HARRIS DECK.)

125 *She was the merchant ship SS* Wild Hunter: Ibid.

125 *This sighting, however, was very much real*: Report of Voyage, SS *Wild Hunter*, Long Beach, California, to Manila, Philippines. Report submitted 31 July 1945 by Lieutenant Bruce K. Maxwell, Commanding Officer. National Archives. College Park, Maryland. (WILD HUNTER.)

125 *sighted a periscope*: Ibid.

126 Wild Hunter *transmitted two messages, six minutes apart*: Ibid.

126 *Granum's office then dispatched* Harris: Memorandum: From Officer in Charge to Commander Marianas. Subject: Radio Transmissions 28 and 29 July 1945 Concerning Enemy Submarines. 28 November 1945. Indiana Historical Society. USS Indianapolis Collection. (RADIO.)

126 *sweeping searchlight sonar across suspect bearings*: Action Report, USS *Albert T. Harris*, 30 July 1945, Record Group 38, Box 800, National Archives, College Park, Maryland. (HARRIS ACTION.)

126 *earning the weapon a nickname, "the hedgehog"*: Destroyer Escort Sailors Association. "Hedgehog." Destroyer Escort Historical Museum. January 24, 2016. Accessed December 1, 2017.

126 *Sonarman Second Class Lefebvre*: HARRIS ACTION. Attack No. 1.

126 *"Bearing width 10° indicated midget submarine"*: HARRIS ACTION. The identity of this submarine is unknown. An examination of records of *kaiten*-carrying IJN subs shows that I-58 was the only such vessel in the southern Philippine Sea on 28 July 1945. According to ULTRA intercepts, I-58 was assigned to patrol the area five hundred miles north of an unrecovered grid. ULTRA analysts speculated that

the area was "[Palau?]," which is borne out by I-58's presence there, both in Hashimoto's own account and in the sinking of *Indianapolis*. However, Hashimoto did not report being repeatedly attacked by a destroyer escort. In addition, according to Hashimoto's court-martial testimony, once he intercepted Route Peddie, he traveled west, never east, which he would have had to do in order to intercept *Indianapolis*. Another Tamon group sub, I-53, which sank *Underhill* on July 24, 1945, *did* report being repeatedly attacked by a destroyer escort firing hedgehogs. The only known record of that attack is on 30 July, however, and the authors were unable to obtain primary sources to confirm the date and I-53's location. Whatever the identity of *Harris*'s target, it was a confirmed submarine in the path of *Indianapolis*, and was attacked by *Harris* and *Greene* a total of seventeen times. In later analysis of *Harris*'s action, Philippine Sea Frontier Commander Vice Admiral James Kauffman, a submarine expert, would say that *Harris* should have dropped depth charges as soon as the target's ten-degree bearing width indicated it was a midget sub.

126   *Dr. Earl Henry decided to split his time*: Henry, Earl O., Sr., letters to his wife, Jane Henry, May 22, 1944–July 27, 1945.

127   *Finally! In two gorgeous photographs*: Ibid.

127   *"All prematures look like the wrath of God"*: Ibid.

127   *the Allies could concentrate on pounding Japan alone*: Ibid.

128   *fired the hedgehog, a twenty-four-missile salvo*: HARRIS DECK, Attack No. 2.

128   *McNulty thought they'd hit the sub*: Ibid.

128   *Each time the hedgehog fired*: Ibid.

128   *King knew he had a sub*: War Diary, Philippine Sea Frontier, July 1–31, 1945, National Archives, accessed online at Fold3.com, July 15, 2016.

129   *backed down his posture*: HARRIS DECK.

Chapter 11

129   *"HARRIS DE FOURFOURSEVEN INVESTIGATING"*: RADIO.

129   *concerned Granum's boss, Commodore Gillette, greatly*: CONEY. Gillette testimony, 552. According to Gillette, the *Wild Hunter* hunter-killer operation led by USS *Harris* was under the immediate direction of Captain Granum.

129   *Wild Hunter in the wee hours of July 29*: RADIO.

130   *"guarding the FOX" was a twenty-four-hour*: "Radio Room." Destroyer Escort Historical Museum. USS *Slater* DE 766. Accessed July 3, 2016.

130   *FOX broadcasts were receive-only and uninterruptible*: Ibid.

130   *Lieutenant Carl Rau relieved Sheperd as officer of the deck*: HARRIS DECK.

130   *Then, at 8:26 p.m.: "Screw beats!"*: HARRIS DECK.

131   *McNulty logged the type of sonar echo: Submarine*: HARRIS ACTION, Attack No. 7.

131   *the ship passed directly over the submarine*: Ibid.

131   *At 9:50 p.m., the hedgehog crew fired a full salvo*: Ibid.

131   *King ordered the gun crew to troubleshoot the weapon*: HARRIS DECK.

Chapter 12

132   *Sam Lopez began the day*: LEGACY: Sam Lopez interviews.

132   *"highly probable," and noted that* Harris *had attacked*: War Diary, Philippine Sea Frontier, July 1–31, 1945, National Archives, accessed online at Fold3.com, July 15, 2016.

132 *dispatching the destroyer transport USS* Greene: Deck Logs, USS *Greene*, 27 July–30 July 1945. National Archives, College Park, Maryland. (GREENE LOG.)

132 *commenced a depth-charge run on various headings*: GREENE LOG.

133 Harris's *crew watched as water plumes*: HARRIS DECK.

133 *Commander Marianas and CincPac Advance received traffic*: RADIO.

133 *his staff at Guam took no action except to move Indy westward*: CONEY. Naquin testimony, 491, 493.

133 *struggling to acquire grid positions*: ULTRA 2. Card dated 29 July 1945: "All positions are unrecovered. We are trying to do something with them."

133 *all Japanese sub operations had localized in home waters*: 7th FLEET.

134 *Japan had added two subs, I-363 and I-366*: ULTRA 2. Card dated 29 July 1945.

134 *That would put him at the dead center of Route Peddie*: SUNK, 218.

134 *the chunky silhouette of a friendly ship*: Hulver, Richard, Ph.D. "Final Contact: USS *Indianapolis* (CA-35) Passes USS *LST-779*, 29 July 1945." Naval History and Heritage Command.

134 *She was the first LST to reach Iwo Jima*: Ibid.

135 *Dinner was steak and strawberries*: FATAL, 52.

135 *The commander usually ate dessert first*: Interview with Paul Everts, grandson of Commander Joseph Flynn and Flynn's wife, Anna. Interviewed by Lynn Vincent, Spring 2017.

135 *"A Jap sub has been spotted along our route"*: CONEY, 306 (McVay). BUMED, 20. Dr. Haynes testified and later wrote that Commander Janney learned of the submarine threat area via the TBS, Talk Between Ships. That may be true. However, it is more likely that he learned of it via the communications office. A message had already made its way to the message board on the bridge, and all such messages were routed through Janney, who would then plot the coordinates of any threat on a chart so that duty officers and the skipper could determine appropriate action.

135 *made his way toward the bridge*: CONEY. McVay testimony. See also, "Record of Proceedings of a General Court-Martial Convened at The Navy Yard, Washington, D. C., By Order of the Secretary of the Navy." 21 December 1945. National Archives, College Park, Maryland. 34. (COURT-MARTIAL.)

135 *careful not to cut any corners*: COURT-MARTIAL. McKissick testimony, 38.

135 *His eye fell on the dispatch Janney had spoken of*: COURT-MARTIAL, 34.

135 *Over the past dozen hours, an equal number of messages*: RADIO.

136 *one or more of the FOX schedules*: Ibid.

136 *the closest it would come to* Indianapolis: COURT-MARTIAL. McKissick testimony, 37.

136 *he could secure from zigzagging*: CONEY, 167. McKissick testimony.

137 *the helmsman began steering a straight course*: COURT-MARTIAL. Ibid. In his court-martial testimony, McKissick could not recall whether he or the oncoming OOD, Commander Lipski, ordered a return to base course. Lipski did not survive.

137 *left orders to be roused at 10:30 p.m.*: SUNK, 218.

137 *A perfect plague, Hashimoto thought*: SUNK, 219.

137 *any man who caught and killed one*: Yamada, Goro. "Sinking the *Indianapolis*: A Japanese Perspective." Interview of Mr. Yamada by historian Dan King. July 30, 1994.

Chapter 13

138   *"Got a submarine report"*: CONEY. Sturtevant testimony, 461.

138   *He clamped on the headphones*: CONEY, 466. Sturtevant testimony.

138   *considered the shacks greatly improved*: CONEY, 461. Sturtevant testimony.

139   *Driscoll seemed bland about the message*: Ibid.

139   *a naval attaché in Helsinki before the war*: Nathan Gorenstien, "Naval Ceremony recalls sad loss for local family." Print. Undated. Publication name obscured.

139   *Janney . . . appeared briefly on the bridge*: COURT-MARTIAL, 48.

140   *Harpo Celaya curled around a woolen blanket*: Account of Celaya and Thorpe on deck before the torpedo strike is based on: LEGACY: Celaya interviews; HARPO, 36; and CELAYA Interview, Florence, Arizona, August 2015.

141   *McVay reviewed the plot and night orders with Janney*: COURT-MARTIAL, 311.

141   *"I want to have a little bit of gravy up my sleeve"*: CONEY, 325. McVay testimony.

141   *Allard couldn't tell his strikers apart*: COURT-MARTIAL. Allard testimony, 190.

141   *Lookout stations were fully manned*: Testimony of Charles McVay, COI, 6.

142   *Having given his stateroom to Captain Edwin Crouch*: MCVAY NARRATIVE, 3.

143   *roused Hashimoto at 10:30 p.m.*: SUNK, 219.

143   *Hashimoto decided to surface and look for enemy ships*: Ibid.

144   *"Bearing red nine-zero degrees, a possible enemy ship"*: SUNK, 220.

144   *"All tubes to the ready"*: Ibid.

Chapter 14

145   *Edgar Harrell got off watch a little before midnight*: DEPTHS, 65.

145   *Santos Pena stretched out on top of a ready-box*: LEGACY: Santos Pena interviews.

145   *Hashimoto still could not determine her class*: SUNK, 221–22.

146   *"Why can't we be launched?"*: SUNK, 223.

147   *an exhilarating thought formed in his mind: We've got her*: SUNK, 222.

147   *Woolston had the 8 p.m. to midnight watch*: Account of Woolston's postwatch activities is based on LEGACY: Woolston interviews as well as telephone, personal, and email interviews conducted between 2012 and 2017.

147   *sonarman thought he heard the clinking of dishes*: YAMADA.

148   *At two-second intervals, six torpedoes ejected*: SUNK, 224.

Chapter 15

148   *violent explosion ejected McVay*: MCVAY NARRATIVE.

149   *first explosion knocked Pena*: "Record of Proceedings of a Court of Inquiry Convened at Headquarters, Commander Marianas, Guam, by Order of Commander in Chief, United States Pacific Fleet and Pacific Ocean Areas," August 13, 1945. Holdings of Naval History and Heritage Command, obtained by the authors on October 24, 2017. (COI.)

149   *it looked to him as if* Indianapolis's *entire bow was gone*: In the decades after the sinking, witness testimony would vary on whether the bow had been blown off, and if so, at what point on the ship. Santos Pena was the eyewitness closest to the bow. His testimony in the Guam Court of Inquiry in August 1945 was corroborated by the discovery of Indy's wreckage on August 19, 2017. However, Troy Nunley's later rec-

ollection that the bow was still hanging by thin threads of steel would also match the discovery. Hashimoto's first torpedo sheered away the bow at the frame 12 watertight partition, but the wreckage showed that it likely hung on to the ship underwater for some unknown length of time. The frames were about four feet apart. The very end of the ship extended to the bowsprit another sixteen to eighteen feet past the waterline. Therefore, the length of bow lost was about sixty-six feet from the bowsprit aft to frame 12 at the top deck, and about forty-eight feet from the waterline and below, aft to frame 12.

149 *Glenn Morgan felt the deck*: Morgan, Glenn Grover. "Torpedoed" Memoir. 1993. 43 pages. Handwritten by G. Morgan. (TORPEDOED.)

150 *Hershberger woke up in midair*: Hershberger, Clarence L. "The USS *Indianapolis* Tragedy" Memoir. 1994. Self-published.

150 *staggered into the smoke-clogged passageway*: "Oral History with Capt. (ret.) Lewis Haynes, MD, USN," U.S. Navy Medical Department Oral History Program, June 5, 12, 22, 1995. (BUMED.)

150 *Whirling caterpillars of flame*: Interview with John Woolston, Legacy on-camera interview. (LEGACY.) Survivor interviews conducted by Sara Vladic, 2005–16.

150 *scene of destruction unfolding quickly before him*: SUNK, 224.

151 *LeFrancis gazed down from the cockpit*: "Witness to the sinking of USS *Indianapolis*," Pappy Boyington Veterans Museum, August 6, 2016. YouTube.com: https://www .youtube.com/watch?v=GKqJdONo9Jc.

152 *Ripped away between frames 12 and 13*: Assisted by mechanical engineer Benjamin Huntley, the authors examined stills and video footage of the wreck of *Indianapolis*, discovered by RV *Petrel* on August 19, 2017, and compared them with a blueprint of the ship.

Chapter 16

152 *"Do you have any reports?"*: MCVAY NARRATIVE, 2.

153 *Witzig saw all hell breaking loose*: Narrative of Robert Witzig, 317, 495–98. Interview with Robert Witzig, LEGACY.

153 *he saw burned men*: DEPTHS, 82.

153 *"Get the commander a life jacket"*: Ibid. 74.

154 *McGinnis heard the keening*: Narrative of Paul McGinnis, 317, 305.

154 *profound hush that followed*: Authors' interviews, 2005–17, with multiple survivors.

154 *Cox jumped to comply*: Interview with L. D. Cox, LEGACY. Narrative of L. D. Cox, 317, 113.

155 *"Do you wish to abandon ship?"*: Testimony of Charles McVay, COI, 3–4.

155 *imprisoning the men in absolute darkness*: The account of events in the engine rooms are based on the testimony of survivors William Nightingale, COI, 31–35, and Norman Roberts. (Narrative of Norman Roberts, 317, 429–34.)

156 *Miner burst through the light-lock*: Narrative of Jack Miner, 317, 333. COI. 19. Investigation of Sinking of USS *Indianapolis*. By order of the Chief of Naval Operations, 6 December 1945, 274. (CONEY.)

156 *"We're in bad shape"*: Testimony of Fred Hart, CONEY, 363.

Chapter 17

157 *Radio 1 was wrecked*: The account of Radio 1 is based on the following sources: Testimony of J. J. Moran, COI, 24; Testimony of Loren McHenry, COI, 29; Testimony of Elwyn Sturtevant, COI, 29–30. CONEY, 461–72; Miner, COI, 19–20.

158 *find a wrench and open the ports*: John Woolston, AUTHORS, 2017.

159 *badly injured Marines were stumbling*: Nightingale testimony, COI, 33–51; Roberts, 317, 429–34.

160 *throttleman yelled down the ladder well*: Nightingale testimony, COI, 33–51.

160 *they had waited too long*: Roberts, ONLY 317, 429–34.

160 *"We need kapoks," Morgan said*: TORPEDOED.

161 *suicide pilots were pleading*: SUNK, 224.

Chapter 18

161 *They crowded behind the ladder*: Roberts, 317, 429–34.

162 *Kirkland turned to look*: Helm, Thomas. *Ordeal by Sea: The Tragedy of the U.S.S. Indianapolis*. New York: Dodd, Mead, 1963, 62–63.

162 *"You better go, kid!"*: Narrative of Harold Bray, 317, 69–72.

163 *He shoved a life jacket*: Narrative of Paul Murphy, 317, 360–63.

163 *"They're crazy!"*: LEGACY Interview with Sam Lopez.

163 *let the jackets propel them up*: Roberts, 317, 429–34.

164 *Redmayne, the engineering officer*: Testimony of Richard Redmayne, COI, 57–60.

164 *Janney then appeared on the bridge*: MCVAY NARRATIVE, 3.

164 *Flynn arrived on the bridge*: Testimony of C. McVay, COI, 4.

164 *"Pass the word to abandon ship"*: MCVAY NARRATIVE, 2.

165 *"XRAY VICTOR MIKE LOVE"*: Testimony of J. J. Moran, COI, 24–26.

166 *Hart clambered over a gun mount*: Testimony of Fred Hart, CONEY, 363.

Chapter 19

166 *Cox didn't want to go down with him*: Narrative of L. D. Cox, 317, 113.

166 *"I'm going down to Radio 1"*: Testimony of McVay, CONEY, 320.

167 *Redmayne made a decision*: Testimony of Richard Redmayne, COI, 58.

167 *remain in the after-engine room*: Ibid.

167 *Miner saw the needle*: Narrative of Jack Miner, 317, 333.

168 *"Don't do it! Don't jump!"*: LEGACY interview with George Horvath.

169 *McVay put his foot on the first ladder rung*: MCVAY NARRATIVE, 3.

169 *Morgan marveled at the young lieutenant's*: TORPEDOED.

170 *Woolston and the steward splashed*: Narrative of John Woolston, 317, 500.

Chapter 20

171 *he remembered Jeremiah*: Narrative of Edgar Harrell, 317, 190.

171 *Driscoll shouted, "Clear out!"*: Testimony of J. J. Moran, CONEY, 486.

172 *"I'll see you later, sir!"*: Glenn Morgan's account of abandoning ship is based on his short memoir, TORPEDOED.

172 *a great pressure released*: Ibid.

173 *to the sailors in Radio 2, "abandon ship"*: Narrative of Jack Miner, 317, 333.

173 *"Where the hell do you think"*: HARPO. 37. Narrative of Santos Pena, 317, 403.

174 *row of welder's oxygen cylinders*: Testimony of Richard Redmayne, COI, 58.

175 *McVay leapt to the fo'c'sle deck*: MCVAY NARRATIVE, 3–4.

BOOK 3: THE DEEP

183 Because the narrative of the men's experiences in the water prior to rescue are anec-
dotal in nature and based on their first-person accounts, we have elected to group the
sourcing information below rather than lengthen these notes exponentially by citing
the same sources each time we returned to an individual or group. The accounts of
the various survivor groups in the water, as well as the water accounts of individual
survivors and Indy crew members lost at sea, are based on the following sources (see
Bibliography for full citations).

Interviews

• "Legacy On-Camera Interviews with Survivors, Survivors Families, and Families of
  Men Lost at Sea," 2005–2016, conducted by Sara Vladic. (LEGACY.) Includes inter-
  views with 108 survivors of the sinking of USS *Indianapolis* conducted over more
  than a decade. Total of 170 hours of footage. (See Bibliography for a list of all indi-
  viduals interviewed.)
• Adolfo Celaya. Interviewed by Lynn Vincent in Florence, Arizona. August 2015.
• Viola Outland, wife of survivor Felton Outland; Felton Outland, Jr., and Theresa
  Outland, survivor Outland's son and daughter. Interviewed by Lynn Vincent on 24
  January 2016.
• Cleatus Lebow, *Indianapolis* survivor. Telephone interview by Lynn Vincent, Octo-
  ber 2017.
• Don McCall, *Indianapolis* survivor. Telephone interview by Lynn Vincent, February
  2017.

Memoirs and Private Papers

• Murphy, Mary Lou, and USS *Indianapolis* Survivors. *Only 317 Survived!: USS Indianapolis (CA-35): Navy's Worst Tragedy at Sea—880 Men Died.* Indianapolis, IN: USS
  Indianapolis Survivors Organization, 2002. (317)
• Hershberger, Clarence L. *Tragedy: As Seen by One Survivor.* De Leon Springs, FL: self-
  published, 1994.
• Private Papers of and interviews with Morgan, Bugler Glenn, USS *Indianapolis* survi-
  vor. "Glenn Morgan's Story of the Suicide Plane Attack." "Glenn Morgan 2006 Inter-
  view." "Glenn G. Morgan—Legacy Interview." Interview by author. February 20, 2011.
  On camera. "Glenn Morgan Diaries." January 1–April 25, 1945. "My Story." Memoir. 28
  September. 2011. "Story of Suicide Plane Attack" Memoir. 28 September. 2011 "Torpe-
  doed" Memoir. 1993. Forty-three pages. Handwritten by G. Morgan. "A WWII Bugler
  Tells His Story." Memoir. 28 September. 2011. (GM—BUGLER)
• Clemans, Charles. *Harpo: War Survivor, Basketball Wizard.* Tucson, AZ: Wheatmark,
  2009.
• Harrell, Edgar, and David Harrell. *Out of the Depths: An Unforgettable WWII Story*

of Survival, Courage, and the Sinking of the USS Indianapolis. 2nd ed. n.p.: Bethany House, 2014. Print.

- USS *Indianapolis* crew members and Philip A. St. John, PhD. *USS Indianapolis, CA-35.* Paducah, KY: Turner Publishing Company, 1997. (WHITE BOOK)
- USS *Indianapolis* families. *Lost at Sea but Not Forgotten.* Indianapolis, IN: Printing Partners, 2008. (LAS)
- Twible, Harlan Malcolm. *The Life and Times of an Immigrant's Son.* Sarasota, FL: self-published, 1997.
- MacGregor, Jill Noblit. *Unsinkable: The Inspiring True Story of USS Indianapolis Survivor: ROBERT P. GAUSE, QM1.* Ed. Julie Gabell. 1st ed. self-published, 2014.

Naval Records

- "An Account of Survivors Following the Sinking of the USS *Indianapolis* with Recommended Changes in Lifesaving Equipment." Haynes, Commander Lewis L., to Naval Inspector General via Captain C. E. Coney. 26 November 1945. Indiana Historical Society. USS *Indianapolis* collection.
- "The Sinking of USS *Indianapolis*: Recollections of Captain Charles B. McVay III." World War II Interviews, Operational Archives Branch, Naval Historical Center.
- Address by R. Adrian Marks (Navy pilot who landed his PBY "Dumbo" in the Philippine Sea and rescued fifty-three *Indianapolis* survivors.) Presented at the first USS *Indianapolis* Survivors Memorial Reunion, Severin Hotel, Indianapolis, Indiana, 30 July 1960.
- Address by Adrian Marks, "I've Seen Greatness," July 1985. Abridged transcript of speech delivered at the fortieth anniversary of the *Indianapolis* sinking and rescue.
- "Oral History with Capt. (ret.) Lewis Haynes, MD, USN," U.S. Navy Medical Department Oral History Program, June 5, 12, 22, 1995.

Additional Notes for Book 3

The following notes refer to scenes that did not take place among the men in the water prior to rescue. See above for sourcing of events in the water prior to rescue.

Chapter 1

188   *attack any enemy survivors*: Address by Atsuko Iida, Commander Hashimoto's granddaughter, at the USS *Indianapolis* Survivors Reunion, 2014.

188   *A ship so badly wounded*: SUNK, 225.

Chapter 2

195   *Any more would push the raft deeper*: The rafts aboard Indy were designed for 40 pounds of buoyancy for each person, meaning that a 10-person raft has 400 pounds of buoyancy, or enough to keep 2 to 3 men fully out of the water. If 10 men were in a 10-person raft, then on average, only 40 pounds of each man would be out of the water, and each man submerged to his chest. Maybe one or two men could be sitting up on the sides, but it would make everyone else float lower. Indy had a number of 10- and 25-person rafts, according to the plans from her final refit. Source: http://www.usmm.org/lifeboat.html. See section 153.4a (dates of Indy plans 4/17/45).

196 *Something about the naval battle*: According to Richard LeFrancis's personal account, two days after it was announced that the *Indianapolis* had been sunk in the area where he reported a possible naval battle, he notified the base intelligence officer of the incident, and was told to forget it, that it was a Navy problem. Not satisfied, LeFrancis writes that he called the FBI in San Francisco, and an agent was sent to his barracks. According to LeFrancis, nothing came of either report. *Witness to the Sinking of* USS Indianapolis. Richard LeFrancis, Jr., director of the Pappy Boyington Veterans Museum and son of Army Captain Richard LeFrancis. Video. Accessed online 10 September 2017 on YouTube.

Chapter 3

200 *Tinian agreed with Major Robert Furman*: "Tinian, July 31." Furman's typewritten account of experiences on Tinian. (TINIAN.)

200 *search the faces of the assembled brass*: Interview with Robert Furman by author Richard Newcomb, Hotel Stacy-Trent, 17 May 1957.

200 *a maneuver Furman found tricky*: FOI, 15.

200 *Birch . . . signed for the canisters*: Ibid.

200 *fifty-one Los Alamos scientists*: Campbell, Richard H., and Paul W. Tibbets. *The Silverplate Bombers: A History and Registry of the* Enola Gay *and Other B-29s Configured to Carry Atomic Bombs*. Jefferson, NC: McFarland, 2012, 155.

201 *scientist received a letter from his father*: FURMAN ATOMIC, 20.

201 *Furman believed using it would save*: DRAFT, 8.

201 *between an ex-policeman and future tree surgeon*: Robert Furman Letter to Parents, dated simply "August," Papers of Robert F. Furman, Library of Congress. Print, 1. (FOLKS.)

203 *"Sinking confirmed. Obtained three torpedo hits"*: Message intercepted 30 July 1945, from Captain, I-58 to Navy Vice Minister and Headquarters Combined Naval Force and others. Print. (ULTRA 1.)

203 *magicians put the intercept into the mill*: Memorandum from Commodore T. E. Van Metre to Admiral Snyder, 2 November 1945. Subject: Progress Report of the INDIANAPOLIS Case, 2.

206 *Guam would simply wipe her off their map*: CONEY, Naquin testimony, 493.

Chapter 5

213 *a conviction that inspired confidence*: Heroic at sea, J. J. Moran would survive the *Indianapolis* disaster only to die less than a year later, on 4 July 1946, in an accident aboard USS *Albemarle*. "Record of Burial Place of Veteran. Joseph John Moran." Pennsylvania Department of Veterans Affairs. Accessed 19 January 2018 at Ancestry .com.

Chapter 6

219 *and if not for Eva*: RHODES, 699.

219 *ready for deployment the day before*: Ibid.

219 *the "Tinian Joint Chiefs"*: "Project Alberta." Atomic Heritage Foundation. Accessed 10 September 2017 at https://www.atomicheritage.org/history/project-alberta.

220 *For Parsons, it was personal*: Christman, Albert B. *Target Hiroshima: Deak Parsons and*

the Creation of the Atomic Bomb. Annapolis, MD: Naval Institute Press, 1998, 174. (TARGET.)

220 *dropped a dummy unit*: RHODES, 699.

220 *Farrell sent a message to Groves*: Ibid.

Chapter 7

223 *Eugene found it merely curious*: On 2 October 2008, aboard the nuclear-powered fleet ballistic missile submarine USS *Ohio*, Machinist Mate First Class (now Chief) Jason Witty stepped onto the deck, preparing himself for the solemn task he was about to perform. Sixty-three years earlier, Witty's grandfather, Eugene Morgan, survived the sinking of *Indianapolis* after having served aboard the ship for nearly four years, earning ten battle stars. With the permission of his commanding officer, Captain Dennis Carpenter, Witty spread his grandfather's ashes into the calm, blue waters of the Pacific—just above the last known coordinates of the *Indianapolis*—fulfilling his grandfather's final wish that he be returned to the waters of the Pacific and the lost shipmates he so dearly loved. Source: email correspondence and interviews with Jason Witty.

Chapter 9

233 *he made a pact with those around him*: Sometimes in real life, heroes and villains wear the same uniform. The burden of the pact plagued these men their entire lives. These sailors shared the horrors they faced in interviews with Sara Vladic and just one other person, imploring them to keep the details to themselves forever. As the survivors aged, the final living members of this group gave their blessing to share what really happened so that it would not be forgotten, but by doing so, saddled two more lives with the burden of carrying the torch. Sara, and the other individual entrusted with this information, determined it was time to share what happened. However, before including this account the authors first verified that all the facts lined up with the sworn testimonies given immediately after the rescue. It is important to help people understand the burden these men shouldered, to convey the tragic heroism it took to carry out these tasks, and the fortitude it took to live with the aftermath. Humanity is revealed at its most primal level when one is forced into an unimaginable situation and made to fight for life. It brings out the very best, or the very worst, in anyone. Out of respect for living descendants, the names of the sailors and the other individual entrusted with the account are withheld.

234 *first noticed Indy's absence*: COI, Gibson testimony, 14.

234 *"frequently becomes bewildered and 'rattle brained' "*: "Report on the Fitness of Officers," Gibson, Stuart Baurland, period from 5 May 1944 to 1 January 1945. Signed by Forrest Tucker, Commander, USNR.

234 *he wrote a rebuttal*: Memorandum from Lieutenant Stuart B. Gibson to BUPERS (Bureau of Naval Personnel), 23 May 1945. Subject: Report on fitness this officer.

234 *he supposed that meant nonarrivals, too*: COI, Gibson testimony, 14.

Chapters 11 and 12

240 *commencing their regular sector search*: "Sighting of Survivors of USS *Indianapolis*; Participation in Air-Sea Rescue and Subsequent Search for Bodies and Debris 2–7 August 1945." Record Group 125, Box 35. National Archives, College Park, Mary-

land. (VPB-152) Also: Transcript of press interviews with the rescue pilots, Lieutenant Junior Grade Wilbur "Chuck" Gwinn, Lieutenant Adrian Marks, and Lieutenant Commander George Atteberry, conducted 6 August 1945 at Peleliu. Record Group 125, Box 35. National Archives, College Park, Maryland, 1. (PRESS.)

240 *cruising at three thousand feet*: PRESS, 1.

240 *reeled out the antenna wire again*: We Were There: The USS Indianapolis *Tragedy, The Rest of the Story as Told by the Men Who Aided the Crew in This Tragedy.* This book is a collection of first-person accounts and official reports from personnel and units involved in the rescue of *Indianapolis* survivors. Compiled by L. Peter Wren, a rescue boat officer at the scene. Richmond, VA: Wren Enterprizes, 2002. Print, 14. (WREN)

241 *"Johnson, Hickman, reel that thing in"*: Letter from Herb Hickman to Peter Wren, 26. (WREN.)

241 *"Look down and you'll see!"*: Ibid., 27.

242 Take the bait, *was all he could think*: Woolston, LEGACY interview.

242 *It took about twenty seconds*: WREN, 27.

242 *"Open the bomb bay doors"*: FATAL, 151.

242 *skimmed the ocean at nine hundred feet*: VPB-152. 1. Also: PRESS, 1.

243 *He thought of the men he knew*: Personal Narrative by Captain Charles B. McVay III, USN, Sinking of USS *Indianapolis*, recorded 27 September 1945. Command File World War II. Indiana Historical Society. In this narrative, recorded on audio after McVay returned to Washington, D.C., he tells the story of his personal experience from the time just before the sinking through rescue. 17. (MCVAY NARRATIVE)

243 *a case of Lucky Strike cigarettes*: 317, Havins narrative, 204.

243 *Morgan felt sorry for him*: TORPEDOED, 34–35.

244 *"Do you see it?"*: TORPEDOED, 36. Also: LEGACY interview.

245 *bumps on a cucumber*: FATAL, 151.

245 *"Secure from bomb run"*: Ibid.

245 *He checked the time—11:18 a.m.*: PRESS, 1.

245 *men waving, splashing, slapping the water*: Ibid., 2.

245 *THIRTY SURVIVORS SIGHTED. SEND ASSISTANCE*: Ibid., 2. Also: VPB-152, 1.

248 *flew straight toward the flotilla*: Morgan account, 317, 351. Also: TORPEDOED, 31–32. LEGACY interview, 23–24.

248 *a large yellow-green blotch*: Account of air crewman Jim Graham, who was aboard Sam Worthington's Mariner. WREN, 22.

248 *Mariner zoomed over a group*: Ibid.

248 *spotted Gwinn's Ventura*: "Bomber Recalls WWII Rescue." *Wayne Independent*, 25 August 2010. In 2008, according to this article, the telephone rang at the home of Gerard Fitzpatrick, another rescuer aboard Worthington's Mariner. The caller identified himself as Paul McGinnis. McGinnis was the Indy signalman who thought everything was going to be okay when one of his buddies started sweeping up spilled sugar after Hashimoto's torpedo strike. In 2008, McGinnis called Fitzpatrick and asked him whether he had been aboard one of the rescue planes that dropped casks of water near him on 2 August 1945. "Yes," Fitzpatrick replied. McGinnis had grabbed one of the casks and held on until *Doyle* picked him up, he told Fitzpatrick. The cask "saved my life," McGinnis said, "and I just wanted to say thank you."

249 *saw objects falling from Gwinn's Ventura*: Bray, LEGACY interview.

249 *to cry, to splash, to pray*: Harrell, LEGACY interview.

250 *to say a farewell benediction*: DEPTHS, 132.

Chapter 13

250 *Atteberry decoded it himself*: PRESS, 2.

250 *Marks would have to leave immediately*: Ibid., 3. Also: VPB-152, 1. And Memorandum for Air Operations Officer, Sub Area, Operations of VPB-23 on *Indianapolis* Rescue, 5 August–9 August 1945. Record Group 125, Box 35, National Archives, College Park, Maryland. (VPB-23.)

251 *The time was 12:42 p.m.*: The PRESS account says Atteberry departed at 12:42 p.m. The squadron record, "VPB-152," says he departed at 12:44 p.m.

251 *Probably one of the carrier boys*: Address by R. Adrian Marks (Navy pilot who landed his PBY "Dumbo" in the Philippine Sea and rescued fifty-three *Indianapolis* survivors). Presented at the first USS *Indianapolis* Survivors Memorial Reunion, Severin Hotel, Indianapolis, IN, 30 July 1960, 1. (MARKS 1960.)

251 *listening to Glenn Miller records*: FATAL, 154.

251 *he had graduated from Northwestern*: Goldstein, Richard. "Adrian Marks, 81, War Pilot Who Led Rescue of 56, Is Dead." *New York Times*, March 15, 1998. Accessed March 15, 2017.

252 *eighty miles north of Palau*: USS *Cecil J. Doyle* Memorandum Report on Rescue of Survivors of USS *Indianapolis* (CA-35) August 2–4, 1945. Record Group 125, Box 35. National Archives, College Park, Maryland. LCDR W. G. Claytor cited his position at the time he reversed course as 8°34'N 135°10'E, about eighty miles north of Palau. (CLAYTOR.)

252 *the ship hailed him on the radio*: AS, 143. Author Richard Newcomb interviewed Claytor.

252 *it could take hours for new routing orders*: Ibid.

252 *He'd worry about the paperwork later*: Claytor's "Memorandum Report" on the *Indianapolis* rescue records that *Doyle* reversed course at 14:18. The Duty Officer's log at Mark's squadron, VPB-23, shows that Claytor was already en route to the rescue site by the time shore radio at Peleliu dispatched him there at 13:55. The Peleliu dispatch occurred almost an hour before Commander Western Caroline Sub Area 020245Z secret dispatch ordering all ships in the area to join the air-sea rescue.

252 *this brave guy trying to swim for it*: WREN, 23.

253 *could he remove* Indianapolis *from the board?*: ADS, 142.

253 *a plainly worded query*: Ibid., 143.

253 *McCormick's reply was equally plain*: Ibid.

Chapter 14

254 *they received a second message*: PRESS, 3. Also: VPB-23, 1.

254 *"What can you do to give me more speed?"*: WREN, 80.

254 *Doyle was wetting down shafts*: Charles Doyle, LEGACY interview.

254 *radio contact with Atteberry at 2:35 p.m.*: CLAYTOR, 1.

255 *a lot of them scattered over a wide area*: PRESS, 1. VPB-152, 1.

255 *NEED ALL SURVIVAL EQUIPMENT WHILE DAYLIGHT HOLDS*: MARKS 1960, 2.

256 *He did not pass the message to Marks's skipper*: Ibid.

256   *the odds that these men would be spotted*: Address by Adrian Marks, "I've Seen Great-
        ness," July 1985. Abridged transcript of speech delivered at the fortieth anniversary
        of the *Indianapolis* sinking and rescue, 1. (GREATNESS.)

256   *a pilot could take in twenty square miles*: Ibid.

256   *Marks considered the odds*: Ibid., 2.

256   *James Bargsley . . . from the Philippine Sea Frontier*: WREN, 39.

256   *"All ahead, flank speed"*: Notes from Albert Lutz made within two days of *Bassett*'s
        participation in the rescue. (LUTZ NOTES.) WREN, 44.

256   *medical department came to full alert*: Ibid.

257   *At 4:05 p.m., the crew opened a hatch*: MARKS NARRATIVE, 1.

257   *Thelen heard Marks's plane*: Thelen's account of losing his friends is based on Thelen,
        LEGACY interview. Also: 317, 473.

258   *He let go of the floater net and swam away*: The account of Hershberger saving Lebow's
        life is based on Lebow and Hershberger LEGACY interviews. Also: Additional inter-
        views with Lebow by Lynn Vincent conducted in 2017.

Chapter 15

259   *Marks made a rebel decision*: PRESS, 4.

259   *little more than a controlled crash*: Second Emergency Rescue Squadron, unknown
        member. "Rescued from the Sea." PBY.org. Accessed March 28, 2017. http://www
        .pbyrescue.com/Stories/rescue%20story.pdf. This article was critical in helping
        describe the physics of Lieutenant Adrian Marks's landing of his PBY-5A Catalina
        flying boat, or "Dumbo," and rescuing fifty-three *Indianapolis* survivors.

259   *many survivors who wouldn't last*: PRESS, 4.

260   *what sort of fool stunt*: MARKS 1960, 3.

260   *He dared the ocean to defy him*: Interview by Sara Vladic with Lieutenant Adrian
        Marks's daughter, Alexes.

260   *executed a power stall into the wind*: PRESS, 4.

261   *rivets popping from her hull*: Ibid.

261   *Hensley worked with the plane captain*: Ibid.

261   *Lefkowitz went aft to organize*: Ibid.

261   *Hensley stood in the open hatch*: Letter from Marks's copilot, Lefkowitz. WREN, 20.
        Also: GREATNESS, 2–3.

261   *a seaman second who had been serving his time*: James Smith had served aboard Indy
        since December 1943—and not without picking up a few tricks along the way. Only
        twenty years old, he obtained a fake ID that said he was twenty-one. The world then his
        for the taking, Smith packed his civilian clothes in a paper bag, went ashore, and hopped
        on a bus to Oakland, where he got drunk, met a girl, and stayed the night. But he also
        failed to check in with the ship every four hours as required. Several days later, Smith
        went to "Captain's Mast," a disciplinary proceeding where Eugene Morgan, the sailor
        who would later brave dangerous waters to retrieve supplies only to have his under-
        wear snatched off by a shark, presided as master at arms. Smith's sentence: five days in
        the brig and a one-hundred-dollar fine. Released just hours before the sinking, he sur-
        vived the five-day ordeal after having eaten only bread and water for the five days before.
        Source: Sara Vladic, telephone and email discussion with James Smith, January 2018.

262   *swam toward his future*: 317, 501. Also: Woolston LEGACY interviews.

262 *Many screamed in agony*: PRESS, 4.

262 *did not have time to code a message*: PRESS, 5.

262 *One of the men yelling was Lyle Umenhoffer*: Umenhoffer LEGACY interview.

263 *"We'll be back to get you!"*: 317, 482.

263 *looked as though they would not be found*: MCVAY NARRATIVE, 8.

263 *Hensley pulled Harrell aboard*: Account of Harrell's rescue and reunion with Spooner is based on DEPTHS, 139–40.

264 *Claytor did receive a secret dispatch*: CLAYTOR, 1.

264 *summa cum laude graduate of Harvard Law*: Phillips, Don. "W. Graham Claytor Jr., 82, Ex–Amtrak President, Dies." *The Washington Post*, May 15, 1994.

264 *At 4:33 p.m., a dispatch from Peleliu*: CLAYTOR, 1.

264 *he had maintained constant contact*: Ibid.

265 *"If they blow, they blow"*: Charles Doyle LEGACY interview.

Chapter 16

265 *the ensign broke away swimming for the Dumbo*: The account of Thomas Brophy, Jr.'s death is based on LEGACY interviews with Harlan Twible, Adolfo Celaya, and Don Howison.

266 *left Leenerman's lifeless body in the raft*: 317, 280. Leenerman, LEGACY interview.

266 *without stepping on survivors*: GREATNESS, 3.

266 *bringing the number of rescued to fifty-three*: Ibid. Also: PRESS, 5.

267 *the captain and his men saw another plane*: 317, 204. MCVAY NARRATIVE, 8.

267 *darkness that was remarkably complete*: MARKS 1960, 5.

267 *Streaming a sea anchor from the bow*: GREATNESS, 3.

267 *a partially full water breaker*: Ibid.

268 *"I've had mine"*: Ibid., 4.

Chapter 17

268 *Claytor had heard that Marks*: CLAYTOR, 1.

268 *"Turn on the searchlight and point it at the sky"*: Wren, 77. Also: Claytor, 1.

269 *Doyle gazed up at this unprecedented beacon*: Charles Doyle LEGACY interview.

269 *he had never seen a finer example of American courage*: GREATNESS, 4.

269 *The reaction on the Dumbo was electrifying*: MARKS 1960, 6.

270 *to avoid running anyone down*: CLAYTOR, 1.

270 *a lookout spotted a pistol flare in the distance*: Ibid.

270 *The transfer operation was wild and precarious*: PRESS, 5. Also: Letter from *Doyle* motorwhaleboat crewman J. W. Brown, WREN, 78.

270 *first survivors arrived alongside* Doyle: WREN, 79.

270 *Leenerman sputtered awake, shocking his rescuers*: 317, 280. Also: Leenerman LEGACY interview.

271 *Claytor had his communications officer draft a secret message*: Naval Message dated 2 August 1945. Passed by Commander in Chief Pacific Fleet Advance Headquarters to Commander in Chief for Action. Pacific Dispatches, Commander in Chief Chart Room Files, November 1945. Record Group 38, Box 86, National Archives, College Park, Maryland.

271 *covered in bold, red pencil marks*: Ibid.

Chapter 18

272 *the quartermaster, steered the ship*: Lutz Notes. WREN, 45.

272 *in the middle of a Hitchcock film*: Ibid.

272 *the whole thing was a Japanese trick*: WREN, 40.

272 *not terribly thrilled to be under Theriault's command*: Ensign Smook and QM1 Lutz's reflections on Theriault are based on interviews by Sara Vladic with Smook and Lutz in 2014. LEGACY.

273 *Van Wilpe, a nineteen-year-old*: The account of Bill Van Wilpe is based on LEGACY interviews. Also: Van Wilpe Letters. WREN, 64, 68–72.

274 *"Life raft, port beam!"*: Lutz Notes. WREN, 40.

274 *Soon a pair of LCVPs was waterborne*: The account of the LCVP rescue boats from *Bassett* is based on the personal recollections of Peter Wren, Jack Broser, Al Lutz, Malcolm Smook, and Bill Van Wilpe. Sara Vladic interviewed all but Broser. Additional information came from letters and recollections included in WREN.

276 *"No way," the officer said*: *Bassett* crew members spoke with author Sara Vladic of a "mutiny" in which the skipper, Theriault, wanted to flee the area, but his officers overrode him in order to rescue survivors. Two men, Sonarman Gunnar Gunheim and Lieutenant Anderson, *Bassett's* chief engineer, witnessed the argument on the bridge. Our account is based on Wren, *We Were There*, 62–63; and author interviews with *Bassett* crew members Van Wilpe, Wren, Smook, Lutz, Jack Paul, and James Bargsley.

276 *At 3:00 a.m., shouts went up*: CLAYTOR, 2.

277 *Peter Wren bounced his LCVP*: The account of *Bassett's* LCVP rescue is based on WREN, 38-71, and author interviews with *Bassett* crew members Van Wilpe, Wren, Smook, Lutz, Jack Paul, and James Bargsley.

279 *It was Van Wilpe again*: Fletcher, Carol. "Lifesaver Honored after 60 Years." *Record* . (Bergen, New Jersey), 2005. The full date on this clipping is obscured, but the article was published in 2005, in conjunction with the sixtieth anniversary of the *Indianapolis* sinking. Van Wilpe had by then worked for decades in the humble job of school district custodian, and few in the town of Wanaque, New Jersey, knew of his courage on that night in August 1945. In 2005, the entire town discovered they had a hero in their midst, and Van Wilpe, at age seventy-nine, was awarded the Navy and Marine Corps Medal, the highest noncombat medal for heroism.

Chapter 19

279 *"Hell, yes!" Bray called back*: Bray LEGACY interviews.

280 *More rescue ships arrived*: CLAYTOR, 2.

280 *he took charge of the scene*: CLAYTOR, 4.

280 *refused the skipper's daily offering of rations.* Havins account. 317, 204.

281 *"Fellas, do I see a ship"*: Ibid.

281 *Meyer said that a report of Ringness's rescue efforts*: Feuer, A. B. "Memories from the USS *Indianapolis*." Warfare History Network. Accessed 28 September 2016. http://warfarehistorynetwork.com/daily/wwii/memories-from-the-uss-indianapolis-ca-35/.

282 *Meyer reminded McVay that a court of inquiry*: Feuer, A. B. "Memories from the USS *Indianapolis*." Warfare History Network.

282 *it was possible that Lieutenant Orr*: CONEY, McVay testimony, 315.

282   *he felt the responsibility lay with himself*: Ibid.

282   *It included the lat/long*: Naval Message from Commander William Meyer, skipper of USS *Ringness*, dated 3 August 1945. Record Group 38, Box 83, National Archives, College Park, Maryland. In this message, Meyer was notifying CincPac Advance and additional addressees that *Ringness* was en route to Peleliu with thirty-nine survivors of *Indianapolis*, including Captain Charles Butler McVay III. The latter part of the message gives the date and approximate location of the sinking and reads, "Speed 17 not zigzagging."

282   *Alcorn was able to take off*: Memorandum for Air Operations Officer, Sub Area, Operations of VPB-23 on *Indianapolis* Rescue, 5 August–9 August 1945. Record Group 125, Box 35, National Archives, College Park, Maryland. (VPB-23)

283   *Marks considered it too hazardous*: Ibid. Also: PRESS, 5.

283   *Ringness also scooped Glenn Morgan's group*: TORPEDOED. Also: 317, 352, and Morgan LEGACY interviews.

283   *the quartermaster he worked with so closely*: Quartermaster Vince Allard would later name his son, Glenn, after Morgan.

283   *Captain McVay wanted to see him*: Ibid.

283   *more search planes streamed into the area*: VPB-152, 1–3. VPB-23, 1–2.

286   *Felton Outland, Giles McCoy, and four raftmates*: Outland and McCoy's raft contained S1c Robert H. Brundige, S1c Willis Gray, SC3c David Kemp, Jr., and S2c Edward Payne. Based on the interview with Felton Outland, Sr., LEGACY.

286   *On August 4, Lieutenant Chuck Gwinn*: VPB-152, 3.

286   *on August 5, the dispatch said*: Ibid.

286   *last* Indianapolis *survivors pulled from the water*: Once launched, the scope of the rescue effort was massive. First on the scene, *Cecil J. Doyle* rescued 93 men including the men from Adrian Marks's PBY, Playmate 2. *Cecil J. Doyle*'s deck logs reported picking up 96 men, in chronological groups of 18, 22, 17, 10, 1, 6, and 22. 53 identified as coming from Marks's PBY and 1 from Alcorn's PBY. In the ship's war diary they adjusted the report to reflect the rescue count as 93, which matches the number of men accounted for by both the Navy and author Sara Vladic's records. Those rescued by *Doyle* originated mainly from the Haynes group. *Bassett* picked up the most men, 151 survivors, with the majority coming from Redmayne's group and Gibson's floater net group. The *Bassett* cohort included survivors Sal Maldonado, Jimmy O'Donnell, Richard Stephens, and Joseph Mikolayek. *Register* left the scene with 37 survivors, 12 of which they rescued, 24 transferred from the *Ralph Talbot*, and 1 from the *Dufilho*. *Ringness* picked up 39 men, including Captain McVay's group, and those in Glenn Morgan's group, including Louis Bitonti, James Belcher, and Adelore Palmiter. *Ringness* also picked up the very last group of men found alive, on the evening of August 3. This was Felton Outland's raft group, which had split apart from Kuryla and the two other rafts earlier in the week. *Bassett*'s load of survivors spent several days recovering at Fleet Hospital #114 at Samar, Philippines. Soon after, they were loaded into planes and flown to Guam to take treatment with the rest of their mates. The survivors initially taken to Base Hospital #20 Peleliu by the other rescue ships later made the voyage to Guam in the gleaming white hospital ship *Tranquility*. With this, the greatly diminished cohort of sailors and marines were at last reunited at Base Hospital #18 on Guam. Of the ship's 82 officers, including passenger Edwin

Crouch, 15 survived. Of the enlisted crew, there were 311. Of the 39 marines, only 9 lived—none of them were officers. Because the steward's compartment took a direct hit from Hashimoto's second torpedo, most of the stewards died instantly. Two more jumped into the ship's screws in front of George Horvath, and neither of the stewards assisted by Woolston survived. Sources (abbreviated; see Bibliography for full citations): SIGHTING. FLIGHT OPS. BASSETT DECK. CLAYTOR. DOYLE WAR. TODD. TODD 2. BODIES. KNOWN. FRENCH. REGISTER. WREN. 317. HULVER/ VLADIC. Memorandum from LT Lee B. Cottrell USNR to Charles McVay, 8 August 1945. Casualty List for U.S. Naval Base Hospital No. 20, Report by Island Command Peleliu, 5 August 1945. Casualty Report prepared by Donald Blum. U.S. Fleet Hospital #114, 5 August 1945.

JANUARY 1999

289   *Toti turned a page*: Author interviews with Bill Toti, 2012–17.

289   *even a sixth-grade kid*: Nelson, Pete, and Preface by Hunter Scott. *Left for Dead: A Young Man's Search for Justice for the USS* Indianapolis. New York: Delacorte, 2002, 12. (LFD.)

290   *graduating fourth in his 1965 academy class*: Department of Defense. "Navy 4-star Admiral and Trident Scholar Dies." www.navy.mil. U.S Navy, 28 May 2008. Web. 306 June 2017. http://www.navy.mil/submit/display.asp?story_id=37463. (PILLING.)

291   *Scott's report was a book in itself*: Cdr. Scott, R. D., JAGC, USN. "Report on the Court-Martial of Captain Charles B. McVay III, USN, Commanding Officer, USS *Indianapolis*." *NJAG* 10.2 (18 June 1996). 149-End. Print. (SCOTT.)

291   *"The Navy has never challenged"*: SCOTT, Footnote 428.

292   *Matsunaga of Hawaii read the* Indianapolis *story*: Congressional Record, Proceedings and Debates of the 98th Congress, Second Session, Washington, D.C., Monday, July 30, 1984. Vol. 130. No. 98.

292   *hope for exoneration flared briefly*: Editorial board, "Justice at Sea." *Honolulu Star-Bulletin*, Monday, July 30, 1990.

292   *the Murphys—Paul and Mary Lou*: LEGACY interviews with Paul Murphy, 2005–16. Author interviews with Mary Lou Murphy, August 2, 2016.

BOOK 4: TRIAL AND SCANDAL

Chapter 1

297   *sixteen reporters crowded around*: Johnson, Malcolm. "Full Sinking Story Isn't Out Yet, Reporter Says: Correspondent Hits Calling of Jap in McVay's Trial, Cites Lack of Search for Cruiser." *Pittsburgh Press*, December 29, 1945: n. Print. (JOHNSON.)

297   *McVay had the presence of mind*: Ibid. McVay asked that a stenographer be present to record his press interview at Peleliu. However, this transcript has not been made public and may be lost to history.

297   *"That is my sixty-four-dollar question"*: Ibid.

297   *"I should think by noon"*: Ibid.

297   *McVay left no doubt in his mind*: Ibid.

297 *young trees in a gale*: Furman, Robert. Handwritten account of events at Tinian Island on August 6, 1945. 7 August 1945. Two pages Box 1. Papers of Robert Furman, Library of Congress. 1. (TINIAN.)

298 *fifteen seconds after 9:15 a.m.*: "Hiroshima and Nagasaki Bombing Timeline." Atomic Heritage Foundation.

298 *Furman broke away and joined the stream*: TINIAN, 1.

298 *The most senior was General*: TINIAN, 2. ALSO: Christman, Albert B. *Target Hiroshima: Deak Parsons and the Creation of the Atomic Bomb.* Annapolis, MD: Naval Institute, 1998, 194. (TARGET.)

298 *"The chimera of one air operation"*: Mets, David R. (1997) [1988]. *Master of Airpower: General Carl A. Spaatz* (paperback ed.).

298 *"Attention to orders!"*: TARGET. 194. Christman writes, "Later, in the briefing room, under plainer circumstances, Brig. Gen. John H. Davies awarded Parsons the Silver Star." When one officer complained that it had really been Parsons, and not Tibbets, running the show, Parsons paraphrased a nineteenth-century adage that seems to have originated among clergy: "There is no limit to the good a man can do if he doesn't care who gets the credit."

298 *"saw a Jap city and wrecked same"*: TINIAN, 2.

299 *"No one could do anything without you"*: Ibid.

299 *equal to what any remote*: TINIAN, 1.

299 *seventy thousand structures in Hiroshima were leveled*: HASTINGS, 477.

299 *"a small number of B-29s" causing "considerable damage"*: LONGEST, 21.

300 *killed between 80,000 and 130,000 people*: Atomic Heritage Foundation, "Hiroshima and Nagasaki Bombing Timeline." Accessed at https://www.atomicheritage.org/history/hiroshima-and-nagasaki-bombing-timeline, July 27, 2017.

300 *"It is an atomic bomb"*: Statement by the President Announcing the Use of the A-Bomb at Hiroshima; Public Papers, Harry S. Truman Library, 6 August 1945.

300 *The tragedy of Hiroshima must not be repeated*: LONGEST, 22.

300 *"more pressing business"*: Ibid.

300 *Newspapers and leaflets*: Given the extent of the effort, it is extraordinary that many Americans are not aware that Japanese cities were warned before being bombed. The Japanese text on the reverse side of the leaflet carried the following warning: "Read this carefully as it may save your life or the life of a relative or friend. In the next few days, some or all of the cities named on the reverse side will be destroyed by American bombs. These cities contain military installations and workshops or factories that produce military goods. We are determined to destroy all of the tools of the military clique, which they are using to prolong this useless war. But, unfortunately, bombs have no eyes. So, in accordance with America's humanitarian policies, the American Air Force, which does not wish to injure innocent people, now gives you warning to evacuate the cities named and save your lives. America is not fighting the Japanese people but is fighting the military clique, which has enslaved the Japanese people. The peace, which America will bring, will free the people from the oppression of the military clique and mean the emergence of a new and better Japan. You can restore peace by demanding new and good leaders who will end the war. We cannot promise that only these cities will be among those attacked but some or all of them will be, so heed this warning and evacuate these cities immediately." (See Rich-

ard S. R. Hubert, "The OWI Saipan Operation," Official Report to US Information Service, Washington, D.C., 1946.)

301 *drop 63 million leaflets over the country*: "The Information War in the Pacific, 1945." Central Intelligence Agency. Accessed at https://www.cia.gov/library/center-for-the -study-of-intelligence/csi-publications/csi-studies/studies/vol46no3/article07.html, May 6, 2009.

301 *on a portico overlooking the Pacific*: Hughes, Paul. "Survivors of the *Indianapolis* had no criticism of McVay." *Louisville Courier-Journal*, 9 December 1945.

302 *Spruance arrived at the hospital*: LEGACY interview with Don McCall. Sudyk, Bob. "Redemption For Sailor Joe." *Hartford Courant*. N.p., 21 June 1998. Web. 15 March 2014. MacGregor, Jill Noblit. *Unsinkable: The Inspiring True Story of USS* Indianapolis *Survivor: ROBERT P. GAUSE, QM1*. Ed. Julie Gabell. 1st ed. N.p.: Self-published, 2014. Amazon Digital Services LLC, 14 March 2014. Kindle.

302 *Lebow read the letter*: LEGACY interview with Lebow.

303 *Horvath wrote lies to his wife*: George Horvath, letter to his wife, Alice Mae, August 9, 1945. Written from the base hospital at Guam.

303 *Was it possible, Johnson wondered*: JOHNSON.

303 *Guam public affairs personnel asked*: Ibid.

Chapter 2

304 *their enemies had increased by one*: *Japan's Longest Day*. 1990 ed. Eighth Printing. Tokyo: Kodansha International, 1968, 22. (LONGEST.)

304 *endless supply of these apocalyptic weapons*: Atomic Heritage Foundation, Nagasaki Mission. Accessed at http://www.atomicheritage.org/history/bombings-hiroshima -and-nagasaki-1945. July 27, 2017.

304 Bockscar *released Fat Man*: Ibid.

304 *Nimitz had ordered a court of inquiry*: Naval Message from Admiral Nimitz, CincPac Advance Headquarters, dated 11 August 1945, ordering the Court of Inquiry at Guam. Record Group 38, Box 83, National Archives, College Park, Maryland.

305 *a series of grim lists took shape*: List of Missing Personnel—USS *Indianapolis*. Record Group 125, Box 35. National Archives, College Park, Maryland. (This list is eighteen pages long and to read it is heart-wrenching.)

306 USS French *reported bodies found*: "Bodies Found by USS *French* (DE-367)." Record Group 125, Box 35, National Archives, College Park, Maryland.

306 *the survivors had two nurses*: Interview with Lyle Umenhoffer.

307 *he had withdrawn $250*: Ibid. $250 in 1945 would be more than $3,000 today.

307 *Each brother learned for the first time*: Martha, R.S. "Eyewitness Story of USS India-napolis Disaster: *Argus-Leader* (Sioux Falls, South Dakota), October 7, 1945.

307 *Furman wanted to at least visit the survivors*: Interview with Robert Furman by author Richard Newcomb, Hotel Stacy-Trent, May 17, 1957.

307 *"if I had asked you about the uranium?"*: Author interviews with John Woolston.

308 *ready to determine the fate of Japan*: LONGEST, 31.

308 *apologized to the emperor for requesting his presence*: According to the Pacific War Research Society, "The tradition was immemorial that the Japanese government never approached the Throne with a problem until the government's own solution to the problem was unanimous. The Emperor himself neither took sides nor stated

his own opinion: he merely approved what the government had already decided. His August Mind was not to be disturbed by party strife and political ambition; the responsibility for decisions made and actions taken was never his. To present him with a divided cabinet was unthinkable." LONGEST, 29.

308 *Suzuki's cabinet divided three ways on surrender*: According to the Pacific War Research Society, "Six members favored acceptance of the Proclamation provided only that the Imperial House be guaranteed, three insisted on the four condition General Anami had outlined [That the Imperial Sovereignty remain untouched; Japan would be allowed a minimal occupation force; Japan, rather than the enemy, would try its own war criminals; and the demobilization of Japanese troops would be done by Japanese officers, not the Allies], while five advocated more conditions than one but fewer then the war-party's four." LONGEST, 32.

308 *annihilation of the Japanese people*: LONGEST, 34.

308 *"That is unbearable for me"*: LONGEST, 34.

309 *"The time has come to bear the unbearable"*: Ibid.

Chapter 3

309 *Lockwood convened the Nimitz-ordered court*: "Record of Proceedings of a Court of Inquiry Convened at Headquarters, Commander Marianas, Guam, by Order of Commander in Chief, United States Pacific Fleet and Pacific Ocean Areas," 13 August 1945. Holdings of Naval History and Heritage Command, obtained by the authors on 24 October 2017. (COI.)

310 *There would be forty-three witnesses*: COI, Index.

310 *to make himself an interested party*: COI, McVay testimony, 2.

310 *the Navy would try to hang the sinking around his neck*: Kurzman, Dan. *Fatal Voyage.* New York: Atheneum, 1990. Print. 188. (FATAL.)

310 *McVay replied, "No, sir"*: COI, McVay testimony, 5.

310 *"I wish to call attention to the interval of time"*: Ibid.

311 *The weather was "excellent"*: COI, Corry testimony, 8.

311 *Naquin took his seat in the witness chair*: COI, Naquin testimony, 12.

311 *"My records indicate we had reports"*: Ibid., 13.

311 *Naquin had been addressed on all message traffic*: From Officer in Charge to Commander Marianas. Subject: Radio Transmissions 28 and 29 July 1945 Concerning Enemy Submarines. 28 November 1945. Indiana Historical Society. USS *Indianapolis* Collection.

312 *"practically negligible," Naquin said*: COI, Naquin testimony, 13.

312 *Jane snatched up the phone*: The account of Jane Henry learning that her husband, Dr. Earl O. Henry, Sr., was missing, is based on author interviews with Earl O. Henry, Jr., conducted 2015–16.

314 *Mary O'Donnell had anxiously waited*: LEGACY interview with Mary O'Donnell.

314 *Emery did not intend to sit still*: Letter from Herb Armitage to Bill Delman seeking information on behalf of Commander John Emery regarding his son, William Friend Emery. 22 August 1945. Armitage's letter quotes Emery's letter to him: "I would like to ask a difficult favor. My son Bill . . . was on the *Indianapolis* and is reported missing . . . I would appreciate it more than I can express if you could talk to any of the survivors and find out if they know or saw anything of Bill." Delman himself wrote to Commander Emery on 24 August after speaking with the quartermaster, Vincent Allard,

who served with Bill in the same division: "Allard remembered Bill very well . . . ," Delman wrote. "He last saw Bill, after the explosions had occurred, standing on the bridge in a life jacket" with several other men. Allard left the bridge and when he returned, "none of the survivors saw Bill's group again."

315 *peaceful end to the war*: LONGEST, 82.

315 *burst into uncontrollable sobs*: LONGEST, 83.

316 *voice of the Crane*: During the night of August 14, the emperor recorded the rescript for radio broadcast the next day. Realizing it would destroy any chance of continuing the war, a cadre of military officers took control of the imperial palace and imprisoned the emperor. Determined not to allow Hirohito's message to reach the airwaves, the coup leaders killed two men in enacting their plan. But a brave chamberlain loyal to the emperor hid Hirohito's recording and would not reveal its location even when threatened with disembowelment by samurai sword. In Yokohama, another rebel faction intended to kill Prime Minister Suzuki, but he escaped, having been tipped off by a friend. Rebels carried out assassination attempts against other cabinet members that night, but none succeeded. Rebels also failed in an attempt to broadcast their own prowar message from the national broadcast center. By 8 a.m. on August 14, all efforts to stop Hirohito's broadcast had failed. Meanwhile, a man loyal to the emperor smuggled Hirohito's recording out of the palace and took it to the radio station, where it was broadcast to millions of Japanese who had waited anxiously to hear their emperor, the Voice of the Crane. Sources: LONGEST, 326–27. JAPAN'S WAR, 410. RACING THE ENEMY, 246.

316 *Under questioning, Gillette did not mention*: COI, Gillette testimony, 113.

316 *"The HARRIS (DE-447) was ordered to the scene"*: War Diary, Philippine Sea Frontier, 1–31 July 1945, National Archives, accessed online at Fold3.com, July 15, 2016.

316 *the failure of Lieutenant Stuart Gibson*: COI, Gibson testimony, 13–16.

317 *Sancho, told the court he did not know* Indianapolis *had not arrived*: COI, Sancho testimony, 37.

317 *Granum blamed this on 10CL-45*: COI, 42.

317 *Carter told the court that both McCormick and Leyte*: COI, Carter testimony, 98.

Chapter 4

318 *Ugaki learned for the first time*: Ugaki, Matome, Donald M. Goldstein, and Katherine V. Dillon. *Fading Victory: The Diary of Admiral Matome Ugaki, 1941–1945.* Annapolis, MD: Naval Institute, 2008, 663. (UGAKI.) In his 15 August 1945, journal entry, Ugaki wrote, "There were various causes for today's tragedy, and I feel that my own responsibility was not light. But, more fundamentally, it was due to the great difference in national resources between both countries."

319 *he headed for Oita airfield*: Ibid., 665. The account of Ugaki's activities at Oita and his departure is based on an epilogue written by Goldstein and Dillon, editors of Ugaki's war diary.

319 *Hashimoto was standing on the bridge of his submarine*: SUNK, 234.

320 *Johnson was livid*: Johnson, Malcolm. "Full Sinking Story Isn't out Yet, Reporter Says: Correspondent Hits Calling of Jap in McVay's Trial, Cites Lack of Search for Cruiser." *Pittsburgh Press*, December 29, 1945.

321 *the court issued a document titled "Finding of Facts"*: COI. "Finding of Facts." These

pages are unnumbered in the copy of the court of inquiry proceedings obtained by the authors.

321 *assembled in four groups of varying sizes*: These early findings did not reflect the true composition and footprint of the survivor groups.

Chapter 5

323 *he was fairly sure his career was over*: FATAL. 201.

324 *his defiant tone had vanished*: North American Newspaper Alliance. "Cruiser's Sinking Laid to Submarine," *New York Times*, September 18, 1945.

324 *Now Purnell told reporters*: Ibid. Purnell and McVay were interviewed on the same day, apparently by the same reporter(s). McVay mentions Purnell as having a more accurate view of events than McVay himself. This, along with McVay's about-face— from indignation in his first press interview in Peleliu and defending himself at the court of inquiry to abject humility in this *Times* interview—raises a question: Was McVay ordered to moderate his public attitude?

325 *The ship was not up to snuff*: Subsequent investigation would show that McVay and his officers "were acquiring a satisfactory state of readiness . . . and [the ship] was approaching top condition as quickly as the ship's officers could retrain." Naval Inspector General to Chief of Naval Operations. "Subject: Your Memorandum 10 November 1945 as to the status of my supplementary investigation into the sinking of the *Indianapolis*." 10 November 1945.

326 *King fired off an acerbic five-page memo*: King, Fleet Admiral Ernest, Memorandum to James Forrestal. Indiana Historical Society. USS *Indianapolis* Collection.

326 *McVay wrote to Lieutenant Commander John Emery*: McVay III, Captain Charles B, letter to Commander John Emery. 29 September 1945. Courtesy of Michael Emery.

327 *manage the onslaught of mail*: LEGACY: Buckett interviews. 317, 82.

327 *Anne adored her father, idolized him*: Paul Everts, grandson of Commander Joseph Flynn and Flynn's wife, Anna. Anne, who adored her father, is Mr. Everts's aunt. The authors interviewed Paul about the effects of the sinking of *Indianapolis* on the Flynn family.

327 *the yeoman agreed, traveling to multiple states*: 317, 82.

328 *presented himself in McVay's temporary office*: FATAL, 212–13. LEGACY, Blum interview.

328 *McVay had asked to see her*: MARU, 162.

329 *Mary's mother had abandoned her*: Interview with Teresa Goldston Brown, granddaughter of Lieutenant Commander Kasey Moore. Teresa is the daughter of Mary, who was abandoned by her mother and, after Moore died, left with Katherine Moore. Interviewed by Lynn Vincent, February 2017.

329 *I lost a $40 million ship*: MARU, 162.

Chapter 6

329 *Snyder was no lawyer*: "ADM Charles Phillip Snyder." Accessed online December 13, 2016. https://www.findagrave.com/memorial/49319414.

329 *supplemental investigation of the sinking*: CONEY. This lengthy record documents the proceeding that would come to be called the "supplemental investigation" conducted by Commodore Thomas Van Metre and Captain Charles Coney.

330 *a veteran of much tougher duty than this*: USS *Nashville*, War Diary, 1 December 1944–31 December 1944. Captain C. E. Coney.

330 *"We knew there were at least four Japanese submarines"*: CONEY, Smedburg testimony, 2.

330 *"I-58 is apparently the one which was closest"*: Ibid.

331 *received fragmentary distress signals*: Commanding Officer, USCGS *Bibb* to Naval Inspector General. "Distress message connection loss of USS *Indianapolis*; report on." 9 January 1946. Indiana Historical Society. USS *Indianapolis* collection. Also: Commander Clark Withers, USNR to Naval Inspector General. "Distress message received by USS Commander Clark Withers, USNR to Naval Inspector General. Distress message received by USS *Hyperion* from the USS *Indianapolis*." January 20, 1946. Indiana Historical Society. USS *Indianapolis* collection. For a fuller explanation of SOS signals reportedly received ashore, see 556–58.

331 *recommended that McVay's court-martial be delayed*: ADS, 178.

331 *Admiral King concurred*: King, Ernest, Memorandum to James Forrestal. "Subject: Court of Inquiry." 9 November 1945.

331 *Snyder received a memo from Van Metre*: Van Metre, T. E., Memorandum to Naval Inspector General. No subject. Begins: "With reference to the memorandum . . ." 10 November 1945.

331 *"necessary to call as witnesses"*: Ibid.

331 *Snyder wrote immediately to King*: Naval Inspector General to Chief of Naval Operations. "Subject: Your Memorandum 10 November 1945 as to the status of my supplementary investigation into the sinking of the *Indianapolis*." 10 November 1945.

332 *Snyder ticked off examples*: Ibid.

333 *how I-58's intercepted message was tracked*: Van Metre, T. E., to Admiral Snyder. "Progress Report of *Indianapolis* Case." 2 November 1945.

333 *Nimitz's intelligence staff had the information*: Ibid.

333 *reached the offices of Admiral King*: Ibid.

333 *including some of considerable seniority*: Ibid.

334 *created a chart in pencil*: "Witnesses." This chart of witnesses, held in the courts of inquiry folder at the National Archives, is handwritten in pencil. Courts of Inquiry, 18 May 1932 to June 1953. Folder 290–96. Box 35. Entry A1-22.

334 *Comment on the feasibility*: Emphasis King's. ADS, 179.

Chapter 7

335 *"entirely feasible to do so"*: ADS, 179.

335 *belonged to the "same small club"*: Lieutenant Commander Thomas Buell's definitive biography of Admiral Spruance, *The Quiet Warrior*, points out the "close, intimate community with common interests and enduring friendships" of naval officers in the early twentieth century. Unlike today, these officers were nearly all Naval Academy alumni. It was Buell who termed their relationship "the same small club." QUIET, 61.

335 *"intimate community with common interests"*: Ibid.

336 *"Naval Aviator No. 22"*: Reynolds, Clark. *The Fast Carriers: The Forging of an Air Navy*. Annapolis, Maryland: Naval Institute Press, 2013. (Digital), 33.

337 *honored Nimitz with a ticker-tape parade*: "Millions Turn Out to Cheer Fleet Adm. Chester Nimitz for NYC Ticker-Tape Parade." Naval History Blog. October 8, 2014.

337 *"Something ought to be done"*: Cunningham, Bill. "Letter to GI Joe and GI Jane." *Abilene Reporter-News*, November 10, 1945. Accessed online May 1, 2017, at News papers.com. (B BAG.)

338 *a shipment of five thousand cases of whiskey*: Perret, Geoffrey. *There's a War to Be Won: The United States Army in World War II*. New York: Ballantine Books, 1991.

338 *"a piece of major Navy criminal negligence"*: B BAG.

338 *"Those agonizing hours my child suffered"*: Ibid.

338 *"get rid of this sensationalism"*: FATAL, 216.

339 *THE SECRETARY DIRECTS THAT GENERAL COURT MARTIAL*: ADS, 180.

Chapter 8

339 *rescued a woman pinned beneath*: Hammer, Joshua. "The Great Japan Earthquake of 1923." Accessed May 30, 2017, at http://www.smithsonianmag.com/history/the-great-japan-earthquake-of-1923-1764539.

340 *Colclough, was busy weighing*: The account of Colclough weighing various charges against McVay is based on ADS, 182–84.

342 *John Parmelee Cady, a Navy captain*: "John Parmelee Cady." *The Lucky Bag: The Annual of the Regiment of Midshipmen*. Annapolis, MD: United States Naval Academy, 1922, 216.

342 *hanging his head out a porthole*: Ibid.

342 *General Snyder boiled it all down*: The litany of blame detailed by Snyder on pp. 439–41 is based on: Naval Inspector General to Chief of Naval Operations. "Report of progress on further investigation of the sinking of the USS *Indianapolis* and the delay in reporting the loss of that ship." Signed C. P. Snyder. 30 November 1945.

344 *Seated with Ryan was Lieutenant Carl Bauersfeld*: COURT MARTIAL, 1.

344 *McVay had been shocked to learn*: CONEY. McVay testimony, 306.

344 *appalled to hear that Commander Janney*: Ibid.

345 *It embarrassed McVay to still be walking*: "Personal Narrative by Captain Charles B. McVay III, USN, Sinking of USS *Indianapolis*." Recorded 27 September 1945. Command File World War II. Indiana Historical Society. 16.

345 *"Negligence" implied knowledge*: The account of Ryan's and Cady's opening day arguments is based on COURT MARTIAL, 1–2.

Chapter 9

346 *his first witness Lieutenant Joseph J. Waldron*: Here begins the court-martial testimony, which is rendered mainly as excerpts and occasionally as dialogue. Witness testimony may be found in the court-martial transcript at the following locations: Waldron, 5–17; Blum, 162–64; McKissick, 30–43; Moran, 94–99; Haynes, 64–70; Jurkiewicz, 125–33; Woolston, 84–93; Hashimoto, 263–76, Reid, 100–105; King, 307–9; Rogers, 120–21; Twible, 324–26; Harrison, 146–51; Naquin, 329–31; Horner, 157–58; Donaho, 334–44.

347 *Naquin had been dodging and weaving*: Naquin's testimony in the supplemental investigation is found at CONEY, 488–508.

Chapter 12

359 *The Navy had called Hashimoto*: Associated Press. "Bring Jap Officer to Trial to Testify in Court Martial." *Palladium-Item*, Richmond, Indiana, December 10, 1945. Newspapers .com.

360 *Hashimoto heard Smith tell reporters*: Associated Press. "Jap Witness to Testify." *Ithaca Journal*, December 10, 1945. Newspapers.com image of original.

360 *United Press elaborated*: United Press. "Hashimoto Called to McVay Trial." *Hartford Courant*, December 9, 1945.

360 *Navy brass used the press to push back*: "May rule out Jap's testimony at trial," *Honolulu Star Advertiser*, December 12, 1945. Newspapers.com image of original.

360 *"was beginning to sag in reader appeal"*: AS, 215.

361 *Inside, a war was under way*: The arguments for and against Hashimoto's being allowed to testify are found in the court-martial transcript, 256–62.

363 *ferocious as a chocolate milkshake*: Edson, Arthur. "'Ferocious as a Milk Shake,' Is Description of Hashimoto," Associated Press, December 14, 1945. Newspapers .com image of original. (MILKSHAKE.)

363 *taking a seat in the witness chair*: The *voir dire* of Hashimoto. COURT MARTIAL, 263.

365 *On the chart, he traced a line*: The chart Hashimoto drew is one of the exhibits appended to the court-martial transcript. The exhibit number is obscured.

368 *That's not what I said, exactly*: Interview with Atsuko Iida, Hashimoto's granddaughter, by Sara Vladic. Atsuko Iida, granddaughter of Hashimoto. LEGACY interview. ALSO: AS, 227.

368 *met with Ryan and Cady*: FATAL, 241.

369 *"I gotta take this monkey back"*: MILKSHAKE.

Chapter 13

369 *When the defense began*: See note for p. 346 for reference to court-martial witnesses' testimony.

371 *"We assumed there were submarines in that area"*: CONEY. Gillette testimony, 548.

371 *Frontier received ULTRA intel on enemy contacts "continuously."* CONEY, 530. Gillette testimony.

372 *"to meet this recognized threat"*: Ibid., 553.

372 *"technically," the ship was still in his area*: CONEY. Murray testimony, 564.

372 *McVay's lack of information was his own fault*: Ibid., 573.

373 *"feel it should have been necessary"*: CONEY. McMorris testimony, 608. McMorris, the most senior admiral to testify during the supplemental investigation, did not do so until 28 December 1945, more than a week after McVay's court-martial had concluded.

Chapter 14

See note on p. 346 for reference to Glynn Donaho's testimony. COURT MARTIAL, 334–44.

Chapter 15

378 *Bower immediately sat down at his typewriter*: Sinking of *Indianapolis* and Survivor Statements. Record Group 24, Box 1, National Archive, College Park Maryland.

378   *"as plenty of other Navy mothers must be"*: Ibid.

379   *written to two senators*: Ibid.

379   *"blot on the Navy that will never be erased"*: Ibid.

379   *Washington had scotched his story*: Johnson, Malcolm. "Full Sinking Story Isn't Out Yet, Reporter Says: Correspondent Hits Calling of Jap in McVay's Trial, Cites Lack of Search for Cruiser." *Pittsburgh Press*, 29 December 1945.

379   *go on to win a Pulitzer Prize*: Johnson would go on to write a series of investigative stories for the *New York Sun* about New York City dock workers and their strong-arm bosses. His series formed the basis for director Elia Kazan's 1954 film, *On the Waterfront*, starring Marlon Brando.

380   *four other officers received letters of reprimand*: ADS, 203.

380   *McVay was awarded the Bronze Star Medal*: Special to the *New York Times*, "Capt. McVay Wins Bronze Star for Valor on the *Indianapolis* in Battle before Loss." *New York Times*, April 27, 1946.

July 1960

385   *dread filled his heart*: Averitt, Jack. "Weeps at Reception: USS *Indianapolis* Captain "dreaded" Survivor Reunion." *Indianapolis News*, 30 July 1960. (WEEPS.)

385   *"extend to you a very special invitation"*: DEPTHS, 202.

385   *still received on a regular basis*: AS, 185–87. IHW, 267.

385   *"do not reserve more than fifteen minutes"*: DEPTHS, 202–3.

385   *comparatively tame world of insurance*: WEEPS.

386   *"degrees" of honesty*: Ibid.

386   *crew of* Indianapolis *snapped to attention*: Thelen LEGACY interview.

386   *Tears welled in McVay's eyes*: WEEPS.

386   *"Let's have it say 'Captain' "*: LaFollette, Gerry. "Tragedy Still Hurts—after 15 Years." *Indianapolis Times*, July 30, 1960. This article includes a photo with the caption, "'Captain' McVay today," in which McVay is asking to have his nametag changed to read "Captain."

386   *A press room was set up in the Severin*: Press, Radio and Television Activities Schedule, 30 July–31 July 1960. Naval Reserve Public Relations Company 9-1, U.S. Naval Reserve Training Center, Indianapolis, Indiana.

387   *McVay sat for a press conference*: Ibid.

387   *whisked off to a formal tea*: "USS *Indianapolis*' Wives Tour Butler, Enjoy Tea," *Indianapolis Times*, 31 July 1960.

387   *gathered on the rooftop of the Severin*: Alice May Horvath LEGACY interview.

387   *Don Howison looked forward*: Howison LEGACY interview.

388   *their welcome was a bit lackluster*: DEPTHS.

388   *"all we've done is lose a ship"*: Woolston LEGACY interviews.

388   *mourned his childhood friend Harry Linville*: Sam Lopez LEGACY interview.

388   *a pair of cold beers*: Erwin and Umenhoffer LEGACY interviews.

388   *"I have returned!"*: Jarvis LEGACY interview.

389   *wrapped his father in a crushing hug*: Thelen LEGACY interview.

389   *whipped up twenty pies at a time*: Maldonado LEGACY interview.

389   *Clarence Hershberger, turned to drinking*: Hershberger LEGACY interview.

390   *a Japanese woman from Sasebo*: James Belcher, Sr., LEGACY interview.

390 *the shame of things he'd done in the water*: Louis Campbell LEGACY interview.

390 *the hardest part of being at the reunion*: The accounts of Outland at the reunion, the first time he shared about the sinking with his wife, Viola, and the Outlands' trip to find Giles McCoy, are based on Felton Outland, Sr., LEGACY interview, as well as interviews with Viola, and two of Outland's children, Felton, Jr., and Teresa.

392 *JoAnne, had a gift for rallying troops*: Dick Thelen LEGACY interviews.

392 *he slept without the recurring nightmares*: Horvath LEGACY interviews.

392 *Outland stood up and walked out*: Viola Outland, wife of survivor Felton Outland, and Felton's son and daughter, Felton, Jr., and Teresa, interviewed by Lynn Vincent on January 24, 2016.

392 *sending him forward on waves of applause*: LaFollette, Gerry. "USS *Indianapolis* Crew Relives War Tragedy." *Indianapolis Times*, July 31, 1960.

392 *as if he were still their commanding officer*: Ibid.

392 *"a feeling of humility and respect"*: "Address by RADM Charles B. McVay." Presented at the first USS *Indianapolis* Survivors Memorial Reunion, 30 July 1960. Reunion material provided to the authors by the family of survivor Felton Outland, Sr.

393 *McCall hadn't wanted to come to the reunion*: McCall LEGACY interviews.

BOOK 5: AN INNOCENT MAN

Chapter 1

397 *Commander William Toti's running shoes*: The narrative related in this chapter, the characterization of Admiral Pilling, and Toti's analysis of Hashimoto's attack are based on interviews with Bill Toti conducted by the authors, 2012–17.

397 *is a nonpartisan forum for debate*: U.S. Naval Institute. Accessed online December 10, 2017. https://www.usni.org/about.

398 *"sound and remedial action is not warranted"*: Scott, R. D., JAGC, USN. "Report on the Court-Martial of Captain Charles B. McVay III, USN, Commanding Officer, USS *Indianapolis*." *NJAG* 10.2 (18 June 1996): 149–End. (SCOTT.)

399 *Donaho had testified at McVay's court-martial*: COURT-MARTIAL. Donaho Testimony, 334–44.

399 *"The Founding Fathers explicitly rejected"*: Toti, William J. "The Legacy of USS *Indianapolis*." *USNI News*, July 30, 2014. Accessed February 15, 2015. (PROCEEDINGS.) https://news.usni.org/2014/07/30/legacy-uss-indianapolis. (Reprinted from 1999.)

400 *"That is why he was found guilty"*: Ibid.

400 *put a .38 revolver to his temple*: Police report, Suicide of Charles B. McVay on November 6, 1968. Connecticut State Police, November 7, 1968.

401 *Some said it was a crumbling marriage*: Lindsey Wilcox LEGACY interview. Wilcox spent time with McVay in New Orleans after the war.

401 *dark dreams that teemed with circling sharks*: Stanton, Doug. *In Harm's Way: The Sinking of the USS* Indianapolis *and the Extraordinary Story of Its Survivors*. New York: H. Holt, 2001, 7. (IHW.)

402 *a school history fair project*: See generally, Nelson, Pete, and Preface by Hunter Scott. *Left for Dead: A Young Man's Search for Justice for the USS* Indianapolis. New York: Delacorte, 2002. (LFD.)

402 *On* NBC Nightly News *with Tom Brokaw*: Biography of Hunter Scott included in "The Sinking of the U.S.S. *Indianapolis* and the Subsequent Court Martial of Rear Adm. Charles B. McVay III, USN," Transcript of Hearing Before the Committee on Armed Services United States Senate. One Hundred Sixth Congress, First Session, September 14, 1999. 24. (SCAS.)

402 *he was also irritating the very people*: Interview with Bill Toti. Personnel in the Pentagon office of the judge advocate general told Toti that Hunter Scott was making the "wrong people" angry in D.C.

Chapter 2

402 *"This is some kid's school project"*: Bob Smith, former United States senator. The authors conducted multiple telephone and email interviews with Senator Smith in 2016 and 2017. We also had the honor of having dinner with Senator Smith at the July 2017 survivors reunion in Indianapolis at which the senator was the keynote speaker. Senator Smith does an excellent Bill Clinton impression. (SENATOR.)

403 *That had been in April 1998*: The narrative of Senator Smith's meeting with John Luddy, then with Hunter Scott and the *Indianapolis* survivors, is based on the SENATOR interviews noted above.

403 *Hunter's interest in* Indianapolis *was triggered*: The narrative of Hunter's getting involved with the survivors and their fight for McVay is based on the preface to *Left for Dead*, which Hunter wrote at age sixteen. (LFD, xi–xx.) Hunter wrote of his fight for Captain McVay, "I think one wonderful thing about being eleven years old is that a letter from the office of the President or the Secretary of the Navy saying something cannot be done doesn't mean too much."

405 *"20 Most Fascinating Men in Politics"*: SASC. Bio of Hunter Scott, 24.

405 *they made a hell of a team*: SENATOR.

406 *"miscarriage of justice that led to his unjust humiliation"*: Senate Joint Resolution 26. Congress.gov. Accessed online December 10, 2017. https://www.congress.gov/bill/106th-congress/senate-joint-resolution/26.

406 *came across Navy documents*: SASC. Testimony of Dan Kurzman, 46–52.

407 *Kimo made a typically audacious move*: McVay, Kimo, letter to Mochitsura Hashimoto, November 1, 1990. Indiana Historical Society. USS *Indianapolis* Collection.

407 *enlisted the help of a wealthy retiree*: Information about Mike Monroney is taken from TOTI and DUCKY interviews.

407 *These senators included John McCain*: SASC. II.

408 *citizen gun rights and unborn children's*: Goldberg, Carey. "Independent Conservative Bob Smith Runs Uphill Race on Principle." *New York Times*, September 20, 1999.

408 *some kid was going to swoop in*: SENATOR interviews.

Chapter 3

409 *going at it for more than an hour*: The account of Bill Toti's meetings concerning the exoneration language for Captain McVay, and Admiral Pilling's response, is based on TOTI INT.

411 *"We cannot change history"*: Taken from the original testimony Toti wrote for Pilling.

412 *Several survivors would testify*: SASC. The full list of survivors and other witnesses, as well as transcripts of oral testimony and copies of written statements, are included.

414 *the question Toti had asked in his* Proceedings *article*: PROCEEDINGS.

415 *Toti's phone rang, a corded landline*: The account of Admiral Pilling's surprise Saturday phone call is based on TOTI INT.

Chapter 4

419 *Monroney had seen them*: Toti, William, fax to Mike Monroney. "Suggested Questions for Navy Witnesses." September 9, 1999. Private papers of William Toti.

419 *Warner was the survivors' contemporary*: Warner, John W, biography. *Biographical Directory of the United States Congress*. Accessed online June 10, 2017. http://bioguide .congress.gov/scripts/biodisplay.pl?index=W000154.

420 *He brought the hearing to order*: The account of the September 14, 1999, Senate Armed Services Committee hearing is based on the complete hearing record. SASC.

420 *"very moving experience for me to go back and shake their hands"*: SASC, Warner, 1.

420 *an inevitable invasion of Japan*: SASC, Warner, 9.

421 *There were twenty-two of those statements*: SASC, Warner, 10–41.

421 *"stand and be accounted for, gentlemen"*: SASC, Warner, 18.

422 *"Charles McVay IV, where are you?"*: SASC, Smith, 20.

Chapter 5

422 *Warner called the first witness, Hunter Scott*: SASC. Hunter Scott testimony, 20–22.

423 *leaned to his right, and whispered to Smith*: SENATOR. Bob Smith interviews.

423 *Murphy's face was deadly serious*: SASC, 27–41. Also, TOTI INT.

424 *iron-chinned journalist of the old school*: Background on Dan Kurzman is based on "Correspondent in Middle East to Speak at IWU." *Pantagraph*, Bloomington, Illinois, November 15, 1953, 6; "Reports Farouk wounded." *News Herald*, Franklin, Pennsylvania, April 29, 1952; "Author says USS *Indianapolis* tragedy a cover-up." *Indianapolis Star*, August 11, 1990.

425 *Kurzman ended his testimony with a pair of powerful questions*: Kurzman testimony and statement. SASC, 49.

Chapter 6

425 *thought the hearing was going well*: SENATOR interviews.

425 *Dudley delivered a lengthy history*: Dudley testimony and statement. SASC, 62–69.

425 *"conclude that the proceedings were fair"*: Hutson testimony and statement. SASC, 69–74.

426 *Pilling said, smooth and polished as always*: SASC. Pilling statement, 74–79. Also, TOTI INT.

427 *"Admiral Pilling, it is weak"*: SASC. Smith and Pilling spar, SASC, 79–81.

428 *"when the Navy talks about their mistakes"*: Smith and Hutson spar, SASC, 81.

428 Bibb *and USS* Hyperion: Commanding Officer, USCGS *Bibb* to Naval Inspector General. "Distress message connection loss of USS *Indianapolis*; report on." 9 January 1946. Indiana Historical Society. USS *Indianapolis* collection. Also: Commander Clark Withers, USNR, to Naval Inspector General. "Distress message received by USS Commander Clark Withers, USNR to Naval Inspector General. Distress message received by USS *Hyperion* from the USS *Indianapolis*." 20 January 1946. Indiana Historical Society. USS *Indianapolis* collection.

428   *sailor named Clair B. Young*: SASC. Appendices C and D, 129–31.

429   *two seagoing tugs were indeed dispatched*: War Diary, Philippine Sea Frontier, July 1–31, 1945, National Archives, accessed online at Fold3.com.

429   *ripped the pages relevant to the distress calls*: Naval History and Heritage Command historian Dr. Richard Hulver researched Russell Hetz's story. Hetz was stationed aboard LCI-1004. The vessel's deck logs, held at the National Archives, appear to be complete.

429   *Another man, Donald Allen*: SASC, Appendix L.

430   *handwritten notes of Lieutenant Carl Bauersfeld*: Bauersfeld, Carl. Handwritten proof matrix prepared for the court-martial of Captain McVay. Papers of Carl Bauersfeld. Private collection. Courtesy of Carl Bauersfeld, Jr. This collection also includes the Navy memorandum assigning Lieutenant Bauersfeld to the case and a laudatory letter dated 2 January 1946, from Captain Ryan, the judge advocate. Ryan wrote that Bauersfeld's performance on the case was "of the highest order" and that he acted as "an associate [counsel] rather than an assistant."

431   *Warner seemed troubled by some of the Navy's assertions*: SASC, 86–93.

431   *"We should change injustices"*: SASC, Smith, 89.

July 2005

435   *At the Westin Hotel in Indianapolis*: The authors' account of the 2005 survivors' reunion is based on author Sara Vladic's experiences at that reunion. Sara was the "young filmmaker" who happened to be present with her camera when Bob Bunai began to speak about the sinking and the days in the water after sixty years of silence.

435   *"Ducky" Hemenway, battled the Pentagon*: Margaret "Ducky" Hemenway," legislative assistant to Senator Bob Smith, interviewed by Lynn Vincent on August 1, 2016. Also: SENATOR. Bob Smith interviews.

435   *"I have met many of your brave men"*: Hashimoto, Mochitsura, letter to Senator John Warner concerning the exoneration of Captain McVay. October 1999.

436   *called Smith to his office to show him the letter*: SENATOR.

436   *England met with Toti to discuss the history*: TOTI INT.

436   *"recognize Captain McVay's lack of culpability"*: Military Service Record of Rear Admiral Charles B. McVay III, obtained from the National Archives via Persons of Exceptional Prominence program. October 2016. Exoneration language added to McVay's record by Captain Bill Toti at the direction of Secretary of Navy Gordon R. England, 11 July 2001.

437   *"Present the medal to Captain McVay's living son"*: TOTI INT.

438   *"You get in and I'll give you a ride!"*: It was author Sara Vladic whom survivor Paul Murphy took for a spin in his wheelchair that day.

438   Only 317 Survived, *a collection of first-person accounts*: Murphy, Mary Lou, and USS *Indianapolis* Survivors. *Only 317 Survived!: USS* Indianapolis *(CA-35): Navy's Worst Tragedy at Sea—880 Men Died.* Indianapolis, IN: USS *Indianapolis* Survivors Organization, 2002. (317.)

439   *"I didn't see the world"*: 317, 85.

BIBLIOGRAPHY

PRIMARY SOURCES

Indianapolis and Sinking: U.S. Navy Documents and Reports

Action Report, Nansei Shoto Operations (Phase 1) 18 March–7 April 1945, USS *Indianapolis*. RG23, Naval War College, Newport, Rhode Island. (NANSEI)

Action Report, Iwo Jima Operations, 8 February–5 March 1945, USS *Indianapolis*. RG23, Naval War College, Newport, Rhode Island. (IWO OPS)

Action Report, "USS *Indianapolis*: 450 miles east of Leyte Gulf, 30 July 1945, Including Circumstances of the Resultant Sinking of the Ship, 26 August 1945." Written from Naval Base Hospital No. 18 at Guam, this is McVay's official report on the sinking to Fleet Admiral King. Indiana Historical Society, USS *Indianapolis* Collection.

Battle Casualty List, U.S. Naval Base Hospital No. 20, 5 August 1945. Record Group 125, Box 35, National Archives, College Park, Maryland.

Compilation of naval message traffic concerning *Indianapolis*, 26 July–3 August 1945. Record Group 125, Box 35, National Archives, College Park, Maryland.

Crew and Casualty List, USS *Indianapolis*, Office of the Judge Advocate General (Navy), Courts of Inquiry, 18 May 1932–June 1953. Record Group 125, Box 35. National Archives, College Park, Maryland.

Deck Logs, USS *Indianapolis*, 1 March–31 March 1945. Record Group 24, Box 4839, National Archives, College Park, Maryland.

Deck Logs, USS *Indianapolis*, 1 April–30 April 1945. Record Group 24, Box 4839, National Archives, College Park, Maryland.

Documents concerning SS *Wild Hunter*, USS *Albert T. Harris*, and USS *Greene* antisubmarine operations, 28 and 29 July 1945:

- Action Report, USS *Albert T. Harris*, 30 July 1945. Record Group 38, Box 800. National Archives, College Park, Maryland. This record, documenting Harris's multiple hedgehog and depth-charge attacks on the enemy sub ahead of Indy's track, was located for the authors by the amazing archivist Nathaniel Patch (who should wear a cape and a big S on his chest). Vice Admiral J. L. Kauffman, commander of the Philippine Sea Frontier (Norman Gillette was acting commander) and a submarine expert, wrote, "This command is of the opinion that a depth charge attack should have been executed after the first two 'runs' showed a definitely narrow width and the strong possibility of a small target."
- Deck Logs, USS *Albert T. Harris*, 24 July–29 July 1945. National Archives, College Park, Maryland.

- Deck Logs, USS *Greene*, 27 July–30 July 1945. National Archives, College Park, Maryland.
- Memorandum: From Officer in Charge to Commander Marianas. Subject: Radio Transmissions 28 and 29 July 1945 Concerning Enemy Submarines. 28 November 1945. Indiana Historical Society. USS *Indianapolis* Collection.
- Report of Voyage, SS *Wild Hunter*, Long Beach, California, to Manila, Philippines. Report submitted 31 July 1945 by Lieutenant Bruce K. Maxwell, Commanding Officer. This report summarizes the periscope sightings that initiated the *Harris/ Greene* hunter-killer operations, along with *Wild Hunter*'s firing on the target. War Diary, Philippine Sea Frontier, 1 July–31 July 1945, National Archives, accessed online at Fold3.com, July 15, 2016.

Haynes, Commander Lewis L., to Naval Inspector General via Captain C. E. Coney. "An account of survivors following the sinking of the USS *Indianapolis* with recommended changes in lifesaving equipment." 26 November 1945. Indiana Historical Society. USS *Indianapolis* collection.

"Leyte Gulf Expected Arrivals list," 31 July–2 August 1945. Record Group 125, Box 35, National Archives, College Park, Maryland.

Naval Message from Bureau of Naval Personnel stating that next-of-kin notification for casualties from USS *Indianapolis* was complete, 13 August 1945. Record Group 38, Box 83, National Archives, College Park, Maryland.

Naval Message dated 14 August 1945 requiring that all reporters' stories about the loss of *Indianapolis* to be forwarded by airmail to the Secretary of the Navy. Record Group 38, Box 83, National Archives, College Park, Maryland.

Pacific Dispatches, Commander in Chief Chart Room Files, November 1945. Record Group 38, Box 83, National Archives, College Park, Maryland.

Pacific Dispatches, Commander in Chief Chart Room Files, 1 July–15 August 1945. Record Group 38, Box 83, National Archives, College Park, Maryland. These records consist mainly of naval messages classified confidential to top secret (since declassified). They tracked hostile submarine sightings and antisubmarine warfare actions, U.S. attacks on Japanese forces and on the home islands, Japanese attacks on U.S. naval forces, and battle damage/casualties resulting from all of the above. In addition, these messages tracked some movement of flag officers throughout the Pacific theater. One very interesting message from CincPac Advance, dated 16 August 1945, states that it is "incumbent on all officers to conduct themselves with dignity and decorum in their treatment of the Japanese and their public utterances in connection with the Japanese race." The message reminds recipients of Japan's treachery and treatment of Allied prisoners, but states that "the use of insulting epithets in connection with the Japanese as a race or as individuals does not now become the officers of the United States Navy. . . . Neither familiarity and open forgiveness nor abuse and vituperation should be permitted."

Personal Narrative by Captain Charles B. McVay III, USN, Sinking of USS *Indianapolis*, recorded 27 September 1945. Command File World War II. Indiana Historical Society. In this narrative, recorded on audio after McVay returned to Washington, D.C., he tells the story of his personal experience from the time just before the sinking through rescue. (MCVAY NARRATIVE)

"Plane Crash and Bomb Damage, USS *Indianapolis* CA 35." Technical drawing of damage done to the ship by 31 March 1945 kamikaze attack. National Archives, College Park, Maryland.

Records of the 7th Fleet, Antisubmarine Warfare Reports. Record Group 38, Box 198, National Archives, College Park, Maryland. (This box contains the 7th Fleet Anti-submarine analysis for July 1945.)

Report of Torpedoing, Resultant Sinking of and Circumstance Subsequent Thereto East of Leyte Gulf, Philippines, USS *Indianapolis*, 30 July 1945–3 August 1945, Charles B. McVay III.

U.S. Fleet Hospital #114, Casualty Reporting, 5 August 1945. Record Group 125, Box 35. National Archives, College Park, Maryland.

War Diary, USS *Indianapolis*, March 1945. Naval War College, Newport, Rhode Island. (MARCH WAR)

War Diary, USS *Indianapolis*, April 1945. Naval War College, Newport, Rhode Island. (APRIL WAR)

War Diary, USS *Indianapolis*, May 1945. Naval War College, Newport, Rhode Island. (MAY WAR)

Intelligence: U.S. Navy Documents and Reports

Office of Naval Intelligence, Intercepted Enemy Radio Traffic & Related Documentation, [Japan] Naval Vessels I-39 to Naval Vessels I-53. Record Group 38, Box 1386, National Archives, College Park, Maryland. (This box contains original "carded" radio intercepts marked "Top Secret-ULTRA.") (ULTRA 1)

Office of Naval Intelligence, Intercepted Enemy Radio Traffic & Related Documentation, [Japan] Naval Vessels I-53 to Naval Vessels I-156. Record Group 38, Box 1387, National Archives, College Park, Maryland. (This box contains original "carded" radio intercepts marked "Top Secret-ULTRA.") (ULTRA 2)

McVay and Court-Martial: U.S. Navy Documents and Reports

I-58 route from Hirao, Japan, to site of attack on *Indianapolis*, an exhibit in "Record of Proceedings of a General Court-Martial Convened at the Navy Yard, Washington, D.C., by Order of the Secretary of the Navy, Case of Charles B. McVay, 3rd." 3 December 1945." National Archives, College Park, Maryland.

Investigation of Sinking of USS *Indianapolis*. By order of the Chief of Naval Operations, 6 December 1945. This lengthy record documents what would come to be called the "supplemental investigation" conducted by Commodore Thomas Van Metre and Captain Charles Coney. (CONEY)

Selected Exhibits:
- Dispatches and correspondence relative to all "Messages transmitted from Guam 28 and 29 July 1945 addressed to ships and referring to enemy submarine contacts."
- Dispatch and Extracts from CincPac War Diary, reference merchant ship *Wild Hunter* sighting of submarine periscope.
- Dispatches on the subject of "Escort Policy."
- Dispatches with reference sinking of *Underhill*.
- Letter from commanding officer, USCGC *Bibb*, dated 9 January 1946, re: "Distress message connection loss of USS *Indianapolis*."

- Memorandum from Captain W. R. Smedburg III to Commodore Thomas Van Metre, relative to a top secret dispatch sent from Commander in Chief and CNO to CincPac Advance Headquarters on 7 August 1945.
- Memorandum from Lt. Stuart B. Gibson to BUPERS (Bureau of Naval Personnel), 23 May 1945. Subject: Report on fitness of this officer.
- PacFleet Confidential Letter 10CL-45, 26 January 1945 (This was the letter issued by Commodore James Carter stating that no arrival reports would be made for combatant ships.)
- Routing orders, USS *Indianapolis*.
- Roster of Officers, list of survivors and roster of surviving officers, USS *Indianapolis*.
- "Report on the Fitness of Officers," Gibson, Stuart Baurland, period from 5 May 1944 to 1 January 1945. Signed by Forrest Tucker, Commander, USNR.
- Secret letter, dated 20 January 1946 from Commander Clarke Withers, USNR, to the Naval Inspector General. Subject: "Distress message received by USS *Hyperion* from the USS *Indianapolis*."
- Transcripts of witness testimony, 616 pages. (Forty-eight witnesses and a total of 5,066 questions. The testimony spanned the period from 31 October 1945 to 28 December 1945.)
- Wartime Pacific Routing Instructions.

Memorandum from Admiral Chester Nimitz re Court of Inquiry into the Sinking of USS *Indianapolis*, September 6, 1945. "The Commander in Chief, U.S. Pacific Fleet, does not agree with the court in its recommendation that Captain Charles B. McVay III, U.S. Navy, be brought to trial by general court-martial . . ." Naval History and Heritage Command. Accessed online 27 November 2016.

Memoranda between the admirals related to the Navy's supplemental investigation of the sinking (listed in date order):
- "Memorandum for Admiral King: Progress Report of USS *Indianapolis* Case." Undated. Courts of Inquiry, 18 May 1932 to June 1953. Folder 290–296, Box 35, National Archives, College Park, Maryland.
- Memorandum, Van Metre, T. E., to Admiral Snyder. "Progress Report of *Indianapolis* Case." 2 November 1945. Courts of Inquiry, 18 May 1932 to June 1953. Folder 290–296, Box 35, National Archives, College Park, Maryland.
- Memorandum, King, Ernest, to James Forrestal. "Subject: Court of Inquiry." 9 November 1945. Courts of Inquiry, 18 May 1932 to June 1953. Folder 290–296, Box 35, National Archives, College Park, Maryland. (Date is handwritten.)
- Naval Inspector General to Chief of Naval Operations. "Subject: Your Memorandum 10 November 1945 as to the status of my supplementary investigation into the sinking of the *Indianapolis*." 10 November 1945. Courts of Inquiry, 18 May 1932 to June 1953. Folder 290–296, Box 35, Entry A1-22.
- Memorandum, Van Metre, T. E., to Naval Inspector General. No subject. Begins: "With reference to the memorandum . . ." 10 November 1945. Courts of Inquiry, 18 May 1932 to June 1953. Folder 290–296, Box 35, National Archives, College Park, Maryland.
- Memorandum, Naval Inspector General to Chief of Naval Operations. Subject:

Progress of *Indianapolis* case. 10 November 1945. Courts of Inquiry, 18 May 1932 to June 1953. Folder 290–296, Box 35, National Archives, College Park, Maryland.

- Memorandum, Naval Inspector General to Chief of Naval Operations. "Subject: Report of Progress on further investigation of the sinking of the USS *Indianapolis* and the delay in reporting the loss of that ship." 30 November 1945. Courts of Inquiry, 18 May 1932 to June 1953. Folder 290 296, Box 35, National Archives, College Park, Maryland.

- Memorandum, Admiral C. P. Snyder to the Secretary of the Navy. "Further investigation into matters connected with the loss of USS *Indianapolis*. This message describes the processing of enemy intelligence, in particular the intercept of Hashimoto's report that he had sunk an enemy ship. Courts of Inquiry, 18 May 1932 to June 1953. Folder 290–296, Box 35, National Archives, College Park, Maryland.

- "Witnesses." List written in pencil listing high-ranking witnesses to be called in the Navy's supplemental investigation of the sinking of *Indianapolis*. Referred to in the court-martial narrative as "the penciled witness list."

Naval Message from Admiral Nimitz, CincPac Advance Headquarters, dated 11 August 1945, ordering the Court of Inquiry at Guam. Record Group 38, Box 83, National Archives, College Park, Maryland.

"Record of Proceedings of a Court of Inquiry Convened at Headquarters, Commander Marianas, Guam, by Order of Commander in Chief, United States Pacific Fleet and Pacific Ocean Areas," 13 August 1945. Holdings of Naval History and Heritage Command, obtained by the authors on 24 October 2017. (COI)

Rescue: U.S. Navy Documents and Reports, Rescue of Indianapolis Survivors

"Bodies Found by USS *French* (DE-367)." Record Group 125, Box 35, National Archives, College Park, Maryland. (FRENCH.)

Deck Log, USS *Bassett*, 4 August 1945. Courtesy of *Bassett* rescuer L. Peter Wren, the ensign who commanded one of the landing craft that picked up survivors. (BASSETT DECK)

List of Known Dead of USS *Indianapolis*. Record Group 125, Box 35, National Archives, College Park, Maryland. (KNOWN)

List of Missing Personnel—USS *Indianapolis*. Record Group 125, Box 35, National Archives, College Park, Maryland. (This list is eighteen pages long and to read it is heart-wrenching.)

List of Survivors of USS *Indianapolis*. Record Group 125, Box 35, National Archives, College Park, Maryland.

"Lt. Adrian Marks Testimony, 2 Aug 1945, Archives Release #967133." Print. (MARKS)

Memorandum for Air Operations Officer, Sub Area, Operations of VPB-23 on *Indianapolis* Rescue, 5 August–9 August 1945. Record Group 125, Box 35, National Archives, College Park, Maryland. (VPB-23)

Memorandum from Commander Western Carolines Sub Area to Admiral King, Commander in Chief, U.S. Fleet: Rescue and Search for Survivors of USS *Indianapolis* (CA-35) and Recovery, Identification and Burial of Bodies, 15 August 1945. Record Group 125, Box 35, National Archives, College Park, Maryland. (BODIES)

Naval Message from Commander Donald Todd, USS *Madison*, to Commander Philippine

Sea Frontier dated 4 August 1945. "*Bassett* returning to Leyte with about 150 survivors . . . Rafts and survivors scattered 50 miles. . . . Continued air search 100 miles from 1–42 133–20 strongly recommended. Will continue search until relieved." Record Group 38, Box 83, National Archives, College Park, Maryland. (TODD 2)

Naval Message from Lieutenant Commander William Claytor, skipper of USS *Cecil J. Doyle*, dated 2 August 1945. This was the message that "landed like a bomb in the upper echelon of the Pacific Fleet." Record Group 38, Box 83, National Archives, College Park, Maryland. Another copy of this message, passed by CincPac/POA) is the one marked in red pencil, "HOLD DO NOT SHOW."

Naval Message from Commander William Meyer, skipper of USS *Ringness*, dated 3 August 1945. Record Group 38, Box 83, National Archives, College Park, Maryland. Meyer is notifying CincPac Advance and additional addressees that *Ringness* was en route to Peleliu with thirty-nine survivors of *Indianapolis*, including Captain Charles Butler McVay III. The latter part of the message gives the date and approximate location of the sinking and reads, "Speed 17 not zigzagging."

"Record of Air Support, 3 August–5 August, 1945." Commander Donald W. Todd, skipper of USS *Madison* and Senior Officer Present Afloat during rescue operations. Indiana Historical Society, USS *Indianapolis* Collection. (TODD)

"Record of Flight Operations in Search for Survivors from USS *Indianapolis* (CA 35), 2 August 1945." Indiana Historical Society, USS *Indianapolis* Collection.

Search Operations of USS *Register* (APD-92) for Survivors of USS *Indianapolis*, 8 August 1945. Record Group 125, Box 35, National Archives, College Park, Maryland. (REGISTER)

"Sighting of Survivors of USS *Indianapolis*; Participation in Air-Sea Rescue and Subsequent Search for Bodies, 2–7 August 1945." Record Group 125, Box 35, National Archives, College Park, Maryland. This is a narrative of air operations in support of rescue operations written by Lieutenant Richard C. Alcorn, who also landed his PBY and rescued a survivor. (VPB-152)

Statement Concerning Sighting of Survivors of CA-35 USS *Indianapolis* on 2 August 1945, Lieutenant Junior Grade Wilbur Gwinn, 3 August 1945. Record Group 125, Box 35, National Archives, College Park, Maryland. (DOYLE WAR)

Transcript of press interviews with the rescue pilots, Lieutenant Junior Grade Wilbur "Chuck" Gwinn, Lieutenant Adrian Marks, and Lieutenant Commander George Atteberry, conducted 6 August 1945 at Peleliu. Record Group 125, Box 35, National Archives, College Park, Maryland. (PRESS)

USS *Cecil J. Doyle* War Diary, 1 August–31 August 1945. Holdings of Naval War College, Newport, Rhode Island.

USS *Cecil J. Doyle* Memorandum Report on Rescue of Survivors of USS *Indianapolis* (CA-35) 2 August–4 August 1945. Record Group 125, Box 35, National Archives, College Park, Maryland. (CLAYTOR)

Navy Documents and Reports (General)

Damage Report, USS *Franklin*, Bomb Damage Honshu, 19 March 1945. Holdings of Naval War College, Newport, Rhode Island.

"Joint Chiefs of Staff 924/15, 25 April, CCS 381 Pacific Ocean Operations. Section 11, Record Group 218. National Archives, College Park, Maryland.

Manual for Buglers, U.S. Navy, Bureau of Naval Personnel, Original edition 1919. Reprinted with minor corrections 1951 and with changes 1953. Accessed online 29 February 2016.

"Naval Material Conditions." Naval Reserve Force Information Service. Accessed at: http://www.usshancockcv19.com/navalmaterialconditions.htm. (YOKE)

Okinawa Operations Record of 32d Army. Vol. 1. Washington, D.C.: n.p., 1949. Print. (JM135)

Pacific Dispatches, Commander in Chief Chart Room Files, November 1945. Record Group 38, Box 86, National Archives, College Park, Maryland.

United States Pacific Fleet Commander First Carrier Task Force. Report. Vol. Serial: 00222. A16-3. 18 June 1945. http://ftp.ibiblio.org/hyperwar/USN/rep/Okinawa/TF58/index.html (PAC-FLEET)

United States. U.S. Navy. Commander in Chief, United States Fleet, and Chief of Naval Operations. *Third Report to the Secretary of the Navy.* By Ernest J. King. N.p., 1945. 1 March 1945–1 October 1945. *U.S. Navy at War, 1941–1945 (Off. Reports to SecNav from CNO) [Third Report].* United States Fleet. Web. (HYPER)

White House and Congressional Documents and Reports

"The Sinking of the U.S.S. *Indianapolis* and the Subsequent Court-Martial of Rear Adm. Charles B. McVay III, USN." Transcript of hearing before the Committee on Armed Services, United States Senate. 106th Congress, First Session, 14 September 1999.

The White House. "Statement by the President of the United States." Press release by the White House, 6 August 1945. Ayers Papers, Subject File. U.S. Army, Press releases, the atomic bomb and atomic energy. (DIARY)

U.S. Congress. Congressional Record, V. 146, Pt. 7, May 24, 2000, to June 12, 2000. 106th Congress, Second Session, Cong. Rept. 146, Pt. 7. http://books.google.com/books?id=z6E993ZslkAC&printsec=frontcover &source=gbs_ge_summary_r&cad =0#v=onepage&q&f=false. (CONGRESS2000)

Warner, John W, biography. *Biographical Directory of the United States Congress.* Accessed 10 June 2017. http://bioguide.congress.gov/scripts/biodisplay.pl?index=W000154.

Primary Source Material about Captain Charles B. McVay III

"Address by RADM Charles B. McVay." Presented at the first USS *Indianapolis* Survivors Memorial Reunion, 30 July 1960. Reunion material provided to the authors by the family of survivor Felton Outland, Sr.

Biography of Rear Admiral Charles B. McVay III, U.S. Navy (Retired) This biography was printed on the letterhead of Headquarters Eighth Naval District, Federal Building, New Orleans, Louisiana.

"Captain McVay's military record should now reflect that he is exonerated for the loss of the USS Indianapolis . . . ," Addition to the Personnel Record of Rear Admiral Charles McVay III by Secretary of Navy Gordon R. England, 11 July 2001. Naval History and Heritage Command. Accessed online 4 August 2016.

Charles B. McVay III, handwritten copy of speech for the *Indianapolis* survivors' first reunion. Delivered at the Severin Hotel, Indianapolis, Indiana. This longhand version is incomplete and appears to be different from the copy of the speech released to the press. Indiana Historical Society. USS *Indianapolis* Collection.

Military Service Record of Rear Admiral Charles B. McVay III, obtained from the National Archives via Persons of Exceptional Prominence program, October 2016.

"The Sinking of USS *Indianapolis:* Recollections of Captain Charles B. McVay III." World War II Interviews, Operational Archives Branch, Naval Historical Center. Accessed online 25 July 2016.

Interviews by the Authors

"Legacy On-Camera Interviews with survivors, survivors' families, rescue crew, and families of men lost at sea," 2005–2016, conducted by Sara Vladic. Total of 119 interviews, 170 hours of footage. (LEGACY)

Includes on-camera interviews with forty-three survivors of the sinking of USS *Indianapolis* conducted over more than a decade, as well as an additional thirty-six audio and in-person survivor interviews completed for research. The following is a complete list of LEGACY interviews:

SURVIVORS: William Akines, Lloyd Barto, Donald Beaty, James Belcher, Maurice Bell, Louis Bitonti, Bryan Blanthorn, Donald Blum, Harold Bray, Victor Buckett, Robert Bunai, Louis Campbell, Loyd Carter, Grover Carver, Adolfo Celaya, Frank Centazzo, L. D. Cox, Granville Crane, Bill Drayton, Louis Erwin, Verlin Fortin, Buck Gibson, Thomas Goff, Edgar Harrell, Lewis Haynes, John Heller, Clarence Hershberger, George Horvath, John Howison, Clarence Hupka, Melvin Jacob, Woodie James, James Jarvis, Tony (A. C.) King, George Kurlich, Michael Kuryla, Kenley Lanter, George Laws, Cleatus Lebow, Arthur Leenerman, Sam Lopez, Donald Mack, Salvador Maldonado, Donald McCall, Paul McGinnis, Robert McGuiggan, Charles McVay, Glen Milbrodt, Donald Miller (former crew), Norval Mitchell, Melvin Modisher, Joseph Moran, Eugene Morgan, Glenn Morgan, Morgan Moseley, Paul Murphy, Troy Nunley, James O'Donnell, Felton Outland, Richard Paroubek, Lyle Pasket, Santos Pena, Gerald Poor, James Denny Price, Earl Riggins, Donald Shown, James Smith, John Spinelli, Florian Stamm, Richard Stephens, Richard Thelen, William Thurkettle, Harlan Twible, Lyle Umenhoffer, George Whiting, Lindsey Wilcox, Robert Witzig, John Woolston. Former crew: Robert Laney, Donald Miller, Hal Weddington.

RESCUE CREW: George Barber, James Bargsley, Eva Jane Bolents-Savel, Charles Doyle, Bill Fouts, Tom Gray, Alfred Lederer, Albert Lutz, Roy McLendon, Jack Paul, Malcolm Smook, William Van Wilpe, L. Peter Wren.

FAMILY MEMBERS: Andrew Barksdale, Toyoko Belcher, James Belcher, Jr., Bonny Campbell, Peggy Campo, Michael Emery, Aurora Garcia, Norma Gwinn, David Harrell, Earl Henry, Jr., Alice Mae Horvath, Ann Kmit, Ethel Leenerman, Mary O'Donnell, Mary Stamm, Mitchell Stamm, Ben Tierney.

FRIENDS: Tom Balunis, Secretary of the Navy Gordon England, John Gromosiak, Sonoe Hashimoto Iida, Atsuko Iida, Oliver North, Hunter Scott, Senator Robert Smith, Captain William Toti.

Adolfo Celaya. Interviewed by Lynn Vincent in Florence, Arizona. August 2015. (LV-CELAYA)

Atusko Iida, granddaughter of Commander Hashimoto. Email interviews by Sara Vladic, May 2014–16.

Bob Smith, United States senator. The authors conducted multiple telephone and email
interviews with Senator Smith in 2016 and 2017.

Captain William Toti. The authors conducted multiple telephone and email interviews
with Captain Toti between 2012 and 2017.

David Furman, son of Army Major Robert Furman. Telephone interview by Sara Vladic on
31 March 2016.

Earl O. Henry, Jr., son of Lieutenant Commander Earl O. Henry, Sr. Interviewed by Sara
Vladic and Sara Cunliffe in Nashville, Tennessee, September 2015.

Mary Lou Murphy, wife of survivor Paul Murphy. Telephone interview by Lynn Vincent on
2 August 2016.

Michael Emery, nephew of Seaman William Friend Emery. Telephone interview by the
authors, 10 May 2016.

Margaret "Ducky" Hemenway," legislative assistant to Senator Bob Smith. Interviewed by
Lynn Vincent on 1 August 2016.

Paul Everts, grandson of Commander Joseph Flynn and Flynn's wife, Anna. The authors
interviewed Paul about the effects of the sinking of *Indianapolis* on the Flynn family, and about Anna's resentment of McVay. Interviewed by Lynn Vincent, Spring
2017.

Teresa Goldston Brown. Granddaughter of Lieutenant Commander Kasey Moore. Teresa
is the daughter of Mary, who was abandoned by her mother and, after Moore died,
left with Katherine Moore. Telephone interview by Lynn Vincent, February 2017.

Viola Outland, wife of survivor Felton Outland, and two of the couple's children, Felton, Jr.,
and Teresa. Interviewed by Lynn Vincent on 24 January 2016.

Private Papers, Diaries, Personal Histories and Correspondence

Armitage, Herb. Letter to Bill Delman seeking information on behalf of Commander John
Emery regarding his son, William Friend Emery. 22 August 1945. Papers of Commander John Emery. Courtesy of Michael Emery, nephew of lost-at-sea *Indianapolis*
crew member William Friend Emery.

Bauersfeld, Carl. Handwritten proof matrix prepared for the court-martial of Captain
McVay. Papers of Carl Bauersfeld. Private collection. Courtesy of Carl Bauersfeld,
Jr. The collection also includes the Navy memorandum assigning Lieutenant Bauersfeld to the case and a laudatory letter dated 2 January 1946, from Captain Ryan,
the judge advocate. Ryan wrote that the lieutenant's performance was "of the highest order" and that he acted as "an associate [counsel] rather than an assistant."

Delman, Bill. Letter to Commander John Emery reporting what was learned about the fate
of Emery's son, William Friend Emery. 24 August 1945. Papers of Commander John
Emery. Courtesy of Michael Emery, nephew of lost-at-sea *Indianapolis* crew member William Friend Emery.

Furman, Robert R. Papers of Robert R. Furman. Box 1. Library of Congress, Washington,
D.C.
- Departure Memorandum written 9 July 1945. (FDN)
- Robert Furman's writing on Manhattan Engineering District, c. 1982. (MED)
- Robert Furman's writing on transporting the atomic bomb aboard USS *India-
napolis*, undated. (FOI)
- Robert Furman letter to parents, dated simply "August." (FOLKS)

- Robert Furman's handwritten account of bomb transport, undated. (FURMAN HW)
- "Tinian, July 31." Furman's typewritten account of experiences on Tinian. (TINIAN)
- Robert Furman's handwritten account of the return to Tinian of the *Enola Gay*. Dated 7 August 1945. (TINIAN 2)
- "How to Carry an Atomic Bomb." Furman's remarks and reflections on the Alsos mission, the Manhattan Project, and his role in both. July 1985.
- "Draft: August 5, 1985." Remarks prepared about the fortieth anniversary of the dropping of the first atomic bomb. (DRAFT)

Hashimoto, Mochitsura. Letter to Senator John Warner concerning the exoneration of Captain McVay. October 1999. www.ussindianapolis.org/hashimoto.htm. Accessed online 20 January 2017.

Henry, Earl O., Sr. Letters to his wife, Jane Henry, 22 May 1944–27 July 1945. Dr. Henry wrote more than 160 pages of letters to Jane. He would pass away three days after his final letter, in which he wrote to Jane that he had finally received photographs of his newborn son, Earl O. Henry, Jr.: "Baby-angel, those two wonderful pictures came today, and I am delighted as I can be over them! Considering that he is a premature baby, he looks mighty good." Letters courtesy of Earl O. Henry, Jr.

Hershberger, Clarence L. *Tragedy: As Seen by One Survivor*. De Leon Springs, FL: self-published, 1994.

Higgins, Anna. Letter to Kimo McVay in response to McVay's letters to President Ronald Reagan and Vice President George W. Bush. 12 September 1983. Indiana Historical Society. USS *Indianapolis* collection.

Horvath, George. Letter to his wife, Alice Mae, 9 August 1945. Written from the base hospital at Guam.

McVay, Charles B., Jr. *Autobiography*. Papers of Admiral Charles B. McVay, Jr. Library of Congress.

McVay, Kimo. Letter to Mochitsura Hashimoto, 1 November 1990. Indiana Historical Society. USS *Indianapolis* collection.

Morgan, Bugler Glenn, USS *Indianapolis* Survivor. "Glenn Morgan's Story of the Suicide Plane Attack." Print. (MORGAN)

Morgan, Glenn Grover. "Glenn Morgan Diaries." 1 January–25 April 1945. Handwritten by Glenn Morgan and typed by Sharon Morgan and Ben Huntley. (GM-DIARIES)

Morgan, Glenn Grover. "My Story." Memoir. 28 September 2011. 3 pages. (GM-MY STORY)

Morgan, Glenn Grover. "Story of Suicide Plane Attack" Memoir. 28 September 2011. 3 pages. (GM-KAMIKAZE)

Morgan, Glenn Grover. "Torpedoed." Memoir. 1993. 43 pages. Handwritten by G. Morgan. (GM-TORPEDO)

Morgan, Glenn Grover. "A WWII Bugler Tells His Story." Memoir. 28 September 2011. 36 pages. (GM-BUGLER)

Murphy, Mary Lou, and USS *Indianapolis* Survivors. *Only 317 Survived!: USS* Indianapolis *(CA-35): Navy's Worst Tragedy at Sea—880 Men Died*. Indianapolis, IN: USS *Indianapolis* Survivors Organization, 2002. (317)

Podoll, Ensign Erling. "LCTs 354 & 991 at Tinian." Ensign Podoll writes about the arrival of *Indianapolis* at Tinian Island and the offloading of the atomic bomb components on 26 July 1945.

Quihuis, Mike. "Mike Quihuis Diary." 22 July 1944–26 November 1945. Handwritten. (KIWI)

Smith, Frances M., "Smitty." "The Tragedy of the USS *Indianapolis* and My Role and Involvement." 1995. (SMITTY)

Spruance, Admiral Raymond. Twenty-page typewritten narrative of island-to-island fighting across the Pacific. The account is partial and begins with Tarawa and proceeds to the end of the war. Holdings of the Naval War College, Newport, Rhode Island.

Twible, Harlan Malcolm. *The Life and Times of an Immigrant's Son.* Sarasota, FL: self-published, 1997.

Wren, L. Peter. *We Were There: The USS* Indianapolis *Tragedy, The Rest of the Story as Told by the Men Who Aided the Crew in This Tragedy.* This book is a collection of first-person accounts and official reports from personnel and units involved in the rescue of *Indianapolis* survivors. Compiled by L. Peter Wren, a rescue boat officer at the scene. Richmond, Virginia: Wren Enterprises. Print. 2002. (WREN)

Speeches

Address by Adrian Marks (Navy pilot who landed his PBY "Dumbo" in the Philippine Sea and rescued fifty-three *Indianapolis* survivors.) Presented at the first USS *Indianapolis* Survivors Memorial Reunion, Severin Hotel, Indianapolis, Indiana, 30 July 1960. (MARKS 1960)

Address by Adrian Marks, "I've Seen Greatness," July 1985. Abridged transcript of speech delivered at the fortieth anniversary of the *Indianapolis* sinking and rescue. (GREATNESS)

Address by Atsuko Iida, Commander Hashimoto's granddaughter, at the USS *Indianapolis* Survivors Reunion, 2005.

Address by George H. Cate, Jr., "USS Indianapolis: A Tennessee Connection," delivered at Old Oak Club meeting, University Club of Nashville, 25 February 1999; Torch Club Meeting, University Club of Nashville, 17 March 1999; Princeton Art Guild, Kentucky, 22 August 1999; Earl Henry Memorial Clinic sponsored by Second District Dental Society, Cherokee Country Club, Knoxville, Tennessee, 27 October 2000; and on numerous other occasions.

Materials from 1960 *Indianapolis* Survivors Memorial Reunion

Press, Radio, and Television Activities Schedule, 30–31 July 1960. Naval Reserve Public Relations Company 9–1, U.S. Naval Reserve Training Center, Indianapolis, Indiana.

Program, 1960 USS *Indianapolis* Survivors Memorial Reunion.

Additional Interviews and Oral Histories

"Corley Haggarton, World War II Veterans History Project." Interview by Jean Reynolds. www.chandleraz.gov. January 21, 2009. https://www.chandleraz.gov/Content/WWII_Haggarton_Transcript.pdf. (HAGGARTON)

"Interview with Robert Furman," Chief of Foreign Intelligence and assistant to General Lloyd Groves, Manhattan Project, February 20, 2008. Voices of the Manhattan Project, a joint project of Atomic Heritage Foundation and the Los Alamos His-

torical Society Online at: http://manhattanprojectvoices.org/oral-histories/robert
-furmans-interview. Accessed on 3/25/2016. (FURMAN ATOMIC)

Interview with Robert Furman by author Richard Newcomb, Hotel Stacy-Trent, 17 May
1957. Papers of Robert Furman. Library of Congress.

"Oral History with Capt. (ret.) Lewis Haynes, MD, USN," U.S. Navy Medical Department
Oral History Program, June 5, 12, 22, 1995.

"Oral History Transcript of Charles F. Barber." Flag Secretary to Admiral Raymond Spruance. Interview by Evelyn M. Cherpak. Archive.org. 1 March 1996. http://archive.org
/stream/oralhistorytrans00barb/oralhistorytrans00barb_djvu.txt. (BARBER)

ADDITIONAL SOURCES

Books

Aitken, Robert, and Marilyn Aitken. *Law Makers, Law Breakers, and Uncommon Trials*. Chicago, IL: American Bar Association, 2007. (LAWMAKERS)

Axell, Albert, and Hideaki Kase. *Kamikaze: Japan's Suicide Gods*. Harlow: Longman, 2002.
(SUICIDE GODS)

Becton, Rear Admiral F. Julian, USN (Retired). *The Ship That Would Not Die*. New York:
Prentice Hall, 1980. (BECTON)

Belote, William. *Typhoon of Steel: The Battle for Okinawa*. New York: Harper and Row, 1970.
(TYPHOON)

Borneman, Walter R. *The Admirals: Nimitz, Halsey, Leahy, and King—the Five-star Admirals
Who Won the War at Sea*. New York: Little, Brown, 2012. (ADMIRALS)

Buell, Thomas B. *The Quiet Warrior: A Biography of Admiral Raymond A. Spruance*. Boston,
MA: Little, Brown, 1987. Print. (QUIET)

Campbell, Richard H., and Paul W. Tibbets. *The Silverplate Bombers: A History and Registry
of the Enola Gay and Other B-29s Configured to Carry Atomic Bombs*. Jefferson, NC:
McFarland, 2012. (SILVERPLATE)

Christman, Albert B. *Target Hiroshima: Deak Parsons and the Creation of the Atomic Bomb*.
Annapolis, MD: Naval Institute Press, 1998. (TARGET)

Clemans, Charles. *Harpo: War Survivor, Basketball Wizard*. Tucson, AZ: Wheatmark, 2009.
(HARPO)

Cracknell, William H. *Profile Warship 28: USS Indianapolis(ca 35)/Heavy Cruiser*. Place of
publication not identified: Profile, 1973. (PROFILE)

Cunningham II, Paul E. *Command and Control of the U.S. Tenth Army During the Battle
of Okinawa*. Thesis (West Point; Master Of Military Art and Science). Fort Leavenworth, KS: U.S. Army Command and General Staff College, 2009. (TENTH)

Feifer, George. *The Battle of Okinawa: The Blood and the Bomb*. Guilford, CT: Lyons Press,
2001. (BLOOD)

Frank, Richard B. *Downfall: The End of the Imperial Japanese Empire*. Random House, New
York, 1999. Print. (DOWNFALL)

Grayling, A. C. *Among the Dead Cities: The History and Moral Legacy of the WWII Bombing
of Civilians in Germany and Japan*. New York: Walker, 2006. (ATDC)

Gromosiak, John G. *Touched by So Many*. Indianapolis: Printing Partners, 2008.
(TOUCHED)

Groves, Leslie R. *Now It Can Be Told: The Story of the Manhattan Project.* New York: Harper and Brothers, 1962. (NOWTOLD)

Hammel, Eric. *Coral and Blood: The U.S. Marine Corps' Pacific Campaign.* Pacifica Military History, 24 January 2010. (CORAL)

Hando, Kazutoshi. *Japan's Longest Day.* 1990 ed. Vol. Eighth Printing. Tokyo: Kodansha International, 1967. (LONGEST)

Harrell, Edgar, and David Harrell. *Out of the Depths: An Unforgettable WWII Story of Survival, Courage, and the Sinking of the USS* Indianapolis. 2nd ed. N.p.: Bethany House, 2014. (DEPTHS)

Hasegawa, Tsuyoshi. *Racing the Enemy: Stalin, Truman, and the Surrender of Japan.* Cambridge, MA: Belknap Press, 2006. (RACING).

Hashimoto, Mochitsura. *Sunk; the Story of the Japanese Submarine Fleet, 1941–1945.* New York: Holt, 1954. (SUNK)

Hastings, Max. *Retribution: The Battle for Japan, 1944–45.* New York: Alfred A. Knopf, 2009. (HASTINGS)

Helm, Thomas. *Ordeal by Sea: The Tragedy of the U.S.S.* Indianapolis. New York: Dodd, Mead, 1963. (OBS)

Hoyt, Edwin P. *How They Won the War in the Pacific: Nimitz and His Admirals.* New York: Weybright and Talley, 1970. (HTW)

Hoyt, Edwin P. *Japan's War: The Great Pacific Conflict.* New York: McGraw-Hill, 1986. (HOYT)

Inagaki, Takeshi. *Okinawa Higu No Sakusen: Itan No Sanbo Yahara Hiromichi* [Okinawa: A Strategy of Tragedy]. Tokyo: Shinchosha, 1984. (INAGAKI)

Isely, Jeter A., and Philip Axtell. *The US Marines and Amphibious War: Its Theory, and Its Practice in the Pacific.* Princeton, NJ: Princeton Univ. Press, 1951. (WAR)

Kelly, Cynthia C. *The Manhattan Project: The Birth of the Atomic Bomb in the Words of Its Creators, Eyewitnesses, and Historians.* New York: Black Dog & Leventhal, 2007. Print. (MANHATTAN)

Kurzman, Dan. *Day of the Bomb: Countdown to Hiroshima.* New York: McGraw-Hill, 1986. (DOTB)

Kurzman, Dan. *Fatal Voyage.* New York: Atheneum, 1990. (FATAL)

Laney, Robert H. *One Lucky Sailor and His Ships.* Chico, *California*: Graphic Fox, 2014. (LUCKY)

Lech, Raymond B. *All the Drowned Sailors.* New York: Stein and Day, 1982. Print. (ADS)

MacGregor, Jill Noblit. *Unsinkable: The Inspiring True Story of USS* Indianapolis *Survivor: Robert P. Gause, QM1.* Ed. Julie Gabell. 1st Ed. N.p.: self-published, 2014. Amazon Digital Services LCC, 14 March 2014. Kindle. (UNSINKABLE)

Mara, Wil. *Harry Truman.* New York: Marshall Cavendish Benchmark, 2012. (PRESIDENTS)

Marston, Daniel. *The Pacific War Companion: From Pearl Harbor to Hiroshima.* Oxford: Osprey, 2005. (PACWAR) Article Contributed by Major Bruce Budmundsson. (BUD)

Marston, Daniel. *The Pacific War Companion: From Pearl Harbor to Hiroshima.* Oxford: Osprey, 2005. (PWC)

McCullough, David G. *Truman.* New York: Simon & Schuster, 1992. (TRUMAN)

Moore, Katherine D. *Goodbye, Indy Maru.* Knoxville, TN: Lori Publications, 1991. (MARU)

Morison, Samuel Eliot. *History of United States Naval Operations in World War II.* Vol. 14: *Victory in the Pacific 1945.* Boston: Little, Brown, 1960. (USNOPS)

Nelson, Pete. Preface by Hunter Scott. *Left for Dead: A Young Man's Search for Justice for the USS* Indianapolis. New York: Delacorte, 2002. (LFD)

Newcomb, Richard F. *Abandon Ship!* New York: HarperTorch, 2001. (AS)

Norris, Robert S. *Racing for the Bomb: The True Story of General Leslie R. Groves, the Man behind the Birth of the Atomic Age.* New York: Skyhorse Publishing, 2002. (RACING)

Okinawa Hōmen Rikugun Sakusen. Boei Kenkyujo Senshishiteu ed. Vol. 11. Tōkyō: Asagumo Shinbunsha, 1968. Print. Senshi Sosho [Okinawa area infantry strategy, War History Series]. (OHRS)

Potter, E. B. *Nimitz.* Annapolis, MD: Naval Institute, 1976. (NIMITZ)

Powers, Thomas. *Heisenberg's War: The Secret History of the German Bomb.* New York: Knopf, 1993. (HEISENBERG)

Pry, Peter. *The Role of Congress in the Strategic Posture of the United States, 1942–1960.* (CONGRESS)

Reynolds, Clark. *The Fast Carriers: The Forging of an Air Navy.* Annapolis, MD: Naval Institute Press, 2013. (Digital.)

Rhodes, Richard. *The Making of the Atomic Bomb.* New York: Simon & Schuster, 1987. (RHODES)

Salmaggi, Cesare, and Alfredo Pallavisini. *2194 Days of War: An Illustrated Chronology of the Second World War.* New York: Mayflower Books, 1977.

Selden, Kyoko Iriye, and Mark Selden. *The Atomic Bomb: Voices from Hiroshima and Nagasaki.* Armonk, NY: M.E. Sharpe, 1989. (ABOMB)

Silverstone, Paul H. *U.S. Warships of World War II.* New York: Doubleday, 1972. (SHIPS)

Skates, John Ray. *The Invasion of Japan: Alternative to the Bomb.* Columbia, SC: University of South Carolina Press, 1994. (ALTERNATIVE)

Sloan, Bill. *The Ultimate Battle: Okinawa 1945–The Last Epic Struggle of World War II.* New York: Simon & Schuster, 2007. (SLOAN)

Stanton, Doug. *In Harm's Way: The Sinking of the USS* Indianapolis *and the Extraordinary Story of Its Survivors.* New York: H. Holt, 2001. (IHW)

Stimson, Henry L., Herman Kahn, Bonnie B. Collier, and Pauline Goldstein. *The Henry Lewis Stimson Diaries in the Yale University Library.* New Haven, CT: Manuscripts and Archives, Yale University Library, 1973. Link to diaries: http://www.doug-long.com/stimson.htm. (STIMSON)

Tibbetts, Paul W., *The Tibbetts Story.* New York: Stein and Day, 1978. (TIBBETTS)

Toland, John. *The Rising Sun: The Decline and Fall of the Japanese Empire, 1936–1945.* New York: Random House. (RS)

Tully, Grace. *F.D.R. My Boss.* New York: Scribner's Sons, 1949. (GRACE)

Ugaki, Matome, Donald M. Goldstein, and Katherine V. Dillon. *Fading Victory: The Diary of Admiral Matome Ugaki, 1941–1945.* Annapolis, MD: Naval Institute Press, 2008. (UGAKI)

USNI. *The Bluejackets' Manual: United States Navy, 1944.* Annapolis, MD: United States Naval Institute, 1944.

USS *Indianapolis* Crew Members, and Philip A. St. John, PhD. *USS* Indianapolis, *CA-35.* Paducah, KY: Turner Publishing Company, 1997. (WHITE BOOK)

USS *Indianapolis* Families. *Lost at Sea but Not Forgotten.* Indianapolis, IN: Printing Partners, 2008. (LAS)

Wiper, Steve. *Portland Class Cruisers: CA-33 USS* Portland *& CA-35 USS* Indianapolis. Tucson, AZ: Classic Warships Pub., 2000. (WARSHIP)

Articles (Print)

Alexander, Colonel Joseph H., USMC (retired). *Naval History.* Vol. 19, No. 2, April 2005. Print. (NH19)

Anderson, Emma. "Foreign Affairs Reporter Dies at Age 88." *The Daily Californian Online,* 24 January 2011. Accessed 26 June 2016.

Aniya, Masaaki. "Compulsory Mass Suicide, the Battle of Okinawa, and Japan's Textbook Controversy." Editorial. *The Asia-Pacific Journal: Japan Focus,* 6 January 2008. http://japanfocus.org/site/view/2629. (KONOE)

Berke, Richard L. "Smith Announces for President." *New York Times,* 2 February 1999.

Borg, Jim. "History Clock Going aboard a New Indy." *Advertiser* (Honolulu), 30 July 1990.

Burlingame, Burl. "A Clock Retells the Story of WWII Sea Tragedy." *Star-Bulletin* (Honolulu), 30 July 1990.

The Chillicothe Constitution-Tribune. 18 December 1945, 5. Print. (EDITH)

Corley, Corporal Angus. "Hometowns in Wartime: San Francisco, Calif." *Yank,* November 1944. Accessed 13 June 2016.

"Cruiser Sunk, 1,196 Casualties; Took Atom Bomb Cargo to Guam." *New York Times,* 15 August 1945. (NYT)

Dayton, Kevin. "Survivors, Japanese Captain in Ceremony." *Star-Bulletin and Advertiser* (Honolulu), 18 November 1990.

Dobbs, Michael. *Six Months in 1945: FDR, Stalin, Churchill and Truman—from World War to Cold War.* New York: Alfred A. Knopf, 2012. (6IN45)

Editorial. Olson, Donald W., Brandon R. Johns, and Russell L. Doescher. "'Ill Met By Moonlight': The Sinking of the USS *Indianapolis*" *Sky & Telescope,* Vol. 104, No. 1, July 2002, 30–36. Faculty Publications-Physics. Web. N.d.: N. pag. Web. (MOON)

Fletcher, Carol. "Lifesaver Honored after 60 Years." *Record* (Bergen, New Jersey), 2005.

Frank, Richard B. "Why Truman Dropped the Bomb." From 8 August 2005 issue: Sixty Years after Hiroshima, We Now Have the Secret Intercepts That Shaped His Decision. 8 August 2005, Vol. 10, No. 44.

Gase, Thomas. "Front and Center: Benicia's Harold Bray Is the Ultimate Survivor." *Vallejo Times-Herald,* 20 September 2014. Web. (HB—NEWS)

Goldberg, Carey. "Independent Conservative Bob Smith Runs Uphill Race on Principle." *New York Times,* 20 September 1999.

Goldstein, Richard. "Adrian Marks, 81, War Pilot Who Led Rescue of 56, Is Dead." *New York Times,* 15 March 1998. Accessed 15 March 2017. http://www.nytimes.com/1998/03/15/us/adrian-marks-81-war-pilot-who-led-rescue-of-56-is-dead.html.

Gordon, William. "A Local Hero: Rescue at Sea." *Star-Ledger* (Newark). (This article is about Bill Van Wilpe, the big farm boy and USS *Bassett* sailor who risked his own life to save multiple *Indianapolis* survivors. The date on this print article was obscured.)

Hawkins, David. *Manhattan District History, Project Y, The Los Alamos Project.* Technical paper no. LAMS 2532. Vol. 1. Los Angeles: U.S. Atomic Energy Commission, 1946. (PROJECT Y)

"Indianapolis Skipper to Speak." *Indianapolis Times*, 17 July 1960.

James, Paul. "Dr. Earl O. Henry, Artist and Naturalist." *The Tennessee Conservationist*, November 2011, 17. (EH—TENN)

"John Parmelee Cady." In *The Lucky Bag*, 216. Annapolis, MD: United States Naval Academy, 1922.

Johnson, Malcolm. "Full Sinking Story Isn't out Yet, Reporter Says: Correspondent Hits Calling of Jap in McVay's Trial, Cites Lack of Search for Cruiser." *Pittsburgh Press*, 29 December 1945.

Kelly, Cynthia. "Robert Furman." *Time*, 31 October 2008. Obituary of Robert Furman, the Army major who shepherded components of Little Boy, the world's first atomic bomb, to Tinian Island aboard *Indianapolis*.

LaFollette, Gerry. "McVay Learned Integrity in the Navy." *Indianapolis Times*, 4 August 1960.

LaFollette, Gerry. "Tragedy Still Hurts—after 15 Years." *Indianapolis Times*, 30 July 1960. (Includes photo with the caption, "'Captain' McVay today," in which McVay is asking to have his nametag changed to read "Captain.")

LaFollette, Gerry. "USS *Indianapolis* Crew Relives War Tragedy." *Indianapolis Times*, 31 July 1960.

Mantho, R. S. "Eyewitness Story of USS *Indianapolis* Disaster." *Argus-Leader* (Sioux Falls, South Dakota), 7 October 1945.

Mok, Michael. "Bethesdan Recalls Trip with A-Bomb's Heart." *Washington Star*. From Papers of Robert Furman, Library of Congress.

"Naval Author to Speak Here." *Indianapolis Times*, 15 July 1960.

"Project Alberta." Atomic Heritage Foundation. Accessed 10 September 2017. https://www.atomicheritage.org/history/project-alberta.

"Reunion Proclaimed." *Indianapolis Star*, 28 July 1960. (Photograph with caption: "Mayor Charles H. Boswell signs a proclamation making Saturday and Sunday 'USS *Indianapolis* Survivors Memorial Reunion Days.'")

"Reunion to Hear Retired Admiral." *Indianapolis Star*, 17 July 1960.

Scott, R. D., JAGC, USN. "Report on the Court-Martial of Captain Charles B. McVay III, USN, Commanding Officer, USS *Indianapolis*." *NJAG* 10.2 (18 June 1996): 149–end. (SCOTT)

Shimpo, Ryuku, Ota Masahide, Mark Ealey, and Alastair McLaughlan. "Descent into Hell: The Battle of Okinawa." *Asia Pacific Journal*, 4th ser., 12, No. 48 (2014). Accessed 10 December 2015. http://apjjf.org/2014/12/48/Ota-Masahide/4230.html.

"The Sinking of USS *Indianapolis*: Navy Department Press Release, Report on Court-Martial of Captain Charles B McVay, III, USN, 23 February 1946." Web. (NAVYPR46)

Special to the *New York Times*. "Capt. McVay Wins Bronze Star for Valor on the *Indianapolis* in Battle before Loss." *New York Times*, 27 April 1946. (This article documents McVay's receipt of a Bronze Star for valor displayed at Okinawa in conjunction with the kamikaze attack. McVay did not even tell his sons about this medal.)

Stillwell, Paul. "Photographer at War." *U.S. Naval Institute's Naval History*, August 2014, 16–23.

Stimson, Henry Lewis. "The Decision to Use the Bomb." *Harper's Magazine*, February 1947, 102–4. (HENRY)

"Ultra and the Sinking of the USS *Indianapolis*," a paper given to the Eleventh Naval History Symposium. 1993. Richard Von Doenhoff. (U&S)

Unbylined. "Adm. Mason to Talk at Memorial Reunion of Survivors of the USS *Indianapolis*." *Indianapolis Star*, 10 July 1960.

"US Naval Institute History Articles." Web. <http://www.usni.org/magazines/navalhistory/1998-08/timeline-justice>. (USNI)

"USS *Indianapolis'* Wives Tour Butler, Enjoy Tea," *Indianapolis Times*, 31 July 1960.

Wells, Randy. "Navy Nurse Recalls USS *Indianapolis* Tragedy." *IUP Magazine*, Summer 2013, 16–18.

Articles and Reports (Web)

Allen, Thomas B., and Norman Polmar. "The Radio Broadcast That Ended World War II." *The Atlantic*, 7 August 2015. http://www.theatlantic.com/international/archive/2015/08/emperor-hirohito-surrender-japan-hiroshima/400328/. (BROADCAST)

Atomic Heritage Foundation. *910 17th St. NW, Suite 408, Washington, DC 20006.* Web. http://www.atomicheritage.org/. (AHF)

Atomic Heritage Foundation. "509th Composite Group." Atomic Heritage Foundation, 4 June 2014. Accessed 18 January 2016. https://www.atomicheritage.org/history/509th-composite-group. (509th)

"Atomic Power in Ten Years." 27 May 1940. *Time*, Accessed 29 March 2016. http://content.time.com/time/magazine/article/0,9171,884111,00.html.

"Attack on the Atom." 16 October 1939. *Time*, Accessed 29 March 2016. http://content.time.com/time/magazine/article/0,9171,762080,00.html.

"Battle of Okinawa." Battle of Okinawa. http://www.globalsecurity.org/military/facility/okinawa-battle.htm. (PHASES)

"Bomber Recalls WWII Rescue." *Wayne Independent*, 25 August 2010. http://www.wayneindependent.com/article/20100825/NEWS/308259996.

"Bombing of Tokyo and Other Cities." World War II Database. Accessed 16 June 2016. Article covers 19 February–10 August 1945.

Bowersmith, John A., and Joshua Hull. "LeBow Leads Survivors' Group from World War II's USS *Indianapolis*." 31 July 2009. http://lubbockonline.com/stories/073109/loc_473111154.shtml#.VuiYaYwrJL8. (CL—LAJ)

Chen, C. Peter. "Mitsuru Ushijima." *World War II Database*. http://ww2db.com/person_bio.php?person_id=306. (USHIJIMA)

"Civilians on Okinawa." PBS. Accessed 16 March 2014. http://www.pbs.org/wgbh/americanexperience/features/general-article/pacific-civilians-okinawa/. (CIVILIANS)

Columbia University. "Japan's Quest for Power and World War II in Asia." Asia For Educators. 2009. http://afe.easia.columbia.edu/special/japan_1900_power.htm. (QUEST)

Cressman, Robert J. "The Official Chronology of the U.S. Navy in World War II—1945." HyperWar. 1999. http://www.ibiblio.org/hyperwar/USN/USN-Chron/USN-Chron-1945.html. (CRESSMAN)

Crum, Jay. "Brief History of the USS *Underhill*." About USS *Underhill*. Accessed 5 October 2016. http://www.ussunderhill.org/html/about_uss_underhill.html.

Dace, Stanley W., Chief Boatswain's Mate. "Brief History of the USS *Underhill* DE-682." About USS *Underhill*. http://www.ussunderhill.org/html/about_the_uss_underhill.html. (UNDERHILL)

Davis, James M. "Operation Downfall—The Invasion of Japan, November, 1945." Novem-

ber 1987. http://www.oocities.org/athens/acropolis/8141/downfall.html. (DOWN-
FALL)

"Decision to Drop the Bomb." Truman Presidency Exhibit—Harry S. Truman Museum &
Library. http://www.trumanlibrary.org/hst/d.htm. (DECISION)

DeFeo, Anthony. "DeLeon Springs Man, USS *Indianapolis* Survivor, Dies at 89." News
-JournalOnline.com. February 16, 2015. http://www.news-journalonline.com/arti
cle/20150216/news/150219533?p=1&tc=pg. (CH—DAYTONA)

Department of Defense. "Navy 4-star Admiral and Trident Scholar Dies." www.navy.mil.
28 May 2008. Accessed 30 June 2017. http://www.navy.mil/submit/display.asp?story
_id=37463. (Obituary of Admiral Don Pilling.)

Destroyer Escort Sailors Association. "Hedgehog." Destroyer Escort Historical Museum. 24
January 2016. Accessed 1 December 2017. https://www.ussslater.org/tour/weapons
/hedgehog/hedgehog.html. Information on the "hedgehog," the antisubmarine
weapons used by *USS Albert T. Harris* to chase the unknown submarine ahead of
Indianapolis's track.

"Destroyer Escorts." Destroyer History Foundation. Accessed 19 October 2016. http://
destroyerhistory.org/de/.

Doody, Richard. "The World at War—Diplomatic Timeline 1939–1945." http://worldat
war.net/timeline/other/diplomacy39-45.html. (DOODY)

Feuer, A. B. "Memories from the USS *Indianapolis*." Warfare History Network. Accessed 28
September 2016. http://warfarehistorynetwork.com/daily/wwii/memories-from
-the-uss-indianapolis-ca-35/.

Ford, Daniel. "The Horror of the Human Bomb-Delivery System." *Wall Street Journal*, 10
September 2002. http://www.wsj.com/articles/SB103162461556052235. (HORROR)

Frank, Richard B. "Why Truman Dropped the Bomb." *Weekly Standard*, 8 August 2005.
http://www.weeklystandard.com/Content/Public/Articles/000/000/005/894mnyyl
.asp#. (DROPPED)

Gandt, Robert. "Killing the *Yamato*." HistoryNet. 4 August 2011. http://www.historynet
.com/killing-the-yamato.htm. (YAMATO)

Garfunkel, Richard J. "FDR—65 Years Ago in Warm Springs 4-12-45." www.richardjgar
funkel.com (blog), 12 April 2010. Accessed 14 March 2014. http://www.richardj
garfunkel.com/2010/04/12/fdr-65-years-ago-in-warm-springs-4-12-45/. (FDR)

Giuggio, Vicki M. "What If You Drink Saltwater?" HowStuffWorks. 16 February 2012.
Accessed 14 March 2014. http://science.howstuffworks.com/science-vs-myth/what
-if/what-if-you-drink-saltwater2.htm. (SALT)

Gogin, Ivan. "'Otsu-gata B3' Cruiser Submarines." IMPERIAL JAPANESE NAVY (JAPAN).
2008. http://www.navypedia.org/ships/japan/jap_ss_b3.htm. (IJN)

Hammel, Eric. "Battle of Okinawa: Summary, Fact, Pictures and Casualties." History
Net. 12 June 2006. Accessed 5 February 2014. http://www.historynet.com/battle
-of-okinawa-operation-iceberg.htm. (ICEBERG)

History Chanel. "Firebombing of Tokyo (This Day in History)." History.com. Accessed 26
June 2016. http://www.history.com/this-day-in-history/firebombing-of-tokyo.

Homans, Lally, Gordon Spector, and Phillip Messineo. "Nazi Sea Water Experiment."
10 October 2009. Accessed 14 March 2014. http://www.slideshare.net/studentwil
sonbiologylab/nazi-sea-water-experiment. (NAZI)

Huber, Thomas M. "Leavenworth Papers—Japan's Battle of Okinawa, April–June 1945."

N.p.,n.d.Web.http://web.archive.org/web/20090214183638/http://www-cgsc.army
.mil/carl/resources/csi/Huber/Huber.asp#contents. Number 18 (JBO)

Hulver, Richard, PhD. "Sinking of USS *Indianapolis*." History.navy.mil. Accessed 4 October
2016. https://www.history.navy.mil/browse-by-topic/disasters-and-phenomena/in
dianapolis.html.

"The Information War in the Pacific, 1945." Central Intelligence Agency. 6 May 2009.
https://www.cia.gov/library/center-for-the-study-of-intelligence/csi-publications
/csi-studies/studies/vol46no3/article07.html. (PEACE)

Ito, Masami. "Guam Native Tells Tokyo Gathering of WWII Atrocities." *The Japan
Times*. 12 December 2004. Accessed 3 March 2017. https://www.japantimes.co.jp
/news/2004/12/12/national/guam-native-tells-tokyo-gathering-of-wwii-atrocities/.

"The Japanese Emperor Speaks." History.com. http://www.history.com/this-day-in
-history/the-japanese-emperor-speaks. (SPEAKS)

"John Chapman and the Kamikaze Attack." 6 April 2015. Accessed 10 March 2016. www
.pbs.org.

Kalafus, Jim, and Cleatus Lebow. "Recalling the *Indianapolis*—Cleatus Lebow." *Encyclo-
pedia Titanica*. 30 July 2007. http://www.encyclopedia-titanica.org/recalling-the
-uss-inianapolis.html. (CL-RECALLING)

King, Lauren. "Sailors of the *Indianapolis* Honored on Veterans Day." *The Virginian-Pilot*. 12
November 2008. http://pilotonline.com/news/military/sailors-of-the-indianapolis
-honored-on-veterans-day/article_1599017a-2f66-56b5-beed-e3415968031e.html.
(VP—SAILORS)

Kingsepp, Sander, and Bob Hackett. "Imperial Submarines." Imperial Submarines. http://
www.combinedfleet.com/Tan%20No.%202.htm. (TAN 2)

MacEachin, Douglas J. "The Final Months of the War with Japan." Central Intelligence Agency. 7 July 2008. https://www.cia.gov/library/center-for-the-study-of
-intelligence/csi-publications/books-and-monographs/the-final-months-of-the-wa
r-with-japan-signals-intelligence-u-s-invasion-planning-and-the-a-bomb-decision
/csi9810001.html#rtoc2. (CIA)

Marble, Joan. "Mathews Man Finds Owner Of Dog Tag Lost In '45." Tribunedigital
-dailypress. 9 December 1992. http://articles.dailypress.com/1992-12-09/news/92
12090224_1_dog-tag-edward-kiser-uss-indianapolis. (SL TAGS)

Masahide, Ota, and Satoko Norimatsu. "'The World Is Beginning to Know Okinawa': Ota
Masahide Reflects on His Life from the Battle of Okinawa to the Struggle for Okinawa." Masahide Ota, Norimatsu Satoko. Accessed 20 September 2015. http://www
.japanfocus.org/-Norimatsu-Satoko/3415/article.html. Ota Peace Research Institute,
Okinawa kanren shiryo—Okinawa sen oyobi kichi mondai, 2010, 2. (OPRI)

"Might-Have-Been." 12 February 1940. Accessed 29 March 2016. http://content.time.com
/time/magazine/0,9263,7601400212,00.html.

Milhomme, Bill. "Chaplain Rev. Thomas M. Conway Remembrance." *Bill Milhomme*
(blog), 20 June 2012. http://milhomme.blogspot.com/2012/06/fr-thomas-m-con
way-chaplain-uss.html. (MILHOMME)

"Militarism and WW2 (1912–1945)." Japanese History: Militarism and World War II.
http://www.japan-guide.com/e/e2129.html. (MILITARISM)

"Millions Turn Out to Cheer Fleet Adm. Chester Nimitz for NYC Ticker-Tape Parade."
Naval History Blog. 9 October 2014. Accessed 28 October 2017. https://www.naval

history.org/2014/10/09/millions-turn-out-to-cheer-fleet-adm-chester-nimitz-for
-nyc-ticker-tape-parade.

Morgan, Sharon, and Tom Morgan. "Glenn Grover Morgan's Obituary on Midland
Reporter-Telegram." *Midland Reporter-Telegram.* 27 December 2012. http://www
.legacy.com/obituaries/mrt/obituary.aspx?pid=161983015#sthash.MPLVXjtv.dpuf.
(GM—OBIT)

Nichols, Chas S., Jr., and Henry I. Shaw, Jr. "OKINAWA: VICTORY IN THE PACIFIC."
HyperWar: USMC Monograph. http://www.ibiblio.org/hyperwar/USMC/USMC-M
-Okinawa/USMC-M-Okinawa-5.html. (BEACHHEAD)

Nichols, Major Chaz. S., Jr., and Henry I. Shaw, Jr. "Okinawa: Victory in the Pacific." Hyper-
War. Accessed 18 November 2014. http://www.ibiblio.org/hyperwar/USMC/USMC
-M-Okinawa/USMC-M-Okinawa-5.html. (USMC)

"Nuclear Files: Timeline of the Nuclear Age: 1945." Nuclear Age Peace Foundation. http://
www.nuclearfiles.org/menu/timeline/timeline_page.php?year=1945. (NAPF)

"Okinawa's History." Okinawa's History. Accessed 4 May 2014. http://rca.open.ed.jp/web_e
/history/story/epoch4/okinawasen_2.html. (BATTLE)

Our Baytown. "Lindsey Z. Wilcox—USS Indianapolis Survivor." Baytown's Historical
Resource. http://www.ourbaytown.com/LindseyZWilcox.htm. (BAYTOWN)

"The Pacific: Photos from WWII." *Denver Post Photo Blog.* http://www.eugenelesslover
.com/The_Pacific.html. (WWII PHOTO BLOG)

Paine, Thomas O. "The Transpacific Voyage Of H.I.J.M.S. I-400." Tom Paine's Journal: July
1945 to January 1946. http://www.pacerfarm.org/i-400/. (PAINE)

Phillips, Don. "W. Graham Claytor Jr., 82, Ex–Amtrak President, Dies." *The Washington
Post*, 15 May 1994. Accessed 10 March 2017. http://www.highbeam.com/doc/1P2
-890812.html?refid=easy_hf.

Pike, John. "Treaty Cruiser." Accessed 8 March 2016. https://www.globalsecurity.org/mil
itary/systems/ship/treaty-cruiser.htm.

Potts, J. R. "IJN I-58—History, Specs and Pictures—Navy Ships." IJN I-58. http://www.mil
itaryfactory.com/ships/detail.asp?ship_id=IJN-I58. (I-58)

"Rear Admiral Thomas J. Ryan, Jr." Ibiblio. Accessed 30 November 2017. https://www.ibib
lio.org/hyperwar/OnlineLibrary/photos/pers-us/uspers-r/t-ryan.htm.

"Recollections of a Vagabonde (Photos)." *The Little White House in Georgia, Part 2.* N.p.,
n.d. Web. http://avagabonde.blogspot.com/2013/05/the-little-white-house-in-geo
rgia-part-2.html. (WHEREFDRDIED)

Rehagen, Tony. "On Duty: A Sailor's Story." *Indianapolis Monthly.* 10 January 2013. http://
www.indianapolismonthly.com/news-opinion/on-duty-a-sailors-story/. (JO-DUTY)

"Remembering the USS *Squalus* 75 Years Later." Naval History Blog. 22 May 2014. Accessed
January 20, 2017. https://www.navalhistory.org/2014/05/23/remembering-the-uss
-squalus-75-years-later.

Ryu, Endo. "Interview with a Zero Pilot." *Rekishi Gunzou*, November 2000, translated by
Gernot Hassenflug of Kyoto. http://www.warbirdforum.com/komachi.htm (ZERO)

Second Emergency Rescue Squadron, unknown Member. "Rescued from the Sea." PBY.org.
Accessed 28 March 2017. http://www.pbyrescue.com/Stories/rescue%20story.pdf.
This article was critical in helping recreate Lieutenant Adrian Marks's landing of his
PBY-5A Catalina flying boat, or "Dumbo," and rescuing fifty-three *Indianapolis* sur-
vivors.

"Science: Big Game." *Time*, 13 March 1939. Accessed 29 March 2016. http://content.time
.com/time/magazine/article/0,9171,760934,00.html.

"Secret Weapons." *Time*, 24 January 1944. Accessed 29 March 2016. http://content.time
.com/time/magazine/article/0.9171.803047,00.html.

Slotnik, Daniel E. "Dan Kurzman, Military Historian, Is Dead at 88." *New York Times*.
24 December 2010. Accessed 1 June 2016. http://www.nytimes.com/2010/12/26
/arts/26kurzman.html.

Smitha, Frank E. "Emperor Hirohito Speaks to His Nation about Surrender." Micro History and World Timeline. http://www.fsmitha.com/h2/ch23ja7.htm. (HIROHITO)

"Sodium: Too Much of a Good Thing." Poison.org. Accessed 29 September 2016. https://
www.poison.org/articles/2013-sep/sodium-too-much-of-a-good-thing.

Sudyk, Bob. "Redemption for Sailor Joe." *Hartford Courant*. 21 June 1998. Accessed 15
March 2014. http://articles.courant.com/1998-06-21/news/9806180129_1_uss-indi
anapolis-charles-butler-mcvay-iii-sofa. (JOE)

"Surrender of Japan—Divisions Within the Japanese Leadership." http://www.worldli
brary.org/articles/surrender_of_japan. (Division)

"Task Force Information." *Task Force 50*. N.p., n.d. Web. http://pacific.valka.cz/forces/tf50
.htm#iceber. (TF)

Thomas, Gordon, and Max Morgan Witts. "Enola Gay: Mission to Hiroshima." Article
also titled "Ruin from the Air." Web. http://www.rulit.net/programRead.php?pro
gram_id=331877&page=1 See also http://www.ourcivilisation.com/smartboard
/shop/tomwitts/index.htm. (ENOLA)

"Thomas John Ryan, Jr." In *The Lucky Bag*, 113. Annapolis, MD: United States Naval
Academy, 1921. Accessed 30 May 2017. https://archive.org/stream/luckybag1921
unse#page/n11/mode/2up/search/Ryan.

Toti, William J. "The Legacy of USS *Indianapolis*." *USNI News*, 30 July 2014. Accessed
15 February 2015. https://news.usni.org/2014/07/30/legacy-uss-indianapolis.

Vladic, Sara. "Lost Survivor of the USS *Indianapolis* (CA-35) Found." *Proceedings*.
14 September 2017. Accessed 29 November 2017. https://www.usni.org/magazines
/proceedings/2017-09/lost-survivor-uss-indianapolis-ca-35-found.

"War in the Laboratories." *Time*, 26 May 1941. Accessed 29 March 2016. http://content
.time.com/time/magazine/article/0,9171,765651,00.html.

"William "Deak" Parsons." Atomic Heritage Foundation. Accessed 14 June 2016. www
.atomicheritage.com.

"William R. Purnell." Atomic Heritage Foundation. Accessed 14 June 2016. www.atomic
heritage.com.

Woodward, Lieutenant Commander C. R., USMC. *The U.S.S. Indianapolis—Tragedy
Amid Triumph*. 1988. Web. http://www.globalsecurity.org/military/library/report
/1988/WCR.htm. (TRAGEDY)

"World War II: Ultra—The Misunderstood Allied Secret Weapon." 4 August 2016. Accessed
21 February 2017. http://www.historynet.com/world-war-ii-ultra-the-misunderstoo
d-allied-secret-weapon.htm.

Wukovitz, John F. "Battle of Okinawa: The Bloodiest Battle of the Pacific War." *World
War II*, May 2000: *History Net Where History Comes Alive World US History
Online*. Web. http://www.historynet.com/battle-of-okinawa-the-bloodiest-battle
-of-the-pacific-war.htm. (SLEDGE)

Yamada, Goro. "Sinking the *Indianapolis*: A Japanese Perspective." HistoricalConsulting
　　.com. 30 July 1994. http://www.historicalconsulting.com/vets_jp.html. Dan King, a
　　Japanese translator and World War II historian/collector, interviewed Mr. Yamada,
　　a former chief petty officer aboard the Japanese submarine I-58. The authors, Vin-
　　cent and Vladic, obtained a print copy of the interview, which is no longer available
　　online. The URL links to a photo of Mssrs. Yamada and King and some additional
　　history.

Film/Video

Video Archive—Witnesses to War. Web. http://www.witnesstowar.org/content/search
　　/search.php?zoom_query=uss+indianapolis. (WTW)
"Video of Truman Being Sworn In." Web. http://www.youtube.com/watch?v=oKsUkRI
　　WbbM. (NEWSREEL)
Day of the Kamikaze, Smithsonian Channel. Traces the origins of kamikaze battle and relives
　　two days of horror in 1945, when the Japanese launched "Operation Heaven" against
　　the Allied fleet in the Pacific. This award-winning documentary details the biggest and
　　bloodiest suicide attack in history, with unforgettable footage and eyewitness accounts.
　　8 February 2008, United Kingdom. Director: Peter Nicholson.
Trinity and Beyond: The Atomic Bomb Movie. Profiles the history of the U.S. nuclear weap-
　　ons program from 1945 to 1963; William Shatner narrates. Director: Peter Kuran.
　　Released 29 September 1995.
USS Indianapolis: *Ship of Doom.* Produced by Bill Van Daalen. Chip Taylor Communica-
　　tions.
Witness to the Sinking of USS Indianapolis. Richard LeFrancis, director of the Pappy Boying-
　　ton Veterans Museum and son of Army Captain Richard LeFrancis. Video. Accessed
　　online 10 September 2017 at https://www.youtube.com.

ACKNOWLEDGMENTS

To God, for choosing us as storytellers for this incredible project, and for always going before us along the journey. Thank you for every little step up the mountain, and each slide in to the valley that brought us here together.

To the USS *Indianapolis* Survivors Organization and the members of the USS *Indianapolis* Legacy group, we give you a million and one thanks. There were so many *Indianapolis* crew and family members who took us in and shared their stories, their love, and their support that we could write another book and fill it easily. To each and every one of you—thank you for allowing us to spend time with your husbands, fathers, grandfathers, brothers, and uncles, so that they would feel comfortable enough to share, some for the first time, their experiences aboard the *Indianapolis.* Suzanne and Craig Baumann, Julia Berg-Stahel, Dale and Rhonda Bogard, the Brays, the Bucketts, Bonny "Sailor" Campbell, Dean Cox, the Draytons, Shirley King Ezel, the Fortins, DeeDee Gutierrez, Cheeky Hampton, the Harrells, Juaneta Hershberger, the Horvaths, the Howisons, the Hupkas, the Jarvis family, Mary Larson, the Lebows, the Leenermans, the Lopez family, the Maldonados, Marcella McGinnis, DJ and Rod Melotte, the Millers, the Modishers and Shores, the Nunleys, the O'Donnells, the Outlands, the Procai and Perchyshyn family, Kaden Streck and Carissa Rosenbhom, Dennis and Adria Smith, the Stamm family, Janet Goff Stefan, Charline Summers, Ryan Summers, the Twibles, Kenny Umenhoffer, Missy Vandyke, Jason and Staci Witty, the Witzigs.

Paul and Mary Lou Murphy deserve some of the biggest thanks possible. For returning the phone call of a naïve twenty-one-year-old, who had only an enormous respect for the story, and the idea to share it with the world. It felt more like a dream than reality for many years. Paul and Mary Lou invited Sara to her first Survivors' reunion in 2001, and stood by her as her biggest champions for years.

We also want to especially thank Mary Lou for her invaluable work as editor of the seminal book *Only 317 Survived*. Authored by the survivors themselves, the book is a collection of first-person accounts. Mary Lou conceived the idea for the book in 2002, collected and typed the men's stories, and found a publisher who bound them into a hardcover book. For us, *Only 317 Survived* provided both first-person accounts of survivors who had already passed on, and crucial details of the men's stories that did not appear in other forms, such as articles, Navy documents, and interviews that we conducted ourselves. Thank you, Mary Lou, for this great work of love that so honors the brave men of *Indianapolis*.

Harold and Steph Bray, when Paul and Mary Lou passed the Survivors Organization torch to you, there was nothing but love, respect (and the best hugs ever) that came our way. Thank you for championing us and always being among the first people to show us you had our backs.

Jim and Sandi Belcher—you both have been tremendously supportive and helpful in our efforts to get the *Indianapolis* story told, and the work you've done to reunite a large and incredibly diverse group of Indy family and friends is nothing short of awe inspiring. Thank you. Toyoko, we thank you for sharing the story of James, and your beautiful love story.

Adolfo Celaya, we still chuckle about the first time Sara showed up at your door to do an interview. You wondered what in the world a young girl like her wanted to know about your story. But you invited her in and shared one of the most incredible stories we've heard. Even better was joking about being fellow high divers. Sara was a platform diver, Celaya jumped off the high side of a ship, seventy-three years earlier. Almost the same, right?

From the first time Sara received a letter from Kayo, thanking her for the milkshake at Steak N' Shake, to the visit to Chattanooga in 2017, the love and support shown by survivor Louis "Kayo" Erwin and his family has been one of the many driving forces that helped get the *Indianapolis* story out there.

To survivor Don McCall and the McCall family. Jeff, thank you for everything you've contributed at the reunions, and for the help you've given to share your dad's story. Skip, your early suggestion of the seminal Spruance biography, *The Quiet Warrior* by LCDR Thomas Buell, served as a foundation and a compass for all that came afterward. And Peggy, we have so much respect and gratitude for your role in the Survivors Organization, and for all the information and assistance you've given us. You've made a huge impact on all the lives you've touched, and we're thankful to you for it.

Survivor Glenn Morgan was one of the very first to begin this journey with Sara, and it took a lot of work to prove to Glenn that Sara was made of the right stuff to tell his story . . . but once that happened, the love and support given by Glenn, and his son, Tom, and Tom's wife, Sharon, were unmatched. Sharon and Tom were among those who embraced Lynn as a dear friend when she entered this journey, and we so appreciate that. Our friendship with the Morgan family will be treasured always.

To Dick Thelen and the Thelen family. We never felt more loved than when we finally made it to the receiving end of your delightful sarcasm and good-natured ribbing. You guys are the best, and we couldn't thank you enough for the support over the years, and all the laughs we've shared. And Dick, thank you for giving us access to all your stories, photos, and albums—we owe an enormous debt of gratitude to your lovely wife, JoAnne, for keeping an incredible collection of *Indianapolis* history.

John Woolston, you started out as an acquaintance and lent us your expertise, both as an eyewitness to this historic event, and an expert witness as the junior damage control officer . . . but you quickly became a dear friend, and like family to Sara. Thank you for everything you gave us to make sure we got the story right. And thank you for the many fantastic conversations we shared over a glass of wine, or our new favorite, shaved ice!

To the survivors, now gone but never forgotten, who called Sara weekly . . . this book is especially for you. You always timed your calls perfectly when she needed an extra kick in the butt: Victor Buckett, Frank Centazzo, LD Cox, Clarence Hupka, Sal Maldonado, Troy Nunley, and Lindsey "Zeb" Wilcox—We know you're all up there keeping an eye on us, and we hope you're proud.

Earl O. Henry, Jr., and his lovely wife, Marilyn, we are so grateful for your faithful support. It was such a privilege reading through the 160 pages of letters that your sweet father, LCDR Earl O. Henry, Sr., wrote to your mother, Jane. Every spring and summer, the oak trees in Lynn's yard come alive with birds of every color—mountain bluebirds, red-tailed hawks, green willow flycatchers, yellow Western king birds. Lynn has named this area the Earl O. Henry, Sr., Memorial Bird Sanctuary in honor of your dad (because, well, she kind of has a historical crush on Earl, Sr.!) Thank you, Earl, Jr., for keeping his legacy alive through group talks and by sharing his bird paintings with the world. We wish we could have known him.

Michael Emery, for everything you do to preserve the story of your uncle, and for traveling around the country to support our efforts, thank you. Sara would also like to add a special thank you for being the first lost-at-sea family member to grant her an interview.

And the many lost-at-sea families who have since shared the stories of their loved ones with us, and who work so hard to keep their legacies alive—Jae Anderson, Michael Annis, the Barksdales, Edwin Crouch, Kristine Connelly, Rebecca Dalrymple, Joni Deaver, Bob Dollins, Michael Emery, Paul Everts, James Fasthorse, Fred Harrison, Kathy Lipski, Katherine Moore, Russ Neal, Jaclyn Bradley Palmer, Tom Rhoten, Cecil Trotter, and Cindy Wilson. Thank you.

Elko Perchyshyn, the "guy who signs the checks for the men who carried the bomb." Your friendship, your sense of humor, and the support you've given us over the years has been essential to this book's success . . . and for everything you do on top of that to help the survivors, as well as to honor your uncle, Earl Procai.

To the rescuers, some just teenagers at the time, who bravely risked your lives to save these men, we thank you repeatedly. Eva Jane Bolents-Savel, George Barber, James Bargsley, Dabny Doty, Charles Doyle, Tom Gray, Bill Fouts, Al Lederer, Albert Lutz, Jack Paul, Malcolm Smook, William Van Wilpe, and L. Peter Wren—thank you for representing your fellow shipmates and giving us this important part of the *Indianapolis* story. And to Tom Balunis, the Houghtons, Etta McLendon, Bill Milhomme, and the friends and family of the rescue crew who work hard to preserve and share their accounts, we thank you.

To the Gwinn and Marks families—if not for Chuck and Adrian, we would not be able to tell these stories today. Beyond discovering and rescuing the men from the water, they were angels who became friends to many. To Alexes Shuman, Norma Gwinn, Jane and Steve Goodall, and Carol Burnside, we thank you for giving us the personal stories of Chuck and Adrian, and for constantly cheering us on, and inspiring us to keep working hard. We are honored to call you all friends. And David Levine—thank you for providing the crucial document that helped us get the record straight. Just like your grandfather, Adrian Marks, you swooped in to save the day.

And then there's Captain William Toti. It is impossible to properly thank Bill Toti without writing an ode or a sonnet. Throughout our research, Bill made himself available at every turn as a subject-matter expert (naval warfare, submarine tactics, naval history and protocol, the exoneration, interpreting ancient midshipman lore found in the *Lucky Bag*, and more.) We interviewed Bill many, *many* times, and he also served as a sounding board for our analysis as we uncovered new details about the sinking, the *Harris* chase, Navy supplemental investigation, and the court-martial. Amidst this gracious donation of his time, Bill continued his work as a tireless advocate for the survivors and families of the lost-at-sea. We also want to thank Bill's wife, the beautiful Karen Toti, for being so gracious as we took up so much of Bill's time. And so, Mr. and Mrs. Toti, we deliver to you a googol of gratitude. Our appreciation for you is literally immeasurable.

To Hunter Scott—now *Lieutenant Commander* Hunter Scott!—thank you for everything you did to help the survivors press their fight to exonerate Captain McVay. You grabbed the world's attention, and did what nobody before you could. And from us personally, thank you for sharing your stories, photos, and friendship with Sara over the years. We sat down together at the survivors' banquet in 2015 and united over the realization that you and Sara shared a bond: that of telling the *Indianapolis* story, and setting the record straight.

Senator Bob Smith, you have been such a blessing to us and to the entire *Indianapolis* family. Thank you so much for helping us with the story, but thanks even more for the unpopular task you took on, putting your reputation on the line to settle a half-century-old question: Was the court-martial of Captain McVay just? It was a question that seemed already to have been answered, repeatedly, by the Navy, an institution that both you and your colleagues held—and still hold—in the highest regard. Your legislative career shows that you always cared more about following your conscience than about how people would judge you for it, and we are so thankful that you took on this great cause. We also very much appreciate the generous spirit and enthusiasm with which you donated your time in providing interviews for this book. Finally, we would like to reprise the applause of hundreds when you warmed up the crowd at the 2017 Survivors' Reunion with a hilarious, spot-on impression of your friend President Bill Clinton. Unlike most impressions of public figures, this one was based on direct experience!

Margaret "Ducky" Hemenway, Senator Smith's former military affairs liaison, who battled valiantly with Senator Warner's staff, as well as with Navy JAG staff, to get the language approved for Captain McVay's exoneration. In the fight for justice for McVay, Ducky took many figurative bullets and withering stares from many unhappy people in government. Though our narrative did not take readers through those skirmishes, we want to acknowledge Ducky's front-line role here, her vital assistance to Senator Smith, and to say, on behalf of the survivors, the lost-at-sea and their families, thank you!

Atsuko Iida, granddaughter of Mochitsura Hashimoto, we are so thankful for the courage you showed in attending that first *Indianapolis* reunion, so many years ago. And to your husband, Jahn, for encouraging you in that decision. We can't begin to thank you enough for being the voice of your grandfather, Commander Hashimoto, and your family.

David Furman, son of Robert Furman and James Nolan, grandson and namesake of James F. Nolan. Thank you for filling in many blanks, and sharing more personal details of the men who helped carry out one of the most important missions in the effort to end WWII. Scott Rifleman, thank you for sharing the notes that your father, Robert Rifleman, recorded about his time on the *Indianapolis*, serving as a communications officer for Admiral Spruance.

To members of Admiral Raymond Spruance's family, including David Bogart and Ellen Holscher—thank you for showing us a side of the admiral that we may never have been lucky enough to learn of: that of a beloved father and grandfather, and a man who you personally admired greatly. It has been a pleasure and an honor getting to know you and call you friends.

Kim Roller, Honorary Survivor, friend above friends, shoulder to lean, laugh, and cry on . . . and the lady who sacrificed an enormous amount of her time (and her flight attendant vouchers) to help Sara visit survivors across the country. The love and care that Kim, and her husband, Steve, give to the Indy families often goes unrecognized, but is nothing short of tremendous. There are not enough thanks out there to be given, and this book wouldn't be what it is without your friendship and help . . . and especially the laughs that served as therapy throughout the journey.

Theresa Goldston Brown, for taking the time to tell the story of your mother, Mary Moore, the daughter of LCDR Kyle "Kasey" Moore. We were honored to tell your grandfather's story and grateful to be able to let readers know that his daughter, Mary, survived him.

Carl Bauersfeld, Jr., son of Lieutenant Carl Bauersfeld, thank you for sharing with us your father's autobiography and Navy papers. Your dad, Carl, went on to become a successful attorney in private practice, as well as a friend of the powerful in Washington, D.C.. We were honored that you brought to our attention your dad's role in the McVay court-martial, even opening your home so that Captain Bill Toti could come by and look at your father's papers in person. We appreciate you!

Bob Hackett and Sander Kingsepp at CombinedFleet.com provided invaluable information on the WWII Japanese submarine fleet. Their amazing website is a go-to spot for anyone seeking more information about this topic. Bob and Sander, thank you!

Our hats are off to Naval War College archivist Dara Baker, who used her historical acumen to unearth informational treasures from the war college's vast stacks at Newport, Rhode Island.

Huge thanks to Ken McNamara, an Indiana War Memorials Foundation board member, for his encouragement and suggestions.

Admiral Samuel Cox, director of the Naval History and Heritage Command, for his kindness, encouragement and responsiveness as we wrote this book.

Giant bouquets of thanks to Nathaniel Patch and Lauren Theodore at the National Archives for SS *Wild Hunter* and USS *Harris* records. The *Harris* deck logs sent us down a storytelling path that had remained hidden for more than seventy years.

Our gratitude to Wilda Reier-Aviles at the Senate Armed Services Committee. Tim Rizzuto, Destroyer Escort Historical Museum, USS *Slater*, Albany, New York. Captain Manny Hernandez and Lieutenant Nick Edmiston of the Arleigh Burke-class destroyer USS *Spruance*.

To our friends to whom we are bonded by a common commitment to preserving the story and a respect for Indy's crew—you took it upon yourselves to help provide research and support in order for us to get the story right. The Ankroms, Jack Barnes, Jody Campbell, the Colvins, Irene Daniels, John Duncan, the Fritzingers, Brian Fruits, Glenn Gray, the Hussey Family, Ken Kebow, Rory Latimer, the Lucas family, Deb Polise, Sarah Cunliffe, Martijn van Haren, Brendan McNally, Pete Pruyn, Ronnie Raines, Anna Runck, Lori Scott, James Theres, Mairead Tucker, Patrick Walmsley. Also, Ryan Gibbons and Kent Fortner at Mare Island Brewery, and the cast and crew of *The Soundless Awe*. John Gromosiak, for your paintings and for the years of advocacy. Stephen Savage, for the countless hours of help you provided in finding research and contact information for the rescue crew, as well as the LAS men and survivors. Leighton Rolley, best storyteller on the Seven Seas. You helped us get to "the bottom of things" with your bathymetry in the sinking area. Paul Brockman, and his team at the Indiana Historical Society— Suzanne Hahn, Corinne Nordin, Melanie Washington, and Nicole Poletika. Thank you for the incredible resources you provided about the *Indianapolis*, and the hours you put in helping us locate and copy the many (boxes and boxes of) documents surrounding the court-martial and exoneration. Ken Wright, Joyce Giles, and Barbara Davis and the volunteers at the Mare Island Museum, thank you for all that you do to preserve the history of the historic shipyards. Scot Christenson and the archivists at USNI who helped us with details about the Navy and Indy's history.

To the many folks who helped us get word out about *Indianapolis*: The team at Tiny Horse (Owen, Jon, Kyle, Jill, Mark, Maria, Marlynda, Aimee, and Kana), A. J. Brooks, Anita Busch, Jodi Cilley, John Cimasko, John Decker, Dan Johnson, Wally Leavitt at IndyCar Radio and USAA, Sheldon Margolis, Ann Marie Price, Peter Rowe at the San Diego *Union Tribune*, Marvin Olasky and Lynn's many friends at *WORLD* Magazine, Pete Daly at *Proceedings*, Denise Scatena, Ray Steele, Nancy Worlie—thanks for helping us share this story with millions!

To Microsoft cofounder Paul G. Allen for making the discovery of the *Indianapolis* possible. Without the find by your *Petrel* crew, so many questions about the ship's final moments would have remained unanswered. Rob Kraft, Paul Mayer, Curt Newport, Janet Greenlee, Carole Tomko, Rocky Collins, Miles O'Brien, Lloyd Fales, David Wulzen, Mika Lentz, and everyone involved in giving the world the chance to see *Indianapolis* once again, thank you.

To the members of Sara's original crew, who filmed the first Legacy interviews in 2005—Tyra Hughes, Jared and Natalie Hankins, Caitlin Hall, and the team at Pathway Productions. Thank you for getting the dream rolling. And to all those who have been there from the very early days. Who helped make further interviews possible, whether it was by covering startup costs, lending interview equipment, sharing ideas, cheering us on along the way, constantly covering us in prayer, or all of the above. We would definitely not be here without you—Michele Barcello; Brian and Courtney Becker; Shalen and Bethany Bishop; the Bodenhausens and Forsmans; Rana Boeckman; Suzy Bohling; Martha Bohuslar; Charlie and Suzi Bradshaw; Blain Breining; Miriam Brijandez; Chris and Amy Brown; Connie Burton; Scott and Sonia Byers; Eileen

Carandang; Jessica Carlton; Leticia Castañeda; Jan Chapman; Brad and Laurie Coleman; Stephanie Connors; Andy and Jenn Cruz; Julie Cox; Olaf and Linda DeKoning; Steve and Jane Diersing; Sean Donohue; Marion Drops; John, Marilyn, Matt and Kim Ebeling; Cecil and Diane Ellison; Josh and Rachel Escalante; Jeff Freeman; Julie Garrett; Tony and Erin Giovanetti; Debbie Gunning; Debbie Hansen; Wade Heimbigner; Tiffany Helfrich, the Hepburns, Christy Hines; Chad and Stacie Hodges; Richard and Kathy Hoefke; Ramie Hong; Adam Hutson; Jim and Lynda Jeffries; Angela Johnson; Ryley and Jenna Johnson; Jon and Melissa Jones; Vince and Megan Joseph; Ben and Emily Kuhnel; Karen Kraft; Hung Lee; Kristina Cook London; Ellyne Lonergan; Amber Longworth; Don and Susan Looney; Ian Lowery; Dimitr and Jennifer Marinov; Vivian Moores; Ingrid Morgan; Bob and Dannye Mason; Yvonne and Summer McCamon; BJ and MacKenzie McLean; Connor McFadden; Denny and Marcy McLarry; Alec and Katie McNayr; Jeanie Meehan; Leah Meinert; the Mills; the Mitchelsons; the Orr family; Bob and Jeanne Peacock; Jim Prechel; Andrea Regalado; Heather Romine; Jenna Sampson; Mike and Sharon Samuelson; Alison Savitch; Paul and Jill Savona; the Siewert family; Mike and Julie Snodgrass; Mila Spasic; Barry and Kathy Spencer; Cody Stenderup; Shirley Tejidor; Rex Thoman; Jill Torres Phillips; Ed and Sandra Townsend; Alan and Lynn Tsunekawa; Beckie Usnik; Lucy Vasquez; Kristen Vassie; Vlada Vladic; Marko and Mikaela Vladic (thanks for always being excited about my projects, and for making me proud to be your big sister); Joyce Warner; Dave and Lynda Williams; Jacquelin Wisniewski; Sha Wit; Kevin and Kendra Witowich, Terry and Kathy Woods, and to the whole Huntley, Siewert and Vladic clans who make up my incredible family—thank you. And to friend and physical therapist extraordinaire Dr. Leslie Desrosiers, who literally got Sara back on her feet and writing again after a back injury. THANK YOU.

Linda Williams, Mary Jenson, Paula Huntley, and the Dear Readers Book Club, if it hadn't been for your small group of San Diego book lovers, this book might never have come to be. Thank you for connecting Sara and Lynn!

Thank you to our agent, Rick Christian of Alive Communications, who has been a stalwart champion of this story and was a valuable sounding board during the development of the manuscript.

To our publisher, Jonathan Karp, Lynn first dreamed of writing for you more than a decade ago, so this project is a literal dream come true. Thank you for your vision for this story and for taking a chance on a couple of California writers. We are so grateful that you put your trust in us.

Jofie Ferrari-Adler, your literary passion and dedication to getting the story just right have been inspiring. We lie awake at night trying to decode your mysterious alchemy—that of a merry and accessible literary savant with equal dashes of coach, advocate, and butt-kicker who never hesitates to say when something doesn't quite ring right or is just downright bad. We very much appreciate your dedication and the fact that you are never satisfied with "good enough." This book is what it is because of your astute sensibilities and expert guidance.

Julianna Haubner, thank you for your uncommon insight and dedication to this story. You had the tricky job of helping us streamline the first 230 pages of the book—absolutely not an easy task for any of us. Your insightful suggestions turned what could have been a painful surgery into a high-five moment for the team.

To Al Madocs, production editor, who in helping us put this giant manuscript through its paces was always helpful, accommodating, and just plain cool.

To Paul Dippolito for this book's fantastic interior design.

And thanks to those who kept us straight with the legal stuff: Jon Pfeiffer, David Oshinsky, Richard Garzilli, and Neal Puckett.

To Sara from Lynn: Six years ago, you called me out of the blue to ask if I might like to team up to write the story of USS *Indianapolis* . . . except that it wasn't out of the blue. A key feature of my writing career is that I've tried to let God guide my work. Since I began writing books in 2005, I have never really "looked" for projects, but rather found myself guided from one to another through prayer and Providence. In 2011, I began praying that God would provide me with an opportunity to write an iconic World War II story. In 2012, you called. I had no idea that, along with the privilege and opportunity of working on this book, I would also be working with a great writer, but is also a woman of industry, faith, good humor, and integrity and, most important, excellent taste in coffee and chocolate. I had no idea that when God guided me to this project, he was also guiding me to a treasured lifelong friend—the kind of friend that you want to work with on *every* project, always.

To Lynn's dear husband, Danny: thank you for supporting a dream that became a calling. Through years, tears ("I can't *do* this!"), and fears ("Okay, I *really* can't do this!), and many takeout dinners (or no food at all), you have been cheerleader, counselor, and conscience. Thank you for putting up with all the deadline crunches, times when I pounded the keyboard until carpal tunnel flared and I zombied for weeks along on a worn-carpet track between desk, refrigerator, and bed. Also, I've said the following before, but will now say it publicly: your wisdom is a guidestar. When I don't quite know my next move, you are the first person I ask, and your advice is always sound, biblical, and wise. I've known you since you were nineteen years old, married you when you were twenty-one. Nearly thirty years later, who woulda thunk you'd mellow into a wise man, and yet you did! It's not easy for you, being married to an obsessive, pie-in-the-sky storyteller, but somehow you make it work. I love you like a rock.

To Lynn's sons, Christian and Jacob: Christian, as you have for every book, you listened patiently every time I said "You've got to hear *this!*" During the writing of this book, Jacob joined the destroyer Navy, reported aboard USS *Truxtun*, and became part of this long, proud tradition. You have both been on many storytelling journeys with me and this one has been *epic.* Thank you for always being there to listen.

To Paula Hough, you mean the world to Lynn and Danny. Thank you for your steadfast love and faithfulness. Lee loved this project and we wish he could've joined us on this journey. We know he is watching—in fact, he has already read the book.

To Lynn from Sara: I couldn't have asked for a better writing partner in this journey. You were more than worth the wait, and I'm so thankful for every step of this process we've shared—the things we've laughed through, got pissed about, discovered, forgot, remember again, and everything between. But more than anything, I'm beyond grateful for the friendship that's formed because of it all. I know that we will do this again someday, and I'm already looking forward to it. Danny, thank you for being the incredible husband you are to Lynn, and the supportive friend you've been to me. I respect you a great deal, and the advice you've always offered us along this road has played a large role in many of the big decisions we made to get here.

To Mel, my (Sara's) sister in this, and friend: I'll never forget sitting on that couch, all those years ago in Pahrump, telling you this story for the first time . . . to your first reunion in 2010, then producing the documentary, traveling the country (and world) together and sharing the story of Indy. What a journey! Thank you for loving the survivors and Indy families like you do, and for believing in me. There is no possible way this would have been accomplished without you. I can't wait to see what's next! And Greg (twin of Ben) . . . and all the Capacias and Johnsons, thank you for inviting me into your family and giving us all the love, support, good food, and good times that made this journey even more enjoyable.

Jen Bodenhausen, Holly Hepburn and Jenn Cruz. The number of urgent prayer requests you've covered over the years is far too many to count, but you were ALWAYS there for me, at full strength. Thanks for the love, the laughs, the walks, the wise counsel, and for all the good food and drinks in between. I love you all dearly and am certain I wouldn't have made it this far without you (and tacos).

To my (Sara's) mother- and father-in-law, Paula and Paul: You are so much more than in-laws to me, and I have such gratitude for all you've done to help us get here. Especially for sharing my journey with your prayer group, who always had my back. From that, to helping to transcribe hours of interview footage, to sharing your home with us during the final book edits together. Thank you.

To my (Sara's) mom: You always wanted me to be a doctor, but finally gave in and embraced my stubborn dream to be a storyteller. Special thanks goes to my stepdad, Don, for his love and encouragement, and for pushing my mom toward that decision. There hasn't been a time when you both weren't by my side, supporting me in every way you could—helping me cover travel costs to do interviews, sending care packages to survivors, volunteering as my research assistants, and just being there to love me. I wouldn't be living this dream without all the help you gave me.

And my (Sara's) husband, Ben: where do I begin? Our joke is that you married in to this journey . . . but the truth is, you became just as much a part of it as Lynn and I did along the way. Your advice and technical knowledge of the ship made all the difference to our story and everything you did to create the maps and help us. But you were so much more than that—best friend, confidant, sounding board, wise counselor, jokester, chauffeur, camera man, audio guy, editor . . . the list goes on and on. Thank you for continuing to live up to those wedding vows that you still keep in your wallet, even after ten years of marriage, and for loving me even when I'm a pain in the butt. There is no possible way I would have survived this without you. Loves you. Pikake!

And to Sara's Labrador retriever, Eli, thanks for the snuggles and for always keeping my feet warm when I write. Who's the best dog ever?

INDEX

Italicized page numbers indicate illustrations

PHOTO CREDITS AND INFORMATION

End Papers—Front

USS *Indianapolis* (CA 35) bow during launching at the New York Shipbuilding Corporation. November 7, 1931. (U.S. Navy photo/Released) NH 0403592.

INSERT 1

Page 1

President Roosevelt receives the salute of the Argentine Navy while standing beneath the eight-inch guns of USS *Indianapolis* (CA-35), during his Good Neighbor cruise to South America, November 29, 1936. (Courtesy of the Naval Historical Foundation, collection of Rear Admiral Paul H. Bastedo) NH 68113.

Passing under the Golden Gate Bridge, San Francisco, California, circa 1938. (Collection of Admiral Thomas C. Kinkaid, USN. U.S. Naval History and Heritage Command Photograph) NH 81893.

Admiral Raymond A. Spruance, Admiral Ernest J. King, Admiral Chester W. Nimitz, USN, and Brigadier General Sanderford Jarman. (U.S. Navy photo/Released)

Page 2

Cooks and bakers on liberty. (Courtesy of Salvador Maldonado)

Officers share a moment of laughter in the wardroom. (USNI Photo. Alfred J. Sedivi Collection)

Page 3

Marine survivors of the *Indianapolis*. (Photo courtesy of Edgar Harrell)

Sailors on liberty. (Photo courtesy of Glenn Morgan)

Adolfo Celaya on Guam. (Photo Courtesy of Adolfo Celaya)

Stewards serving as a gun crew on USS *Indianapolis*, July 1942. (U.S. Navy photo/Released) National Archives Photo #80-G-21743.

Page 4

CDR Stanley Lipski. (Courtesy of the Lipski family)

LT (jg) Charles McKissick. (U.S. Navy photo/Released)

LT Richard Redmayne. (U.S. Navy photo/Released)

Officers aboard *Indianapolis*. (U.S. Navy photo/Released)

CWO Leonard Woods. (U.S. Navy photo/Released)

ENS John Woolston. (U.S. Navy photo/Released)

Capt. Edwin Parke. (Photo courtesy of MCRD, San Diego. U.S. Marine Corps)

Page 5

Japanese plane shot down near USS *Essex*. (USNI Photo. Alfred J. Sedivi Collection)

Earl Procai's obituary. (Courtesy of Elko Perchyshyn, nephew of Earl Procai)

Spruance visits a wounded sailor in sick bay. (USNI Photo. Alfred J. Sedivi Collection)

Funeral for men who were killed in kamikaze attack. (USNI Photo. Alfred J. Sedivi Collection)

Page 6

Jimmy and Mary O'Donnell. (Photo courtesy of Mary O'Donnell)

Dick Thelen with his father. (Photo courtesy of the Thelen family)

Earl and Jane Henry. (Photo courtesy of Earl Henry, Jr.)

Harlan and Alice Twible. (Photo courtesy of Harlan Twible)

Kasey and Mary Moore. (Photo courtesy of Teresa Goldston Brown)

Page 7

Van Kirk, Tibbets, and Ferebee. Members of the *Enola Gay* crew taken August 6, 1945. (U.S. Military/D.O.D.)

Manhattan Engineering District group photo. (Atomic Heritage Foundation) This work is in the public domain in the United States because it is a work prepared by an officer or employee of the United States Government as part of that person's official duties under the terms of Title 17, Chapter 1, Section 105 of the U.S. Code.

Robert Furman. This work is in the public domain in the United States because it is a work prepared by an officer or employee of the United States Government as part of that person's official duties under the terms of Title 17, Chapter 1, Section 105 of the U.S. Code.

Page 8

Japanese Submarine I-58. (U.S. Navy photo/Released) National Archives #80-G-260244.

Hashimoto aboard I-58. (Courtesy of the Hashimoto family)

Young Hashimoto with family. (Courtesy of the Hashimoto family)

ULTRA intercept message. (National Archives. Declassified) NND 957001.

INSERT 2

Page 1

Rescue Pilot Chuck Gwinn. (Photo courtesy of the Gwinn Family)

Rescue Pilot Adrian Marks. (Photo courtesy of Nancy Hart of the Clinton County Historical Society)

Claytor & *Doyle* crew. (Steve Smith, a cousin of W. Graham Claytor's, via findagrave.com)

Rescuer Bill Van Wilpe—Courtesy of William Van Wilpe. (U.S. Navy photo/Released)

Troy Nunley and Joseph Van Meter on rolled-up floater net. (U.S. Navy photo/Released)

Page 2

Base Hospital #20, Peleliu. (U.S. Navy photo/Released)

Nurse Eva Jane Bolents treats survivor Vincent Allard. (Courtesy of Eva Jane Bolents)

Purple Heart presentation. (U.S. Navy photo/Released) National Archives #80-G-490311.

Survivors Bernard Bateman, A.C. King, and Erick Anderson, recovering at Peleliu. (U.S. Navy photo/Released) National Archives #80-G-336799.

Page 3

Hirohito with his war council. The only known rendering of this event was included in the 1968 book *Japan's Longest Day*. The book, a detailed reconstruction of the tense hours preceding the surrender announcement of Emperor Hirohito, is based on material gathered by the Pacific War Research Society, a panel of distinguished Japanese authors and journalists. Authors Vincent and Vladic thoroughly investigated the source of this photograph, finding that the publisher, Kodansha USA, and Pacific War Research Society have since dissolved. The photo comes from page 191 in the 1990 paperback edition.

Ugaki before his final flight, August 1945. Public domain in the United States because copyright in Japan expired by 1970.

Japanese forces surrender in the Philippines. (U.S. Navy photo/Released) NH 97276.

Page 4

Hashimoto draws maps at court-martial. (Getty Images)

McVay during his court-martial. (Getty Images)

Survivor witnesses at McVay's court-martial. Left to right, called as witnesses for McVay's court-martial: (seated) Lieutenant (jg) Charles McKissick, McKinney, TX; Warrant Gunner Durward Horner, Vallejo, CA; Ensign Harlan Twible, Gilbertsville, MA; Ensign Ross Rogers, Jr., Paris, TN; Warrant Machinist Harley Hanson, Bronx, NY. Standing, left to right: Ensign John Howison, New Albany, IN; Ensign John Woolston, Needham, MA; Radioman Second Class Elwyn Sturtevant, Los Angeles, CA; and Seaman Loren McHenry, Jr., Fall River, MO. (Getty Images)

Thomas Ryan, the Navy judge advocate. (U.S. Navy photo/Released) NH 46075.

Fleet Admiral Ernest J. King, Secretary of the Navy James Forrestal, and Fleet Admiral Chester W. Nimitz pose together at the Navy Department, Washington, D.C., on November 21, 1945, as it was announced that Fleet Admiral Nimitz would succeed Fleet Admiral King as Chief of Naval Operations. (U.S. Navy photo/Released)

Page 5

McVay shakes hands at the 1960 reunion. (Photo courtesy of Edgar Harrell)

McVay with his wife, Louise, at the 1960 reunion. (Photo courtesy of Edgar Harrell)

Indy's "5th Division" at the 1960 reunion. (Photo courtesy of survivor Felton J. Outland's family)

Page 6

Senator John Warner. This work is in the public domain in the United States because it is a work prepared by an officer or employee of the United States Government as part of that person's official duties under the terms of Title 17, Chapter 1, Section 105 of the U.S. Code.

Senator Bob Smith. (Getty Images)

Hunter Scott speaking during the exoneration efforts. (Photo courtesy of Hunter Scott)

Admiral Don Pilling. (U.S. Navy photo/Released)

Captain William J. Toti. (Photo courtesy of William Toti)

Page 7

Indianapolis survivors at the deactivation ceremony of SSN-697. (Photo courtesy of William Toti). In order to name all the survivors pictured, an extensive search was made by author Sara Vladic, inquiring with family members, posting photos across social media platforms, and speaking with those who attended. All but one man was named. If you know the name of the unidentified man pictured first on the left, please contact the survivors organization at www.ussindianapolis.com.

Mochitsura Hashimoto as a Shinto priest. (Photo courtesy of Atsuko Iida, grand-daughter of Hashimoto)

Jason Witty spreads his grandfather's ashes in the Pacific. (Photo courtesy of Jason Witty)

Page 8

Photos from the 2005 reunion were taken by Natalie Hankins and Sara Vladic as part of the documentary project *USS Indianapolis: The Legacy*. 2016.

Art Leenerman and Earl Riggins with the survivors' book. (Reproduced by permission of the *News-Gazette*, Inc. Permission does not imply endorsement). Publication date 2/27/2011.

End Papers—Back

5" gun—In remarkable condition after more than seventy years underwater, one of Indy's starboard side 5"/25 caliber AA guns is lit by the R/V *Petrel*'s ROV. Even the rifling inside the barrel is still visible. The crew of the R/V *Petrel* discovered the wreckage of the USS *Indianapolis* 5,500 meters below the surface of the Philippine Sea on August 19, 2017. (Photo courtesy of Paul G. Allen)

Maps & Diagrams

Map data was compiled and analyzed by Ben Huntley, allowing the authors to show a bigger picture of the events that transpired during the final days in the water and during rescue efforts. Ben was also largely responsible for the ship's diagram and labeling, helping the authors understand the engineering and structural aspects of the ship's design.

Japanese Home Islands (Map)

Profile photos on this map are public domain in the United States because their copyright in Japan expired by 1970.

Philippine Sea Commands (Map)

Profile photos on this map have been released by the U.S. Navy for public use.

This military insignia are public domain in the United States because they contains materials that originally came from a United States Armed Forces badge or logo.

Sketch by I-58 Captain Mochitsura Hashimoto

Battle diagram of I-58 Submarine 20th Year (Showa) July 29. The diagram shows magnetic north, and then depicts the location of the moon to the east. The scale in the corner is in meters (the scale is 50,000 to 1). The submarine appears to be heading 190 at time 2305 on July 29 when it spots the ship at approximately 10,000 meters off its starboard side. Apparent course and speed of the target is 260 at 11 knots. The submarine maneuvers into position 1500 meters off the starboard beam, where it takes six shots at time 2332. The dotted line is the apparent location of where the ship was sunk. The submarine performed a starboard, then port, then starboard turn before settling out on course 045 at approximately 0030 on July 30. (Source: Naval History and Heritage Command)

ABOUT THE AUTHORS

U.S. Navy veteran Lynn Vincent is the #1 *New York Times* bestselling author or coauthor of eleven nonfiction books with more than sixteen million copies in print. Her best-known titles are *Same Kind of Different As Me* (with Ron Hall and Denver Moore) and *Heaven Is for Real* (with Todd Burpo), both of which were released as major motion pictures. Lynn is a senior writer for *WORLD Magazine*, where she covers politics, culture, and current events. Her investigative work includes exposés of criminals and cranks, corrupt industries, and government agencies, as well as the longest-running federal case in U.S. history. Her articles have been cited before Congress and the U.S. Supreme Court. Lynn has been profiled in major media outlets, including *Newsweek* and *The New Yorker.* She lives in the mountains east of San Diego with Danny, her husband of twenty-nine years, her Heritage Softail, and three Labrador retrievers.

Sara Vladic, an acclaimed documentary filmmaker and honorary USS *Indianapolis* survivor, is one of the world's leading experts on the USS *Indianapolis*, having become obsessed with the story at the age of thirteen. She is a member of the Producers Guild of America, and has for years worked on and off set as production manager, editor and post supervisor, writer, and director for both commercials and live news. She has also worked as talent coordinator, live event producer, and even a stunt woman. She has earned awards for camera work, and has spoken on panels for screenwriting and documentary filmmaking. During all of this, and over nearly two decades, Vladic met and interviewed more than one hundred *Indianapolis* survivors and rescue crew members, and in 2016 she released an award-winning documentary film, *USS* Indianapolis: *The Legacy.* She has published new research on the *Indianapolis* in *Proceedings*, the flagship journal of the U.S. Naval Institute, and appeared as an expert commentator for National Geographic, the Smithsonian, and PBS's *USS* Indianapolis: *Live from the Deep*, which explored the ship's wreckage. She and her husband, Ben, live in San Marcos, California.